THUNDER IN THE EAST

D1564249

Modern Wars

Series editor: Hew Strachan

Chichele Professor of the History of War, All Souls College, University of Oxford (UK)

Advisory editor: Michael Howard

Emeritus Fellow of All Souls College, University of Oxford (UK)

Covering the period from 1792 to the present day, the *Modern Wars* series explores the global development of modern war. Military history is increasingly an integrated part of 'total history', and yet this is not always reflected in the literature. The *Modern Wars* address this need, offering well-rounded and balanced synoptic accounts of the major conflicts of the modern period. Each volume recognizes not only the military, but also the diplomatic, political, social, economic and ideological contexts of these wars. The result is a series that ensures a genuine integration of the military history with history as a whole.

Published:

The South African War, Bill Nasson (1999)
The Crimean War, Winfried Baumgart (1999)
Allies in War, Mark A. Stoler (2005)
The First World War (Second Edition), Holger Herwig (2014)

Forthcoming:

New Order Diplomacy, Martin Folly (2016)

THUNDER IN THE EAST:
THE NAZI–SOVIET WAR 1941–1945

SECOND EDITION

Evan Mawdsley

Bloomsbury Academic
An imprint of Bloomsbury Publishing Plc

B L O O M S B U R Y
LONDON · NEW DELHI · NEW YORK · SYDNEY

Bloomsbury Academic

An imprint of Bloomsbury Publishing Plc

50 Bedford Square	1385 Broadway
London	New York
WC1B 3DP	NY 10018
UK	USA

www.bloomsbury.com

BLOOMSBURY and the Diana logo are trademarks of Bloomsbury Publishing Plc

First edition published 2005

This second edition published 2016

© Evan Mawdsley, 2005, 2016

Evan Mawdsley has asserted his right under the Copyright, Designs and Patents Act, 1988, to be identified as Author of this work.

All rights reserved. No part of this publication may be reproduced or transmitted in any form or by any means, electronic or mechanical, including photocopying, recording, or any information storage or retrieval system, without prior permission in writing from the publishers.

No responsibility for loss caused to any individual or organization acting on or refraining from action as a result of the material in this publication can be accepted by Bloomsbury or the author.

British Library Cataloguing-in-Publication Data

A catalogue record for this book is available from the British Library.

ISBN: HB: 978-1-4725-1166-9
PB: 978-1-4725-0756-3
ePDF: 978-1-4725-1008-2
ePub: 978-1-4725-1345-8

Library of Congress Cataloging-in-Publication Data

Mawdsley, Evan, 1945-
Thunder in the east: the Nazi-Soviet war 1941-1945 / Evan Mawdsley. – Second edition.
pages cm. – (Modern wars)
Original edition published: 2005.
Includes bibliographical references and index.
ISBN 978-1-4725-0756-3 – ISBN 978-1-4725-1008-2 (ePDF) – ISBN 978-1-4725-1345-8 (ePub)
1. World War, 1939-1945–Campaigns–Eastern Front. 2. World War, 1939-1945–Campaigns–Soviet Union. I. Title.
D764.M377 2015
940.54'217–dc23
2015006334

Series: Modern Wars

Typeset by Deanta Global Publishing Services, Chennai, India
Printed and bound in India

For Gillian, Michael and Robyn

CONTENTS

List of Illustrations   viii
List of Maps   ix
List of Tables   x
List of Abbreviations   xi
General Editor's Preface   xii
Preface   xvii

Part I   The Nazi Onslaught, 1941–2   1
1   Hitler's War   3
2   Preparations and Perceptions   17
3   Operation BARBAROSSA, June to September 1941   54
4   Moscow and the End of BARBAROSSA, October to December 1941   86
5   The First Soviet General Offensive, December 1941 to May 1942   115
6   Moscow, Stalingrad, Leningrad, June 1942 to January 1943   144

Part II   The Soviet Victory, 1943–5   179
7   Total War I: Wartime Arms and Armies   181
8   Total War II: Occupation and Diplomacy   220
9   The Red Army Takes the Initiative, January to September 1943   244
10   The Ukraine and Leningrad, August 1943 to April 1944   268
11   To the Soviet Frontiers, June to October 1944   285
12   The March into Eastern Europe, July 1944 to May 1945   307
13   The Destruction of Nazi Germany, October 1944 to May 1945   349
14   Conclusion   383

Chronology of Events, 1939–45   393
Glossary   416
Notes   419
Select Bibliography   487
Index   498

LIST OF ILLUSTRATIONS

1 Hitler talks with Ion Antonescu, the Romanian dictator. Behind Hitler's right shoulder is Field Marshal Wilhelm Keitel; to Hitler's left (with spectacles) is General Franz Halder   4

2 German troops enter a burning Russian village in the first days of the war   58

3 Russian T-26 tanks, with their crews, July 1941   73

4 German troops evacuate wounded in the mud of March 1942   105

5 German soldiers drive a horse and cart through a snowstorm   119

6 German tanks ford a shallow reach of the Don in the drive on Stalingrad   153

7 German armour supports the last push in Stalingrad in November 1942   155

8 A battery of Soviet 'Katiusha' rocket launchers, mounted on Lend-Lease Studebaker trucks   192

9 German prisoners at Stalingrad   234

10 Soviet infantry advances across the steppe of southern Russia in 1943   263

11 Red Army forces cross a river in the western Ukraine, near L'vov   316

12 Marshals Rokossovskii and Zhukov with Field Marshal Montgomery in Berlin, July 1945   325

13 The Red Army enters Prague on 9 May 1945. The Soviet soldiers ride in Lend-Lease American M3 half-tracks   346

14 A column of 'Stalin' heavy tanks in Germany. Alongside, French liberated forced labourers make their way home from Germany   354

15 Stalin and Molotov at the Yalta Conference, February 1945. In the background is A. Ia. Vyshinskii, the Deputy Foreign Commissar   357

16 A Soviet self-propelled gun firing in a Berlin street, 1945   370

17 Soviet T-34s fight their way into Berlin in April 1945   371

18 Soviet soldiers in Berlin, May 1945. The men who destroyed the German Army   379

LIST OF MAPS

Map 1	The German invasion, 1941	56
Map 2	The Moscow theatre, 1941–2	90
Map 3	The Leningrad theatre, 1941–4	126
Map 4	The Soviet winter offensive, 1941–2	132
Map 5	Hitler's second offensive, 1942	151
Map 6	The Soviet home front	186
Map 7	The Soviet winter offensive, 1942–3	245
Map 8	The Battle of the Ukraine, 1943–4	270
Map 9	Belorussia and the Baltic, 1943–4	291
Map 10	Southeastern Europe, 1944–5	330
Map 11	Poland and Eastern Germany, 1945	353

LIST OF TABLES

Table 2.1	Operation BARBAROSSA: forces directly involved	18
Table 2.2	Location of German Army divisions, end of May 1941	34
Table 2.3	Distribution of Soviet and German divisions, June 1941	40
Table 2.4	Soviet pre-war weapons production, 1937–41	43
Table 2.5	Comparative armaments production, January 1941 to December 1942	43
Table 2.6	Soviet military equipment, June 1941 to December 1942	44
Table 3.1	Soviet equipment losses, June–September 1941	84
Table 4.1	Personnel of the Red Army, September 1941	109
Table 7.1	German and Soviet war production, 1942–4	184
Table 7.2	Soviet artillery production, 1941–5	190
Table 7.3	Soviet tank and SP losses	191
Table 7.4	Soviet combat aircraft losses, 1941–5	197
Table 14.1	German and Russian military personnel losses in the Second World War	390

LIST OF ABBREVIATIONS

AA	*anti-aircraft (gun)*
AFV	*armoured fighting vehicle*
AT	*anti-tank (gun)*
C-in-C	*Commander-in-Chief*
GKO	(*Gosudarstvennyi Komitet Oborony*) State Defence Committee
GULAG	*Soviet Main Administration of Labour Camps*
KTB	*Kriegstagebuch* (war diary)
MD	*military district*
NCO	*non-commissioned officer*
NKO	*People's Commissariat of Defence*
NKVD	*People's Commissariat of Internal Affairs*, i.e. the secret police
OKH	(*Oberkommando des Heeres*) German Army High Command
OKW	(*Oberkommando der Wehrmacht*) German Armed Forces High Command
OO	(*Osobyi otdel*, Special Section) NKVD counter-intelligence within the Red Army
PVO	(*Voiska Protivovozdushnoi oborony strany*) Air Defence Forces
Pz Kpfw	(*Panzerkampfwagen*) German abbreviation for 'tank'
RSFSR	*Russian Soviet Federative Socialist Republic*
SMERSH	(*Smert' shpionam*, Death to spies) counter-intelligence organ in the Red Army
SP gun	*self-propelled gun*

GENERAL EDITOR'S PREFACE

When, in 1970, Basil Liddell Hart's *History of the Second World War* was published in Britain, it marked the end of an era. One reason was that it was published after the death of its author. More importantly, it represented an approach to its subject that even then looked dated. Liddell Hart's war was one fought and won in the West; he paid more attention to the North African campaign, to which the Germans had allocated two divisions in 1941, than to Russia, to which they had devoted seventy-five times that number. This was a story of the war that travelled from Dunkirk to D-Day, by way of El Alamein.

In those days the English-speaking historians who did write about the war on the Eastern Front approached their subject from the perspective of the Germans, and especially that of the German generals. Liddell Hart himself had interviewed many of them after the war, and he and others had been midwives in the translation of their memoirs into English. Here was a Wehrmacht that was politically innocent, a supremely able but also honourable fighting force, unsullied by the worst excesses of Nazism, the professional competence of its officers constantly subverted by the interventions of Hitler, especially in the conduct of the defensive battles which the German Army was condemned to fight after 1943. The Cold War made the lessons the Germans had learnt in combating a Soviet invasion of Europe of greater moment than historical context. Atrocities were not a necessary part of this narrative, and if they were acknowledged, they were blamed on the Nazi Party and its military arm, the Waffen-SS, not the Wehrmacht: such a demarcation made life easier for everyone, for Germans anxious to draw a line under the past and for NATO needing the manpower of a new West German Army, the *Bundeswehr*.

The Wehrmacht was complicit in war crimes and particularly so on the Eastern Front. The massive ten-volume history of Germany in the Second World War, *Das deutsche Reich und der zweite Weltkrieg*, prepared by the *Bundeswehr*'s own military history section, makes this clear, particularly in the contributions of Jürgen Förster. The German public has been confronted with the acts of its fathers and grandfathers in a deeply controversial and profoundly unsettling touring exhibition, originating in Hamburg, whose catalogue was published in 2002. Neither Heinz Guderian, the panzer general appointed chief of the General Staff in the wake of the bomb plot against Hitler in July 1944, nor Erich von Manstein, who devised the plan that led to the breakthrough against France in May 1940, and who commanded, first, an army and, then, an army group in Russia, look as innocent now as they managed to do in the 1950s. Both of them were generals whose reputations were refurbished by Liddell Hart, and yet Guderian was a committed Nazi and Manstein ordered the extermination of Jews and Bolsheviks.

Today our picture of the German Army of the Second World War is therefore very different from that which was shaped by Rommel's Afrika Korps and the notion of a war without hate (to use Rommel's own description of the North African campaign). The war in the East was fought with a bestiality and ferocity by both sides that raise questions about its links to totalitarianism and its methods. As Evan Mawdsley makes clear in his conclusion, this was a deeply politicized war, even if it was not a rational one: politics and reason are, unfortunately, not synonymous. Professor Mawdsley does not let himself get drawn into the Holocaust itself, but he points out that the 'solution' to the Jewish question proposed by the Nazis in 1941 was the forced resettlement of European Jewry in Asiatic Russia. This proposal was undermined by Germany's failure to defeat the Soviet Union in short order, and thus the path was opened to another more 'final' and even more awful 'solution'. Moreover, whether violence begets more violence is a moot but highly relevant point. The vocabulary used to motivate the soldiers of the Wehrmacht in battle could be transferred to those – policemen as well as soldiers – tasked with extermination. War legitimizes behaviour in the individual that is beyond the pale in peacetime. Did the extraordinary losses inflicted on the Eastern Front make it easier to carry out murder in the death camps?

The Soviet Union was also a totalitarian regime. Moreover, before the invasion of 1941, it had shown itself even readier than Germany to inflict massive losses on its own peoples in the name of progress and political conformity. It was Russia's war about which Liddell Hart was particularly ill-informed. By 1970 the combination of linguistic ignorance, tainted historical writing and deep distrust had erected an impenetrable barrier between the peoples of the West and their appreciation of the achievements of the Red Army. In 1975, John Erickson began to tear down these obstacles with the publication of *The Road to Stalingrad*, followed in 1983 by *The Road to Berlin*. Since then, other scholars, notably Earl Ziemke and David Glantz, have written prolifically on the subject, and Antony Beevor has shown that it is one which appeals to an English-speaking readership on a massive scale.

Evan Mawdsley is first and foremost a historian of modern Russia, but in *Thunder in the East*, he achieves a balance between his first love and the history of Germany; it is a military history written from both sides of the hill, and one whose operational accounts are set in the context of economic mobilization, an appreciation of geography and a refreshing readiness to reject historical fashion for its own sake. Recent work on the war on the Eastern Front, anxious to come to grips with the motivations of those who fought it, has focused on its 'de-modernization'. Here is the most costly and unrestrained conflict of modern times – indeed, of any epoch – fought by a state which had been ranked second in the world in terms of GNP by 1914 against a state which had undergone a forced march to industrialization in the 1930s. But by 1945, the first of those states, Germany, put panzer divisions into the field which possessed few, if any, tanks, and fought operations almost totally devoid of air cover; the second, Russia, suffered casualties which seemed to rate masses of men over quality in technology. (In reality, the Red Army made good its manpower losses in 1943–5 by better use of firepower.) One ostensible symptom of this 'de-modernization' was the importance of the horse not only for transport but also for fighting itself. Most of the German Army's transport in 1941 was horse-drawn, but the Red Army went further, possessing as many as eight cavalry corps in 1943. In addressing the issue, Professor Mawdsley achieves balance and insight by stepping back from the theoretical vocabulary of modernism into the hard-headed world of pragmatism. The Soviet Union made particularly effective use of cavalry because the terrain, the size of the front and the operational conditions all favoured it.

The awareness of the Soviet Army's operational strengths, its development of the ideas of 'deep battle' in the 1930s, colours *Thunder in the East*. Evan Mawdsley connects the performance of the Red Army in 1944–5 with the doctrines of the previous decade, developed through the writings of thinkers like V. K. Triandafillov and applied by M. N. Tukhachevskii as chief of the Red Army's General Staff. Tukhachevskii was one of three Soviet marshals executed between 1937 and 1939, in a purge of the army which convinced many European observers, not least the Germans, that the Red Army was not capable of maximizing its own potential. To make the connections with the innovations in operational thought pioneered by the Soviet Union in the interwar period and its triumphs in the later years of the Second World War, Evan Mawdsley puts the 1937 army purges into context. The cull was particularly severe in the highest ranks, but the majority of middle-rank commanders came through unscathed. Those who led the Red Army to victory in 1943–5 were the colonels of 1937, still young men as they entered Berlin. Zhukov, already a corps commander in 1937, was only forty-eight as the war ended, and most of the army group commanders were of a comparable age. The causes of the Russians' early and well-nigh catastrophic defeats in 1941 lie not in the purge but elsewhere. In his opening two chapters, Professor Mawdsley has produced a major re-interpretation of the interaction between Soviet and German plans and doctrines. The Red Army was committed to fighting a war offensively, but the posture of its foreign policy in 1941 was defensive, as Stalin remained determined not to provoke Germany. Moreover, it was deployed on territory newly acquired in 1939–40, and as yet poorly integrated into the defensive arrangements of the state. By committing its resources close to the frontiers, it played into German hands, creating great pockets to be encircled, and failing to exploit the inherent advantages of time and space which geography had vouchsafed Russia.

The Germans, Hitler among them, tended to blame their setbacks on the weather, as though this was something that, because it was outside their control, they could not predict. Again, Professor Mawdsley tends to be impatient of such orthodox truisms. The Russians used the weather as the backdrop to their defensive successes before Moscow in 1941–2 and at Stalingrad in 1942–3, but they also managed to sustain their advances through the winters of 1943–4 and 1944–5. In this they surprised even themselves. The fact that the war ended when it did represented a paradox: after the Normandy landings in June 1944, the Western Allies thought it would be over by the end of the year; as they launched the greatest advance of the war, Operation BAGRATION, in July, the Russians never expected to be on the doorstep of the Reich so soon.

In 1956 Stalin's successor, Nikita Khrushchev, delivered a speech in which he attacked Stalin's legacy, and in particular denigrated his war record. Judging Stalin as a war leader and military commander becomes harder as the record of human suffering inflicted through the purges, collectivization and the GULAG mounts. Moreover, he cannot escape his measure of responsibility for what happened in 1941: intelligence was misread and surprise was handed to the enemy. But by the same token, he is entitled to his share of the credit for the victory of 1945. Indeed, in 1944 he took over direct command of the Red Army in the central sector, and his erstwhile representatives at the front, Zhukov and Vasilevskii pre-eminent among them, became army group commanders. Unlike either Churchill or Roosevelt, Stalin had a hands-on role in military operations and yet maintained it without any diminution of his political authority either domestically or internationally. The liberal democracies could only achieve the same effects by co-ordination through joint organizations. It was what the Germans imagined a *Führer* would be capable of in the waging of 'total war', and yet ultimately Hitler failed. Stalin's success defied the scale of the war – indeed of modern, industrialized war as a whole.

The Second World War was not won and lost solely on the Eastern Front. Explanations of the comparative ease with which the Russians advanced in the second half of 1944 have to include the impact of the Allied landings in Europe and of strategic bombing. This was a coalition war. Germany had allies in its invasion of the Soviet Union, but by 1945 they had all been defeated and in most cases had actually thrown in their lot with the other side. The Soviet Union, by contrast, was part of an alliance, which grew progressively stronger over time and whose members fed off each other's contributions. The deep battle fought by the Red Army depended, as *Thunder in the East* stresses, on American trucks, supplied through Lend-Lease, to sustain its logistic needs.

Ultimately, in Evan Mawdsley's view, the demands of waging the war broke the Soviet Union. Its economic demands set back its growth ten years, and Russia's acquisition of territories in eastern Europe created an ongoing military burden which forestalled growth and reform in subsequent decades. Each generation has its own interpretation of the past. Self-evidently, that was not how things looked to Liddell Hart and to his contemporaries in the immediate post-war years. For them, waging war had made the Soviet Union a superpower to rival the United States and had brought Russia into the heart of Europe. Germany had tried to kill the Bolshevik viper, but in the process it had turned into a hydra. As in the First World War, war could be the midwife of revolutionary change.

Since the end of the Cold War, the war on the Eastern Front has acquired different connotations. Situated roughly in the middle of the twentieth century, it played a key role in defining that century, but for most Europeans it does now belong there. Germany is reunited and has confronted its crimes: indeed, its determination to do so is one reason why the memory of the war on the Eastern Front remains politically so important. Despite its central position in Europe, both geographically and economically, Germany resists the strategic responsibilities of its latent hegemony. Its politicians refuse to use the word 'war' to describe the deployments of today's *Bundeswehr* and in doing so reflect the mood of the German public.

For Russia, on the other hand, the memory of the 'Great Patriotic War' remains the high point of recent national history, not least because of the sense of loss which the

Cold War has bequeathed. The veterans of the Red Army enjoy a status in Russia denied those of the Wehrmacht, the justice not only of the cause for which they fought but also the manner in which they did so having become well-nigh unimpeachable. The territories which the Germans overran in 1941 were not in the main, as Evan Mawdsley points out in his conclusion, ethnically Russian. Germany's initial success was predicated, like the later stages of American strategy in the Cold War, on the fragility of the Soviet Union. The lands lost in 1941 were regained thanks to the victory of 1945, but forfeit again in 1990. The Soviet Union no longer exists. One immediate consequence of its demise was the opening of sources that were both fresh and frank, and they proved very valuable to Evan Mawdsley when he was writing the first edition of this book. That flow was not sustained after 2000. The legacy of Stalin may be fraught but that of his military triumphs matters to Putin's Russia, and to his and its sense of self-worth.

For many western Europeans, what *Thunder in the East* tells us about modern war and its lessons has also lost immediacy. In 1945, as in 1815 and 1918, the big battalions won. Those powers which could best harness the resources available to them won, and did so because they also had more men and material available to them. When viewed from this perspective, conflict is not the realm of chance but of certainty. Its outcome, at least when states embark on major war, seems so assured that an economically inferior power should never countenance using it as a tool of policy. And yet the military history of the world since 1945 shows that many powers continue to reject that logic.

They do so using methods and tools which, while not absent on the Eastern Front in 1941–5, were not centre stage. The battles fought in Russia between 1941 and 1945 were fought by industrialized societies equipped with tanks and aircraft, both of them technologies which, although still central to armed forces today, are no longer at the cutting edge of innovation in warfare. Even more significant is the fact that Europe is turning its back on the mass army. What is different about the war then and war now is less the diminished status of the tank or the manned aircraft than the decline in the numbers of those platforms deployed in national arsenals. The defining characteristic of twentieth-century warfare in Europe was that it married mass mobilization to national industrialization. States could not only form large armies, they could also equip them. The Eastern Front stands at the acme of this development, a point made all too graphically by the casualties sustained by both sides and by their civilian populations. Between 1941 and 1945, the armed forces of the Soviet Union alone suffered ten million deaths, a total equivalent to the overall military losses in the First World War for all belligerents. This is the potential of interstate war waged in the name of ideology: the fact that it may be increasingly remote from current perspectives on war, at least within Europe, is no reason to forget it.

Hew Strachan

PREFACE

Seventy years have now passed since the soldiers of Marshal Georgii Zhukov's 1st Belorussian Army Group fought their way into Berlin and raised the Red flag over the Reichstag. The Cold War with Soviet Union has come and gone; the wheel of history has made another full turn; yet May 1945 is still a crucial moment of the last century.

Before the victory, the cruel war had lasted for four years. The aim of this book is to cover the entire Nazi–Soviet conflict, not only Hitler's onslaught and the desperate Soviet struggle for survival in 1941–3, but also the huge Red Army counter-attack in 1943–5 and the destruction of the Third Reich. Achieving this within the covers of a relatively short book is a real challenge, and it is also important to do more than simply outline events. I try to answer the big questions: Why did the military conflict in the East develop as it did? Why did the Germans lose? Why did the Red Army win? Why did the Russians pay such a high price for victory?

Who is this book intended for, and why have I taken the opportunity to write a second edition? General readers interested in history will get a readable – and hopefully thoughtful – account of the largest land war ever fought. Even those who know something about military history or about the Nazi–Soviet war may learn something new, and perhaps have some assumptions challenged. For a more 'specialist' audience, I engage with what others have written about the war, and I provide references to books, articles and documents. Writing a second edition has allowed me to use the impressive body of work produced by other historians over the last decade and to guide readers towards it. On the military side, there are too many good new works to give details in this preface – see the notes and bibliography – but I would mention the extraordinary output on the Red Army by David Glantz (often written in collaboration with Jonathan House), and also the newly completed 'official' German account, most volumes of which are now available in English as *Germany and the Second World War*.[1] My overall interpretation of the Nazi–Soviet war has not changed fundamentally over the past decade, but I have certainly 'refined' my views on specific events and aspects.

The general histories of the Nazi–Soviet war, even the larger ones, have tended to look at one side or the other. This is not to say that all the historians involved were myopically pro-Germany or pro-Russia (although some of them certainly were); German civilian historians have often been preoccupied – not unreasonably – with the guilt rather than the glory of their countrymen. But in any event, Russian and German historical 'schools' unfolded, independently of one another, with an abyss of misunderstanding and wartime animosity between them that was deepened by the Cold War.

This divide is even evident in books by 'outsiders', historians based neither in Russia nor in Germany. Some outstanding books have been written by English-language historians, but individuals tend to fall more within one school than the other. To oversimplify the situation a little, the books written in English in the first two or three decades after the war were clearer on Germany, thanks to the availability of captured German documents and the flow of accounts by unemployed Wehrmacht generals.[2] Later another school arose in Britain and America which owed more to memoirs and histories produced on an industrial scale in the USSR of Khrushchev and Brezhnev.[3] In striving for a happy medium, my aims include, alongside keeping the account to a manageable length, giving each side comparable attention.

I would not push this claim too far. My expertise is in Russian history, not German. My primary sources are mainly Russian. I certainly would not pretend single-handedly to have bridged the two national schools. Nevertheless, I have tried to get to grips with the German perspective on the war, and I have found especially interesting the chance to compare this with what I know from the Russian side. Having said that, I also bring to this study of military history some useful personal intellectual baggage, including a background in the history of the Russian Civil War of 1917–20 (vital for understanding Stalin and the Red Army of 1941–5) and a grasp of the general (non-military) history of Stalinist Russia. Since writing the first edition, I have worked more broadly on the history of the Second World War, and this has helped clarify my sense of how the Russian–German campaign fits into the larger conflict and how it compares with events elsewhere.[4]

The treatment of the Eastern Front by historians is odd because, in some respects, the German 'story' has been forty or fifty years ahead of the Russian one. The Germans lost in 1945; the Nazis were totally discredited and their crimes documented for war crimes trials; Wehrmacht records became available (and some were physically moved to other countries).[5] Two or three generations of good secondary works on the 'German' war have been written from this source base, and it has been possible to create a synthesis from these accounts.[6] Moreover, there was largely a consensus about what had happened. Few serious historians in Germany did not want to damn Hitler and his senior military advisers as war leaders, or to condemn the extreme criminality of Himmler and the Nazi SS. There was a prominent debate among West German intellectuals in the late 1980s – known as the *Historikerstreit* – about whether Nazi Germany was actually any worse than Communist Russia, and whether the Germans were not themselves victims – but both sides in the debate accepted the criminality of Hitler and the Nazis.

More contentious (especially in a high Cold War context, with West Germany's vital military role in NATO) was the conduct of the German armed forces, especially on the Eastern Front. For decades, the concept of a 'clean' Wehrmacht – distinct from Hitler and the Nazi regime – held sway. In the 1980s, however, a number of history books began to document the issue of grass-roots criminality in the German Army in Russia, including occupation policy and treatment of Soviet prisoners of war (POWs). There was a controversy specifically about the armed forces in the late 1990s, when a touring museum exhibition (the *Wehrmachtsausstellung*) detailed crimes committed by German troops in Russia and elsewhere. But by the time the first edition of *Thunder in the East* was published in 2005 the consensus, at least among serious historians, was that the wartime German Army – its commanders and many of its soldiers – had been deeply complicit in 'Nazi' crimes.[7]

On the Russian side, things were different. The political system that fought the Second World War remained in power in Moscow for over four more decades, until 1991. The Soviet government did sponsor the publication of a flood of histories and memoirs about the war.[8] But it also tightly controlled information about an event that was both a legitimization of Communist rule and a national tragedy. Unlike the post-war German view of Hitler, there was (and still is) a great ambivalence in Russia about Stalin and his role in the war.[9] The Red Army had driven out the Nazi invaders and won the Second World War, but the country was still seen to be surrounded by enemies. The 1939 Nazi–Soviet Pact was not mentioned, and the Soviet annexation of territories in the West in 1939–40 (the Baltic states, eastern Poland and Moldavia) was, until the 1980s, an irreversible liberation.

The powerful Soviet military establishment was jealous of its reputation and that of its veteran leaders. The opening months of the war in 1941 had been catastrophic. Stalin and his army and air force were caught by surprise, and the early defeats were followed by mass surrenders of Red Army troops and the German occupation of vast territories. These events were used by Khrushchev in the 1950s in his 'de-Stalinization' campaign, but after he fell from power in 1964, they were largely ignored. Only triumphal advances by the Red Army were discussed – and to be sure there had been plenty of those in 1943–5 – but setbacks and stalemates were 'forgotten battles' (to use the apt term of the historian David Glantz).[10] The huge losses suffered by the Red Army throughout the war were neither enumerated nor explained. The harsh disciplinary structures – the punitive units and 'blocking detachments' – were not mentioned, nor the large number of Soviet citizens who collaborated with the occupiers. The criminal behaviour of some Soviet troops in Eastern Europe and Germany in 1944–5 – including looting and mass rape – was also forgotten.

Still, much of value was produced in the USSR after the mid-1950s. Historical enterprise did, moreover, change drastically in the 1980s and early 1990s, first with the Gorbachev policy of *glasnost'* (openness) in about 1987 and then with the end of Communist rule in 1991. Many of the taboo subjects relating to the war were now open to discussion. One reason I undertook the first edition of *Thunder in the East* was the availability of this hitherto unavailable Russian material.

These 'new' Russian-published primary sources are detailed in the notes and bibliography. Especially important for the first edition, and not used in previous general works, were the twenty-five or so large volumes of military documents published in the late 1990s and the early 2000s in the series *Velikaia Otechestvennaia* [The Great Fatherland (War)].[11] These allowed the historian to compare the intentions of Soviet military operations with their outcomes, and to obtain a more objective view of how Stalin and the Soviet high command judged the performance of their forces. Another important source from this period was a remarkable set of documents relating to the eve of the war and the first months of the fighting, *1941 god* [The Year 1941].[12] This was especially informative on the vital but poorly understood question of the Red Army's pre-war plans. Many other documents were made available in printed collections. Published documents are not as good as the real thing. As one wise historian of the Cold War has pointed out, with reference to documents which modern states make available, 'there is no such thing as an historical free lunch'.[13] Nevertheless, what was made available genuinely allowed us to know much more about Soviet operations than we used to.

Less censored military memoirs were also printed in Russia in the 1980s and 1990s, and these had not been available for earlier histories. The 1990 edition of Marshal Zhukov's memoirs was especially valuable, as were a number of posthumously published interviews with him; Zhukov was Stalin's military deputy and the outstanding field commander of the Second World War.[14] Also now available were diaries and memoirs of civilian war leaders with access to Stalin, notably Khrushchev, Molotov and Mikoian (all Politburo members), Dimitrov (head of the Comintern) and Malyshev (People's Commissar of the Tank Industry).[15]

A wide range of topics were dealt with in individual books and in the Russian history journals. In trying to get an overview of the war as a whole, I made particular use of a new four-volume Russian official history, *Velikaia Otechestvennaia voina, 1941–1945: Voenno-istoricheskie ocherki* [The Great Patriotic War, 1941–1945: Military-Historical Essays], published by the Ministry of Defence and the Academy of Sciences of the Russian Federation in 1998–9, under the editorship of V. A. Zolotarev, G. N. Sevast'ianov and others. Also important was the statistical information on Red Army losses and strengths published under the editorship of Professor G. F. Krivosheev, and the 'order of battle' material edited by A. N. Grylev.[16]

The 1990s were indeed a rich period for historical writing in the Russian Federation about the war, but since about 2000 the situation has been less good. Post-Soviet governments in Moscow, like their USSR predecessor, have used Russian nationalism and the memory of the 'Great Patriotic War' as a means of political legitimization. The military establishment, weakened and embattled even in the new century, has increased its guard over access to documents and publication programmes. But even in the last ten years, some new material has appeared in mainstream sources, and – alongside some sensationalist nonsense – there has been interesting work on aspects of the war written by Russian historical 'outsiders'.[17]

Meanwhile, in Germany over the past decade, there has been less controversy than in the 1980s and 1990s, and the dominant interpretation of the history of the war has not changed. The completion of the official history, *Germany and the Second World War*, has already been mentioned. On the operational side, vol. 8 deals in depth with the Wehrmacht's campaigns of 1943–4, while the first part of vol. 10 covers the final battles in Eastern Europe and Germany (both volumes were published in 2008, but neither has yet been translated). Vol. 9 (published in 2004 and available in English since 2008) is important for non-operational aspects like the social structure and ideology of the German Army, occupation policy and treatment of POWs.

* * *

For the sake of clarity, the structure of this book is broadly chronological, and 'campaign history' is the meat of nine of the thirteen chapters. The book is, however, split into two parts, each of which begins with two introductory chapters. The logic of this is that the first half is largely about Soviet defeats and German victories, but it is also about a period when the struggle was based on the military, political and economic situation that was in place in June 1941. The second half is about the years of Soviet victory, but it begins (in Chapters 7 and 8) by looking at *wartime* 'internal' developments in the USSR and Germany, mostly from 1942 to 1943 onwards. In several other places I found it best to stray from a straight chronological narrative. Chapter 4 is essentially about the clash of armies from October to December 1941, but it is here that I also deal with the Holocaust in Russia and the fate of the Soviet POWs (from 1941 to as late as 1995); both topics relate most closely to these last months of 1941. And the two chapters near the end of the book cover the last twelve months of the war on geographical rather than chronological lines. Chapter 12 is about operations on the territories of the East European states which were satellites or victims of Hitler. Chapter 13 is about fighting in the core Reich, the land of the ethnic Germans. My argument for doing this is that the Soviet 'liberation' of Eastern Europe involved a different set of problems than the smashing of Nazi power in the ethnic German lands, what Stalin called 'killing the Fascist beast in its own den'. I think this odd approach works, but one result is that the capture of Prague, which took place on 9 May 1945, comes in the book before the first Soviet raid into East Prussia in August 1944.

There is no preoccupation here with battles, armies and weapons for their own sake. I am not a military professional with a vocational interest in considering any 'lessons' that the events of 1941–5 might have for future wars. Nevertheless, if this book has heroes and villains, successes and failures, they are the planners and senior commanders. There are a number of books about the experience of small units and of individual German or Soviet soldiers in their foxholes, but that subject is not a practical option for a work that tries to give a bird's-eye view of an immense war.[18] However, morale and motivation relating both to military effectiveness and to war crimes are important elements for this book, and much continues to be written about them.[19]

Military historians – both official and unofficial – often overlook the overall human cost of war. We now know much more about casualties on both the Soviet and the German sides, and this question is dealt with throughout the book.[20] War crimes, perpetrated both by Nazi organizations and the Wehrmacht, were a central rather than a peripheral feature of Hitler's war in Russia. The barbaric treatment of enemy POWs is an issue that a few German historians have confronted and the Russians are beginning to consider. The 'home front' is also important, both for war production and for political developments, but treating that fully would have demanded a much longer and very different book. The diplomacy of the war is sketched in only as far as is necessary. My argument would be that after November 1940, at the latest, diplomats had little part to play in the Nazi–Soviet confrontation. They had rather more work to do in smoothing the edgy relations between allies.

* * *

The terms 'Russia', 'Russian', 'USSR' and 'Soviet' are all used, and pretty much interchangeably. This usage has its pitfalls. In particular, 'Russia', as employed here, sometimes includes the territory not just of the post-1991 Russian Federation but also that of the new states of Ukraine and Belarus and, indeed, the entire 'space' of the state formerly known as the Union of Soviet Socialist Republics. Likewise, the word 'Russian' is inaccurate for that half of the population of the USSR whose first language was not Russian. At the same time, the word 'Soviet' has its uses, even though it has been obsolete for twenty-five years; it gets around this ethnic complexity.

On the other side of the battle line, I have often used the term 'German' as a shorthand for all the Axis forces fighting in Russia. It is not intended by this to minimize the involvement of the numerous Finnish, Romanian, Hungarian, Italian, Slovak and Croat forces, not to mention the very large crowd of 'volunteers' from among the population of the occupied USSR. It has been estimated that even in the first phase of the war, non-German troops made up a quarter of the forces deployed against the Red Army.[21]

Russian-language versions of place names are used for locations within the Soviet borders as of 22 June 1941 (L'vov rather than the Ukrainian L'viv or the Polish Lwów). Similarly, I have used contemporary German names for places within the borders of the Third Reich on 1 September 1939 but non-German names for places beyond those borders (so Breslau rather than Wrocław, but Poznań rather than Posen). I realize that all this is arbitrary and will probably cause offence to someone; I continue to apologize. Where clarity is required, I have put in two versions of place names. The Cyrillic alphabet is transliterated rigorously into our Latin alphabet using the standard American Library of Congress system; there are a handful of exceptions (e.g. Moscow rather than Moskva, Beria rather than Beriia, Yak aircraft rather than Iak).

Not all readers will be familiar with the language of mid-twentieth-century war. Many military writers now make a distinction between 'grand strategy' and the lower level of 'military strategy'. The important concept of 'operational art' is used to describe a level of war below military strategy but above the 'tactics' of the battlefield. As General Svechin, one of Russia's most important military thinkers put it, 'Tactics takes the steps that make up an operational leap, and strategy points the way.' This book might be called in German 'ein operativer Überblick' (an operational-level overview), to repeat the subtitle of an earlier work.[22] To give a relevant example of these different levels, many historians would argue that in 1941, Hitler's Germany had a very poor grand strategy, and a military strategy that was almost as bad; it had armed forces that excelled, however, at the 'operational' and tactical level. Hitler's Wehrmacht was good at fighting battles but not at winning wars.

The Russian word *front* is translated here as 'army group'. For some historians, rank titles such as *General der Panzertruppen*, and so on, roll off the tongue, but I will not differentiate between gradations and flavours of general officer on either side – except when the distinction has some special meaning. There are also technical differences between an *Oberbefehlshaber* and a *Befehlshaber* and a *glavnokomanduiushchii* and a *komanduiushchii* that I will not burden the reader with. I have generally used the abbreviation 'C-in-C' (commander-in-chief) for the head of the armed services or a branch of service and have called everyone else a 'commander'. I follow the Russian practice of using simple Arabic ordinal numbers for all levels of military formations and units (the 37th Army, the 48th Corps, the 51st Division, rather than the Thirty-Seventh Army, the XXXXVIII Corps, the 51st Division, which is often found in Western military usage). The simpler version makes sense where there were on the Soviet side so many army-level formations, and where on the German side corps numbers were very high. (More details of military and political terminology are provided in the Glossary.) On the diplomatic and political side, the word 'Allies' (with a capital) is applied to all the partners in the anti-Nazi alliance. Some Cold War accounts take 'Allies' to mean just the 'Western' Allies and leave out the big eastern one. Occasionally, I refer to the British and Americans as the 'Western Allies'. To avoid confusion, Germany's 'allies' (Finland, Romania, etc.) are referred to without the capital letter.

* * *

Authors owe many debts. Colleagues have provided formal and informal advice, and I am particularly grateful to Hew Strachan for proposing the subject of the Nazi–Soviet war to me 'way back when'. Jürgen Förster, Bruce Menning, Geoff Roberts and the late John Erickson, each an outstanding expert on the wartime period, provided inspiration, encouragement and background advice for the original project. For the second edition, I have had repeated useful discussions with Alex Marshall, Phillips O'Brien and Ben H. Shepherd. John Ferris was especially helpful with intelligence matters, and Ilya Grinberg with Lend-Lease and aviation. The University of Glasgow library has few rivals in the UK for its holdings in Russian History and War Studies; the library staff, especially Tania Konn-Roberts, excelled at providing resources. For the second edition, I have made extensive use of the National Library of Scotland. As well as its superb general holdings, the NLS now includes the John and Ljubica Erickson Collection. The patience and support of my editors at Hodder Arnold and later Bloomsbury have sustained work on the two editions. I am especially grateful for the generosity of the British funding body, the Arts and Humanities Research Board, which made possible two periods of extended research leave from my university while working on the first edition.

PART I
THE NAZI ONSLAUGHT, 1941–2

CHAPTER 1
HITLER'S WAR

The annihilation of that state under present conditions would mean one fewer bourgeois fascist state to contend with! What would be the harm if as a result of the rout of Poland we were to extend the socialist system onto new territories and populations?

Joseph Stalin, 7 September 1939

We have a war of annihilation on our hands.

Adolf Hitler, 30 March 1941

The German–Soviet campaign opened with terrible defeats for the Red Army but with victories for the Wehrmacht that were less than decisive. This is one of the most controversial episodes in the whole history of the Second World War. Why did Hitler attack the USSR? Why was Stalin caught by surprise, and what effect did this have? Making sense of all this requires looking at the historical situation on the eve of the invasion. The more general features are dealt with here and the specifically military ones in the chapter that follows. Of the general points, the first would be that the invasion was planned and carried out on the initiative of Adolf Hitler, and that it was a project over which he had a remarkable degree of control. The professional leadership of the German armed forces also enthusiastically supported it. Second, the German invasion was not just a huge military operation. It had, from its conception, a character that was both imperialistic and ruthlessly ideological. Third, the Germans were able in 1941 to devote most of their army and air force to the invasion; this concentration was made easier, and the initial Soviet defeats made worse, by the Kremlin's diplomatic blunders in 1939, 1940 and 1941.

HITLER DECIDES ON WAR WITH RUSSIA

Hitler and the German high command

In September 1939 Hitler had not wanted war with a major power; in June 1941 he did. Planning for an invasion of Russia began in the German high command soon after the fall of France in June 1940. The results of the staff studies were outlined in Hitler's Directive No. 21 of 18 December 1940. In that month, Hitler personally chose the operation's code name, recalling Friedrich I 'Barbarossa' ('Red Beard'), the twelfth-century Holy Roman Emperor who had campaigned in the East. The Führer's grandiose and pathologically misconceived strategic ideas were remarkable enough. More striking still was how little resistance they met among military and civilian leaders in Berlin.

Hitler's regime was based on the irrational and on his personal power. Neither before the war, nor during it, did Germany have state structures suited to rational military planning at the strategic level. There was nothing like the British War Cabinet or even the Russian wartime State Defence Committee (GKO). A short-lived defence council was set up at the end of 1939 under Hermann Goering, the second most important person in the Nazi state and C-in-C of the Luftwaffe, but this body had restricted powers and seldom met. By definition, the Führer was central to the decision-making process, and his power could not be shared. Hitler had a powerful personality and the ability to browbeat even senior generals; he also had a prodigious memory for technical and military-economic detail. He dominated the German military establishment, both formally and in reality. He had been 'Supreme C-in-C' of the German armed forces since the death of President Hindenburg in August 1934; by decree he had also combined the posts of president and prime minister, and became *Führer* (Leader) of the German Reich. Hitler took the most direct interest in war preparations and strategy. During the campaigns of 1939–40 in Poland and France, he left the capital for a headquarters train. This was a pattern he would repeat in 1941, with the establishment of his Russian campaign headquarters at Rastenburg (now Kętrzyn) in East Prussia.[1]

FIGURE 1 Hitler talks with Ion Antonescu, the Romanian dictator. Behind Hitler's right shoulder is Field Marshal Wilhelm Keitel; to Hitler's left (with spectacles) is General Franz Halder.

On the surface, the armed services of Nazi Germany were organized along more rational lines than those of any of the other powers. The Army, the Navy and the Air Force (Luftwaffe) together formed the 'Armed Forces' or the Wehrmacht. Soldiers, sailors and airmen were subordinate to a tri-service headquarters, the Armed Forces High Command or OKW (*Oberkommando der Wehrmacht*). Early in 1938 Hitler's position with respect to the armed forces was strengthened by the fall, on the grounds of real or contrived personal scandal, of Generals Blomberg and Fritsch. Fritsch had been the C-in-C of the Army since February 1934. Blomberg had been the operational C-in-C of the Armed Forces (Wehrmacht); when he resigned, Hitler himself took his place. In August 1938, General Beck, chief of the Army General Staff, resigned; he had been the third key member of the command triumvirate. Beck quit over Nazi encroachments on Czechoslovakia; he (rightly) thought they would lead to a European war which Germany could not win. The officer corps did not rally around their three generals, and Hitler found others eager to work under him. Hitler's chief of staff within the OKW was General Wilhelm Keitel, whom he inherited from Blomberg. The other key member of the OKW was General Alfred Jodl, eight years younger than Keitel, who would be wartime head of the OKW Operations Department. Keitel and Jodl stayed at Hitler's side to the end.[2] They were among the main defendants at the 1946 Nuremberg Trial. Both men were hanged.

Even without the toxic effects of Hitler's leadership, there were massive structural problems in the Wehrmacht. The army was much the largest service in terms of personnel, equipment and experience. The Wehrmacht High Command lacked an effective planning organization and had to rely for much of its preparatory work on the Army General Staff. The OKW initially concerned itself with broad strategy, but it came to have a leading role at the operational level from the time of the German invasion of Norway – a genuine tri-service operation – in early 1940. By the summer of 1941, a situation had evolved in which the OKW was taking control over Nazi Germany's western and southern fronts, leaving to the Army High Command (*Oberkommando des Heeres* or OKH) control over the eastern one.

General Walther von Brauchitsch replaced Fritsch as Army C-in-C in February 1938.[3] Hitler himself would replace Brauchitsch during the crisis in front of Moscow in December 1941. Within the army, the General Staff occupied a particularly important place, as it had since the Prussian wars of the mid-nineteenth century. This organization was led from 1938 to late 1942, by General Franz Halder, Beck's replacement.[4] Halder would leave the General Staff, on the eve of the Stalingrad disaster, in September 1942. He had connections to the anti-Nazi generals and ended the war in Dachau concentration camp; this saved him from post-war prosecution, and he went on to produce some influential writings. In truth, the Chief of the Army General Staff had been an unreserved supporter of military aggression against Poland in 1939 and a leading advocate of Operation BARBAROSSA, the invasion of Russia. Beyond his moral responsibility, Halder must bear much of the blame for three of the strategic shortcomings of the campaign in Russia: (1) for the faulty overall concept; (2) for the continued prosecution of the campaign in late 1941 (when it should have been clear that the Wehrmacht was overextended in front of Moscow); and (3) for the over-optimistic 'second campaign' in south Russia in 1942. Halder's dismissal in 1942 came from personal difficulties with Hitler, not from disagreement over basic strategy. The Luftwaffe, meanwhile, although nominally subordinate to the OKW, was led by a powerful Nazi politician in the bulky form of Hermann Goering, who was not about to subordinate himself or his air force to the Prussian aristocrats of the German Army.

German grand strategy

This rickety command structure gave Hitler room to make fatal strategic mistakes. His early initiatives were relatively limited and fitted within the context of German nationalism. For many Germans, the remilitarization of the Rhineland, the annexation of Austria, the occupation of the Sudetenland in Czechoslovakia and the demand for the Polish 'Danzig corridor' were intended to right the wrongs of the 1919 Versailles Treaty settlement, after Germany's defeat in the First World War. Hitler's actions led to wars which the Wehrmacht won, against Poland and France. By the late summer of 1940, thanks to these victories, thanks to his own prestige and thanks to the subordination of the generals, Hitler had a freer hand to make decisions and take action; he now thought that he could attempt something even more daring.

Hitler had a number of reasons for deciding to invade the Soviet Union, some of which were shared by his military advisers. One objective was political, the destruction of 'Jewish Bolshevism'. As a goal, it was originally as fantastic as the Soviet Communist Party's goal of bringing about a socialist Europe – or indeed the American goal of making the world 'safe for democracy'. The apparent feasibility of this project changed, however, with the sudden achievement of Nazi military domination over western continental Europe following the fall of France in the summer of 1940.

The political destruction of 'Bolshevism' was more plausible, because strategic and diplomatic objectives of a more conventional type could be dovetailed with it. It was these conventional aspects that Hitler cited in his fullest attempt at self-justification, included in his *Testament* of early 1945:

> We no longer had any hope of ending the war in the West with an invasion of the British Isles. That ... country would balk at the recognition of our leading role and at making an honourable peace as long as there remained undefeated one European power that was inherently hostile to the Reich. The war would have gone on forever; a war in which the Americans in the background would have taken an increasingly large role. The weight of the human and material potential of the USA, the development of military technology ... the threatening proximity of the British coast, all this compelled us to try with all means to avoid a prolonged war. Time – always time! – would increasingly work against us. The only way to force the English to make peace was to take away their hopes of confronting us on the Continent with a comparable opponent through the annihilation of the Red Army. For us there remained no other choice but to strike the Russia factor out of the European equation.[5]

Hitler's thinking – thinking shared by key military leaders – was that the defeat of Russia would make London see reason.

This roundabout route to the defeat or neutralization of the British Empire was all the more attractive to Hitler because it also fitted in with other military objectives. The German Führer envisaged eventual war with the United States. To compete on this global scale, to win such a conflict, Nazi Germany needed a European, continental, empire. Hitler's famous concept of *Lebensraum* ('living space' for the German people) is confused with Nazi ideologues' dreams of the colonization of Russia by Germanic soldier-farmers. Of much more immediate importance to the German military and economic elites was direct access to the food and mineral resources of Russia, the Ukraine and the Caucasus. For these elites, as for Hitler, autarky (self-sufficiency) was a rational strategy, and one all the more necessary in light of what had happened to Germany in the First World War and in the Great Depression. In the first case, landlocked Germany's lack of access to minerals and foodstuffs had led to military defeat; in the second, it had led to unemployment and poverty. This view was not incorrect; Hitler's failure in late 1941 to successfully establish an autarkic 'empire' in eastern Europe – due to the partial failure of Operation BARBAROSSA – would turn out to be of crucial importance when Germany's ultimate rival, the United States, did enter the Second World War in December 1941. In terms of this grand strategy, invading Russia was not *the* fatal mistake of Nazi Germany. After all, what was Hitler's alternative? *Not* to invade Russia? Inaction would have allowed Germany's enemies to become stronger and would have left Germany economically dependent on Russia. The lethal mistake had been made earlier, when Hitler's adventures in Czechoslovakia and Poland led Germany into a general war.

Hitler's Russian adventure was not a preventative war, although Hitler also claimed this in his 1945 *Testament*: 'There was a second compelling reason, which would have been enough on its own: that from the very existence of Bolshevism there was a threatening danger. From this side one day must inevitably come an attack.' Three years before, early on the morning of 22 June 1941, the note handed to Foreign Commissar Molotov by Germany's ambassador had given the same grounds: German action was justified by the 'steadily growing concentration of all available Russian forces on a long front from the Baltic to the Black Sea'. This note charged that 'reports received in the last few days eliminated the last remaining doubts as to the aggressive character of this Russian concentration and completed the picture of an extremely tense military situation'. Later in the day, in a radio message to the German *Volk*, Hitler spoke of a build-up of 160 Russian divisions on 'our border' and described the Axis task as the 'defence of the European continent'. The accusations continued right through the war. Goebbels, in one of his 'Total War' speeches after the Battle of Stalingrad, would declare that for Germany in June 1941, 'it was two minutes before twelve!'[6]

The Nazi arguments were repeated by the Russian émigré writer Rezun-Suvorov in the late 1980s and incorporated into the arguments of German right-wing writers.[7] This extreme 'revisionist' historical argument has two distinct sides to it. One is that the USSR was planning offensive operations against Germany, the other is that the German attack was therefore pre-emptive and, at its heart, defensive. A discussion of the first part requires a closer look of Soviet military and political preparations (see Chapter 2). The second part, however, can readily be dismissed right here. Germany did not invade Russia because its leaders knew about, or feared, an imminent Soviet onslaught. Goebbels summed up the perception of the top Nazi leaders in a diary entry of early May 1941: 'Stalin and his people remain completely inactive. Like a rabbit confronted by a snake.'[8] The Nazis had other reasons for the attack on Russia.

The German military seemed to provide an 'operational' means to achieve Hitler's grand political, strategic and economic dreams. (The distinction between 'operational' and 'strategic' is discussed in the Preface; basically, the idea was that the Wehrmacht could quickly win decisive battles that would determine the overall outcome of the struggle.) From the late-nineteenth-century German Imperial tradition of strategic thought, from Prussian leaders and thinkers such as Moltke and Schlieffen, came the concept of the 'battle of annihilation' (*Vernichtungsschlacht*). This meant a decisive battle of rapid destruction aimed at the flanks and rear of the enemy; it was contrasted with a prolonged war of attrition. The June 1941 invasion of Russia was another 'battle of annihilation', aimed this time against Red Army forces concentrated in the western part of European Russia.[9] The BARBAROSSA directive of December 1940 began with the statement that 'the German Armed Forces must be prepared . . . to overthrow Soviet Russia in a rapid campaign'.[10] Hitler and the generals believed that the Red Army was concentrated west of the line of the Dvina and Dnepr rivers.

Under the heading 'General Intention', the BARBAROSSA directive stated that 'the bulk of the Russian Army stationed in Western Russia will be destroyed by daring operations led by deeply penetrating armoured spearheads. Russian forces still capable of giving battle will be prevented from withdrawing into the depths of Russia.' Unlike the previous German operations in France in 1940, BARBAROSSA was planned from the start as a short campaign; outsiders called it a *Blitzkrieg*, a lightning war. Germany needed a quick victory because her population and resources were limited; she could not fight on two fronts.

In any event, according to the BARBAROSSA directive, the battle of annihilation was to be followed by an easy pursuit of shattered remnants of the Red Army far to the east of Moscow. The target line was to run from the northern port of Arkhangel'sk and down the long Volga River to the port of Astrakhan at the mouth of that river, on the Caspian Sea. The December 1940 BARBAROSSA directive appeared in Hitler's name, but the overall concept, a summer–autumn campaign whose objective was the destruction of the mass of the Red Army in the western borderlands, dated back to the very first project for the attack developed within the German Army in June 1940; this had been commissioned by Halder and drafted by General Erich Marcks. The concept was further worked on from early September 1940 by a clever staff officer named General Friedrich Paulus. Two years later, at Stalingrad, Paulus would himself become a famous victim of the war he helped plan.[11]

THE NAZI WAR OF ANNIHILATION

With its panzer divisions and Stuka dive-bombers, its pace and daring operations, the Wehrmacht attack on Russia looked very similar to the military campaign in France and the Low Countries in 1940. In both its aims and conduct, however, Operation BARBAROSSA was very different. The aims of the invader partly explained the nature of the war. Hitler planned it as a 'total' struggle to occupy all of European Russia. He intended nothing less than the extinction of the USSR/Russia as a state. Although the Führer had grandiose long-term plans for using Russia's territory, the actual military campaign was supposed to be very short. Within a few months, victory was to have given the Reich the potential to do whatever it wanted in the vast Russian expanse from the old western border to the Arkhangel'sk–Volga–Astrakhan line.

The character of the occupation was set out in the spring of 1941, side by side with the military preparations.[12] First of all, the treatment of defeated Russia was planned by Hitler and the highest civilian and military authorities in the Third Reich to involve ruthless economic exploitation. The objectives of BARBAROSSA were genuinely imperialistic, more so than Lenin could have imagined back in 1916 when he wrote *Imperialism: The Highest Stage of Capitalism*. Although the campaign also had important diplomatic purposes, the object was not just to stun the USSR in order to bring about a settlement with Britain. Europe's rulers had for centuries been seizing one province or another at the expense of their neighbours; Hitler's aims went far beyond that. Adam Tooze aptly described the invasion as 'the last great land grab in the long and bloody history of European colonialism'.[13]

From the outset, it was planned that conquered Russia would provide food and other raw materials to give Germany autarky (self-sufficiency). The Third Reich would then have a 'large-scale economy' (*Grossraumswirtschaft*) as vast as the economic systems of the United States and the colonial great powers. Hitler had never made any secret of *Lebensraum*, of his vision of the Ukrainian 'breadbasket' as an economic panacea for Germany. He echoed here traditional ideas of the German nationalist Right. In the months before the invasion on 22 June 1941, elaborate projects for the economic exploitation of Russian territory and the Russian people were put forward, and overall responsibility was given to Goering as head of the Nazi 'Four-Year Plan' administration.[14] The short-term proposals envisaged a German Army of several million strong living off the land in Russia and the export to the German Reich of 8–10 million tons of grain a year. This exploitation would be at the expense of the population in the conquered territories where, with extraordinary callousness, the Reich authorities expected mass starvation. This ruthless and pre-planned policy of looting ruled out, in advance, any genuine 'collaboration' on the part of the Soviet population.

Imperialism in practice means not only economic exploitation but the oppression of some ethnic groups by others. The Nazi plan for Russia centred on the subjugation of an 'inferior race', the Slavs. In the autumn of 1941, enthusiastic planners in Heinrich Himmler's SS would draw up a *Generalplan Ost* (General Plan for the East), which envisaged the deportation over the course of several decades of thirty-one million people, mostly Slavs, to Asiatic Russia. Even in the immediate campaign and its aftermath, however, the population of Russia were to be treated as slaves, their leaders wiped out.[15]

The German 'project' of economic and ethnic exploitation was independent of the political system existing in Russia in 1941. The territory to be taken could have been Coptic Christian rather than Communist. Nevertheless, it was still most important that the 'Jewish-Bolshevik' system in Russia was seen as the fundamental enemy of Nazism. The Soviet system could not be allowed to survive, the war was also one against this insidious force, and there could be no negotiated peace. This was the most immediate 'political' task of the invaders and the one that involved the planning of criminal acts. Numerous planning documents demonstrated the complicity of the 'conventional' German armed forces. On 30 March 1941, at a conference of high-ranking military officers, Hitler laid out the German position. Halder, the Chief of the Army General Staff, transcribed it in his notes:

> Bolshevism is antisocial criminality. ... The Communist has never been a comrade and will never be a comrade. We have a war of annihilation [*Vernichtungskrieg*] on our hands. If we do not conceive of it as such, we shall indeed defeat the enemy, but in thirty years the Communist foe will face us again. We are not going to wage war to preserve the enemy. ... Commissars and GPU [secret police] officials are criminals and must be treated as such.[16]

The army planners thought in terms of a 'battle of annihilation' (*Vernichtungsschlacht*), a decisive military battle. Hitler now spoke of a '*war* of annihilation', a concept with the most sinister implications.

The radical political arm of the Third Reich, Himmler's SS organization, was also brought into the planning. Detachments of the SS were to operate behind the German Army as they had in Poland, subduing resistance and implementing racist policies. Verbal instructions were given to murder Communists, Jews and other 'radical elements' found on Soviet territory. As the plans for military invasion began to take shape, the Nazis also came to see the conquest and occupation of the Soviet Union as a way to resolve the whole European Jewish 'problem'.[17] Russia would be the final destination for the Jews of western and central Europe, especially those who in 1940–1 were being held in limbo in Nazi-occupied Poland. The Jews were to be deported further east and worked to death. This vile project was not, however, the main reason for Hitler's invasion of Russia, and in the end the path to a 'territorial solution' of the Jewish 'problem' would be blocked by the Red Army. The Nazis turned to another type of 'final solution' for Europe's Jews in 1942–4.

From the start, the Nazis planned to kill not just the Jews living in the USSR but also officials of the Soviet state and the Communist Party (who were expected often to be Jews). 'Special tasks' were to be undertaken by the SS within the Wehrmacht's operational zone. Hitler evidently issued no specific written directives, although he undoubtedly inspired many of his underlings' orders. The SS took charge of the detailed planning of the occupation regime.

Hitler gave no thought to positive political warfare. He did not try to 'win the hearts and minds' of even *part* of the population of the USSR by mounting a political attack on Stalinism or by rallying the ethnic minorities like the Baltic peoples or the Ukrainians against ethnic Russian domination. The German planners never made clear what the post-conquest political structure of the territory of the former Soviet Union would be. Hitler was reluctant to commit himself. Alfred Rosenberg was initially the most 'sensible' of the senior Nazis about winning over the population, at least outside the ethnic Russian core. He was the Baltic German and racial theorist whom Hitler would put in overall charge of the political administration of the East. But his political influence was limited, and even he had no plan for winning over the ethnic Russian majority. The Germany of Kaiser Wilhelm II had followed an astute policy of creating vassal states in the East in 1918, after the Peace of Brest-Litovsk with Bolshevik Russia; nothing like this was considered by the Germany of Hitler.

The commanders of the Wehrmacht were extensively briefed in the months before the invasion on the nature of the campaign, which was to include measures for the economic exploitation of the population and for the murder of political opponents. Some German commanders had complained about atrocities in Poland in 1939–40, but there was little of that now. Field Marshal Keitel's 'jurisdiction decree' was issued on 13 May 1941, six weeks before the invasion. Drafted by the legal branch of the OKW, it permitted the harsh German treatment of hostile civilians outside normal military law. It also allowed group reprisals against the population of the occupied territory even on suspicion of guerrilla activity. Even more radical in legal terms was the later notorious 'Commissar Order' of 6 June 1941, which ordered that captured Red Army political officers should be shot out of hand. This order was actually instigated by the German Army High Command.[18]

The expected nature of the Russian campaign played a decisive part in all this. The barbaric plans of the invaders came from the expectation *not* of a persistent Soviet military resistance, but of an easy German victory. The brutal and exploitative occupation regime planned before 22 June would be made worse by the bloodlust of the actual fighting, with atrocities on both sides and with the Soviet government's declaration of its own war of ideology. But before a shot was fired in Russia, the German onslaught was planned – both at the front and the rear – to be the cruellest military campaign ever fought.

STALIN'S WORLD

Stalin and the Soviet high command

On 22 June 1941, most of the army and air force of the Third Reich were massed against the USSR. This was one of the few times in the Second World War when one of the combatants would have such an advantage. It was of crucial importance to the initial German success. Russia's dismal isolated situation came from successive and successful acts of Nazi aggression, but serious mistakes by the leaders in the Kremlin also played a crucial part.

The Russian blunders were of a different order from those of the Germans. Hitler had thrown himself into foolhardy ventures of aggression in September 1939 and was doing so again in June 1941. Stalin's mistake was not to pursue a policy which would effectively deter such aggression. But the USSR was in no way a 'normal' state, and Moscow and Berlin had fateful similarities. Supreme authority was concentrated in the hands of a dictator.[19] Foreign policy was highly ideological. Structures for co-ordinating the activities of different agencies and for fully rational decision-making did not exist. Joseph Stalin had consolidated sole power since the defeat of his major rivals within the Communist Party in 1929–30 and the purge of tens of thousands of senior officials (and hundreds of thousands of ordinary people) in 1937–8. Among those murdered in the late 1930s were the more independently minded Soviet military commanders and diplomats. By 1939–41 fundamental issues of foreign and security policy were decided arbitrarily, not even by the party Politburo but only by Stalin and selected members of the Politburo. Especially important was premier and foreign minister, V. M. Molotov, described as 'one of the most inexorably stupid men to hold the foreign ministership of any major power this century'.[20] Stalin and Molotov were both ignorant of the outside world and, remarkably, they had little understanding of Hitler's National Socialism. As in Germany, the country's elite accepted, through conviction or fear, the radical programmes of the ruling dictator.

The USSR and the great powers

Soviet policy, like that of Germany, can be split into two parts: relations with the great powers and relations with smaller neighbours. Relations with the great powers take in the Kremlin's overall orientation. Here, historians continue to argue. Was Stalin's policy driven by ideology or *Realpolitik* (power politics)? Was Nazi Germany the only rogue power in pre-war Europe? Terms like 'revolutionary-imperial paradigm', 'revolutionary patriotism' and 'national Bolshevism' have been coined to sum up the paradoxes.[21]

Stalin's approach to foreign policy was based on that of Lenin, the founding father of the Russian Communist state, who had died fifteen years before 1939, in 1924. Lenin had created the Communist International (the Comintern) in 1919, with the aim of bringing about a European revolution. It is doubtful, however, if in the 1930s the Soviet leaders worked in any practical way towards this aim or if they expected sudden results – in the way that Hitler did. Nevertheless, Stalin's ideology and mindset involved a fundamental divide between 'socialism' and 'imperialism', from which came his core concept of the 'two camps'.[22] Moscow felt under threat, not only from Germany but from all the other 'capitalist' powers. In this mindset, Soviet Russia (like Nazi Germany) could have no permanent friends, and the country had ultimately to rely on its own resources. Diplomatic co-operation with Britain and France in 1934–9, diplomatic co-operation with Nazi Germany in 1939–41 – and military co-operation with Britain and America in 1941–5 – were temporary expedients.

The Munich crisis in the autumn of 1938 was a missed opportunity for joint action by Russia, Britain and France against Hitler. How ready the USSR was to take an active part in a coalition war against Germany in 1938 is still debated.[23] The USSR was ignored during the Munich negotiations between Germany, Britain, France and Italy. In the end, the British and French governments gave way to Hitler's pressure and effectively surrendered part of Czechoslovakia. They did not call on Soviet support. They distrusted the Communist government and doubted the Red Army's fighting value; Stalin's army purges of 1937–8 had greatly reduced Russia's value as a military ally.

Meanwhile, what has been aptly called Stalin's 'isolationist concept of security', coupled with the tactical cynicism of a totalitarian state – where alliances could be reversed overnight – lay behind the infamous August 1939 Nazi–Soviet Pact.[24] In the summer of 1939, after Munich, the British and French only discussed military co-operation with the USSR in a listless fashion. From the Russian point of view, Munich showed the British and French to be only too willing to do a deal with Hitler. Soviet writers made much of an impending 'second Munich', where the British and French would make further concessions – at the expense of Russia. Stalin did not, however, *have* to accept the offer put to him by Hitler's foreign minister, Ribbentrop, in August 1939: a non-aggression pact and the division of eastern Europe into German and Soviet spheres of influence. Contemporaries were certainly astonished by the Soviet dictator's decision. The 'second Munich' never happened; however ineffectual the British and French were in saving Poland, they did actually go to war in September 1939. The August 1939 Soviet pledge of neutrality freed Germany's hands to invade Poland (although Hitler would almost certainly have invaded that country with or without the Pact).

Contrary to the historical 'revisionists', Stalin was not the hidden instigator of the Second World War, nor did he use Hitler as an 'icebreaker' against the frozen sea of western capitalism.[25] For the Kremlin leaders, another world war between the capitalist states was inevitable. Such a war presented a grave danger to the USSR; it might be drawn in, or used by one side or other as a prize. Yet, war also presented opportunities, as Stalin explained to his close comrades:

A war is on between two groups of capitalist countries … for the re-division of the world, for the domination of the world! We see nothing wrong in their having a good hard fight and weakening each other. It would be fine if at the hands of Germany the position of the richest capitalist countries (especially England) were shaken.[26]

As things turned out, the consequences of the Nazi–Soviet Pact and the successful German invasion of Poland and France were nearly fatal for the USSR. Stalin expected a prolonged war between Germany and the Allies, which would wear both down. Instead, on 22 June 1940, a year to the day before the BARBAROSSA campaign opened, the French Republic signed an armistice with Nazi Germany. In the desperate situation of May 1940, the beleaguered British and French Armies had had no relief in the form of what would be called, two years later, a 'Second Front'. The defeat of France and the entry of Italy into the war in June 1940 produced a very different European correlation of forces. The balance of power had shifted, and not in a way that the Kremlin had expected. Germany no longer seemed to need Russia the way it had in August 1939. The Reich now had no active enemies on the continent in the West. Its army and air force were fully mobilized and proven in large-scale fighting. In addition, the Nazi–Soviet Pact gave Germany a common border with Russia, across which the Wehrmacht assault of June 1941 would come. Finally, the Kremlin leaders made fatal mistakes in guessing Hitler's intentions, something which will be discussed more fully in the next chapter.[27]

The USSR and its neighbours

The second part of the Kremlin's foreign policy concerned relations with Russia's smaller neighbours. Here there was little to distinguish Moscow's actions from those of Berlin. Both the German and Russian empires had lost extensive border territories when they were defeated in 1917–20. Both were trying to turn the clock back to before those years, using the justifications of history, ethnicity and strategy. 'Western Belorussia' (eastern Poland), to take one example, was to Russia what the Danzig corridor (northern Poland) was to Germany. One attraction of the Nazi–Soviet Pact was that it gave Moscow a free hand to make these border 'readjustments'. In early September, Georgi Dimitrov, the Bulgarian leader of the Comintern, recorded Stalin's extraordinary comments about Poland:

> Formerly … the Polish state was a nat[ional] state. … *Now [Poland] is a fascist state, oppressing Ukrainians, Belorussians and so forth.* The annihilation of that state under present conditions would mean one fewer bourgeois fascist state to contend with! What would be the harm if as a result of the rout of Poland we were to extend the socialist system onto new territories and populations?[28]

Successive Moscow leaders were to be so ashamed of the secret Nazi–Soviet territorial agreements to partition Poland and other parts of eastern Europe that they lied about their very existence until 1991. The USSR did not just stand aside from the invasion of Poland; it undertook the military occupation of the eastern half of its neighbour in September 1939. Treaties of 'Friendship and Co-operation' were signed under duress by Estonia, Latvia and Lithuania in September 1939. Although these Baltic states were still independent, the governments in Tallin, Riga and Kaunas now allowed the basing of Soviet forces in their territory. There was also a military dimension to the talks held with Finland, a fourth Baltic country which had been part of Imperial Russia: in October 1939, Helsinki was asked to give up territory and bases. When the Finns refused, the Red Army attacked, on 30 November 1939, and the 'Winter War' began. In a treaty signed in mid-March 1940, after the short but very costly Soviet–Finnish War, the Russians gained their basic objectives, essentially a band of territory protecting Leningrad, and a naval position at the mouth of the Gulf of Finland. In mid-June 1940, a few days after the French government fled Paris, the Red Army occupied the Baltic states; within a matter of weeks, these had become the Lithuanian, Estonian and Latvian Soviet Socialist Republics (SSRs) and were incorporated into the USSR. Also in June 1940 the USSR presented an ultimatum to Romania and annexed its northeastern region, which had been a province of Bessarabia in the Tsarist Empire; this became the Moldavian SSR.

These territorial advances against small neighbours turned out to have a number of very harmful consequences for the USSR. Russian aggression antagonized the surviving small states of northern and central Europe. Hungary and Slovakia might have allied with the Reich in any event, but Soviet actions pushed Finland and Romania, on either flank of the Soviet front, fully into the German camp. Furthermore, much of the fighting in 1941 (and 1944) would take place in this newly annexed zone. In June 1941, Soviet rule had been in place for only twenty months in the western Ukraine and western Belorussia (i.e. eastern Poland), and for a little over twelve months in the case of Moldavia and the Baltic countries. The local population was antagonized by crude Sovietization in which tens of thousands of 'class enemies' from the local elites were arrested, deported or even shot. The benefits to the Red Army by 1941 were much less than expected, as Soviet military engineers had little time to fortify the new frontier, develop military communications and supply facilities, or build a system of air and naval bases.[29]

CONCLUSION

There was one other aspect of Soviet diplomacy. In mid-April 1941 the Soviet–Japanese Neutrality Pact was signed. Moscow's worst strategic fear, a simultaneous attack by European enemies and by the Japanese, was not realized, and Soviet ground and air forces could be concentrated in Europe. The Red Army had helped to deter a Japanese attack by its fighting in border battles at Lake Khasan (Changkufeng) in 1938 and especially at Khalkhin Gol (Nomonhan) in 1939 – the latter operation under one General Zhukov. Other factors also contributed to Tokyo's decision, notably the lack of key resources to plunder in the Soviet Far East, compared to what could be gained by aggression in Southeast Asia. The Japanese military decided to 'wait until the persimmon ripened and fell' rather than take offensive action against the USSR. Hitler's own grand strategy initially supported this decision. Because he underestimated the USSR, he believed Japan would make a greater contribution to Axis victory in the war by attacking the British Empire and by tying down American forces in the Pacific than by attacking Siberia. Near the end of his life, the Führer changed his mind:

> It is certainly regrettable that the Japanese did not enter the war against Soviet Russia alongside us. Had that happened, Stalin's armies would not now be besieging Breslau and the Soviets would not be standing in Budapest. We would together have exterminated Bolshevism before the winter of 1941.[30]

The accommodation with Japan, however, was the one long-term success of Soviet foreign policy. In the main, Soviet inability or unwillingness to work within the European state system pushed its policy of self-reliance to the ultimate test.

CHAPTER 2
PREPARATIONS AND PERCEPTIONS

The German Wehrmacht must be prepared, even before the conclusion of the war against England, *to crush Soviet Russia in a rapid campaign* (Case Barbarossa).

OKW Directive No. 21, 18 December 1940

The Red Army is a modern army, and a modern army is an offensive army.

Joseph Stalin, 5 May 1941

Germany has a Treaty of Non-Aggression with us. Germany is involved up to its ears in the war in the West, and I believe that Hitler will not risk creating a second front for himself by attacking the Soviet Union. Hitler is not such a fool as to think that the Soviet Union is Poland, that it is France, that it is England, and even that it is [just] all of them put together.

Joseph Stalin, mid-June 1941

GERMAN MILITARY SUPERIORITY

Military leadership and doctrine

Numbers had much to do with the early German successes in Russia. Hitler was able to concentrate a huge force against the Soviet Union in June 1941. German sources give a figure of 3,100,000 German soldiers involved in Operation BARBAROSSA, plus several hundred thousand more personnel from the Luftwaffe and the Navy. The Axis allies contributed 650,000 troops. Russian sources make Axis strength even higher, with 4,100,000 Germans, plus a further 900,000 from Axis allies (Table 2.1). Put another way, each of the ten German motorized corps sent to Russia was larger than Rommel's famous Afrika Korps, and they were only the advance guard of a huge phalanx of German infantry. Operation BARBAROSSA involved more German soldiers than would be used in active campaigns against Russia later in the war: Army Group South mounted the main German effort in 1942; even taking (high) figures cited by Russian historians, it marched with only 900,000 troops towards Stalingrad and the Caucasus.[1]

And yet the Wehrmacht did not win its early victories because it overwhelmed its opponents with numbers. In the 1940 campaign in France, the Germans had deployed

Table 2.1 Operation BARBAROSSA: forces directly involved

	USSR	Axis
Divisions	186	153
Personnel	3,000,000	3,767,000
Artillery	19,800	7,200
Tanks	11,000	4,000
Combat aircraft	9,100	4,400

Source: *VOV/VIO*, vol. 1, p. 123, *GSWW*, vol. 4, pp. 318, 364.

Note: These are forces directly engaged in June 1941: Axis forces in East Prussia, Poland, Romania and Finland, and Soviet forces in the first and second 'strategic echelons' (including reserve forces being moved to the western border). These figures are as calculated by Russian historians, except those for Axis personnel and artillery, which are from a German source; the Russian version was 4,400,000 Axis personnel and 39,400 'guns and mortars' for the USSR and 39,000 for the Axis.

141 divisions against 144 Allied ones. In Operation BARBAROSSA, the Wehrmacht was able to mass a huge strength, but the Russians were stronger than the Western Allies had been in 1940. The German Army had a slight numerical advantage in terms of immediately available manpower, but nothing like the correlation of forces that would normally be required to guarantee decisive offensive success. Indeed, the Wehrmacht was at a significant disadvantage to the Russians in terms of the quantity of artillery, tanks and aircraft. In early October 1941, Marshal Voroshilov, the pre-war commander of the Red Army, would speak frankly about the situation at the front to Dimitrov, head of the Comintern. It was 'awful', despite better Soviet equipment and braver Soviet soldiers: 'But our organisation is weaker than theirs. Our commanding officers are less well trained. The Germans succeed usually because of their better organization and clever tricks.'[2] The German armed forces would indeed not have achieved what they did, in 1940, in 1941, and in much of 1942, without 'clever tricks'. Objectively, this might be taken to mean superior military effectiveness, bringing in the interlinked elements of leadership, doctrine, organization, equipment and personnel.[3]

A central explanation of the Wehrmacht's early offensive successes in 1939–42 – and of its stubborn defence in 1943–5 – was outstanding professional leadership, at least at the operational and tactical levels. The German General Staff, the brain of the army, might formally have been banned by the victorious Allies at Versailles in 1919, but for successive German governments this ban was the easiest of the Versailles restrictions to get around. In 1940 and 1941, the German campaign planners and the field commanders of army groups, corps and divisions were experienced and well prepared. Many of the senior generals had gained command experience in the First World War. At the middle levels of the military hierarchy, the Germans retained the pick of long-service career officers. As for battalion and company officers, they could be recruited from a well-educated and nationalistic population.

At all levels the German Army stressed education and initiative. A 'mission-oriented' command system (the so-called *Auftragstaktik*) gave commanders flexibility in carrying out tasks; they did not simply have to follow detailed orders from above. German military doctrine, developed by generals like Moltke and Schlieffen before the First World War, and Seeckt after it, gave these commanders a framework for operational success. Decisive, offensive, action was emphasized, in campaigns of rapid movement and 'annihilating' victory; these campaigns were to involve the close co-ordination of the different arms of service (originally infantry, artillery, cavalry, etc.). Crucially, commanders and doctrine had been tested in the Wehrmacht's victorious campaigns before June 1941. German generals had learnt how to organize armoured advances, and the Army and Luftwaffe developed methods to fight together on the battlefield. The Wehrmacht also trained intensively during the 1939–41 period and made great efforts to learn and incorporate the operational and tactical lessons of real combat.

The German leadership and doctrine have to be compared with their Red Army counterparts. The Russians had a military tradition of their own. The reputations of commanders from the history of old Russia, Aleksandr Nevskii, Suvorov and Kutuzov, would be used to the hilt by the Stalinist state, especially after June 1941. The Russian Empire, however, had suffered defeat after defeat from the second half of the nineteenth century, just when Prussia/Germany was demonstrating its military pre-eminence. Russia was beaten by the British and French in the Crimean War, and then by the Japanese. The huge Russian Army of 1914 was broken in battle and its remains scattered by the revolutionary winds of 1917–18. A new Red Army was created in 1918–19, but on a very different basis, and it was hurriedly demobilized at the beginning of the 1920s. Compared with the Wehrmacht, the Red Army leadership possessed less stability and command experience. Soviet commanders were granted less freedom of action on the battlefield – certainly in 1941. Very few of the experienced staff officers of the pre-revolutionary army – the contemporaries of the Wehrmacht's supreme leaders – survived the revolution or the dismissals of the early 1930s. Most of the senior Red Army commanders of 1941 earned their spurs (often literally – in the Red Cavalry) in the two or three years of civil war which followed the 1917 Revolution.[4]

Communist Party control was central to the whole Soviet structure; it became still more comprehensive in the late 1930s. Stalin's purges of the Red Army were an extraordinary factor here. The first closed trial of senior leaders of the Red Army took place on 11 June 1937, nearly four years to the day before BARBAROSSA. Many arrests followed. In the end, according to the most reliable figures available, 34,000 army and air force 'commanders' and commissars were dismissed; of these about 12,000 were reinstated. Some 20,000 leaders were arrested, and a majority of them were executed. It is sometimes suggested that half the leadership of the Red Army was wiped out, but this was certainly not the case. There had been 142,000 commanders and commissars in 1937, and tens of thousands of new men entered service in the following years; the command staff numbered 282,000 in 1939. The Red Army commanders who were executed were not proven military leaders, at least not in a mechanized war. Many able middle-level commanders survived the purges. For example, 276 Red Army commanders who held the rank equivalent to that of a colonel died in the purges in 1937–41, but 1,713 men had held that rank in 1936. Stalin, in the army and elsewhere, made much of the need to promote 'young cadres'. In February 1941 he toasted the 'young cadres', contrasting the Russian situation with that in Britain and France, where 'the young cadres are kept [back] for twenty or thirty-five years …. This was one of the reasons for France's downfall.' 'Replacing the old men with the young at the proper time is very essential. The country that fails to do that is doomed to failure.'[5]

However, the purges certainly played a most important part in what happened on and after 22 June 1941. Although the Red Army commanders and commissars who were shot made up a minority – relative to the size of the whole leadership corps – the execution of even a few hundred officers would be a traumatic event in any army, and in Russia the officer victims seem to have numbered in the tens of thousands. Moreover, the Red Army toll was particularly devastating at the uppermost levels. Among those murdered were three of five marshals. The generals also suffered heavily: 20 men with the rank of 'army commander' were shot between 1937 and 1941, compared to 15 men who held that rank in 1936; for 'corps commanders' the victims numbered 64 (compared to 62 on strength in 1936), for 'division commanders' 131 (compared to 201) and for 'brigade commanders' 217 (compared to 474).[6] These men possessed the fullest professional, educational and operational experience that the Red Army had accumulated. They had overseen the spectacular modernization of doctrine and matériel of the early 1930s. Despite professional and personal rivalries among themselves, these leaders had formed a fairly cohesive command structure. The paradox is that this was precisely why Stalin mistrusted them. The worst of the terror occurred in 1937–8; nevertheless, high-level arrests and executions continued right up to the eve of the war, notably in the Red Army Air Force. The purges of the Soviet military had three results, each devastating. Indispensable trained leaders were lost at a time when the Red Army was rapidly expanding. Second, the initiative of Red Army leaders was reduced, and a mental state was imposed which was the very opposite of the German 'mission-oriented command system'. Finally, the purges made foreign governments – potential allies as well as potential enemies – assume that the Red Army was a broken shell.

The pre-war Stalinist 'leader-state' lacked effective overall military leadership. This paradox was not just a product of the purges. The People's Commissar (Minister) of Defence from 1925 and up until May 1940 was Kliment Voroshilov, an incompetent political crony of Stalin's.[7] An uneducated worker who had joined the Bolsheviks long before the 1917 Revolution, Voroshilov became one of Stalin's 'team' in the Civil War and helped the dictator in his rise to power. He was rewarded by a seat on the party Politburo from the 1920s and by lavish praise from Soviet propaganda. It was 'Marshal' Voroshilov who oversaw the Red Army purges of 1937–8. Stalin held him responsible for the Red Army's poor performance in the Winter War with Finland and sacked him as People's Commissar, but he kept his position on the Politburo and was one of the five members of the State Defence Committee (GKO) that was formed in July 1941. Voroshilov's successor as People's Commissar of Defence, serving to the outbreak of the war and promoted to the rank of Marshal, was Semen Timoshenko. The new People's Commissar was a professional by Red Army standards, but like most of the Soviet military leaders, he had been only an enlisted soldier in the First World War. In the coming Nazi–Soviet war, he would prove to be a commander of limited abilities. Also, while Voroshilov had been a member of the party Politburo, Timoshenko lacked this political status.

The other important 'professional' command post was that of the Chief of the General Staff, and here there was damaging instability. From the 1937 purge to August 1940, the General Staff was headed by Boris Shaposhnikov, but he was replaced by Kirill Meretskov, who had been the main planner of the final stages of the Finnish War. Meretskov was in turn replaced in January 1941 by Georgii Zhukov; Zhukov, whatever his other abilities, lacked staff experience, and in post-war unpublished memoirs he was frank about his own failings in organizing Red Army mobilization.[8]

The most striking feature of this command system was the position of Stalin. While Hitler was head of the Armed Forces High Command (OKW), Stalin initially had no specific titular role in the military. (Until May 1941 he did not even have a formal post in the Soviet state; he was General Secretary of the Communist Party.) Stalin's drive for ultimate authority meant that he tolerated no independent head of the military, but at the same time he did not put himself in supreme command until July 1941. Meanwhile, the Soviet dictator had a great deal of other business to attend to. No one had bothered to prepare a physical central headquarters, and the top-level command organization held no exercises; this would prove an acute problem on and after 22 June.

Soviet military doctrine was more stable than Soviet military leadership. It was a 'combined-arms' offensive doctrine, which had much in common with that of the Wehrmacht. Red Army doctrinal innovation was driven forward by considerations which were not solely military, notably enthusiasm for the advance of the Communist revolution and for mechanization. In the early 1930s the Soviet Army had been ahead of the other armies in thinking about new ways of overcoming the strategic gridlock of the First World War and of reviving offensive war. This doctrine has been linked to Voroshilov's one-time deputy, Marshal Mikhail Tukhachevskii, and was built on the concept of 'deep battle': the enemy would be attacked simultaneously in depth, with tanks and aircraft paralysing his defences.

The Kremlin had been generous in providing the appropriate equipment for such a war. With huge – for the time – tank, artillery and aircraft programmes, Russia was the first of the European powers to rearm. Some historians argue that the problem in 1941 was that Soviet offensive doctrine was watered down after the trial and 'liquidation' of the Tukhachevskii group in 1937, and in light of the failures of Russian 'volunteers' in the Spanish Civil War in 1936–9 and the chaotic advance into Poland in 1939. But in reality the Red Army held true to its offensive doctrine, and if anything this orientation was reinforced following the triumphs of the German panzer campaigns in Poland and France in 1939 and 1940. The real problem was the mismatch between doctrine and capability. On paper, a large amount of equipment was available, but the Red Army did not have the leadership or organization – especially after the purges – to carry out offensive operations against a first-class enemy. The offensive doctrine, as we will see later in this chapter, also exposed the Red Army to a surprise attack. Meanwhile, serious thought about, and training for, defensive operations were neglected.

Soviet military planning, both for offence and defence, was greatly confused by the movement of the frontier 200 miles to the west, following the annexation of the Baltic states, eastern Poland and Bessarabia in 1939–40. Before 1939 the Red Army had prepared defensive positions on the Soviet Union's existing border, in what the Germans would call the 'Stalin Line'. With a border stretching 800 miles and relatively level terrain, it was impossible to create a defensive position comparable to the French Maginot Line or the German *Westwall*. Instead, there was a string of 'fortified zones' (*ukreplennye raiony*), each with bunkers, artillery and machine gun positions, and tank traps. The annexations made by the USSR in the west presented Stalin and the Red Army leadership with hard choices. They decided on a high priority programme to build twenty fortified zones along the new border (what the Germans called the 'Molotov Line'), using matériel from the old border defences. Marshal Shaposhnikov, the former Chief of the General Staff, was made responsible for this work. Defensive positions did not mean a defensive doctrine. The fortified zones provided part of the 'screen' behind which the main offensive force of the Red Army could mobilize – so the further west this screen was sited the better. The fortified zones also freed mobile troops for a general offensive, by covering that part of the frontier where Soviet troops would not be attacking.[9]

There was, to be sure, a more pessimistic side to Soviet strategic planning, which would explain why in May 1941 work began on renovating the Stalin Line and building a new 'rear' defensive line (the Ostashkov–Pochep Line) just west of Moscow. The Russians would not in the end be given much time to prepare the new fortified zones. From the point of view of fixed defences, the Red Army was in the worst possible position in June 1941: the 'Molotov Line' was far from finished, and the 'Stalin Line' had been partly dismantled.

Military structures

Despite the difference in experience, the German and Soviet Armies were organized along similar lines.[10] A June 1941 Soviet 'rifle' (infantry) division had the same structure as a Germany infantry division; both had three infantry regiments and an artillery regiment. The 'establishment' of a Soviet division was 144 artillery pieces (including 54 anti-tank guns); the German version had 149 (75 anti-tank). In 1941, the Germans had more operational *motorized* infantry divisions, which were capable of keeping up with and supporting armoured divisions. The Red Army had in 1939 begun to form motorized divisions, but these lacked equipment; in late 1941 they would be converted into normal rifle divisions. In June 1941 Soviet and German divisions were organized conventionally into corps and then into armies, but the post-BARBAROSSA shortage of Soviet commanders and communications facilities led to a big reduction in the corps 'echelon' for the first half of the war. Meanwhile, the Soviet 'armies' became smaller and much more numerous than their German counterparts. There were fifty-eight headquarters of Soviet infantry armies (i.e. excluding a handful of 'tank armies') at the start of 1942 and seventy-three at the start of 1943. In contrast, the enemy had only ten army headquarters and four panzer-group headquarters in the East at the time of Operation BARBAROSSA (panzer groups later became panzer armies); the Germans added one army headquarters in the autumn of 1941 (the 2nd Army) and another in 1943 (the 8th Army).[11]

In June 1941 both Germany and the USSR left the rest of the world far behind in the number of their armoured divisions. On 22 June, the Germans had 21 of them, of which 19 were deployed against Russia. Their elements were a panzer regiment, two 'panzer-grenadier' (motorized infantry) regiments and an artillery regiment. Standard strength was now 118 tanks and 99 artillery pieces (45 anti-tank guns). On paper, a 1941 Soviet 'tank division' had many more tanks (375 in two regiments) and less infantry (only one regiment) and artillery (28 pieces). Unlike the French in 1940, the Soviets were by 1941 well aware of the need to concentrate their armoured forces in large formations. There was still, however, a great discrepancy between awareness of the task and the ability to deal effectively with it.

In June 1941, the Russians were in the middle of a hugely ambitious reorganization plan aimed at creating sixty tank divisions by the end of the year. These tank divisions would be combined with thirty motorized divisions to form thirty 'mechanized corps'. To achieve this, existing tank brigades were regrouped into divisions, but the process was far from complete in June, and the organized brigades that *had* existed were thrown into disarray. In one of the first wartime analyses of the faults of the Red Army, the Stavka (the Soviet high command) concluded that the mechanized corps (and large air formations) had been 'unwieldy' and that it was necessary instead to stiffen the infantry by giving each rifle division a company of 20–30 tanks.[12] The whole process might have been smoother had the four huge 'tank corps' created at the end of the 1930s not been broken up in November 1939, but the Red Army would still have lacked the training and communications to make effective use of such large formations.

The Germans, in contrast, had sorted out the organization problem: they attacked Russia with ten panzer ('motorized') corps, each normally having a couple of panzer divisions and one or two motorized divisions. These were massed into four panzer groups, each of two or three panzer corps. Compared to their Soviet equivalents, the German formations were better structured and led, they were more experienced, and they were generally better equipped – albeit with a hodge-podge of German and captured vehicles. The Soviets would not deploy a formation comparable to a panzer corps – they would call them 'tank armies' – until 1942; they would not begin to use the tank armies effectively until 1943–4.

There was one surprising anomaly. Along with armour, airborne troops were seen by both the Germans and the Russians as a key element in modern mobile warfare. The Russians held the world's first large exercises of parachute troops in the mid-1930s while testing the 'deep battle' concept, and the Germans used parachutists and glider troops in some of their invasions of 1940–1. In the Russian campaign, both sides had, on paper, large airborne formations, but neither used them much in the role for which they were intended. Hitler's December 1940 BARBAROSSA directive mentioned the 'bold use of parachute and airborne troops'. The Red Army command took the German airborne threat very seriously at the start of the war, for example, warning in July about possible airborne landings at Odessa and Leningrad. But German airborne forces were never used en masse, partly because of the mauling they had received in the Battle of Crete in May 1941. The Russians, for their part, gave a high priority to forming airborne forces in the months immediately before 22 June, but would only deploy them in small numbers in the battles around Moscow in December. The first and last serious Soviet airborne operation to be mounted as part of the 'deep battle' concept came in the autumn of 1943.[13]

The opposing air forces, like the armies, were organized on broadly similar lines.[14] The Luftwaffe building blocks, the *Gruppe* and *Geschwader* (respectively about thirty and ninety aircraft of the same type), were matched by the air regiment and air division of the Red Army Air Force (VVS). The Luftwaffe, however, was in 1941 better organized to mass its forces, with large air corps and air fleets (*Fliegerkorps* and *Luftflotten*). This complemented the Germans' advantages in equipment, training and communications. Larger Soviet formations did exist, air corps of medium bombers tasked for semi-independent operations under the direction of the Red Army high command. These, however, would be thrown away without fighter support, in June and July 1941. Only from the summer of 1942 did the Russians concentrate their air strength effectively: an 'air army' would be comparable to a German *Fliegerkorps* but was attached to one particular army group. As the fighting began in 1941, the air forces on both sides accepted that in this campaign at least their main task would be to assist ground forces with close support and with the interdiction of enemy supply lines; they would not fly long-range 'independent' operations against strategic economic targets deep in the enemy's rear. As with the panzer forces, the Germans had gained vital practical experience of ground–air co-operation in the Polish and French campaigns. The main task for the Luftwaffe was the concentrated support of masses of aircraft at the centre of gravity of the attack, the *Schwerpunkt*. In the Russian campaign, this would mean supporting the panzer groups.

Military equipment

The ground forces on both sides had weapons of similar quality, and the Russians had more of everything.[15] Most of the German and Russian infantry were armed with bolt-action rifles dating back to before the First World War. The automatic infantry weapons of the two sides were similar. The standard German field artillery pieces were of 75mm, 105mm and 150mm. Soviet artillery was comparable, with 76mm, 107mm, 122mm and 152mm types, a mix of guns and howitzers, and a range of obsolete, modernized and new models. Most of the Soviet artillery was horse-drawn in 1941, and there were very few tracked artillery pieces (self-propelled guns) that could operate off roads. This, however, was also true of the Wehrmacht. Altogether, the German Army in Russia initially fielded about 7,000 light and heavy artillery pieces. Red Army strength for the whole of the USSR was four or five times that, at 33,200 artillery pieces. Stalin seems to have been a believer in the importance of artillery, and he once commented on the enemy's relative weakness. 'The German Army is really an army of mortars and tank guns', Stalin told one of his industrial ministers in 1942. 'It is a light army.'[16]

On both sides, line infantry divisions consisted of marching men heavily dependent on horse traction. The great bulk of the German Army was not motorized; the BARBAROSSA force took 625,000 horses with them.[17] However, the invaders also had 600,000 motor vehicles. This was substantially more than what the Red Army had available: 272,600 vehicles both in Europe and the Far East – and 204,900 mobilized from the civilian economy. The Soviet lorry park was more standardized than its German equivalent, but the basic vehicles, such as the ZIS-5 and GAZ-AA, were copies of outdated Western designs and relatively small. Another significant Red Army shortcoming was the lack of armoured personnel carriers (APCs) for the infantry, vehicles comparable to the German SdKfz 251 half-track. Some 4,650 of the latter were built between 1939 and 1943 to carry German infantry into battle, with even larger numbers of a simplified model later in the war.[18] If Soviet infantry rode to the battlefield, it was on the hulls of tanks, or sitting in unarmoured civilian lorries.

One of the myths of Operation BARBAROSSA is the German advantage in mechanized equipment. The tanks the Wehrmacht used in Russia in 1941 (and in Poland and France in 1939–40) were small, lightly armed and thinly armoured, if compared against what would become the world 'standard' in 1942, the Russian T-34; this was a 29-ton vehicle armed with a 76mm gun. The German tanks available in largest numbers were the 9-ton Pz Kpfw II and the 20-ton Pz Kpfw III.[19] The Pz Kpfw II mounted a 20mm gun, the Pz Kpfw III a 37mm or 50mm one. The German 6th Panzer Division was actually equipped with Czechoslovak tanks. On paper, the main Russian tanks of 1941, the 11-ton T-26 and the 14-ton BT, were comparable at least to the Pz Kpfw II, and most carried a gun similar to that of the Pz Kpfw III, a 45mm. Both tanks were available in far greater numbers than their German equivalents.

Of much higher quality were two bigger Soviet tanks, the T-34 medium tank and the 45-ton KV heavy tank. Both were products of pre-1941 Soviet combat experience, which had shown the importance of heavy armour and a powerful gun, regardless of the higher cost and the technical challenges involved. Of the two tanks, the thickly armoured KV probably came as the greater shock to the Germans in 1941; it was at that time available in similar numbers to the T-34. The 'medium' T-34, however, mounted the same 76mm gun as the KV but cost less and was more mobile. Fortunately for the Germans, neither big Soviet tank was concentrated in sufficient numbers in June 1941 to prevent the Red Army catastrophe. In the summer of 1941, then, the Germans were much inferior in tank numbers and were about equal in basic tank quality (i.e. gun, armour, mobility). They had to make up for this by better operational and tactical skill, by better communications equipment and by greater mechanical reliability.

Taking the story forward to the end of 1941 and into 1942, the German position was helped in the short run by the speed of their advance. This quickly threatened Khar'kov and Leningrad, where the two 'lead' Soviet medium and heavy tank factories were located. The tank assembly lines had to be moved to the Urals, and initially no facilities existed there for producing diesel motors or rolling heavy tank armour. As a stopgap, large numbers of the 6.4-ton T-60 light tank were produced over the winter of 1941–2. Powered by a lorry petrol engine (rather than by a diesel engine), the T-60 could be built by automobile plants, but it was smaller even than the T-26 and the BT and mounted only a 20mm gun. KV production was especially hit by the shift of production from Leningrad, and 1942 output was only 1,800 vehicles. In contrast, T-34 production leapt to 12,600 in 1942.[20]

In 1941 the availability of some excellent towed anti-tank guns enabled the Germans to cope with large numbers of enemy tanks. The 88mm, which was actually a heavy anti-aircraft gun, provided the high-velocity firepower to knock out even the T-34 and KV. The standard Soviet 45mm Model 1937 anti-tank gun (like the German 50mm) had limited effectiveness against newer tanks, but the Red Army had 15,000 of them (of which 12,000 were lost in 1941). Nevertheless, it became clear very soon after the war began that 'tank-panic' (tankoboiazn') was a major problem in the Red Army. In early July the GKO had to order the production of 120,000 'Molotov cocktails' a day, for use against tanks.[21]

There was one crucially important area where the myth of German qualitative superiority was correct. In contrast to tanks and artillery, Soviet aircraft were, even on paper, inferior to those of the Luftwaffe.[22] The Messerschmitt Bf 109 (and – for comparison – the British Hurricane) first flew in 1935. Comparable Soviet fighter types, the Yak-1, LaGG-3 and MiG-3, first flew as prototypes in March–April 1940, five years later. Only the MiG was actually in service on 22 June, and it was an unsuccessful design removed from production in 1942. Many regiments of 'Stalin's Hawks' were in the throes of re-equipment when the Germans attacked. This technical backwardness was especially surprising in view of Stalin's personal interest in the Red Army Air Force, the massive funds granted to the Soviet aviation industry and its technical achievements in the early 1930s. One underlying problem was the Soviet system's preoccupation with numbers, which led to premature standardization and to the output of older designs to keep production numbers up (the factories at least learnt valuable production lessons).

In 1941 the Luftwaffe gained air superiority using large numbers of Messerschmitt Bf 109 fighters, and it would have achieved this – more slowly – even without the successful surprise attack on Soviet airfields. The numerically most important Russian fighter was the little I-16 monoplane, of which the best version had a speed of about 300 mph. A total of 9,450 I-16s were built, a colossal number in terms of the 1930s. For the British Empire the closest equivalent was the Gladiator fighter, built between 1934 and 1940 with a production run of 550. In 1941 the I-16 was 50 mph slower than a Bf 109E and only as fast as a German Ju 88 bomber. The 'new' I-153 fighter entered service in 1939; it was a biplane, albeit with retractable landing gear. The I-153 had a maximum speed of 265 mph and could barely catch up with a German He 111 medium bomber or even a Ju 87 Stuka dive-bomber. No fewer than 1,000 of these useless biplanes came off Soviet assembly lines in 1939, and 2,400 in 1940. Neither the I-16 nor the I-153 was able to climb to high altitude – which was one reason German reconnaissance planes could roam at will over western Russia before and after 22 June.

The most numerous Soviet bomber type, the SB, was a light bomber, which had neither the bomb load nor the range of the German Do 17, He 111 or Ju 88, nor the ground attack capability of the Ju 87 Stuka. The bigger Soviet Il-4 (DB-3) was then available only in small numbers. The outstanding Soviet ground attack aircraft of the mid-war years, the Il-2 *shturmovik* and the Pe-2 twin-engined dive-bomber, were just entering service in June 1941. In 1941 and 1942 the production for the Red Army Air Force was badly hit by the decision to evacuate the airframe and engine factories that were concentrated around Moscow.

The Red Army Air Force, then, had serious problems of equipment and organization; as we shall see, much of it would be caught by surprise and destroyed on the ground on 22 June. The paradox was that the Kremlin leadership in the 1930s had been very 'air-minded': scarce resources were lavished on the flyers and the aircraft industry, and they enjoyed Stalin's special patronage. The explanation of this paradox was that too much had been expected of the Red Army Air Force and the aviation industry by the Soviet leadership – and the NKVD. Many of the leading aircraft designers were in prison. The head of the People's Commissariat of Aircraft Production, the brother of Politburo member Lazar' Kaganovich, had been driven to suicide in 1940. Like that of the other services, the leadership of the Red Army Air Force had been decimated in the purges of 1937–8, but it was also affected by continuing persecution going on into the weeks right up to June 1941. Even more than in the ground forces, young and inexperienced commanders were put in charge. These were mostly veterans of air battles over Spain and China, flyers with no staff experience. P. V. Rychagov was twenty-nine years old when he was made a lieutenant general, head of the whole Air Force and Deputy People's Commissar. General Kopets, the doomed head of the Western MD Air Force in June, was thirty-three. Even Rychagov only lasted until April 1941; he was reassigned to the Academy of the General Staff and arrested there shortly after the war began. General G. M. Shtern, Chief of the Air Defence (PVO) Administration, and General Ia. V. Smushkevich, Deputy Chief of the General Staff for Aviation, were arrested on 14 June 1941, eight days before Operation BARBAROSSA.[23]

Raw numbers and paper specifications for Soviet tanks and aircraft were in any event misleading. The arms industry, like other Soviet industrial sectors, was rewarded for the highest possible gross output, what the Russians call *val*.[24] Numbers were stressed, at the expense of less tangible qualities such as reliability, spare parts, repair facilities and communications equipment. A more confident and better qualified military leadership would have been necessary to ensure that the balance was correct; the other test would be war. The availability of trained personnel was not taken fully into consideration, and Russian educational backwardness, primitive infrastructure and severe climate made it hard to maintain complex weaponry. The Red Army thus had a huge tank park, but tanks with motors that required frequent overhaul, and a large proportion of vehicles that were under repair. Most tanks did not have radios, and the mechanized corps based in western Russia lacked fuel and equipment depots. Meanwhile, in the spring of 1941 it was noted at Politburo level that the Red Army Air Force was losing 2–3 aircraft a day (600–900 a year) in accidents.[25]

Finally, the communications network of the Red Army – radio and land lines – was woefully inadequate. Three weeks after the war began, in the chaos of the early defeats, the head of the Signals Directorate (*Upravlenie sviazi*) of the Red Army, General N. I. Gapich, would be demoted and then sentenced to ten years in prison; the chief of signals troops of the Western Army Group, General A. T. Grigor'ev, was shot. A week after that, an order sent out over the names of Stalin and Zhukov stated that 'the underestimation of radio, as the most reliable form of communications, and the basic means of administering forces, is the result of the backwardness of our staffs, the fact that they do not understand the significance of radio in the mobile forms of modern battle'. A hurried programme to train radio operators was set up. But the real source of the problem in this vital area was inadequate pre-war provision of equipment, personnel and training.[26]

The Third Reich, meanwhile, was a world leader in automotive, aviation and communications technology. The vehicles and aircraft of the Wehrmacht were equipped with radios and more reliable engines. Germany also had formidable advantages in operational and tactical radio intelligence which gave it a good knowledge of the deployment of Soviet forces, at least in in the western part of Russia. This facilitated many of the invaders' early victories – especially their ability to anticipate Soviet counter-attacks.[27]

Military personnel

In weighing up the two armies, the military effectiveness and motivation of the fighting troops themselves are all-important. The total armed forces of the Third Reich at the start of 1941 included 3,800,000 in the Field Army (*Feldheer*), 1,200,000 in the Replacement Army (*Ersatzheer*), 150,000 in the Waffen-SS, 1,680,000 in the Luftwaffe and 404,000 in the Navy.[28]

The German military had been greatly limited by the 1919 Treaty of Versailles; the terms of the treaty were specifically intended to prevent the rebuilding of powerful forces, and they attempted to block the Germans from expanding their army rapidly in wartime by calling up reservists. The small post-Versailles German Army was a long-service force (normally with a twelve-year period of service for enlisted personnel). This provided highly experienced cadres; the non-commissioned officers were outstanding. On the negative side, there were the thirteen 'white years' for the year-groups 1901 to 1913; in compliance with the 1919 treaty terms, the great majority of men born in these years had received no military training and so could not provide a pool of trained reservists. Once conscription was resumed in 1936 and the training system began to expand the army, it was an efficient system. But training facilities could not be created overnight, even with the assistance of paramilitary organizations like the *Reichsarbeitsdienst* (Reich Labour Service) and the Hitler Youth.

The qualities, morale and motivation of the young men who came into the Wehrmacht have been the subject of much study, because of their readiness to serve an authoritarian regime, because of their remarkable success in offensive and defensive combat, and because of their perpetration of criminal acts.[29] They reflected the qualities of the German population; as Hitler's army expanded, the rank and file remained well educated, highly disciplined and highly motivated. Effective training and replacement systems made for high morale and tight unit cohesion.

Most of the German troops accepted and even supported the policies of the Third Reich. The soldiers came from a society that was nationalistic, relatively affluent and ethnically homogeneous; the Nazi regime attempted to foster its version of social integration – for ethnic Germans – in the so-called *Volksgemeinschaft* ('People's Community').[30] The 1933 Nazi government appeared to have dealt with the economic crisis of the Great Depression, especially mass unemployment. For nearly a decade the political outlook of the German population and their attitude to the outside world had been dominated by Nazi propaganda; for the soldiers of 1941, this decade had often coincided with their formative years. The Nazis catered to German nationalism and to a common sense that Germany had been hard done by after 1918. To quote the historian Steven Fritz, 'The staying power of the average German soldier, his sense of seriousness and purpose … depended in large measure on the conviction that National Socialist Germany had redeemed the failures of World War I and had restored, both individually and collectively, a unique German sense of identity.'[31] Nazi theory, however repulsive in the abstract, provided a powerful integrating force and reinforced a sense of superiority. Although Hitler's regime was highly repressive, it was minorities like Jews and Communists that had been targeted, rather than any large category of the ethnic German population.

In addition, by the time of the invasion of Russia in June 1941, the Wehrmacht had experienced two years of unbroken military victory, in Poland, Norway, France, the Low Countries and the Balkans. This, on top of assumed racial mastery, made many a German *Landser* (common soldier, the German version of 'GI') think himself invincible. Fortunately, the Germans were not actually supermen.

The main military forces of the USSR were officially known as the Workers' and Peasants' Red Army (RKKA) and were renamed the 'Soviet Army' (*Sovetskaia armiia*) in 1945. The 'Red Army' included the air force. On the eve of the war, in 1941, the Soviet armed forces, taking in the whole of the USSR, consisted of 5,373,000 personnel, of which 4,261,000 were in the ground forces, 618,000 in the Red Army Air Force (VVS), 183,000 in the Air Defence Force (PVO) and 312,000 in the Navy.[32] Assessing the qualities of the 'Red Army man' (*krasnoarmeets*, the Tsarist term *soldat* was still 'politically incorrect' in the USSR) is even more complex than assessing those of the Wehrmacht soldier.[33]

Unlike Germany, the USSR had been able to carry out mass military conscription throughout the 1920s and 1930s. The size of the army rose from 500,000 to a million in the late 1920s and early 1930s; young men most normally served for a short period, but it is evident that a large number were given at least basic military training. This was at a time when the German Reichwehr was limited to 100,000 long-service men.

There was also a considerable amount of Soviet paramilitary training in the youth-based *Osoaviakhim* organization, established in 1927; it had boasted as many as 10,000,000 members in the mid-1930s.

The Russians were not without recent combat experience. Small numbers of Soviet aviators and ground troops served in Spain and China in the late 1930s. Significant engagements were fought with the Japanese at Lake Khasan and Khalkhin Gol on the Far Eastern borders in 1938 and 1939. The Red Army advance into eastern Poland and the Baltic states in 1940 provided some experience of large-scale troop movement. The war with Finland over the winter of 1939–40 ultimately achieved its objectives, although the Soviet campaign was fought clumsily and at very high cost.[34]

Leaving aside, for the moment, broader 'political' issues, the rapid pre-war expansion of the Red Army – from 1.5 million men on active service at the start of 1938 to 5 million in June 1941 – created huge problems. The Red Army before the war had difficulties keeping trained personnel, especially junior officers and NCOs. Unit-level commanders had received excessively accelerated training, especially six-month courses for junior lieutenants. These, in turn, were the men who were supposed to train NCOs and soldiers within units.

Last-minute expansion increased manpower but reduced quality. In 1941 two-thirds of the ordinary soldiers in the military districts on the western border were in their first year of service. Of these, half were untrained raw recruits, from the special spring draft of April–May 1941. The historian Roger Reese argues that the quality of the army declined after the Finnish War, when it was 're-peasantised' and swollen with recruits from the newly annexed western border territories.[35] From the point of view of the Soviet government, conscripts called up from the new borderlands were politically unreliable. In July 1941 General Zhukov would report 'mass desertion and treason to the Motherland' among conscripts from the western regions of the Ukraine and Belorussia, and from Bessarabia.[36] Some 5,300,000 reservists were called up in the first eight days after 22 June 1941, but it was often very hard to transport them to their units. The NKVD reported that in the first month of the war 104,000 disoriented servicemen had been rounded up and sent to combat units.[37]

The morale and motivation of the Red Army, especially in 1941–2, would raise some different questions than those relevant to the advancing Germans, especially during the grim months of encirclement and mass surrender in 1941 and 1942. As with the Wehrmacht, the personnel of the Red Army were a product of their society Urbanization, the spread of education, the rapid dash to industrialization and growth of the state machinery in the 1930s had created 'winners' in Stalin's Russia as well as 'losers'. As in Germany, there were reasons why people supported a repressive system in power. The Soviet regime fostered its own version of social integration (socialism) and related it to a mission of rapid economic and social modernization. The government had indeed made progress in industrializing the country. It had provided education for both children and adults, and an expanding industry and bureaucracy provided employment. As with the people of the Third Reich, the core (pre-1940) Soviet population had been subject to a 'propaganda state', which possessed a monopoly of information. Indeed, the Communists had controlled the mass media not for eight years (as with NSDAP up to 1941), but for two decades; most of the generation of young men who entered military service in the later 1930s had no memory of life before the Communists. Propaganda also provided these people with their only view of the outside world. From the late 1930s the propaganda line aimed at the mass of the population was based more on Russian nationalism and history (and on Stalin as leader) than on revolutionary internationalism.[38] Once the German invasion began, of course, all this became much more concrete. With many of these considerations in mind, the American historian Robert Thurston, has argued that pre-war Soviet society was reasonably well integrated, and he has used the Soviet–German military campaign of 1941 as evidence of such integration.[39]

On the other hand, the USSR was different from Nazi Germany. Despite the rapid changes in the 1930s, it was still a 'backward' rural country. Life was harder for the average Soviet citizen than for the average German, and the population in general suffered from severe shortages. Recent comparative figures put wealth per capita for Russia at about a third that of the United States, Britain and Germany, and the standard of living had probably fallen in the 1930s.[40] Relative to Germany, education levels were still low. Most of the Red Army's conscripts came from the countryside, and the negative social impact of the 'peasant rear' was significant. Furthermore, everyday life in the villages had been badly hit by the fiasco of collectivization in 1929–30 (the creation of a vast system of collective farms and 'state' farms), and deportation of better-off peasants (*kulaks*) and others who opposed state policy. Famine reigned in parts of the countryside, especially the Ukraine, in the early 1930s. All this must have engendered large-scale peasant hostility to the Communist government in Moscow.[41]

As already suggested, the population of the USSR was more diverse than that of the Third Reich. About half the Soviet citizens were not ethnic Russians, and only about two-thirds were Slavs (Russians, Ukrainians and Belorussians). Although none of the non-Slav groups was large enough to challenge the Russians, the diversity created training problems in the army.

The late 1930s was also a time of Stalinist terror which was worse for the core population of the USSR than the Nazi terror was for the core population of Germany. The most spectacular feature were the show trials of party, government and army leaders, but 1937–8 also saw the execution of almost 700,000 people, in the so-called 'mass operations'. Millions more unfortunates were consigned to a vast system of labour camps and prisons, of which the GULAG is the best-known component. In June 1941 the population of Soviet 'corrective labour camps' had risen to 2,300,000. Some 1,300,000 more Soviet citizens would be arrested in the second half of 1941, and most of them were held in confinement.

Very soon after the start of the war, the Soviet leadership put into place harsh control mechanisms. 'Blocking detachments' (*zagraditel'nye otriady*) were intended to stop mass flight and desertion. Zhukov also complained that 'a very large number of commanders and soldiers are leaking through to the deep rear'; 'they disorganize the population and sow panic'. Punitive measures seem to have gone to extremes; in October 1941 the

Stavka (Soviet high command) would actually have to issue special orders instructing commanders to use persuasion rather than brute force.[42]

The other Allied armies – especially the British and the American ones – had to expand even more quickly. These armies, however, were not face-to-face with masses of experienced and highly motivated German troops from the moment their war began. At the same time, social, cultural and educational factors certainly should not be made too much of in assessing the Soviet soldier. In 1943–5 Soviet troops fought effectively and mastered advanced weapons.[43] However, the process of learning and adaptation had to be carried out under fire. The cost would be enormous.

Over time, hatred of the Germans, Russian nationalism, the survival of the Stalinist system, effective propaganda and the scent of possible victory would bolster Red Army morale. But in the short term, in 1941, the collective mentality of the rank and file of the Red Army was a source of weakness. Many Soviet soldiers fought badly or surrendered without a fight in 1941, demoralized troops in a demoralized society. Hundreds of thousands of them would even fight *alongside* the Wehrmacht in the next three years. The Wehrmacht did not fight with these handicaps. German soldiers and airmen were better organized, better trained and more experienced. This goes a long way towards explaining why Hitler's forces were able to achieve so much without decisive numerical superiority.

THE ELEMENT OF SURPRISE

German preparations and Soviet intelligence

The military effectiveness of the Wehrmacht, honed by the combat experience of 1939–41, was probably the most important single factor in the success of Operation BARBAROSSA; second was the concentration of German forces against Russia. Third, but far from unimportant, was the element of surprise. Soviet ground forces on the border were not on full alert on Sunday, 22 June, and in the first few days, many divisions were overrun or encircled. Most Soviet planes at forward bases were destroyed or immobilized on the ground early on the morning of the invasion; others were abandoned in the precipitate retreat.

Surprise had been a central consideration for the German planners. They believed the Red Army had to be destroyed and prevented from withdrawing behind the line of the Dvina and Dnepr rivers and into the interior of Russia. As we have seen, planning for an attack on Russia began in June 1940, soon after the French campaign. The build-up of German forces on the eastern frontier of the Reich was at first slow. By the end of the year, there were still only thirty-four German divisions there. As the implementation stage of BARBAROSSA began, more and more troops were moved east, up to the final total of approximately 110 divisions in Poland and East Prussia. The first three waves moved from mid-February 1941 through mid-May. The final group of forces were moved to their attack positions only after 3 June 1941. This comprised the key striking force, twelve panzer divisions (out of a total of seventeen/nineteen in the German Army) and twelve motorized divisions (out of a total of thirteen). The Luftwaffe hid the expansion of its airfield network in the east, and short-range air units were only flown into their forward bases on 21 June.[44]

The Germans masked their preparations well, but they could not completely conceal the movement of very large forces. The failure to detect the change of Nazi intentions, or to respond to those Wehrmacht deployments that *could* be seen, came in part from shortcomings on the Soviet side. Stalin's terror again had a great impact: the USSR had two major foreign espionage organizations, one civilian and one military, but both had been heavily purged of agents and analysts. Timoshenko's 1940 overall report on the state of the Red Army was damning here: 'The organization of intelligence (*razvedka*) is one of the weakest sectors of the work of the Commissariat of Defence. There is no organized intelligence and systematic gathering of information on foreign armies.' General F. I. Golikov, who took over the military intelligence organization in July 1940, had no previous experience of such work.[45]

Three closely related elements were involved: (1) the *scale* of the potential threat; (2) the general *intentions* of Germany; and (3) the actual *timing* of the attack. Whatever its failings, Soviet intelligence provided Stalin and the Red Army high command with abundant and chilling information about the scale of the German force built up on the border. This goes against the popular misconception of an ignorant Soviet leadership. Churchill despatched a famous letter of warning to Stalin on 3 April 1941, based on intercepted German signals. He actually told the Russians little that was new to them. The key piece of British evidence was that three panzer divisions had been ordered to southern Poland.[46] Golikov's intelligence 'appreciation' of 11 March 1941 had credited the Germans with 123 divisions in the east (East Prussia and Poland) and southeast (Romania), including 12 panzer divisions and 9 motorized divisions. In his final pre-war appreciation, on 31 May 1941, Golikov placed 120–22 German divisions facing the USSR: 23–4 German divisions in East Prussia (including 2 panzer and 3 motorized divisions), 81 divisions in Poland and Slovakia (10 panzer and 6 motorized) and 17 divisions in eastern Romania (2 panzer and 4 motorized). A final British warning, handed to Ambassador Maiskii in London on 16 June, cited a figure slightly *lower* than Golikov's: 80 German divisions in Poland, 30 in Romania, and 5 in Norway and Finland. The actual German strength in the East on 22 June was 121 divisions, plus 14 in reserve (see Table 2.2).[47]

Contrary to what is often suggested, then, the Russians did *not* underestimate the potential scale of the threat; their estimates of German division strengths in the East were very close to reality. The Soviet appreciation of scale was misleading but not in the way that historians have described it. First of all, Soviet intelligence had *exaggerated*, not minimized, the pace of the early German build-up in the East. In a September 1940 war plan, the General Staff placed 'up to' 94 German divisions on the Soviet border. If accurate, this estimate would have implied a great build-up of German troops in the two months since mid-July 1940, when the estimate had been only 13 divisions in East Prussia and 'up to' 28 in Poland. In reality, even in December of that year, only 36

Table 2.2 Location of German Army divisions, end of May 1941

	Soviet estimate 31 May 1941	Actual 22 June 1941
West	76–80 (na, na)	38 (0, 0)
Norway	17 (na, na)	8 (0, 0)
Africa/Italy	17 (na, na)	2 (1, 1)
Balkans	12 (na, na)	7⅓ (0, 0)
East	**120–2 (14, 13)**	**139⅙ (17, 14⅙)**
Reserve	44–8 (na, na)	15 (2, 1)
Total	286–96	209⅙

Source: *1941 god*, vol. 2, p. 289; Müller-Hillebrand, *Das Heer*, vol. 2, p. 111.

Note: Bracketed figures are, respectively, panzer divisions and motorized divisions.

German divisions were facing Russia, out of a total of 140 combat-ready divisions in the German Army. In March 1941 the Soviet estimate had already risen to 111 German divisions. As a result, the figure of 120 divisions produced by Golikov at the end of May 1941 did not seem – as it should have done – an alarming increase; it was only 8 per cent more than in March. More fundamentally, the Russians failed to see that the eastern build-up represented the majority of German divisions. This was because Soviet intelligence greatly exaggerated the overall size of the German Army. It assumed a total strength of 286–96 German divisions, of which 40 per cent were in the East. In reality, the Germans even by this time had only 209 divisions, and 66 per cent were in the East.[48]

Another Soviet miscalculation was underestimating the *quality* of the Wehrmacht. Zhukov, Chief of the General Staff in 1941, later admitted that what surprised him was the power of the sudden German blow and the tight concentration of panzer and motorized divisions on all the main axes of attack. The Russians had studied the German experience of 1939 and 1940, but they assumed that the Red Army was superior to the Polish Army or the French Army, and would put up a better fight. As Stalin apparently put it to Zhukov: 'Hitler is not such a fool as to think that the Soviet Union is Poland, that it is France, that it is England, and even that it is [just] all of them put together.'[49]

The lessons of military history suggest that a significant numeral advantage is needed for a successful attack; this the Germans did not have. The four Soviet frontier military districts possessed on paper 149 divisions, including 36 tank and 18 motorized ones. Stalin and the Soviet high command were aware of the scale of the German build-up, but they believed they had matched it and that the Red Army could deal with an invasion, if it came to that. I would argue, then, contrary to a number of recent historians, that Stalin and his generals believed that they were dealing with Hitler from a position of strength, not from one of weakness. Stalin's sense of inferiority to Germany is central to the arguments in Gabriel Gorodetsky's book *Grand Delusion*, which stresses the dictator's policy of appeasement. It is important to the thesis of David Glantz's *Stumbling*

Colossus, which (like Gorodetsky's book) is partly a polemic against Rezun-Suvorov's *Icebreaker* argument; Rezun-Suvorov, as we have seen, had claimed that Stalin planned to attack Hitler. Gorodetsky and Glantz were right about the actual shortcomings of the Red Army, but it is not clear to me that Stalin saw these shortcomings before the catastrophe of late June 1941.

So Stalin knew that large German forces had been deployed along the Soviet frontier. What he did not know was what Hitler intended to do with them, and he made a fatal misjudgement: he assumed that there was no plan to attack Russia in the near future. After his death, Stalin was blamed for this misjudgement by his immediate political successors, and retired Soviet generals threw in criticism in the memoirs they were now allowed to publish. We know from hindsight that Stalin's view was foolish, but even at the time the sequence of diplomatic events should have alarmed Moscow. A German–Soviet honeymoon followed the signing of the Non-Aggression Treaty in August 1939, but relations then soured. The Wehrmacht defeated France in May and June 1940 and drove the British from the Continent. Germany's overall strategic position was now much better than it had been in 1939, and it must have been obvious to the Kremlin that Hitler needed the USSR less as partner or a neutral than it had before. Moscow and Berlin had already come into conflict over spheres of influence in Eastern Europe. German troops had openly moved into Romania. Molotov, who was both prime minister and the head of the People's Commissariat of Foreign Affairs, went to Berlin in November 1940 (it was his first ever trip abroad). Even such a high-powered visit had not smoothed out relations; Berlin ignored Moscow's subsequent proposals for the solution of various issues. In April 1941, the Germans had invaded Yugoslavia despite Russian diplomatic support for that country. The failure of the Luftwaffe in the Battle of Britain in the autumn of 1940 had shown significant limits of German power. If an invasion of Britain was not possible, where else could the mass of the German Army be employed?

The Kremlin also received intelligence reports about German intentions to attack the USSR. Some of these reports were accurate and were based on knowledge of detailed planning that had begun with the BARBAROSSA directive in December 1940. A report from the military intelligence agent Ilse Stöbe ('*Al'te*') in Berlin, in February 1941, correctly named the commanders of the three German army groups and reported a planned invasion date of 20 May, which was very near what was then the scheduled attack date (15 May). There would be other warnings.[50]

Several factors – some logical, some not – prevented a proper reading of German intentions. To start with, the decision-making structure in Moscow was over-centralized. A great deal depended on Stalin's personal judgement. Accounts vary, but it appears that the Soviet high command did not receive all of the information that Stalin and key Politburo leaders did. It has also been argued that the information and assessments sent to Stalin were tailored by Golikov, the head of military intelligence, to tell the dictator what he wanted to hear. Much came down to Stalin's personal view. Of course, we do not know what Stalin thought. As an old man, Molotov correctly urged caution on this subject, in a critique of other veterans' memoirs of the war: "'Stalin believed this,

Stalin thought that." As if anyone knew what Stalin thought about the war.'[51] It would seem, however, that Stalin was both cautious and suspicious. In the background was his perception of the German power structure. Stalin may well have believed that the leaders of the Third Reich were divided between those who wanted immediate war with the USSR and those who did not, and he may have placed Hitler in the latter group. Stalin's key assumption was perhaps that German policy was undecided, but that rash Soviet action could bring about an unnecessary, or at least premature, war with the Reich. Such action would include precipitate mobilization and concentration of the Red Army or changes in the propaganda line towards Nazi Germany. This was also the reason for the harmful military decision not to man the security zone (*predpol'e*) immediately adjacent to the border; indeed, the NKVD was instructed to ensure that Red Army units obeyed this directive.

Stalin may also have taken as a basic factor Hitler's unwillingness to fight another world war on two fronts. Stalin was not alone in assuming this. The important American warning given to the Soviet ambassador in Washington on 1 March 1941 stated that the US government had reliable information that detailed German plans existed for an attack on the USSR; this was to be 'after the achievement of victory over Britain'. The Soviet leadership received an accurate outline of the BARBAROSSA plan in mid-March 1941, but Golikov's conclusion was, 'I consider the most likely (*vozmozhnoe*) time for the beginning of action against the USSR to be immediately after victory over Britain or the conclusion with her of a peace acceptable to Germany.' 'Germany is involved up to its ears in the war in the West', Stalin reportedly told Zhukov in mid-June, 'and I believe Hitler will not risk creating a second front for himself by attacking the Soviet Union.'[52] As we have already seen, Soviet intelligence overestimated the number of German divisions deployed against the British. Meanwhile, the fighting fronts in the West and the Mediterranean – on land, on sea or in the air – were indeed far from quiet. The warnings received about German intentions, like those about the force build-up on the frontier, could also be interpreted by the Kremlin as the Nazis' diplomatic pressure to force territorial or economic concessions or Churchill's 'provocation' to drag the USSR into war. German 'disinformation' certainly also played its part. The Wehrmacht went to great lengths to mask the preparations for BARBAROSSA, and the major element in their 'deception planning' was to make the Kremlin think the German focus was on continuing operations in the West and in the Mediterranean.

The Kremlin's assessment of the scale of the threat and intentions of the German leadership was related closely to a third element, timing. Stalin and his close comrades probably assumed Nazi intentions were hostile *in the long term*, but they did not expect an attack when it came in June 1941. Soviet spies produced accurate information about the timing of the attack. Famously, 'Ramsay' (Richard Sorge), who had access to the indiscreet German ambassador to Tokyo, warned on 1 June that war would begin in the second half of the month. '*Starshina*' ('Foreman', Harro Schulze-Boysen), a spy holding a senior post in the German Air Ministry, was quoted in a report of 11 June as saying that 'the question of the attack by Germany on the Soviet Union has been definitely decided', and that it might come without any ultimatum. On 17 June a report from

'*Starshina*' stated that 'all military preparations . . . are fully completed' and 'the blow can be expected at any time'.

To understand why Stalin did not take these reports seriously, they must be seen in their entirety and in context. The 11 June report from '*Starshina*' also included an armchair strategist's fantasy of a vast pincer movement involving East Prussia and Romania; his second report predicted an air attack on the power stations near Leningrad and on Moscow aircraft component factories, neither of which was a practical possibility. More important, in a previous report dated 9 May, '*Starshina*' had predicted 20 May as the date of the outbreak of war; on 21 May 'Ramsay' had mentioned the possibility of war at the end of May.[53] Hitler did not, in any event, set the final invasion date (22 June) until 1 May, and he confirmed it only on 10 June. The Kremlin leaders may have thought – correctly, as it would eventually turn out – that the end of June was too late to mount a war-winning attack in 1941, and that the Germans would not attempt it.

There were, to be sure, some last-minute warnings on the night of 21–22 June from anti-Nazi defectors serving in the army of 3,800,000 poised on the Soviet border. A few brave and committed souls crossed the frontier after their units had been briefed about the following day's attack. Late on the evening of 21 June, Stalin finally allowed the military to take action. The forces of the Leningrad, Baltic, Western, Kiev and Odessa Military Districts were ordered to full combat readiness. Fortified border positions were ordered to be manned in the few hours of the night remaining; by dawn, front-line aircraft were to be dispersed and camouflaged.[54] Even then, the alert order was prefaced, at Stalin's insistence, by sentences saying that any attacks might be 'provocative' and calling for a 'hidden' response; any other measures were forbidden. The order was sent out at 12.30 am on 22 June. It is very doubtful if many front-line units actually received it during the night, let alone that they took action. The attacks began at 3.00 am.

The Red Army could have been better deployed on the morning of 22 June 1941. Front-line units could have been at full readiness, with adequate stocks of fuel and ammunition. Front-line air regiments could have been dispersed and camouflaged. Such preparations, however, would have required at least several days' notice, and the Wehrmacht was too skilled to give that. Putting the Red Army on alert a few hours earlier might have saved lives, but it would not have affected the looming military catastrophe.

Soviet war plans

Most historians writing about the Russians' BARBAROSSA disaster have made too little of one crucial factor, Red Army war plans.[55] In an extraordinary example of strategic blindness, the Soviet political and military leadership prepared for war on a false assumption: that there would be time to mobilize and concentrate the Red Army before the main fighting began. *Vnezapnost'* ('suddenness', the element of surprise) was for Soviet commanders a key element in warfare. The USSR would choose when war would break out – as had been the case with Finland in 1939. The Soviet generals could not grasp that it was *the Red Army* that could be caught by surprise. They also expected – at least until the late spring of 1941 – that it would take several weeks for the Germans to concentrate their forces for an attack. They believed that this concentration could not be carried out secretly. It was also assumed that Soviet covering forces on the border could hold any enemy attack for three or four weeks, while the Red Army was mobilized and concentrated. These assumptions were not consistent with the intelligence that was coming in, nor with the knowledge of the sudden attacks that had been mounted against Poland, Scandinavia and France. By May 1941 the Red Army had finally concluded that the German armed forces were *already* mobilized and that a large force had been concentrated in East Prussia and Poland. But Stalin still did not order a change to existing plans.

Behind the planning of 1940–1 was the Red Army's offensive doctrine. Under Marshal Timoshenko, the high command developed a series of war plans from September 1940. The initial plan was for a massive counter-offensive into German-held southern Poland (to be mounted after a thirty-day mobilization period). By May 1941, the planners were proposing a pre-emptive surprise attack, a 'sudden blow on the enemy, both from the air and on land', following a 'hidden mobilization'.[56] Offensive action was tested in the war games of January 1941, and the offensively minded General Zhukov was appointed Chief of the General Staff after his success in those games. Stalin's own preference was for the offensive. In May 1941 he outlined this to a large gathering of Red Army leaders:

> Defending our country, we must act offensively. From defence to go to a military doctrine of offensive actions. We must transform our training, our propaganda, our agitation, our press in an offensive spirit. The Red Army is a modern army, and a modern army is an offensive army.[57]

An early Red Army counter-offensive, and even more, a pre-emptive attack, demanded advance preparation. Ground and air forces, and their supplies, had to be in place near the western border. The Russian railway system has significant limitations, and there were special shortcomings with the lines running from the old western border (i.e. the border before the annexations began in September 1939) to the new one; this made proactive movement of troops and supplies essential. Armoured units had to be located near their start points. Aircraft – which had short range – had to be based as far west as possible to be able to strike at enemy air bases and supply lines in East Prussia, Poland and Romania. As already mentioned, it was in order to cover these forward positions that the fortified regions had to be moved from the Stalin Line to the new border.

Plans and capabilities were fatally mismatched. An offensive doctrine required much better intelligence than the Red Army was actually able to obtain. A more basic problem was that, for reasons already mentioned, the Red Army was ready neither to attack nor to defend itself. Above all, however, Stalin was not prepared to take the preliminary steps required to set in motion an offensively oriented war plan, for fear of precipitating war with Germany. He refused to allow a full-scale 'hidden' general mobilization, despite the requests of Timoshenko and Zhukov. The question came back to intentions and timing. Whether a counter-offensive or a pre-emptive strike was planned, what was crucial to the Kremlin was knowing if and when the Germans were going to attack. Stalin thought that Hitler probably did not intend to attack Russia in the summer of 1941. He opposed measures that might provoke early German aggression, before Red Army force modernization had been completed.

Some steps were taken. In March 1941 the Politburo approved the calling up of 900,000 reservists over the coming summer. In mid-May, four 'High Command Reserve' armies (the 16th, 19th, 21st and 22nd Armies) were ordered to move from the deep interior of the USSR to the Western and Kiev Military Districts. Their strength totalled twenty-eight rifle divisions. At the same time, the military districts on the European border were ordered to draw up 'covering plans'.[58] This was a precaution against a German attack, but it was also a measure for screening the mobilization and concentration of the bulk of the Red Army. Also following Stalin's speech, central party organs prepared two draft propaganda directives which referred to 'a fundamental change in party-political work in the Bolshevik indoctrination of the personnel of the Red Army and of the whole Soviet people in the spirit of burning patriotism, revolutionary decisiveness, and constant readiness to go over to a crushing offensive against the enemy'.[59]

None of this, however, had actually been put in place by 22 June. The secret concentration had not been completed. The cover plan orders had not been drafted by all the border military districts, and there had been no order to put them into effect. The 'offensive war' propaganda directives had not yet been approved by Stalin. What had been issued – on 13 June – was an important communiqué from TASS (the Soviet press agency). Far from creating an 'offensive' mood in the Red Army and among the Soviet population, TASS announced that Germany was not making demands, that it was observing the non-aggression pact and that movement of its forces to the Balkans was not connected with Soviet–German relations. Russia, in accordance with its 'policy of peace', had every intention of observing the non-aggression pact. Any Red Army troop movements were normal summer manoeuvres.[60]

The Soviet offensive doctrine meant not only that Red Army forces were deployed too far forward. It also resulted in a concentration on the wrong part of the border; the planners in Moscow failed to foresee where the fighting would start. The main potential battle front was along a 400-mile line running from the Baltic to the Carpathian Mountains.[61] East Prussia and Poland lay to the west; Belorussia and the Ukraine lay to the east, separated by the Poles'e (the Pripiat' Marshes). The question was whether it was the northern or southern sector of this main front, north or south of the Poles'e, that would be more important. Nearly all historians have discussed this only in terms of a *German attack*. We now know that Hitler decided to attack on a broad front, but with the largest concentration of strength in Belorussia, between the Poles'e and the Baltic. Here were concentrated two of the Wehrmacht's three army groups and, more importantly, three of the four panzer groups. Of 117 German divisions deployed in the East, 76 divisions were in Army Groups North and Centre, and only 41 in Army Group South. The Red Army intelligence figure of some 114–16 German divisions facing Russia was, as we have seen, remarkably close to reality. But there were estimated to be only 53–4 divisions of the potential enemy facing the Baltic and Western Military Districts,

Table 2.3 Distribution of Soviet and German divisions, June 1941

	Soviet divs.	German divs. (Soviet estimate)	German divs. (actual)
Baltic MD	25 (4, 2)	23–4 (2, 3) [E Prussia]	26 (3, 3) [AG North]
Western MD	44 (12, 6)	30 (4, 1)	50 (9, 6) [AG Centre]
Kiev MD	60 (16, 8)	44–5 (6, 5)	
			41 (5, 3) [AG South]
Odessa MD	22 (4, 2)	17 (2, 4) [Romania]	

Source: Zhukov, *ViR*, vol. 1, p. 367; *1941 god*, vol. 2, p. 289 [31 May]; *GSWW*, vol. 4, *Maps*, No. 2.

Note: This table shows the forces deployed in the sectors of the four Soviet border military districts (MDs). Bracketed figures are, respectively, tank/panzer divisions and motorized divisions, separated by a comma. German AG (Army Group) South was divided between the main element based in southern Poland (facing the Kiev MD) and a smaller element in Romania (facing the Odessa MD).

and 61–2 based from the Polese to the Black Sea (see Table 2.3). The March 1941 Red Army plan suggested for the first time that the Germans might concentrate their forces in southeastern Poland and Hungary 'in order by means of a blow in the direction of Berdichev and Kiev to occupy the Ukraine'. In reality, it was at just this time, in March 1941, that Hitler abandoned plans for a southern envelopment of the Soviet forces in the Ukraine, by a German 12th Army moving across the Pruth River.[62]

However, fear for the Ukraine was not the main reason for the concentration of the Red Army there, in the Kiev Military District. From the Russian point of view, the question was not where to defend but *where to attack*. The alternatives lay between attacking the Germans in East Prussia and northern Poland (*out of* Belorussia), and attacking them in southern Poland (*out of* the Ukraine). The problem with the northern axis was that it meant attacking through the lakes and forests of East Prussia, in which there were prepared German defensive fortifications. The Russian Army had stalled there in 1914–15; meanwhile, the strength of modern field fortifications had become clear in the Red Army's 1940 attacks on the Finnish 'Mannerheim Line'. The southern axis, in contrast, allowed an advance into relatively open country, without long-built German fortifications, and with the attacking Red Army's left flank covered by the Carpathian Mountains. A drive into Poland, through Lublin to Kraków and Upper Silesia, would outflank from the south the German concentration in Poland and threaten German links to the Balkans. The Red Army planners looked at the options and recommended an attack along the southern axis. This variant was approved by Stalin in October 1940. A large force, heavy in tanks and aircraft, was built up in the Kiev Military District, which would form the offensive fist of a wartime Southwestern Army Group. The plan was tested in the January 1941 war games. It was developed by Zhukov in the form of the March 1941 and May 1941 war plans when he became Chief of the General Staff.[63]

The ground and air forces of the Red Army *were* caught by surprise on the morning of 22 June. The Soviet leadership made terrible mistakes. It mistook German short-term intentions and capabilities. As for timing, it had no inkling of an imminent attack until a few hours before it began. The element of surprise, however, is not as simple as it is often made out to be. It was certainly not the only reason for the Soviet defeats in 1941. The Wehrmacht, for example, achieved a huge new victory in the Battle of Viaz'ma–Briansk in October 1941, over three months after war started and well after the initial shock had worn off. Far from ignoring the general German threat in the late spring of 1941, Stalin and the Red Army high command were preoccupied with it. The Russians were scrambling to reorganize their forces on the ground and in the air. They believed they had a means of dealing with the German threat, through a counter-offensive or even a pre-emptive attack. What existed by June, however, was a half-baked strategy for offensive actions by Soviet mechanized formations and aviation regiments concentrated near the border. The USSR could not simultaneously prepare a defence in depth and an offensive spearhead; in the end, it had neither. Given Soviet problems of training and deployment, it would not have mattered if the leadership of the USSR had had a week's warning of the date, hour and thrust lines of the invasion. By the summer of 1941, it was already too late to avoid a very serious defeat.

FAILURES OF GERMAN INTELLIGENCE AND STRATEGY

The fallacy of quick victory

Three great failures of strategic intelligence and planning occurred in the summer and autumn of 1941. The mistake of Stalin and the Red Army leaders was the most obvious. Less immediately apparent were two mistakes made by Hitler and the German high command. One was belief in a quick victory over the Soviet Union. The other was the belief that when victory was not won quickly, it could still be achieved in a longer war.

The German planners did not originally think in terms of a *prolonged* war with the USSR. The beginning of Hitler's directive of December 1940 encapsulated the concept: 'The German Wehrmacht must be prepared, even before the conclusion of the war against England, *to crush Soviet Russia in a rapid campaign* (Case Barbarossa).'[64] To Hitler and the planners, it did not matter if Russia had abundant natural resources, a huge population, muddy roads for much of the year or severe winters. It did not matter if it was 700 miles from the Dvina–Dnepr line to the Volga. It did not matter how many tanks and aircraft the USSR could produce in a month. Under the BARBAROSSA plan, victory was to be decided at an operational level *in a few weeks*. The French campaign was the prototype. There, a decisive battle on the frontiers had destroyed the effective forces of the enemy. The resistance of the French government was broken before Paris fell – and after only a tenth of the territory of France had been brought under German control. The central concept, as we saw in Chapter 1, was the 'battle of annihilation' (*Vernichtungsschlacht*), the decisive victory.

The German planners' assumption of a quick victory was, however, fatally flawed, and flawed in its own terms. The two main Wehrmacht thrusts into Poland in 1939 had to cover 65 and 150 miles (from East Prussia and Silesia, respectively). In the seven-week campaign against France in 1940, the depth of the longest advance was 250 miles, the panzer drive west across the Meuse River to the English Channel. The breadth of the active front against France and the Low Countries was only 150 miles. In contrast, even for the 'borderland' battle of annihilation in Russia, the anticipated theatre of operations was vast. The Dvina–Dnepr line, west of which the *Vernichtungsschlacht* was to take place, was some 200 to 350 miles from the 1941 Soviet border, and the German Army had to attack along a breadth of 750 miles. A Soviet defeat within the western border zone would not expose Moscow in the way that the German drive to the Channel had exposed Paris. The distance of the pursuit from the line of the Somme and Aisne rivers to the French capital had been only 75 miles; in contrast, Moscow was 350 miles east of the Dvina–Dnepr line.

The German planners also greatly underestimated the forces required to win the decisive 'battle of annihilation'. Whether or not the Wehrmacht could win such a battle depended on its strength and the enemy's weakness at that time and in that particular region. The German generals may not have known how strong the Red Army was, but they should have been aware of their own limitations. The Wehrmacht began the Russian campaign with forces little stronger than those available in May 1940, especially in terms of tanks and aircraft. There was not even a concentration of effort; the Wehrmacht fought another campaign just before it invaded the USSR, against Yugoslavia and Greece.

The German planners also underestimated the forces the Russians would have available for the battle of annihilation. As we have already seen, the Soviet forces in the western USSR comprised 186 divisions (including the 'second strategic echelon'). German intelligence estimated that the Russians had 147 divisions and 39–40 independent brigades in the four border (western) military districts, out of 180.5 Red Army divisions and 44–5 independent brigades in Europe. There was a much greater discrepancy in the German estimate of the total forces available across the USSR, put at 222.5 divisions and 49–50 independent brigades. In fact, the planned mobilization strength of the ground forces of the Red Army in June 1941 comprised 303 divisions, although a significant proportion of these were only in the early stages of formation. The Germans, even more seriously, underestimated the quantity of equipment available to their enemy at the start of the war. German intelligence estimated that there were 10,000 Soviet tanks, while the total Russian tank park numbered 23,100 vehicles. The Soviets were estimated by the Germans to have a grand total of 6,000 aircraft, 5,000 of them first-line types, and 3,300 in European Russia. The number based on airfields immediately in front of the invaders was actually 9,100, with a total for the whole USSR of 20,000.[65] Soviet pre-war production of key weapons was extraordinary. It is outlined in Table 2.4.

The Germans did not grasp the importance of the pre-war build-up of the Red Army. They did not correctly estimate the number of equipped divisions that the Russians could quickly put into the field. They did not foresee the damage the existing Red Army could inflict on the Wehrmacht, even while retreating and suffering heavy defeats.

In November 1941 Stalin would speak of the 'lack of tanks and – to some extent – of aviation', compared to the enemy; 'in this lies the secret of the temporary successes of the German army'. Khrushchev, in his influential 1956 'Secret Speech' denouncing Stalin, actually said much the same thing. Military preparations, he claimed, were neglected under Stalin: 'From the first days of the war it was apparent that our army was poorly equipped, that we did not have enough artillery, tanks, and aircraft to repel the enemy.'[66] Tables 2.4, 2.5 and 2.6 show the falsity of both Stalin's excuse and Khrushchev's accusation. We now know much more about the pre-war military build-up of the Soviet Union, and descriptive terms like 'Proletarian Sparta' and 'Soviet warfare state' are far from irrelevant. This build-up applied not just to mobilization potential; it applied to actual production in the pre-war years. Soviet factories turned out as many military aircraft in 1939 as German ones did in 1942. It has been justly argued that the whole 'raison d'être of the Soviet warfare state was ... to wage war from a running start.'[67] The Red Army did not succeed in doing that (or it turned out to be running in the wrong direction), but the effort could not but have an impact. The USSR produced 9,600 tanks in 1937–40, as well as 50,000 artillery pieces and 31,000 military aircraft. The total personnel of the Soviet armed forces rose from 1,600,000 in January 1938 to over 5,000,000 in mid-1941. These 'objective' figures make much more understandable how

Table 2.4 Soviet pre-war weapons production, 1937–41

	1937	1938	1939	1940	1941 (Jan.–Jun)
Tanks	1,600	2,300	3,000	2,800	1,700
Artillery	5,400	12,300	17,100	15,100	7,900
Mortars	1,600	1,200	4,100	37,900	10,500
Rifles	567,400	1,224,700	1,396,700	1,395,000	792,000
MGs	31,100	52,600	73,600	52,200	na
Aircraft	4,400	5,500	10,400	10,600	6,000
Munitions	na	13m	20m	33m	19m

Source: VOV/VOI, vol. 1, p. 508.

Note: MGs are machine guns. Munitions are shells and mines.

Table 2.5 Comparative armaments production, January 1941 to December 1942

	1941		1942	
	Germany	USSR	Germany	USSR
Rifles	1,359,000	2,421,000	1,370,000	4,049,000
MG	96,000	149,000	117,000	356,000
Artillery	22,000	41,000	41,000	128,000
Tanks/SPG	3,800	6,600	6,200	24,700
Combat aircraft	8,400	12,400	11,600	21,700

Source: J. Barber and M. Harrison (eds), The Soviet Defence-Industry Complex from Stalin to Khrushchev (Basingstoke: Macmillan, 2000), p. 100.

Note: Figures cover the period from January 1941. Artillery includes mortars. MG = machine guns, SPG = self-propelled guns.

Table 2.6 Soviet military equipment, June 1941 to December 1942

	On hand 22 June 1941	Entered 22 June 1941 to 31 Dec. 1941	Lost 1941	On hand 1 Jan. 1942	Entered Service 1942	Lost 1942	On hand 1 Jan. 1943
Rifles	7,740,000	157,000	5,550,000	3,760,000	4,040,000	2,180,000	5,620,000
SMG	100,000	100,000	100,000	100,000	1,560,000	550,000	1,110,000
MG	248,900	55,100	190,800	113,200	238,200	106,100	245,300
AT	14,900	2,500	12,100	5,300	20,500	11,500	14,300
AA	8,600	3,400	4,100	7,900	6,800	1,600	13,100
Artillery	33,200	10,100	24,400	18,900	30,100	12,300	36,700
Mortars	56,100	42,400	60,500	38,000	230,000	82,000	186,100
'Katiushas'	0	1,000	0	1,000	3,300	700	3,600
Heavy tanks	500	1,000	900	600	2,600	1,200	2,000
Medium tanks	900	2,200	2,300	800	13,400	6,600	7,600
Light tanks	21,200	2,400	17,300	6,300	11,900	7,200	11,000
Fighters	11,500	6,000	9,600	7,900	10,700	7,000	11,600
Attack aircraft	100	1,400	1,100	400	7,200	2,600	5,000
Bombers	8,400	2,500	7,200	3,700	4,100	2,500	5,300
Motor vehicles	273,000	205,000	159,000	318,000	153,000	66,000	404,000
Radios	37,000	6,000	24,000	19,000	27,000	7,000	40,000

Source: Poteri, pp. 473–81.

Note: Rows do not always exactly add up, due to rounding. SMG = submachine guns, MG = machine guns, AT = anti-tank guns, AA = anti-aircraft guns, attack aircraft = *shturmoviki*, 'Katiusha' = multiple rocket launcher. Motor vehicles 'entered service', especially for 1941, includes mobilization of existing civilian trucks, etc. Figures include Lend-Lease supplies, but this was only a small component in 1941–2. Aircraft losses include accidents.

the Soviet leadership could discount the importance of the purges. An example of this overconfidence is Stalin's private statement on the occasion of Marshal Voroshilov's 60th birthday in February 1941:

> At one time the Tsarist government dreamt of having in peacetime an army of 1,700,000 and was able to bring the army up to 1,100,000. We have an army of over 4,000,000 and it is well equipped. It is a force that cannot be ignored in deciding questions of international relations, and therefore we are able to occupy a neutral position; we can achieve successes in the realm of foreign relations, because we have a mighty arm.[68]

The question, then, was not: Why did the Red Army not have 'enough artillery, tanks, and aircraft'? It was: Why was the Red Army defeated *despite* having been so lavishly equipped?

The Germans expected their swift and decisive military victory in western Russia to coincide with the collapse of Communist rule. The serious flaws in the Soviet system and deep popular dissatisfaction have already been mentioned. However, the Stalinist apparatus of control, in the form of the Communist Party and the NKVD, was much more resilient than the German planners expected, even in the short term. As Stalin put it in November 1941, 'any other government which had suffered such losses of territory as we did would not have stood the test and would have collapsed'.[69] This Nazi blindness to the strength inherent in another police state is extraordinary. The Stalinist political terror of the 1920s and 1930s had wiped out any organized political opposition, and much more besides. Equally, the Germans underestimated the degree of active popular support that the economic and state-building achievements of the Soviet system had won, and they underestimated the effect of the Communist Party's absolute monopoly of power and of nearly twenty-five years of political propaganda. The Nazis also had little inkling of the extent to which Moscow would be able to rally the population, even in the summer of 1941, around a traditional 'Brothers and Sisters' policy of Russian patriotism, and around Stalin as a 'national' figurehead. The Germans might have had more political impact had they depicted the invasion from the outset as a war of liberation, against Stalinism and Bolshevism or against Russian oppression of the minorities. But that, put at its simplest, was not what the Nazi regime was about.

The war of attrition

Within about six weeks of the start of the BARBAROSSA campaign, it was clear that the Wehrmacht had indeed won a brilliant 'operational' victory and perhaps – in Napoleon's or Schlieffen's sense – a battle of annihilation. But Germany had not won the war. The Red Army had not been destroyed, the Nazi–Soviet conflict had become a war of attrition, and longer-term factors had come into play. Hitler and the generals did not despair then. Even with the serious military setback at the Battle of Moscow in December 1941, only a few German leaders saw the writing on the wall. Wishful thinking about the battle of annihilation was replaced by wishful thinking about a war of attrition. German Supreme Headquarters could see that the Wehrmacht had advanced deep into the USSR and had inflicted much heavier losses on the Red Army than it had itself suffered. German intelligence underestimates of Red Army strength continued into the summer campaign of 1942. The assumption – repeatedly made and repeatedly incorrect – was that the Red Army and the USSR were on the brink of exhaustion.

The strategic calculus had changed. For a battle of annihilation, divisions and air squadrons, in place, at the start of the fighting, were all that mattered. For a war of attrition, it now *did* matter that Russia had abundant natural resources, a huge population, muddy roads and severe winters. It did matter that it was 700 miles from the Dvina–Dnepr line to the Volga. It did matter how many tanks and aircraft the USSR could produce in a month. For a protracted war, fundamental comparisons came into play. The first of these was population. In September 1939, Germany had a population of 80 million, while that of the USSR was 171 million.[70] Germany, unlike Russia, would have allies directly involved in the fighting in the East. Romania had a population of 16 million, Hungary 9 million, and Finland 4 million. Fascist Italy, with a pre-war population of 43 million, would commit a large 'expeditionary force'. Those allies would become an important factor in 1942, as the front line in Russia held by German divisions stretched to unmanageable lengths. Later in the war, German manpower was freed for the Wehrmacht by the conscription of foreign labour. But these factors did not alter the basic demographic reality: the Soviet population was more than twice that of pre-war Germany. Population distribution also had critical implications. In the period 1941–2, about 65 million citizens of the 1941 USSR would live in the German-occupied zone, but the majority of these were not ethnic Russians[71]; they were Ukrainians, Belorussians or members of the Baltic nationalities. Nearly half the people in the occupied zone had been Soviet 'citizens' for only a year or two. At the height of the Wehrmacht's advance, the Soviet government still controlled a huge population of well over 100 million people, and that population now contained a much higher proportion of ethnic Russians than it had before June 1941.

The enormous size of the territory that the Wehrmacht had to conquer in a prolonged war (rather than to occupy after a quick battle of annihilation) also shows the impossible demands facing the Germans. The area of the European part of the USSR alone extended over 2,110,000 square miles, with a further 6,460,000 square miles in the Asiatic part. Hitler liked to make comparisons between Russia and India, but even the European part of USSR could have swallowed up the 1,630,000 square miles of British India. By comparison, previous German conquests seemed trifling: the territory of Poland was 120,000 square miles, that of France 213,000. Overall, the Germans are officially reckoned to have taken 693,000 square miles of Soviet territory by November 1942.[72] Rough terrain, a harsh climate and a poor infrastructure made the German task more difficult. European Russia is not the endless grassy plain of the 'steppe'. Its territory is divided into three vegetation belts. Thick forests are common in the north, further south there is wooded steppe and only south to the Black Sea does the steppe proper open out. It was no accident that the 1942 German advances (towards Stalingrad) were across the steppe, while from the winter of 1941–2 a static war of positions was the norm in the wooded zone. Rivers blocked the invaders' path, first of all the Dvina and the Dnepr, further east the Don, the Donets and the Volga. Large territories were swampy; the Poles'e separated Army Groups Centre and South in 1941; marshland protected Leningrad, and numerous small glacial lakes covered the northern approaches to Moscow. Dense woods like the Briansk Forest provided bases for partisans.

Modern roads were few in Russia, and movement was brought to a halt during the spring and autumn thaws, the *rasputitsa*. Dirt roads turned to mud, and swollen rivers became major obstacles. Winter snow blocked roads, and frost disabled vehicle motors. The railways were potentially the best means for moving troops and supplies, but the Germans could expect to have to rebuild the system slowly as they advanced. Their engineers would have to narrow broad-gauge Russian track (5 feet) to the European standard gauge (4 feet 8.5 in) before it could take German supply trains. The Russian railway system was not dense by European standards, but it was sizeable and had been further lengthened in the 1930s. The defenders would be able to use their railway system to move troops and goods to and from the deep hinterland, and from one part of the front to another; they would do this at a time when the invading force was still repairing the lines on the other side of the front.

The low population density of Russia added to the problem of moving and supporting large bodies of troops; fewer inhabitants per square mile meant fewer roads, less shelter and less food for troops living off the land. The modern UK has an average population density of about 660 people per square mile; the part of Soviet territory lost to the Germans in 1941–2 had a density of only 115. By the end of the first phase of the war, the Wehrmacht would be fighting in territory that was very sparsely inhabited indeed: Rostov and Stalingrad Regions in the southeast had a population density of only 49 people per square mile.[73]

Demography, geography and climate were factors that had worn down invaders of Russia throughout history. What was new, and what was still not taken seriously by the Germans at the end of 1941, was the economic potential of the USSR. When the Nazis thought of Russia in economic terms at all, it was as a crude object of looting. To repeat: underlying Russian economic potential did not matter *if victory was swift*. Economic potential became vital when the conflict was dragged out to become a war of attrition and production. A comparison of Soviet and German armaments production in 1941–2 is given in Table 2.5. In each category of weapons production, the Russians were ahead. Procurement and losses on the Soviet side are given in Table 2.6.[74] This second table is long and detailed, but essential for understanding the course of the first two years of the Nazi–Soviet war. It emphasizes, first of all, that the Red Army enjoyed a remarkably high level of equipment in June 1941. Second, it makes clear the staggering losses of this equipment in 1941–2 suffered by the Russians (in 1941, 41,000 out of 57,000 artillery pieces, 20,000 out of 23,000 tanks). Finally, Table 2.6 shows that a quite remarkable production effort made good the larger part of those huge losses of matériel by December 1942. Nothing, unfortunately, could make good the human losses.

What lay behind the success of Soviet equipment build-up after June 1941? Supply from abroad was not initially a big factor. Little aid from the United States and Britain reached the fighting front of the Red Army in the first eighteen months of the war. It needs to be stressed again that Soviet production had been steadily climbing in the final pre-war years (see Table 2.4). Huge investments had been poured into the arms production industries, and this led to a large number of new plants coming on stream in 1941–2. Molotov was right when he recalled that 'the growth of our military industry in the years before the war could not possibly have been greater!'[75] Both before and after June 1941, factories producing civilian goods converted quickly to military production, following pre-war mobilization plans.

By the end of 1941 the Wehrmacht had occupied key manufacturing centres of the USSR. Leningrad had been reduced to a starving shell, while Khar'kov in the Ukraine was actually in German hands. It is perhaps not surprising that the Germans thought Soviet arms production had been shattered. Another strength of the Soviet system, unanticipated in Berlin, was the ability to evacuate industrial plants from the threatened western and central zones. Contrary to myth, the USSR had made no special effort before the war to concentrate armaments production in the eastern part of the country. The Five-Year Plans (especially in 1927–37) had opened up the natural resources of Asiatic Russia, but that was for overall economic development. The Soviet planners had had some awareness of the vulnerability of factories to air attack, including gas attack, but little sense that a deep invasion was likely. The pre-war priority was to maximize current weapons production by concentrating it in the *developed* (western) parts of the country. Even many of the new war plants established in 1938–40 were sited in central European Russia and the Ukraine. There were no pre-war plans for the evacuation of industry to the East.[76]

Evacuation took place in two major waves, in July–August 1941 and from September 1941. Figures vary, but probably some 2,500 'enterprises' were moved. Half went to the Urals, the rest to the Volga region, to western Siberia and to Kazakhstan in Central Asia. In terms of distance, this would be like the Germans moving the munitions plants of the Ruhr to Spain. The best Western source estimates that the Soviet move took in 8–10 per cent of pre-war 'capital stock' (productive capacity).[77] The success of *evakuatsiia* should not be exaggerated. Much of Soviet war industry was already in the eastern part of European Russia (between Moscow and the Urals) and did not need to be evacuated; examples would be the big complex of aircraft plants on the middle Volga, or the weapons plants at Gor'kii. Evacuation also involved terrible waste, as trainloads of equipment were bombed or simply lost. Also, trains that were evacuating factories to the rear could not effectively move forward troops and supplies. Industrial production slumped temporarily in the winter of 1941–2, partly from a fuel crisis and partly because it took time to get the evacuated plants working.

Beyond evacuation was something much more fundamental: the extraordinary growth of the Soviet economy in the interwar years. The Russia that Hitler had written about in *Mein Kampf* in the mid-1920s produced some 4 million tons of steel a year, roughly what it had produced before the First World War. Soviet factories built fewer than 500 motor vehicles in 1927. In 1940 annual Soviet steel production had risen to 18.3 million tons, and the motor industry turned out some 200,000 vehicles (mostly trucks). The Stalin government had prioritized the development of heavy industry – and the armaments industry – at the end of the 1920s. In assessing the position of the USSR in 1929, the Red Army strategist V. K. Triandafillov bemoaned the potential contradiction for the USSR between 'the mechanized front and the peasant rear', but a remarkable change took place in the 1930s.[78] The USSR now had the components of a successful war economy. This system had, at its heart, a brutal but effective economic planning system. The Germans had an inherent advantage in their military general staff system; the Russians had the advantage of a 'command' economic administrative system.

As its many critics have pointed out, the Soviet economy was not 'planned' in an overall rational sense; there was no balanced economy. On the other hand by 1941 the Stalinist state had gained over a decade's experience of setting targets and allocating scarce resources. The war required little change to the formal structure of the 'military-industrial complex'. A cohort of able and experienced young economic administrators had emerged from the confusion of the 1930s, and they would lead the wartime economy. As Stalin himself put it late in 1943:

> The lessons of the war are that the Soviet structure is not only the best form of the organization of the economic and cultural advance of the country in the years of peaceful development, but also the best form of mobilization of all forces of the people to drive off the enemy in wartime.[79]

For the war economies of all the combatant powers, a critical factor was labour, the availability of men and women to work in factories and on building sites. Russian industry faced a severe shortage of industrial workers after the start of the war. At the end of 1941 the labour force had shrunk to 18.5 million men and women, or about 60 per cent of what it had been six months before.[80] The Soviets were able to bring additional labour into the workplace, especially women, teenagers and pensioners. The government lengthened working time and applied the most severe discipline; job-leaving was equated with desertion. Some factories, especially in the aircraft industry, were already run on a semi-military basis, with uniformed managers and foremen. By the end of 1941 about 700,000 people were serving in construction battalions. A compulsory mobilization of the whole urban population for war work was ordered in February 1942. This applied to men from age sixteen to fifty-five, and women from sixteen to forty-five. As with Nazi Europe, forced labour (or 'slave labour') was an important component. Some of the most difficult construction tasks were undertaken by the forced labourers from the NKVD's prison camp system, the GULAG. The camps had over two million inmates at the start of the war. Forced labourers were especially important in the repair and expansion of the railway system, military roads and airfields. They were also used for the construction of new plants, especially in remote and difficult locations.[81]

Labour was one key factor in production, two other factors were raw materials and fuel. By November 1941 the Wehrmacht had occupied territory from which two-thirds of the USSR's coal and iron ore had been mined before the war.[82] Key resources had been in the Ukraine. Iron ore was mined around Krivoi Rog (west of the Dnepr River bend), coal in the Donbass (Donets *bassein* or 'basin') (east of it). An extensive metallurgical industry had been created around them. The fact that the Soviets had lost this region, and that the Germans controlled it, would be a reason for misguided optimism at the Führer's headquarters in the second half of 1942. As it happened, the invaders were never able to exploit these Ukrainian resources effectively, due to distance and wartime damage. Meanwhile, the Soviets, who had begun the war holding the better part of a continent, still had access to vast resources beyond the line of German control. The eastern part of European Russia, especially the Urals, had been a centre of mining and metallurgy since Tsarist times. In the 1920s and 1930s further development of major mining and manufacturing took place there, and even further east in Uzbekistan in Central Asia, and in central and southern Siberia. The huge iron ore mines and blast furnaces around Magnitogorsk in the southern Urals had been one of the showpiece developments of the Five-Year Plans. The mines of Karaganda in Central Asia and the Kuzbass (Kuznetskii *bassein*) of central Siberia were available to make up for the coal of the Donbass. These enterprises provided raw materials and energy for factories which had been founded in the eastern part of the USSR in the 1930s, or which were evacuated there in 1941.

Another Russian mineral resource advantage was huge reserves of petroleum. For the Germans the Soviet oil fields were a vital economic objective, but the distance to them from the western frontier was as far as the distance to the Urals. In the end, the Wehrmacht would get nowhere near the most important oil-producing area, near Baku, on the Caspian Sea. As one German spearhead was fighting in Stalingrad, in the autumn of 1942, another approached Groznyi on the route to Baku. But the Wehrmacht was already stretched to its limits, and the attempt to grasp both Stalingrad *and* Groznyi proved disastrous. The continental Soviet economy in any event possessed another oil region east of the Volga, between Kuibyshev and Ufa. This was the so-called 'Second Baku', developed in the 1930s. Wartime problems reduced total Soviet crude oil production from 33 million tons in 1941 to 22 million in 1942 and 18 million in 1943. German production, however, was only 5.7 million tons in 1941, of which 3.9 million was synthetic oil. The Romanian oil fields were vitally important to Germany, but they produced only 5.5 million tons in 1941 and 5.7 million in 1942.[83]

Food supply had been the Achilles' heel of the war effort of both Russia and Germany in the First World War. As already discussed, for Hitler's project of a self-sufficient – autarkic – Reich, the food resources of the USSR were deemed to be essential. As a result of its operations, the German Army came to occupy by the end of 1942 about half the cultivated land in the USSR. In the first campaign alone, up to November 1941, the enemy occupied territory which had produced 38 per cent of the Soviet Union's grain and held a large proportion of its livestock. The most important region, again, was the Ukraine.[84] The German occupiers attempted ruthless exploitation of food resources, at the expense of the local population. In the end, however, Soviet agriculture was not easily exploited by Germany, although the large occupying army was fed, and some food was shipped back to the Reich. Soviet 'scorched earth' policy, wartime disruption and the lack of rewards for the farmers of the occupied territories prevented the level of 'exports' the Nazis had hoped for. The Germans had access to three Ukrainian autumn harvests; the first, however, took place in the chaotic conditions of 1941, and by the autumn of 1943, the Wehrmacht had already lost half the region.

After the retreats of 1941, the Soviet government faced terrible difficulties in agriculture and food procurement. It still held most of northern and central European Russia, but before the war much of the food for this area had come from regions that were now occupied by the Wehrmacht. Agriculture also suffered from a lack of labour, as *kolkhozniki* (collective-farmers) were called up for the Red Army or to jobs in the war industry. The grain harvest available in 1942 was only a third of that in 1940.[85] The continental scale of the USSR was again a saving grace. The Moscow government still controlled the farmland of the Volga basin and the newer agricultural regions of Kazakhstan and western Siberia. The state also had much more direct control over agriculture and supply than its Tsarist predecessor had had in 1914–17. The collectivization of agriculture from 1929 to 1930 had been a disaster both for the peasants and for the rural economy. It had, however, put in place the administrative machinery required to control production and supply. Meanwhile, the Soviet state had been able to accumulate large reserves of grain.[86]

The Nazi leaders failed correctly to assess Russian economic potential for a prolonged war of attrition; they also failed to prepare Germany's own industry for such a conflict.[87] The German lands had industrialized half a century before Russia. If the Five-Year Plans boosted Soviet annual steel production to 18.3 million tons by 1940, German production, even within the 1937 borders, was 19.1 million. The steel output of Germany and occupied Europe averaged no less than 33.4 million tons a year in 1941–4, compared to 11.3 million a year for the USSR.[88] All the same, German production of the basic types of weapon was smaller than that of Russia, let alone that of the whole anti-German alliance, including the United States and Britain. The notion that Hitler set out to fight a series of short wars, and organized his economy accordingly, is not now generally accepted by historians.[89] He actually began preparations for a long-term general war, but that conflict came earlier than expected – in the autumn of 1939. Even twenty months later, in June 1941, the Reich economy was prepared 'in breadth' but not 'in depth'. German factories produced a range of advanced weapons, but facilities did not exist for long-term production on a massive scale. As for the Russian campaign, it had been expected to be a short one which would not, in itself, require the acceleration of German war production. Ground forces were needed to defeat the USSR; this required tanks, trucks and massed army personnel. In contrast, aeroplanes and warships would be required to fight the expected longer war against Britain and, potentially, America. The second type of war demanded different specialist forces, and it demanded factory workers. A month after the beginning of BARBAROSSA, with the Russian campaign still seemingly going very well, Hitler would actually order a switch of resources away from army production.[90]

Administrative inefficiency also held back the war economy of the Reich. Hitler was an economic illiterate, and Goering, head of the Nazi 'Four-Year Plan', a poor co-ordinator. The situation improved after 1940, when technocrats were put in charge of war production, first Fritz Todt, and then, in early 1942, Albert Speer. Production was rationalized; more effective use was made of available labour, machinery and raw materials. This was partly a response to shortcomings that had become evident at the *beginning* of 1941 (after the 1940 French campaign but before BARBAROSSA); it also came partly from the realization at the end of 1941 that the war in Russia was going to be a long one. In 1942–4, the Germans achieved a 'production miracle'. Soviet tank production, for example, was four times greater than German tank production in 1942, but only twice as great in 1943, and one and a half times greater in 1944.[91]

In any event the Reich war economy could not have been rationalized earlier. If the Germans had known their main priority was going to be a prolonged land war in Russia, they might have emphasized tank production earlier. But that would have meant giving up other global goals. The point of Nazi grand strategy was *not* to fight a prolonged land war in Russia. Also, a large factor in the increased 'German' output of 1943–4 was the development of a Europe-wide scale of production. Such a process could only be in its early stages in 1940–1, as the Reich had to consolidate its hold over the occupied countries. This leads to a final paradox. For Hitler the original strategic point of the BARBAROSSA campaign had been to tap Russian resources for a general war against Britain and the United States. But the failure of the 'battle of annihilation' meant that Russia unexpectedly became the biggest of Germany's *problems*. The vast lands in eastern Europe were still largely beyond German control, and so a different kind of 'wide-scale economy' (*Grossraumwirtschaft*) had to be created. To fight a war against an industrialized Soviet Russia, Germany had to attempt to exploit the resources of western and central Europe.

The Nazis and the German military, then, made fundamental errors in the preparation of their own forces and in their assessment of Soviet strengths and weaknesses. They underestimated the difficulties of campaigning in the expanses even of western Russia. They underestimated the strength of the Red Army, and they misunderstood its deployment. Even as the campaign dragged out into a war of attrition, over the summer and autumn of 1941 and into the following winter, most of the German leadership thought that the war was still winnable. In this they showed themselves poorly informed about the broader economic potential of Soviet Russia and the adaptability of the Soviet system. They were ignorant too of the ability of the 'Bolshevik' government to rally the population around the cause of national defence. What can explain these fatal errors of German intelligence and strategic planning – which applied both to the war of annihilation and to the war of attrition?

The misperception by the Germans (and by other governments) came partly from the closed nature of the USSR. (The British and American intelligence services also got things wrong, assuming after 22 June a quick Soviet collapse.) But there were also shortcomings on the side of the Wehrmacht. Intelligence work, it has been argued, had never been its strongest feature, and there seem to have been particular shortcomings with respect to Soviet Russia. The Army General Staff officer responsible for co-ordinating intelligence about the Red Army, General Kinzel, was not a Russian specialist.

In April 1942 Kinzel was replaced by the later-famous Colonel Reinhard Gehlen, but Gehlen too lacked expertise on Russian affairs. A deeper problem was arrogance about German military prowess and about racial superiority in a war of Teuton against Slav; this arrogance came partly from Nazi ideology, but it also had more traditional origins in German nationalism.[92]

CONCLUSION

Operation BARBAROSSA was one of history's most carefully premeditated and planned invasions, developed by German staff officers over eight or nine months, and thought about even longer. In the Second World War, only the planning for Operation OVERLORD, the British-American invasion of France, was comparable. Nevertheless, the German planning for the attack on the Soviet Union contained fatal flaws. From the beginning of the war in the East there were for both sides certain inevitabilities. The Soviets were to fight at a severe disadvantage, due to weaknesses in their armed forces and in their society and to misperceptions of their own strength and of the strength and intentions of Nazi Germany. Hitler, famously, told his generals in January 1941 that Russia was a colossus with feet of clay, and there was some truth in this assessment. But in November 1938 General Beck, the former chief of the Army General Staff, had used the same metaphor to describe the war potential of the Third Reich. 'The Wehrmacht', he noted, 'is comparable to a colossus on earthen feet, if it is not supported by the other factors necessary for total warfare.'[93]

Before the war began, numerous factors were in play that would make the struggle much longer and harder than Hitler or the German military ever expected. At 3.00 am on 22 June 1941, as the Luftwaffe began its first attacks on Soviet airfields, many things – more than either side knew – had already been decided.

CHAPTER 3
OPERATION BARBAROSSA,
JUNE TO SEPTEMBER 1941

I have decided today to put the fate of our state and our people in the hands of our soldiers. God help them in the great struggle.

Adolf Hitler, 22 June 1941

The State Defence Committee must recognize that individual commanders and rank-and-file combatants display unsteadiness, panic, shameful cowardice, they are throwing away their arms and, forgetting their duty to the Motherland, completely breaking their [military] oath, and becoming a herd of sheep running in panic before an insolent enemy.

GKO Decree, 16 July 1941

The 1941 campaign in Russia was without doubt one of the most remarkable in all military history. The border defeats began a cascade of misfortune for the Red Army, leading to the loss of vast territories and, presently, of millions of lives. And yet this year was also probably the turning point of the Second World War. The initial German offensive in Russia lasted for five and a half months. It began with the start of Operation BARBAROSSA on 22 June 1941, and it ended when the Russian counter-attack in front of Moscow began on 5 December.[1] The present chapter deals with the first three months of this period, when the Germans achieved their greatest advances and inflicted the heaviest casualties.

THE DESTRUCTION OF THE RED ARMY AIR FORCE

Some events were repeated up and down the front. Accounts of BARBAROSSA often pass quickly over one of the most extraordinary events of the Second World War, the destruction of the Red Army Air Force in the first hours and days of the campaign.[2] Nothing else like this occurred between 1939 and 1945. The most recently published sources show that the air units of the Western Military District lost 740 combat aircraft out of a total of 1,540 at the very start of the war; the local air commander, General I. I. Kopets, shot himself in despair. The destruction was even worse in the Baltic Military District, which lost 920 out of 1,080 aircraft in the first three days. Only the Kiev Military District lost a smaller number, 340 aircraft (of which 230 were destroyed on the ground) out of a total of 1,760. Compared to this total of about 2,000 Russian aircraft, the Germans lost 330 aircraft (up to the end of June).[3] Heads rolled in the Red Army Air Force command. General

Rychagov, who had headed the VVS until April 1941, was arrested on the second day of the war; a few days later he was followed into prison by P. S. Volodin from the Air Force staff; both men were shot, with a number of other commanders, in October.

Many of the Russian aircraft were destroyed on the ground by Luftwaffe strafing and bombing attacks in the early morning of 22 June. But even repairable aircraft had to be abandoned when their forward airfields were overrun or surrounded by German ground forces. In the air battles of the following days, the relatively inexperienced Russian fighter pilots, flying their little I-16 monoplane fighters or even I-15 and I-153 biplanes, could hardly catch up with the Luftwaffe's bombers, let alone shoot them down. Russian medium and light bombers were thrown against enemy airfields and advancing ground troops without fighter escort. Without radios, without co-ordination, without modern tactics, and without experience of operations against a large, modern enemy air force, Russian fighters and bombers fell easy victim to the Messerschmitt Bf 109 and Bf 110 fighters of the Luftwaffe. The German ace, 'Vati' Mölders, shot down his 100th enemy plane on 16 July, having destroyed thirty aircraft over Army Group Centre since the start of the Russian war.

The Luftwaffe achieved air superiority and within three days was able to shift over to an army-support role. German control of the skies was an essential prerequisite for the disaster which befell the Red Army over the following summer and autumn. Soviet troops were at the mercy of Luftwaffe attack aircraft, and Soviet commanders operated with very little air reconnaissance. The psychological impact of Luftwaffe air superiority was telling, and the Soviets reckoned 'aeroplane panic' (*samoletoboiazn'*) to be a major problem among their troops. The closely co-operating German motorized and air units surged ahead. Russian air losses mounted throughout the 1941 campaign, totalling nearly 3,990 combat aircraft on the three main fronts up to the first week of July (compared to a total of 550 German aircraft lost) and a further 2,950 up to the end of September. All told, the Red Army Air Force would lose 10,300 warplanes (5,100 fighters and 5,200 bombers and attack planes) in battle in 1941, with a further 7,600 lost due to other causes (accidents or written off). In addition, 3,600 trainers and transports were lost, for a grand total of 21,200 aircraft; this was from an initial strength of 32,100. German losses in the East in the same period totalled 2,180 planes lost in combat and 330 from non-combat causes. These German losses were not insignificant: by comparison, Luftwaffe losses in the three and a half months of the Battle of Britain in 1940 had been 1,290 aircraft (the British lost 790 fighters).[4]

BELORUSSIA AND SMOLENSK: GERMAN ARMY GROUP CENTRE

German victories in Belorussia

The German ground forces struck their heaviest blow on the centre of the Soviet front, first of all in Belorussia, and then further east on the distant approaches to Moscow.[5] The commander of Army Group Centre, Fedor von Bock, was a very experienced soldier.[6] He had led the northern pincer into Poland in 1939, and he won his field marshal's baton

MAP 1 The German invasion, 1941.

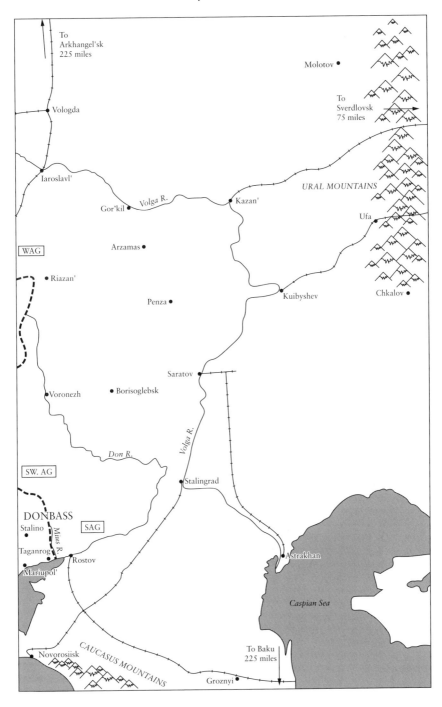

for the lightning strike into Holland in 1940. Bock was a third-generation officer from the Prussian military elite. The National Socialist Hitler fundamentally distrusted such aristocratic officers on class grounds, but he clearly placed great confidence in Bock. Even after he failed to take Moscow, Bock would be assigned to the main attack again, in 1942 in south Russia. In 1941 Bock had two field armies (the 9th and the 4th) and two panzer groups (the 3rd under Hermann Hoth and the 2nd under Heinz Guderian).[7] The defending Soviet Western Army Group, the forces of the pre-war Western Military District, were about to suffer sudden and devastating defeat. A month after the outbreak of war, the army group commander, General D. G. Pavlov, would be executed by his own government, along with his chief of staff and several subordinates.

German Army Group Centre carried out a devastating double encirclement in Belorussia. By the seventh day of the war Soviet forward forces stationed on the border around Belostok (now Białystok) had been encircled by Bock's infantry. The second and deeper encirclement was achieved during the same week by the tank forces operating on the flanks of Army Group Centre. Hoth's 3rd Panzer Group had attacked near Grodno (on the north flank) and Guderian's 2nd Panzer Group at Brest (on the south flank); they linked up at Minsk, 200 miles to the east. This deep 'cauldron' (*Kessel*) trapped nearly all Pavlov's remaining forces. It was the 'Cannae' operation – inspired by Hannibal's 216 BC battle of encirclement and annihilation – that classically educated Prussian staff officers had dreamt of since the time of Field Marshal von Schlieffen. About thirty Red Army divisions were trapped in what had now become the Belostok–Minsk pocket. Organized Soviet resistance continued until about 8 July. Not the least of the dangers facing the trapped Soviet soldiers was the forest fires set off by combat and spread by

FIGURE 2 German troops enter a burning Russian village in the first days of the war.

the dry weather. Red Army losses included 4,800 tanks and 9,400 guns and mortars. A high proportion were evidently abandoned rather than destroyed by the enemy; the Germans claimed as captured 3,300 tanks and 1,800 artillery pieces. Russian figures for killed, missing and captured personnel come to 340,000, which needs to be compared to the total strength of 680,000 in the Western Army Group at the start of the war. A very high proportion of these losses were soldiers taken prisoner, rather than killed on the battlefield; the Germans claimed 324,000 POWs.[8] These prisoners were just the first wave of a great flood of misery.

The reasons for Soviet failure

In the Baltic theatre of the huge Russian–German front, fragments at least of the border armies would escape; this will be described later in this chapter. In the southern theatre, in the Ukraine, stubborn resistance would continue into August. In contrast, almost all General Pavlov's Western Army Group was swallowed up within a matter of a week. Why did the battle go so terribly badly for the Red Army in Belorussia?

Pavlov was dismissed on 30 June and replaced by Marshal Timoshenko. Stalin's decision to put the People's Commissar of Defence himself in command of the Western Army Group showed the extreme gravity of the crisis in the central theatre and the primary importance that was now attached to it. Within days the unfortunate Pavlov was arrested, tried and executed. His chief of staff, V. E. Klimovskikh, and several subordinates suffered the same fate. The original indictment against Pavlov and Klimovskikh included the charge that they were 'participants in an anti-Soviet military conspiracy' and had *allowed* themselves to be defeated. In the end the charges – though still fatal for the accused – were reduced to cowardice, panic and incompetence.[9] Crucially, Stalin had intervened to hold the NKVD in check; he needed a scapegoat but not a witch-hunt. Interrogated on 7 July, Pavlov refused to accept any personal responsibility for the debacle, although he did criticize defecting Lithuanian units on the border with the Northwestern Army Group. He also accused his own 4th Army commander of panicking. (The 4th Army, deployed around Brest, had been overrun by the Germans; the army commander, General A. A. Korobkov, was arrested and shot by the Soviet authorities.) Above all, Pavlov complained about the 'huge advantage of enemy tanks, his [the enemy's] new equipment, and the huge advantage of the enemy air force'. He protested, too, that Soviet forces in the Ukraine had been given more personnel and equipment than he had.[10]

General of the Army Dmitrii Pavlov was only forty-four when he was shot. Molotov, who knew Pavlov well, described him patronizingly as a 'sturdy peasant', loyal and brave, but 'not clever enough, and something of a blockhead'.[11] Pavlov had unusually wide experience of war, and his personal courage was proven. A veteran of the Russian Civil War, he had also led Republican tank forces outside Madrid in 1937, for which he was made one of the first 'Heroes of the Soviet Union'. During the Winter War with Finland, Pavlov led one of Timoshenko's corps in a daring march across the frozen Vyborg Bay to outflank the defences of the Mannerheim Line, an action which forced the Finns to make peace. By pre-war (and post-purge) standards, Pavlov was well trained. He had had a 'proper' military education at the Frunze Military Academy. He was brought back from Spain at the height of the purges in mid-1937 to take over the Directorate of Armoured Forces. The future Marshal Zhukov was impressed by the speech he made on armoured warfare at the December 1940 Moscow conference. We can only speculate what kind of 'war' Pavlov would have had, had he been stationed somewhere else on 22 June. Like Zhukov, he had been an example of the kind of brave, energetic, youthful – and ruthless – middle-level leader that Stalin liked to pick out and promote. Pavlov was probably no better and no worse than the other generals commanding army groups and armies on the western frontier in June 1941.

Pavlov's blunders before, during or after 22 June were not the root cause of the debacle. Pavlov had indeed been head of the Western Military District since June 1940, but he had not been complacent about what was needed to fight a war in Belorussia. The disastrous forward deployment of the Western Military District's armies in the months before 22 June was ordered not by Pavlov, but by Timoshenko and the Soviet General Staff. The deployment was the same as that on the other regions of the long border, from the Baltic to the Black Sea. The level of training and equipment readiness in the Western Military District was equivalent to that in other parts of the Red Army. The low level of alert on 21–22 June was dictated by Moscow, which wanted above all not to provoke Hitler. Pavlov was later criticized for going to the theatre in Minsk on the night of 21 June, but that made very little difference; he was in direct communication with Moscow shortly after midnight.[12]

Once war began, Pavlov was in an impossible situation. The signals network of the Western Military District was put out of action almost immediately. The headquarters of the three forward-based armies in the Belostok salient could not communicate with their divisions. Pavlov in turn, 150 miles to the east in Minsk, could not reach the three army commanders; he could neither obtain situation reports nor give appropriate orders. On 22 June he received orders from Moscow to counter-attack, but he could not even pass these on. In any event, from the first day Pavlov had not been operating on his own. A high-powered team arrived from Moscow; looking over Pavlov's shoulder in Minsk were Marshals Shaposhnikov, Kulik and Voroshilov, as well as Generals Sokolovskii and Malandin, from the General Staff.

Pavlov was a victim, in part, of the decisions made by the Soviet high command about where it would deploy its forces. Those decisions, in turn, came from the failure of Soviet intelligence to predict where the main fighting would take place. On paper, Pavlov's forces were very impressive: 678,000 men, 2,200 tanks and 1,550 combat aircraft. The 17th Mechanized Corps, with which he attempted a counter-attack against the Grodno breakthrough, was the best-equipped formation in the Red Army. It had 1,022 tanks, including 352 of the new KV and T-34 types.[13] Pavlov's Western Army Group was not, however, the centre of gravity of the Soviet deployment, and substantially larger Red Army forces were located further south, in the Ukraine (the pre-war Kiev Military District), ready for offensive operations into southern Poland. But in reality it was Pavlov who faced the main German force, Bock's Army Group Centre. Bock had two big mobile formations, the 2nd and the 3rd Panzer Groups, compared to just one panzer group in each of German Army Groups North and South.

Pavlov's Western Army Group was also in a particularly dangerous geographical position. The Soviet army groups to the north and south at least had their flanks covered, one by the Baltic and the other by the Carpathian Mountains and the Black Sea. In contrast, both of Western Army Group's flanks were open to attack. What made the situation much worse was the particular deployment of the army group. Three of Pavlov's four armies, with three of his four mechanized corps, were crammed into the large salient around the border town of Belostok, which jutted into German-occupied Poland. Belostok was strategically important to the Red Army as a rail hub, and tank and aviation units in the salient were poised there to support a possible advance into southern Poland. The Belostok salient was some 80 miles deep and 125 miles wide. This was about the same size and shape as the famous Kursk bulge, but in contrast to the situation in July 1943, the Red Army in 1941 had not had three or four months to anticipate the German blow, nor two years of full-scale combat experience. It was Stalin and the high command who put these forces in the trap at Belostok. Pavlov was right in his testimony: 'I am not a traitor. The defeat of the forces that I commanded took place for reasons beyond my control.'[14]

The nineteenth-century fortress at Brest, the southern anchor of Pavlov's front, was surrounded by the Germans on the first day of the war. It was at Brest – then Brest-Litovsk – that Lenin's Bolshevik government had capitulated to Imperial Germany twenty-two years earlier in March 1918. The defenders in 1941 originally numbered 3,500 men, a mix of soldiers, border guards and NKVD men. The Germans stormed the main part of the fortress on the first days of the war, but some of the garrison may have survived until late July, when the nearest friendly unit was 300 miles to the east. Russian propaganda made Brest into a potent symbol of resistance, much as the Americans would use Bataan and Corregidor in a similar military shambles in the Pacific.[15]

Brest, however, was a footnote to history. The General Staff would note in November that 'practical experience on all fronts has shown that [commanders] are paying little attention to the potential of towns and villages for stubborn defence'.[16] Everywhere else the German battle of annihilation seemed to be unfolding according to plan. Army Group Centre had trapped Pavlov's army group. As we will see, German Army Group South was making steady progress towards the Dnepr in the Ukraine, and leading elements of German Army Group North had taken the Dvina bridges off the march and were well to the east of them. Thursday, 3 July, was the twelfth day of the war. On that day Halder, chief of the German Army General Staff, made the following entry in his war diary, one that historians frequently quote:

On the whole, then, one can even now say that the objective of shattering the bulk of the Russian army in front of the Dvina and Dnepr has been accomplished. I believe the statement of a captured Russian general that east of the Dvina and Dnepr we will have only fragments of forces to worry about, and these are not strong enough to decisively hinder German operations. So it is probably not too much to say, I suggest, that the campaign against Russia has been won within 14 days.[17]

Stalin made his famous radio speech on that same Thursday, explaining the character of the war and laying down the measures to be taken. The Soviet dictator did not suffer a psychological breakdown on 22 June; this is a myth. His appointments diary shows that he was fully occupied in meetings with generals and party leaders in the week after the attack. War had always been a possibility for Stalin, if not the most likely or most welcome one. At first – I would argue – he had confidence in the abilities of the Red Army. Nevertheless, Stalin could not help but be devastated as events unfolded in the first week – the loss of aircraft, the failure of the counter-attacks and the deep Belostok–Minsk encirclement. The last straw was the breakdown of communications with Western Army Group on Sunday, 29 June (D + 7). A stormy meeting of political leaders and generals took place that evening, a week after the war began, in the Commissariat of Defence. Zhukov, the Chief of the General Staff, burst into tears. Stalin withdrew in despair to his *dacha* outside Moscow. The dictator's frightened Politburo comrades had to drive out and coax him back to the Kremlin.[18]

Measures – belated ones – began to be taken. On Monday, 30 June, Stalin set up a State Defence Committee (GKO) to direct the war effort; aside from the dictator himself, the GKO included four other Politburo members (Beria, Malenkov, Molotov and Voroshilov).[19] Stalin ordered Timoshenko to replace Pavlov as commander of the Western Army Group. On 10 July (D + 18) Stalin would take the place of Timoshenko as head of the Stavka, the supreme headquarters. The same day, three big regional military commands or 'theatres' would be created.[20] Nine days after that, Stalin also took over from Timoshenko the post of People's Commissar of Defence.

Stalin opened his 3 July address with extraordinary words: 'Comrades! Citizens! Brothers and sisters! I appeal to you, my friends!' He laid down the party 'line' on what had happened, admitting defeats and explaining why the Red Army had had to pull back. He stressed German perfidy and Russia's incomplete mobilization. He listed Soviet strengths and claimed the Germans had suffered heavy losses. In an extraordinary break from tradition, he stressed the importance of allies and friends like Britain and the United States. Stalin also laid out what had to be done next. The people had to see both the extent of the threat and the danger of panic. A 'patriotic war of all the people' (*vsenarodnaia otechestvennaia voina*) would involve all-out support for the Red Army and also the waging of a partisan war behind enemy lines. Russian cities would be defended with the help of a People's Militia (*Narodnoe opol'chenie*); the best-known model were the *opol'chenie* who fought Napoleon in 1812.[21]

Three weeks into the war, the Stavka, over Zhukov's name, issued a directive to senior commanders about the main organizational lessons learnt so far from the battle in Belorussia (and the western Ukraine). The implied lesson was that the Red Army's leaders had been much too ambitious. They now received a healthy dose of 'de-modernization'. The big mechanized corps (two tank divisions and a motor rifle division) were now said to be unwieldy, hard to manoeuvre and 'a very easy target for enemy aviation'. The tank divisions of these corps were now put directly under army-level command. Their motorized divisions were converted into regular rifle divisions, and their lorries were transferred to army-level lorry battalions. Another extraordinary development in this 'war of motors' was the revival of the cavalry horse.

> Our army has somewhat under-estimated the significance of cavalry. Given the present situation at the front, where the enemy's rear is spread out over several hundred kilometres in wooded locations and has not been at all secured against major diversionary action by our side, raids by Red cavalrymen against the extended rear of the enemy might play a decisive role in disorganizing the administration and supply of the German forces, and in consequence, in bringing about the defeat of the German forces.

The army was to form light cavalry divisions which would harass the enemy's rear. More generally, the armies were to be reduced in size; the small new armies were to have a maximum of six divisions and no corps echelon. Much the same criticism was made of large Red Army Air Force formations. They were hard to use and they were vulnerable. Rather than big air corps and air divisions, the most important element would be the small air regiment (thirty aircraft), with at most two regiments in an air division and no air corps echelon. In reality, losses had been so massive that formation size had to be drastically reduced anyway.[22]

Discipline in the army was tightened. Stalin installed Lev Mekhlis, one of his most trusted party hatchet men, as head of the army's Main Political Administration on 23 June. In a secret order of 16 July, the GKO declared that it would take the 'strictest measures against cowards, *panikery* [panic-mongers], and deserters'. It ordered that nine senior officers including Pavlov and his Western Army Group subordinates be brought before the Military Tribunal.[23] Pavlov's was the only Soviet army group staff to be arrested and executed during the war. Their fate reflected the shock and scale of the military disaster in Belorussia. Some terrorization of the upper ranks of the Red Army continued, with the arrest by the NKVD of suspect generals. General N. I. Trubetskoi, chief of the Red Army's Directorate of Communications (*Upravlenie voennykh soobshchenii*), who had warned Stalin in May 1941 about the inadequacies of the railway system in the newly annexed western territories, was dismissed and executed. The most important victim was General Meretskov, Zhukov's predecessor as Chief of the General Staff, who was apparently compromised by his relations with General P. V. Rychagov, the former head of the Red Army Air Force; Meretskov was arrested and only released in September 1941.[24] On 16 July political commissars were reinstated in the Red Army at division and regiment level, with 'political leaders' (*politruky*) in smaller elements; commissars had previously been abolished after the Winter War with Finland.

The following day the GKO formally revived another Civil War institution, the Special Section (OO, *Osobyi otdel*). It was now subordinated to Beria's dreaded secret police, the NKVD, rather than the People's Commissariat of Defence (NKO). Under the deputy head of the NKVD, V. S. Abakumov, the task of the OO was to combat espionage and treason and to liquidate desertion, using the most extreme measures. The NKVD blocking detachments (*zagraditel'nye otriady*) were fiercely active throughout the summer and autumn of 1941. Abakumov's deputy reported that up to 10 October, the OO and NKVD blocking detachments had arrested over 650,000 servicemen and shot 10,201 of them, a third in front of their own comrades.[25]

Confusion in the top level of the Soviet command structure was a basic problem of the early war months. No personal or organizational arrangements for a high command had been made before 22 June; there was not even a proper physical command post. When the war started, there was for a few days a vacuum of professional authority at the top. Timoshenko and Shaposhnikov left Moscow to oversee the Western Army Group, Zhukov (the Chief of the General Staff) flew to the Southwestern Army Group, and General N. F. Vatutin (Zhukov's deputy) went to the Northwestern Army Group. The self-appointment of Stalin to the post of Supreme C-in-C (the so-called *Verkhovnyi*) on D + 18 did create a centre, but the Soviet dictator was a military amateur prone to impulsive orders for offensive action – and for radical changes of personnel. On Zhukov's return to Moscow, he was probably Stalin's main military adviser, but the two men soon fell out. Zhukov's dismissal on 29 July came in part from his recommendation to give up the city of Kiev in the Ukraine, but it may also have been due to the poor results of the Red Army's July counter-offensive in the centre of the front.

After Zhukov left, Marshal Boris Shaposhnikov became Stalin's main military adviser. The new Chief of the General Staff, whatever his intellectual and personal qualities, was not prepared to stand up to the *Verkhovnyi*; Shaposhnikov also suffered from ill health.[26] In the background was the able General Aleksandr Vasilevskii, who became head of the Operations Directorate of the General Staff in August, but he was still too junior to carry much influence. As for the three new theatre commands, they were directly under the Moscow Stavka, but they were not militarily effective. The commanders were, above all, politically trusted comrades with personal links to the dictator. The appointment of Voroshilov, Timoshenko, and Budennyi, to the Northwestern, Western and Southwestern Theatres, was the last victory of the clique of veterans of the Civil War 1st Cavalry Army (*Konarmiia*). Budennyi had commanded the *Konarmiia* as a whole; Voroshilov had been the main commissar; and Timoshenko had led one of the army's divisions. None of the three would turn out to be a fully competent commander in the new war. Very senior party leaders, Politburo members, watched over the Theatre headquarters: Zhdanov in the northwest, Bulganin in the west and Khrushchev (from August) in the south. In the event the authority of the Stavka and the three Theatre commands overlapped, and Moscow tended to give orders directly to the army group and army commanders.

The Battle of Smolensk

Some essential first steps had been taken by the Soviet government, but exhortation, popular mobilization and repression were not enough. After the disaster in the Belostok salient and around Minsk, the Red Army failed to make a stand further east, on the Berezina River at Bobruisk. Then the focus in the centre of the Russian–German front turned to what Halder had written about on 3 July, the main natural defence of the region, the line of the Dvina and upper Dnepr rivers. These were about 300 miles west of Moscow. Especially important was the 50-mile gap between the rivers, the Orsha 'land bridge' or the 'Smolensk gate'. The latter name comes from the ancient town on the Dnepr which covers this weak spot in Russia's natural defences. The highway from Minsk to Viaz'ma and Moscow ran through the gap. The long Battle of Smolensk was fought around here between the second week of July and the second week of September.[27]

The place that the Battle of Smolensk occupies in the history of the war is complex. Smolensk was a very big battle, but until recently it was largely forgotten. It was not like the later Battles of Moscow or Stalingrad, where the Red Army successfully defended a big city. Smolensk was a relatively small town of 170,000 inhabitants; it fell early in the battle. Even the outcome of the Battle of Smolensk is debatable. Some historians, including Soviet-era Russian historians, argue that at Smolensk the Red Army stopped Hitler's BARBAROSSA plan of 'daring operations making extensive use of the panzer spearheads'. The Battle of Smolensk is bound up with another momentous development, Hitler's decision to shift the main attack from the centre of the front – the Moscow axis – to the flanks. This was not a simple case of cause and effect, as Hitler's decisions were made in late July and early August, in the middle of the Battle of Smolensk. Furthermore, some of the heaviest fighting of the Battle of Smolensk took place *after* Hitler's decision, when the Red Army tried to hit the flank of General Guderian's 2nd Panzer Group as he carried out the order to move south from the Smolensk area into the Ukraine.

The first weeks of the battle were a time of stiffening Soviet resistance in the Smolensk gate, something Halder had not anticipated. It was roughly here, on the line of the Dvina and upper Dnepr, that the Soviet 22nd Army had commenced forming up, following orders issued in mid-May 1941; this was the northern part of the Red Army's 'second strategic echelon'. In the second week of the war a 'group of reserve armies' had begun to assemble here. These were (from left to right) the 21st, 20th, 19th and 22nd Armies. The 20th had been rushed west from the Orel Military District after 22 June; the others had started their transfer in May, the 19th and the 21st having gone originally to the Ukraine. With the collapse of Pavlov's command, these four armies were incorporated into the Western Army Group. The 16th Army, another of the formations that had begun its transfer in May, was moved north to near Smolensk.

After Smolensk came under German attack, a short-lived 'front of reserve armies' was established behind Smolensk on the Staraia Russa–Briansk line. This front was made up of NKVD paramilitary forces (border guards, etc.) and put under the command of the former head of the NKVD Belorussian Border Region, General I. A. Bogdanov; it had four new armies, each commanded by a senior NKVD general. A new 'front of the Mozhaisk defence line', even further back and directly in front of Moscow, was created by the State Defence Committee on 16 July; the front consisted of three armies of People's Militia and NKVD divisions under NKVD General P. A. Artem'ev, the commander of the Moscow Military District.[28] Throughout the summer, new forces of greatly varying qualities were raised or redeployed: reserve divisions, converted NKVD divisions, plus some better divisions from the eastern military districts. As they became available, the Stavka sent them to fight here, on the distant approaches to Moscow.

Command of Western Army Group was now held (until early September) by the tall bullet-headed Marshal Timoshenko, who also commanded the new Western Theatre.[29] In some respects, this was Timoshenko's finest hour. He was then Stalin's favourite soldier, seemingly combining loyalty with training, authority in the army and proven modern combat experience (in Finland). Zhukov was a protégé of Timoshenko but was ambivalent about his patron's abilities. In August 1944, in a candid letter to General Golikov, he spoke of army group commanders at the start of the war 'who messed up one affair after another', and he specifically included Timoshenko in this group. On the other hand, in 1965 Zhukov denied that Timoshenko was a weak-willed man who followed Stalin's whims: 'He was a stubborn and resolute commander, who was well trained at the tactical and operational level. And there is no basis for comparing him with Voroshilov and Budennyi, as is not infrequently done.' Despite failure in 1941, catastrophe at Khar'kov in 1942 and secondary appointments after 1942, Timoshenko would in June 1945 be awarded the 'Victory' (*Pobeda*) medal for conduct of major operations; he was one of only ten generals to receive this award. He had personal links to Stalin; his daughter was at one time married to Stalin's tearaway son Vasilii.[30] Timoshenko remained a member of the Stavka committee until February 1945.

Timoshenko's first chief of staff was Marshal Shaposhnikov, the most experienced planner in the Red Army. A number of other commanders who would distinguish themselves later on in the war appeared in the Smolensk battle. General Andrei Eremenko, another *Konarmiia* veteran and famous later as the defender of Stalingrad, was deputy commander of the Western Army Group. Commander of the 16th Army, moved into the centre of the sector, was General Konstantin Rokossovskii; he had escaped the destruction of his mechanized corps in the Ukraine. Ivan Konev, who was to race Zhukov to Berlin in 1945, commanded the 19th Army, having formerly been in charge of the North Caucasus Military District.

Russian counter-attacks grew in scale as the Wehrmacht approached the Smolensk gate in the third week of the war. One of the most spectacular attacks took place on the eve of the battle itself. The Soviet 5th and the 7th Mechanized Corps had moved west with the 20th Army. On 6 July (D + 14) hundreds of Soviet tanks were thrown into a deep penetration on the flanks of Hoth's 3rd Panzer Group as it crossed the upper Dvina River, near Lepel'. The Russian armoured group had little air cover and few anti-aircraft guns. It suffered badly from Stuka attacks before its attack was broken up by German armour. The two corps were virtually destroyed; 832 tanks were lost in the four-day battle. Among those captured, near Vitebsk ten days after the battle, was Senior Lieutenant Dzhugashvili, a battery commander from the 14th Tank Division of the 7th Mechanized Corps – Stalin's elder son, Iakov. Dzhugashvili apparently complained to his captors about the poor training and weak leadership of these formations: 'In my view the army was well equipped, it just did not know how to use this equipment, that's that.' In 1965 Zhukov told an interviewer that the destruction of the two mechanized corps 'sobered up' him and Timoshenko, from their early 'dreams' about the possibility of early Soviet counter-attacks; unfortunately, Stalin himself did not take this lesson on board.[31]

Timoshenko's forces arrived piecemeal. As the next phase of the German advance began in the second week of July, Timoshenko had twenty-four divisions in his first line of defence, with 275,000 men and only 135 tanks (compared to Pavlov's 2,200 tanks on 22 June).[32] Vitebsk, on the north side of the Smolensk gate, was taken on 9 July (D + 17). Six days later, a German motorized division cut the main rail and road line east from Smolensk, hemming in three Russian armies (the 16th, Konev's 19th, and the 20th). The town of Smolensk itself fell on the following day, 16 July (D + 24). The Germans had to fight harder, however, than they had to in the frontier battles of late June.

Meanwhile, the offensively minded Soviet strategy which had led to such terrible consequences at the beginning of the war was still in place. Zhukov would later claim that this was Stalin's fault, rather than his or Timoshenko's. On 20 July (D + 28) Stalin had told Timoshenko, 'I think that the time has come for us to change from pettiness to action with large forces (*ot krokhoborstva k deistviiam bol'shimi gruppami*).' A Stavka order of 20 July talked about 'an operation to encircle and destroy the enemy's Smolensk grouping'. By the end of July, Timoshenko had formed an arc of 'operational groups' to patch the holes in the front and to mount a counter-offensive converging on Smolensk. These operations were attempted in the last week of July and the first week of August. They failed to achieve their objectives; Stalin seriously considered sacking Timoshenko at the end of July, having been advised to do so by the Western Theatre commissar, Bulganin.

Timoshenko told the Comintern leader Dimitrov in early August that the battles had had positive results: 'We gave the Germans a good beating. Smashed a few of their divisions. They do not come straight for me any more. They try to go around.' (Dimitrov noted his impressions of Timoshenko in his diary: 'Robust and energetic, good man!')[33] In truth, the unexpected Soviet resistance did stall the advance of German Army Group Centre, and it made possible the breakout of some troops from the three armies trapped around Smolensk. The Red Army's secret weapon, the '*Katiusha*' multiple rocket launcher – known to the Germans as the 'Stalin organ' – was used for the first time here. Each truck-mounted BM-13 launcher fired salvoes of 16 132mm rockets, but only a few 'Katiushas' were available.

Hitler looks to the flanks

It was at this point, at the end of July and August, that fateful choices began to be made by Hitler and the German high command. Many historians have regarded these as decisive for the BARBAROSSA campaign, and even for the outcome of the Second World War. After closing the Smolensk pocket in mid-July, German Army Group Centre did not push further east, although Moscow was only 200 miles away. Not until 6 September, some seven weeks later, would Hitler issue his directive (No. 35) ordering a decisive operation against the Russian forces in front of the Soviet capital.[34] Three more weeks would pass before that advance, Operation TYPHOON (TAIFUN), could be set in motion (on 30 September). Operation TYPHOON would be first slowed by the weather and then reversed by the Russian counter-offensive of 5 December.

Hitler's earlier directives of 19 and 23 July, at the end of the fourth week of the war, had specified that *infantry* formations could continue the advance in the centre towards Moscow. The German army's mobile forces, however, would be used not on the direct route to Moscow, but on the flanks. With Directive No. 34 (30 July), Hitler ordered Bock's Army Group Centre to go over to the defensive. The German Army's leaders, especially Halder and Bock, but also Brauchitsch, Rundstedt (Army Group South) and the panzer group commanders (Guderian and others), argued for an advance on Moscow. The generals, reared in the tradition of the Prussian military thinker Karl von Clausewitz, were drawn to the enemy's supposed 'centre of gravity' (*Schwerpunkt*), which they took to be the Soviet capital. Hitler did not see things that way; he flew to the headquarters of Army Groups Centre and South at the start of August and rejected the recommendations of both Bock and Rundstedt. In mid-August Hitler confirmed the order moving the panzer groups to the flanks, overriding his professional advisers.[35]

There were several strands to this decision. Grand strategy played its part. The Führer prided himself on seeing the 'big picture'. The war, both in Russia and against Britain, was going to drag on longer than expected. Resources were now vital; what mattered was depriving the enemy of them, gaining them for Germany and protecting what the Reich already had. Hitler's attention was drawn to Leningrad as a centre of Soviet war industry, and a base for a naval threat to Germany's shipping routes to the iron ore of Sweden. He was also being consistent with the December 1940 BARBAROSSA directive, according to which Leningrad was to be taken before Moscow. Meanwhile, the Ukraine had long been seen by the Nazi leader – and other German ultra-nationalists – as an important resource base of foodstuffs and minerals for Germany. Through the Ukraine, too, ran the route to the Caucasus and the oil riches of the USSR. What would become Hitler's 1942 strategy emerged here for the first time; it would lead to the lunge for the oil of the Caucasus – and the disaster at Stalingrad. In 1941 Hitler also cited the danger of Soviet air attacks mounted from the Crimea against the Romanian oil fields. The defensive side of Hitler's 'strategy', protecting the Baltic ore trade and the Romanian oil wells, greatly exaggerated the potential of the Soviet Navy and the Red Army Air Force. Hitler misunderstood the importance of Moscow and its region. Leaving aside its political value, Moscow was by 1941 at least as important to the Soviet war economy as Leningrad or the Ukraine. Moscow was now a leading industrial centre, especially for the Soviet motor vehicle and aircraft industries, and nearby was an important coal field. The capital was also the hub of Russia's railway network. In any event, the 'resource' side of Hitler's argument made little sense in the short or medium term. If the war was to be won in 1941, then Russian resources did not matter.

Hitler's decision to move to the flanks might also be explained by a kind of strategic 'opportunism'. Strategic possibilities were opening up for the Germans in the northern and southern theatres. In the north, at the end of July, the motorized spearheads of German Army Group North had broken through the old (1939) border defences, driven the Red Army back and crossed the Velikaia River at Pskov (9 July, D + 17). They had even reached the Luga River line, only 80 miles from Leningrad. A few weeks later, Field Marshal Rundstedt finally broke the Soviet Southwestern Army Group in the Ukraine. The remnants of what had been the main pre-war Soviet field force were trapped in a pocket west of the Dnepr River at Uman' (3 August). Final German victory in the north and south seemed possible – if forces advancing there could be reinforced from the centre. However, this 'opportunism' argument also made only limited sense: there was little point in winning battles for their own sake, if these battles did not destroy the main force of the Red Army.

Arguably the flanks of German Army Group Centre had to be taken to secure a further advance on Moscow. Hitler's Order No. 34a, although it called for the capture of the Soviet capital 'before the coming of winter', specified that the threat to the flanks of Army Group Centre had to be eliminated. An advance towards Moscow with strong Soviet forces still active to the north and south would have been even riskier than the offensive the Germans actually attempted in November and December, Operation TYPHOON. With hindsight, when he finally ordered the TYPHOON attack in early September, Hitler could note that successes achieved around Leningrad had created 'the prerequisites' for a further advance in the centre.[36]

Another reason for the pause in the centre was the need to 'mop up' after the early victories. Hitler was concerned with the number of Soviet stragglers behind German Army Group Centre. It took considerable effort for the Germans to eliminate the remains of Western Army Group; this was the first task of a new German 2nd Army established under General Weichs. German logistics, maintenance and deployment were a final explanation for the pause at Smolensk. Bock's Army Group Centre had ploughed ahead hundreds of miles and fought difficult battles. The motorized spearheads needed to be refitted. Meanwhile, the bulk of the German infantry, marching on foot, had to catch up. The Germans now had very long supply lines stretching across Poland and then 450 miles across the western USSR, where the roads were poor and the railways had to be repaired and converted to take German rolling stock. Truck-borne supplies had to move great distances from the railheads along bad and damaged roads. The supply system had been set up to support all three German army groups, and it could not be quickly or easily rejigged for a narrow drive on Moscow.[37]

Hitler's pause at Smolensk and his transfer of forces to the flanks were the result of several factors. But they all come back to the essence of the BARBAROSSA fallacy – that the whole effective strength of the Red Army would be destroyed on the frontiers. Contrary to the expectation of both Hitler and the generals, the victories west of the Dvina–Dnepr line had not eliminated the resistance of the Red Army. In the northern and southern theatres, the Red Army had effected a fighting withdrawal, albeit with huge losses. In the centre, in the area of Smolensk, fresh Soviet reserves had been brought forward, and the Red Army was mounting vigorous counter-attacks. The Stalinist political system of the USSR had not collapsed. In reality, the Russians still had forces available to block the German advance. Soviet resistance did indeed contribute greatly to the German pause in the centre. Hitler's 30 July directive (No. 34), after the first phase of the Battle of Smolensk, had cited 'the appearance of strong enemy forces on the front and to the flanks of Army Group Centre' (this would be Timoshenko's reserves), and the 12 August directive (No. 34a), which sent Guderian to the south, mentioned 'the strong enemy forces which have been concentrated for the defence of Moscow'.[38]

The Führer's decision had been made before the second part of the Battle of Smolensk began. This second phase was marked, if anything, by greater Red Army activity in the centre. By August, Timoshenko's Western Theatre had three components: Central (later Briansk) Army Group, Reserve Army Group and Western Army Group – running from south to north. Part of the Smolensk fighting, in the middle of August, was actually a Soviet response to Guderian's turn to the south. General Eremenko, who had been appointed to the Briansk Army Group, promised Stalin he could stop Guderian by hitting his flanks. Eremenko was able to mount only ineffective and costly attacks. The Red Army Air Force set up its first large-scale concentrated 'air operation', as 460 aircraft were thrown against Guderian and the 2nd Panzer Group. Unfortunately, it had little effect. Pushes by Western Army Group to take the region north of Smolensk were also unsuccessful.[39]

A local victory, one of the first successful Russian counter-attacks of the entire war, was won between Western and Briansk Army Groups, in the sector of the new Reserve Army Group. At the end of August this army group's 24th Army mounted a concentric attack on the small town of El'nia (sometimes transliterated as Yelnya), 75 miles southeast of Smolensk, and an important German bridgehead over the Desna River. El'nia was retaken by the Red Army on 6 September. The operation was overseen by none other than General Zhukov, the new commander of the Reserve Army Group. Zhukov had been sacked as Chief of the General Staff at the end of July for urging Stalin to abandon Kiev. 'The El'nia operation', Zhukov later recalled, 'was my first independent operation, the first test of my personal operational–strategic abilities in the great war with Hitler's Germany'.[40]

The first of the famous Soviet 'Guards' units was created on 18 September. The 100th, 127th, 153rd and 161st Rifle Divisions had distinguished themselves at El'nia; they were re-designated as the 1st, 2nd, 3rd and 4th Guards Rifle Divisions. The Guards were held up as models of how to fight – in contrast to other units. Stalin's order of 18 September 1941 explained their qualities. They were supposed to show better use of reconnaissance, they aimed to envelop the enemy rather than just break through his lines, they dug in once they had taken territory, and they defended actively what they had gained.

> When attacked by the enemy, these divisions did not panic, did not throw down their guns, did not run and hide in the woods, did not cry out 'We are surrounded!', but rather they answered their enemy blow for blow in an organized way, they kept the panic-mongers under strict control, dealt mercilessly with cowards and deserters, ensuring by this the discipline and organization of their units.
>
> The commanders and commissars in these divisions conducted themselves as brave and demanding leaders, able to get their subordinates to obey orders and not being afraid to punish disobedient and undisciplined personnel.[41]

Historians on both sides of the Iron Curtain ignored – for different reasons – the Battle of Smolensk. It now seems clear that Soviet operations in both phases of the battle, in July and the first half of August, and in late August and early September, had a very serious impact on the advance of the German Army. The overall verdict by David Glantz was emphatic: 'Instead of a mere "bump in the road" on the way to Moscow, in fact, the Battle for Smolensk derailed Operation Barbarossa, ultimately paving the way for the *Wehrmacht*'s December defeat.' David Stahel, who has written another recent account, did not disagree with this, seeing the Battle of Smolensk as being – for Germany – more a propaganda victory that a military one. Moreover, he argued that the battle 'is perhaps best represented less in terms of a rousing victory for either side but rather as a defeat for both', although the strategic ramifications for failure were greater for the Germans than for their opponents.[42]

The energetic, if costly, resistance of the Red Army may have had an even wider impact. On 2 July 1941, in the weeks after the German invasion, the Japanese government had ordered a preliminary army mobilization for possible operations from Manchuria against eastern Siberia. Nine weeks later, however, on 6 September 1941, an Imperial Conference in Tokyo decided that Japanese efforts should be concentrated against Southeast Asia, and the troops mobilized were to be made available for a campaign there, rather than used immediately against Siberia. The leaders of the Imperial Japanese Army had a higher estimation of the capability of the Red Army than did their German counterparts, and they expected that the campaign in Russia might be prolonged. This expectation seemed to be confirmed by the battles raging at the end of August and the beginning of September, with the Wehrmacht apparently stalled on the high road to Moscow. The Battle of Smolensk, then, may have played a part in the decision made in Tokyo on 6 September.[43]

However, the question was not just whether the battle stalled the German offensive or deterred Japanese involvement against Russia. The bloody Soviet counter-offensives also weakened the Red Army and made possible dramatic new German victories in October and November. The Battle of Smolensk might even be classed with the Battle of Khar'kov in May 1942 as an abortive Soviet offensive which exposed the Red Army to a devastating German counter-attack.[44] At the end of September Shaposhnikov, the Chief of the General Staff, issued a directive to the Soviet army group commanders noting that unsuccessful operations were 'a direct result of their poor organization and preparation'. The reasons for failure were assessed in detail. Shaposhnikov emphasized the lack of reconnaissance by Soviet commanders, their failure to check the readiness – military and political – of attacking forces, the poor co-ordination between the various arms, including tanks and aircraft, and the inability to make sure that orders were issued promptly and that they were fulfilled. However Smolensk is assessed, the two-month battle cost the Red Army dear. Official Russian figures for the period 10 July to 10 September were 490,000 personnel lost, as well as 1,350 tanks and 900 aircraft. As in the first weeks of the war, a high proportion of these losses were Red soldiers who surrendered; German figures list 400,000 POWs taken in the fighting around Smolensk, including

309,000 in the Smolensk pocket itself.[45] The Soviet losses, then, were as big as those of the first frontier battles.

In late September, Army Group Centre would launch a remarkable drive on Moscow (Operation TYPHOON), wiping out yet another row of Soviet armies at Viaz'ma–Briansk. Could this attack have been mounted in early August? That it could was the conclusion of the famous British strategist Basil Liddell Hart after post-war talks with captured German generals: 'Hitler's gamble in Russia failed because he was not bold enough. He wobbled for weeks at the critical phase, losing time he could never regain.'[46]

Liddell Hart's verdict was influential, but wrong. In reality, the military situation at the beginning of August was quite different from that at the end of September.[47] First of all, in the intervening eight weeks, German Army Group Centre had been reinforced, not least by the addition of the 4th Panzer Group and the Luftwaffe's 8th Air Corps from the Army Group North area. The flanks of the attack on the Moscow axis were now not seriously threatened, and German forces could be concentrated in the centre. The supply situation behind German Army Group Centre had been improved. Some of the panzer divisions had been refitted. Infantry divisions moving east on foot had been able to catch up with the panzer and motorized divisions. The Russians, for their part, were now distracted by the Kiev disaster suffered by Budennyi's Southwestern Theatre (see below), and they had been forced to send reserves there. The blood of Timoshenko's Western Army Group had been drained by the Battle of Smolensk, especially its massive final phase.

An August German offensive against Moscow can only be speculation. The balance of probabilities was against its success. In the end, of course, Operation TYPHOON itself did not get Army Group Centre to Moscow in November–December 1941. We know that the decision Hitler took at the beginning of September ended in German failure. That does not mean that another decision, an earlier move on Moscow, would not also have failed. In any event, the main German battles in August and September 1941 would be fought somewhere else.

THE FIRST BATTLE OF THE UKRAINE: GERMAN ARMY GROUP SOUTH

German victories in the western Ukraine

The summer 1941 campaign in the Ukraine took a different form than the fighting in Belorussia.[48] The Southwestern Army Group under General Kirponos put up a much stouter initial resistance than the defenders of Belorussia, mounting large-scale armoured counter-attacks in the Ukraine–Poland border zone. When Marshal Timoshenko began his counter-offensives in late July during the Battle of Smolensk, the Southwestern Army Group was still well to the west of the Dnepr, and Kirponos avoided big encirclements of his forces until the Battle of Uman' in early August. Kiev, the capital of the Ukraine, came under direct German threat from the middle of July, but the city and the long line of the Dnepr River were held until the beginning of September. Tragedy came for the Soviets at the end of this campaign. The Germans encircled Kiev and the region behind it in late September. This was their greatest triumph of the war in the East and the Red Army's greatest single military disaster. Kiev cost the Russians twice as many losses as the Belostok–Minsk encirclement.

Several factors explained the Russian defenders' relative early success in the south. The Southwestern Army Group was perhaps better led, but there is no way of fully comparing Kirponos and Pavlov. General Mikhail Kirponos would be killed in action in September 1941. He had led a regiment in the Civil War and had completed his education at the Frunze Academy. Kirponos, like Pavlov, was an example of the new blood promoted to senior commands after the Winter War with Finland. He had successfully commanded one of Timoshenko's divisions in the final attack on the Mannerheim Line in early 1940, and for this action he had been made a Hero of the Soviet Union. Kirponos was advanced extremely rapidly from division commander to be head of the Leningrad Military District, and then, in February 1941, he replaced Zhukov as commander of the Kiev Military District. At 49, Kirponos was relatively old for a Soviet senior commander, but he was not greatly experienced; his main post before Finland had been five years as commandant of the Kazan' Infantry School (1934–9), one of over a hundred such schools.

More important than the ability of the army group commander was the greater strength of the Red Army in the Ukraine, relative to other Soviet theatres, and relative to the German invaders. It was Kirponos's good fortune that the largest concentration of the Red Army had been stationed in the Ukraine. The 1940–1 offensive strategy of the Red Army, as we have seen, involved a possible thrust (or counter-thrust) into southern Poland from the Ukraine. As a result, the Kiev Military District (the core of the wartime Southwestern Army Group) had been the military district provided with the strongest

FIGURE 3 Russian T-26 tanks, with their crews, July 1941.

forces. Kirponos had 960,000 personnel (compared to 678,000 for Pavlov in Belorussia), 12,600 guns and mortars (compared to 10,300), 4,800 tanks (compared to 2,200) and 1,750 combat aircraft (compared to 1,550).[49]

Meanwhile, on the German side, Rundstedt's Army Group South was not as strong as Bock's Army Group Centre. Field Marshal Gerd von Rundstedt was the Wehrmacht's outstanding commander. In 1939 he was recalled from retirement to command the Wehrmacht's southern thrust into Poland; in 1940 his army group mounted the main attack in the French campaign. At the time of D-Day in 1944, when Rundstedt was nearly seventy, he would command the Nazi defences of western Europe; he would also lead Hitler's last offensive in the West, the Battle of the Bulge in the Ardennes. In 1941 Rundstedt commanded three field armies, the 6th, 17th and 11th, but the last was far to the south facing Odessa. Rundstedt was given only one big mobile formation (General Ewald Kleist's 1st Panzer Group) – compared with two for Bock at Army Group Centre. He had only five panzer divisions and two motorized divisions, against nine and five for Bock. An encirclement like Belostok–Minsk in Belorussia could not quickly be brought off in the Ukraine; Rundstedt had a hammer, but no anvil. Even Russian figures give their own forces in the Ukraine a 6:1 advantage over the Germans in tanks and a 2:1 advantage in aircraft.[50]

Geography also favoured the Soviet defenders of the Ukraine, compared to those of Belorussia. Kirponos, like Pavlov, had an exposed salient jutting into German-occupied Poland; his was around the city of L'vov. But the L'vov salient was in the event only seriously attacked by the Germans from one side. The southern flank of the salient faced the territory of Hungary, and Hungary was neutral, at least at the very start of the war. This flank was protected, too, by the Carpathian Mountains. In March 1941 Hitler had abandoned the original intention to add a southern pincer – the 12th Army – to Army Group South. The Ukrainian front was also relatively deep. The distance from the border to Kiev was 350 miles, compared to 200 miles from the border to Minsk. The wide expanse of the middle Dnepr River provided a backstop for the Red Army, making easier the defence of the Kiev region (although most of the city itself lay on the west side of the river). The invading German Army Group South had to operate on a much wider front than Army Group Centre, starting from three different territories, Poland, Hungary and Romania. The distance from the L'vov salient down to the Black Sea, the operational span of German Army Group South, was 450 miles. In comparison, the width of the German Army Group Centre sector was 200 miles. The headquarters of the German 11th Army, in northeastern Romania, was 300 miles from that of its 'neighbour', the 17th Army, in southeast Poland; between them were the Carpathians. Meanwhile, the nearly impenetrable expanse of the Poles'e marshes provided a base from which the northern flank of Rundstedt's advance into the Ukraine could be threatened by the Russians.

All the same, once the invasion began, Kirponos's Southwestern Army Group was thrown into great confusion. Moscow's Directive No. 3, of 22 June, ordering the Red Army to counter-attack into enemy territory, probably had a more harmful effect on the Southwestern Army Group than elsewhere.[51] In Belorussia Pavlov was already doomed when he received the order; Kuznetsov, the Soviet commander in the Baltic area, was already retreating. In Kirponos's case, the order to strike into the enemy rear at Lublin with five mechanized corps and all air strength – a scaled-down version of the pre-war offensive plan – at least matched the balance of forces and the concentration of Russian armour. On paper, the five Soviet mechanized corps were comparable to two or three panzer groups, and the Southwestern Army Group had three more mechanized corps in reserve. But preparation for this hasty counter-blow distracted Kirponos from what would have been the more sensible option of concentrating his armour for a mobile defence deeper in Soviet territory.

Rundstedt's armoured commander, Kleist, was able to make a penetration with the 1st Panzer Group between two Russian frontier armies (the 5th and the 6th). The reaction of the Russian mechanized corps was piecemeal, despite the presence of at least two effective commanders, A. A. Vlasov and K. K. Rokossovskii, in the 4th and the 9th Mechanized Corps. (The first of these generals would be hanged as a traitor in 1946; the other – released from the GULAG in 1940 – became a Marshal and one of the Red Army's two or three outstanding field commanders.) Lack of preparation time, disrupted Soviet communications and dispersed Red Army formations contributed to the failure, and so did the low readiness state of many units. Large numbers of Russian vehicles broke down on the way to their assignments or ran out of fuel and ammunition. Soviet co-ordination was weak. The confused fighting in the western Ukraine – the same place where Tsarist General Brusilov had mounted his famous offensive against the Austro-Hungarians in 1916 – lasted for over a week. The biggest tank battle (so far) of the Second World War was fought out. In the end the huge Soviet force was able to achieve nothing. On 30 June (D + 8, and two days after the Minsk encirclement was completed in Belorussia), the Stavka ordered Kirponos to fall back 125 miles to the pre-1939 border – and to the partially dismantled Stalin Line.[52]

The Soviet Southern Army Group, further south in the Ukraine and facing north-eastern Romania, was more successful. Formed at the outbreak of war from the Odessa Military District, the Southern Army Group was commanded by General I. V. Tiulenev, yet another Civil War Red Cavalry veteran. Tiulenev had some impressive subordinates: A. N. Antonov (a future Chief of the General Staff) was on his staff, and R. Ia. Malinovskii (the future Marshal) was one of his corps commanders. The Axis advance in the far south began a week after the main invasion, so the element of surprise was less. The balance of forces was also favourable to the Red Army. The Germans and Romanians nevertheless soon made rapid progress across the open steppe, crossing the Dnestr River around Tiraspol' and bypassing the major port of Odessa. At Nikolaev, 75 miles east of Odessa, the Germans captured the unfinished hull of a 59,000-ton super-battleship, the *Sovetskaia Ukraina*, which was to have been the pride of Stalin's ocean-going navy. (A sister ship survived on the stocks in Leningrad, but work stopped during the siege of the city, and it was eventually dismantled.) The Red Army abandoned the rich iron ore mines at Krivoi Rog. The Dnepr Power Station, a huge dam and a showcase of Stalinist industrialization, was blown up. Unlike the formations further north, however, Tiulenev's divisions were eventually allowed by the Stavka to pull back east across the lower Dnepr River. By the end of September the German 11th Army had reached Melitopol', not far from the Sea of Azov and on the main railway line from Moscow to the Crimea. Soviet resistance continued in besieged Odessa until many of the defenders were evacuated by sea in mid-October, well after the beginning of German Operation TYPHOON against Moscow. The Romanians and Germans inflicted terrible atrocities on captured civilians. Although on the periphery, the siege was later treated in a very positive light: Odessa was decreed one of the first four 'hero cities' on 1 May 1945, alongside Leningrad, Stalingrad and Sevastopol'.

Soviet disasters at Uman' and Kiev

The Stavka set up the Southwestern Theatre on 10 July as headquarters to co-ordinate the Southwestern and Southern Army Groups. In command was Marshal Budennyi, whose post was comparable to the one Marshal Timoshenko held in the Western Theatre. Marshal Semen Budennyi was the extraordinary Tsarist trooper who had risen from the ranks to command the war-winning cavalry formation of the Civil War, the Konarmiia.[53] For Stalin, Budennyi's assets were his known reliability and his aura of victory. Budennyi was aged 58 and belonged to an older generation than most other Red Army leaders; he was, however, still seven years younger than von Rundstedt. A forceful and probably a genuinely popular figure, Budennyi was in over his head as a strategist. He cannot personally be blamed for the operational failures, but the eventual disaster in the Ukraine would tarnish his reputation. Politically, the Southwestern Theatre was overseen by Nikita Khrushchev, Party '1st Secretary' in the Ukrainian SSR, and from early August a member of the theatre's Military Council.

Meanwhile, Kirponos's belated attempt to form a new defensive position along the Stalin Line was not successful. By 11 July (D + 19) the leading panzer divisions had broken through that barrier too, and lurked on the approaches to Kiev. Historians have speculated that the panzers could have taken Kiev 'off the march', but the probabilities are against this. The German infantry was still far behind, and Russian resistance hardened in front of the Ukrainian capital. Local propaganda styled Kiev the 'second Tsaritsyn', after the Volga city – later Stalingrad – that had held out against the Whites in the Civil War. Kiev was a great city of 850,000 people, mostly situated on the high western bank of the river, but with suburbs on the eastern bank. The local inhabitants formed emergency military units, the People's Militia. The Red Army mounted a vigorous defence. General M. I. Potapov's 5th Army, operating from the Poles'e, threatened the left flank of the German Army Group South. The energetic General Vlasov, whose mechanized corps had been dispersed, took over a new 37th Army in front of Kiev.

In fact, the initial German objective was not to take the Ukrainian capital, but to roll up the Red Army west of the Dnepr River – in accordance with the BARBAROSSA directive. This it did. Budennyi and Kirponos (and Zhukov) anticipated the danger, but Stalin forbade them to withdraw behind the river. At the beginning of August, most of the forces originally based in the northwestern Ukraine, the 6th and 12th Armies, some twenty-four divisions, were surrounded and destroyed just west of the Dnepr, at Uman'. Both army commanders (Generals Muzychenko and Ponedelin) were taken prisoner; the Germans claimed to have captured 103,000 POWs.[54]

The Uman' disaster, the worst for the Red Army since the Belostok–Minsk encirclement, triggered the Stavka's notorious Order No. 270 (16 August). Encircled units were
ordered to fight to the last. The directive, like some of those from the purge period, made
scapegoats of 'careerist' intermediate leaders, among whom were 'cowards and deserters'.
Commanders and commissars who left the front or surrendered were to be considered
as deserters; their families were subject to arrest. The families of soldiers who surrendered were to be denied state allowances. Three generals were condemned by name.
One of these was General P. G. Ponedelin, commander of the 12th Army, who was also
sentenced in absentia to be shot, along with one of his corps commanders. The sentence
was not to be carried out until 1950; brought back from a German POW camp in 1945,
the unfortunate generals sat in a Soviet prison for five years before their execution. The
third 'coward' named was V. Ia. Kachalov, whose 28th Army had been destroyed south of
Smolensk, in Timoshenko's Western Theatre. Kachalov had in fact been killed in action
but was only exonerated in 1954. At the time, however, even Zhukov believed something
worse than cowardice was involved, to judge by a report he sent to Stalin on 19 August:
'Among the most senior [military] leaders . . . the enemy has his people. It seems that a
criminal role . . . was played by Kachalov and Ponedelin . . . Everyone says that Kachalov
knowingly went over to the enemy.'[55]

Something even worse for the Stavka than Uman' now began to take shape around
Kiev. It was to be one of the most devastating encirclement of the Second World War.
In the last week of August the German high command ordered Guderian to implement
the turn to the south of his 2nd Panzer Group from Army Group Centre, threatening
the defenders of Kiev from the northeast. A few days later, Field Marshal Rundstedt
established a bridgehead across the Dnepr on the other (southern) flank of German
Army Group South; this was at Kremenchug, 180 miles downstream from Kiev.
Rundstedt quickly put more tanks across the river. On 15 September his 16th Panzer
Division (General Hube) met the 3rd Panzer Division (from the panzer corps of General
Model and the panzer group of General Guderian), coming down from the north; the
meeting place was at Lokhvitsa, 125 miles behind Kiev.

Four Soviet armies were caught in the *Kessel*: the 5th and 26th Armies which had
fought their way back from the frontier, the 21st which had been part of the May–
June 'second strategic echelon' and Vlasov's new 37th. The Germans even trapped
the headquarters of the Southwestern Army Group. Who was responsible? Six weeks
before the encirclement, on 29 July and before Guderian began his move south,
Zhukov had recommended that Kirponos's northern flank should be supported. He
urged giving up Kiev, on the *west* bank of the Dnepr, and shifting all forces behind
the Dnepr River line. His advice was ignored, with the result that some of Kirponos's
strongest forces were tied down in the defence of the exposed city. They would have
been better employed covering the fatal gap between the Western and Southwestern
Theatres. Stalin, however, could not accept giving up the Ukrainian capital, and this
was one of the reasons Zhukov was dismissed as Chief of the General Staff (on 29 July).
Zhukov, who remained a member of the Stavka, repeated his warning in the middle of
August.[56] Stalin, as Supreme Commander, saw a bigger picture. Kiev was politically very

important as the centre of medieval Russia, capital of the Ukraine and the third biggest city in the USSR. Khrushchev, the Ukrainian party chief, was among those urging that the city be held. Stalin also had to inspire the defenders of Leningrad and Odessa, and he was desperate to maintain his standing with the British and the neutral Americans. Stalin was concerned above all about Moscow, and he initially interpreted Guderian's move as the first part of a manoeuvre to approach the capital indirectly, rather than as a turn south into the Ukraine. This judgement might be seen as part of Stalin's fixation on Moscow (something similar would happen in 1942); it might also be another example of Stalin's crediting the German high command with more strategic sense than it deserved. As we have seen, another factor was Stalin's overestimation of the Red Army's ability to counter-attack; he had counted too much on the offensive of General Eremenko's Briansk Army Group (from the Western Theatre) stopping Guderian.

Faced by threats to the north and south, Budennyi (commander of the Southwestern Theatre) and Kirponos (commander of the Southwestern Army Group) called for a withdrawal not only from Kiev but back from the whole middle Dnepr line. Stalin sacked Budennyi on 11 September, four days before the jaws of the German trap closed behind Kiev at Lokhvitsa. Marshal Timoshenko had foolishly assured Stalin that Kiev could be held; Stalin shifted him from the now (apparently) quiet Western Theatre to replace Budennyi. But Timoshenko could not work miracles, and this change of leaders further confused the Russian chain of command, in both the Southwestern and Western Theatres. Stalin dictated inflexible 'stand fast' orders to Marshal Shaposhnikov, the Chief of the General Staff, and sent them out over his (Shaposhnikov's) name to Timoshenko; Shaposhnikov did not resist. A remarkable exchange took place by teleprinter between Shaposhnikov and the chief of staff of the Southwestern Army Group (Tupikov). Tupikov reported, 'The beginning of the catastrophe which you know about is only a couple of days away.' Shaposhnikov signalled back accusing him of panic.[57] On 16 September Timoshenko transmitted to Kirponos oral permission to break out, but the general refused to pull back without written orders. No doubt the baneful influence of Stalin's vicious anti-cowardice Order No. 270 played its part here.

By then, in any event, events had gone too far. The attempted Soviet withdrawal to the east began on the following day, but the trapped armies could not break out of the pocket. Kiev, the 'second Tsaritsyn', fell to the German 6th Army (itself lost a year later at Stalingrad) on 19 September 1941. Fragments of the defending forces escaped. Among them was Vlasov, making his second breakout from an encirclement; another survivor was the future Marshal I. Kh. Bagramian, Kirponos's operations chief. A large column of headquarters staff was trapped in a wood near Lokhvitsa on 20 September. Kirponos was first wounded in the leg, and then finished off by a mortar shell. Killed at this same time was the most senior Communist Party leader to die in the war: M. A. Burmistenko, the commissar attached to Kirponos, was a full member of the Central Committee of the CPSU, and Party 2nd Secretary of the Ukraine, under Khrushchev. The badly injured General Potapov, commander of the 5th Army, was captured; he survived German imprisonment and – unusually – returned to Red Army service after 1945. Timoshenko and Khrushchev, meanwhile, were safe at the headquarters of the Southwestern Theatre, which was some distance east of the pocket. The Germans claimed 665,000 prisoners. As in Belorussia, a very high proportion of Russian losses were men who chose to surrender, rather than fight to the death. From 7 July to 26 September, 620,000 Russian troops were recorded as killed, missing and captured in the fighting in this area, and, given the German figures, the majority must have fallen in the third category of captured.[58]

The 'right bank' Ukraine, west of the Dnepr, was now in German hands. For the moment, few Soviet forces survived to prevent the Wehrmacht seizing the rich economic resources of the 'left bank' Ukraine and the Caucasus. Soviet replacements had now to be sent from the centre to cover the wide breach in the southern defences. Nothing protected Moscow from the southwest. Guderian and the 2nd Panzer Group were free – supply lines permitting – to join in an attack on the Soviet capital from that direction.

THE BALTIC STATES AND LENINGRAD: GERMAN ARMY GROUP NORTH

German victories in the Baltic region

The 65-year-old Field Marshal Wilhelm Ritter von Leeb led the German attack in the north.[59] Leeb had to concern himself, at least at the start of the campaign, with a relatively narrow front of about 175 miles along the Neman River. This was about the same width of front as his 1940 army group had faced against the Maginot Line and in Alsace-Lorraine. Army Group North had limited resources, just one Panzer Group (the 4th, under Hoepner) and two infantry armies (the 18th and 16th).

General Fedor Kuznetsov commanded the forces of the Soviet Baltic Military District, renamed the Northwestern Army Group on the outbreak of the war. Kuznetsov was a well-educated and experienced general who had taught at the Military Academy and successfully led a corps in the Winter War with Finland. In 1941 he commanded three armies including, near the frontier, two mechanized corps with 500 tanks. On paper, Kuznetsov's defensive task should have been easier than that of Pavlov or Kirponos. His initial front was narrow, he did not have exposed salients like those at Belostok and L'vov, and his right flank was covered by the Baltic. The region offered several natural lines of defence. The Neman River and its tributaries lay along the border or just behind it. Some 150 miles further back was the Dvina River, where the Tsarist armies had held out for two years in 1915–17. A further 150 miles to the east were Lake Chud (Lake Peipus) and the Narva and Velikaia rivers, on the line of the old border between the USSR and Estonia and Latvia.

Kuznetsov (and his successor) were not, however, able to take advantage of the terrain. One of Leeb's advantages over Bock and Rundstedt was that he was starting from long-held German territory, East Prussia, which had good military bases and an efficient transport system. Meanwhile, unlike Pavlov and Kirponos, Kuznetsov was based entirely on the 'foreign' territory of the former Baltic states, with an unfriendly population. It cannot have helped that the NKVD had begun a mass deportation of 'hostile elements' from here on 14 June. As elsewhere, the momentum of the initial German attack and the Russian failure to go onto alert contributed to early enemy successes. The most spectacular German coup was the capture intact on the fourth day of the war of the bridges across the Dvina at Daugavpils (Dvinsk), before a Russian second echelon could move into position behind it. This dash to the Dvina was executed by a motorized corps commanded by General Erich von Manstein, who began his career here as one of the most successful Eastern Front generals. Kuznetsov's two mechanized corps tried to mount counter-attacks, but the Soviet tanks began to move only when they were well to the rear of the German spearheads, and their attacks were broken up. The only positive feature of the situation in the northern theatre was the absence of German mass encirclement of Soviet forces, nothing like the *Kessels* at Belostok–Minsk and Smolensk in the centre, or at Uman' and Kiev in the south. This was, however, only because of the rapid retreat of the Northwestern Army Group. A week after crashing through the Dvina line, German leading troops reached the third Russian line of defence on the Velikaia River at Ostrov (2 July, D + 10) and posed an imminent threat to Leningrad. One of Kuznetsov's two border armies (the 8th) retreated north into Estonia, the other (the 11th) withdrew to the east, and the two formations were now cut off from one another.

Kuznetsov had clearly lost control, and the Stavka dismissed him on 4 July, two weeks into the war. His fate was happier than that of Pavlov and Kirponos: neither a firing squad nor death in battle. Kuznetsov would go on to hold a number of less prominent commands, as well as heading the Academy of the General Staff in 1942–3. He was replaced as commander of the Northwestern Army Group by General P. P. Sobennikov (one of his army commanders). The Stavka sent the very able General N. F. Vatutin – Zhukov's former deputy at the General Staff – to serve as Sobennikov's chief of staff. It gave overall command on 10 July to a new Leningrad-based headquarters, the Northwestern Theatre. The Theatre command was under Politburo member Kliment Voroshilov, but the 'Red Marshal' was now in his sixtieth year and had no professional military qualifications. In any event, the limited resources of Voroshilov's Northwestern Theatre were pulled in several different directions. The Theatre headquarters – until wound up at the end of August 1941 – was responsible not only for the Northwestern Army Group but also for the Northern Army Group. This second formation faced another – and seemingly more immediate – threat to Leningrad, coming from the Finnish Army in the Karelian Isthmus north of the city. Northern Army Group also had to hold the very long front stretching 700 miles north from Leningrad to Murmansk; this covered the potentially vital supply route from Britain and America.

By the middle of July, the Northwestern Army Group had lost 75,000 men, over 2,500 tanks, 3,600 guns and mortars, and 1,000 aircraft. Fortunately for the Russians, the pace of the advance in the Baltic region now slowed, as the defence began to become more coherent and the German motorized spearheads had to stop, refit and wait for their infantry to catch up.[60] The Red Army had begun to create a defensive line on the Luga River, running south from the Gulf of Finland, between Lake Chud and Leningrad.

One forgotten tragedy was the Soviet attempt to evacuate forces by sea from Tallin, the capital of Estonia, at the end of August 1941. This turned out to be one of the costliest convoy battles of the whole Second World War, and perhaps the worst disaster in Russian naval history – with twice the losses of the Battle of Tsu-Shima against the Japanese in 1905. The eastbound convoy, commanded personally by the Baltic Fleet commander, ran at night into a German minefield off the Estonian coast. On the following day, the larger covering warships made for the safety of the naval base at Kronshtadt (off Leningrad), and the defenceless surviving transports were picked off by German bombers. More than 12,000 soldiers and sailors perished, many of them wounded victims of the fighting in Estonia. All except two of the large transport ships in the convoy were sunk, as well as five destroyers. The root causes of the calamity were the inept leadership of the convoy and the Stavka's refusal to allow the evacuation until the last moment.[61]

Leningrad blockaded

The German high command was now discussing how best to exploit the victories won in the East. Leningrad had been an important objective in the BARBAROSSA directive. Hitler wanted the conquest of 'economic' objectives on the flanks of the vast Russian–German front. He ordered the movement of Hoth's 3rd Panzer Group from Army Group Centre to cover the right flank of Army Group North and to help to cut Leningrad off from central Russia. Halder, the Chief of the Army General Staff, opposed this diversion of forces from the Moscow axis, but two panzer and two motorized divisions (half of the 3rd Panzer Group) were able to join in the attack south of Leningrad. The transfer of 400 aircraft of the German 8th Air Corps to the Army Group North area (the 1st Air Fleet) gave much more weight to the attack there. In fact, Hitler's concentration on Leningrad made a certain amount of sense within the context of the invasion – had the attack in the north been pursued to its conclusion. Leningrad was indeed a major industrial centre and port. The city's geographical position meant that its capture would finish off the whole northern part of the BARBAROSSA campaign (the region behind Leningrad was sparsely inhabited, unlike that behind Moscow and Kiev). With the capture of the city, many units of Army Group North could have been released for other fronts. On the other hand, Hitler greatly exaggerated the city's importance as a Soviet naval centre. There was an irrational political factor too, going back to the 1917 Bolshevik Revolution in St Petersburg (the former name of Leningrad). This was evident in Hitler's comment of mid-September: 'The "venomous nest Petersburg" out of which Asiatic poison had so long "gushed" into the Baltic Sea would have to disappear from the face of the earth.'[62]

In any event, after a few probing attacks the German armour was able to break through the Luga River line in mid-August, before the Russians could mount a planned counter-blow. The position around Leningrad now became desperate. More than any other great European city, St Petersburg-Leningrad had an artificial character. It was founded by Peter the Great in the early 1700s as a sea port in the empty wilderness of the Neva River delta. Although now the second biggest city in the USSR, its hinterland was still sparsely inhabited. Leningrad's geographical position between the Gulf of Finland and Lake Ladoga was both a disadvantage and an advantage. It was relatively easy to isolate the city from Moscow and the rest of Russia, but Leningrad was better situated for defence than Kiev or Moscow. The western approaches were covered by the Gulf of Finland, the northern by the narrow Karelian Isthmus, the eastern by the expanse of Lake Ladoga, and the southeastern by the upper Neva River. Much of the region bordering the city to the south was swampy and hard to move through.

Leningrad initiated on 30 June the national mass mobilization of the People's Militia. Ten militia divisions and other units totalling 135,000 personnel were formed in the city from late June through August. But the militia wasted skilled industrial manpower and had little military success. The German vanguard cut the main rail line southeast from Leningrad to Moscow (on 20 August) and then the last branch line from Leningrad to the east at Mga (31 August). When the Soviet 34th Army (on the southern flank of the Northwestern Army Group) broke and fled, its commander, General K. M. Kachanov, was tried and shot under the provisions of Stalin's Order No. 270. The Stavka issued a stinging rebuke to the 'heroes of retreat' of the Leningrad Army Group.[63] Finally, the Germans took (8 September) the last land link with the mainland at Shlissel'burg, where the waters of Lake Ladoga enter the Neva. Directly south of Leningrad, German units were pressing in, beginning a long-range artillery bombardment of the city (4 September). The Soviets' unwieldy Northwestern Theatre had been abolished at the end of August, after seven weeks. At about the same time, the military defence of the city was entrusted to the new Leningrad Army Group, formed (along with a new Karelian Army Group) from the old Northern Army Group. Voroshilov was in charge of the Leningrad Army Group for a few days, but this was effectively the end of the career of the 'Red Marshal' as a field commander.[64] For Stalin the fall of Shlissel'burg, which Voroshilov did not immediately report to Moscow, was evidently the last straw (it came at the same time as the Kiev encirclement). General Zhukov was ordered to fly north to take over the Leningrad Army Group and the defence of the city.

This episode became part of the Zhukov legend. Sacked as Chief of the General Staff, Zhukov had just thrown his Reserve Army Group into a successful counter-attack at El'nia in the central front. In the months ahead, in December 1941, lay his great victory in the Battle of Moscow. What happened at Leningrad is, however, less clear-cut. On his arrival, on 10 September, Zhukov certainly threatened draconian punishments and put in place more successful commanders. By that date, however, the defenders already had their backs to the wall, and within three weeks Zhukov would be on his way back to Moscow. Most importantly, Hitler had already, on 5 September, before Zhukov's arrival, decided to remove key offensive forces from Army Group North.[65]

Leningrad appeared to have been neutralized, so forces from German Army Group North could be moved to the centre of the front. As we have seen, Field Marshal Leeb's main mobile formation (the 4th Panzer Group) and much of his air support (the 8th Air Corps) were ordered south for the proposed attack on the Moscow axis. In any event, Leeb's army group was stopped just south of the built-up area of Leningrad, and there it would sit for 900 days. Although eliminated as a major production centre, the huge city would still tie up large numbers of German troops, and it helped protect the Soviet supply lines to the Arctic ports. Hitler made the capture of Leningrad an objective of his

April 1942 campaign directive. Leon Goure, in one of the fullest western histories of the battle, argued that the Germans could have taken Leningrad in September 1941.[66] We can only speculate what would have happened had Leeb's forces not been reduced. It is at least possible that a tighter blockade could have been imposed by pushing German forces across the Neva into the open country east of the city, between it and Lake Ladoga. Such a position would have made impossible the later 'road of life' across the frozen lake to the Russian 'mainland'. Of course, the German troops required for further operations around Leningrad would not have been available for use against Moscow. There would have been even less chance of taking the Soviet capital in October–November. In any event, the terrible siege of Leningrad, the *blokada*, had begun.

CONCLUSION

Stalin claimed in the 3 July radio address that 'the best divisions of the enemy and the best units of his air force have been destroyed and have found their grave on the battlefield'. This was fantasy. But although the German Army won great victories in the first months of Operation BARBAROSSA, it had done so at heavy cost. German losses *before* the Russian campaign – from 1939 to June 1941 – had totalled 102,000 dead and missing. This figure included 15,000 in September 1939 (the period of the Polish campaign) and 50,000 in May–June 1940 (the time of the campaign in the Low Countries and France). In contrast, German losses on the Eastern Front in the three and a quarter months through to the end of September 1941 numbered 185,000. Not until August 1942 would monthly German losses in the East exceed those of July, August and September 1941.[67]

By the end of September 1941, fourteen weeks into the Great Fatherland War, the position of the two sides had developed dramatically. The Wehrmacht had won great victories and driven 400 miles into Russia. It had reached and crossed the initial territorial objective of the BARBAROSSA project, the line of the Dvina and the Dnepr rivers. Nevertheless, the advance had taken longer than the German planners expected. The Red Army had suffered enormous losses, but was still fighting. The Germans had run into the Red Army's 'second strategic echelon', which in turn was reinforced by wave after wave of Russian reserve divisions from the interior. The German intelligence blunder regarding Russian strength was now evident. Halder wrote another memorable diary entry, this time in mid-August:

> In the general situation what stands out is that we have underestimated the Russian colossus, which has consciously prepared for war with all the effort a totalitarian state can muster. This assertion applies to general organizational and industrial power, to the communications infrastructure, but above all to pure military power. At the start of the war we had counted on about 200 enemy divisions. We have now counted 360. These divs. are not as well armed or equipped as ours, they are often poorly led. But they are there. And if we knock out a dozen of them, then the Russian puts up another dozen.[68]

Devastating defeats had not shaken Soviet Russia politically. A battle of annihilation had become a war of attrition.

The paradox was that although the Red Army had not been destroyed in the initial onslaught, it had suffered near mortal damage. The early days, weeks and months of the war determined the character of its next years. Territory and population had been lost which it would take the Russians three years to claw back. The USSR would have to defend central Russia and fight the campaign of 'liberation' with virtually a new army. It is hard to grasp just how much damage the Red Army had suffered in the encirclements and costly counter-attacks. All told, the Red Army lost 177 divisions in 1941, the majority of them in the June–September period.[69] Soviet military losses up to the end of September 1941 have been given as at least 2,050,000. This was over twice the military losses that would come later, in October through to December 1941 (950,000), and it was nearly three times any comparable period of the war. (To give a scale of comparison, British war dead for the entire six years of the war numbered 350,000.) Perhaps 70–80 per cent of these Soviet losses were prisoners-of-war, rather than soldiers killed on the battlefield; by the middle of December 1941 the German Army claimed to have taken 3,350,000 POWs. As prisoners they would suffer a terrible fate at the hands of their captors. But alive or dead, these soldiers were still lost to the Red Army.[70]

Casualties among the Soviet officer corps were especially important. In little more than three months, the Red Army had lost 142,000 officers, compared to 440,000 'command staff' in service at the start of the war (and to 20,000 who died in the 1937–8 purges). Some forty generals were killed and forty-four captured.[71] This devastation of the middle and lower ranks was especially great when added to the losses at the upper levels in the purges. The leaders of a new 'cadre army' would have to be built, if not from scratch, then from a very low level.

Stalin would complain for the next year that the Red Army was losing because it lacked weapons. It had not, in truth, lacked equipment on 22 June, but this strength had been thrown away. The losses have already been mentioned (see Chapter 2), and Table 3.1 breaks them down between the three main theatres.

Table 3.1 Soviet equipment losses, June–September 1941

	Tanks	Artillery/Mortars	Aircraft
Baltic/Leningrad	4,000	13,500	2,700
Belorussia/Smolensk	6,100	18,700	2,700
W Ukraine/Kiev	4,800	34,200	1,600

Source: Poteri, p. 484.

Note: Russian statistics lump rather different weapons – proper artillery (orudii) and mortars – together. If the artillery:mortar loss ratio in each of these theatres was the same as that for the whole Red Army (about 40:60), then the Soviet losses of artillery pieces would have been about 5,400 in the north, 7,500 in the centre and 13,700 in the south.

'Our army … is still young', Stalin would complain in November, by which he meant it was inexperienced.[72] In reality this was so, not because the USSR had failed to prepare for war, but because the Wehrmacht had been so successful in the early months and destroyed most of the Soviet cadre army. The ineptitude of the Stalin regime and the Red Army had led to it being mauled by a weaker enemy. And at the end of September 1941, the German ability to inflict damage was far from spent.

CHAPTER 4
MOSCOW AND THE END OF BARBAROSSA, OCTOBER TO DECEMBER 1941

It is not true that the army's fighting capacity decreases in wintertime. All the Russian Army's major victories were won in wintertime. Aleksandr Nevskii against the Swedes, Peter I against the Swedes in Finland, Alexander I's victory over Napoleon. We are a northern country.

> Joseph Stalin, 28 March 1940

The war with fascist Germany cannot be considered an ordinary war.

> Joseph Stalin, 3 July 1941

Although [we are] weak in the knees … the enemy is worse off than we are; he is on the verge of collapse.

> General Halder, 13 November 1941

By the end of September 1941, despite great successes, it was clear that Hitler and the German generals had not achieved their original BARBAROSSA objective of destroying the bulk of the Red Army in a decisive battle in the western borderlands. The estimated six-week period had come and gone, and the Red Army was still desperately fighting. One of the most dramatic periods of the war now began, with both deepening barbarity and pivotal action. This period opened in the middle of September, after the end of the Soviet counter-attacks on Smolensk and the encirclement at Kiev. It ended in early December, with the halting of the German offensive. The autumn of 1941, when the Germans were most successful in their drive into the western USSR, was a time of spectacular panzer victories. It was also a time of terrible atrocities; Hitler's terrible project was put into reality, with the complicity of the Wehrmacht.

The German advance in the summer of 1941 underwent frequent changes of emphasis. By September Hitler had made his decision to destroy the Soviet forces defending Moscow. But some fighting continued on the flanks of the great advance, around Leningrad, and in the Ukraine, in the Crimea and in the lower Don region. Field Marshal Rundstedt's German Army Group South had broken the Dnepr River line in September; it now moved deeper into the 'left-bank' Ukraine on a wide front.[1] The Russians call the northern part of this drive, by Reichenau's German 6th Army (later of Stalingrad fame), the 'Sumy–Khar'kov defensive operation'. They call the southern part, by the German 17th Army and Kleist's 1st Panzer Group, the 'Donbass–Rostov strategic defensive operation'. These advances threatened the Ukrainian industrial city of Khar'kov, the vital coal-mining region of the Donets River Basin (the Donbass) and the strategic city of Rostov, the gateway to the Caucasus.

German Army Group South at first made steady progress into the eastern Ukraine. The bulk of Red Army reserves were now being committed to the Moscow theatre, where Operation TYPHOON smashed through the Soviet front at the start of October. As a result, in the south the German 6th Army took Sumy (10 October) and then Khar'kov (25 October). Khar'kov, a great city of 840,000 inhabitants before the war, was soon in the grip of starvation. Further south, the 1st Panzer Group advanced to the industrial centre of Stalino (now Donetsk) on the western edge of the Donbass (20 October), although the Germans' movements were now slowed by the onset of the *rasputitsa*, the autumn rains, and by continuing supply problems.

The Germans won another major victory at the far southern end of the line, near the Sea of Azov. Elements of two Soviet armies were trapped east of Melitopol' by Manstein's 11th Army and Kleist's 1st Panzer Group. This happened in early October, and the Germans called it the 'Battle on the Sea of Azov'. The commander of the Soviet 18th Army, General A. K. Smirnov, was killed in action, and the Germans claimed to have taken over 100,000 prisoners and captured over 200 tanks and nearly 700 artillery pieces.[2] Coming as it did at the same moment as even greater disasters in front of Moscow (the Battle of Viaz'ma–Briansk, see below), this southern battle is often ignored by historians. In fact, it was certainly one of the half dozen great Red Army defeats of 1941. This new Soviet failure left Manstein free to push south into the Crimea, and it opened the way for Kleist's tanks to move east towards Rostov.

In mid-October Manstein broke through the Soviet positions at the neck of the Crimean peninsula. Within four weeks, the poorly led Russian forces had abandoned the whole peninsula except for the big naval base and fortress at Sevastopol', on the southwestern tip. During the following month, Hitler's attention turned to Rostov. With the end of the *rasputitsa* and the onset of the first mild frost in November, the way was opened for a German advance. Mackensen's corps, from Kleist's panzer group, had raced ahead to take Rostov off the march; on 21 November 'Sepp' Dietrich's 'Adolf Hitler' motorized division entered the city. This first notable victory of the Waffen-SS was short-lived. The Germans had overextended themselves, and Rostov became one of the first setbacks to BARBAROSSA. The Soviet defending forces of the Southern Army Group, now led by General Cherevichenko, put heavy pressure on the overextended enemy salient. The local German commanders wanted to pull back to a more defensible position 30 miles west of Rostov, on the Mius River, which runs into the Sea of Azov at Taganrog. Field Marshal Rundstedt backed this withdrawal; when Hitler disagreed he resigned as commander of Army Group South (Field Marshal Reichenau replaced him). Not by accident, the setback at Rostov showed the first cracks in the German command structure. Hitler, for his part, already attached great importance to the southern theatre, with the coming 1942 campaign in the Caucasus in mind. On 2 December he flew from Rastenburg to Mariupol', only 60 miles behind the front line, in an attempt to resolve the situation. In the end, Hitler had to accept the retreat. As for Stalin, he sent his personal commendation to the local Soviet commanders. This was a new phenomenon for the Red Army in 1941, and Stalin's words were published in *Pravda*: 'I congratulate you on the victory over the enemy and liberation of Rostov from the German-fascist aggressors.'[3]

Another part of the background to the Battle of Moscow was the continued fighting around Leningrad, where in October and November the Red Army's position still appeared to be at risk.[4] The immediate crisis the Soviets faced was now at Tikhvin, 110 miles east of Leningrad, which forces of the German 16th Army moved towards in late October and which they took on 8 November. The remote little town – only 16,000 inhabitants in 1939 – was important because it controlled the last railway line to Lake Ladoga; across this lake Soviet supplies could be transferred into Leningrad. In the course of late November and early December, the Soviet armies, co-ordinated from mid-November by General Meretskov in a new Volkhov Army Group, were able to push the enemy back from the railway. Desperate battles were fought in the sparsely inhabited woods of the eastern Leningrad Region. On 9 December, the Russians recaptured Tikhvin. By the end of December 1941, the German Army Group North had been pushed back to the Volkhov River, where the front stabilized. In the northern theatre, as in south Russia, the *Ostheer* had now receded from its high-water mark.

THE BATTLE OF VIAZ'MA–BRIANSK

The German victory

The battles on the flanks, at Rostov and Tikhvin, were literally sideshows; the German campaign's centre of gravity was now the advance towards Moscow. On 5 December 1941 the Red Army's central formations would be able to begin their first sustained and successful counter-attack of the war. This military blow would signal the doom of the whole Nazi adventure. Before that, however, there would be over two months of desperate fighting, from the start of the first German attack on 30 September.

In early September Hitler still dreamt of a decisive battle of annihilation against the Red Army, but he had now moved the Soviet Armageddon several months forward in time and several hundred miles to the east in space. In his Directive No. 35 of 6 September, he outlined an operation which would commence in three or four weeks' time. Successes on the flanks, he declared,

> have provided the basis for a decisive operation against the Timoshenko Army Group (*Heeresgruppe Timoschenko*), which is committed to offensive action against our central forces. This [army group] must be beaten to destruction in the limited time available before the onset of winter weather. To this end it is necessary to concentrate all the strength of the Army and the Luftwaffe which can be spared from the flanks and which can be moved up in time.

Note that the stated objective was the 'Timoshenko Army Group', not Moscow. The Soviet capital itself was covered in the directive under the heading 'further course of operations'. The same point was made in Hitler's order to the soldiers of the Eastern Front as the main battle opened on 2 October. This was to be 'the last powerful blow that will smash this enemy before the onset of winter'.[5]

The fighting in the central theatre developed very badly for the Russians. With it came the last great German *Kesselschlacht* (battle of encirclement) of the 1941–5 war, the Battle of Viaz'ma–Briansk.[6] At the end of September, the Russian forces were drawn up on a relatively straight north–south line, drawn 30 miles to the east of Smolensk (and 200 miles to the west of Moscow). In all, this defensive line in the centre of the Russian defences was about 600 miles long. The position was roughly where the German Army Group Centre had halted in July. It was a predictable, even necessary, place for covering the distant approaches to the Soviet capital. As early as May 1941, when the peacetime Soviet high command had contemplated the growing Nazi threat, work had begun here on a third, Ostashkov–Pochep, line of defence (behind the 'Molotov' and 'Stalin' Lines). In July, a 'front of reserve armies' had been created on this line. Anchored in the north around Ostashkov, in the glacial lakes and hills of the Valdai Uplands, the line ran south to Pochep (west of Briansk) and beyond to Glukhov.[7] Behind the Soviet front lay the small town of Viaz'ma, the centre of a district (*raion*) of Smolensk Region. The history of Viaz'ma went back to early medieval times, but its population was only 34,000 in 1939, and the place was of little economic importance. Viaz'ma, however, had great value to the generals as a railway junction on the direct route from Smolensk to Moscow; strategic railways also ran north from Viaz'ma to Rzhev and south to Briansk. The Germans and Russians would fight huge and largely forgotten battles for Viaz'ma over the next eighteen months; the Red Army would lose it and then expend hundreds of thousands of lives in desperate attempts to take it back.

The forces of what Hitler had called *Heeresgruppe Timoschenko* were by late September organized into three army groups. Marshal Timoshenko, who had commanded both Western Army Group and the (higher level) Western Theatre, had actually departed for the Ukraine two weeks earlier. The Western Theatre headquarters was wound up, and command of the Western Army Group, in the direct path of the Wehrmacht's drive to the east, was given to one of Timoshenko's army commanders, General Ivan Stepanovich Konev. The new commander of the Western Army Group was an officer destined in the long term for great things; by the end of the war Marshal Konev would race Marshal Zhukov to Berlin.[8] In the short term, in 1941, Konev was faced with disaster and near disgrace. Konev's Red Army career up to September 1941 suggested that he was a leader in whom Stalin and his senior military advisers had a great deal of confidence. This was true despite the fact that Konev was not a member of the 1st Cavalry Army clique and had not proven his abilities in combat in Spain or Finland. A peasant boy from northern Russia, born in 1897, Konev was conscripted into the Tsarist Army too late to see action in the First World War (he was an NCO in the artillery). However, he took a very active part in the Civil War fighting in Siberia, where he served mainly as a Red Army political commissar; he joined the Communist Party in 1918. A commander of various

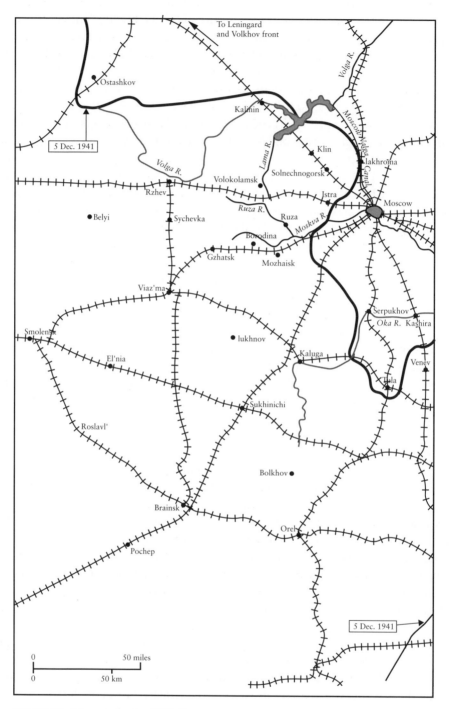

MAP 2 The Moscow theatre, 1941–2.

divisions in the 1930s, he also received abbreviated higher military training, at which he excelled. *Komdiv* Konev came under some suspicion in 1937 due to his previous service connections and his suspected social background. His father was said to have been a *kulak* (better-off peasant) and his uncle a Tsarist policeman. Konev survived this and the Red Army purge, and the confrontation with Japan opened his route to higher posts. In 1938 he was given command of a rifle corps in Mongolia, in 1938–40 of the 2nd Army in the Far East and in 1940–1 of the whole Transbaikal Military District.

In 1941 Konev came back to Europe to take charge of the North Caucasus Military District, with the rank of Lieutenant General. He brought the 19th Army from the North Caucasus to the Western Army Group at the start of the war. This formation fought effectively under Timoshenko's overall command in the Battle of Smolensk. Konev famously came into conflict with Zhukov in the later stages of the war, and in the post-war 'battle of memoirs'. If Zhukov can be believed, however, it was he himself who recommended to Stalin that Konev take Timoshenko's place in the Western Army Group. Zhukov and Konev were well acquainted from having served together as middle-level commanders in Belorussia at the height of the purges.

In September–October 1941 General Konev's Western Army Group consisted of the 20th, 16th, 19th, 30th, 29th and 22nd Armies (counting from south to north). They held the northern half of the line, with the left-flank 20th Army astride the highway and the railway running from Smolensk to Moscow. General Eremenko's Briansk Army Group, the 13th, 3rd and 50th Armies, covered the southern third of the line. Behind Eremenko, and 150 miles south of Viaz'ma, was the larger town of Briansk (174,000 inhabitants in 1939). Briansk, where three major lines criss-crossed, was an even more important railway hub than Viaz'ma. Between Konev and Eremenko were the 43rd and the 24th Armies of the so-called Reserve Army Group, now commanded by Marshal Budennyi. Four other armies of this army group (the 33rd, 32nd, 49th and 31st) formed a potential second echelon behind Konev.

On the other side of the front stood Field Marshal Bock and German Army Group Centre. For the first time in the campaign, three German panzer groups were assembled in one theatre. For the first time, too, a double encirclement was possible. Hoth's 3rd Panzer Group, was concentrated north of the Smolensk–Viaz'ma–Moscow railway. Some 150 miles to the south was the main concentration of Hoepner's 4th Panzer Group, shifted down from the Leningrad front; 290 miles south of Hoepner was Guderian, with the 2nd Panzer Group, refitting after the Kiev campaign. The slower infantry divisions of German Army Group Centre, in the 9th, 4th and 2nd Armies, had now caught up with the panzer spearheads. Luftwaffe air groups had been concentrated behind the German front.

The first German action came at dawn of Tuesday, 30 September, as Guderian began his attack with the 2nd Panzer Group at the southern end of the German line; the aim was partly to distract the Russians' attention. The main German drive, known as Operation TYPHOON, began 300–450 miles to the north, on Thursday, 2 October. Hoepner's 4th Panzer Group, in the centre of the attack, smashed through the Russian lines and curved up to take Viaz'ma from the south. A drive of about 100 miles took Hoepner's tanks through the Soviet Reserve Army Group to Viaz'ma on Tuesday, 7 October. There they met Hoth's 3rd Panzer Group, which had sliced through Konev's lines and driven down to the south. Behind the Germans and west of Viaz'ma was now a huge pocket; it contained most of the Soviet 19th, 20th, 24th and 32nd Armies.

The Germans claimed some 660,000 POWs were taken here – a number matching that of the Kiev encirclement in the previous month. Three of the Soviet army commanders were captured: Ershakov, Vishnevskii and Lukin from the Western Army Group (commanding, respectively, the 20th, 32nd and 19th Armies); another army commander, Rakutin, was killed on the battlefield (he was the commander of the 24th Army in the Reserve Army Group, and had been Zhukov's subordinate at El'nia). The first 'Katiusha' rocket battery, which had entered service in July 1941, was trapped near Viaz'ma; the launchers were destroyed by their crews and Captain Flerov, the battery commander, was killed. In the other part of the 'twin' encirclement, at Briansk, the Germans claimed a further 100,000 POWs. The advance here was more daring, involving a deeper drive by Guderian's 2nd Panzer Group. This took Briansk from the rear, as the infantry of the German 2nd Army marched forward from the west. The Soviet 13th and 3rd Armies were trapped south of Briansk. The 50th Army pulled back, but its commander, M. P. Petrov, was killed in action.

The most recent multi-volume Russian history accepts that casualties from the end of September until the middle of October were extremely heavy. Of the 1,250,000 troops deployed at the start of these battles in the Soviet Western, Reserve and Briansk Army Groups, up to a million were lost, 690,000 of them prisoners. The grand total of Soviet formations trapped at Viaz'ma–Briansk came to sixty-four rifle divisions, eleven tank brigades and fifty artillery regiments.[9] The great twin battle for Viaz'ma and Briansk, what the Germans called the *Doppelschlacht*, has been something of a forgotten event. It was overshadowed historically by the Soviet disaster on the frontiers in June, and by the sudden change of fortunes in Russia's favour at Moscow in December; 'Victors aren't judged', as the Russian saying has it. In fact, the Battle of Viaz'ma–Briansk was one of the greatest successes of German arms in the entire Second World War. It was perhaps, too, the most ignominious defeat suffered by the Soviets. The last major Red Army concentration on the approaches to Moscow was largely eliminated.

On the morning of Sunday, 5 October (D + 5 of the whole German operation), a Soviet fighter plane spotted a 15-mile-long column of German vehicles heading towards Iukhnov. This town was 90 miles east of the TYPHOON start line, and about a third of the way from that line to Moscow. Stalin's 'Black Sunday' had begun. At a meeting that afternoon with Marshal Shaposhnikov and General Vasilevskii, Stalin decided to pull the main Soviet defensive position covering Moscow back 120 miles, to a north–south line running in front of the towns of Volokolamsk, Mozhaisk and Kaluga. This 'Mozhaisk Line of Defence' was about 75 miles west of the Soviet capital, and had originally been set up under NKVD General Artem'ev back in July, at the time Smolensk was encircled. When Stalin's October order was issued, there were almost no regular forces left to man the Mozhaisk Line, as so much had been trapped at Viaz'ma–Briansk. All that could be done in the first days was to throw in officer cadets, 'destroyer' battalions, People's

Militia (*opolchentsy*), and NKVD and police units to cover the most vital points. It was on this fateful day, too, that Stalin sent General Zhukov an order calling him back from Leningrad.[10]

An even more portentous measure was taken that Sunday, in the name of the GKO. It was decided to create a new 'strategic echelon' on the line of the Volga River, stretching from Vytegra to Astrakhan. Vytegra is a little town in north Russia, 225 miles east of Leningrad, near where the Volga–Baltic Canal enters Lake Onega; the sector of the canal near here covered the approaches to the strategic railway running south from the northern port of Arkhangel'sk to Vologda and Moscow. Astrakhan is at the other end of European Russia; the river port is 1,150 miles to the southeast of Vytegra, at the mouth of the Volga, and 400 miles east of Rostov (see Map 1). For the Russians this new 'strategic echelon' covering the Volga was to consist of nine new 'reserve armies'. At the same time the GKO decided to form a number of 'Engineer Armies' (*sapernye armii*) to dig fortifications behind the existing positions and on the Volga Line. Ominously, the Soviet line was essentially what Hitler had described ten months earlier, in December 1940. Directive No. 21, for Operation BARBAROSSA, declared that '[t]he final objective is to erect a barrier against Asiatic Russia on the general line Volga–Arkhangel'sk'.[11]

Early on Wednesday, 8 October (D + 8), Zhukov described the situation over the telephone to Stalin. 'The main danger now is that nearly all routes to Moscow are open, the weak covering forces on the Mozhaisk Line cannot be a guarantee against the sudden appearance of enemy tank forces in front of Moscow. It is necessary quickly to gather forces from wherever possible for the Mozhaisk line of defence.' The lead elements of Hoepner's 4th Panzer Group reached the edge of the Mozhaisk Line on Friday, 10 October, meeting only scratch Soviet units. A GKO decree was passed on 11 October putting the NKVD in control of the Moscow region and ordering construction of inner defences on the line Khlebnikovo–Moskva River.[12]

Politically, this string of disasters marked another low point for Stalin. On 2 October he had, in the name of the Politburo, summoned a plenum (plenary meeting) of the Central Committee of the Communist Party; it was to open in Moscow on 10 October. The CC was a most important body, representing the power elite of the USSR, the most important regional party leaders from across the country, the main government ministers from Moscow, as well as a number of the generals. Plenums were infrequent; only one plenum had met since the March 1939 Party Congress. Stalin's objective was presumably to rally the party and the nation for a winter campaign. All this was overtaken by the Viaz'ma–Briansk disaster and the threat to Moscow, a misfortune which had not been anticipated on 2 October. The plenum delegates arrived in Moscow, many from very long distances, only to be told that the meeting had been postponed 'for a month'; in fact, a plenum would not meet until January 1944.

Early on Wednesday, 15 October, Stalin signed a GKO decree ordering the evacuation of Moscow. The main government ministries (under Molotov) and embassies were ordered east 650 miles to Kuibyshev (Samara) on the Volga. The Red Army's Political Administration (GPU) was moved to Kuibyshev; most significantly, the General Staff was also moved out, to Arzamas, 260 miles east of Moscow and halfway to Kuibyshev. Dimitrov, whose Comintern organization was evacuated to Kuibyshev and Ufa, recalled a conversation with Stalin and Molotov on the 15th, when it was said that the government was being evacuated: 'Moscow cannot be defended like Leningrad.' On Thursday morning the Metro stopped running. From the 16th to 18th there were unprecedented scenes of panic in the streets and railway stations of Stalin's capital. On Saturday, 18 October, panzer spearheads broke through the Mozhaisk Line, two hours' drive west of the Kremlin. The following day a state of siege was declared. Stalin instructed Beria, the head of the NKVD, to prepare some one thousand locations in the Soviet capital for demolition.[13]

The reasons for Soviet defeat

The outcome of the Battle of Viaz'ma–Briansk is harder to explain than earlier Soviet defeats. The Belostok–Minsk encirclement was inflicted on the Red Army in the shock and chaos of the first weeks of the war. Justifiably or not, the element of surprise was important, as was the forward basing of Soviet forces in the newly annexed territories. Even the Kiev debacle of the Soviet Southwestern Army Group in September was explicable. It came about from the unexpected movement of Guderian's 2nd Panzer Group, from Stalin's obstinate demand to hold Kiev, and from the wear and tear of months of non-stop battle. In contrast, at the beginning of October there was now nothing unexpected about the use of the German armoured concentrations, and the soldiers of the Red Army had had some quiet weeks to prepare for an attack on their line east of Smolensk.

There is some disagreement about the relative strength of the two sides. Official Russian sources maintain that German Army Group Centre had 1,800,000 personnel, 1,700 tanks, 14,000 guns and mortars, and 1,390 aircraft; this was in contrast to the three Soviet defending army groups (Western, Briansk and Reserve), which had a reported strength of 1,250,000 personnel, with 990 tanks, 7,600 artillery pieces and mortars, and 670 aircraft. Recent Western sources suggest the two sides were actually about equal in manpower terms.[14] It is clear that the number of operational German tanks was substantially less than the Russian claim, given the wear and tear of the previous months' operations. There is no doubt, however, that this was a maximum German effort, and a basic factor was the concentration of enemy fighting power. In contrast, the German 6th Army in the advance on Stalingrad a year later in 1942 would number only 270,000 men, and German troops involved in the dual offensive at Kursk in mid-1943 would come to 700,000.[15]

Another basic reason for the Viaz'ma–Briansk defeat was the low quality of the Russian formations, lower even than those on the frontier in June. Many were composed of poorly trained reservists; some were manned by armed workers recruited through the People's Militia.[16] Although the weeks immediately before the start of Operation TYPHOON had been quiet, the two months of Timoshenko's abortive offensives towards Smolensk had knocked the stuffing out of the 'regular' Soviet divisions. All were demoralized by defeat, terrified of German superiority and incapable of complicated operations. Konev argued that a controlled retreat – as opposed to panicky flight – was a very difficult manoeuvre to carry out. 'Before the war our forces very rarely trained for this form of action, considering retreat a sign of weakness.' In contrast, the *Ostheer* was intact and now highly experienced in fighting the Red Army. German morale was still high.

Undoubtedly a major part of the German success was a concentration of air strength in the central theatre under Field Marshal Kesselring's 2nd Air Fleet. Especially important were the ground attack specialists of 8th Air Corps under Richthofen, brought back from the Leningrad theatre. The Luftwaffe's 1st Air Corps was transferred from the south. Konev complained on the eve of the attack that he was crucially weak in air power; he had only 106 fighters (44 of them obsolete), 28 light bombers and a handful of attack aircraft; he requested 350–400 additional aircraft. The arrival of the first batch of American P-40 fighters in mid-October (diverted from shipments to Britain) made little difference. In his analysis of the causes of defeat, published 25 years later, Konev put at the top of his list German air superiority.[17]

The three Soviet army group commanders each bore a degree of responsibility. Marshal Budennyi was a commander of limited abilities, but he had only arrived at the Reserve Army Group from the Ukraine in mid-September. General Eremenko was easier to criticize. He had been responsible for the Briansk Army Group since its creation in mid-August; he had also failed to stop Guderian's turn to the south behind Kiev. Eremenko was probably fortunate to be badly injured in a German air attack on 12 October. Despite the devastation suffered by his army group, he would return as one of the victorious commanders at Stalingrad, and then in the great offensives of 1944–5.

As for General Konev, his army group took the main brunt of the attack in early October, and it suffered the highest losses in men captured and killed. Konev had been commander of the Western Army Group for only two weeks when the Germans struck, and he was there because Timoshenko had been moved south. He was only forty-three; his high-level command experience had been limited to leading the 19th Army during the Smolensk battles.[18] Konev's career, and perhaps his life, were on a knife-edge. According to Zhukov, Stalin at first suspected the worst: 'Konev, like Pavlov at the start of the war, opened the front [*otkryl ... front*] to the enemy here.' (General Pavlov, commander of Western Army Group, had been tried and shot three months previously.) A GKO commission, including Molotov, Voroshilov and General Vasilevskii, was sent to examine the causes of the October collapse. In the end, there was no trial. Stalin issued no draconian orders, nothing like what came from the Kremlin following the surrender of the Uman' pocket in August. Zhukov apparently intervened with Stalin on Konev's behalf: 'I saved Konev's life', he would later claim. (Konev's failure – or treason – placed Zhukov himself in danger, as it was probably he who had proposed Konev for the Western Army Group post.) Rather than being dismissed, Konev was briefly made Zhukov's deputy, moving on almost immediately to take over the Kalinin Army Group northwest of Moscow. For Konev, too, this would be a shattering experience. He had had unlimited confidence in Stalin. Having to deal with a confused and nearly hysterical dictator shook his faith.[19]

The Viaz'ma–Briansk disaster was, however, less the responsibility of the local commanders than of Stalin, Shaposhnikov and the Red Army high command. The Stavka had overall responsibility for the assignment of local commanders, the assessment of the overall military situation and the deployment of forces. As would happen again and again in the first two years of the war, Soviet intelligence did not provide an accurate picture of German intentions. On 26 September Konev did apparently send out a message warning his command about an imminent German attack towards Viaz'ma, using tanks and aircraft. In their report of 1 October, he and his commissar (Bulganin) complained, 'It has not been possible to get information about the objectives of the enemy's offensive operations from our intelligence organs'. Zhukov maintained in a 1965 interview that by the middle of July 1941, after the initial defeat near Smolensk and the loss of the Orsha land bridge, he had come to the conclusion that the Red Army would have to fight in front of Moscow. He claimed that at that point even Stalin had concluded that 'in the winter months the front would get near Moscow'.[20] Zhukov's recollection may or may not have been affected by hindsight, but in any event developments after that July, notably the German advances in the Ukraine and at Leningrad, distracted the attention of the Soviet high command. Stalin and the Stavka were preoccupied with the fall of Kiev, the threat to the Donbass and the imminent fall of Leningrad. This was an unintended benefit to the Germans of Hitler's erratic strategy. Marshal Vasilevskii admitted after the war that the General Staff did not expect the German attack in the central part of the front in early October.[21] The Soviet high command may have assumed that German losses had been so high that another major enemy attack was not possible. In any event, in mid-September, two weeks before the Germans attacked, Timoshenko was transferred to the Ukraine and Zhukov was sent to Leningrad.

Stalin, according to Zhukov, was still 'in a trance' after the Kiev catastrophe, and Shaposhnikov was not prepared to stand up to him.[22] Both Stalin and Shaposhnikov must also be heavily criticized for allowing a muddled command structure to develop in the region in front of Moscow. Winding up the Western Theatre on 10 September was a blunder, as it was not replaced by anything else. The three army groups covering the capital were now co-ordinated only by the Stavka, and the Stavka had other national responsibilities. Stalin came to realize that there was a command problem and, on 5 October, he recalled Zhukov from Leningrad. By then, however, it was much too late. Unity of command was only established on the eleventh day of the German attack, on 10 October, when the remnants of the three Soviet army groups were merged into an enlarged Western Army Group, and Zhukov was put in overall charge.[23]

There was no clear plan for defence or withdrawal. The Ostashkov–Pochep Line, where the Soviet armies were drawn up at the end of September, was not one that the Stavka wanted to abandon. The position covered a vital lateral railway (Briansk–Viaz'ma–Rzhev), and kept the enemy at arm's length from Moscow. Stalin was probably thinking, too, of holding this forward position for future counter-offensives against Smolensk. For months, preparations had been made to fight here, and some field fortifications had been constructed. The Stavka also reacted slowly to TYPHOON once it had begun. Orders to retreat, as in June 1941, were issued five or six days too late, when the front-line Russian troops were trapped 50 miles or more behind the lead panzers. Konev, in his plausible account, spoke of a vacuum of authority and of a panicky and confused Stalin whose indecision, especially about falling back to the Mozhaisk Line, led to disaster. The Germans were satisfied with the result. 'Operation TYPHOON is following an altogether classic course', commented Halder at a conference in early October, 'The enemy is standing fast on all parts of the front not under attack, which gives high hopes for the creation of pockets.'[24]

THE WAR OF IDEOLOGY: SOVIET JEWS AND RED ARMY POWS

The Holocaust in the USSR

Military campaigns are the main subject of this book. Political–ideological developments, however important, can be mentioned only in passing. Nevertheless, campaigns and ideas were closely linked, in what was a most 'political' war. Hitler conceived of the invasion of Russia as a war of ideologies and of annihilation. It was a war against the 'Bolsheviks', against the Jews, against the Slavs. Two aspects of the sinister Nazi war of ideology have a special relevance to the first period of the war: the genocide of the Jews and the murder of Soviet POWs.

The invasion of Russia was the only act of German aggression where the Jews were mentioned as an excuse for action. This was true from the outset, but shortly after the Battle of Viaz'ma–Briansk, Hitler made a major speech in which he returned to the theme of 'the international Jew' as the firebrand of the war and the 'inspirer of the world coalition against the German people and the German Reich'. The Soviet Union was the 'greatest servant of Judaism'; 'If Stalin can be seen on the stage in front of the curtain, behind it stand Kaganovich and all the other Jews, who in tens of thousands of ways lead this powerful state'; it was 'a regime of commissars, 90 per cent of Jewish extraction, who rule this whole slave state'.[25] The Holocaust in the USSR was perhaps most intense in the period from September to December 1941, and the atrocities were perpetrated in the regions of heavy Jewish settlement that had just been conquered by the armies of Field Marshals Leeb, Bock and Rundstedt.[26] Most of the 5,000,000 Jews of the USSR in 1941 lived in the western regions of the country. About 380,000 had lived within the pre-1939 borders of Soviet Belorussia, and another 1,500,000 in the regions of the pre-1939 Soviet Ukraine, mostly west of the Dnepr River. A further 1,300,000 Jews were added to the 'Soviet' population with the annexation of eastern Poland in 1939. To the south, 250,000 Jews had lived in the Bessarabia and Northern Bukovina, newly annexed from Romania. A smaller number, about 230,000, were incorporated into the USSR with the annexation of the Baltic states; most were in Lithuania and Latvia.

The most infamous agents of destruction were the four *Einsatzgruppen* ('task forces'), mobile SS killing units which followed closely behind the advancing panzers. The 'operational' elements were a dozen or so *Einsatzkommandos*. Given their lethal impact, the numbers of personnel of the *Einsatzgruppen* were very small, with only a grand total of about 3,000 police officials initially. Although the *Einsatzgruppen's* place in infamy relates to the genocide of the Jews, the role the Nazi leadership originally intended for them was quite different; they were to destroy the Soviet political leadership. Only when that task proved to be impossible were these death squads turned on the remaining Jews. After the first few months, these *Einsatzgruppen* were reinforced by police units from the Reich, and locally conscripted militias.

The horror emerged in stages. In the initial advance the *Einsatzkommandos* killed groups of Jews, initially younger males, but they did not attempt everywhere to destroy whole communities of men, women and children. At the very end of September 1941, the infamous Babii Iar (Babii Yar) massacre of 34,000 Jews – men, women and children – was carried out in Kiev, 'justified' by the detonation of a large delayed-action bomb (planted by the Soviet NKVD) in a government building later used as a Germany Army headquarters. The 'reprisal' killings were carried out by units of *Einsatzgruppe* C, assisted by the Wehrmacht.[27] At this moment, just 200 miles to the north, German Army Group Centre was beginning its offensive towards Moscow, Operation TYPHOON. Probably the worst single atrocity of the whole Eastern Front took place a few weeks later in another Ukrainian city, Odessa. The port had been held by the Russians during a long siege. Six days after it fell, in late October, Romanian troops began a pogrom in which tens of thousands of Jews were killed (as in Kiev, the massacre of innocent Jews followed the detonation of an NKVD bomb in a military headquarters).

One authoritative source estimates that 500,000 Jews were killed outright by the *Einsatzkommandos* and other Nazi police units in the 'first sweep' of killing in the USSR. This has been called 'Holocaust by bullets' – rather than by gas chambers in death camps.[28] Other Jews, however, had been trapped far behind the advancing German front line, in the western regions of the USSR. They were completely at the mercy of the Nazis. These unfortunates had from the autumn of 1941 been concentrated in ghettos in some of the larger towns. The killing of the Soviet Jews continued in 1942 and even in 1943 and 1944, in what has been called the 'second sweep'. By this time there was some argument on the German side between those who wanted quickly to carry through genocide, and those who wanted to use Jews capable of work to support the war economy in a prolonged war.[29] Mass murder won out, in a combination of 'anti-bandit' operations and the gradual killing of the ghetto residents. This process was rapid in the Ukraine in the autumn of 1942 as, further east, the German Army marched towards Stalingrad and the Caucasus. The killing was slower in the Baltic and Belorussia, but it was still carried through to a final conclusion. There are different estimates of the number of Jews who were murdered. Yitzhak Arad counted 946,000 to 996,000 'direct victims' from the pre-September 1939 USSR, and 1,561,000 to 1,628,000 from territories annexed in 1939–40. Raul Hilberg estimated that about 700,000 Jews from the pre-1939 Soviet Union perished as a direct result of Nazi mass killing policies, and as many again from territories annexed by Moscow in 1939–40.[30] Even by his calculation, a quarter of the five or six million European Jews who were murdered by the Nazis in 1941–4 came from Soviet territory.

The Nazis did not, as is sometimes argued, stumble into the Holocaust because of unexpectedly stiff Red Army resistance or because of Stalin's declaration of partisan war in July 1941 (although the Jews were associated in German propaganda with partisan activity). Nazi policy was also not a reprisal for the Soviet deportation of 400,000 'Volga Germans', ethnic Germans, from European Russia to Siberia and Central Asia. News of this event reached the German side by September, but Nazi policies of mass murder were in place on 22 June 1941. It is worth recalling, too, that between 500,000 and a million Jews from the USSR had been killed before the Wannsee Conference met in Berlin in January 1942 to discuss the 'final solution' in central and western Europe. The German military setback before Moscow in the winter of 1941–2 may have affected the time and location of the mass murder of the western and central European Jews; their killing ground would be in Poland, not in Russia. But the Russian campaign did not affect the essence of the atrocity.

The German Army – senior commanders and front-line soldiers – must bear a major share of responsibility for the perpetration of the Holocaust.[31] It co-operated with the killing of the Jews. Its commanders did not protest; some of them issued baldly anti-Semitic orders. One of the most quoted was a 10 October 1941 order of Field Marshal Reichenau, the commander of the German 6th Army in the northern Ukraine. Reichenau endorsed reprisals against 'Jewish subhumanity'. Hitler approved this order, and Field Marshal Rundstedt forwarded it to the other Army Group South commanders.

The murder of Soviet POWs

The second aspect of the Nazi war of annihilation which related especially to 1941 was the tragedy of the Soviet POWs.[32] In his order at the start of Operation TYPHOON, Hitler announced to the soldiers of the Eastern Front that 'this enemy is made up not of soldiers, but for the most part only of animals'. In his November 1941 speech, in which he had attacked the Jews, Hitler also announced, as a sign of victory, that Germany had captured no fewer than 3,600,000 POWs. This was only a slight exaggeration of the official figures. Altogether the Wehrmacht claimed an astonishing total of 3,300,000 prisoners taken before the end of 1941. German Army Group Centre had captured the largest numbers: 323,000 in June and July at Belostok and Minsk, and 348,000 at Smolensk and Roslavl' by the beginning of August. Army Group South claimed 103,000 at Uman' in early August, plus 665,000 at Kiev.[33] In October the Wehrmacht claimed another 660,000 POWs in the Battle of Viaz'ma–Briansk, as well as 100,000 in the far south at Melitopol' and Berdiansk. Further Soviet prisoners would be taken by the Germans later, especially in 1942 and early 1943. A Russian-published figure of 1,653,000 POWs has been given for 1942, and 585,000 for 1943, but only 147,000 for 1944.[34] In 1942 the Germans would claim to have taken 265,000 POWs in the Crimea, 240,000 after the Battle of Khar'kov, 32,000 in the 2nd Shock Army near Leningrad, 88,000 in the Battle of the Donbass (in July 1942), and 57,000 in the advance on Stalingrad. A Russian state commission in the 1990s, while admitting that exact data for Red Army POWs was lacking, suggested that there had been a grand total of some 4,100,000 Red Army POWs: 'nearly 2,000,000' in 1941, 1,339,000 in 1942, 487,000 in 1943, 203,000 in 1944, and 41,000 in 1945.[35] Whatever the precise figure, it would seem that twice as many Soviet soldiers were captured between June and November 1941 as would be captured for the entire remainder of the war. Of these unfortunates of 1941, most would be dead before the following spring.

In terms of scale, the fatalities among Red Army POWs were second only to the mass murder of the European Jews. Although an important part of the charges at the Nuremberg Trials, the story was far less prominent in the Cold War years.[36] A quarter to a third of all the USSR's ten million military deaths were soldiers who died in captivity. The exact figure can never be calculated, but the most commonly accepted German figure is 3,300,300 Soviet POWs dying in captivity, some 58 per cent of the 5,700,000 taken prisoner. The Russians accept a lower figure of Red Army POWs, 4,559,000, and 2,500,000 deaths, but with a similar death rate of 55 per cent.[37]

There were two aspects to the criminality of the Nazis and the Wehrmacht as far as Soviet POWs were concerned. The first, involving a relatively small number of victims, was the pre-planned murder of certain categories of prisoner. The Wehrmacht and the SS collaborated in this selection and summary execution. This was a direct consequence of Hitler's 'war of ideology'. The best-known aspect was the 'Commissar Order' of 6 June 1941, sanctioning the shooting on the spot of captured Red Army political commissars (as well as civilian Communist officials). And in the process of 'sorting out' at the various camps, any POWs identified as Jews were handed over to the Nazi security services. This process evidently involved at least several hundred thousand Soviet POWs, with the greatest number of victims at the end of 1941.[38] The first large-scale experimental use of poison gas for mass execution was actually undertaken against Soviet POWs; this was at Auschwitz in early September 1941, when several hundred were killed.

The second, even more lethal, aspect of the treatment of Soviet POWs by the German Army was that it was both extremely brutal and extremely negligent. Many of these Soviet soldiers were captured in a weakened state, having been cut off and unsupplied for perhaps weeks in the final stages of battlefield defeat. Some were wounded. They were then force-marched into captivity, and stragglers were shot on the way. The transit camps (*Dulags*) and the main camps (*Stalags*) in conquered territories and in the Reich were hugely overcrowded in the early months. Often thousands of Soviet POWs were simply encircled with barbed wire and ordered to dig their own shelters. Those sent to the Reich had to travel in open freight wagons. Food supplies were low. Starvation, epidemics and cold killed a very high percentage of Red Army personnel passing through the system. Those captured deepest in Russia, and at the onset of the severe winter, had the lowest chance of survival. In this category were soldiers captured at the Battle of Viaz'ma–Briansk.

The situation of the Soviet POWs did improve somewhat, from an extremely low point, in the spring of 1942. The German camp system had been stabilized, with the construction of at least primitive facilities. Paradoxically, the very high death rate over the winter meant there was now somewhat better food and shelter for the survivors. Meanwhile, the German authorities also began to realize that the war was going to be drawn out and that labour power of all kinds would be needed. The POWs became part of a pool of forced labour under the auspices of the Wehrmacht and the SS, notably in the coal mines, but also in many other sectors of the Reich's war economy. By the end of the war only 930,000 of the surviving 2,000,000 Soviet POWs were actually in POW camps; the others were working as forced labour or had been recruited into the German armed forces.[39] Another factor, later in the war, was that Russians began to hold large numbers of German POWs, and Berlin had to worry about reprisals. Nevertheless, even in 1942–5, Soviet POWs were still held under atrocious conditions involving heavy labour, poor diet, inadequate housing and minimal medical treatment. Overall, the death rate among Soviet POWs was much higher than among Western POWs in German hands; British and American deaths amounted to only some 3.6 per cent of 232,000 POWs.[40]

Although the Soviet government condemned those Red Army soldiers who surrendered, it also made propaganda about German mistreatment of POWs. The visible mistreatment of the columns of POWs and the terrible conditions in the *Dulags* helped turn the population of the occupied regions against the invaders. The German policy also hardened the resistance of the Red Army; one post-war German account of the Battle of Moscow argued that fear of being captured was the main thing that improved Soviet morale in front of Moscow.[41] German mistreatment played a part, too, in the cruel way that Russian soldiers, and the Soviet authorities, dealt with German personnel who fell into their hands later in the war.

There is another sinister twist to the story of the Soviet POWs: they were treated very badly by their own side. The USSR had not signed the 1928 Geneva Convention on POWs. Red Army regulations forbade surrender. The mass surrenders of the summer of 1941 made the Soviet government adopt an even harsher policy. Stalin's Order No. 270 of August 1941, after the capitulation at Uman', declared that surrender was a form of treason. Stalin first spoke sympathetically about the plight of the POWs in his Order of the Day of 7 November 1942. There had, however, been a Soviet diplomatic note about POWs in late November 1941. The April 1943 Supreme Soviet decree on war crimes specified violence not only against the civilian population but also against 'imprisoned Red Army personnel'.[42]

When the Red Army began to recapture territory in December 1941, it came upon large numbers of former Soviet soldiers who had been held by the Germans. An order of late December 1941 set up NKVD 'filtration' camps to deal with them.[43] Three and a half years later, immediately after the German capitulation, the seven Soviet army groups in Central Europe were ordered to form a huge network of camps to receive former POWs and Soviet citizens from western Germany. Each transit camp was to hold 10,000 people, with 100 camps in Germany and Poland. Screening of POWs was to be carried out by SMERSH (military counter-intelligence) and was to be completed in 1–2 months.[44]

Most of the POWs were glad enough to be going home. And not all were simply thrown into the Soviet labour camp system, the GULAG. According to figures released in the 1990s, 1,550,000 POWs were repatriated to the USSR, up to March 1946.[45] The *repatrianty* were treated with suspicion. They were restricted as to where in the USSR they could reside, and they had limited career opportunities. In the Khrushchev years of de-Stalinization, the government noted the wrongs suffered by returned POWs and their families. In a draft speech of May 1956, written during the anti-Stalin campaign (but a speech which he did not actually deliver), Zhukov devoted considerable space to the unfair treatment of returned POWs. He called for the removal of their 'moral oppression of mistrust, the rehabilitation of those who had been illegally condemned, and the end of restriction in relation to former POWs'. Discrimination, however, continued until after the fall of Communism; only in 1994 did a Presidential Commission pass a decree granting the former POWs full formal rehabilitation.[46]

THE BATTLE OF MOSCOW

The Soviets counter-attack

The Soviet calamity at Viaz'ma–Briansk in early October 1941 did more than yield another vast haul of prisoners for the Wehrmacht. The defeat of Konev, Eremenko and Budennyi also blasted away the main defences of Moscow. Zhukov would later see the period from 10 to 20 October – rather than November – as the most dangerous moment for the Red Army. This was when the road to the Soviet capital lay open.[47] By 5 October, the scale of the disaster at Viaz'ma–Briansk had sunk in. As we have seen, there was a belated Soviet attempt to hold a new line about 75 miles west of Moscow, but this Mozhaisk Line too was overwhelmed. One anchor of the Soviet position was temporarily lost when the enemy took Kalinin (Tver') on 14 October. On 19 October Zhukov proposed pulling back to a position 35 miles further east, and only 40 miles from the centre of Moscow. Stalin gave his approval.[48]

Although Moscow had survived the October crisis, a new danger threatened when the ground froze in November.[49] The Wehrmacht was once again able to exploit its greater mobility. The second phase of Operation TYPHOON and the last gasp of Operation BARBAROSSA began on 15 November. Six weeks had passed since the start of Operation TYPHOON; it was still three weeks before Zhukov's December counter-attack. On the second day of the new advance, a dramatic skirmish was fought out at the village of Dubosekovo. A detachment of the 316th Rifle Division, under General Panfilov, held off the German drive along the Volokolamsk Highway. The *panfilovtsy*, twenty-eight soldiers, were later reported to have fought to the death. The Soviet press reported that they fought under a slogan of resistance: 'Russia is vast, but there is nowhere to retreat – Moscow is behind us!' In the years that followed, the slogan was known to every Soviet schoolchild.[50] All the same, the panzers rolled eastwards.

The deepest German advance was achieved, as Hitler intended, on the wings. To the left, the 3rd and 4th Panzer Groups (Reinhardt and Hoepner) pushed eastward through the towns of Klin and Istra to the line of the Moscow–Volga Canal.[51] The canal runs 60 miles south to north, from the capital to the Volga River. Early on Friday, 28 November, the German units nearest Moscow established a bridgehead over the canal at Iakhroma, only 35 miles north of the Kremlin. The German advance here, however, was slowing. On the right wing, 170 miles to the south, Guderian's 2nd Panzer Group was attempting to get to the Oka River, but it was blocked by continuing Soviet resistance at the city of Tula.

The first German setback was in southern Russia, at Rostov, but at Moscow the Red Army counter-attack came just seven days later, on Friday, 5 December. On that day the forces of Konev's Kalinin Army Group (northwest of Moscow) began their attack. General Zhukov's Western Army Group launched the main attack on the following day, Saturday, 6 December. Soon there was bitter fighting across the central theatre. German Army Group Centre was stopped; it began slowly to withdraw to the west. The easternmost German forces, with Hitler's armoured spearheads, were at first the least stable position. Reinhardt's 3rd Panzer Group was by 16 December pushed 35 miles back from the Moscow–Volga Canal. It was under heavy pressure from two new Soviet formations, General A. A. Vlasov's re-formed 20th Army and General V. I. Kuznetsov's 1st Shock Army.[52] Soviet cavalry in the form of the 2nd Guards Cavalry Corps also played a prominent part, raiding the German rear; the corps commander, General Dovator, was killed near Ruza in mid-December. Further out on the right flank, the 31st Army, from Konev's army group, threw the German 9th Army out of Kalinin (16 December). It gradually pushed the enemy back to the outskirts of Rzhev. The recapture of Klin and Kalinin was vitally important, as these victories reopened the direct Soviet rail link from Moscow to the Volkhov front (near Leningrad). Meanwhile, Guderian and the 2nd Panzer Group had been pushed back from the bulge southeast of Tula by General Golikov's new 10th Army. Here an important part was played by the 1st Guards Cavalry Corps under General Belov. By 26 December the Germans had been driven west beyond the city of Kaluga. On the far flanks, Kurochkin's Northwestern Army Group and the right wing of Timoshenko's Southwestern Army Group put pressure on the forward German positions.

The Soviet Moscow counter-attack had begun on 5 December. Three days later Hitler secretly admitted that the 1941 campaign was over. In his secret Directive No. 39 of 8 December 1941, the Führer stated that the circumstances in the East 'make essential the immediate adjustment of all major offensive operations and the transition to the defensive'. 'The mass of the Eastern Army is to go over to the defensive on a [more] easily defended front and then the refitting of formations is to begin, with panzer and motorized divisions being pulled out first.' As for the Russians, they restrained themselves from celebration until they were sure of the situation. Five days later, however, on 13 December, the announcement of *Sovinformburo* was published on the front page of *Pravda*, under a bold heading: 'Failure of the German plan for the encirclement and capture of Moscow. Defeat of the German forces on the approaches to Moscow.'[53]

The tone of Soviet orders changed. On 13 December, Stalin told Zhukov and Konev to deal ruthlessly with encircled German forces: 'Trap the enemy … give the Germans a chance to surrender and promise to spare their lives, and if they do not accept, destroy them to the last man.'[54] Over the next two or three weeks, as the weary German troops retreated tens of miles through the deep snow, Hitler and his generals debated how to respond to the unexpected reverse. Some wanted to fall further back to more readily defendable positions, although Hitler and General Halder feared this would mean abandoning their snowbound heavy equipment, in a kind of winter Dunkirk. Hitler's decision was for 'fanatical resistance'. Army Group Centre was to hold on, and as close as possible to its starting point. This task the army group was, for the most part, able to fulfil. By the end of December the northern flank of the Moscow force (the 3rd Panzer Group) had withdrawn only about 50 miles. The southern wing, however, had to pull back 150–175 miles from the bulge created by Guderian in late November.

The reasons for the German failure

'General Winter' is often used to explain the German setback at Moscow. When Hitler on 8 December ordered that the *Ostheer* go over to the defensive, he blamed the weather by saying, 'the winter in the East, which has come surprisingly early, and the resulting supply problems'. In speeches made during the following months, explaining the crisis in Russia, he repeatedly stressed the severity of the winter. He maintained that it had been the worst in 150 years, and had come on four weeks earlier than expected.[55] Writing in February 1945, with Zhukov and Konev now commanding huge Soviet army groups in front of his own capital, Hitler blamed his predicament on the 1941 Balkan campaign. This had 'led directly to the calamitous delay of the attack on Russia'. But for this, Hitler claimed, Germany could have attacked on 15 May 1941 and 'we would have been in a position to end the campaign in the East before the onset of winter'.[56]

The Russians, in contrast, have often played down the effect of the weather on their victory. In reality, the Soviet leaders did not discount the climate. On 6 November 1941, no doubt with the Napoleonic experience in mind, Stalin had stated that 'the winter promises [the enemy] nothing good'. In 1940, after the Soviet–Finnish War, he had stressed that the climate could favour the Red Army:

> It is not true that the army's fighting capacity decreases in wintertime. All the Russian Army's major victories were won in wintertime. Aleksandr Nevskii against the Swedes, Peter I against the Swedes in Finland, Alexander I's victory over Napoleon. We are a northern country.[57]

The defence of Moscow was certainly helped by changes in the weather. The fate of Hitler's offensive is commonly associated with deep snow drifts and frozen German motors, with the bitter cold of December and January. The first snow fell in the centre of the Eastern Front in early October. What, however, gave the Red Army its first respite was the autumn season of rain and snow, and alternating freeze and thaw which began shortly afterwards, the *rasputitsa*.

> We had anticipated this of course [one German general recalled], for we had read about it in our studies of Russian conditions. But the reality far exceeded our worst expectations. In the Viaz'ma area it began, slowly enough, in mid-October and

became steadily more intense until mid-November. It is hard to convey a picture of what it was like to anybody who has not actually experienced it. There are only very few metalled roads in this part of the world. All others, and the open country too, become a sticky morass. The infantryman slithers in the mud, while many teams of horses are needed to drag each gun forward. All wheeled vehicles sink up to their axles in the slime. Even tractors can only move with great difficulty.[58]

Indeed, it was only with the onset of the early winter frost in late November that German (and Soviet) movement became easier. On the other hand, the *rasputitsa*, like the final freeze of winter, was not something that was unexpected for either side. Zhukov maintained that the *rasputitsa* period was relatively short in 1941, and this seems to have been the truth.[59] The rain and mud made operations as difficult for the Russians as it did for the Germans. It hampered Red Army efforts to pull equipment out of the Viaz'ma–Briansk trap and to bring up replacement units by road to cover Moscow. The change of the weather did, however, on balance, favour the Red Army. Unlike the Germans, the Russians had a working railway system behind their front line. Soviet planes, meanwhile, were operating from prepared airfields, while the Luftwaffe now had to make do with improvised muddy landing strips.

Opinions also vary about the effect of the December frost. The evidence would seem to suggest it was severe but not out of the ordinary for central Russia.[60] Expectation of a cold snap may have played some part in Stalin and Zhukov's calculations for the timing of a counter-offensive, but they could not have predicted a particular day. The freeze affected events later in December, when it prevented German withdrawal of heavy equipment; this dilemma drove Hitler to deliver his 'stand fast' order. Still, planners have to plan for the existing climate. The Germans did not fail to get to Moscow because the weather broke; they were caught by the freeze because they had failed to reach Moscow.

FIGURE 4 German troops evacuate wounded in the mud of March 1942.

Historians blame Hitler and the German high command for making two quite different mistakes. First of all, the *Ostheer* failed to advance on Moscow in October after the great victory at Viaz'ma–Briansk. Second, it rashly advanced on Moscow five or six weeks later, and it drove on in the teeth of increasing Russian resistance. The failure of the Germans to take Moscow in later October and early November had several explanations. First of all, the German attack at Viaz'ma–Briansk had been less deep than the earlier penetration in Belorussia and the Ukraine. Viaz'ma was only about 75 miles from the nearest point on the German front line. It needs to be compared to Minsk, which had been 200 miles away from the start point in the June battle. After the Battle of Viaz'ma–Briansk, the Führer assumed for some weeks that the defending Soviet armies had been annihilated and the objectives of Directive No. 35 (6 September) achieved. The head of the Reich press agency, the DNB, told a press conference on 9 October that 'with the smashing of Army Group Timoshenko the campaign in the East has been decided'.[61] Probably with the bad experience of Napoleon in mind, Hitler claimed never to have been preoccupied with the city of Moscow. He resumed his interest in the northern and southern theatres, which he assumed were now more vulnerable than ever.

The Germans also needed to digest the huge number of Red Army formations that had been swallowed up at Viaz'ma and Briansk. Soviet resistance in the northern *Kessel* (west of Viaz'ma) continued until 13 October, and that in the two southern ones (east and south of Briansk) continued until 17 and 20 October. Zhukov mentioned this in his memoirs (in a passage cut by Brezhnev's censors from early editions): 'The most important thing then was to gain time to prepare the defence of our front. If you evaluate the actions of the formations surrounded west of Viaz'ma from this point of view, then you have to give the credit that is due to them for their heroic struggle.'[62] Time was needed, too, to bring up the infantry armies and supplies of German Army Group Centre.

The second German mistake was to continue on towards Moscow in November. At a German staff conference at Orsha (west of Smolensk) on 13 November, presided over by Halder, the decision was made to push on. In fact, the Chief of the General Staff tried to convince the army group representatives of the need to go *beyond* Moscow to get the best starting point for the spring campaign; Halder assumed the *Ostheer* would be able to operate until the end of December. The army group representatives were more realistic, but they too agreed to continue the next stage of an advance towards Moscow.[63] There would be panzer spearheads on either side of the city, and the infantry of General Kluge's 4th Army aimed at Moscow itself. With this, Halder followed through to the point of exhaustion what had been his *idée fixe* throughout 1941. Hitler did not impose a strategy on the OKH. Halder, as late as the middle of November, assigned much too ambitious tasks to German formations in Russia, especially to Army Group Centre. When the front approached crisis at the end of November 1941, Halder did not allow the preparation of a German defensive line. Field Marshal Bock, for his part, did not put a brake on the attack. The commander of Army Group Centre was driven by personal ambition to get the credit for taking Moscow, and in the last weeks he ignored the practical problems of his overextended forces. In this he can be contrasted with the more prudent Rundstedt in Army Group South.[64]

Central to this faulty strategy was another intelligence failure, one that would bedevil the Germans again and again in the war. Hitler and his generals underestimated the quantity of forces that the Russians still had available for a counter-attack. This was evident in Halder's comment at the Orsha conference: 'Although [we are] weak in the knees . . . the enemy is worse off than we are; he is on the verge of collapse.'[65] Hitler himself attached great weight to the Russian POW figures, from which he extrapolated total Red Army losses. In his speech of 8 November, he announced that the capture of 3,600,000 Russian POWs meant that overall Red Army losses (captured, dead and seriously wounded) were 'at a minimum eight to ten million'. 'No army in the world, including the Russian, can recover from that.'[66] In the final stages of the German attack on Moscow, in late November 1941, Hitler, Halder and Bock were convinced that one last effort could and would destroy the shattered Russians. Halder and Bock discussed events in terms of the campaign against the French in 1914: 'Von Bock makes a comparison with the Battle of the Marne, where the last battalion that can be thrown in will be decisive.'[67] In 1914 the German Army had not made the final effort, it had been blocked from Paris, the war of movement ended, and the Kaiser ultimately lost the war. It would not be incorrect to speak here of a 'Marne complex'. In the opinion of the historian Ernst Klink, in the German official history, the decisive factor was 'the complete misjudgement of the remaining fighting power of the Red Army and its equipment'.[68] Meanwhile, it was actually the Germans who had run out of reserves. Despite all the propaganda, Stalin was basically right to argue, on 6 November, that the Germans were using up their last strength. When Zhukov attacked in December, the *Ostheer* had nothing with which to back up the line and fill the gaps, and Hitler had to take a momentous gamble on 'standing fast'.

One result of the Moscow crisis in December would be the shake-up in the German high command. The resignation of Rundstedt in Army Group South has already been mentioned. Brauchitsch, the C-in-C of the German Army, was dismissed on 19 December, and this was even more ominous. To some extent Brauchitsch's replacement by Hitler only confirmed a de facto situation, but it led to fatal confusion in the administration of the German Army. The previous day Field Marshal Bock, who had presided for five months over the momentous campaign from Belostok to Moscow, had been sent on indefinite leave. He handed Army Group Centre over to the commander of his 4th Army, General Kluge (who would lead the army group until late 1943). The third army group commander, Field Marshal Leeb in Army Group North, was removed in January. Among the other victims of Hitler's shake-up were outstanding field commanders. On 25 December General Guderian was dismissed; he was the architect of Germany's armoured forces and an enthusiast for National Socialism who had been allowed a direct line to Hitler. In the crisis Guderian refused to pass on Hitler's order to stand fast and fell out with the new commander of Army Group Centre. Later, in mid-January 1942, General Hoepner, who had commanded the 4th Panzer Group in Army Group North and in front of Moscow, was sacked; he would be shot in 1944 for his part in the July bomb plot. Even Stalin would comment on this turmoil in the German high command in his Red Army Day speech of February 1942.[69]

Stalin, Zhukov and the Red Army

The weather was not the basic reason for the Moscow turnaround. Soviet reserves and resistance were the critical factors. Political will was part of this. Stalin's presence in the capital, even though many ministries and factories were evacuated east to the Volga, the Urals and Siberia, carried great moral weight. On 15 October a special train and a Douglas transport plane had been standing by, ready to evacuate the Soviet leader. In the end he had decided to stay. When told of the disorders in Moscow on 16 October, he is reported to have replied, 'Well, that's nothing. I thought it would be worse.'[70] The decision to hold the annual military parade 'as usual' in Red Square on 7 November – the twenty-fourth anniversary of the Bolshevik Revolution – was psychologically a most important gesture. This came only three weeks after the Moscow panic of mid-October.

Soviet ruthlessness played a part. In mid-November Stalin issued fierce orders for a policy of 'scorched earth' behind the enemy: 'Deprive the German army of the possibility to quarter itself in villages and towns, drive the German aggressors out of all inhabited places into the cold fields, smoke them out of all lodgings and warm shelters and force them to freeze under the open sky.' All villages up to 25–35 miles behind the enemy front line, and 10–20 miles on either side of the roads, were to be burned to the ground; this was to be done by aircraft and artillery, and teams of 'hunters' recruited from each regiment. If Soviet units had to retreat, they should take the population with them, and burn down the abandoned villages. Two weeks later Zhukov reported that in his Western Army Group, nearly 400 villages had been destroyed.[71] There was some partisan activity behind German lines, mostly poorly trained *Komsomol* (Young Communist) groups sent out from the cities. One tragic result of this was the capture and public hanging of the schoolgirl *partizanka* Zoia Kosmodem'ianskaia at Petrishchevo (near Mozhaisk) on 29 November. When the Red Army recaptured Petrishchevo a few days later, they found the young girl's frozen body. The photographs taken became a powerful propaganda symbol.[72]

The backbone of the resistance, however, was the Red Army. In his statements of 6 and 7 November, Stalin had also cited the importance of 'human reserves' (*liudskie rezervy*), relative to the Germans. The accumulation of 'strategic reserves', raising and organizing fresh formations in the hinterland, had been the main activity of the Soviet high command in October and November.[73] The human resources were still very large. A secret GKO decree of mid-September (before the Kiev disaster) had outlined the overall ration strength of the Red Army (see Table 4.1). It also showed the troops that were 'in the pipeline' for the battles of October, November and December.

While the Red Army was suffering repeated losses at the front, a mammoth and ultimately successful effort was taking place behind the lines to reconstruct the Red Army; this is a vital but neglected subject. Some 156 new divisions began formation in June and July (some in the weeks before the invasion), but they were thrown into battle before completion of their training, and very many were lost. On 11 August, as the fighting around Smolensk intensified, Stalin's State Committee of State Defence had set out a grandiose programme to form 85 new rifle divisions, and 25 (smaller) cavalry

Table 4.1 Personnel of the Red Army, September 1941 (1,000s)

Front-line formations (e.g. Army Groups)		**4,059**
Arkhangel'sk MD	104	
Leningrad MD	45	
Moscow MD	392	
Orel MD	245	
Total European Russia (North)		786
Khar'kov MD	356	
N. Caucasus MD	228	
Transcaucasus MD	390	
Total European Russia (South)		974
Urals MD	221	
Volga MD	268	
Total European Russia (East)		489
Central Asian MD	170	
Siberian MD	176	
Transbaikal MD	320	
Far Eastern Army Group	511	
Total Eastern USSR		1,177
Total		*7,485

Source: Kudriashov, *Voina*, pp. 69–70 [11 September]. For comparable figures for 15 October 1941, see ibid., p. 83. At that time Red Army front-line strength had fallen from 4,049,00 to 3,465,000, but that in the MDs had risen by over a million personnel, from 3,426,000 to 4,541,000.

Note: MD = Military District, a large administrative region used for raising and training troops. In the document the grand total for Red Army personnel is given as 7,400,000; this is evidently a mathematical error. Front-line formations comprised the Karelian, Leningrad, Northwestern, Western, Briansk, Reserve, Southwestern and Southern Army Groups, the Odessa 'group', and the newly formed 51st, 52nd and 54th Armies.

divisions; 35 of the rifle divisions were to be formed by mid-October and the other 50 by mid-December. As of 13 October, in the depths of the crisis after Viaz'ma–Briansk, only ten combat-ready rifle divisions had been formed, due to the lack of weapons. In the following weeks, the GKO ordered the establishment of 75 'independent' rifle brigades.[74] The historian Walter Dunn argues convincingly that it was the divisions and brigades which began formation in August 1941, and the independent rifle and tank brigades which began formation in August, September and October, that played a crucial role in the Moscow counter-offensive in December. They were, he argued, relatively better trained than the formations raised in June and July.[75] Soviet forces equivalent to 99 new divisions were brought up into the central theatre in October, November and early December.[76] Many of these were incorporated in eight new armies set up on 5 November to form defensive positions *behind* Moscow.[77] This build-up meant that the Germans' task would have been very hard even if they had succeeded in taking Moscow; in the event a number of these big formations were thrown into the counter-attack on 5–6 December.

Some of the forces ordered to defend Moscow came from Siberia. On 12 October, for example, in the immediate aftermath of Viaz'ma–Briansk, the Stavka had ordered the Far Eastern Army Group to begin movement of five divisions.[78] However, one of the myths of the Battle of Moscow is the supposedly decisive role played by fresh Siberian troops, made available because Stalin's spies had revealed that Japan was not going to attack the Soviet Union. In reality, formations transferred from Siberia made up only a fifth of tank strength in the defence of Moscow, and perhaps 15 per cent of the infantry. The thirteen 'Siberian' divisions in the Battle of Moscow in late November and early December comprised two tank and eleven rifle formations, from the Far Eastern Army Group and the Transbaikal and Siberian Military Districts. The total strength of the Kalinin and Western Army Groups on 1 December included fourteen tank division-equivalents and seventy-four rifle division-equivalents (three tank divisions, twenty-two tank brigades, sixty-six rifle divisions, seventeen rifle brigades), as well as seventeen cavalry divisions. (Other Siberian divisions fought elsewhere in European Russia at this time, notably in defence of Leningrad.)[79]

Probably an equally important factor involving a German ally – Italy rather than Japan – was the transfer of much of the Luftwaffe striking force away from Army Group Centre to the Mediterranean, due to the threatened position of Italy (as a result of British successes). After the victory of Viaz'ma–Briansk, Hitler decided to send the headquarters of Kesselring's 2nd Air Fleet and many of its aircraft to the south in order to support the embattled Italians.

To move these reserve forces in European Russia and Siberia, the Red Army possessed a superior transport network, at least once it had retreated behind the old borders of the USSR (i.e. those before September 1939). The invaders struggled with repairing the railways (and converting track gauge) on the lines required to transport supplies and reinforcement to forward depots. The Russians had been able to withdraw the great majority of their locomotives and rolling stock to the east, despite losing a great deal of territory in the west in 1941–2, with about 40 per cent of the existing railway network (by length of track). At the start of 1943 some 85 per cent of pre-war locomotives and 80 per cent of freight cars were available, and running on a shorter railway system.[80] As a result, the Russians had adequate equipment to operate on the compressed network that was still in their hands. Although the Germans mounted air attacks, they were not able seriously to limit the system's carrying capacity.

Extraordinary steps were also taken to restore discipline in the Red Army. The commander of the 17th Rifle Division was shot for the unsteadiness of his troops, and there were other such incidents. Available information is still sketchy, but one example is perhaps indicative. In 3 divisions of the Soviet 10th Army, which was re-formed under General Golikov in November 1941 and which advanced from Riazan' to a position south of Viaz'ma, some 233 soldiers were condemned to death in the period November 1941 to February 1942; a further 507 were sentenced to terms of confinement from 3 to 10 years. The most numerous charges involve 'counter-revolutionary crimes' (189 soldiers), desertion (168) and 'fleeing the field of battle' (105). In the same period, these divisions reported losses of 4,292 killed, 10,062 wounded and 6,097 missing.[81]

The Battle of Moscow brought together many of the able Soviet commanders who would lead the Soviet Army throughout the war, even in Eastern Europe and Germany in 1944 and 1945. Konev and Eremenko held army group commands. Rokossovskii commanded the 16th Army. At division or brigade level were commanders like Generals Leliushenko and Katukov, who would lead tank armies in 1943–5. Above all, however, the Battle of Moscow was identified with General Georgii Konstantinovich Zhukov.[82] On 19 October 1941, on the day that martial law was declared in Moscow, Stalin called the editor of the Red Army newspaper, *Krasnaia zvezda*, and asked that he print Zhukov's photograph in the next day's issue. A large photograph of Zhukov also appeared with the 13 December victory announcement in *Pravda*; it was flanked by smaller portraits of Zhukov's army commanders.[83] A new statue of Zhukov on horseback now stands at the entrance to Red Square, and he was undoubtedly the outstanding military commander of the Second World War.

This critical moment, after the Battle of Viaz'ma–Briansk, was when the military reputation of Zhukov was really established. He was summoned back from Leningrad on 5 October, and three days later he was ordered to take over the Reserve Army Group from Marshal Budennyi. On 11 October he was made commander of a new Western Army Group, which included the remnants of Konev's and Budennyi's commands. Zhukov was just forty-three years old, two decades younger than his opposite number, Field Marshal von Bock. The son of poor peasants, with little formal education, Zhukov had served with distinction as a rank-and-file cavalryman in the First World War. In his mid-twenties he fought as a squadron commander in Budennyi's Red Cavalry in the Civil War. He was a demanding and committed leader, and by the start of the 1930s he had risen to command a cavalry division. He had faults; he could be vain, and he was brutal. Molotov later called him a 'bellower' [*gorloplan*].[84] His accelerated promotion owed much to the 1937–8 destruction of the top tier of commanders of the Red Army. The 1st Cavalry Army veterans like Zhukov were the army faction that Stalin and Voroshilov most trusted. *Komdiv* Zhukov was made commander of the 3rd Cavalry Corps in Belorussia in July 1937. It was important, too, that Zhukov had served in the 1930s under Budennyi and Timoshenko. This protected him during the purges, and it favoured him for advancement when Timoshenko (who was only a year older) became the new broom in the Red Army after the Winter War of 1939–40.

What had done most to advance Zhukov's career was his victory over the Japanese in the division-level battles at Khalkhin Gol in eastern Mongolia in the summer of 1939. Using tanks, aircraft and artillery, Zhukov achieved the tactical envelopment of a Japanese division. In the command shake-up of the summer of 1940, following the Winter War,

Stalin and Timoshenko gave Zhukov one of the Red Army's three most important field commands, the Kiev Military District. This was followed by an even more extraordinary jump to the post of Chief of the General Staff in January 1941, replacing General Meretskov. Zhukov combined a sound tactical sense with self-confidence, energy and a demanding personality. He had established the all-important personal link with Stalin; he also had the courage to disagree with the Soviet dictator on military questions.

One of Zhukov's strengths – and perhaps part of his attraction to Stalin – was his ruthlessness. He made examples of people; on 3 November 1941, Zhukov announced, with Commissar Bulganin, that the commander and commissar of the 133rd Rifle Division, which had given way before the Germans the week before at the town of Ruza (60 miles west of Moscow on the Mozhaisk Line), had been shot in front of their assembled men:

> Announcing this for the information of commanders and political workers, the Military Council of the [Western] Army Group demands of all unit and formation commanders an unrelenting struggle with all occurrences of cowardice, especially on the part of command staff and [it] insists on the unquestioning fulfilment of the orders of the Military Council of the army group, [prohibiting] retreat without written orders from the commanders of the army and the army group.[85]

A forceful and self-confident commander, enjoying Stalin's confidence, was what the Red Army desperately needed at the end of 1941. One crucially important element for the turning of the Nazi tide was now in place.

The Battle of Moscow is sometimes depicted as a carefully timed Soviet counter-attack. The extreme Soviet myth, which was really only taken seriously in Stalin's old age, concerned the strategy of the 'counter-offensive' (*kontrnastuplenie*), luring the enemy into the depths of one's country and destroying him there. Some historians, even in the West, have shared this view.[86] The Soviet Moscow operation was quite different from the Stalingrad counter-offensive of November 1942, which was planned over a month in advance, and used carefully prepared armoured thrusts to effect an encirclement. According to Zhukov, in early November 1941 Stalin and Shaposhnikov pushed him into premature and unsuccessful spoiling counter-attacks against Army Group Centre, intended to disrupt the imminent German offensive. It was only with difficulty that Zhukov got Stalin to accept a more cautious policy of building up his forces.[87]

As we have seen, the first Soviet reaction after the defeats suffered at the hands of the Germans in TYPHOON in October 1941 was to create eight new armies. In early November six of these armies were ordered to begin preparing defences on a line from Lake Onega and in the front of the Volga all the way south to near Saratov.[88] These new formations were not of high quality, but it was possible to man and arm them, and the Germans did not suspect they would be available. The critical decision to deploy some of these formations in the defence of Moscow was evidently made on 24 November, a few days after German Army Group Centre resumed its attack.[89] Zhukov recalled

Stalin seeking assurances that Moscow could be held, and himself (Zhukov) giving these assurances.

> *Stalin:* Are you sure that we will hold Moscow? I ask you about this with an aching heart. Tell me honestly, as a Communist.
>
> *Zhukov:* We will, without fail, hold Moscow. But I need at least two more armies and 200 tanks.

This discussion probably took place, by telephone, in the third week of November.[90]

The gamble was a monentous one, as another defeat in front of Moscow would destroy the forces needed to defend the Volga Line. On the other hand it was essential not to allow the Germans to consolidate their position and go into winter quarters in front of Moscow. Timing was all-important. It was not so much a question of the frost; the invaders needed to be hit once they had reached the point where they could no longer attack – but before they had dug in. As we have seen, Konev's Kalinin Army Group, northwest of Moscow, actually began the counter-offensive on 5 December. This, however, was after a number of local counter-attacks by him which were criticized by the Stavka as 'ineffective'. It was only early on 1 December that Konev was ordered to make a somewhat deeper attack behind the 3rd Panzer Group. 'Your task: come out in the rear of the enemy Klin group [the 3rd Panzer Group] and co-operate in the destruction of the latter by the forces of Western Army Group.' From the Stavka, General Vasilevskii (Deputy Chief of the General Staff) had a teleprinter exchange with Konev later that morning. Konev complained of his weaknesses, of divisions with 2,500–3,000 men, of his lack of tanks. Vasilevskii insisted on decisive action:

> Comrade commander, have you heard about the events at Rostov? [Rostov had been re-captured by the Red Army on 29 November.] Breaking up the German offensive against Moscow, which will not only save Moscow, but set the basis for the serious defeat of the enemy, is possible only by active operations, with decisive goals. If we do not do this in the next few days it will be too late.[91]

The Red Army's counter-blow, when it came, was not elegant. The main Soviet effort on 6 December was a head-on attack by four armies of Western Army Group: the 16th, 20th, 1st Shock and 30th. In the south the 10th and 50th Armies, supported by the Belov Group, were thrown against Guderian. There seems to have been no formal overall plan, although Zhukov sent the Stavka a map outlining what he wanted to do with the Western Army Group, and Stalin approved that. Retired Soviet generals later argued about who should get the credit. Zhukov's account gives the impression that the plan, such as it was, came from him; Vasilevskii gave more credit to the Stavka and General Staff.[92] The important thing is that the Germans were caught by surprise. Operation TYPHOON, Operation BARBAROSSA and Hitler's Blitzkrieg war all came to a halt. The Battle of Moscow showed that the USSR was not going to be defeated in 1941 and that Operation BARBAROSSA had failed.

CONCLUSION

Soviet personnel losses, despite Zhukov's initial victory at Moscow, were much heavier than those of the invader. Losses in all Soviet theatres from 1 September 1941 to the end of the year have been given as 926,000, although to be sure this was better than the 2,068,000 lost in the previous two and a half months.[93] German losses on the Russian front in the last quarter of 1941, despite the onset of winter and the drama of the drive on Moscow, were lower than those in the summer: 41,000 in October, 36,000 in November and 40,000 in December, compared to 50–60,000 in each of the preceding three months. These fourth-quarter figures represented a ratio of losses between the Russians and Germans of as much as 8:1. Overall, however, German losses in the 1941 campaign were very great. Some 302,000 German service personnel had been killed, or twice the losses for the period from September 1939 to May 1941. General Haider himself admitted that there was now a break (*Zäsur*) in the course of the war and that this affected Germany's available means: 'They are naturally limited by use and by the enormous stretching of the space which our forces have to cover. We will not again have available the army we had at our disposal in June 1941.'[94]

In his Munich speech of 8 November 1941, Hitler claimed great successes, while declaring himself surprisingly ambivalent about the Blitzkrieg concept: 'I have never used the word Blitzkrieg, because it is a completely idiotic word. But if it can be applied to any campaign, it can be applied to this one. Never has a giant state been defeated and overthrown in such a short time as Soviet Russia.'[95] By the middle of December, however, it was clear to the whole world that the Blitzkrieg had failed, and with it Hitler's hopes for a quick decisive victory.[96] Later German operations in the USSR, in 1942 and 1943, would be based on a protracted war. In these desperate days Hitler had also found time to declare war on the United States. Pearl Harbor was attacked on Sunday, 7 December, about forty hours after Zhukov's counter-attacks in the Moscow area began. The weekend of 6–7 December can be seen as the turning point of the Second World War as a whole.[97]

CHAPTER 5
THE FIRST SOVIET GENERAL OFFENSIVE, DECEMBER 1941 TO MAY 1942

Commanding generals, commanders, and officers are to intervene in person to compel the troops to fanatical resistance in their positions without regard to the enemy broken through on the flanks or in the rear. This is the only way to gain the time necessary to bring up the reinforcements from Germany and the West that I have ordered.

Adolf Hitler, 18 December 1941

It is a fact that thanks to the successes of the Red Army the Fatherland War has begun a new period, the period of the liberation of the Soviet lands from the Hitlerite filth.

Joseph Stalin, 1 May 1942

In 1942 we will achieve the decisive defeat of the German-fascist forces.

Red Army May Day 1942 slogan

We cannot help but see the Second World War as it really was. The Battle of Moscow would be followed by two and a half more years of desperate fighting deep in Russia – at Stalingrad, at Kursk, in the Ukraine and in Belorussia.

The leaders of the two sides in the winter of 1941–2 had a different perspective, one based on the experience of 1812. Napoleon had crossed into Russia in late June, hoping for a quick victory. In early September he finally engaged the main Russian Army 75 miles west of Moscow, at Borodino; it was a bloody but inconclusive battle. The Russians let the French enter Moscow, but the deserted city was soon ravaged by fire. With the Russian Army under Kutuzov still intact, with his own lines of communication threatened, Bonaparte abandoned Moscow after five weeks' occupation. The withdrawal took the weakened and increasingly undisciplined Grande Armée through areas ravaged by its original advance. The *rasputitsa*, winter snows, and harsh cold slowed the retreat march. Napoleon's forces were increasingly harassed by Russian irregulars. Retreat degenerated into rout. At the ice-laden Berezina River in late November 1812 the French were nearly trapped by two Russian armies. Some of Napoleon's troops fought their way through, but half the surviving army had been lost. On 5 December Napoleon left the remnants of the Grande Armée and set off on his own for Paris. The Napoleonic Empire never recovered. The myth of French invincibility had been shattered. Napoleon's enemies at home began to work against him. In the following months Prussia and Austria changed sides, and in 1813 Napoleon's raw new armies were defeated in battles in Germany. Pursued into France, in April 1814, the Emperor was forced to abdicate. Some 140 years later, Stalin's hope was that Hitler's *Ostheer*, and Hitler's own prestige, would prove as brittle as that of the Grande Armée and Napoleon. Hitler himself was fully aware that his defeat in front of Moscow could turn into a rout like that of 1812.[1]

In January 1942 Stalin set in train operations all along the vast Nazi–Soviet front. The Soviet dictator had come to the conclusion that victory was going to be possible in the coming year. This would be the line of Soviet propaganda until at least late June 1942.[2] In the first two weeks of the new year, instructions were given for various offensives. On 10 January the Stavka issued an extraordinary 'directive letter' to the military councils of all Soviet army groups and armies. Although the main part of the letter was advice, in Stalin's rhetorical style, on the use of 'shock groups' and 'artillery offensives',[3] it was clear about strategic perceptions. The Germans, the directive stated, had been worn down by their autumn 1941 offensive. They now hoped to play for time.

> Our task is to deny the Germans this breathing space, to drive them to the west without a halt, to force them to expend their reserves before spring, when we will have new and large reserves, and the Germans will have no large reserves, and to thus secure complete defeat of the Hitlerite forces in the year 1942.

General Zhukov, commander of the Western Army Group, had attended a meeting of the Stavka a few days before this, to work out plans for the general offensive. Following on from the successes of the army groups in front of Moscow, Stalin proposed that there should be Red Army attacks right along the 800-mile front, from Leningrad in the north to the Donbass and the Crimea in the south. These attacks were to be mounted at very short notice. According to Zhukov's memoirs – written, to be sure, with hindsight – he alone dared to voice criticism. Zhukov argued that it was more important to concentrate the sparse resources available against the enemy centre of gravity. Marshal B. M. Shaposhnikov, the Chief of the General Staff, was bending with the wind, at least according to Zhukov's account of a conversation they had on leaving Stalin's office: [Shaposhnikov:] 'You argued for nothing; the Chief (*Verkhovnyi*) had decided this in advance.' [Zhukov:] 'Why, then did he ask our opinion?' [Shaposhnikov ('taking a deep breath'):] 'I don't know, my dear boy [*golubchik*], I don't know!'[4]

THE CENTRAL THEATRE

The Soviet failure in front of Moscow

At the start of 1942 Stalin had nine army groups lined up along the main front: the Caucasus Army Group (Kozlov), Southern Army Group (Malinovskii), Southwestern

Army Group (Timoshenko), Briansk Army Group (Cherevichenko), Western Army Group (Zhukov), Kalinin Army Group (Konev), Northwestern Army Group (Kurochkin), Volkhov Army Group (Meretskov) and Leningrad Army Group (Khozin).[5] The major Soviet success had occurred in the centre in December 1941, and here also was the main concentration of German forces. In a complex – over-complex – set of attacks in the centre of the front, the Soviet Briansk Army Group was to push the 2nd Panzer Army back from Briansk. The Western and Kalinin Army Groups were to cover the area west of Moscow. Finally, the Northwestern Army Group was to effect a deep penetration to the southwest to get behind German Army Group Centre.

The blocking of Operation TYPHOON was followed by a confused dogfight in front of Moscow.[6] It lasted for five months, in the first two of which (December and January) the Germans were under deadly Soviet pressure and threatened with catastrophe. In February and early March the front was more stable for the Wehrmacht, despite continuing Soviet attacks. In late March and April the spring *rasputitsa* brought action to a halt. Russian historians usually call the two periods of this central battle the 'Moscow offensive operation' (5 December 1941 to 7 January 1942) and the 'Rzhev–Viaz'ma strategic operation' (8 January to 20 April).

The fighting in the central theatre covered an expanse of rural Russia in Moscow, Kalinin and Smolensk Regions. This zone ran 340 miles from Lake Il'men in the north to Briansk in the south; it was about 150 miles in depth. In the end the Wehrmacht held on to a convoluted double line of defence here. In essence, German Army Group Centre and the right flank of Army Group North retained a rear line just east of the north–south Orsha–Vitebsk–Leningrad railway, and just north of the main east–west Orsha–Smolensk–Viaz'ma–Moscow railway. The German high command thus protected the lines of communication of both Army Group Centre and Army Group North. It could move its forces up and down the front and bring reinforcements from the West. In this general position Army Group Centre would stand until the autumn of 1943. The eye of the storm early in 1942, as in October 1941, was further forward, at the small town of Viaz'ma, on the Moscow railway line. Viaz'ma was linked by lateral (north–south) rail lines to Rzhev, 70 miles to the north, and to Briansk, 140 miles to the south.

Stalin, Shaposhnikov and Zhukov were probably as surprised as Hitler, Halder and Bock by the sudden and drastic change of fortunes on the battle front in early December 1941. Stalin's mood quickly turned to one of militant enthusiasm. As we have seen, the Stavka issued orders in mid-December to 'destroy' the encircled Germans 'to the last man'. Most of the German generals, for their part, wanted to pull Army Group Centre back to the so-called 'K' or KÖNIGSBERG line, which was 50–75 miles west of the German high-water mark of early December. The line stretched from Rzhev south through Gzhatsk (east of Viaz'ma) to Iukhnov. Hitler and Halder opposed this withdrawal, and with some justification. Little work had been done to prepare the 'K' line. Also, German vehicles and heavy artillery were stuck fast in the deep snow, and retreat would only be possible if they were abandoned. Hitler's famous response was the so-called 'stand fast' order (*Haltebefehl*) of 18 December:

> Commanding generals, commanders, and officers are to intervene in person to compel the troops to fanatical resistance in their positions without regard to the enemy broken through on the flanks or in the rear. This is the only way to gain the time necessary to bring up the reinforcements from Germany and the West that I have ordered.[7]

Zhukov only gradually pushed the 3rd and 4th Panzer Armies (as the Panzer Groups were renamed on 1 January) back from the Moscow–Volga Canal and then from the Moscow–Sol'nechnogorsk–Klin–Kalinin railway. His main drive was parallel to the two central railways; one ran from Moscow to Rzhev (past Volokolamsk) and the other from Moscow to Viaz'ma (past Mozhaisk and Gzhatsk). Soviet pressure was, however, also building up at the start of January around the flanks of the central German position, from north of Rzhev and – 200 miles to the southeast – through the city of Kaluga. Stalin and the Stavka had high hopes of a grand encirclement dwarfing those achieved by the Germans at Belostok–Minsk, Smolensk, and Viaz'ma–Briansk, but this time trapping the bulk of German Army Group Centre. On 7 January General Zhukov's Western Army Group and General Konev's smaller Kalinin Army Group were ordered to destroy 'the Mozhaisk–Gzhatsk–Viaz'ma enemy group', essentially the German 3rd and the 4th Panzer Armies, eliminating at the same time the group around Rzhev (the German 9th Army). Konev's Kalinin Army Group was reinforced and ordered to drive southwest. Two new shock armies, the 3rd and the 4th, set up following Stalin's directive of 10 January to establish striking forces, were transferred to Konev's command from the Northwestern Army Group on 19 January. Konev was ordered to use them for the very ambitious task of cutting off Smolensk from the west; Smolensk was 95 miles west of Viaz'ma.[8]

Soviet spearheads were indeed able to thrust through gaps in the thinly held German lines. Early in January some of Konev's forces (the 39th and 29th Armies) turned around Rzhev and headed south, on the far side of the northern spine of the German defence, the Rzhev–Viaz'ma railway. Meanwhile, southwest of Kaluga, other Soviet armies swept forward against the German 4th Army. A small German force was encircled at the important rail junction of Sukhinichi. As part of the 'fanatical resistance', Hitler ordered this town held, just as the Alcázar of Toledo had been held by a Francoist garrison in an epic siege for two months at the start of the Spanish Civil War.[9] Sukhinichi was relieved after three weeks, but the Germans had to evacuate it at the end of January. Nevertheless, Sukhinichi was something new for the German Army in the Second World War, the forerunner of a string of embattled 'Alcázars', from Demiansk and Kholm in 1941–2, through Stalingrad in 1942–3, Kurland and Crimea in 1944, an archipelago of 'fortified places' in 1944, and finally East Prussia in 1945. On the other hand, this dual crisis did lead Hitler in mid-January to relax his demand for fanatical resistance and to allow a slow withdrawal to the shorter 'K' line. As he angrily pointed out, this was the first major retreat he had had to order in the whole war. It would not be the last.

Meanwhile, a mix of Soviet airborne forces and cavalry were sent deep behind German lines. The newly revived Soviet cavalry arm was to play a prominent role that winter. Zhukov, it will be recalled, was a cavalryman, and he had commanded a cavalry corps in 1937. In an operation reminiscent of the Russian Civil War, massed cavalry was sent around the German flanks. Two cavalry corps, the 11th coming from the north and Belov's 1st Guards coming from the southeast, were ordered to meet behind Viaz'ma, cutting German communications. On 26–27 January, horsemen from the 11th briefly cut the railway between Smolensk and Viaz'ma while the 1st Guards harassed the Warsaw–Moscow highway south of Viaz'ma. At the other end of the technological spectrum, the Russians mounted their first parachute operation. Soviet airborne forces had been developed in the 1930s (and revived in early 1941) as part of the 'deep battle' concept. Now they were dropped into the rear of German Army Group Centre south of Viaz'ma. Their objective was to secure strong points for the advancing Soviet ground troops.[10] Operations included brigade-strength drops (2,000 men) from the 4th Air Landing Corps, and then the flying in of reinforcements to improvised airfields in the captured zones. The Soviets, as it would turn out, lacked sufficient transport aircraft and means of co-ordinating the elite parachute troops on the ground.

At the beginning of February the German high command began to restore the situation. It did this partly by dismissing exhausted commanders and inserting energetic, able and self-confident replacements. General Walter Model was appointed to take over the 9th Army on the northern face of the German position. As he was being briefed on the precarious situation by his new staff, someone enquired, 'And what, sir, have you brought to restore the situation?' Without hesitation and in a deadpan manner, Model replied, 'Myself'.[11] An officer of extraordinary abilities, Model began a meteoric rise, and would establish himself as the German Army's best defensive specialist, Hitler's 'fireman'. Within a few weeks he had closed the gap in his front, cutting off much of the Soviet 29th Army west of the Rzhev–Viaz'ma railway. Meanwhile, General Heinrici, the new commander of the German 4th Army, resealed his eastern front and cut off Efremov's

FIGURE 5 German soldiers drive a horse and cart through a snowstorm.

33rd Army and Belov's 1st Guards Cavalry Corps deep behind his lines south of Viaz'ma. (In the last days of the war in 1945, Heinrici would defend the centre of the Reich, as commander of German Army Group Vistula.) By the second week of February, Field Marshal Kluge could finally make a more positive report about the situation of the five armies of his Army Group Centre. Indeed, the worst of the ten-week crisis was over for the Germans. In the middle of February, Hitler told his army group commanders that the 'danger of a panic in the 1812 sense' had been 'eliminated'.[12]

The Soviets still did not see things so pessimistically. They were still keeping external pressure on the Germans' outer front, and their forces behind German lines threatened the enemy's communications and Viaz'ma itself. Early in February 1942, the Soviet Western Theatre headquarters was revived, under Zhukov, to co-ordinate the attack of Kalinin and Western Army Groups. In mid-February the Stavka again ordered Zhukov to destroy the Rzhev–Viaz'ma group of the enemy, this time by 5 March. The offensive made little progress. The mobile phase of the campaign was over, with the Soviet front stalled and with the greater part of three Soviet armies (the 29th, 33rd and 39th) still trapped behind the enemy lines. Another major offensive directive followed from the Stavka on 20 March, which Zhukov found foolish and wasteful, as the spring *rasputitsa* was about to set in. The *rasputitsa* in October 1941 came from the autumn rains, but the *rasputitsa* in the last weeks of March 1942 was more elemental. The melting of the winter's snowfall was combined with the gradual thawing of the sodden ground which had been frozen to a depth of several metres. For up to two months movement was very difficult, especially on unpaved roads.

Red Army units held out behind the German lines. They lived off the land or were supplied as far as possible over back trails through the woods and by the occasional air drop. After the worst of the *rasputitsa*, German Army Centre was able to deal with the weakened Soviet survivors. Efremov's 33rd Army, cut off in early February in the woods south of the Smolensk–Viaz'ma railway, was finally destroyed in April 1942. Only a few survivors made good their escape; General Efremov shot himself rather than fall into German hands. On 20 April Kalinin and Western Army Groups were apparently ordered to shift to defence, and with that the 'Rzhev–Viaz'ma operation' sputtered out.[13] The great Battle of Moscow was finally over. Zhukov's Western Theatre command was disbanded on 5 May.

Unfinished business remained. The 'Belov Group', based on the 1st Guards Cavalry Corps, was also trapped south of Viaz'ma, but it was more fortunate than the 33rd Army. Belov's troopers escaped German Operation HANNOVER in May–June 1942, and the haggard and bearded survivors were able to break out in mid-June. General Belov himself was flown to safety. Some survivors of the 4th Airborne Corps also got out. The last act was the destruction of Maslennikov's 39th Army, which had ended up stranded northwest of Viaz'ma. For months this force had been supplied though forest trails back to the rest of the Kalinin Army Group. The Germans finally cut the link and in early July 1942, in Operation SEYDLITZ, they eliminated the pocket. Army commander Maslennikov, an NKVD general, escaped, but thousands of Soviet troops were captured. As a result of this mopping up, the German-held area of the Rzhev–Viaz'ma salient was much expanded.

It would feature prominently in the terrible battles of the coming summer and autumn. The reduced Toropets bulge further to the west, however, remained in Soviet hands, and powerful Red Army forces would gradually be built up there.

The flanks of the Moscow front

The Stavka attempted to mount offensives on either side of Zhukov's Central Army Group, with Kurochkin's Northwestern Army Group (on the right flank) and Cherevichenko's Briansk Army Group (on the left) – see Map 4. These did not achieve decisive success. Stalin paid much attention at this time, and later, to the southwestern approaches to Moscow, through the towns of Briansk and Orel, held by the German 2nd Panzer Army. Cherevichenko attempted an advance aimed at the town of Bolkhov, about 40 miles north of Briansk, but he made little progress, probably because of the limited forces at his disposal. In March 1942 this sector was identified by the Stavka – incorrectly – as the most likely avenue for the main German advance in the coming summer campaign (the actual route would be in southern Russia). In April 1942, Golikov, a general in whom Stalin seems to have put special trust, replaced Cherevichenko as commander of the Briansk Army Group. He was sent powerful reinforcements, including four tank corps and seven rifle divisions, along with the new 5th Tank Army.

Much more was happening on the right flank, by Lake Il'men. General Kurochkin's Northwestern Army Group was trying to destroy German elements at Staraia Russa, Kholm and Velikie Luki – near the demarcation lines of German Army Groups North and Centre. These towns blocked the Red Army's way to the west, and in particular to Dno and Pskov on the railway lines that supplied German Army Group North around Leningrad (see Map 3). The chief of staff of the Northwestern Army Group from December 1941 to May 1942 was the very able General Vatutin, who would play a prominent part later in the war. Kurochkin's Army Group was actually the most successful of any that winter. In January he advanced about 100 miles south and west from his starting point in the Valdai hills. This drive cut the Moscow–Rzhev–Velikie Luki railway west of Rzhev and put in place a big salient, centred on the small town of Toropets and hanging over Vitebsk and Smolensk. After this advance the 3rd and 4th Shock Armies were transferred to the Kalinin Army Group, soon to be part of Zhukov's Western Theatre. Kurochkin was left to concentrate on the western face of his front, which ran about 100 miles down from Lake Il'men. In late January and early February 1942, Kurochkin encircled considerable German forces first around Kholm and then around the village of Demiansk.

Unlike the earlier Sukhinichi pocket, Demiansk and Kholm were not abandoned by the Germans.[14] The Luftwaffe mounted a major operation to supply them by air, with dozens of big Ju 52 tri-motor transport planes flying in supplies and reinforcements; the Germans had more success than the Russians did with the air supply of their own forces south of Viaz'ma. Demiansk, just a big village with a population of only 2,500 in 1926, became an extraordinary focus of fighting. Six divisions of the German 2nd Corps

(95,000 troops) held a pocket about 35 miles in diameter. Demiansk itself was not on the railway, but the area around it was an important strategic position. The northern edge of the pocket blocked the east–west rail line from Bologoe to Staraia Russa, Dno and Pskov, and the eastern edge threatened the Soviet-held railway running southwest into the new Toropets salient. The worst threat for the Russians would be if the German forces at Demiansk and Rzhev could cross the 110 miles between them, and join hands; by doing so they would cut off the whole territory of the Soviet Toropets salient and trap many Soviet divisions there. Hitler was enthusiastic about this plan, which he provisionally called Operation BRIDGE-BUILDING (BRÜCKENSCHLAG). As it turned out there were too few German forces and too little time.

In any event, in the following summer the German garrisons (and Luftwaffe ferry crews) were awarded special 'Cholm' and 'Demjansk' arm shields, a type of badge issued for only a handful of the Wehrmacht's battles.[15] The Germans made a major effort to relieve Demiansk, and drove a thin corridor through to the pocket in early March 1942. The breakout, in April 1942, was commanded by General Seydlitz-Kurzbach, who would later be captured at Stalingrad and become a figurehead of the anti-Nazi movement. The smaller Kholm pocket was relieved on 1 May, after a three-month siege. Demiansk and Kholm were important as a dangerous precedent for Stalingrad in the following winter; Hitler thought he could repeat them on a much grander scale on the Volga. After the *rasputitsa*, on 3 May 1942, another offensive was mounted against Demiansk by Kurochkin's Northwestern Army Group, this time supervised by General Vasilevskii. It was probably intended to be co-ordinated with the other operations in the Ukraine and around Leningrad, but it did not achieve its objective. Very heavy fighting was involved; altogether, 90,000 Soviet troops were lost in the fighting around Demiansk that winter and spring.[16]

Just northwest of Demiansk the Russians planned an ambitious operation to coincide with the drive of the Volkhov Army Group towards Leningrad. The Soviet intention in late January was to use elite formations here. General V. I. Kuznetsov's 1st Shock Army (taken from Zhukov's army group) was to be assembled by 8 February. It was supposed to drive west, from Staraia Russa through the Dno rail junction and then on to Pskov and Ostrov, reaching the latter places by the end of February (see Map 3). With this advance Kuznetsov was to cut the lines of communications of German Army Group North. The plan did not work out, and on 2 March Stalin sent a critical signal to Kuznetsov: 'It seems to me that you are disobeying the order of the Stavka and of the commander of the [Northwestern Army Group] about an offensive. I ask you to send me your explanation by coded telegraph of the reasons for your shift from offence to defence.'[17] At least Kuznetsov avoided the fate of the 2nd Shock Army, whose offensive 75 miles to the north would eventually leave it trapped in the bogs beyond the Volkhov (see next section).

In the end, Kurochkin's Northwestern Army Group was more successful than its neighbours to the south. It advanced west to the line held in September 1941 (before the Battle of Viaz'ma–Briansk), with the important exception of the Demiansk pocket. Unlike the Volkhov Army Group, Kalinin Army Group and Western Army Group, General Kurochkin did not have whole armies and corps trapped behind German lines and eventually destroyed. The considerable territory gained, however, was mostly sparsely inhabited forest and swamps of little immediate military value. Most importantly, Kurochkin's forces did not advance as far as the north–south railways and the lines of communication of German Army Group North; this would not happen until early 1944.

The reasons for the failure of the Soviet winter offensive

In a draft of his memoirs, Zhukov was bitter about what had happened to the Red Army in the winter of 1941–2:

> The History of the Great Fatherland War still comes to a generally positive conclusion about the winter offensive of our forces, despite the lack of success. I do not agree with this evaluation. The embellishment of history, one could say, is a sad attempt to paint over failure. If you consider our losses and what results were achieved, it will be clear that it was a Pyrrhic victory.

The Soviet operations in the central theatre had not been a success. The maximum goal, the destruction of Army Group Centre, had not been achieved, and neither had the more practical goal of getting back to the line held in September 1941 at the start of German Operation TYPHOON. The fighting was extremely costly for the Red Army. Zhukov's Rzhev–Viaz'ma operation alone, from January to April 1942, cost 272,000 lives.[18]

This failure of the Soviet counter-offensive had several explanations. For the Russians, as for the Germans, it was difficult to move rapidly in the depths of winter, through snow-covered forests, and the Red Army no longer had enough mechanized mobile forces. Soviet ski troops, cavalry, and even parachutists could move around the front and threaten enemy communications, but they could not permanently block the railways and roads or take the villages the Germans had fortified. The Russians had suffered huge losses. In early February one of his commanders [Belov] explained the problem to Zhukov: 'I have already reported about the reasons for the slowness of the offensive. Snow a metre deep, and enemy resistance. That is the main reason [sic].' The Germans had occupied vast territories with short devastating bursts of activity in the summer and early autumn; this possibility was not open to the Russians. As Zhukov complained, you cannot encircle without tanks, and the reason for the lack of armour was partly that some resources were sent elsewhere, and partly that there was no longer enough armour in the whole Red Army to go around.[19] Another problem was that the Soviet command structure was still muddled. There was no overall commander or even co-ordinator for the four Army Groups engaged in the centre: the Northwestern, Kalinin, Western and Briansk. Everything was run from the Stavka, which had three other major operations to look after. At the start of February (when the impetus was already fading), Zhukov was given control of both the Western and Kalinin Army Groups, but he was not given responsibility for the Northwestern or Briansk Army Groups.[20]

The Stavka made the same mistake that Hitler and his high command had made in 1941, assuming the enemy to be exhausted and shattered. It also attempted, as the Germans did in Operation BARBAROSSA, to attack everywhere at once. Zhukov's view was that it would have been much wiser to concentrate resources on the central part of the front and advance to the line Staraia Russa–Velikie Luki–Vitebsk–Smolensk–Briansk (see Map 4). To achieve this, however, he needed the reserve armies that were being raised by the Stavka. Later in January he was to complain that he had lost 276,000 troops and only received 100,000 reinforcements.[21] In fact, important formations and headquarters were actually removed from Zhukov's control in mid-January. The 1st Shock Army was shifted to the Northwestern Army Group for the promising operations due west towards Pskov. Rokossovskii's 16th Army headquarters was shifted south of Zhukov's sector to strengthen the effort around Sukhinichi. As the winter progressed, armies, rifle divisions and tank brigades that could have been used on the Moscow–Viaz'ma–Smolensk axis were deployed towards Leningrad, towards Pskov, towards Khar'kov and in the Crimea.

Soviet loss figures show where the winter's fighting was heaviest. Zhukov's Western Army Group did carry out the brunt of the Soviet counter-offensive. It lost 101,000 troops in the month after 5 December, compared to 27,000 for Konev's Kalinin Army Group. In the next phase, from early January to mid-April, the losses of the two army groups were more similar, although those of Western Army Group were still heavier: 149,000 versus 123,000. In the same period losses of Briansk Army Group on the left flank, were lower, 21,000 in the Bolkhov operation. Greater, as we have seen, were losses on the Soviet right flank, with 89,000 troops lost by Northwestern Army Group in the fighting around Demiansk.[22]

The Germans had been remarkably successful in holding a deep, if exposed, position in front of Moscow. The Rzhev–Viaz'ma salient remained as a sword pointing at Moscow. The survival of the German position at Briansk and Orel presented another credible threat to the Soviet capital, and one that would distract the Stavka from the real danger further south. But the 'fanatical resistance' had been a great gamble on the part of Hitler and Halder. Aside from the Russians' problems, the quality and morale of the German infantry were undoubtedly a big factor in preventing disaster. The *Ostheer* did receive some fresh forces, but German and Russian sources differ on the scale and effect of those.[23] The Germans certainly did mount an effective defence, mainly with the troops they had to hand. It is worth remembering that Army Group Centre was still the strongest formation in the German Army. Field Marshal Günther von Kluge was one of Hitler's most talented and effective leaders.[24] A senior commander in Poland in 1939 and France in 1940 (for which he received his marshal's baton), he would be sent to replace Rundstedt as C-in-C West after the 1944 Normandy landings. By late January 1941 Kluge had, as we have seen, outstanding subordinate commanders in the form of Generals Model and Heinrici.

It probably would have been impossible to trap German Army Group Centre, in view of the weather and the overall quantity and quality of Soviet forces. Nevertheless, the Germans might have been forced into a desperate withdrawal, giving up much of their heavy equipment. They might have been pushed back at least to Smolensk. German Army Group Centre would eventually be encircled and largely destroyed, in a rout comparable to that of Napoleon and the Grande Armée, but this would not happen until the summer of 1944.

THE BLOCKADE OF LENINGRAD

Attempts to relieve Leningrad

With all the drama in front of Moscow, Leningrad seemed less important.[25] In October 1941 the position of Russia's second city had looked very grim. At that time General Vasilevskii from the General Staff had sent a pessimistic signal to General Khozin (commander of Leningrad Army Group). It was important, he said, to ensure a link with the 54th Army, to the east of the city, on the Volkhov River

> to give a way out for the forces of the Leningrad Army Group to retreat to the east, to avoid imprisonment if necessity forces us to abandon Leningrad. Either you break through in the next week or so and give your forces a chance to withdraw to the east in the event of the impossibility of holding Leningrad, or you will fall into captivity.[26]

The Stavka must have had in mind the terrible experience of the Kiev encirclement. By December, however, the Germans had been pushed back from their advanced position at Tikhvin, and this was to be crucially important. Although for the defenders of Leningrad the route – via Tikhvin – to the central Russian 'mainland' was indirect and poor, it prevented the complete starvation and surrender of the city. Meanwhile, the Finns were not inclined to move on Leningrad and its supply lines from the north, especially in view of Hitler's reverses at Moscow and the now uncertain course of the war. They stood on the Svir' River, between Lake Ladoga and Lake Onega, and awaited events.

But the most direct routes to Leningrad, especially the railways and metalled roads, were still blocked. As it happened, the worst period of the Blockade of Leningrad for the civilian inhabitants would be from January to March 1942. This was a time when the main German armies in Russia were in retreat or fighting desperate defensive battles, and when Stalin and the Stavka thought there was a possibility of an early victory in the war as a whole. If the Soviet recapture of the exposed position at Tikhvin was important, so was the failure of the Red Army's attempts to relieve Leningrad during the winter.[27] In June 1942, Field Marshal Küchler's German Army Group North still held the line it had fallen back to at the end of December 1941. The German 18th Army (General Lindemann) kept control of the so-called 'Shlissel'burg corridor', a broad wedge of territory with the Neva River on the left, the Volkhov River on the right, and Shlissel'burg and Lake Ladoga at the north end. Although the Germans had not gone the last mile, they had made extremely difficult the supply of Leningrad and evacuation of its civilians.

Why did Soviet attempts to relieve Leningrad fail in the first months of 1942? It was very difficult for the defenders of the starving city to mount offensive operations outwards against the besiegers. The main Red Army pressure had to come from outside, mainly from the forces along the Volkhov River, which flows north from Lake Il'men into Lake Ladoga. From the river to Leningrad, the distance is some 75 miles (see Map 3). In mid-December 1941 the Stavka ordered an offensive to relieve Leningrad. Stalin urged the Volkhov Army Group forwards, using the same ambitiously

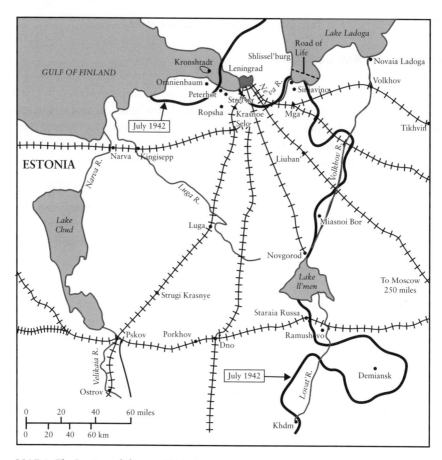

MAP 3 The Leningrad theatre, 1941–4.

blood-curdling words he was now using on the Moscow front. With the aid of the Leningrad garrison, Volkhov Army Group was to turn the tables on the besiegers. It was 'to surround and capture [the enemy], and in the event of the enemy's refusal to surrender, to destroy him'.[28] Although the initial objectives of the Soviet offensive had been broad, taking in three of the railways running north into Leningrad, in the end the attack concentrated on the main line from Moscow to Leningrad, the 'October' Railway. On this line, the station at Liuban' was the key German position. Liuban' was also vulnerable to an attack from the Soviet 54th Army of Leningrad Army Group. This army was not in Leningrad itself but west of the Volkhov on the 'mainland' side of the German-held Shlissel'burg corridor. The Soviet operation could also be supported as far as possible from the side of the besieged northern capital. The whole offensive, if successful, would cut off the German sector southeast of Leningrad and open a rail link into the city.

The Soviet Volkhov Army Group had a numerical superiority over its opponents, except in air strength. According to a recent Russian account, it outnumbered the German units facing it by more than 2:1 in personnel, and more than 3:1 in tanks.[29] Volkhov Army Group was also given an experienced and reasonably competent commander in the form of General Kirill Afanas'evich Meretskov. Almost all of Meretskov's war career was to be linked to the northwest (aside from command of the main attack against Japan in 1945). As the youthful commander of the Leningrad Military District (aged 43), he oversaw the first abortive attacks on the Mannerheim Line in the Winter War of 1939–40. In September 1941 he was put in charge of the line facing the Finns between Lake Ladoga and Lake Onega. After commanding the Volkhov Army Group, between December 1941 and February 1944, he would take over the new Karelian Army Group which knocked Finland out of the war. Meretskov was, in the end, evidently well thought of by Stalin. Of Russian peasant origin and with very limited formal education, he had served in the 1st Cavalry Army, after an abbreviated course at the General Staff Academy. He made his career in senior staff posts in the 1930s and as an adviser in Spain. In August 1940 he had shot up to the post of Chief of the General Staff. Four months later, in January 1941, he was replaced by Zhukov after his lacklustre performance in the December war games. When the war began, his career took a more shocking decline. He was suddenly arrested, not for military incompetence (he was then a Deputy People's Commissar, in charge of training), but because of his personal links with General Pavlov, the former commander of Western Army Group who was accused of leading a defeatist conspiracy. Meretskov was thrown into prison and tortured into confessing his 'crimes'. In mid-September 1941 he was suddenly summoned from his prison cell to the Kremlin. Stalin apparently made no comment about his prolonged absence and haggard appearance, and sent him off to fight the Finns.[30]

Moscow attached great urgency to Meretskov's campaign. On 7 January his Volkhov Army Group, formed three weeks earlier, began an abortive attack against the 16th Army of German Army Group North before a full force had been assembled; Meretskov had only two infantry armies. More progress was made a week later when one of Stalin's new reserve armies was added to the order of battle. This was the 26th Army, which was renamed the 2nd Shock Army. This doomed army attacked out of a 15-mile front on the Volkhov River and through a weak point in the German position about 20 miles southwest of the Moscow–Leningrad main line.[31] The 2nd Shock Army got across the Novgorod–Leningrad railroad. It failed to turn northeast towards Liuban' to cut the Moscow–Leningrad line, probably because its initial goals were too ambitious. Unfortunately, the armies flanking the 2nd Shock Army failed to penetrate the German lines to anything like the same depth. This was a tragic failure, in view of the weakness of the Germans and their exposed position. The Liuban' offensive was the last chance to relieve Leningrad before the human catastrophe of the deep winter.

The Volkhov front degenerated into fighting typical of this period of the Eastern Front. There was no clear front line. Small forces, exhausted and – literally – bogged down, tried to encircle one another in the woods and swamps. Stalin was evidently dissatisfied with the progress and in February ordered Voroshilov, who was the Stavka 'representative' in the northern theatre, to take over. Voroshilov (sensibly) refused, and would later be criticized for this in a Politburo resolution.[32] In any event the main Soviet emphasis now became the capture of Liuban', with the 2nd Shock Army being turned inward in that direction. If the 2nd Shock Army and the 54th Army (from the north) could have joined up at Liuban', the German 1st Corps would have been trapped, and the breaking of the blockade made nearer. It was a close thing. As it was, the Germans were gradually able to bring up reinforcements and in the middle of March 1942, Küchler's Army Group North carried out Operation BEAST OF PREY (RAUBTIER), in which sharp attacks by the flanking German corps, backed by concentrated Luftwaffe support, cut off the 2nd Shock Army. General A. A. Vlasov, who had recently arrived as Meretskov's deputy in the Volkhov Army Group, was in mid-April sent into the pocket to take over the 2nd Shock Army. In his earlier commands in 1941 and 1942, Vlasov had developed a reputation for dealing effectively with difficult situations.[33] Although the Germans were pushed away from the 2nd Shock Army's lines of communications, the onset of the *rasputitsa* immediately after the start of Operation BEAST OF PREY had a severe effect on Vlasov's supplies. These battles were very expensive for the Russians; between the start of January and the end of April 1942, the Liuban' operation cost 95,000 Russian lives.[34] Worse was yet to come.

One of the reasons for the Russian failures had been poor coordination between the forces attacking Liuban'. This allowed the Germans to defeat them in detail. The 54th Army, approaching from the northeast (i.e. from south of Lake Ladoga), was under Khozin's Leningrad Army Group, while the 2nd Shock Army (attacking from the southwest) and the 59th and 4th Armies (attacking from the southeast) were under Meretskov's Volkhov Army Group. The headquarters of the Leningrad Army Group proposed that it take over the whole front. Stalin, apparently against the advice of Shaposhnikov, the Chief of the General Staff, accepted the proposal. In late April 1942, with the attack on Liuban' stalled and the 2nd Shock Army terribly exposed, the Stavka disbanded the Volkhov Army Group. Meretskov was effectively dismissed, and the armies of the Volkhov Army Group were made part of Khozin's Leningrad Army Group. Unfortunately, the creation of this new enlarged Leningrad Army Group also had no positive effect. The formation was unwieldy (with nine armies, three independent corps and two 'groups of forces'). Khozin's attempt to continue offensive operations west of the Volkhov was foolhardy. The 2nd Shock Army was neither reinforced nor allowed to withdraw. The 1998 Russian official history blames Khozin, and says that the Stavka ordered withdrawal in mid-May.[35] At the end of May the Germans were finally able to close the ring around the 2nd Shock Army. (This was at the same time that the Red Army was suffering disaster in the Crimea and at Khar'kov.)

Neither the return of the now-vindicated Meretskov nor the re-creation of his Volkhov Army Group – both implemented at the start of June – could save the situation. Khozin was replaced as commander of Leningrad Army Group by the artilleryman General Govorov, who had distinguished himself in the Battle of Moscow. Khozin served on in the Red Army, but he would never again command an army group; from early 1944 he held only rear-echelon posts. Meretskov launched major operations to support the withdrawal of the 2nd Shock Army, but to no avail. The cost was enormous. Some 55,000 personnel were counted as lost in the battles fought to save Vlasov's 2nd Shock Army from mid-May to early July 1942. The Germans claimed over 33,000 prisoners were taken in late June 1942; most famous of them all was General Vlasov himself.[36]

Leningrad starves

The Soviet 2nd Shock Army was finally crushed at the end of June 1942. As tragic as that defeat was, it was overshadowed by the fate of the civilian inhabitants of Leningrad over the previous winter. By October 1941 the Germans had given up on a head-on assault on Leningrad, and they attempted to achieve their ends through a siege.[37]

Leningrad was one of the great cities of Europe. As St Petersburg, the city had been the Imperial Russian capital until 1918. It was larger than Moscow at that time. By 1939 Leningrad was still the second city in the USSR, with 3,100,000 inhabitants, compared to 4,500,000 in Moscow. It was much bigger than Kiev, the third city, which had a population of 850,000. In December 1941 there were still no fewer than 2,500,000 civilians in Leningrad. Rations were progressively cut throughout the months of early winter – to a low of 125 grams of bread per day for the mass of the population. Fuel ran out, and the power stations closed down. Famine reigned.

Although Leningrad was, more than any other, a front-line city, it was only affected to a limited degree by air attacks and artillery bombardment. Goering had promised to neutralize Leningrad with air power, but this proved impossible; air attacks were light from December 1941 onwards. The constant artillery bombardment, which continued – unlike the bombing – on a considerable scale through 1943 (in which year 68,000 shells were recorded), was more lethal to Leningrad's civilians. It probably accounted for three-quarters of the total 15,800 civilians recorded as being killed by shelling and air raids combined.[38] However, the Germans had failed in August–September 1941 to reach a line where they could hit Leningrad city centre with their medium-range artillery. They had only limited amounts of heavy siege artillery, and until mid-1942 much of that was tied up in the attack on Sevastopol' in the Crimea. The historic town centre of Leningrad was 20,000–25,000 yards away from the main German artillery positions – although of course the industrial suburbs in the south were much more vulnerable. As time passed, the Russian artillery developed effective counter-battery tactics.

Leningrad's economic potential had been 'neutralized' by other means. Without forgetting them, the victims of air raids and shells were minimal compared to losses due to starvation. The Russian northern capital had always had to bring in most of its food from distant regions, and even in June 1941 stocks had been limited. By August, the regular supply lines had been cut. The bread ration rapidly fell. For a time the city was completely cut off except by air, and only in late November 1941 did lorries begin to bring in small supplies of food and fuel via the 'road of life' (*doroga zhizni*) across the frozen Lake Ladoga. At the end of the war, the Russians claimed no fewer than 632,000 civilian deaths 'from hunger' in Leningrad. There is good reason to believe that the total number of dead was nearer a million. In any event, the great majority of deaths took place between December 1941 – when the first cases of starvation were reported – and June 1942. Some 1,094,000 burials were recorded from July 1941 through June 1942. In an incomplete listing of 517,000 registered deaths in all of 1942, 475,000 took place in the first six months of the year. The deaths in the later months were much fewer, with the figures for September to December 1942 all under 5,000 a month (compared to 107,000 in February 1942).[39] The numbers are hard to calculate with any precision; a large number of refugees from the Baltic states and Leningrad Region – several tens of thousands of people – had taken refuge in the city during the German 1941 summer onslaught; more importantly, later on, the deaths registration system collapsed. There is also no way of knowing just how many Leningraders died of the consequences of malnutrition on 'the mainland' after they had been evacuated. As for the military side, the losses of Leningrad Army Group were recorded as 144,800 in 1941, 83,700 in 1942 and 88,700 in 1943. Probably about two-thirds of these soldiers came from the garrison of the encircled city, as opposed to units of the army group fighting their way in from south of Lake Ladoga. Losses of the Volkhov Army Group alone from December 1941 to February 1944 were 298,000.[40]

Put baldly, the reason for perhaps the worst single demographic catastrophe of the Second World War was that there were too many inhabitants for the available food supplies. From hindsight, what was crucial was the failure rapidly to evacuate civilians to central Russia before the winter of 1941–2. The population should have been brought down to the sustainable 600,000 civilians who stayed on after the summer of 1942. This failure did not stem simply from negligence or incompetence on the part of the Soviet authorities, or even from the great speed of the German advance. Evacuation began on 29 June 1941 and by the end of August, when the Germans closed the ring, nearly 490,000 people had been evacuated, including 220,000 children and 164,000 workers who had been moved out with their factories. Many Leningraders did not want to be evacuated, seeing refugee trains and refugee status in the hinterland of north central Russia as a worse option than staying put in the great city. In the end, mass evacuation was only decreed at the start of December 1941, and it began to be implemented towards the end of January 1942. When evacuation did become the policy of the city administration, it was already too late for many Leningraders. All the same, between mid-January 1942 and mid-March 1942, 554,000 people – two-fifths dependants – were evacuated over the ice of Lake Ladoga, and in the summer of 1942 the final large wave of evacuees were sent out.[41]

The Soviet government was responsible for the generally inept defence of the whole state, which allowed the Germans so quickly to attack the great northern city. The Red Army's failure to break the siege was also important, although even if the Volkhov Army Group had advanced successfully in February 1942, the number of civilian deaths in Leningrad would still have been in six figures. Leningrad might, hypothetically, have been surrendered to the Wehrmacht – as Minsk, Riga, Kiev and Khar'kov were – but it is hard to see how this would have saved lives. The Germans could not have fed Leningrad in the winter of 1941–2 even if they had wanted to. The Third Reich ultimately bore responsibility for the war of aggression and for the imposition of the blockade. Hitler made various private pronouncements about levelling Leningrad (and Moscow), and the experience of Leningrad fits within the general monstrous policy of starving the Russian population and in particular the cities. The German Army ordered that the starving population, even women and children, should not be allowed to cross its lines. Even if the population of the city had attempted to surrender, this would have been refused by the Germans.[42]

Two final points can be made about the siege of Leningrad. One is that the Soviet government maintained control of the population; some twenty-five years earlier, the collapse of another government, that of the Tsar, had been set off by food riots in this city. Rigorous discipline was enforced. Taking just the period from the invasion to October 1942, some 9,574 people were arrested by the NKVD and another 22,166 by the regular police (militsiia); of these, 5,360 people were executed by Leningrad Region NKVD in the period up to October 1942.[43] A second point is that the blockade was endured largely by women. Many of the men had been called up for the Red Army or the People's Militia (and often died serving there), or were evacuated with their factories. Women made up 75 per cent of the 790,000 population registered in July–August 1942 and 75 per cent of the 569,400 in July 1943. Of 254,000 war industry workers in Leningrad in April 1942, 181,000 were women.[44]

THE CRIMEA

The siege of Sevastopol' remains one of the epics of the Nazi–Soviet campaign.[45] The Crimea is a peninsula roughly the size of Sicily, about 100 miles from north to south and 200 miles from east to west, but with about a quarter of the population of the Italian island. Of the pre-war population of 1,100,000, about half were ethnic Russians, and over 200,000 were Tatars. The peninsula was an 'autonomous' republic, the Crimean ASSR, within the Russian Federation (RSFSR). With its Mediterranean climate, the south coast of the Crimea was a Russian Riviera favoured as a resort by the Tsarist aristocracy; the Soviet elite, too, spent summer months in sanatoria here. The eastern part of the Crimea is another and smaller peninsula, that of Kerch'; this Kerch' Peninsula is about 60 miles long and its western entrance is a 10-mile wide isthmus. At the far end are the Kerch' Straits, 3–10 miles wide, with the Taman' Peninsula and the North Caucasus on the other side. Hitler placed high value on the Crimea. In the long term, it was a place for German settlement. In the short term, it had immediate strategic importance. The Crimea could be used as a base for the Red Army Air Force to raid the vital Romanian oil fields, which were only 375 miles to the west. The peninsula was also a German route, via the Kerch' Straits, to the oilfield regions of the North Caucasus. This route bypassed the seemingly strong Soviet position at Rostov. Diplomatically, possession of the Crimea was a factor in influencing neutral Turkey. For the Russians, Sevastopol' was the main base of the Black Sea Fleet. It had much historical significance; the Crimea was the site of campaign of 1854–6 against the British and French, and the anti-Bolshevik White Armies had made their last stand here in 1920.

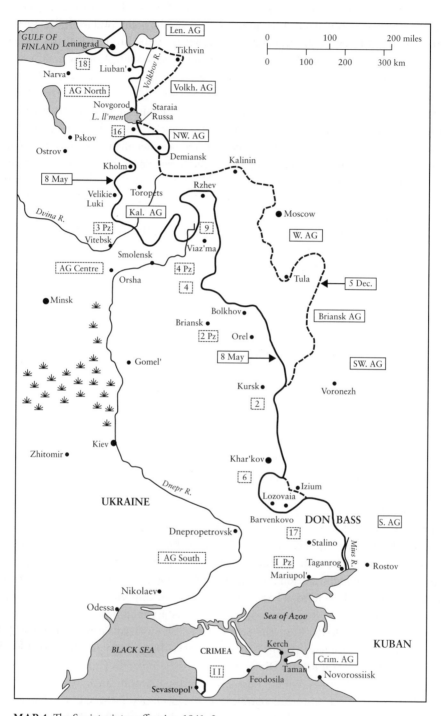

MAP 4 The Soviet winter offensive, 1941–2.

The German campaign is often identified with Erich von Manstein, who received his field marshal's baton from Hitler at the end of it.[46] Manstein was one of the German Army's most able – and self-confident – field commanders. In a relatively junior post (the chief of staff of an army group), he had been the architect of the *Sichelschnitt* (sickle cut) plan, the daring panzer offensive which led to the rapid defeat of France in 1940. With this, Manstein made his name and won Hitler's favour. He was seen as a possible successor to Halder as Chief of the Army General Staff. In June 1941 he proved his talent as a front-line commander when his motorized corps made a daring advance over the Dvina and into the Baltic region. It was only by chance, however, that Manstein ended up leading the 11th Army in the Crimea. The original commander, General Schobert, was killed in September 1941 when his light aircraft landed in a Russian minefield; Manstein was transferred down from Army Group North to replace him.

German and Romanian forces, latterly with concentrated Luftwaffe air support, broke into the peninsula against considerable Russian resistance. The breakthrough of the Perekop Isthmus, covering the northern entrance to the Crimea, had taken some weeks: from the end of September 1941 to the end of October. The defenders were the Russian 51st Army, commanded by the unfortunate General F. I. Kuznetsov, the June 1941 commander of the Northwestern Army Group. The attackers were a relatively weak German infantry formation, the 11th Army. The isthmus was readily defendable; the Whites had held it for ten months in 1920, and the Germans would do so for five months in 1944. To a degree, the loss of the isthmus can be explained by Red Army chaos in the campaign further north, in the Ukraine and in front of Moscow. In any event, having lost the Perekop Isthmus, the Russians were then unable to hold the open central plain of the peninsula. Sevastopol', on the southwestern tip, came under siege. The next Russian failure was on the eastern side of the Crimea, and was even less excusable than the loss of Perekop; in November 1941 the Red Army gave up the readily defendable entrance (from the west) to the Kerch' Peninsula. The town of Kerch' itself, the last Russian toehold on the eastern end of the Crimea, fell on 15 November; German squads proceeded to murder all the 40,000 Jews living in the towns and villages of the peninsula, outside Sevastopol'.[47]

Red Army recorded losses in the Crimea over the previous month had been great, some 48,000 troops. The local Stavka representative, Marshal Kulik, was severely punished for the Kerch' fiasco. A member of the Civil War 1st Cavalry Army Group, Kulik had been one of only four marshals in the Red Army in June 1941. Stalin now demoted him to the rank of major general, stripped him of his award of Hero of the Soviet Union and expelled him from the Central Committee of the Communist Party. A Commissariat of Defence directive in February 1942, over Stalin's name, accused Kulik of drunkenness and cowardice:

I make the warning, that henceforward decisive steps will be taken against those commanders, whoever they are and whatever their past achievements, who do not fulfil orders, or who do not fulfil them wholeheartedly, who show cowardice, who demoralize the forces by their defeatist attitude and are frightened of the Germans, who sow panic and undermine the confidence in our victory over the German aggressors.[48]

Soviet operations in the Crimea were to be a striking mix of incompetence, courage and occasional inspiration. Stalin and the Stavka attached high priority to the Crimea, and the Russians were in the unusual situation of possessing local naval superiority. Their Black Sea Fleet included a modernized battleship, two new cruisers, two older cruisers, several dozen destroyers, and numerous torpedo boats and submarines. The Germans, for their part, had to rely on small craft and the Luftwaffe. It is rarely noted that the first major Allied amphibious landing of the Second World War, the Kerch'–Feodosiia operation, was carried out by the Russians at the end of December 1941. The British landings in Vichy Madagascar came only five months later, in May 1942, and the seaborne assaults at Guadalcanal and Dieppe were mounted three months after that. The Kerch'–Feodosiia operation was originally suggested by General Kozlov of Transcaucasus Army Group. It was one of the largest Russian naval operations of the Second World War. The ambitious Soviet objectives were Kerch' and the port of Feodosiia, which lies on the south side of the entrance to the Kerch' Peninsula. The Russians took advantage of their much superior fleet and of Manstein's concentration on Sevastopol', and they caught the Germans by surprise. Although some of the Soviet attackers were ferried in small craft across the Kerch' Straits, others had to make a 130-mile crossing west to Feodosiia, in difficult winter weather conditions. Three days after the initial Christmas Day landings, two cruisers and three destroyers put a landing party ashore in Feodosiia, and within a few days this lodgement had expanded to 40,000 personnel in two armies. Stalin extended his personal congratulations to the victorious commanders. Hitler meanwhile court-martialled General Sponeck, the commander of the German corps which gave way before the Russian advance. Later – in the different political atmosphere of 1944 – Sponeck would be executed.[49]

The landings at Feodosiia and Kerch' broke off Manstein's first assault on the Sevastopol' fortress, which had begun in mid-December 1941. The Crimea had been one of the few areas on the Eastern Front where the Wehrmacht had kept the initiative in December 1941. In other respects the initial promise of Kozlov's Kerch'–Feodosiia operation was not fulfilled. On 2 January 1942 the Stavka had approved an ambitious operation to recapture the whole of the Crimea. This was to be mounted in the middle of the month. As Kozlov put it, 'The idea of the operation: with a blow by a mobile motor-mechanized group in the direction of Perekop to completely encircle and isolate enemy units in the Crimea from the Tauride region [north of Perekop] … with a simultaneous offensive against Simferopol' and along the coast of the Black Sea'. Perekop itself was to be seized by a parachute drop.[50] Stalin urged that the attack be launched on schedule, but severe weather delayed the build-up of forces. Kozlov failed to consolidate the territory he had gained, partly because he underestimated the Germans and partly because he was preparing his grand offensive. At the end of January 1942, under the pressure of Manstein's counter-attacks to the east, the Soviets had to abandon Feodosiia and withdrew further east into the Kerch' Peninsula, back to the ancient 'Turkish wall'.

Moscow, meanwhile, still attached great importance to the Crimea, and to Red Army offensive action there (and elsewhere). At the end of January, the Kerch' forces, Sevastopol' and the Black Sea Fleet, were joined together as the Crimean Army Group, under Kozlov's command. Four days later Kozlov prepared orders to retake Feodosiia and relieve the pressure on Sevastopol'. Much blame for this stage of the Crimean tragedy is heaped on Lazar' Mekhlis, who arrived on the scene in February 1942, assigned as Stavka representative to the Crimean Army Group. Mekhlis headed the Main Political Administration of the Red Army and since the 1930s had been one of Stalin's key agents (or hatchet men). Many leading party officials were assigned to front-line formations as 'members of the Military Council' (i.e. senior commissars). Most seem to have worked reasonably well with the line commanders, even in 1941–2. Mekhlis proved unable to work effectively with General Kozlov. This may have been because of his abrasive personality, his position as 'Stavka representative' (rather than as commissar) or the difficulty of the tasks Stalin had set him. In any event Mekhlis sacked Kozlov's able chief of staff, General Tolbukhin; in 1944 as commander of the 3rd Ukrainian Army Group, Tolbukhin would lead the re-capture of the Crimea. Jewish commissar Mekhlis is a bête noire of Russian memoirists and military historians, partly because he had been deeply involved in the 1937–8 Red Army purge.[51]

Many Soviet troops and much equipment were eventually brought into the Kerch' Peninsula via a road laid across the frozen Kerch' Straits in January–February 1942. By May 1942, the main force of the Crimean Army Group in the Kerch' Peninsula had grown to three infantry armies, with 21 divisions, 260,000 men and 350 tanks. Under Mekhlis's prompting, Kozlov's offensive had finally begun on 27 February, but it made little progress, and neither did attacks launched in mid-March and mid-April. Preoccupied with planning the attack, Mekhlis had forbidden digging trenches. On the German side, Manstein received his first armoured unit. Even more important, he was from April given massive air support in the form of General Richtofen's 8th Air Corps from the German Army Group Centre area. Richtofen's formation, along with other air units, enabled the Luftwaffe to keep air superiority, carry out devastatingly effective ground support missions, and block the Russian naval supply routes into the Kerch' Peninsula – and later into Sevastopol' itself. On 8 May 1942 (four days before the Soviet Khar'kov offensive began – see below), Manstein finally went over to a decisive attack against the Kerch' group in Operation BUSTARD HUNT (TRAPPENJAGD). The Russians' command, control and communications were paralysed by air strikes, and their forces out-manoeuvred.[52] The tension between Kozlov and Mekhlis compounded the problem. Stalin had to send a signal to Kozlov on 15 May: 'You command the army group, and not Mekhlis. Mekhlis must help you. If he does not help let me know.'[53] In less than a week, Kozlov had abandoned the line of the Turkish wall, fallen back to Kerch', and begun evacuating across the straits to the Kuban' those forces that had not already been trapped. All of the eastern Crimea now fell into enemy hands. It was one of the greatest Soviet defeats of the war. The Russians recorded a loss here of 162,000 personnel in the middle two weeks of May. This was a debacle nearly comparable to that in the Battle of Khar'kov, which was being fought and lost at the same moment. The Germans claimed to have captured 170,000 prisoners, 1,100 guns and 260 tanks. Marshal Zhukov thought Kozlov's performance very poor: 'Having at his disposal twenty-one divisions and reinforcements, the army group command was not able to organize a firm defence of the Kerch' region.'[54]

Manstein's decisive victory in the Kerch' Peninsula now left him free to besiege Sevastopol', with no danger to his rear. The Sevastopol' fortress area was about 16 miles from east to west, and 14 from north to south. It was held by General Petrov's Coastal (*Primorskaia*) Army, with 7 divisions and 106,000 men. The defenders' supply line was now a long 240-mile sea crossing to Novorossiisk. Manstein, meanwhile, had by now been given some 600 guns, including super-heavy siege artillery of 420mm, 530mm, and even 800mm, the largest concentration of German artillery in the Second World War. The 8th Air Corps kept control of the skies. Manstein's final attack began on 7 June and lasted for nearly a month, until 4 July. Eventually, the defenders ran out of ammunition. Only a few escaped in the last days, although these included, on the Stavka's orders, Petrov and senior officers; they were brought out by aircraft or submarine. The Germans took another 95,000 prisoners.[55] General Petrov would go on to hold senior commands in 1943–5. Mekhlis, the Stavka representative, was removed from his post of head of the Main Political Administration of the Red Army (and also from that of Deputy People's Commissar of Defence). He spent the rest of his – very active – war career as an army group commissar and kept his place on the party's Organization Bureau (Orgburo). Manstein himself was promoted to field marshal on 2 July 1942, after the fortress of Sevastopol' had fallen.

Manstein needed seven months to take Sevastopol', and perhaps his troops could have been better used elsewhere.[56] But the campaign was certainly catastrophic for the Russians. The Crimea turned out to be a sinkhole into which the Stavka threw masses of personnel and equipment. Some 150,000 Soviet personnel were lost in the course of the nine-month siege of Sevastopol' itself, perhaps a third of them as POWs. The relief attempts, on the Kerch' side of the peninsula, were much more expensive, costing nearly 240,000 troops from the first landing in December 1941 to the disaster of May 1942.[57] These forgotten losses would cost the Red Army dear over the next few months, during the campaigns in the Donbass, in the North Caucasus and at Stalingrad.

THE BATTLE OF KHAR'KOV

Stalin's grand strategy

The Stavka considered its overall strategy twice before the summer of 1942. The first time was in early January, when Stalin put forward the concept of wearing down German resistance during the rest of winter. The second time was in March, when the Stavka considered operations for the period after the spring *rasputitsa*. Again, Stalin led the discussion. He had publicly committed himself to a decisive and successful offensive in his late February Red Army Day speech:

> The day is not far when the Red Army with mighty blows will throw the brutal enemies from Leningrad, will clean them out of the towns and villages of Belorussia and the Ukraine, of Lithuania and Latvia, of Estonia and Karelia, and will free the Soviet Crimea, and in the whole Soviet land red banners will again wave victoriously.

Privately, Stalin also had worries about losing the initiative. As he put it to Zhukov, 'We can't sit on the defensive with our arms folded and wait for the Germans to get in the first blow!'[58]

The Stavka's decision in March was to continue with a range of local offensive actions. Zhukov maintained that he himself had again opposed the dispersal of effort. He recalled that Shaposhnikov shared his views, but the elderly Marshal was still not prepared to argue with Stalin.[59] We have already seen some of the results of the decisions made that March: local offensives on the Volkhov, around Demiansk, towards Viaz'ma and Rzhev, towards Briansk and Orel, and into the Crimea. The Stavka's most important decision, in retrospect, was to support a local offensive to recapture the region north and west of the Donbass, with the main objective being Khar'kov. The eastern Ukrainian city was held by General Paulus's German 6th Army. This operation had evidently grown out of proposals made by Marshal Timoshenko and the local commanders in the Southwestern Theatre, and they had a strong presence at the late March 1942 Stavka meeting, including Timoshenko, General Bagramian and Nikita Khrushchev; Khrushchev, the future leader of the USSR, was at that time Timoshenko's commissar. Zhukov was very unhappy about this plan, as it conflicted with his own preference to consolidate the position in front of Moscow.

The initial version of the Southwestern Theatre plan was extremely ambitious. It involved a general offensive to go beyond the line of the Dnepr, from Gomel' in Belorussia to Nikolaev on the Black Sea – a line the Red Army would not reach until the spring of 1944. After objections by Shaposhnikov and the General Staff, this was scaled down to an attack on Khar'kov. The planning had thus become muddled, with Stalin accepting Timoshenko's proposals for an offensive, and at the same time agreeing with Shaposhnikov about the need to regroup. Vasilevskii later recalled this to have been 'a decision to defend and attack at the same time'.[60]

The Khar'kov plan

The background to the Battle of Khar'kov lay in the events of the previous winter.[61] The first check to Hitler's Operation BARBAROSSA had been at the southern city of Rostov in November 1941. Two months later the forces of the Soviet Southwestern Theatre had attempted another ambitious operation to cut off the German 1st Panzer Army (Kleist) on the lower Don River. The Southern Army Group was tasked in January 1942 with cutting off the German 17th Army and 1st Panzer Army, by driving behind them to the Sea of Azov. In January 1942 Marshal Timoshenko, reinforced with several hundred new tanks, mounted an ambitious deep advance west across the middle Donets River and on towards Barvenkovo and Lozovaia, towns about halfway between Khar'kov and Stalino. This Soviet thrust did not reach its final objective of Lozovaia but it did gain much ground, and it was one of the two deep and (relatively) lasting successes of Stalin's winter offensive (the other was the Toropets salient, hacked out by the 3rd and 4th Shock Armies northwest of Moscow). The southern operation created the Barvenkovo salient, around a little town 80 miles southeast of Khar'kov; German sources often referred to this sector as the Izium salient after the nearby town on the Donets River. The Barvenkovo salient was about 60 miles wide and 60 miles deep (roughly a quarter the size of the Kursk bulge of 1943). (See Map 4.)

The Barvenkovo salient played a critical part in Timoshenko's plan to attack Khar'kov. Khar'kov was certainly an important political, economic and strategic objective. Before much of its industry and population were evacuated to the east, Khar'kov had been the fourth biggest city in the USSR (population of 840,000) and the largest industrial centre in the Ukraine. The Khar'kov Tractor Works had been the home of the Russian tank industry; the T-34 was developed there. Strategically, too, Khar'kov was important. If the Red Army could capture the city it would shorten the front line between the Southwestern and Briansk Army Groups and reduce the vulnerability of the Barvenkovo salient. Politically, the capture of Khar'kov would begin the liberation of the Ukraine.

Timoshenko's plan involved a pincer attack, mounted by the Southwestern Army Group. On 12 May 1942 three Soviet infantry armies attacked towards Khar'kov from the east. At the same time the Russian 6th Army (General Gorodnianskii), with a concentration of tanks, attacked from the south, out of the Barvenkovo salient. The Soviet offensive plan, as watered down by the Stavka, was not really all that daring. One Russian force started from 25 miles east of Khar'kov and another about 35 miles to the south. All the same, Timoshenko's attacks made less progress than had initially been hoped for. Much worse, and for the Russians a complete surprise, the Germans on 17 May quickly put into effect an already-prepared plan called FRIDERICUS; this was for an attack by 'Army Group/Detachment Kleist' (Kleist's own 1st Panzer Army and Hoth/ Salmuth's 17th Army). This German offensive from the south was mounted against the neck of the Barvenkovo salient, in the sector of Malinovskii's Southern Army Group. The Soviet 6th Army striking forces were forced to reverse direction to meet the new German threat, and this then turned into a desperate Soviet move east to scramble out of the trap. The Russians did not succeed. Supported by an attack from the German 6th Army of General Paulus in the north, the enemy on 23 May choked off the 50-mile neck of the Barvenkovo salient. Many Russian units were trapped here, including the striking force which had been trying to take Khar'kov from the south. By 29 May, two and a half weeks after it began, the Battle of Khar'kov had ended in overwhelming Russian defeat. It was a catastrophe on the same scale as 1941. Some 18–20 Russian divisions were destroyed. The recorded Russian losses were 171,000 personnel, but the Germans claimed to have captured 239,000 prisoners, and captured or destroyed 1,200 armoured vehicles and 2,000 guns.[62] Among those killed were Gorodnianskii and Podlas, who had commanded the 6th and the 57th Armies. Another victim was General Kostenko, Timoshenko's deputy, who had been sent in to take command of the forces in the Barvenkovo pocket.

The reasons for the Soviet failure

The first Battle of Khar'kov later aroused in Russia a major historical controversy. As we have seen, Nikita Khrushchev, in 1957–64 the dominant political figure in the USSR, was in 1942 the 'political member' (i.e. commissar) of the Military Council of the Southwestern Theatre. In his famous 'Secret Speech' of 1956 denouncing Stalin, Khrushchev went into detail about the Soviet dictator's personal responsibility for the Khar'kov disaster, especially for not allowing the Russian 6th Army to pull back out of the Barvenkovo pocket in time.[63] Other senior generals – successful marshals later in the war or after it – became enmeshed in the debate. General Bagramian had been Timoshenko's chief of staff and planner. General Moskalenko had been unable to develop his 38th Army's attack on Khar'kov. General Malinovskii, commander of Southern Army Group, was accused of having done too little to hinder Kleist's southern attack. And from the 'centre', Zhukov and Vasilevskii were eager to exonerate themselves.

The situation may have been complicated by the illness of Shaposhnikov, the Chief of the General Staff, and his replacement at the end of April by General Vasilevskii (the head of the Operations Section). Vasilevskii at that time had less influence with Stalin. But Marshal Timoshenko was most to blame for the fiasco. He was commander of the Soviet Southwestern Theatre and at the same time commander of one of its constituent formations, the Southwestern Army Group. (The other elements of the Southwestern Theatre were Golikov's Briansk Army Group and Malinovskii's Southern Army Group.) Timoshenko was in charge of planning and implementing the ill-fated Khar'kov operation. He, more than anyone else, was responsible for the fatal delay in moving from offensive to defensive and for the delay in pulling the Red Army out of the Barvenkovo trap.

More general reasons existed for the Soviet failure. There were problems co-ordinating the operations and intelligence of the Southwestern and Southern Army Groups, although both were under Timoshenko's Southwestern Theatre. The most thorough analysis of the battle confirms that the Germans did not have any numerical advantage in personnel or equipment, either on the front as a whole or in the Khar'kov sector.[64] There was an element of Soviet bad luck in that the Germans were already planning an operation (FRIDERICUS) at the crucial point and time. Russian intelligence, as in 1941, did not accurately forecast German strategic intentions. The evidence suggests that the Stavka was expecting the main German effort to come in the central theatre, and to be directed against Moscow. This expectation was the result partly of the Stavka's inherent priorities and partly of a successful German deception plan code-named KREML. For this and other reasons, the Russians underestimated both the number and capabilities of German formations in the southern part of the front and did not build up reserves here.[65] The Soviet reserves that were accumulated went further north to protect the southern approaches to Moscow.

At the operational level the Battle of Khar'kov showed the Red Army's command weaknesses. The Russians had been able to assemble for the Khar'kov offensive armour in greater strength than at any time since June–July 1941. There were 925 tanks in the Southwestern Army Group (and another 209 in the Southern Army Group area), compared to only 774 tanks available in front of Moscow in early December 1941. The Russians also fielded large tank formations again, the 21st and 23rd Tank Corps with, all together, 269 machines; the Russian 6th Army also had four independent tank brigades. The two tank corps had only been formed from independent brigades in April 1942. The original Soviet offensive developed at too slow a pace, and the Red Army's ponderous response to the German counter-attack showed that the Russians still had a great deal to learn about the use of armour.

The superior air power of the Luftwaffe was a very important element in allowing the Germans to master the situation. Despite the deployment of 656 Russian aircraft, the Luftwaffe's 4th Air Corps achieved superiority over the Khar'kov battlefield on the second day of the Russian offensive. The open steppe gave little cover for the Red Army. Air power could be applied by the Germans quickly to any part of the front. It was instrumental in the paralysis of the communications and mobility of the Russian units defending the southern side of the Barvenkovo salient.

And in general – as elsewhere – the quality of Russian forces had not recovered after the losses of first-line strength in 1941, despite the breathing space of a few months in the winter of 1941–2. Enemy units still had greater coherence. There were desperate battles as the victorious Germans tightened the noose around the Barvenkovo pocket, but the high number of prisoners indicates that the Red Army still had problems of troop motivation, discipline and morale.

The other side of the coin is that at Khar'kov, the Wehrmacht again demonstrated the operational and tactical skills that had led to the victories of the summer and autumn of 1941. Paulus and his 6th Army, doomed to destruction at Stalingrad seven months later, successfully held off the numerically superior Russian attack against Khar'kov. Kleist's major counter-attack through the southern side of the Barvenkovo salient, the rapid implementation, under threat, of FRIDERICUS, was an act of daring, fully supported by Hitler. It was one of the Führer's last 'correct' military decisions. The defeat at Khar'kov left a huge hole in the front, through which the German 6th Army could now advance to Stalingrad. The Germans were now in a stronger position to implement the southern offensive that they had been planning since December 1941. The only positive result for the Russians of the Khar'kov debacle was that it led Stalin and the Stavka to take a more realistic approach. It also raised the influence of the General Staff in Moscow, which had been more hesitant about the whole operation than the theatre commander. This led to more control from the centre. (Stalin had taken military advice before Khar'kov from Timoshenko.)

CONCLUSION

When the German drive on Moscow was stopped in December 1941, and as the Wehrmacht was driven back in the snow, the Soviet high command had hopes for a complete reversal of the campaign. There seemed a parallel with the Napoleonic campaign of 1812. At the start of the new year both Hitler and Stalin thought deeply about the overall war situation. As Army Group Centre looked in danger of being outflanked and overrun in late January, Hitler told his intimates that Germany might fail but that then the German people would deserve their fate: 'If the German people lost its faith, if the German people were no longer inclined to give itself body and soul in order to survive – then the German people would have nothing to do but disappear.' Stalin's public perception, four weeks later, was uncannily similar, but based on the hope that the Führer's position had been fundamentally weakened by the Moscow debacle: 'The Hitlers come and go, but the German people, and the German state, they remain.'[66] Stalin appealed to the German people, and hopefully to disgruntled German elites, over the Führer's head. Both perceptions proved premature; the rout of the Grande Armée had not been repeated.

The military casualty figures suggest a way of looking at these winter and spring 1942 battles that is different from the conventional one. Historians have paid most attention to the crisis of German Army Group Centre in January and February 1942, and the Battle of Khar'kov in May 1942. The three and a half months of fighting against German Army Group Centre from 7 January cost 270,000 Soviet troops – 150,000 in Zhukov's Western Army Group and 120,000 in Konev's Kalinin Army Group. Meretskov's offensives on the Volkhov, in front of Leningrad, were also extremely costly. If losses in the Liuban' offensive are added to those lost trying to extract the 2nd Shock Army (mainly in May and June 1942), the total is about 150,000. Also striking are losses – about 90,000 – suffered between Leningrad and Moscow, where Kurochkin's Northwestern Army Group tried to eliminate the Demiansk pocket and break out to the west at Staraia Russa. The Red Army suffered especially devastating losses in the Crimea. The relief operation in the eastern part of the peninsula through May 1942 cost about 240,000 soldiers – leaving aside the fate of the garrison of Sevastopol' itself. The Crimea was, in terms of Soviet losses, much costlier than the Khar'kov battle and on the same scale as the Moscow offensive. In terms of human cost, the Battle of Khar'kov, coming at the end of the period, was actually rather less expensive, at 170,000, although it swallowed up more new equipment, especially new armoured formations.[67]

Russian figures give total Red Army losses from January to March 1942 as 620,000; from April to June they were 780,000.[68] As for the Germans, the desperate winter defence of forward German positions, which Hitler insisted upon, did not cause unprecedented losses. German deaths on the Eastern Front have been estimated as 48,000 in January 1942; they were 44,000 in both February and March 1942, before dropping to 23,000 in April, 16,000 in May and 13,000 in June. Total German losses came to 188,000, on the face of it *one-seventh* of Soviet ones.[69] Stalin's January 1942 strategy of wearing down German reserves before the spring did not work. As Hitler himself prophetically put it in mid-March 1942, 'History will in the next few months show whether the [wastage] of hecatombs of Russian lives in this battle was militarily a correct or a false decision.'[70]

For these huge losses the Red Army regained little territory. Stalin in November 1942 said that if only there had been a 'second front' in Western Europe, the Red Army would stand not where it did now, 'but somewhere around Pskov, Minsk, Zhitomir, Odessa. It would mean that even in the summer of this year the German-fascist army would have stood on the brink of catastrophe.' In fact, however, on much of the front the Germans were able to hold on to the territory they had reached in early December 1941. Even at Rostov and Moscow they had only had to fall back 50 to 150 miles. They were still very deep in Soviet territory. In the north and centre they would hold this line until late 1943. In the south they would make great advances further east, to Stalingrad and the North Caucasus.

Stalin has received much of the blame for the wastage of troops and matériel and the lack of territorial gains. The Russians faced in the winter of 1941–2 the same dilemmas and strategic confusion that Hitler and his generals had faced during Operation BARBAROSSA. Twice, in January and March 1942, Stalin and the Stavka decided to encourage general offensives that in the end proved to be both too costly and too thinly spread. The Red Army could not be strong everywhere, and decisions should have been made about concentrating on only part of the front. From hindsight it would probably have been wiser for the Red Army to have concentrated even greater forces for the attack on German Army Group Centre. Given Hitler's stand-fast order the Germans would have been particularly vulnerable there.

However, due to the failures of the Soviet armies in 1941, Stalin and the Stavka had unenviable and extremely difficult choices to make. Besieged centres of Soviet strength, at Leningrad and Sevastopol', gave an incentive to commit forces *immediately* to the northern and southern flanks. A failure to act at once might doom those besieged centres. There was also a rational Soviet desire to regain the economic resources of the eastern Ukraine and to block any further German access to the Caucasus; indeed, that was where the main German threat would come in 1942, in the form of Operation BLUE. As for the central theatre, Zhukov made much of this in his writings. Like any field commander, he had a personal interest in the reinforcement of his own armies. Taking the Stavka's point of view, and looking at the front as a whole, the central sector was less promising. An advance to the west – to Smolensk – offered the Red Army relatively few short-term rewards, other than a straightening out of the line. The Red Army lacked the mobile forces that would have been required to encircle and destroy Army Group Centre. In any event, the terrain here was not very suitable for offensive tank warfare – compared to the open steppe further south. With hindsight, we know that the Red Army would have very long and difficult battles to fight in 1942, 1943 and 1944 in this central theatre, and would only show great progress with Operation BAGRATION in Belorussia in June 1944.

Stalin was also criticized for too offensive a strategy. This bore similarities to Hitler's strategy in 1941, and was likewise based on an underestimation of enemy resources and perhaps an overestimation of Russian ones. But the Germans did seem to be particularly exposed in December 1941 and January 1942. In reality, the Red Army was still a very weak instrument in the winter of 1941–2, manned by untrained conscripts and poorly equipped. In January 1942 the whole Red Army had only 600 heavy tanks and 800 medium tanks, plus 6,300 light tanks; in contrast, the figure for January 1943 would be 2,000 heavies, no fewer than 7,600 mediums and 11,000 lights. The relative figures for artillery to equip the new rifle divisions were similar, only 18,900 field guns in January 1942, compared to 36,700 in January 1943.[71]

Hitler came out better from these winter battles than Stalin did, at least within his own short-range terms. The 'stand-fast' policy saved his Eastern Front. Ironically, the disaster at Moscow probably enhanced in the short term his reputation (and his self-estimation) as a war leader, although in a different way from the 1940 campaign in France. He could claim to have saved the German Army from its own errors. There was a degree of truth in this, as the foolhardy exposure of Army Group Centre (and the related intelligence and supply failures) had been as much the responsibility of the German Army high command as it had been that of the Führer. Of course, Russian stand-fast orders had led to disasters for the Red Army – especially at Kiev in September 1941 – and for the Germans such a tactic would create disasters in the winter of 1942–3 and later. Hitler's tactic worked in the winter of 1941–2; this was partly because the weather aided the German defence and made Russian movement difficult, and partly because the Russians had been bled white in the battles of the first summer and autumn of the war. The tactic would not work in the winter of 1942–3.

CHAPTER 6
MOSCOW, STALINGRAD, LENINGRAD, JUNE 1942 TO JANUARY 1943

Not a step backwards! This must now be our main slogan. It is necessary steadfastly, to the last drop of blood, to defend each position, each metre of Soviet territory, to hold every patch of Soviet soil, and to hold it as long as possible.

Joseph Stalin, Order No. 227, 28 July 1942

The day is not far away when the enemy will know the strength of the new blows of the Red Army. *Budet i na nashei ulitse prazdnik!* [We too will have something to celebrate!]

Joseph Stalin, 7 November 1942

To think that I will come back here again [to Stalingrad] next time is madness. … We won't come back here, so we cannot leave. Also too much blood has been shed to do that.

Adolf Hitler, 12 December 1942

After the crisis in front of Moscow during the winter of 1941–2, it was quite remarkable that Hitler and the Wehrmacht were able to grasp the initiative again. The year 1942, however, was far from a simple repeat of 1941. Hitler's Directive No. 41 of 5 April 1942 was the equivalent of his BARBAROSSA directive (of 18 December 1940), but it showed more limited – and realistic – aims. The BARBAROSSA goal had been 'to crush Soviet Russia in a rapid campaign'. The goal of Directive No. 41 was 'definitively to destroy any military strength remaining to the Soviets and as far as possible to deprive them of the most important sources of strength of their war economy [*kriegswirtschaftlichen Kraft quellen*]'. The geographical objectives of the 1942 campaign were also more restricted than those of 1941:

> In pursuit of the original plan for the Eastern campaign, the armies of the Central sector will stand fast, those in the North will capture Leningrad and link up with the Finns, while those on the southern flank will break through into the Caucasus.
>
> In view of conditions prevailing at the end of the winter, the availability of troops and resources, and transport problems, these aims can be achieved only one at a time.

First, therefore, all available strength will be concentrated on the *main operations in the Southern sector*.[1]

Stalin and the Stavka had their own expectations of how the campaign of 1942 would develop, even after the disaster of the Khar'kov offensive in May. There were operations all along the front in the second half of 1942. Even in terms of the battles in the south, the street fighting in Stalingrad would be only a small part of the picture. The Red Army suffered huge losses in the summer and early autumn of 1942, even before the Battle of Stalingrad began.

The fighting on the other land fronts in Europe was still on a relatively small scale. The British and Canadians did mount a division-sized 'raid' on the port of Dieppe on 19 August, at about the time that the German 6th Army was approaching the outskirts of Stalingrad. Moscow had, however, already been told there would be no cross-Channel invasion of France in 1942. Meanwhile, in North Africa Rommel's Axis forces inflicted a serious defeat on the British, pushing them back well beyond the Egyptian frontier. Only at the very end of the 1942, in November, would the Germans have really serious problems to worry about in Africa, with Rommel's defeat at Alamein and the British–American landings in Morocco and Tunisia.

DEFENDING MOSCOW

Stalin's fears

Hitler may have intended the central sector only to 'stand fast'. All the same, the Stalingrad epic can only be understood against the background of the Soviet high command's concerns about the central part of the front, 700 miles to the north, in front of Moscow. The Red Army mounted two major offensives here, one in July–August 1942 (the first 'Rzhev–Sychevka operation'), and the other in November–December 1942 (Operation MARS). The Stavka also tried to wear down strategic German salients at Demiansk and Velikie Luki. At the end of winter of 1942–3 the German position finally cracked, but only after the Russian victory at Stalingrad. Even then, the Germans were able to carry out a controlled withdrawal.[2]

For Stalin and the Stavka the greatest potential threat was to Moscow. The main German blows had in the end been directed there in late 1941. The centre of Moscow was still only 100 miles from the most forward enemy positions. The Germans encouraged this fear and, as already mentioned, they created a deception plan, KREML, about an offensive against Moscow. The plan was put in place at the end of May (a month before 28 June, when the real offensive began in the south). It is not clear how far KREML affected Soviet deployments. Meanwhile, the Stavka had also long been interested in the central sector as a place to mount a decisive offensive. The greatest successes of the Red Army had been achieved against the Germans here in the winter of 1941–2, and the positions the Wehrmacht withdrew to were still ragged and apparently vulnerable. Here it was, too, that the most important German force could be trapped; the destruction of Army Group Centre would also open the shortest route to the Reich.

There is no doubt that Stalin continued to attach great importance to the forces in the central sector in front of Moscow. He made this clear in a public speech of 7 November 1942 (when Stalingrad was under serious German threat, but when the Soviet operation to encircle the German 6th Army was in its final stages of preparation). 'The main aim of the Germans' summer offensive', Stalin said, 'was to encircle Moscow and end the war in this year.' He argued that the main area of German strategic interest was not the Caucasus but Moscow, and that Hitler's intention was to swing around Moscow from the south.

This emphasis on Moscow was not just rhetoric. General Zhukov, Stalin's key commander and the victor of the 1941 Battle of Moscow, remained the commander of the Western Army Group until late August 1942 (when he was replaced by Konev). Zhukov would return to the central part of the front in early November 1942 and remain there through most of the winter of 1942–3. The deployment of Red Army reinforcements across the whole of the year 1942 showed a concentration on the central theatre defending Moscow: the Briansk, Western and Kalinin Army Groups were sent some 3,435,000 reinforcements from outside. This can be compared to 3,260,000 reinforcements sent in 1942 to the southern part of the front (extending south from the Voronezh Army Group to the Stalingrad Army Group). In addition, some 630,000 reinforcements were sent to the Caucasus/Transcaucasus Army Group and 1,505,000 to the forces facing German Army Group North.[3] On 19 November 1942, the moment the Stalingrad counter-offensive began, Soviet forces in the central theatre numbered 2,530,000 men, compared to 1,100,000 in the south. Equipment was also concentrated in the centre, 4,260 tanks (compared to 1,463) and 1,400 aircraft (930).[4]

On the other side of the line, two of the outstanding German field commanders were active in this central sector. Field Marshal Günther Kluge commanded Army Group Centre, while the very able General Walter Model commanded Kluge's key 9th Army, in the Rzhev–Viaz'ma salient in front of Moscow. In the second half of 1942, Kluge and Model successfully dealt with the kinds of Soviet challenges that would destroy General Paulus at Stalingrad.

Stalemate in the centre

The central theatre of the Eastern Front began south of Lake Il'men, and the line of the front now ran to just south of the German-held town of Orel, a distance of 400–450 miles as the crow flies (see Map 4). The situation in the northern part of this central theatre was much as it had been when the fighting stopped in the winter of 1941–2, with static fronts interlocked like the pieces of a giant jigsaw puzzle. The terrain of the pre-war Novgorod, Velikie Luki, Smolensk, Kalinin and Kaluga Regions was more heavily forested than in the south of European Russia, and both sides now had time to build defences in depth there: log-lined blockhouses and artillery positions, trench systems, and so on. Overall, the nature of the fighting here bore a closer relationship to the trench fighting of the First World War, than it did to the Blitzkrieg notions of Hitler's war or to Soviet 'deep battle'. This was true both of the physical appearance of the battlefield and the results of combat – small progress achieved at enormous human cost.

Two big salients, locked together, dominated the position. The first was held by the Red Army and centred on the small town of Toropets; this salient was about 200 miles deep and 250 wide. No fewer than eight armies of the Kalinin Army Group were crowded into it. Bordering the Soviet Toropets salient, to the southeast, was a German one, the similarly sized Rzhev–Viaz'ma salient. Armies in the two salients had the potential to encircle and destroy each other. The German Rzhev–Viaz'ma salient was vulnerable to being partially or fully crushed by Soviet forces advancing from either side, from the Kalinin Army Group (in the Toropets salient) to the west and from the Western Army Group (in front of Moscow) to the east. The Germans, meanwhile, held a strong position on the western rim of the Soviet Toropets salient, at Velikie Luki; here they blocked a Soviet breakout to the west. The Wehrmacht also held a smaller but deep salient around Demiansk (between the Toropets salient and Lake Il'men). From Demiansk they threatened, together with the German forces in the Rzhev–Viaz'ma salient, to decapitate the Russian Toropets salient, or at least to cut its main supply railway (at Ostashkov).

The southern part of the central front was different. The battle line from the Rzhev–Viaz'ma salient to the latitude of Kursk and Voronezh was 350 miles long and much less convoluted. It covered the southwestern approaches to Moscow. This was the route from the Briansk–Orel area to Tula, the direction along which Guderian had taken his 2nd Panzer Group in 1941. This relatively open unwooded country of Orel, Tula and Voronezh Regions seemed particularly vulnerable to another panzer attack from the three German armies here, the 4th, 2nd Panzer and 2nd. This sector was also important to the Soviets as a possible route for their own offensive against German Army Group Centre. (It would become just such a route in July–August 1943, after the Battle of Kursk. In Operation KUTUZOV Soviet forces smashed through the German lines here to take Orel.) In the summer of 1942 the Soviet forces deployed here were the three left-flank armies of the Western Army Group and the three armies of the Briansk Army Group, but this force made little progress. As it turned out, there would be less movement here than at Rzhev–Viaz'ma or Stalingrad.

On the German side the central theatre was mostly the operational responsibility of Field Marshal Kluge's Army Group Centre; the left wing (north of Velikie Luki and including Demiansk and Kholm) came under Army Group North's right-flank army (the 16th). Kluge had at his disposal (running north to south) four armies, the 3rd Panzer, 9th (in the Rzhev–Viaz'ma salient), 4th and 2nd Panzer. The 'panzer' armies – a legacy of two of the 1941 BARBAROSSA panzer groups – were now tank formations in name only, and they lacked equipment and potential for rapid movement. Facing the Germans were four Soviet army groups, the Briansk, Western, Kalinin (in the Toropets salient) and Northwestern. The best known of the Soviet generals was Konev, commanding the Kalinin Army Group.

Throughout the summer and autumn of 1942, German Army Group Centre suffered from a lack of troops and equipment, as priority was given to the army groups operating against Stalingrad and the Caucasus. German divisions were sent south from April to June 1942. Individual formations were less fully manned and equipped than those in the south. Unlike the situation further south, there were virtually no troops from the German allies involved in the Army Group Centre theatre. Army Group Centre also received little support from the Luftwaffe, the bulk of air strength having been concentrated on the *Schwerpunkt* in the south. Kluge did not even have a full Luftwaffe Air Fleet in support of his Army Group until May 1943.

A key Soviet objective in the summer of 1942 was the railway from Viaz'ma north to the town of Rzhev (pronounced Rzh*y*ov) on the upper Volga River, with the small town of Sychevka (Sych*y*ovka) – headquarters of General Model's 9th Army – between them. The armies of the Soviet Kalinin and Western Army Groups mounted a series of offensives here over the summer, and this was the focus of General Zhukov's attention until mid-August. The Red Army's Rzhev–Sychevka offensive in August 1942 made some progress, crushing in the east side of the German Rzhev–Viaz'ma salient but failing to take Rzhev or Sychevka or even to cut the railway. The German 9th Army had, however, been on the brink of defeat. Hitler, on General Model's insistence, committed strong tank reinforcements to hold Rzhev. Red Army attacks in the Rzhev–Viaz'ma salient petered out in late September and early October 1942 with the *rasputitsa*.

In the middle of November, just as the Stalingrad counter-offensive was beginning, Zhukov came back to the central front to co-ordinate the operations of the Kalinin and Western Army Groups, in the offensive called Operation MARS. Zhukov later maintained that this new Rzhev offensive was designed to prevent the Germans from sending reserves to the south. Another plausible explanation is that the Stavka gave this operation as much attention as the one in the south, at Stalingrad. Zhukov was a great adherent of seizing the strategic initiative. The operations around Stalingrad could be seen, in contrast, only as a response to a German attack. In the centre the Red Army would be dictating the terms. The November 1942 Soviet MARS offensive repeated the Rzhev–Sychevka offensive of August 1942, but this time the attack came from both sides of the northern part of the Rzhev–Viaz'ma salient, from the west (General M. A. Purkaev's Kalinin Army Group) and the east (Konev's Western Army Group).

Operation MARS has been called 'Zhukov's greatest defeat'.[5] The Soviet operation had been originally scheduled for October 1942 but was evidently delayed by the *rasputitsa*. When it actually came, on 25 November (six days after the Stalingrad counter-attack), the Germans had brought up armoured reserves (five panzer divisions were employed), and they parried or even pinched off the four local Soviet advances. Unlike the August–September 1942 Rzhev–Sychevka attack, Operation MARS gained no ground; it cost more Soviet lives – at least 70,000 men. There is speculation that an even larger Soviet attack was in the offing, Operation JUPITER (IUPITER). In the south, Soviet Operation SATURN (the trapping of all of Army Group 'A' and 'B' west of Rostov) was a larger version of Operation URANUS (encircling the 6th Army at Stalingrad). So JUPITER (destroying a large part of Army Group Centre) was perhaps an enlarged version of MARS, taking in the capture of Viaz'ma.[6] The failure (at an operational level) of MARS – the Stavka wound it up in mid-December – made a further development of the offensive in the centre – JUPITER or whatever – impossible.

Operation MARS did play an important role in overall Soviet strategy at the end of 1942, as it restricted the forces the Germans could move to the southern theatre. It also tied up Red Army troops that might have been used elsewhere. The attack eventually helped convince Hitler to agree to make a planned withdrawal of forces from the exposed positions in the central theatre. On balance, MARS was probably an expensive failure for the Red Army. It was certainly a remarkable 'blank space' in the Soviet history of the war. Zhukov's presence as Stavka representative (and his absence from the Stalingrad front) indicates the importance of the operation. The failure of MARS presumably contributed to the temporary eclipse of General Konev. He was later removed as commander of Western Army Group in February 1943 as 'not up to the duties of an army group commander'.[7]

Another Soviet setback in the centre, although not one on the scale of Operation MARS, was the failure of Northwestern Army Group's repeated efforts to take the exposed German strongpoint at Demiansk.[8] This place had remained in German hands through the winter of 1941–2, even when the land route to the main forces of German Army Group North was completely cut. The failure to take Demiansk in the second half of 1942 was a final nail in the coffin of Marshal Timoshenko's military reputation; he had been Stavka representative in the north, and then commander of the Northwestern Army Group. The attack on the German salient at Demiansk, which had been under pressure since November 1942, was finally abandoned; it was described in the 1998 official history as 'one of the most unsuccessful offensive operations of the ... war'.[9] The Germans then abandoned the salient in mid-February 1943, effecting a phased withdrawal to the Lovat' River, and as a result shortening and strengthening their defensive line.

The Red Army achieved one important local success on the western side of the Toropets salient, with an offensive mounted in late November 1942 by the armies of Kalinin Army Group to encircle the German strongpoint at Velikie Luki. After prolonged fighting to permit a withdrawal, the town was surrounded, and German attempts to reinforce it beaten off. Velikie Luki finally fell to the Russians in January 1943.[10]

The German Army Group Centre was in a weak position by the late winter of 1942–3, as a result of its own lack of reserves, and with the defeat suffered by German army groups on either strategic flank – the Battle of Stalingrad and the partial breaking of the Leningrad blockade. On 26 January 1943 – a few days before Paulus's surrender, but when the issue at Stalingrad was no longer in doubt – Field Marshal Kluge, commander of the army group, proposed the withdrawal from the big Rzhev–Viaz'ma salient. Shortly after the Stalingrad surrender, Hitler agreed. Operation BUFFALO (BÜFFEL) was a drastic planned retreat and straightening of the German line (reducing it from 340 to 110 miles). The operation began on 1 March 1943 and was completed by the 24th. Rzhev and Viaz'ma (and Sychevka), over which the two sides had been battling since October 1941, were finally given up by the

Ostheer. With BUFFALO ended any remaining possibility of a successful German attack on Moscow or even of a serious threat in that direction. No fewer than 190,000 Soviet civilians were moved west with the retreating German Army; many of these people were being forcibly deported as part of a German 'scorched earth' policy.[11]

HITLER'S SECOND OFFENSIVE: STALINGRAD AND THE NORTH CAUCASUS

Into the Don bend

In the middle of 1942, the Germans were deep in Soviet territory in southern Russia (see Map 5). The Red Army's offensive at Khar'kov had ended in late May 1942. The Wehrmacht now held a line running 375 miles from just beyond Kursk straight down to Taganrog on the Sea of Azov. On 28 June 1942, a year after BARBAROSSA, Germany began a second major offensive in Russia, on this southern part of the front, under the general name of Operation BLUE (BLAU).[12] Russian historians call the first stage of these vast and confused battles the 'Voronezh–Voroshilovgrad defensive operation' (28 June to 24 July 1942). The onslaught involved all German forces then available to Bock's Army Group South – the 4th Panzer, 2nd, 6th, 1st Panzer and 17th Armies, as well as the Hungarian 2nd Army. On the other side were Timoshenko's Southwestern Army Group, with five infantry armies, and Malinovskii's Southern Army Group with four. The German advance began with a battle for Voronezh, at the northern end of the Soviet line (6 July), and it ended with the fall of the key city of Rostov at the southern end (23 July). The initial attack in the north was code-named BLUE I; the drive south across the Donets River basin (Donbass) to Rostov was BLUE II (later Operation CLAUSEWITZ). Voronezh was on the upper Don, Rostov at the mouth of the river, but in between the river makes a huge bend to the east, some 300 miles at its deepest. As they began to fill in the Don bend (*izluchina Dona*), the Germans captured the Donbass, centred on Voroshilovgrad (Lugansk). This was a region that had produced 60 per cent of the USSR's coal.

The Briansk Army Group commander, General Golikov, badly parried the northern advance of the German 4th Tank Army and 6th Army to the upper Don River; he lost the important town of Voronezh (situated on the western bank of the river) at the end of the first week, on 6 July. The Stavka threw in massive reinforcements, including three reserve armies and the 5th Tank Army, removed Golikov and created a new Voronezh Army Group under General Vatutin. During heavy counter-attacks in the early weeks of July, the Russians were unable to recapture Voronezh, but they held the critical Don River line stretching hundreds of miles below the city; from here they would be able to launch the decisive counter-attack five months later, in November. In mid-July, however, German forces, now designated as Army Group 'B', continued their offensive. The Panzer spearheads drove rapidly to the southeast, with the Don and Chir rivers on their left flank, in a wide turning movement.

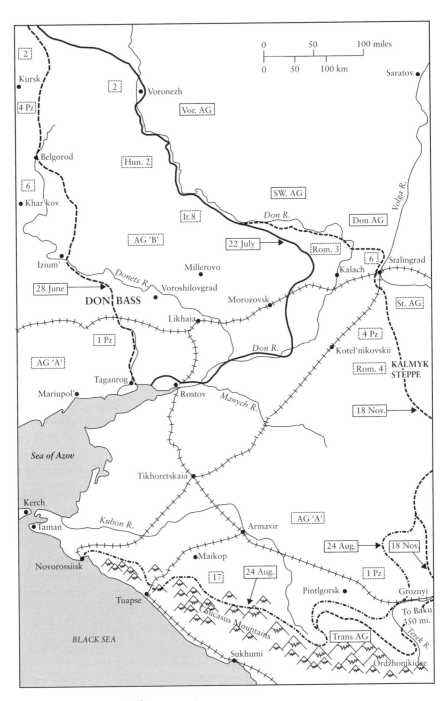

MAP 5 Hitler's second offensive, 1942.

Meanwhile, in early July the southern armies of German Army Group South, the 1st Panzer Army and 17th Army, overwhelmed Timoshenko's Southwestern Army Group and Malinovskii's Southern Army Group. Russian historians call these battles the 'Donbass defensive operation'. The fighting lasted from 7 to 24 July. In the middle of the month, with Soviet forces threatened by a big encirclement around Millerovo, the Stavka ordered a retreat south to the lower Don. The pursuing Germans were able to reach the river east of Rostov, and took the critical southern city on 24 July. The Russians had made a major effort to turn Rostov into a fortress, but it fell without a fight. The remnants of the Southern Army Group withdrew south across the Don and were incorporated into the North Caucasus Army Group. The armies of the Southwestern Army Group were largely destroyed, and the formation was reconstituted from 12 July as the Stalingrad Army Group; Timoshenko remained in command for ten days and then was replaced by General V. N. Gordov.

On 9 July German Army Group South had been divided into two new formations. In the northern sector was Army Group 'B' (originally the 2nd Army, 4th Panzer Army and 6th Army) and in the southern sector was Army Group 'A' (the 1st Panzer Army and 17th Army). After the success of early and mid-July – especially the fall of Rostov on the 23rd – the two reorganized German army groups moved in different directions. Under the terms of Hitler's Directive No. 45 of 23 July,[13] Army Group 'A' was to advance southeast across the Don and then along the north side of the Caucasus mountain range in the direction of the Caspian Sea and the oil wells and refineries of Baku. It was commanded by Field Marshal Wilhelm List. Army Group 'B' was very briefly commanded by Field Marshal Bock, until General Weichs replaced him in mid-July. Army Group 'B' was to continue east; it would be involved in the next, and better-remembered phase of the campaign, which the Russians call the 'Stalingrad strategic defensive operation'. This is dated from 17 July to 18 November, the second date being the eve of the great Soviet counter-offensive.

General Friedrich Paulus's 6th Army was to be the spearhead of Army Group 'B'. Slowed and worn down by Soviet resistance, limited by lack of fuel and other supplies, the 6th Army advanced in August towards the eastern part of the Don bend. Facing it, west of the middle Don and covering Stalingrad, was Gordov's Stalingrad Army Group, with fresh forces thrown in by the Stavka, including the new 62nd, 63rd and 64th Armies and the new 1st and 4th Tank Armies. General Eremenko was brought in to oversee operations at the start of August, effectively demoting Gordov, and by September he was in direct command of the armies of the Stalingrad Army Group.[14] In the meantime, however, after weeks of heavy fighting, German troops on 21 August forced the first major crossing of the middle Don, which was here only 40 miles from the Volga and Stalingrad. On the 23rd the 14th Panzer Corps cut a narrow corridor through to the great river just north of Stalingrad, although it was unable to take the city off the march and was soon seriously threatened by heavy counter-attacks. The breaching of the middle Don line and threat to Stalingrad caused intense alarm at the Stavka in Moscow. Three days later, on 26 August, General Zhukov was appointed Deputy Supreme C-in-C, with responsibility for the south.

Into the North Caucasus

The German march on Stalingrad was originally a secondary operation, intended to cover the conquest of the Caucasus. Hitler's grand strategic emphasis was on the capture of economic resources, and his main preoccupation in the late summer 1942 campaign in the south was not Stalingrad but the North Caucasus and the oil centres of Maikop and Groznyi. The German Army planners originally code-named the advance of the forces of Army Group 'A' into the North Caucasus Operation BLUE IV, and then Operation EDELWEISS. Russian historians call this the 'North Caucasus strategic defensive operation', and date it from 25 July to 31 December 1942.[15]

The North Caucasus was a huge and sparsely inhabited expanse of contrasting terrain – steppe, desert and mountain range. It stretched east from the Sea of Azov and the lower Don, taking in the Rostov, Krasnodar and Ordzhonikidze Regions, and the Kalmyk ASSR. The area was linked to the main part of Russia by railways to Rostov and Stalingrad, but both of these lines were soon cut by the enemy. The Soviet defenders of the North Caucasus now had to rely on new supplies brought across the Caspian from Russia or from Iran (from the Lend-Lease shipments of the Western Allies). The three Caucasian Soviet republics of Georgia, Armenia and Azerbaidzhan, with a population of about eight million, did form a southern hinterland for the theatre, south of the Caucasus Mountains. Available Soviet forces were strictly limited in the North Caucasus; even on 19 November 1942 they numbered only 820,000 men, and a mere 320 tanks and 260 aircraft.[16]

The commander of Army Group 'A', Field Marshal Wilhelm List, was experienced and talented, but new to the Russian Front. He had led armies in the Polish campaign and then in the fighting in France (where he was promoted to Field Marshal), but he really made his name with the lightning conquest of Yugoslavia and Greece in the spring of 1941. List then remained in the West until early 1942, when he was ordered to prepare a new army group headquarters for the campaign in the Caucasus. The two formations under List's command, the 17th Army (General Ruoff) and the 1st Panzer Army (General Kleist),

FIGURE 6 German tanks ford a shallow reach of the Don in the drive on Stalingrad.

made extremely rapid progress in the open steppe of the Kuban' (in the North Caucasus) in late July and August, fanning out in a 200–300-mile radius south and southeast of Rostov (see Map 1). List was weakly opposed by Marshal Budennyi's North Caucasus Army Group. In 1919–20 Budennyi had won some of his greatest Civil War victories just here in the North Caucasus against the 'White' Volunteer Army, but in 1942 he was not able to stop the German advance, and this was to be his last combat command. Budennyi was recalled to Moscow, and his forces were merged into the Transcaucasus Army Group. General I. V. Tiulenev was put in charge, with the Politburo member Lazar' Kaganovich as a member of the army group military council.

By the end of August 1942, just as Paulus and the 6th Army neared Stalingrad, the columns of the 1st Panzer Army moving southeast towards the Caspian were slowed by increasing Soviet resistance, supply problems and the weather. At the same time, List's infantry divisions reached the natural barrier of the Caucasus Mountains in the south. The Soviet 'Black Sea Group', with four infantry armies, held the mountain passes and the 40-mile coastal strip from the mountains to the sea. A German detachment scaled Elbrus, the highest mountain in the USSR, but the main forces of the German 17th Army could not break through the passes of the Caucasus to the coastal plain (to the ports of Tuapse and Sukhumi), or drive southeast down the coast from Novorossiisk. The Germans mounted a landing east across the Kerch' Straits from the Crimea in early September with the 11th Army (Operation BLÜCHER II).

For Hitler things were not moving fast enough, and in his annoyance he sacked List in September and took over 'direct' control of the army group – from his field headquarters at Vinnitsa, far away in the western Ukraine.[17] North of the Caucasus Mountains, General Kleist's 1st Panzer Army reached the outskirts of Ordzhonikidze (Vladikavkaz) at the beginning of November, but with very little momentum left. The 'Northern Group' of the Soviet Transcaucasus Army Group, with four infantry armies, made a stand along the Terek River. The German spearhead was still well short of the oil centre of Groznyi and 150 miles from the Caspian. At the end of November, with the start of the Stalingrad crisis, Kleist took over Army Group 'A' (with General Mackensen replacing him in the 1st Panzer Army). A few weeks later, at the very end of the year, Hitler allowed Kleist to pull Army Group 'A' back; the defeats suffered around Stalingrad had made its position untenable. The retreating Germans were only feebly pursued by the weak Transcaucasus Army Group. In the new year, the only remnant of Hitler's Caucasian adventure would be a bridgehead on the Taman' Peninsula, facing the Crimea on the east side of the Kerch' Strait.

The German battle for Stalingrad and the Red Army counter-attack

All this, however, lay months in the future. The operations with the greatest consequences involved the city of Stalingrad, and they were fought out from late August 1942 to January 1943.

Stalingrad stretched along the western shore of the Volga River. The town of Tsaritsyn was named after Stalin in 1925 – because he had played a part in its defence in 1918, when anti-Bolshevik cossacks had attempted to take it from the south. Tsaritsyn (the 'Red Verdun') became a symbol of Bolshevik powers of resistance, and of the martial qualities of Stalin (and of the future Marshal Voroshilov, who was another of Tsaritsyn's defenders). Stalingrad was the administrative centre of a huge agricultural region and an important industrial centre, but not one of the very largest towns in Russia; in 1939 the population was 445,000, smaller than that of Rostov. The city had been heavily developed before the war, and in 1941–2, as a 'safe' war production centre, and by August 1942 it was crowded with refugees. Stalingrad was an important communications hub, near strategic railways and pipelines, but especially important was the river. In his directives and speeches, Hitler made much of the Volga as an economic artery.

As the 6th Army's lead panzers reached the Volga on 23 August, the bombers of Richtofen's 4th Air Fleet mounted a large air raid on Stalingrad.[18] Heavy fighting soon began inside the built-up area of the city now defended by the 62nd Army, commanded from 12 September by General Chuikov. The Stalingrad Tractor Factory (the STZ, a centre of T-34 production), the Barrikada artillery factory, the Krasnyi Oktiabr' steel plant and the administrative centre of the city to the south were reduced to ruins. Stalingrad had not been evacuated in time, and many inhabitants and refugees were caught up in the fighting.

From the middle of September through October, the German infantry tried to push General Chuikov's 62nd Army out of the ruins of the city and into the Volga. Eventually, the 62nd Army's hold was reduced to bridgeheads on the steep river bank. There the defenders dug in, however, supported by Soviet reinforcements and by masses of artillery sited on the far shore of the great river.

Many accounts of the Battle of Stalingrad concentrate on the desperate house-to-house fighting between Germans and Russians in the ruined city, and ignore the large-scale fighting in the open country around the city; in reality Stalingrad was a huge battle. By mid-September 1942, Stalingrad was actually defended by two large formations, designated from the end of the month as the Stalingrad Army Group

FIGURE 7 German armour supports the last push in Stalingrad in November 1942.

(under Eremenko) and the Don Army Group (under Rokossovskii). Chuikov's 62nd Army is the most famous element of the defence, as it fought in the city itself, but it was only one of four armies in General Eremenko's Stalingrad Army Group. The 64th, the 57th (under General Tolbukhin) and the 51st Armies were positioned south of the city on the right (west) bank of the Volga. North of Stalingrad, on the Don and covering the gap between the Don and the Volga, stood three more armies (the 65th, 24th and 66th) from Rokossovskii's Don Army Group. They took part in the early attempts to break through to Stalingrad from the north, and they blocked a German advance further up the Volga.[19]

Hitler had thrust the German forces into a huge bulge, taking in both the Don bend and the North Caucasus. This position was exposed and in strategic terms extremely dangerous. In the Stalingrad direction, the cutting edge of the German divisions, fighting in the ruins of Stalingrad, was 250 miles east of Rostov; this was the German 6th Army (General Paulus) and the German–Romanian 4th Panzer Army (under the German General Hoth). The strength of the German divisions had been worn down by months of fighting, and most of them were now committed to the battle for the city and its immediate outskirts. The long flanks were covered by second-rate forces from Hitler's satellites. In the north the Don was covered by the Romanian 3rd Army (nearest Stalingrad), the Italian 8th Army and the 2nd Hungarian (both further west along the Don). On the eastern face of the Stalingrad salient, stretching far into the empty Kalmyk steppe south of the city, was the Romanian 4th Army.

On 19 November, as the winter set in, the Russians began a huge encirclement, Operation URANUS (URAN).[20] The 'Stalingrad strategic offensive operation' is dated by Russian historians from that day until 2 February 1943, when the last Germans in the Stalingrad pocket surrendered. For URANUS, a third – and secret – Soviet army group had been deployed west of Rokossovskii's Don Army Group, on the upper Don. This was General Vatutin's Southwestern Army Group (the 21st and the 63rd Armies, and the rebuilt 5th Tank Army). Cutting through Romanian positions, bypassing German strong points, Vatutin's mobile forces wheeled around Stalingrad, but 100 miles west of the city. A southern pincer, from the left flank of Eremenko's Stalingrad Army Group, attacked a day later, on 20 November. The two Soviet spearheads met near Kalach on the middle Don River on 24 November. By the time the Russians had consolidated the outer edges of their encirclement, Paulus and the German 6th Army were trapped in a huge pocket, about 75 miles from the nearest friendly units. (In 1941 the German term *Kessel* was used; more appropriate now was the Russian equivalent, *kotel*.)

Hitler ordered Paulus to stand fast in Stalingrad, rather than to attempt a break out. The newly promoted Field Marshal Manstein, conqueror of the Crimea, was put in charge of a hurriedly formed Army Group Don, composed of the Axis armies in and around Stalingrad. Manstein was in overall command of the Romanian 3rd and the German 6th Army and 4th Panzer Army, plus reinforcements arriving from the West. General Weichs, still in command of Army Group 'B', handled the more northerly armies; these were the German 2nd Army (west of the crucial Voronezh hinge-point), and the Hungarian 2nd and Italian 8th (covering the long gap between Voronezh and Stalingrad).

German Operation WINTER STORM (WINTERGEWITTER) was mounted on 12 December (D + 23, twenty-three days after the start of Operation URANUS) from southwest of the Stalingrad pocket. Manstein's forces were unable to break through. Four days later (D + 27), the Red Army began an outer encirclement, LITTLE SATURN, which shattered more of the Axis-satellite forces and threatened Manstein's rear. Manstein had to fall back, and the Russians deepened their encirclement, overrunning the forward Luftwaffe airfields which were being used in an attempt to supply the besieged 6th Army by air. By the middle of January 1943 the Stalingrad *kotel* was 200 miles behind the Soviet front line. As the siege of the city continued, Soviet forces drove rapidly westward, in Operation DON. They did not, however, go as fast as the Stavka wanted, and were unable to prevent the eventual escape from the North Caucasus of German Army Group 'A' through the Rostov area. Rostov was finally captured on 14 February 1943 – two weeks after the capitulation of Stalingrad – and by which time the Russians had retaken most of the North Caucasus and the Donbass.[21]

It took the Red Army longer than planned to eliminate the Stalingrad pocket, because it originally contained well over the twice number of enemy troops that had been expected. In any event the pocket was gradually ground down by Rokossovskii in Operation RING (KOL'TSO), Soviet artillery taking a major part. The famous surrender scene was played out on 31 January 1943, after a siege of over two months. Paulus, promoted to Field Marshal only the day before, emerged from his basement headquarters at the Stalingrad *Univermag* (Department Store). Ten years, almost to the day, had passed since Hitler became Chancellor of Germany, on 29 January 1933. German troops in the northern part of the city surrendered separately, on 2 February. Altogether, the Axis had lost 200,000 personnel at Stalingrad, including 91,000 who surrendered in the final capitulations.[22] An entire Axis field army had been trapped, commanded by a field marshal and with five corps headquarters, 22 German divisions and many troops from the Axis allies. The disaster was unprecedented in the history of the German Army.

The reasons for the German defeat at Stalingrad

Much of the 1942 German campaign in southern Russia was brilliantly successful at the operational level. With weaker forces the Wehrmacht achieved what seemed to be decisive victories in the Donbass, in the North Caucasus and on the approaches to Stalingrad. On balance, however, it is only the last six weeks of 1942 that mattered, and this – along with the first months of 1943 – was a time of failure for the Third Reich.

The German command system contributed to the Stalingrad fiasco. It was increasingly confused and strained, and this was a new development compared to the beginning of Operation BARBAROSSA. Even in 1941 there had been no overall Eastern Front commander, but Brauchitsch as C-in-C of the Army High Command (OKH) had provided a professional centre point for the campaign. In 1942 Hitler himself was in direct overall control of the Eastern Front. General Halder, Chief of the Army General Staff since 1938, fell out with Hitler over the conduct of the war in Russia and as a result of the strain of constant interaction with the Führer. Halder himself, however, bore responsibility for the basic – and unrealistic – concept of Operation BLUE. He was replaced in September 1942 by a general more acceptable to Hitler, General Kurt Zeitzler. The new Chief of the Army General Staff was eleven years younger than Halder, a relatively junior officer by German standards (although he was in fact a contemporary of Zhukov's). Zeitzler had distinguished himself as General Kleist's chief of staff in France in 1940 and had most recently been chief of staff to Field Marshal Rundstedt, the C-in-C West; there the August 1942 British–Canadian Dieppe raid had just been successfully dealt with. Zeitzler was an energetic and capable commander, but more under Hitler's spell than some of the Army old guard. Zeitzler was, for all that, a defender of the prerogatives of the Army General Staff and specifically of his responsibility for the Eastern Front. It was at this time, the autumn of 1942, that the German High Command effectively splintered into two major parts, the theatres of the Armed Forces (Wehrmacht) High Command (the OKW) in the West and South and the theatre of the German Army High Command (the OKH) in the East. There was no competent German overview of the situation as a whole, and a continual tug of war existed between the two theatres.[23]

Hitler was his own superior at the OKW, with Keitel as his Chief of Staff and Jodl as Chief of Operations. General Jodl was efficient in a technical sense, but he and Keitel were notable above all for their slavish compliance with Hitler's wishes, especially after the crisis over the movements of Army Group 'A' in September 1942. In the language of the 1990s, the Führer was attempting to 'micro-manage' the entire war from his WOLFSSCHANZE headquarters near Rastenburg in East Prussia or from an advanced headquarters, WERWOLF, at Vinnitsa in the western Ukraine (from mid-July 1942). In addition, there was a vacuum of authority at a critical time in the Stalingrad fighting. On 7 November Hitler left Vinnitsa for Germany, and he only returned to an eastern HQ (Rastenburg) on the 23rd. For much of the key period, he was on the Obersalzberg in the Tyrol. As well as 'planning' the conduct of the war as a whole, the OKW also had direct responsibility for all forces in western and southern Europe and in North Africa. At the time of Stalingrad – the key date being 19 November – Hitler and the OKW were also tied up with Rommel's defeat at El Alamein (23 October to 4 November), with the Anglo-American TORCH landings in Morocco and Algeria (8 November), and with the German occupation of Vichy France (from 11 November).

The shuffling and reshuffling of German commanders were superimposed on top of structural confusion. Field Marshal Bock, removed from Army Group Centre at the time of the 1941 Moscow crisis, had taken over Army Group South early in 1942. He was unexpectedly removed from his new command on 15 July 1942, shortly after the army group had been split into Army Groups 'A' (List) and 'B' (Bock). Hitler's ostensible reason for sacking Bock was a brief delay to Operation BLUE at Voronezh, an extraordinary decision on his part, given the German triumph in the Donbass. The real cause was long-standing friction with the sexagenarian and aristocratic Prussian field marshal and Hitler's desire to assert his own authority.[24] It was the end of Bock's career. He lived out the last two years of the war in semi-disgrace, until he was killed in an Allied strafing attack near Hamburg. The details of the southern offensive had been developed by Bock. Had he stayed on at Army Group 'B' headquarters, Hitler's overall campaign would still not have been successful, but the worst of the operational humiliation at Stalingrad might have been avoided. Bock's replacement at Army Group 'B' was General Maximilian von Weichs, who had ably commanded the 2nd Army (between Army Groups Centre and South) in 1941, but who was neither a brilliant leader nor an officer prepared to stand up to the Führer. Hitler did eventually – in November 1942 – install one of his most gifted operational commanders, Manstein, at the head of the new Army Group Don, but only after the crisis had begun.

Meanwhile, the German command muddle was even worse in the North Caucasus. As we have seen, Hitler precipitately removed Field Marshal List from command of Army Group 'A' and took over the army group command post himself for two and a half months. There was much more command stability in German Army Groups North and Centre, where Field Marshal Küchler and Field Marshal Kluge, respectively, were to stay in charge until January 1944 and October 1943.

Going beyond these systemic problems, the elements of the Stalingrad blunder can be broken down into several levels. First of all, the overall conception of the 1942 campaign was flawed. Although Hitler is rightly blamed for some of the final decisions, the German High Command – especially Halder and Bock – endorsed the general plan of operations, and did not begin to worry until the Wehrmacht stalled at Stalingrad in September. The German 1942 campaign was less ambitious than that of 1941, but it was still attempting to do a great deal with limited resources. In both years, plans were based on faulty assumptions and intelligence. This time the basic assumption was that the Red Army had been sufficiently weakened in the campaigns of the summer of 1941 and the winter and spring of 1942 that it would not be able to block a German drive to the Soviet oil resources.

Another important factor, at the level of general strategy, was Hitler's growing dependence (for raw manpower) on his Axis allies.[25] The year 1942 was the time when Romania, Italy and Hungary were of greatest importance in the war against 'Bolshevism'. The southern allies had had little role in Russia in 1941 (the exception was the Romanians around Odessa); after the third month of 1943, the Axis allies would hardly be able to play a front-line role at all. In November–December 1941, with the delay to BARBAROSSA and significant German losses, Hitler put personal pressure on the leaders in Bucharest, Rome and Budapest to make a much greater contribution to the coming campaign; the results have already been mentioned. Marshal Antonescu reinforced the two Romanian field armies (the 3rd and 4th), which had marched across the southern Ukraine and the Crimea in 1941. From Hungary, Admiral Horthy replaced token forces with a full army (the 2nd). Mussolini did the same, expanding an 'expeditionary corps' into the Italian 8th Army. Some of the Axis leaders believed in the Bolshevik peril; all were subject to German political and economic pressure. The ordinary soldiers of Romania, Italy and Hungary, for their part, had very little motivation to fight in Russia, and their equipment was much worse in terms of quantity or quality than that of the Germans or the Russians; their training was also poor. The planned mission of these armies turned out to be covering 'quiet' sectors of the expanded southern front, mostly along the line of the upper Don, or on the open steppe south of the Stalingrad bulge. The satellite armies eventually allowed Weichs – and Paulus – to concentrate the limited German forces available at the *Schwerpunkt*, Stalingrad itself.

The Soviet attacks in November 1942 were initially and intentionally concentrated on the weak flanks held by the satellite armies. Stalin once described these to Zhukov as a *nitochka*, a 'thin thread'.[26] The Romanian forces were hit directly by the Soviet Operation URANUS in November 1942. The Hungarian and Italian armies, and some of the Romanians, were positioned far enough up the Don or out in the Kalmyk steppe to escape the initial attack and encirclement, but they were smashed in LITTLE SATURN or in the Soviet pursuit of the following three months. The cost to the three Axis allies was very high. In the Italian case alone, with large-scale involvement in Russia mostly confined to 1942, Soviet figures for Italian losses in Russia are 44,900 killed and missing, and 49,000 captured (of whom 27,700 died in captivity).[27] Involvement in Russia ran against the rational interests of the satellite leaders, except in the sense that the survival of their political system depended on the victory of Germany, and the victory of Germany depended on knocking Russia out of the war. In the Italian case, Mussolini's commitment to Russia bled men and equipment from what was really the most threatening theatre for Italy, North Africa. In the end, however, the most significant thing about Hitler's reliance on second-rate allied armies was what it said about the threadbare nature even of his 'limited' southern strategy in Operation BLUE.

Not only were the overall objectives of the campaign of 1942 unfeasible, but the Germans were the victims of their own early successes in the high summer of that year. Hitler accelerated, expanded and muddled what was already a faulty strategic concept. The original plan had been for a phased sequence of four operations (BLUE I–IV) taking into account the gradual arrival of German reinforcements from western and central Europe. The city of Stalingrad had not originally been a major objective, or at least not one that would require any more of a German effort than the capture of Voronezh, Voroshilovgrad or Rostov. The line of the upper Don would be secured (albeit anchored on Stalingrad) and then – in BLUE IV – there would be an advance over the lower Don into the North Caucasus. The abortive Soviet Khar'kov offensive had unexpectedly opened a huge hole in the Soviet lines. Hitler was also excessively impressed by the effect of Richtofen's 4th Air Fleet in Manstein's campaign in the Crimea.[28] A third success in the Donbass in early July, with the rapid retreat of the defending Soviet armies, encouraged Hitler to accelerate operations (Bock had by this time been dismissed). Hitler split his forces and fundamentally reoriented the operation under Directive No. 45 of 23 July.[29] The advance towards Stalingrad, Operation BLUE III, renamed Operation HERON (FISCHREIHER), and the advance south into the Caucasus, Operation BLUE IV, renamed Operation EDELWEISS, would now begin *at the same time*. The assumption seems to have been that the rapid advance in the north could be continued to the Volga, and that Stalingrad could be taken off the march. Symptomatic of the confusion was the movement of General Hoth's 4th Panzer Army. Hoth was detached on 13 July to take part in the advance to the Caucasus, and then on 31 July most of his divisions were redirected back towards Stalingrad, approaching the city from the southwest. The critical but numerically limited air support of the 4th Air Fleet had to be spread across a huge front.[30]

At a number of points the Germans could have taken different decisions that would have reduced their losses, but they could never have taken both the Caucasus and Stalingrad at the same time.[31] Paulus's 6th Army was only able to create a deep salient and never to take Stalingrad itself. In the Caucasus, especially, the 1st Panzer Army never got to Ordzhonikidze, let alone Makhachkala and the distant approaches to Baku. Well before the Soviet counter-offensive in November 1942, the German double drive had stalled.

What turned a strategic and operational failure into the disaster of the 6th Army and the precipitate collapse of Hitler's whole southern adventure was another – fatal – German misperception. This was that the Red Army could not launch a serious counter-offensive in the south. Although the long Don River flank to the north was obviously exposed, the assumption in the late autumn of German Army intelligence was that the Russians were still concentrated more in the central theatre – in front of Moscow – than the south, and that they did not have forces for a major southern counter-offensive. The same ignorance of the Red Army order of battle prevailed as in 1941. The Germans also believed that even if the Red Army did make attacks, they could be repelled by qualitatively superior Axis forces. Soviet failures in the centre in August 1942 (at Rzhev) reassured Hitler about the continuing powers of the German defence.[32]

The local commander at Stalingrad, General Paulus, was not responsible for this intelligence failure, but he has been criticized for many other things. He was a gifted staff officer but lacked experience as a field commander. As Army Deputy Chief of Staff in 1941, he had been an important BARBAROSSA planner. In September 1942, he had been tipped eventually to replace Jodl as operations chief at the OKW. His promotion to command of a major operational formation had been unexpectedly accelerated by the fatal heart attack of Field Marshal Reichenau, the former 6th Army commander, in January 1942. Paulus had no command experience at division level, let alone that of a corps or an army. His 6th Army – with sixteen divisions in September 1942 – was one of the largest formations in the German Army. Much has been written over the years about his mistakes in the conduct of the battle within Stalingrad. He let himself be drawn into street fighting. His army was cut up and immobilized. He failed to leave enough of a mobile reserve. When the Soviet breakthrough began on 19 November, he reacted slowly and passively. Above all, he compliantly accepted Hitler's orders not to attempt a breakout to the west with his army.

At a higher level, political considerations distorted the conduct of the final operations around Stalingrad. The name of the city came to have symbolic importance. Hitler staked his prestige on the success of the fighting, and this made it harder for him to back down. Speaking at the Berlin Sportpalast on 30 September, he promised that Germany would never be driven from Stalingrad. On 8 November in a speech in Munich he claimed Germany already held the city: 'We have it. There are only a few tiny places [left] there.'[33]

Finally, once the Stavka had mounted its Operation URANUS, the Germans perhaps had the chance to extract some, perhaps most, of their forces at Stalingrad.[34] Hitler and others, however, saw an analogy with the battles of the previous winter. Then, the Führer's firmness, and the success of his 'stand fast' order, had meant that withdrawal did not become a rout. Some of the pockets in the central theatre, like Demiansk and Kholm, held out for long periods, supplied by air. Paulus was already at the end of a very difficult supply line when the ring around him was sealed at Kalach in late November. Military historians still argue about whether Paulus had sufficient resources to pull the 6th Army out of the pocket. Probably he could have done, had he acted immediately, but he certainly would have had to leave much of his heavy equipment and perhaps his wounded behind. Field Marshal Manstein's role is controversial, as his initial optimism (and promise to relieve the city) encouraged Hitler to order Paulus to stand fast. Even if Manstein's December Operation WINTER STORM had succeeded, its aim was to create a line of communications *into* 'Fortress Stalingrad', not to facilitate a breakout.[35] Much has been made of the failure of the air bridge. Goering promised, against the advice of his subordinates, that the Luftwaffe could keep the pocket supplied. The Luftwaffe C-in-C reckoned without the terrible weather and the eventual loss of advanced airfields west of the Don. In reality, the Luftwaffe fell well short of its supply targets, and it lost 500 aircrafts in the airlift.[36] It would be an exaggeration, however, to say that Hitler ordered Paulus to stand fast *because* of Goering's promise; it was more a justification for a decision he had made for other reasons.

There was a terrible logic in this chain of German blunders. From the point of view of Hitler's overall strategy, the 6th Army (and the 1st Panzer Army in the Caucasus) had to be placed in an exposed position and could not be withdrawn. In a sense, the final mistakes were irrelevant. Even if Paulus had extracted himself, the BLUE campaign, and with it the war as a whole, would have been doomed. As Hitler told Zeitzler, at the start of Operation WINTER STORM: 'To think that I will come back here again next time is madness. ... We won't come back here, so we cannot leave. Also too much blood has been shed to do that.'[37]

The background to the Soviet victory at Stalingrad

Soviet successes are the other side of the coin to German defeats, but the reasons for success are perhaps more complicated.

Some historians explain the Russians' stand on the Volga from August 1942 and their successful counter-attack in November by a new determination in the ranks of the Red Army. The basis for this is often said to be Stalin's famous 'Not One Step Backwards!' order. This Order No. 227 was issued on 28 July, immediately after the loss of Rostov and Novocherkassk on 23 and 24 July, and shortly after the loss of Voronezh and Voroshilovgrad.[38] 'The German occupiers', Stalin declared, 'are struggling to get to Stalingrad, to the Volga and they want at any cost to grab the Kuban', [and] the North Caucasus with its wealth of oil and grain.' As for the Soviet Southern Army Group, 'panic-mongers gave up Rostov and Novocherkassk without serious resistance and covered their banners with disgrace'. The USSR had already lost too much territory and resources:

> To retreat further means to doom yourself and with it to doom our Motherland. ... Not one step backwards! This must now be our main slogan. It is necessary steadfastly, to the last drop of blood, to defend each position, each metre of Soviet territory, to hold every patch of Soviet soil, and to hold it as long as possible.

The central theme of Order No. 227 was discipline, but that was to be created by two different methods, appeals to patriotism and threat of punishment. The latter methods involved an enhanced apparatus of repression in the Red Army. Stalin actually praised the harsh measures taken to restore order in the German Army in the winter of 1941–2 including, he claimed, penal (*shtrafnye*) battalions for cowards and deserters and 'blocking detachments' (*otriady zagrazhdeniia*) behind unsteady units 'to shoot on the spot panic-mongers and cowards'. There followed a striking example of a Stalinist rhetorical question: 'Is it appropriate to learn in this matter from our enemies, as our forefathers learned from their enemies, and in that way achieved victory over them? I think it is appropriate.'

Although great importance was attached by the Soviet government to the punitive side of Order No. 227, the specific effect of the order can be questioned. The Red Army of totalitarian Russia had hardly been a loosely structured force. It had lived through the purges of 1937–8, and the crisis measures of 1941 with the reintroduction of commissars and the OO (Special Section). Stalin had condemned cowards and panic-mongers in his 3 July 1941 speech and his order of 16 August 1941.

Paradoxically, the most positive feature of Order No. 227 was probably the Soviet government's admission of failure. Stalin emphasized that the USSR did not have unlimited resources and empty territory. He frankly detailed what had been lost – seventy million people and vast resources of grain and minerals. The Soviet propaganda line changed in a fundamental way. The slogans following Stalin's 1942 May Day speech had included complacent themes: 'The weakening of Fascist Germany in the course of the war and the strengthening of the USSR', 'The new period of the Fatherland War – the period of the liberation of the Soviet lands from the Hitlerite filth' and 'The Red Army has all it needs to destroy the German-Fascist Army in 1942'. After that came the disaster of the Soviet Khar'kov offensive (12–29 May), but a *Pravda* keynote article a month later on the first anniversary of BARBAROSSA (22 June) still declared that '1942 will be the year of the final defeat of the enemy, the year of our final victory'. After Order No. 227 all this changed. The slogans for 2 August included 'Not one step backwards! Every metre, every scrap of our Soviet land given up strengthens the enemy and weakens our Motherland', 'A threatening danger hangs over the Motherland' and 'The coward and the panic-monger is a traitor to the Motherland. The coward gets the first bullet!'[39]

It would also be a mistake to be too rigid and to treat the end of July as a turning point in the history of the Red Army. The Southwestern Army Group did indeed fall apart in July – resulting in the loss of Rostov. Elsewhere, however, Soviet troops fought with determination, in the battle around Voronezh in early July and in a number of battles across the Don bend from late July to late August, as fresh formations were thrown into combat.[40] It is true that the number of Soviet prisoners captured in the Don bend was less than the high hundreds of thousands taken in each of the mass surrenders in Belorussia, in the Ukraine and at the Battle of Viaz'ma–Briansk in 1941, or even at Khar'kov in 1942. Glantz and House recently suggested a plausible figure of 'only' 150,000 Soviet prisoners in the June and July phases of Operation BLAU in the western part of the Don bend.[41] The lower POW figure probably had much to do with the expanse of the theatre of operations and the limited strength of the German mobile forces engaging them (eight panzer and two motorized divisions across a front 350 miles wide).[42] In addition, Soviet troops were more experienced and had a greater fear of falling into German hands. But the number who surrendered was not small.

Strategic geography was perhaps a more significant factor than Order No. 227, for explaining the apparent stiffening of Soviet resistance. When Operation BLUE began in late June, Soviet units were hard put to find a geographical line of resistance to fall behind within the Don bend. The Germans was moving more or less parallel to the rivers as they advanced from north to south, in the huge sweep behind the Russian Southwestern and Southern Army Groups. Stalin wanted to make a stand at Rostov and the lower Don, but the dangers of this exposed position were obvious (see Map 5). Rostov could be (and was) outflanked from the east. If cut off, the city could not be supplied, reinforced or evacuated by sea (unlike Odessa or Sevastopol'). The supply line back from Rostov to central Russia would have been very tenuous, even had the Stalingrad–Tikhoretskaia–Rostov railway line remained in Soviet hands. The reluctance to defend the town is understandable. Geography also played a part in the sparsely populated steppe of the North Caucasus, where there was no natural line to hold between the Don and the Caucasus Mountains. The Soviet defenders there were able to make a stand only when they fell back to the mountains and to the Terek River line – and with the Germans at the end of a logistical bungee rope. The onset of winter in the mountain passes made the defenders' task easier.

At Stalingrad, too, geography would be crucial. The very wide Volga River behind the city made it impossible for the Germans to advance further east to outflank the Stalingrad garrison. The wider flanks of the Soviet position were covered to the north by the line of the upper Don River (with rail lines and central Russia behind it), and to the south by the waterless and empty Kalmyk steppe.

Accumulation of Red Army strength was another basic factor explaining ever greater resistance. Russian forces, even in the south, outnumbered the enemy in manpower and equipment. This was partly the pay-off for the pre-war rearmament and training, and it has been discussed at length earlier. The Red Army and Soviet industry had after eighteen months begun to overcome the crisis caused by the destruction of the cadre army in 1941, and the evacuation of industry. The Red Army, for example, received 5,600 tanks and 3,400 artillery pieces in the second half of 1941, and 14,800 tanks and 6,800 artillery pieces in 1942.[43] More and more rifle divisions and tank corps were trained, organized and sent to the front.[44] Some 100,000 sailors were taken from the navy. More first-rate divisions were moved from the Far East (a transfer perhaps facilitated by the American naval victory over Japan at Midway in early July).[45]

The Stavka deployed fresh troops to the south, at least from the time of the fall of Voronezh in early July. As already mentioned, three new armies (the 60th, 6th and 63rd, formerly the 3th, 6th and 5th Reserve Armies) were thrown in to cover the Don front, as well as the 5th Tank Army.[46] Three combined-arms armies (the 62nd, 63rd and 64th, formerly the 7th, 5th and 1st Reserve Armies) and two tank armies (the 1st and 4th) were deployed to cover the eastern extremity of the Don bend, and two combined-arms armies (the 24th and 66th, formerly the 8th and 9th Reserve Armies) and the new 1st Guards Army were deployed for attacks north of Stalingrad in September. And this is not even counting the three armies secretly assembled in the Southwestern Army Group for Operation URANUS in November. In all, some fifty divisions and thirty-three independent brigades were sent to the Stalingrad theatre between mid-July and the end of September. (This was also partly the explanation for the much better Red Army performance at Stalingrad than in the North Caucasus, to which it was physically difficult, after July 1942, to transport fresh reserves from central Russia or Siberia.) After the decision in September to proceed with Operation URANUS, the Stalingrad area was assigned four tank corps and two mechanized corps from the Stavka reserve. Marshalling this force, especially in secret, was a major achievement.

The final element in the changing Soviet fortunes was the growing competence at the strategic and operational level of the Red Army command. This contrasted not only with 1941, but also with the first half of 1942. Just when this improvement occurred is open to debate. Some Western historians have argued that the Soviet decision to retreat, made in early July 1942, marked a fundamental shift in Soviet strategy and doctrine.

The difference between late 1942 and 1941, it is suggested, was that the Germans were no longer able to achieve huge encirclements like Belostok–Minsk, Uman', Kiev or Viaz'ma–Briansk. The American historian Earl Ziemke argued that 'Stalin stopped playing Terentius Varro to Hitler's Hannibal'. (Terentius was the Roman general whose army was encircled and destroyed by Hannibal at the Battle of Cannae in 216 BC.) Bernd Wegner made a similar argument, identifying the new flexibility with General Vasilevskii at the Soviet General Staff and citing a captured directive from Timoshenko. The Russian historian A. M. Samsonov took the same line, but followed the German historian (and general) Kurt von Tippelskirch, rather than citing a specific Timoshenko directive from the Russian archives.[47]

This argument, however, is largely incorrect; rather than retreating without a fight, the Stavka threw in fresh divisions to mount counter-attacks around Voronezh and in the eastern part of the Don bend.[48] This is not to deny that the Germans outfought the Russians, nor that they inflicted much heavier losses. At the end of June 1942, Timoshenko and Malinovskii (commanding the Southwestern and Southern Army Groups) had, on paper, powerful forces. These numbered 1,310,000 troops, including 6 tank corps, 68 rifle divisions and a large number of smaller formations.[49] Despite this strength, and despite receiving a warning about Operation BLUE when orders relating to it were recovered from a crashed German aircraft (on 20 June), the Red Army was unable to respond to the German threat.

Timoshenko was personally devastated by the initial onslaught on his Southwestern Army Group, according to his commissar, Khrushchev. He lost touch with the Stavka and his subordinate armies. Meanwhile, the career of General Rodion Iakovlevich Malinovskii was almost ended. Malinovskii had made a name for himself as an adviser in Spain and was in command of a rifle corps in the Kiev Military District when war broke out. He was rapidly promoted to command an army and then – from December 1941 – the whole Southern Army Group. His army group performed badly on the southern flank of the Battle of Khar'kov in May 1942 and was devastated in the July disaster. Malinovskii fell into deep disfavour with Stalin and was demoted to command of a reserve army. But like Konev (after the Viaz'ma–Briansk defeat in October 1941), Malinovskii was an officer of substantial ability and was eventually able to redeem himself. He won major victories later during the war and in 1957 would be Khrushchev's Minister of Defence – replacing the dismissed Marshal Zhukov.[50]

Overall, the July 1942 fighting (28 June to 24 July) was extremely expensive for the Red Army, much more so even than the better-known Battle of Khar'kov. According to Russian statistics, some 371,000 troops were lost, as compared to 171,000 in May at Khar'kov (and 324,000 in the much longer and more famous 'Stalingrad defensive operation' (which lasted four times as long, from 17 July to 18 November). The Red Army also lost 2,436 tanks, compared to the 1,426 it would lose later in the 'Stalingrad defensive operation'.[51]

Stalin's July Order No. 227 also contradicts the idea that the Soviet high command was following a flexible policy. Indeed, Order No. 227 was essentially identical to Hitler's 'stand fast' doctrine of the previous winter, which Stalin even cited as a model. And in practice there was little such flexibility. A bitter stand was made for Voronezh. Budennyi was given the impossible orders to stand fast on the lower Don with his North Caucasus Army Group (just as he had had been ordered to do on the Dnepr in 1941).[52] Several armies were shattered in August in a vain attempt to hold the Germans west of the Don in front of Stalingrad.

And yet there *was* a critical new maturity in the Red Army command in the late summer of 1942. General Zhukov had finally replaced Timoshenko as Stalin's key military executive. He was made Deputy Supreme C-in-C in August 1942; he also became 1st Deputy Commissar of Defence, replacing Marshal Budennyi. The quality of advice being given to the Soviet dictator probably improved in May 1942 with the final retirement of Shaposhnikov as Chief of the General Staff. This was on genuine grounds of ill health; Shaposhnikov died in 1945. His replacement was General Aleksandr Vasilevskii; in October 1942 Vasilevskii also became a Deputy Commissar of Defence, but unlike Zhukov, he was not made a member of the Stavka.[53] Vasilevskii was forty-six at the time of his appointment – fourteen months older than Zhukov but younger than his eventual German opposite number Zeitzler. He had been a wartime subaltern in the Tsarist Army. More remarkably, he was a priest's son and (like Stalin) had studied in an Orthodox seminary.[54] In Stalin's time, such a background could block a man's promotion – or even send him to the GULAG. Vasilevskii was only admitted to the Communist Party in 1938. Zhukov, Konev and Rokossovskii – his contemporaries – had joined twenty years earlier. Vasilevskii's survival and ascent through the General Staff was a product of formidable ability, of unimpeachable loyalty to the system and – in the later stages – of Stalin's personal favour.

Vasilevskii seems to have been a true believer in Stalin's martial qualities, as he did not take the opportunity to attack the dictator's memory after 1953. Stalin probably saw him as a safer figure than the charismatic Zhukov, and a counterbalance to him. When Zhukov was reduced to secondary posts after the war, Vasilevskii was promoted to be Minister of Defence and held that post from 1949 to 1953 – the height of the Cold War. Vasilevskii's abilities as a planner had been evident in 1941–2, but unlike Paulus – another planner – Vasilevskii emerged as an able field commander at Stalingrad and later. When the war began, Vasilevskii was three tiers down in the General Staff structure, while Zhukov was at the top. He was only a major general (a 'one-star' general, roughly a western brigadier) compared to the four-star General of the Army Zhukov – not to mention the (in effect five-star) Marshals. Promoted to (three-star) Colonel-General rank immediately following the Stalingrad victory, Vasilevskii was promoted a few weeks later to the rank of Marshal of the Soviet Union; this was on 6 February 1943.

Finally, of course, there was the Supreme Commander-in-Chief. Stalin, like Hitler, was directly involved in the details of operations. Stalin's evolution as military commander will be discussed in greater depth in the following chapter. For the moment, it can be said that he was now much more experienced in day-to-day command, he was more realistic and he was better advised. He certainly took the credit for success. On 6 March 1943, a month after Paulus's surrender, and after the breaking of the blockade of Leningrad and the beginning of the German withdrawal from the Rzhev–Viaz'ma salient (in front of Moscow), Joseph Stalin too became a Marshal of the Soviet Union.

Stalin also had a more flexible and effective top-level command system than before. The 1941 echelon of the theatre command had been removed, the Southwestern Theatre having been disbanded on 21 June 1942, shortly before Operation BLUE began. An effective means of communication between the centre and field armies emerged in the form of the 'Stavka representative', a plenipotentiary from Moscow who could focus command talent – like artillery and other material assets – in a key sector. For the rest of the war, it would be the Stavka representative who co-ordinated the operations of several army groups, but of course he always kept in close teletype and telephone contact with Stalin and the centre.

The operational Soviet leaders, the army group and army commanders, were men who had emerged from a process of Darwinian natural selection in the first year of the war, although there was still an element of high-command politics. This was an incremental process, and it varied from front to front. Zhukov installed 'his' people in the important posts, the headquarters of the army groups on the Don. His old friend Rokossovskii commanded the Don Army Group. A key figure was General Nikolai Vatutin, Zhukov's deputy when he was Chief of the General Staff in June 1941; Vatutin commanded the secret striking force, the Southwestern Army Group. Less important, and probably less able, was the commander of the Stalingrad Army Group, Eremenko, who enjoyed Stalin's personal favour rather than Zhukov's. Zhukov caused particular offence to Eremenko at the end of December 1942 by making Rokossovskii responsible for the final reduction of the Stalingrad pocket. Eremenko's Stalingrad Army Group became (again) the Southern Army Group and was committed to operations towards Rostov (and Eremenko was replaced as head of this formation by Malinovskii at the start of February 1943).[55] Malinovskii was another able officer whose role in the defeat of Manstein in December 1942 (as commander of the 2nd Guards Army) made up for his loss of Rostov six months earlier. At lower levels, in the tank corps and rifle divisions, the commanders were now increasingly officers of experience and proven ability.

The structural shortcomings of the Soviet high command, even in the second half of 1942, should not be forgotten. Both Zhukov and Vasilevskii were absent from Moscow for much of the last three or four months of 1942. In the autumn, commanders were constantly reshuffled. The new Stalingrad Army Group (created on 12 July 1942) was commanded for the first few weeks by Timoshenko, who was replaced by General V. N. Gordov (executed in 1950), and finally – after the army group had been split in two – by Rokossovskii and Eremenko. According to Khrushchev, Stalin thought seriously about replacing Eremenko. An untested and inexperienced senior staff officer was initially assigned to co-ordinate the two (later three) army groups. (Fortunately, that officer, Vasilevskii, turned out to be very able.) In Stalingrad itself, the key commander, Lopatin, had to be replaced as commander of the 62nd Army by Chuikov (in September). There was a particular command problem in the far south, where Beria and the NKVD became involved in command arrangements; in the later stages of the campaign, the armies of the North Caucasus Army Group were commanded by an NKVD general of limited abilities, I. I. Maslennikov.

The Red Army comes of age: Operation URANUS

The failures of the later summer, and the confused arrangements of the autumn, make the Soviet defence and counter-attack at Stalingrad stand out all the more clearly. The most famous aspect of the Stalingrad fighting was the fierce resistance of General Chuikov's 62nd Army within the city itself during September, October and November 1942. This was dramatic and symbolic, but, without demeaning the heroism of the defenders, it was only one part of the battle.[56] A courageous Soviet defence was also not in itself new; the fighting at Sevastopol' had shown the readiness of Soviet soldiers and sailors to fight to the end.

What was really striking, indeed revolutionary, about the Battle of Stalingrad was Operation URANUS, the deep encirclement operation of German 6th Army that began on 19 November. Attacking a considerable distance away from the city reduced the danger of counter-attack from Paulus's forces within the trap. Meanwhile, the encircling Soviet formations would be covered by the Don River against an early German response from the west. The Russians were aware that there were no concentrated German reserves behind Paulus's 6th Army and that the flanks of the huge salient were thinly held by armies from Germany's weak allies.

Well known to historians of the Red Army is a passage in General Zhukov's memoirs in which he describes a 12 September 1942 conference in Moscow with Stalin.[57] Zhukov was Deputy Supreme C-in-C; according to him, Vasilevskii, Chief of the General Staff, was also present. Zhukov's attack from immediately north of Stalingrad with the 24th Army, 1st Guards and new 66th Army had just been stopped in the difficult terrain and the entrenched German positions on the northern edge of the city. There seemed no point in repeating this. Zhukov and Vasilevskii whispered to one another during Stalin's briefing about the need to find 'another solution' (*inoe reshenie*).

'What "other solution"?' asked Stalin, suddenly raising his head [from the map table].

I [Zhukov] never thought that I. V. Stalin had such sharp hearing. We approached the table.

'Well look', he continued, 'go to the General Staff and think through thoroughly what has to be done in the Stalingrad area. ... Tomorrow at 21:00 we will meet again here.'

According to Zhukov's account, this led to a plan for a deep encirclement. A preliminary draft plan of Operation URANUS, with a map, was presented to Stalin on the following evening.

The American historians David Glantz and Jonathan House have very recently accepted a different version of the origins of the all-important Stalingrad counter-offensive. They maintain that Zhukov's account is 'patently incorrect'. Instead, they agree with claims made by the then Marshal Eremenko in 1961, eight years before the publication of Zhukov's memoirs. Eremenko, commander of the 1942 Stalingrad Army Group, maintained that he was the originator of the concept of a broad encirclement. Glantz and House came to their conclusion partly because there is no archival evidence of a meeting between Stalin, Zhukov and Vasilevskii on 12 September, and partly because a proposal for a large-scale encirclement was indeed put to Stalin by Eremenko (and Nikita Khrushchev) in early October.[58]

The Stalingrad plan was one of the most important military decisions of the whole Second World War. Glantz and House may well be correct about its origins. There is probably no way, however, to verify with certainty either the Zhukov or the Eremenko version. The absence of archival evidence for the meeting on 12 September does not mean that no such event took place. The occurrence of the meeting was accepted by Vasilevskii in his 1973 memoirs, by a published chronology of Zhukov's activities, by the 1998–9 Russian official history, and by Zhukov's most recent biographer, Geoffrey Roberts.[59] Glantz and House admit that the proposals by Eremenko and Khrushchev, based on existing documents, were for a more limited operation.[60] The concept of a deep double encirclement went back to Hannibal and Cannae, and it was certainly not new to Soviet doctrine. Zhukov's attack against the Japanese at Khalkhin Gol in 1939 had been conceptually similar, although on a much smaller scale. His Moscow counter-offensive of 6 December, although hastily improvised, had many of the same features. The Soviet threat from the upper Don line south to the east–west railway line supplying Stalingrad (from Likhaia through Morozovsk) was obvious to the Germans (although the southern prong of the Soviet pincers was not).

Nonetheless, the URANUS concept was very daring. The Red Army had contemplated large encirclement operations in 1941 and early 1942, but never brought them off. The main striking force would have to travel 75 miles southeast behind enemy lines to reach the Kalach-on-Don region. The southern arm of the pincers had to drive northwest 50 miles. Practical preparations began in the middle of September 1942, some nine weeks before URANUS was actually carried out (the operation was postponed two weeks). It was apparently given national first priority. Zhukov and Vasilevskii inspected the deploying forces (one in the north, the other in the south). The American historian Earl Ziemke has suggested that URANUS was delayed to follow the TORCH landings in North Africa on 8 November.[61] The Soviet attack, however, would have been launched in any event, and there were more plausible reasons for the postponement, notably the need to complete the concentration of Soviet forces using railways and roads with limited capacity.

It was, by the way, evidently at about this time that Soviet operations began to be given code names like URANUS. The astronomical theme was evidently chosen by Stalin himself. The first recorded name of this type was evidently the small Operation VENUS (VENERA), which the Stavka prepared for the Kalinin Army Group in mid-September 1943. Operation MARS was set up on 1 October (originally for the 10th). Operations SATURN, POLAR STAR (POLIARNAIA ZVEZDA) and STAR (ZVEZDZA) followed later in the winter. As a young man, Stalin had worked as caretaker of the Tiflis astronomical observatory, and it is intriguing to speculate whether this affected his choice of language.[62]

General Zhukov took part in the desperate (and unsuccessful) battles around Stalingrad in late August and early September. Whatever did or did not happen on 12 September, he certainly had a part in developing and extending the initial proposals for Operation URANUS. However, one of the most surprising features of the Stalingrad plan was that Zhukov did not have a direct role in implementing it. According to Zhukov, on the eve of 19 November Stalin asked who should co-ordinate the whole operation. Zhukov replied that he and Vasilevskii had discussed the matter and agreed that Vasilevskii would take over the task. Zhukov himself would take charge of preparing the MARS offensive in front of Moscow. It seems most likely that Stalingrad was not seen by the Stavka as the uniquely important operation that it became in hindsight (partly because of the failure of Operation MARS). The central theatre still had great importance attached to it, both in terms of resources committed and the perceived threat to the capital. The end result was that Stalingrad was more Vasilevskii's victory than Zhukov's.

It was not just the daring concept of URANUS that was so extraordinary. As significant was the ability of the Soviet command to take the operation through the stages needed to bring it off: to keep the Germans in an exposed position, to mass superior forces without detection and to maintain control of the fluid battle that began on 19 November.

The only contentious part is how far the siege battle in the city was the conscious Soviet baiting of a trap. Chuikov's defence had pinned Paulus down in Stalingrad and drawn in his reserves. Certainly, one feature of the situation was that the Red Army did not initially have to hit a moving target. Like the Germans, the Soviet leaders seemed to have made mental calculations about the real potential of their enemy. They concluded that the Germans did not have the resources to achieve their objectives in 1942 and that the Red Army could methodically organize a complex operation on the flanks of the 6th Army. It had time for a set-piece preparation – two months (and there was a two-week postponement).

Another sign of the Russians' skill was their deployment of reserves to the south of the bulge without alerting the Germans. They cleverly camouflaged their movements (*maskirovka*), and they achieved an extraordinary degree of surprise. Part of the preparations was the creation of a 15-mile (25-km) 'front-line zone', from which all civilians were excluded. The concentration area north of the Don, including that of the new Southwestern Army Group, was out in the open steppe. The same was true out in the Kalmyk steppe, and on this side there was the even greater problem of moving forces around Stalingrad and ferrying men and vehicles secretly across the Volga and into their concentration areas.

The Soviet conduct of the mobile battle west of Stalingrad in December 1942 was especially striking. The situation was made more challenging by the need for the Soviet encirclers to have both an inner face (to contain and destroy the 6th Army) and an outer one (to prevent the arrival of a German relief force from the west). Even the decision to scale down Operation SATURN (changing it from an overambitious drive on Rostov to a counter-attack against Manstein's relief expedition, Operation WINTER STORM) was symptomatic of genuinely greater command flexibility and of the maturity of the Stavka's system.

The Red Army's conduct of operations in the south, even in the last months of the year, was far from perfect. It took much longer than expected to reduce the Stalingrad pocket – some ten weeks. This was partly because the encircled German force was much larger than expected, partly because Paulus's men put up a stiff resistance, and partly because Soviet forces – especially Malinovskii's 2nd Guards Army – had to be diverted to deal with Manstein and WINTER STORM. The Stavka was forced to abandon Operation SATURN (as opposed to Operation LITTLE SATURN), which would have driven south to Rostov and cut off all Axis forces in the North Caucasus. After the threat from Manstein was eliminated, the pursuit in January 1943 was too slow. Operation DON took a month longer than expected to block the German escape routes through Rostov, and Tiulenev's Operations SEA (MORE) and MOUNTAINS (GORY) failed to prevent the orderly withdrawal of the German 17th Army into the Taman' Peninsula opposite the Kerch' Straits. As we will see, the Soviet pursuit of the Wehrmacht to the Donbass would suffer serious reverses in February and March 1943. Soviet operations in the North Caucasus from November 1942 through February 1943 were much less impressive, due to poor leadership and the difficulties of concentrating well-equipped and well-organized troops there. The German extraction of Army Group 'A' was made possible by the feeble pursuit of the Soviet Transcaucasus Army Group. On 4 February 1943, the Stavka ordered the re-formed North Caucasus Army Group 'to surround the group of the enemy and destroy it, just as it was (*sic*) surrounded and destroyed by our forces at Stalingrad'. But for the Red Army, only one Stalingrad proved possible.

But if the southern campaign did not end in decisive victory, the Battle of Stalingrad was still a military classic. One traditional Western school of history blames Stalingrad on blunders by Hitler or his generals.[63] Russian historians, in contrast, rightly stress the fact that the Red Army *won* the Battle of Stalingrad. Greater determination, better organization, equipment and supply, better training, and more realistic commanders won the day. All these elements which had been developing since the wreck of the pre-war 'cadre' army at the outbreak of the war now came together to make a qualitative change on the Russian side. Stalin would note this in February 1943, when he called the Red Army a 'cadre army'.

OPERATION SPARK: THE RELIEF OF LENINGRAD

The German attack planned for the autumn of 1942

The great military drama of late 1942 was played out at Stalingrad in the southern theatre. Both the Germans and the Russians attached much more importance to Moscow and the central theatre than historians generally allow. But the northern theatre was also a major battlefield in 1942 and early 1943.[64] Hitler's last serious attempt to take Leningrad was forestalled in August 1942. Partly as a result of victories elsewhere, the situation around Leningrad finally improved at the very beginning of the new year, 1943, when Operation SPARK restored a land link to the city. And at the Stavka, preparations were being made for the complete destruction of German Army Group North.

German plans for the whole 1942 Russian campaign had included not only a main offensive in the south but a second, if smaller, operation in the north intended to finish off Leningrad (see Map 3). Hitler's April Directive No. 41 laid down the task 'in the *North* to bring about the fall of Leningrad and to establish a land link with the Finns'. The attraction for the German High Command was that its troops around Leningrad were already geographically very near their objective – the nearest positions were within 10 miles of the centre of the city. Capturing Leningrad would allow Axis operations against the vital supply lines to Murmansk and Arkhangel'sk, not least by increasing Finnish involvement there. The Russian northern capital would be a great prestige victory; Hitler himself still saw the city as a political objective and still aimed to level it to the ground.[65]

Hitler's operation against Leningrad was scheduled for September 1942, under the code name Operation FIRE MAGIC (FEUERZAUBER), later NORTHERN LIGHTS (NORDLICHT). The overall commander of German Army Group North was still Georg von Küchler, from July 1942 a Field Marshal. Under Küchler was General Lindemann, whose 18th Army was actually besieging Leningrad. In late August, however, Field Marshal Manstein, the conqueror of Sevastopol', was sent north to finish the job. As already mentioned, five divisions from Manstein's 11th Army, having successfully completed the siege of Sevastopol', were committed to the Leningrad operation, as well as the super-heavy siege artillery. Manstein's plan was to avoid fighting in the built-up areas of Leningrad. After an initial advance to the southern edges of the city proper, he planned a sweep around Leningrad to the east. Crossing the Neva outside the city, he would effect a close encirclement. This would once and for all cut the great city off from its supplies.

As it happened, Operation NORTHERN LIGHTS was pre-empted by the Soviet 'Siniavino operation', begun in mid-August 1942.[66] This was a less ambitious version of what the Red Army had attempted at the beginning of 1942 with the Liuban' offensive. The southeastern part of General Govorov's Leningrad Army Group attacked across the middle and upper Neva River into the swamps and forests of the Shlissel'burg corridor. A week later, the 8th Army and a new 2nd Shock Army from Meretskov's Volkhov Army Group attacked from the east, towards the high ground at the village of Siniavino (3 miles south of Shlissel'burg and 10 miles north of Mga). Manstein was able to cut off many of the attackers. The Russians pulled back to their initial positions after heavy losses – more than they would suffer in the successful January 1943 relief operation. Govorov did not succeed in breaking the blockade, although he kept a small bridgehead south of the Neva at Moskovskaia Dubrovka. The real importance of the Siniavino operation was that it pre-empted NORTHERN LIGHTS. The arriving elements of Manstein's 11th Army had to be thrown in to contain the Soviet attack, and the Germans suffered significant losses.

It is doubtful if, in any event, Manstein had much chance of taking Leningrad. The new Field Marshal was gifted, but he was not a miracle worker. He had taken seven months to reduce Sevastopol'. Manstein may have prevented an early Soviet relief of Leningrad, but on balance his armour and infantry could have been put to better use elsewhere. As it was, at the end of November 1942, Manstein was flown off to the south to take command of the forces trying to relieve the 6th Army at Stalingrad. He never returned to Leningrad.

Finland and north Russia

Hitler ignored the far north of the Russian–German front in his April 1942 directive. On 21 July 1942, after the new victories won in the Don bend, the Wehrmacht high command put forward Operation SALMON CATCH (LACHSFANG).[67] This was a renewed corps-level German advance in north central Finland to reach the Murmansk–Vologda railway at Kandalaksha. In grand strategic terms, severing the main northern Allied Lend-Lease supply line would complement the expected cutting of southern Allied supply lines through the Caucasus.

The far north had been a secondary theatre for both sides since the start of the war. The Germans had controlled northern Norway since April 1940. In June–July 1941, they had mounted an attack east towards Murmansk with small forces, but the robust Soviet defence and the extreme difficulty of the terrain stopped them. During that year they also attempted, some 200 miles to the south, the first unsuccessful advance with a German corps east towards Kandalaksha. In October 1941, after the apparently decisive success of the German armies in front of Moscow at the Battle of Viaz'ma–Briansk, Hitler issued a directive calling off further attacks on Murmansk. The Germans did make very effective use of air and naval forces based in Norway to attack the British supply convoys. The biggest success was against convoy PQ17 in early July 1942, just as Hitler launched Operation BLUE in south Russia. The Germans succeeded in reducing the convoys in the winter of 1942–3, and halting them entirely in the summer and autumn of 1943.

Operation SALMON CATCH always had limited chances for success, in view of the lack of German troops and the problems of getting reinforcements and supplies into the Arctic theatre. Above all, however, the operation depended on the Wehrmacht first taking Leningrad (by means of Operation NORTHERN LIGHTS); this was the Finns' requirement for participation. Finland, the fourth Axis 'ally', had a quite different position from Romania, Italy and Hungary. With a limited population and economic base, the country made a supreme effort in 1941 to regain territories lost in the Winter War of 1939–40, but it could not sustain this. The United States put diplomatic pressure on the Finns to restrain them from further offensive action, beyond the gains of 1941. Marshal Mannerheim, the Finnish C-in-C and a former general in the Tsarist Army, had a more realistic view of the likelihood of German ultimate success against Russia than other Axis leaders such as Antonescu in Romania or Mussolini in Italy. Hitler, for his part, treated Mannerheim and the Finns with respect. The Germans never expected that the Finns would participate directly in an attack on Leningrad in 1942, although early in the year there was some hope that the Finns might advance to Belomorsk (Sorokka), 200 miles south of Kandalaksha, to cut the Murmansk–Vologda railway. The Finns did not move then, nor later in 1942. In the end, Operation SALMON CATCH, like NORTHERN LIGHTS, came to nothing. The far north remained a static front, which it would remain until the Red Army mounted a counter-offensive in the summer of 1944.

Leningrad breakthrough

The third major Russian attempt to liberate Leningrad (after the Liuban' and Siniavino operations) was Operation SPARK. In the depths of the winter of 1942–3 Generals Govorov and Meretskov in effect repeated the Siniavino operation against Lindemann's 18th Army. Once again, the main Russian formation on the east (mainland) side of the Shlissel'burg corridor was the 2nd Shock Army; meanwhile, a new 67th Army attacked from the Leningrad side. Voroshilov had been the Stavka representative in the Leningrad theatre, but Stalin sent the ubiquitous Zhukov north to make sure the operation was as well prepared as possible. It was on his arrival at the Leningrad front that Zhukov learnt he had been promoted to the rank of Marshal. The Soviet attack began on 12 January 1943, as the German 6th Army was being ground down within the Stalingrad ring. Six days later the two arms of the Soviet pincers joined, and Shlissel'burg fell. This was the first time in the war that the Red Army had broken through a heavily fortified German position. Russian attempts to drive further to the south were, for the moment, unsuccessful. Nevertheless, a narrow corridor 5–7 miles wide had been hacked out along the south shore of Lake Ladoga. Through this, a rail line was quickly laid to run from the 'mainland' to Leningrad, albeit under German artillery fire. Given its importance, Operation SPARK was achieved at relatively low cost for the Russians: 34,000 personnel, 41 tanks and 41 aircraft.[68] One of the trophies of this fighting was the first captured German 'Tiger' (Pz Kpfw VI) heavy tank.

With hindsight, given the crisis in the whole German front at the time of Stalingrad, it was surprising that the Red Army did not make even more progress around Leningrad. The German Army Group North sector remained static for another ten months, until January 1944, when the 900-day blockade was fully broken. Even then, the Germans would be able to extricate themselves. The fighting in the northern theatre, even more than that in the centre, took the form of trench warfare reminiscent of the First World War. This slow progress was also dictated by the limited resources committed by the two sides to what could never be a decisive theatre.

CONCLUSION

There was an element of strategic confusion on both sides of the Eastern Front in the second half of 1942. Stalin – and his highest military advisers – misread overall German strategic intentions in the East. They exaggerated the importance of the Moscow theatre, both as an area to defend and as the most profitable line of advance. Hitler, for his part, assumed that the southern theatre could be decisive.

On 6 November 1942, only two weeks before the great counter-offensive at Stalingrad, the Soviet dictator made his annual address on the anniversary of the revolution. In this speech was an extraordinary public statement of Soviet strategic perceptions. Hitler's head-on attack against the Soviet capital had failed in December 1941, Stalin noted:

> The main goal of the German [1942 summer] offensive was to go around Moscow to the east, to cut it off from its rear, the Volga area and the Urals, and then to strike at Moscow. The advance of the Germans to the south towards the oil regions had a secondary objective, which was not so much the occupation of the oil-producing regions as the diversion of our main reserves to the south and the weakening of the Moscow front, in order to make it easier to deliver a blow against Moscow. This explains the fact that the main concentration of German forces is now not in the south [i.e. the North Caucasus] but in the region of Orel and Stalingrad.[69]

This *may* have been a piece of very highly placed disinformation to distract the Germans from the forces massing for Operation URANUS around Stalingrad. Another explanation is that this was a morale-building speech, a speech of self-justification; Stalin may have been attempting to make the military situation seem as positive as possible: if the German intention had been a roundabout attack on Moscow, then it had been thwarted by the Red Army. The speech may also, however, accurately have reflected the preoccupation of Stalin and the Stavka with the Moscow axis. Stalin was certainly right about one thing, however. The Germans had tried to do too much: 'Thus the tactical successes of the German summer offensive were not followed through in view of the completely unrealistic nature of their strategic plans.'[70] The 'two hares' were not, as Stalin suggested, Moscow and Baku, but Stalingrad and Baku, the fatal split between Army Groups 'A' and 'B'.

The later part of 1942 is often seen as the single turning point in the war, but this is arguable. The Red Army had not suffered its last defeat, and it would not fully gain the strategic initiative until six or seven months after Paulus's capitulation at Stalingrad. Stalin had certainly expected the 1942 campaign to be more decisive than it was. He did not, as he ordered in January 1942, bring the war to a complete victory in 1942 and drive all the invaders from Soviet soil. In net terms, even in February–March 1943, the line of the front had only shifted fractionally back from where it had been in January 1942. In the north and centre, up to the end of 1942, the front had been static. In the south the Germans had been pushed west 350–400 miles, but only back to where they began in the winter of 1941–2. This year of 1942 had been extremely costly to the Russians.

Meanwhile, the static situation in the north and centre of the Soviet–German fronts in 1942 showed how important as a turning point the Battle of Moscow in 1941 had been. It stopped the Wehrmacht in front of Moscow and Leningrad, and Army Groups North and Centre never moved any closer to those vital objectives.

The winter battles of 1942–3 were extremely costly for the Axis forces, both in absolute terms and compared to what had gone before. The 180,000 Germans lost in January 1943 amounted to a death toll three times that of any previous month in the East, and would only be exceeded in October 1944. Losses in December 1942 had been 79,000, and in February 1943 they would be 68,000 for a total of 327,000 over the winter.[71] Nazi Germany could not sustain this. Meanwhile, Hitler's attempt to fill the manpower gap with Axis-satellite armies – Romanians, Hungarians, Italians – had failed miserably. The blow to the prestige of the Wehrmacht, of National Socialism, of Germany, of Hitler, was devastating. The myth of German invincibility, which Stalin had been debunking since his May and July 1941 speeches, was now really in tatters. This was true for the Battle of Stalingrad in a way that had not been true for the Battle of Moscow, where German losses had been lower and the retreating Germans had stood fast after giving up only a month's worth of their sensational BARBAROSSA advance. As for Stalin and the Russians, never again after Stalingrad would their position be so desperate.

Even more important, however, at Stalingrad Hitler's strategic plan had failed – again. Directive No. 41 (5 April 1942) and Operation BLUE made a grim strategic sense for Hitler. The strength and endurance of the Red Army were an unknown quantity. From Hitler's point of view, every gamble, even at long odds, was justifiable if a lucky win would make the southern operation succeed. If this ambitious operation was not attempted, Germany would lose the war anyway; the Wehrmacht could not stand still.

But the run of the cards resulted in defeat, and because of the way Hitler raised his stakes, the defeat that followed was catastrophic.

The German Operation BLUE was now as much a failure as Operation BARBAROSSA. The 'military strength remaining to the Soviets' had not been destroyed, nor had the Russians been deprived of any of the 'sources of strength of their war economy' (to quote the BLUE directive of 5 April 1942). Hitler had achieved none of his objectives; even Leningrad had survived in Soviet hands. His 'breathing space' of 1942, the period before American troops and matériel entered the war in force, had come and gone.

In itself, the German defeat at Stalingrad was not all that different from the Axis capitulation to the British and Americans in Tunisia. This was true in terms of the scale of loss of forces, of strategic position (and of physical distance from the heart of the Reich), and even of impact on Italy and the smaller Axis military partners. But Stalingrad also represented the failure of Hitler's second grand offensive. The destruction of the German 6th Army at Stalingrad and the precipitate retreat of Army Group 'A' from the Caucasus signified the utter wreck of Hitler's grand strategy in a way that his defeat in North Africa did not. Indeed, Germany no longer had a grand strategy. The Battles of Smolensk and Moscow in 1941 were costly engagements that demonstrated the failure of Hitler's first campaign. The Battle of Stalingrad showed the failure of the second. Despite the spectacular clash of armour at Kursk in 1943, Hitler would mount no comparable third campaign.

PART II
THE SOVIET VICTORY, 1943–5

CHAPTER 7
TOTAL WAR I: WARTIME ARMS AND ARMIES

Modern war is a war of motors. The war will be won by whichever side produces the most motors.

Joseph Stalin, 6 November 1941

One must be clear, *mein Führer*, that the extremely critical situation in which we find ourselves cannot be put down just to the enemy's undeniable superiority [of numbers]. It is also due to the way in which we are led.

Field Marshal Manstein, 4 January 1944

From the point of view of historians, Stalingrad may or may not have been the turning point in the Nazi–Soviet War. The beginning of 1943, however, was certainly a psychological moment of telling importance for both sides. Stalin issued his annual Red Army Day order on 23 February 1943:

Three months ago the Red Army began an offensive on the approaches to Stalingrad. From that time the initiative of military action has been in our hands, and the tempo and force of the offensive operations of the Red Army are not weakening.[1]

The tempo would slacken in the spring of 1943; the Stavka decided to switch to the defensive against two last German assaults (at Khar'kov and Kursk); but in essence the Red Army held the initiative until the end of the war.

For the Nazi leaders Stalingrad was, as Propaganda Minister Goebbels put it, an *Alarmsignal*. The Nazi leaders put the situation in stark terms. On 30 January 1943, with Paulus's surrender imminent (and on the tenth anniversary of the Nazi seizure of power), Hitler issued a proclamation. Russia, he declared, was a state that wanted

to conquer Europe, to destroy its culture, to exterminate its people, and to gain slave labour for the Siberian tundra. ... Either there is a victory of Germany, of the German Wehrmacht, of our allies, and of Europe, or the Asiatic-Bolshevik wave will break into our continent whose culture is the world's most ancient.

Three weeks later, in Berlin, Nazi Propaganda Minister Goebbels made his most important address to the Reich population. 'The assault from the steppe [*der Ansturm der Steppe*] against our noble continent has broken out this winter with a force beyond human and historical imagination.' The Wehrmacht was the only bulwark against this assault. At one level this was all the direst Nazi hypocrisy; in reality, Germany had launched a terrible war of aggression against her neighbour. At another level, Goebbels' words were true enough. The tables had turned, and Nazi Germany and its empire was now under deadly assault. Stalin was right to say, in May 1943, that Goebbels', call for 'total war' was evidence that Hitler's original intention, the Blitzkrieg, had failed.[2]

There were other ways in which the second part of the Nazi–Soviet war, the two and a half years after the Battle of Stalingrad, was different from the first. In the eighteen months after 22 June 1941, both sides had fought the war, in effect, using no more than what they had possessed at the start. The Soviet Union had the benefit of its pre-war military armaments production spurt, but it had actually lost assets since the invasion. These losses included much of its standing army and many of the USSR's economic resources. The country also fought in isolation in this first part of the war, facing the bulk of the German Army and the Luftwaffe and receiving little material support from its wealthy allies. For the Germans, the invasion was intended to be a quick 'battle of annihilation' using forces in being. As we have seen, in the euphoria of mid-July 1941, Hitler had actually planned the partial demobilization of ground forces. While the Germans gained further vast territories in the East, they had not gained new assets there which they could put to effective use in 1941 or 1942. In 1942 the two sides settled into a prolonged war of attrition, for which neither was yet ready. In contrast, in 1943 and 1944, both sides had been able to carry through the expansion of their industry, and the re-equipment of their armed forces was working its way through. Finally, in 1943–4, Britain and the United States were playing a much more important part in the war both operationally and logistically.

WAR INDUSTRY AND LEND-LEASE

Economic resources

'The correlation of forces on the Soviet–German front has changed', Stalin said in his February 1943 speech. 'The fact is that Fascist Germany is more and more exhausted and is becoming weaker, and the Soviet Union is deploying its reserves more and more and is becoming stronger.' Stalin was speaking, in the first place, about equipment. In the course of the winter of 1942–3, he said, there had been a combination of the gearing up of Soviet factories and losses by the Germans. The Wehrmacht, he claimed, had lost 7,000 tanks, 4,000 aircraft and 17,000 guns. Now things were fundamentally different. 'Of course the Germans will try to make good these losses, but that is not so easily done, since it demands no little time to make good these huge losses in equipment. And time does not wait.'[3]

The Nazis, for their part, now portrayed the production situation in the Soviet Union differently. In his January 1943 proclamation, Hitler described the threat: 'With the aim of invading Europe, Bolshevism pursued a planned arms build-up of truly gigantic proportions'; this build-up began a decade before the Nazi seizure of power. In a speech made on the same day, Goebbels described the winter battles as being 'for the German nation a searchlight [*Fanal*] for total war':

The Soviet Union built up its arms for 25 years to prepare itself for this. The Bolsheviks make people into war robots. In 1936 we had the motto 'First guns, then butter!' Bolshevism had for 25 years outdone this with a motto of its own: 'Social misery, hunger, and mass hardship, but from that weapons, cannon, and war matériel'. This abnormal military threat we must resist with our whole national strength.

In February 1943, in his 'total war' speech to the German people, Goebbels elaborated on this theme:

In the East a whole people are forced to go into the struggle; men, women, and even children are driven not only into armaments factories but into battle itself. Two hundred million stand against us here, part under the terror of the GPU, part holding stupidly to devilish views. The masses of tanks that are attacking our Eastern Front this winter are the result of the twenty-five years social misfortune and hardship of the Bolshevik *Volk*.

The Germans, Goebbels went on, could win by making a similar commitment. 'Do you want total war? Do you want it, if necessary, more total and more radical than we can imagine it today?' The answer from the huge audience in the Sportpalast arena was a stormy '*Ja!*'[4]

Each of these statements, by Stalin, Hitler and Goebbels, contained an element of truth. Developments, however, had followed a more complicated path than Stalin suggested. As discussed in Chapter 2, the USSR had thrown away an initial advantage. The Russian forces started the war in June 1941 numerically much better equipped than those of Germany. The Red Army had then lost vast amounts of matériel in the summer of 1941. However, it *was* true that by the winter of 1941–2, the Red Army had been worn down to a relative disadvantage in terms of numbers of tanks, aircraft and guns. The Soviet forces had lost battles in late 1941, and in 1942 they could not regain the initiative. It was also not true to say, as Goebbels did, that Germany had been complacent before January 1943. Stalin was also wrong to suggest that Germany could not expand its war industry.

The Third Reich did not lose the Second World War solely because it was negligent in gearing up its economy for war in time. This was not a winnable production race between a Nazi hare and Soviet tortoise. Even if Germany and Nazi-occupied Europe had produced 50 per cent more of everything, this production would still not have matched that of the United States, the British Empire and the Soviet Union. Germany could not have won, but the production gap hastened its defeat. The basic problem throughout the war was that the economy of the Third Reich was too small.[5]

Table 7.1 German and Soviet war production, 1942–4 (1,000s)

	1942		1943		1944	
	Ger.	USSR	Ger.	USSR	Ger.	USSR
Rifles, submachine guns	1,602	4,619	2,509	4,081	3,085	3,006
Machine guns	117	356	263	458	509	439
Artillery	41	128	74	130	148	122
Tanks/SPG	6	24	11	24	18	29
Combat aircraft	12	22	19	30	34	33

Source: Barber and Harrison, *Defence Industry*, p. 100.

Note: German figures cover only Germany. Occupied territories like the Czech lands contributed significantly to production totals. Artillery ('guns' in the source) supposedly excludes mortars. Soviet artillery figures in this source are much higher than those published elsewhere, and these are cited in Table 7.2. In 1942, for example, production of field artillery, anti-tank guns and anti-aircraft guns was 57,000, not 128,000. The numbers above perhaps include other categories of artillery.

Although most of 1942 was a time of sensational victories for the Wehrmacht, it was also the year that the Germans had their greatest production disadvantage relative to the USSR (see Table 7.1). After 1942 the Third Reich achieved a remarkable expansion of its war economy. The leadership in Berlin had begun dealing with economic inefficiencies before the war with Russia, but the Wehrmacht's failure at Moscow in December 1941 speeded this up. Under Fritz Todt, and then under Albert Speer, the administration of the Nazi war economy was shaken up. By September 1943, Speer held all authority for the German war economy, with the – significant – exceptions of labour and of factories controlled by the SS. The summer of 1944 saw another – and more desperate – reorganization of German industry, in response to the successful D-Day landings, the military crisis in Belorussia and the attempted assassination of Hitler. Goebbels himself then oversaw the 'total war' effort.

Why could this improvement not have been implemented earlier? First of all, as was shown in the first chapter, the German economy was already geared to war from the late 1930s. The curve of production could only slope upwards at a certain angle. Second, some of the German advantage came from the control of the assets in other parts of Europe which only slowly became available after the conquests of the summer of 1940.

On the negative side, the Allied strategic bombing campaign from the west and south had begun. Axis war industry and civilian morale were the main targets. The British night bombing campaign became a significant factor in the spring of 1942, and the American daytime campaign in the course of 1943. In May 1944, when deeper and more accurate air raids provided the opportunity to target and cripple synthetic oil production, the situation became really difficult for Nazi Germany. Although the output of Reich industry continued to grow, production was increasingly affected; without the air attacks, output would have expanded even more rapidly.

Goebbels' image of twenty-five years of Soviet preparation was much exaggerated. Nevertheless, it is true that from about 1927–8, the Soviet economy had been built up, and on the military side it was perhaps five years ahead of Germany (although the Russians started from a lower general economic level).[6] The very considerable strengths of the Soviet economy, in the 1930s and in 1939–42, were outlined in Chapter 2. It proved easier for the USSR to mobilize its economy than it was for other countries, and indeed the problem was one of avoiding excessive mobilization. However, not only was the USSR a much poorer country than Germany, on a per capita basis, but in the course of 1941 and early 1942 the Soviets lost access to raw materials and a large amount of their productive capacity. Diversion of resources to the military eventually wore the whole economic system down. Despite the Red Army's victories at Stalingrad and the beginnings of a production upturn in the last months of 1942, the Soviet economy was still under great strain in 1943. There was a marked decline in the first quarter of that year – the very time of the Stalingrad victory. In this period the Soviet population suffered its worst shortages in terms of food and consumer goods. At the start of 1943, the planners' attention had to be turned to the imbalances in the economy, especially the lack of raw materials, fuel and power. Resources, especially labour, were now channelled to the civilian sector. Indeed, the Soviet economy was set on a more planned basis only in 1943, thanks to the breathing space won by victories at the front. As the best Western historian of the Soviet home front has pointed out, the planned economy of the USSR was a *consequence* of victory, rather than a cause of it. Even in 1945 the Soviet economy was smaller than it had been on the eve of the war.[7]

Food supply needs to be considered too. The breakdown of this system had been a major reason for the collapse of Russia, Austria–Hungary and Germany in 1917–18. In the Second World War, Germany could draw on foodstuffs from other parts of central and western Europe, and the population of the Reich only faced serious problems in the winter of 1944–5.[8] On the Russian side, maintaining the food supply throughout the war was a basic cause of victory. This was achieved despite great handicaps. Much of the best Soviet farmland was occupied or subjected to a policy of 'scorched earth'. Even in the Soviet-held zones the agricultural sector was stripped bare during the war. The collective farms were largely worked by women, and they were left few draught animals or tractors. In January 1945, when the liberation of Soviet territory was complete, the labour force of the collective farms was reckoned to be twenty-two million, fourteen million less than it had been at the start of 1941.[9] Although Soviet industry began to improve in the middle of 1942, agriculture did not show signs of positive change until 1944. The 'victorious' year of 1943 was especially difficult for farmers because of a drought in the centre of the country which was as severe as the catastrophic drought of 1921. This, coupled with the need to provide emergency food for the recaptured territories, led to a lowering of the food ration.

The economic underpinnings of the Nazi–Soviet war after 1942 did not involve just a simple comparison between Germany and Russia. A global war was being fought between two great coalitions, of which the USSR was only part. The Allies as a whole were substantially richer than the Axis. One historian has estimated that the area controlled by the Allies in 1942 had had a pre-war (1938) GDP of $2,070,000,000, compared to $1,550,000,000 for the territory controlled by the Axis (including Japan), and the Allied

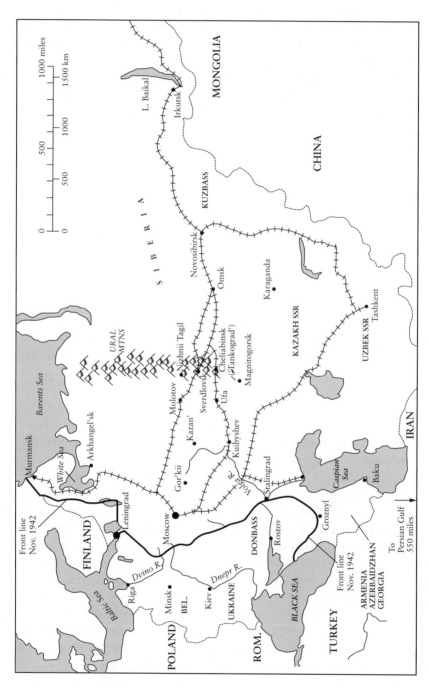

MAP 6 The Soviet home front.

figure left out the extraordinary growth of the American GDP after 1938.[10] Russia's main enemy, Germany, had to devote a larger and larger part of its production to fighting the Americans and the British. The challenges for Germany increased significantly by the start of 1943. They included waging the U-boat war, fighting the British and American ground forces in the Mediterranean, preparing the coastal defences of northwestern Europe, defending the Reich against air attack, and devising and deploying 'revenge' weapons (the Vl and V2 missiles). Meanwhile, part of the production of Russia's Allied partners, especially America, could be transferred to the Red Army and the Soviet civilian economy. The shipment of weapons and supplies from America and the British Empire went from a trickle to a torrent in 1943.

Some aid had been given to Russia by Britain at the very beginning of the Nazi–Soviet war, but within a few months – before Pearl Harbor – this had been put under the umbrella of 'Lend-Lease' and was provided mainly by the United States.[11] Lend-Lease supply to the USSR eventually fell into four periods. The period covered by the First Protocol (the inter-Allied agreement) ran from October 1941 to the end of June 1942, and the remaining three protocols covered successive 12-month periods (1 July to 30 June). Under the First Protocol, the British and Americans promised to send 400 aircraft and 500 tanks each month, plus a large range of other supplies.

The Western powers did ship what they promised under the First Protocol, despite the entry of the United States into the war and the defeats suffered in Asia by both Britain and America. Nevertheless, a significant proportion of these supplies were lost en route. The bigger promises made under the Second Protocol were harder to keep, and there were also shipping problems. Both the Western Allies and the Russians preferred the Arctic convoy route, from Britain and the North American east coast to Murmansk and Arkhangel'sk in North Russia. Unfortunately, this route was partly cut by German air and naval attacks mounted from northern Norway. The disaster of convoy PQ17 in July 1942 – 24 of 35 merchant ships were sunk – was only the worst. Meanwhile, Allied shipping and naval escorts were everywhere in short supply, what with losses from enemy action and the unfolding American and British overseas campaigns in the Mediterranean and the Pacific.

The shipping situation improved in mid-1943, and deliveries under the Third and Fourth Protocols were at or above what had been agreed. Lend-Lease is often associated with the drama of the Arctic convoys, and it is true that in 1941–2 they accounted for about 40 per cent of shipments (by tonnage). In 1943, however, the Pacific route, from the west coast of North America to the Siberian ports, made up nearly half the shipments, and a further 30 per cent came via the Persian Gulf; the share for North Russia was now only 14 per cent.[12] As America and Japan were at war, and the USSR was a neutral, the Pacific sea route could be used for oil and food, but not for weapons. Many American warplanes, however, were flown from the United States across the North Pacific via Alaska and Siberia, the ALSIB route; this opened in the summer of 1942. The decision in the autumn of 1942 to upgrade the supply route from the Persian Gulf across Iran (and to transfer control from the British to the more efficient Americans) was to prove a most important step. It was also a belated recognition that the war was going to last a long time.

During the Cold War the Russians minimized the impact of Lend-Lease and the West exaggerated it. (There was no such argument about the great role of American Lend-Lease supplies in the *British* war effort. Britain received substantially more American Lend-Lease aid than the USSR, 43 per cent of the total – by value – compared to 29 per cent.) Hitler alluded to Lend-Lease to Russia in 1945 in part of his *Testament*:

> At a time when Europe is fighting desperately to ward off the Bolshevik peril, the United States, guided by the Jew-ridden Roosevelt, can think of nothing better than to place its colossal material resources at the disposal of the Asiatic barbarians, the barbarians who want to annihilate Europe, the motherland of the New World!

Stalin's verdict, at about the same time (at the Yalta Conference), was balanced. 'Lend-Lease', he told Roosevelt, 'was a remarkable invention without which victory would have been delayed'; he gave 'his opinion of the extraordinary contribution of Lend-Lease to the winning of the war'.[13]

The peak periods of Lend-Lease were the fourth quarter of 1943 and the third quarter of 1944. Of about $9,500,000 of US Lend-Lease aid to Russia, some 85 per cent was accounted for in the period after Stalingrad (i.e. after 1 January 1943), and 54 per cent in the period after 1 January 1944. Having said that, Lend-Lease had an intangible morale impact from the earliest stages of the war. Even bare promises were important then. The Red Army's political organs in July 1941 ordered that the new Anglo-Soviet agreement be given the widest circulation, including 500,000 copies in German and, interestingly, a million copies in Finnish.[14]

It is difficult to calculate the effect of economic aid, as opposed to the supply of military equipment; the former actually made up the larger part of Lend-Lease. About 30 per cent of the Lend-Lease total (by value) was machinery and raw materials, and about 20 per cent agricultural products. To take one example, in 1944, the USSR received 1,100 main-line railway locomotives through Lend-Lease and produced only 32 of its own. Supply of foodstuffs and raw material was very important in sustaining the Soviet economy after two or three years of a draining total war. The best estimate is that external resources, essentially Lend-Lease, contributed 10 per cent of Soviet GDP in 1943 and 1944.[15] The Soviet Union would probably still have held its own, without internal social turmoil like that of 1917. However, the war, for Russia and her allies, would have lasted longer, and the death toll of Soviet soldiers and civilians would have been even higher. It is one thing to say that the Red Army had such and such a number of American and British tanks in a particular battle, or even that British and American aircraft made up such and such a proportion of a certain type. It is harder to calculate the weight of transport or communications resources, harder still to evaluate the importance of explosives, high octane fuel or aluminium. Most difficult of all is factoring in the importance of aid to the Soviet home front, which sustained Soviet production and recruitment, and prevented discontent.

It is sometimes argued that the West should have used control of the Lend-Lease pipeline to secure more co-operative Soviet policies, for example, over Poland and

Eastern Europe. Aside from the fact that such diplomatic pressure would probably have been counterproductive, it misses the basic point about aid to Russia: it worked in the interests of the Western Allies. Lend-Lease kept the Russians fighting, and it kept pressure on the Wehrmacht. What the Western Allies lost in terms of equipment, the Red Army lost in terms of human lives.

However the overall contribution of Lend-Lease is evaluated, it did not have a crucial effect on the survival of the USSR in the *first* period of the war, through the winter of 1942–3. In contrast, the Soviet counter-offensive, which ran for two and a half years from early 1943 in the second part of the Nazi–Soviet war, owed a great deal to Lend-Lease. Particularly important here was the supply of heavy lorries from the United States. The fact that the Soviet economy did not collapse in 1941–2 was due to pre-war Soviet organization and investments, but those things would not have allowed the long and continuous offensive of 1943–5.

In one of the worst periods of the war for Russia, in November 1941, Stalin listed the critical factors that made Germany's defeat inevitable. One was the 'coalition' of the USSR, Britain and the United States, and the productive power this unleashed. 'Modern war is a war of motors. The war will be won by whichever side produces the most motors. The combined motor production of the USA, Britain, and the USSR is at least three times that of Germany.'[16] The advantage was masked by production and supply problems in 1941 and 1942, but by 1943 and 1944 the power of the Allied coalition in the 'war of motors' was fully evident.

Equipment for war

Production and economic mobilization translated into weaponry; weapons in turn affected the changing fortunes of the two sides as the war progressed. The quality of weapons changed incrementally. On the Soviet side, equipment that had been available in prototype form, or in small numbers, in June 1941 became available in massive quantities. This was not a war like some of those of the nineteenth century, where a better rifle could turn the tide. The most numerous weapons, basic infantry arms, changed, but the advances of the two sides cancelled one another out. Some infantry on both sides had more and cheaper automatic weapons, but only one soldier in ten carried a submachine gun. Small arms were not a category where Lend-Lease was of great importance. The United States, Britain and Canada supplied Russia with only 152,000 small arms.[17] The Russians produced more than enough to equip their new infantry divisions. As for the Germans, they succeeded in producing a huge amount of small arms. Although they overtook Soviet production in 1944 (see Table 7.1), the Germans had fallen behind in 1942 and 1943, and by 1944 they needed all the small arms they could get to cope with campaigns on three land fronts.

Towed artillery also changed less than some other kinds of weapons over the course of the war. As with rifles, the Germans overtook Soviet production here in 1944, but the Russians had also been well ahead in 1942 and 1943, and they were progressively able to equip their new divisions with artillery. (On the other hand, the Wehrmacht had the considerable advantage of Soviet artillery pieces captured in 1941–2.) The Red Army began the war with 33,200 artillery pieces and lost 24,400 in six months; another 12,300 were lost in 1942, and at the start of 1943 the Soviet artillery park was only slightly larger than it had been in June 1941. In 1942, and to a lesser extent in 1943, the Russians resorted to the production and use of the relatively simple mortar (mostly 50mm and 82mm) to supplement proper field artillery pieces. The Soviet position with respect to towed artillery improved in 1943, due less to production (which was actually lower than in 1942) than to lower losses. By January 1944 the Red Army had 53,100 field artillery pieces, and in January 1945, 62,300.[18]

As can be seen in Table 7.2, the Soviet production of the famous 'Katiusha' or 'Stalin organ' rocket launchers was relatively small and was actually reduced in 1944. Production was counted in terms of launcher vehicles. In 1944–5, the most common launcher vehicle was the BM-31. BM stands for *boevaia mashina* (combat vehicle); this version had 12 launcher rails for 310mm rockets mounted on a lorry. The standard lorry was the American Studebaker US6. A BM-31 'Guards Mortar' division (3 brigades) comprised 288 launcher vehicles and could lay down 3,456 rockets in one salvo.[19] The Germans developed a comparable weapon, the six-barrel 150mm and the five-barrel 210mm *Nebelwerfer*, but did not use them on such a massive scale.

A major problem for the Red Army in the early war years had been the lack of effective anti-tank (AT) guns. In January 1943 the Red Army, after heavy losses, had fewer AT guns on hand (14,300) than in June 1941 (14,900, mostly 45mm). In the course of 1943 the situation greatly improved, with the number of guns doubling by January 1944 (to 32,200). The Germans, for their part, developed light and heavy anti-tank rockets, the *Panzerfaust* and *Panzerschreck*, which could be carried by infantrymen. The Russians had nothing like these or like the American bazooka. The Soviet wartime development was a pair of large-calibre (14.5mm) anti-tank rifles, the PTRD and the PTRS, but these elephant guns were ineffective against later and better armoured enemy tanks.

Table 7.2 Soviet artillery production, 1941–5

	1941	1942	1943	1944	1945
Artillery (76–203mm)	10,100	30,100	22,100	21,500	5,800
Anti-tank guns	2,500	20,500	23,400	6,400	1,400
SP guns	0	60	4,400	13,600	5,000
AA guns	3,400	6,800	12,200	13,400	2,600
Mortars (50–160mm)	42,400	230,300	67,900	2,000	1,400
Katiushas	1,000	3,300	3,300	2,600	800

Source: Poteri, pp. 473–4, 477–9.

Note: Artillery includes guns and howitzers. Artillery pieces mounted on SP (self-propelled) mounts are probably not double-counted in the 'artillery' or the 'anti-tank gun' rows. 'Katiushas' numbers refer to launcher vehicles, not individual launch rails.

A weapon that became important only in the second half of the war was the self-propelled gun (SP gun). This was an artillery piece mounted on a tracked chassis; it could keep up with, and support, rapidly advancing tanks and infantry.[20] The Germans introduced the StuG III in February 1940, a 75mm gun mounted on a Pz Kpfw III tank chassis. They built later versions on a very large scale: some 7,700 of the 24-ton 'G' variant of the StuG III were produced between late 1942 and early 1945. The Germans also produced numerous small batches of other SP guns, based on an array of German and captured tank chassis, and using many different field guns and anti-tank guns. In the Soviet case, SP gun production was negligible in 1941 and 1942, and less than a quarter of conventional field gun production in 1943. In 1944, by contrast, production had risen to nearly 70 per cent of towed artillery production (see Table 7.2). Much the most common Soviet SP gun was the 11-ton SU-76 (SU standing for *samokhodnaia ustanovka*, or 'self-propelled mount'); this was a 76mm field gun on a T-70 tank chassis. The SU-76 entered service in early 1943, some three years after the StuG III; some 1,900 were built in that year, no fewer than 7,200 in 1944, and 3,600 in 1945. More potent Soviet SP guns, mostly based on the T-34 chassis and KV/IS chassis and often used in a tank-destroyer role, also entered service in smaller numbers.[21]

In the later years of the war much of Red Army artillery in all its forms – heavy and medium guns, heavy mortars, rocket launchers, and heavy AA and AT guns – was deployed on critical parts of the battle front from the huge central pool of the High Command Reserve (*RVGK*). By the end of 1944, this numbered 105 divisions, including 31 artillery breakthrough divisions (*artilleriiskye divizii proryva*) and 7 rocket-launcher divisions. There were also 147 independent brigades, and numerous independent battalions (*diviziony*) and regiments.[22]

As with infantry weapons, artillery equipment did not make up a substantial proportion of Lend-Lease aid, even in 1943–5. On the other hand, the numerous trucks and other vehicles supplied by the Americans and British were important for towing Soviet artillery pieces. Ammunition requirements for all these small arms and artillery pieces were very high. According to one Russian estimate, in the Battle of Moscow in 1941,

Table 7.3 Soviet tank and SP losses

	1941	*1942*	*1943*	*1944*	*1945*
Tanks and SPG available	28,200	35,700	47,900	59,100	48,900
Losses					
Heavy tanks	900	1,200	1,300	900	900
Medium tanks	2,300	6,600	14,700	13,800	7,500
Light tanks	17,300	7,200	6,400	2,300	300
SP guns	0	100	1,100	6,800	5,000

Source: Poteri, pp. 475, 479.

Note: 'Available' is number of tanks and SP guns on hand on 1 January (22 June in 1941) plus vehicles entering service in the course of the following year. Heavy tanks are mainly KV and IS, medium tanks mainly T-34, light tanks mainly T-26, BT, T-60 and T-70, and SP guns mainly SU-76.

FIGURE 8 A battery of Soviet 'Katiusha' rocket launchers, mounted on Lend-Lease Studebaker trucks.

ammunition expenditure was 700–1,000 tons a day; in 1944, the 1st Belorussian Army Group alone was expending 20–30,000 tons a day. After the war Marshal Zhukov identified explosives provided by the Western Allies, along with lorries, as key war-winners.[23]

The central weapon of the war on the Eastern Front was the tank. The Russians had lost the armoured battles of 1941 mainly with the 11-ton T-26 and 14-ton BT light tanks. A new generation of Soviet tanks, which had been appearing in small numbers in 1941, replaced them en masse in 1942 and 1943. The most important were mentioned in Chapter 2, the 29-ton T-34 medium tank and the 45-ton KV heavy. Both were armed with a 76mm gun, which was a much larger weapon than what was fitted to foreign tanks of the time. Even two years later, at Normandy, the biggest British or American tank gun would be a 76mm. As the second part of the war began, the T-34 became available in very large numbers – 12,600 were built in 1942 and 15,700 in 1943, thanks to the completion of giant plants in the Urals.

Stalin made much of the need to stay up to date: 'To stand still in military affairs means to fall behind. And those who fall behind, as is well known, get beaten.' On the other hand, he also saw the value of mass. Malyshev, the People's Commissar of Tank Production, noted a conversation in the Kremlin in January 1942: 'Com. Stalin emphasized several times that what was needed now were those weapons which had done well in battle; they were to be produced on a massive scale, without making any modifications.' Stalin said this was a mistake the Germans had made.[24] The result of this approach, however, was that in terms of quality – but not quantity – the Germans began to catch up in certain categories of weapon, especially tanks. By 1943 the original version of the Soviet T-34 medium tank was being outclassed by new German tanks and SP guns. The T-34 with its 76mm gun had entered service in the autumn of 1940; not until early 1944 did the 32-ton T-34-85 begin to take its place on Soviet production lines. The new model mounted the heavier 85mm gun – with a bore close to that of 88mm gun of the German Tiger tank and a high muzzle velocity (enabling penetration of the thick armour). It had better radio equipment than the older version and a three-man turret which greatly enhanced the tank's combat potential. Nevertheless, the original T-34 had emerged as the mass weapon in the Red Army in later 1942 and early 1943, in the new tank corps. It was not until the middle of 1943 that the Germans fielded in any strength tanks able to match it, and by that time the Russians had a huge numerical advantage. In any event, some 11,000 of the up-gunned T-34-85s were produced in 1944 (alongside 3,700 of the 76mm model), and no fewer than 18,300 T-34-85s came off the assembly lines in 1945.[25]

Other Soviet tank models were less important than the T-34, which became a 'universal' tank, a vehicle able to fulfil any battlefield role. As the war progressed, the KV heavy was built in smaller numbers than the T-34 medium; only some 1,800 were delivered in 1942. The basic KV design continued throughout the war and, like the T-34, it was progressively modified and up-gunned. The name was changed from 'KV' (Kliment Voroshilov) to 'IS' (Iosif Stalin); the reputation of Voroshilov had become somewhat tarnished during the war. The 46-ton IS-2 'Stalin' mounted what was, for a tank of the Second World War, a large-bore 122mm gun (replacing the 76mm of the KV). Series manufacture of the new model began in the autumn of 1943 and the IS-2 entered service in the western Ukraine in the spring of 1944. The 'Stalin' was, like the KV, built in relatively small numbers (in Russian terms): 2,300 in 1944 and 1,500 in 1945, although another 4,000 IS chassis were used for big SP guns. In 1941–2, a significant proportion of Soviet tank production had taken the form of light tanks, the 6-ton T-60 and 9-ton T-70, replacing the T-26. In 1942 4,500 T-60s and 4,900 T-70s were produced, the latter with a 45mm gun. Even in 1943, 3,300 T-70s were built, but from then on the chassis was used only for the SU-76 SP gun.

Russian tank losses were very high in 1941: some 20,500 vehicles. The number of tanks and SP guns available in the Red Army rose rapidly, especially in 1943, but losses were also heavy. In the victories of 1944 the Red Army lost twice as many tanks as in the disastrous year of 1942. Throughout the period 1943–5, the Red Army was losing an average of about 1,000 T-34 medium tanks a month (see Table 7.3).[26]

The Germans were not outclassed. Their tank force had come a long way since the 20-ton Pz Kpfw III with its 50mm gun. This vehicle had made up the largest part of the *Panzerwaffe* in 1941–2. The famous 57-ton Pz Kpfw VI (Tiger I), heavily armoured and equipped with what was for the time a big gun, the 88mm, appeared in Russia in small numbers in the autumn of 1942. It continued in production until the summer of 1944, but only 1,400 were built. The 46-ton *Jagdpanther* SP gun and the 68-ton Tiger II – both armed with improved 88mm guns – entered service only in June 1944, and a mere 390 examples of the first type and 500 of the second were built.

Much more important was the excellent German 'medium' tank, the Pz Kpfw V Panther, which the German Army designed as a reply to the T-34 and rushed into service at Kursk in the summer of 1943. At 43 tons, the Panther was nearer in size to a KV or an IS than a T-34. Total Panther production was only 6,000 vehicles, which was a small number by Russian or American standards. The 25-ton Pz Kpfw IV, a type dating back to 1938, was (in up-gunned versions) a significant element of the German armoured forces even in the later stages of the war; the total production run was 6,800. The 20-ton Pz Kpfw III was phased out of production by the summer of 1943 after a total of 5,500 had been built.

In contrast to the situation with respect to infantry weapons and artillery, the Russians maintained a numerical edge over the Germans in tank production throughout the war years, producing 24,000 tanks and SP guns in 1943, compared to 10,700 in Germany, and no fewer than 29,000 in 1944, compared to 18,300 in Germany (see Table 7.1). British and American tanks were inferior to those of the Russians and Germans, at least in their technical specifications. The Americans produced a standard medium tank in even larger numbers than the T-34, building 41,500 of the 31-ton M4 Sherman, as well as 7,400 of the earlier 27-ton M3 Grant. The Russians were sent 4,100 Shermans and 1,400 Grants under Lend-Lease. Compared to the United States, a higher proportion of British Empire tank production went to Russia: 3,900 of 8,300 18-ton Valentines, 1,100 of 4,700 27-ton Matildas, and 300 of 5,600 40-ton Churchills. Altogether, the Americans, British and Canadians supplied the USSR with 11,900 tanks and SP guns.[27] Although more important as a contribution than small arms and artillery, Western tanks still made up a relatively small part of the Red Army's tank park, and their quality was inferior to the T-34 (either variant).

Even in the later part of the war, and despite their emphasis on 'deep battle', the Russians did not produce armoured personnel carriers (APCs) like the German SdKfz 251 half-track or the American equivalent (M2, M3, M5). The Germans produced 15,300 such APCs, and the Americans no fewer than 41,200. Typically these vehicles carried about ten infantrymen or other equipment. The Russians did receive 5,000 APCs from the British and Americans, but the most common Red Army practice was to carry infantry as 'tank-riders' (*tankodesantniki*), sitting on top of tanks.

The German Army had only limited provision of transport and support vehicles, and was far from being a motorized army. The army that invaded Russia in 1941 had had an awkward mixture of military, civilian and captured vehicles. Nevertheless, the Germans had a large motor industry, plus access to European production. German output was gradually rationalized, and in October 1943 it was reduced to three classes of truck and five makes; these were based on civilian models. Germany produced more trucks than the USSR in every war year except 1945; the greatest advantage was in 1942, when Germany produced 58,000 trucks to 30,000 produced in Russia.

In the autumn of 1942, motor transport was one of the most important weaknesses of the Red Army. This was a time when the northern (Leningrad) and central (Moscow) sectors of the Soviet front were stalemated, and in the southern sectors (towards Stalingrad and the North Caucasus) the Red Army was still retreating. In a general report of 10 September, General E. A. Shchadenko, in charge of forming and manning new units, reported to Stalin that the Red Army was prone to passivity and static-defensive operations: 'The army at the present time does not have enough motor transport [*avtotransport*] which makes it difficult to move, incapable of rapid action and maneuver. Such an army will not be in a position to mount decisive offensive operations without fundamental reorganisation.'[28]

A great change was evident in the second half of 1943 and throughout 1944 and the spring of 1945: the Red Army proved fully capable of highly mobile and long-range operations, in all seasons of the year. The number of trucks (*gruzoviki*) on hand in the Red Army rose steeply, from 274,000 in November 1942 to 330,000 in June 1944, and to 379,000 in January 1945; for the same dates the quantities for other vehicles (jeeps, cars, etc.) were 103,000, 130,000 and 153,000.[29] Soviet truck production did recover from 35,000 in 1942 (a quarter of pre-war production) to 61,000 in 1944 (although not all went to the Red Army). Also extremely important were motor vehicle deliveries under Lend-Lease, the great bulk from the United States, but some from Britain and Canada. Two different totals for this have been given, 312,600 and 409,500, but even the lower figure is very impressive.[30] The bulk of these vehicles only became available to the front-line Red Army in late 1943 and 1944.[31]

The Red Army was not carried mainly by American Lend-Lease trucks even in 1944–5. In May 1945, apparently only a third of the Red Army's motor transport vehicles had come from Lend-Lease; 58 per cent was Soviet produced, and 9 per cent had been captured.[32] But if the number of Lend-Lease vehicles was smaller, their total carrying capacity was probably at least as great. The Studebaker US6 was much more capable than the most common Soviet truck, the GAZ-AA (itself a licence-built version of a 15-year-old Ford design). Not only did the Studebaker have over 50 per cent more capacity (2.5 tons vs. 1.5 tons) and power (87 hp vs. 50 hp), it also had 6 axles, and in many cases 6-wheel drive, greatly improving its off-road performance and the mobility of Red Army formations. Only 3,800 Studebakers were received in 1942, but 34,800 arrived in 1943 and 75,600 in 1944–5.

It was the growing availability of motor transport that allowed the rapid and sustained forward movement of Soviet armies in 1943–5, and which kept those armies supplied.[33] The Red Army had to advance over very long distances. The big American trucks were especially important where the Soviet forces were advancing in regions with poor roads and where the railway network had been devastated by the retreating Germans. 'In fact', Marshal Zhukov admitted in an unpublished post-war interview, 'they [American Studebakers] to a considerable degree provided our transport in the forward area [*frontovoi transport*].'[34]

On the other hand, it is important to remember that the Red Army relied heavily on horse traction throughout the war. According to official statistics, there were 1,275,000 horses in May 1942 and 1,054,000 in January 1945 (the number dropped to about 935,000 in mid-1943).[35]

One of the reasons why the Germans could not match the Russians in the production of tanks and other ground vehicles was that they devoted a large part of their limited resources to equipment for the air war, both in the first and second periods of the war. The Red Army Air Force had been technically inferior to the Luftwaffe at the start of the war. Nevertheless, the huge aircraft plants on the middle Volga (constructed by Soviet forced labour just before the conflict) now began to produce very large numbers of modern fighters and attack aircraft. By the winter of 1942–3, new Soviet aircraft were roughly comparable in quality to those of the Luftwaffe. The Yakovlev fighters, just entering service in June 1941, now became available in substantial numbers; they improved in performance through gradual changes. By the late autumn of 1942, the relatively simple Yak-1 (8,700 built in total) and Yak-7 (6,400) were being replaced on the production lines by the numerically most important Russian fighter of the war, the Yak-9 (14,600 delivered before the end of the war). The lightweight, air-superiority version of the same basic design, the Yak-3, entered service in the summer of 1944 (4,100 being delivered during the war). The unsuccessful LaGG-3 fighter, also just entering service at the time of the invasion, was transformed into the excellent Lavochkin La-5 by fitting the basic airframe with a new engine; the modified fighter entered service in the winter of 1942–3. Some 9,900 were built plus, from the end of 1944, some 5,800 of the refined La-7.

The most numerous German fighters in the later part of the war were the 'G' version of the Messerschmitt Bf 109 and the 'A' and 'F' versions of the newer Focke-Wulf Fw 190. While these aircraft were not inferior to the Yaks and Lavochkins, they were available over the Eastern Front in much smaller numbers. The Germans did produce various 'miracle' air weapons, which were more advanced than those of the Russians (or of the British and Americans). The most important was the Messerschmitt Me 262 jet fighter. However, only 1,100 of these jets were produced, just a small proportion actually entered service, and they were used almost exclusively in the West.

Russian fighter production was much higher than German production and higher than British production. Britain produced 14,200 Hurricanes and 22,300 Spitfires – of which 2,800 and 1,300, respectively, were sent to the USSR. American fighter production was higher than that of Russia. Some of the older American types were actually kept in production throughout the war solely to supply the USSR. Factories in the United States produced 9,600 Bell P-39 Airacobras and 13,800 Curtiss P-40s, of which 4,700 and 2,100, respectively, went to the USSR. The Airacobra was the more significant plane; Stalin personally requested this type, and it was flown by a number of leading Russian aces right through to the end of the war.

The most important Soviet aircraft were two battlefield attack aircraft (light bombers) the Il-2 and Pe-2. The twin-engined Petliakov Pe-2 dive-bomber was in service in very small numbers in 1941 and continued in production through 1945; some 10,600 were built. The two-seat version of the Il'iushin Il-2, the famous *Shturmovik*, entered operational service in October 1942; the provision of a rear gunner greatly improved its survivability. Some 36,200 of these heavily armoured Il-2 aircraft left the factories during the war, making it numerically the most important aircraft type of the Second World War (the Messerschmitt Bf 109 took second place, with over 33,000 produced). In contrast, production of the main Luftwaffe ground attack aircraft, the Junkers Ju 87 Stuka, was only 5,700; the Ju 87 was a design dating back to 1934. German factories failed to provide an effective replacement. A heavily armed and armoured battlefield aircraft, the twin-engined Henschel Hs 129, underwent protracted development. Some were used at the Battle of Kursk, but only a small number (900) were ever built, and they suffered from technical shortcomings. The main 'new' German ground attack aircraft was the fighter-bomber version of the Fw 190 fighter, of which 6,600 were produced.

Purpose-built ground attack aircraft (*shturmoviki*) made up only 0.5 per cent of Soviet aircraft in June 1941, but 27 per cent in January 1944. In contrast, at the start of 1944, bombers made up only 21 per cent of Russian combat aircraft, compared to 42 per cent in June 1941. The main Russian medium bomber was the twin-engined Il'iushin Il-4, roughly comparable in age, performance and production numbers to the German He 111; some 6,800 were built. American production of medium bombers was much higher than Russia's, with 7,400 A-20s ('Boston' or 'Havoc') and 11,000 B-25s ('Mitchell'). Of these, 3,000 A-20s and 900 B-25s went to the USSR.

There was one great difference between the various Allied air forces. Very few four-engined Soviet heavy bombers were built, despite a strong pre-war bomber tradition. Only 93 of the Petliakov TB-7/Pe-8 heavy bombers left the factory, and the type is perhaps best known for ferrying Molotov to Britain and America in 1942. The Western Allies, in contrast, built over 50,000 four-engined bombers (none of which were supplied to the USSR). Fortunately for the Russians, the Luftwaffe also did not invest in a heavy bomber force, and the mainstay of Goering's bomber force in the Russian–German front throughout the war remained the Heinkel He 111 (first flown in 1935, with 7,300 built) and the Junkers Ju 88 (14,700 built, plus 1,100 similar Ju 188) medium bombers. With another 3,000 Dornier Do 17 and Do 217 medium bombers completed, the Germans significantly out-produced their eastern enemy in this one category of aircraft. Even here, they fell behind the Allies taken together. The Germans also suffered serious medium-bomber losses in the abortive Stalingrad air bridge. The four-engined Heinkel He 177 heavy bomber was built in relatively small numbers (1,100 machines) and was unreliable; it was one of the failures of Reich technology.

Soviet air losses were very high, even in the victorious later years of the war, and non-combat losses (accidents, aircraft retired) made up a large proportion. It must be assumed that some of the 'other losses' in 1944 were worn-out aircraft that were scrapped, but there still would seem to have been – as was the case in foreign air forces – a high accident rate. Non-combat losses were particularly high for fighters in 1944, 8,600 out of 12,700.

Table 7.4 shows that aircraft combat losses decreased from 34 per cent of available aircraft in 1942 to 14 per cent in 1944. The absolute total of Russian combat aircraft

Table 7.4 Soviet combat aircraft losses

	1941	1942	1943	1944	1945
Total combat a/c available	29,000	33,000	55,000	68,100	58,300
Losses					
Combat losses	10,300	7,800	11,200	9,700	4,100
Other losses	7,600	4,300	11,300	15,100	6,900

Source: *Poteri*, pp. 475–6, 479–80.

Note: 'Available' is aircraft on hand on 1 January (22 June in 1941) plus aircraft entering service in the course of the following year. The Russians also had 10,000–15,000 training aircraft and transports.

losses in 1944, however, was nearly as large as that in the catastrophic year 1941. In the first year of the war, the loss figure had included aircraft destroyed on the ground and abandoned on forward airfields. The 1944 figure reflected the greater activity of Russian aircraft and their exposure in large numbers to Axis fighter and AA guns. The Russian losses are also consistent with some of the very high number of Russian aircraft claimed shot down by the Luftwaffe '*Experten*'. Erich Hartmann, the top German ace, claimed 352 aircraft, nearly all Russian and nearly all after Stalingrad (his combat flying career began in October 1942). The second top Luftwaffe ace, Barkhorn, claimed 301 aircraft destroyed, mostly in Russia, and there were a large number of other German fighter pilots who claimed to have shot down more than 100 aircraft over the Soviet–German front. In contrast, the leading Russian '*asy*', Kozhedub and Pokryshkin, claimed 62 and 59 enemy aircraft, and the claims of the top American and British aces were only 40 and 38. The German pilots' claims were apparently not especially exaggerated by Nazi propaganda; the long tours of duty which German fighter pilots served were a factor. The Luftwaffe veterans also had a very large number of targets in the later part of the war.

Overall, Lend-Lease was more important for the provision of aircraft than it was for the provision of ground force combat equipment. Altogether, the Red Army Air Force received 18,300 aircraft from the Americans and British, about 15 per cent of all its aircraft.[36] Nevertheless, they were not of war-winning importance. Of much greater significance was the concentration of the Luftwaffe in the West, which was forced on the Germans by the British and American bomber offensive.

Space does not allow a discussion of all kinds of military equipment. Radio sets, however, although less 'visible' than tanks, or guns, or aircraft, are worthy of mention. The German Army was well equipped with radios, which were vital for combined arms operations. For the Russians, in contrast, communication failures were an important reason for the Red Army's disasters in 1941. The Russian armed forces reportedly began the war with 37,400 radio sets and lost two-thirds of them in the course of the year. The pre-war level was only reached again in January 1943. By January 1944, however, the figure had doubled to 71,600 sets, and it increased by a third by January 1945. A considerable proportion of these radio sets were provided under Lend-Lease. Put another way, in January 1942, there was one radio set for 218 personnel in the active army and navy; in January 1944, the figure had improved to one set for 88 personnel, and in January 1945, it was one for 60. At an operational level, this meant more effective command of troops; at a tactical level, it reflected the fitting of radios to most tanks and aircraft.[37]

The overall picture of production and supply in the last three years of the Nazi–Soviet struggle is not a simple one. Russia was still a poor and backward country, and it had now been devastated by war. Unlike America, Britain and Germany, the USSR did not in 1941–5 introduce fundamentally new weapons like strategic bombers, radar, jet aircraft, long-range rockets or landing craft. Instead, the Russians effected the incremental improvement of weapons available in 1941.[38] The Soviet record in the 1930s had been more impressive; in that decade the Red Army pioneered extensive use of fast tanks, heavy bombers and parachute troops; Soviet technical innovation would also be much greater in the 1950s. The Soviet government did, however, achieve a concentration of effort. Beyond standard infantry equipment and munitions, Soviet factories in the second half of the war produced great quantities of medium artillery, medium tanks and battlefield aircraft. They did not produce significant naval or long-range bomber forces, and they relied heavily on imports for transport vehicles. The Germans showed greater innovation, and had a more complex mix of weapons, driven partly by the multi-front nature of their war. They devoted too many of their resources to the Luftwaffe, without producing war-winning air weapons.[39] The war in the East might have been prolonged if the Third Reich had mimicked the USSR, building more tanks, artillery and ground attack aircraft. But in that case, the Wehrmacht would have lost – even sooner – crucial battles in the Atlantic and in the skies over Germany. Those Germans, including Hitler, who thought the Third Reich could not win an extended war on two fronts were proved right.

THE WEHRMACHT AND THE RED ARMY IN 1943–5

The high commands

Victory was not just about 'producing the most motors'. Well-equipped armies can still be beaten by better-organized ones. Levels of organization depended on leadership from high command to unit level, on training and organization, on discipline, on doctrine. Stalin argued in May 1942 that the Red Army had enough equipment (he might have added, 'again'). The problem, as the dictator put it, was 'knowing how fully to use this first-class equipment'. The Red Army succeeded in doing this. Stalin reinforced the point in February 1945: 'In the fourth year of the war [i.e. from the summer of 1944] the Red Army became stronger than it had ever been, its military equipment became still more modern, and its skill on the battlefield [*boevoe masterstvo*] many times higher.'[40] The story was rather more complex than that, but there was an essential truth there. After Stalingrad the Germans had a new and healthier respect for the Red Army. As we have seen, in his speech of 18 February 1943, Goebbels spoke of 'motorized divisions of robots [*Roboterdivisionen*]', and this was a backhanded compliment to the discipline and equipment of the Red Army after twenty months of war.[41]

The history of the German high command in the second period of the war is well known. There were two related problems: the confused command structure and Hitler's inflexibility. Some memoir writers and historians see these as the chief reasons for the Wehrmacht's catastrophe, with Hitler as an all-powerful and inflexible individual, refusing especially to make timely withdrawals. Field Marshal Manstein, for example, recalled a conversation he had with Hitler at Rastenburg in January 1944, as the position in the Ukraine began to disintegrate: 'One must be clear, *mein Führer*, that the extremely critical situation in which we find ourselves cannot be put down just to the enemy's undeniable superiority [of numbers]. It is also due to the way in which we are led.' Germany needed, in particular, a C-in-C of the Eastern Front 'who should have complete independence within the framework of general military leadership [*Gesamtkriegführung*].[42] What Manstein was asking for was both a different commander and a different structure.

It would be nearer the truth to say that these command problems were inherent to the National Socialist state, and that the catastrophe came before the worst of the disorganization. The pre-eminent political leader, the Führer, had personally to undertake the defence of the state. Numerous attempts have been made to get inside the mind of Hitler the strategist. If in 1938–42 he took rash risks, in 1943–5, he was reluctant to give anything up. The interaction between structures and circumstances was important. The German command structure was in chaos, at least from 1942, because the Third Reich was losing the war. It was not losing the war because of its chaotic command structure. The Wehrmacht had exhausted its chances for military victory at least by the time of Stalingrad, and possibly by the end of 1941. The Red Army had survived, it was steadily getting stronger, and by October 1942, it was clear Germany could advance no further to the East. Hitler's decision to take sole command of the German Army from Field Marshal Brauchitsch had not come out of the blue, at the Führer's whim. It followed the grievous – probably mortal – German military setback in front of Moscow.

Likewise, the defeat at Stalingrad in the winter of 1942–3 did not stem purely from Hitler's leadership style or blindness. It followed the perverse logic of an 'all-or-nothing' victory. Seeking peace was not for the Third Reich a 'rational' choice. Hitler and those around him – including some of the generals – may also have acted in the spirit of what has been called 'catastrophic nationalism'. The *Endkampf* (final battle) *had* to be fought whatever the cost, and the *Endkampf* began at Stalingrad.[43] Later on, Hitler ignored calls to find a 'political' solution; he also ignored advice that might perhaps, in military-technical terms, have given Nazi Germany another six months or so of existence, but no more than that. Even if Manstein or some other field marshal had been given sole command of the eastern theatre, it would have made little difference. In short, if Hitler was indecisive from 1942 onwards, this was because for the Third Reich the outcomes of all decisions had become unacceptable.

The professionals at the top of the German armed forces had less excuse than Hitler for holding on to delusions in 1943–5. For most of them, neither making peace nor removing Hitler were options. Manstein explained his own decision in 1943–4 not to take part in the conspiracy against Hitler:

> It was clear to me that any attempt to make the necessary changes by force would lead to the collapse of our front. The thought that the Russians would get through to Germany ruled out violent change as much as did the Anglo-Saxon demand for unconditional surrender.[44]

The senior generals were too committed to the Nazis and to the Nazi wars of aggression. The Armed Forces (Wehrmacht) High Command (the OKW) did not change in the second half of the war. It was still led, under Hitler, by the team of Keitel and Jodl. For the Army (as opposed to the Wehrmacht as a whole), the leadership change had come in December 1941, when Hitler replaced Field Marshal Brauchitsch as head of the Army High Command (OKH). The removal of Halder as Chief of the Army General Staff in September 1942 came about, as we have seen, because of frustrations with the slowing pace of operations in Russia. Halder's replacement in this key organization, General Kurt Zeitzler, was eleven years younger. Zeitzler had distinguished himself as General Kleist's chief of staff in France in 1940 and had most recently been chief of staff to Field Marshal Rundstedt, the C-in-C West. Under Rundstedt and Zeitzler the Dieppe raid had been successfully dealt with. Zeitzler was an energetic and capable officer, although he apparently came to his post with high confidence in the Führer. He was prepared to defend his own sphere, the Army General Staff and, more specifically, the Eastern Front for which he effectively had responsibility.

The next big formal change would not come until the summer of 1944, when the burned-out Zeitzler was dismissed. The sacking again followed a front-line crisis, this time in Belorussia. The replacement of Zeitzler as Chief of the Army General Staff by the famous panzer commander Heinz Guderian in late July 1944 made little practical difference. The General Staff lost a number of experienced officers with the arrests after the July 1944 bomb plot. In late March 1945 Guderian was replaced by General Krebs. Finally, after July 1944 the SS was given direct control over a quarter of the German Army when Himmler was put in charge of the Replacement Army.

The command structures of the German armed forces remained confused, with the continuing distinction between the Army High Command (OKH) running the war in Russia and the Wehrmacht High Command (OKW) running the campaigns in other theatres. These difficulties were, again, not so much a whim of Hitler as a response to changing reality. Western Allied fronts now represented a real and more active danger to the Reich, first in the Mediterranean, and then in France. There was no overview of the situation as a whole (aside from what was in Hitler's head), and a continual tug of war was carried on between the eastern and western theatres. There was still no overall commander in Russia to provide a counterbalance to Hitler.

A number of proposals after Stalingrad to unify the various commands and even the OKW and OKH staffs came to nothing. In early September 1943, as the German front east of the Dnepr River in the Ukraine faced being overwhelmed, Field Marshals Kluge and Manstein (C-in-Cs of Army Groups Centre and South) went to Hitler at Rastenburg to propose concentration of all fronts under the Army Chief of Staff. We have seen how in February 1944 Manstein proposed a theatre command in the East like those held by Field Marshals Rundstedt in western Europe and Kesselring in the Mediterranean. A more rational structure would have had a professional high command – in the image of Hindenburg and Ludendorff from the First World War – and three tri-service theatre commands. That was incompatible with the Führer state, and by 1943 it would have made little difference to the outcome of the war.

The German high command was greatly affected when some senior officers organized a plot to assassinate Hitler on 20 July 1944, and followed this with a bungled attempt to seize power. A bomb planted by a staff officer, Count Claus Schenk von Stauffenberg, went off during one of Hitler's conferences at Rastenburg. Hitler, who for many months had blamed his military failures on the incompetence of his commanders, now accused them of treason. The Stauffenberg *attentat* was the one that came nearest success, but there was also a plan to assassinate Hitler on a visit to Army Group Centre headquarters in Smolensk in March 1943.[45] Many of the conspirators had links to the Eastern Front, although that is not so surprising; most of the German Army was concentrated in Russia. The conspirators were not necessarily so much anti-Nazi as anti-defeat. This was a phenomenon of the second part of the war, after Stalingrad, when for some German nationalists Hitler came to symbolize the destruction of the Fatherland.

The Red Army high command changed less than did the German one, but partly because – for other reasons – the war was going more successfully for the USSR. As with the Third Reich, the dictator figure held a multiplicity of posts. Stalin was Supreme Commander-in-Chief and chairman of the Stavka; he was also chairman of the State Defence Committee (GKO), chairman of Sovnarkom (i.e. prime minister), People's Commissar of Defence and General Secretary of the Central Committee of the Communist Party. Like Hitler, Stalin's activities even went down to operational level in special cases. The German dictator took over direct command of the vital invasion of the North Caucasus in 1942; the Soviet one took over direct operational control of three army groups during the Battle of Berlin.[46] A Soviet Manstein, had he dared, could have complained to Stalin about the lack of a 'professional' head of the Soviet armed forces or even – in the second half of the war – about the lack of a resident Chief of the General Staff, about the lack of inter-service co-ordination, and about the lack of theatre commands.

The personality of the supreme leader was, of course, important. Stalin's military abilities, even in the second phase of the war, are still a matter of controversy. One difficulty is explaining how Stalin could have made so many mistakes in the first eighteen months or so of the war, and then have improved. Khrushchev, in a typically colourful passage, said that from 1943 onwards, 'Stalin got into combat uniform and was sure we would win'; he contrasted this with the earlier period of the war when 'he went around like a wet chicken'. Marshals Vasilevskii and Zhukov worked most closely with the *Verkhovnyi* [Supreme C-in-C] throughout the war. Vasilevskii thought Stalin was 'reconstructed' in November 1942. The Soviet leader calmed down and realized he could make mistakes.

Zhukov's view, in a lecture delivered in 1966, divided Stalin's command activities into three periods. In the first, up to Stalingrad, Stalin showed a naive interest in modern military technology but dealt poorly with the demands of modern strategy; he remained fixed in the traditions of the Civil War of 1918–20:

In the second period of the war, which went from the preparation of the Battle of Stalingrad and up to Kursk, inclusive, I must say that Stalin showed definite flashes of insight into modern war. And as far as the third period of the war is concerned ... I must say to you – and here Zhukov's voice took on a special tone – here was a real military commander [*polkovodets*] of modern world war on a large scale. And coming to a general conclusion, said Zhukov, in this war we had a worthy Supreme C-in-C.[47]

In a part of his memoirs that was censored in early editions by Soviet editors, Zhukov claimed:

> Up until the defeat of the German forces at Stalingrad [Stalin] had a superficial understanding of combined arms operations. Not having a strong grasp of the complexities, methods, and potential of modern army-group level operations I. V. Stalin frequently demanded patently unrealistic periods of time for the preparation and carrying out of operations.

The comment of Zhukov's that seems most telling is that about the greater realism of the Soviet leader. Stalin's wishful thinking had, after all, been at the root of Hitler's ability to achieve surprise in Operation BARBAROSSA; Stalin's wishful thinking also explained the unsuccessful Soviet winter counter-offensives in 1941–2 and the retreat of the summer of 1942. As Zhukov put it, 'The notion "what I decide can and must happen" was replaced by a more sober notion, based on an objective assessment of reality. "It is only possible to do what can be done, what can't be done, can't".'[48]

The historian David Glantz convincingly dismissed the myth that victory came because Stalin was more ready to follow the advice of his senior generals. Glantz has a greater command of the military documentation than any other historian in the West. Writing in 2009, he stated that he found

> no evidence indicating that Stalin ever relinquished his role as chief architect of the military strategy the Soviet Union and its Red Army pursued during the war. On the contrary, close examination of key wartime documents … show [sic] that the dictator dominated military decision-making as much in the spring of 1945 as he had during the initial period of the war, often on matters tactical and operational as well as strategic.[49]

Stalin did evolve during the war into an effective military executive. He was in day-to-day control of the Stavka; the armies that he controlled were victorious. There was some attempt to take the formal load off Stalin in November 1944 when the 'political general' N. A. Bulganin was made Deputy Commissar of Defence, with responsibility for the preliminary consideration of questions raised by various directorates of the Commissariat. However, the key organs, the General Staff and the Main Political Administration, were still to report directly to Stalin.[50] This measure coincided with Stalin's decision to take direct command of the three army groups on the main front, against eastern Germany.

Stalin found different subordinates in the second half of the war, men who would achieve better results than their predecessors.[51] Marshal Shaposhnikov and Marshal Timoshenko have not come in for much criticism from historians, but their departure from the centre of the high command in the middle of 1942 coincided with a marked improvement in the Red Army's fortunes. Zhukov and Vasilevskii were probably more talented commanders, and they were certainly more able to win Stalin around to their point of view. The membership of the Stavka VGK (High Command of the Supreme Commander-in-Chief) from the middle of 1942 to the beginning of 1945 did not accurately reflect who actually ran the Soviet armed forces. The Stavka was not like the Chiefs of Staff Committees in the United States or Britain. Its membership did not change for most of the war; the Stavka formally included Stalin, Molotov and Zhukov, but also Marshals Budennyi and Voroshilov and, as late as February 1945, Marshals Timoshenko and Shaposhnikov. The Stavka VGK was only shaken up in February 1945, when Timoshenko and Voroshilov were removed, and Vasilevskii, Bulganin and General Antonov (the new Chief of the General Staff) were made members.[52] There was no naval presence on the Stavka for nearly the entire war; Admiral Kuznetsov was removed in early July 1941 and only returned in February 1945. The Red Army Air Force never had representation. According to Zhukov, the Stavka never met with its full membership.[53] As with so much of Stalinist Russia, the 'system' did not rely on formal bureaucratic structures. It depended on a key central individual, that is Stalin, and on subordinates he delegated power to.

More important was the 'motor' of the Stavka, the Red Army General Staff.[54] The Stavka had no personnel or communications system beyond what was provided by the General Staff. Marshal Vasilevskii's view was that there had been no war in which general staffs were more important; he called it a 'war of staffs'. Both Vasilevskii and Zhukov argued, however, that in the first part of the war Stalin underrated the General Staff.[55] They were probably right that Stalin's greater readiness to listen to the professional advice of the General Staff was an important reason for the success of Red Army operations in the second part of the war. The Soviet General Staff system, too, did not work the way that it was supposed to on paper. Vasilevskii had replaced Shaposhnikov as Chief of the General Staff in the summer of 1942, and he was undoubtedly an able officer. But by his own reckoning, during his thirty-four months as Chief of the General Staff, Vasilevskii had spent twenty-two months at the front, as a Stavka co-ordinator, in effect as a field commander. Writing from an army group commander's point of view, in memoirs not published in his lifetime, Marshal Rokossovskii was highly critical of this system and of the ambiguous position of the Stavka representatives.[56]

A third key military adviser to Stalin fitted closely into this system, an officer whose time was clearly in the second half of the war. Vasilevskii would only step down as Chief of the General Staff in February 1945, but for over a year the day-to-day running of the General Staff in Moscow had been looked after by General Aleksei Antonov. Although about the same age as Zhukov and Vasilevskii, Antonov had held relatively junior staff posts in the field in 1941–2. It was only in December 1942, after the Stalingrad encirclement, that he was brought into the Operations Directorate of the General Staff, evidently on Vasilevskii's urging. Although Stalin was wary of a new face, Antonov soon became the Soviet leader's indispensable day-to-day military adviser. It was he who now counter signed most of Stalin's orders. A sign of his importance is the personal access he had to the Soviet leader. In 1944, for example, there were 102 meetings between Antonov and Stalin in the latter's Kremlin offices, compared to 16 with Vasilevskii and 18 with Zhukov (and compared to 137 with Molotov).

Zhukov accorded General Antonov high praise: 'Aleksei Innokent'evich was to the highest degree a capable and well trained military man, a man of high culture and charm.'[57] Antonov has remained somewhat in the historical shadows, despite the fact that he played a prominent part at the Yalta and Potsdam Conferences. This was partly because he died early (in 1962) and did not produce memoirs. It was also partly because of his very close association with Stalin, which was a liability in the Khrushchev years of de-Stalinization. Antonov never held a major front command, and (like Halder and Zeitzler) he was never promoted to the rank of Marshal.

We have seen how the system of 'Stavka representatives', one unique to the Red Army, developed from the start of 1942. This system effectively replaced the old theatre (*napravlenie*) commands. Theatre headquarters lacked staff and, as an intermediate tier, slowed the passing back and forth of reports and orders. Under the new system, the military talent was doled out to the key fronts on an ad hoc basis as required for particular operations. Zhukov reckoned that he and Vasilevskii had each been sent out about fifteen times as Stavka representatives. There was still friction. In the middle of August 1943, Vasilevskii was Stavka representative for the critical Donbass operation. On the second day, as his armies were moving rapidly forward, Stalin sharply criticized his failure to make a daily report and contrasted him with Zhukov who was more 'disciplined': 'I am warning you for the last time. If you once more allow yourself to forget your duty to the Stavka you will be removed from your post of Chief of the General Staff and you will be recalled from the front.' A related, and important, mechanism in the later part of the war was the attachment of General Staff officers to formations, down to division level. They reported back directly to Moscow and could bypass the local commander.[58]

Strategic intelligence can logically be linked with high-command functions. Historians' accounts of the campaigns in the West had to be rewritten after information was revealed about the ULTRA system of reading and exploiting Wehrmacht signals. Despite some new research, Red Army intelligence remains largely hidden. Very few relevant Soviet intelligence assessments have been published. (The exceptions are some reports relating to the immediate pre-war period.) Meanwhile, the Western Allies did not provide the USSR with war-winning intelligence; they did not even let the Russians know, on a regular basis, what they were learning about the German order of battle on the Eastern front from decrypted signals, mainly from the Luftwaffe.[59] It is unlikely that even in the later stage of the war, Red Army intelligence was reading Wehrmacht signals in the way that the British and Americans were, although they were able to analyse aspects of German radio traffic. The Red Army Air Force also lacked fully effective air reconnaissance; Zhukov blamed this on Stalin, with his emphasis on combat air units.[60] In the second half of the war, the Russians evidently did develop thorough systems for interrogating POWs, and they gained some operational and tactical intelligence from partisans, at least until the middle of 1944, when the fighting was still on Soviet territory.[61]

Meanwhile, German military intelligence did not markedly improve in the second half of the war. The central figure, General Gehlen, was frequently incorrect, especially in his attempts to anticipate the next Soviet move. The Wehrmacht was especially caught out by the June 1944 offensive in Belorussia. The Germans still had great difficulties obtaining concrete information on Soviet industrial potential or resources of military personnel. Although they were able to gain considerable information about the strength and deployment of Soviet troops from radio traffic analysis and from direction finding, the highest-level Russian radio communications were secure, at least from 1943. The

Luftwaffe seldom flew reconnaissance missions deep into Soviet territory, and with the growth of Red Army Air Force, even short-range reconnaissance was more limited.[62]

German personnel

The position of the officers and men of the two armies evolved during the course of the war. The composition and power of the German officer corps at formation level did not change fundamentally. Hitler had new favourites among the more junior generals, men like Walter Model or Ferdinand Schörner, but these individuals were, as a rule, energetic and effective. There was almost no 'political' appointment of militarily incompetent leaders to operational commands at theatre or formation level; the exception was Hitler's choice of the SS leader Heinrich Himmler to command Army Group Vistula in 1945.

At a lower level, Hitler had made much of the democratization of the officer corps. In November 1942, before the Stalingrad disaster, he stressed the qualitative change in the German army, distinguishing it from its previous incarnations. It was now based on what the Nazis called the 'people's community' (*Volksgemeinschaft*): 'You will see ... how month by month the Wehrmacht will become more and more National Socialist, as it takes on the shape of the new Germany, as privileges, class prejudices, etc., are eliminated.'[63] Political education was more stressed in the German armed forces. National Socialist 'leadership officers', comparable to Soviet commissars, were introduced. At the end of 1943 the Nazi Party became directly involved in the selection and training of new officers.[64]

Officers made up only a small proportion of the Wehrmacht; the great majority were enlisted personnel. It was here that the Third Reich was especially at a disadvantage, with its smaller population base. When Stalin spoke of the changing 'correlation of forces' in 1942–3, he was talking partly about losses to the German rank and file. He maintained that the enemy had suffered nine million casualties in the twenty months of the war, four million of these killed in battle. 'The weak spot in the German armies is the lack of reserves of personnel.' Stalin's assessment of German losses was greatly exaggerated, but the Wehrmacht certainly had severe personnel shortages due both to losses and to the expanse of conquered territory that had to be defended. As it happened, the total strength of the German armed forces peaked in 1944 at 12,070,000 personnel, but the front-line army had gone down to 4,000,000 personnel, from 4,250,000 in 1943.[65] Even keeping the German Army at this level could only be achieved by reducing its quality.

Some historians have stressed the 'de-modernization' of the German Army, especially under the conditions of the Russian front, and the way the development contributed to the barbarity of warfare there. This was not altogether inconsistent with the remarkable cohesion of the rank and file of the German Army, on the Russian front and elsewhere, who fought on under extremely disadvantageous conditions.[66] There are certainly questions to be asked about the motivation of the ordinary German soldier (*Landser*) in the later years of the war. The continued resistance of the regular German Army was as remarkable as its extraordinary victories of 1939–42 (and the qualities of the German soldier then were discussed in Chapter 2).[67]

The July 1944 coup attempt led to Himmler's SS taking control of the 'Replacement Army' from the regular military authorities, some of whom had been implicated in the plot. To stress the 'popular' nature of the post-coup army, new infantry divisions were henceforth given the title of *Volksgrenadier* ('People's Grenadier' or *VG*) divisions. It was also hoped to keep these divisions under the supervision of the SS to ensure they were not misled by reactionary officers. Fifty of these *Volksgrenadier* divisions existed on paper.[68]

The German front line had to be fleshed out with second-class units of various types. One expedient was use of the troops of Germany's allies, Romania, Hungary and Italy, but this was shown to be of little value after the battles of the winter of 1942–3. Another source of personnel was from the occupied areas of the USSR, although men recruited there were used as internal security troops or as non-combat service troops in Wehrmacht units, the ubiquitous *Hiwis*.[69] Combat forces were brought in from other parts of the Wehrmacht. In September 1942, some fifteen Luftwaffe Field Divisions began formation: ground forces made up of excess Air Force personnel. In late 1943, they were incorporated into the Army, but they evidently were not as effective in combat as the regular ground forces. An even less effective manpower improvisation was Hitler's creation in October 1944 of the last-ditch militia, the *Volkssturm*. This organization was under the control of the local Nazi Party leaders. It was made up of men who were too old, too young or too unfit for the regular army.[70] The *Volkssturm* were poorly armed and probably inferior in quality even to the similar Soviet *Narodnoe opolchenie* of 1941.

The expansion of the Waffen-SS was the most striking development in Hitler's ground forces; the organization played a much more prominent part in the second half of the war than the first.[71] Himmler had been given permission to develop the organization as a combat force in mid-1938. In 1940, national strength had been just 50,000, and only a few Waffen-SS motorized divisions took part in the 1941 Russian invasion force. By March 1945 the Waffen-SS numbered no fewer than 830,000 troops. At that time only 40 per cent of its personnel were German nationals, and it did not represent a force qualitatively any better than the regular Army. On the other hand, the best-manned and best-equipped Waffen-SS formations had played a distinct and significant part in the campaigns in Russia and elsewhere. Waffen-SS motorized divisions were converted into armoured divisions, equipped to the highest standard and staffed with fit and highly motivated personnel. Most important were the famous 'Adolf Hitler' (*Leibstandarte Adolf Hitler*), 'Das Reich' and 'Totenkopf' divisions. These were especially prominent from the second Battle of Khar'kov in early 1943; they fought en masse at Kursk in 1943 and in Hungary in 1945.

Whatever the forces the Germans were able to assemble from the middle of 1943, the great difference from the earlier period was that they were deployed on the defensive. They could not show off their panzer tactics (the Blitzkrieg) in the East after the Battle of Kursk. Hitler's approach to this was largely unimaginative; he increasingly stressed point defence, with 'fanatical resistance', on the model of Sukhinichi or Demiansk. In early 1944 he made the creation of 'fortified places' the effective basis of his strategy. Field Marshal Manstein later stressed the potential of 'mobile defence', which he claimed foundered on Hitler's refusal to give up territory in order to consolidate reserves. In practice, however, 'mobile defence' only worked against the Red Army at the tail end of its offensives, when it had lost momentum. Hitler, probably correctly, thought that the days of 'elegant' operations were gone. They were possible only with first-class troops. Now improvisers with 'will', men like Field Marshal Model and General Schörner, could make more of the odds and ends the Wehrmacht scraped together than could 'technicians' like Manstein. 'Operations' largely disappeared after Kursk, with the only serious offensive being planned not against the Russians but against the seemingly more vulnerable British and Americans, in the Ardennes in December 1944.

Soviet personnel

Developments on the Soviet side of the front line were more positive. In February 1943, Stalin reported that 'in the course of the war the Red Army has become a cadre army [*kadrovaia armiia*]'. As victory loomed in May 1945 he could report that the Red Army has become a 'first-class cadre army'.[72]

Even more than Hitler, Stalin put a premium on rejuvenation of the high-level officer corps. There was public criticism of overconfident and underprepared commanders from the Civil War era, and in 1942 a play, A. E. Korneichuk's *The Front*, was staged to stress this theme.[73] In an NKO order of April 1942, Stalin bemoaned the fact that Soviet commanders, from the level of a regiment to that of an army, were trained as infantrymen or cavalrymen, and lacked a knowledge of the specialist arms like aviation, artillery and tanks. Meanwhile, he argued, the Voroshilov General Staff Academy produced planners with limited practical knowledge of the various arms. As a result of this, the Voroshilov and Frunze Academies were reformed.[74]

One important feature of Stalin's cadre army was the increase in the prestige and power of the officers corps as a whole. In early October 1942 the dual-command system was replaced by one of single command [*edinonachalie*] and the institution of commissar was removed; this was on grounds of greater military efficiency. This certainly did not mean the end of the Communist Party's involvement in the Red Army. The commissars became 'deputy commanders (political)', and at the army-group level the Military Councils (*voennye sovety*) included a senior party official, alongside the commander and his chief of staff. The abolition of the commissar came before the Stalingrad encirclement, but at a time when the Red Army's front was relatively stable.[75] An important factor behind the change was the more efficient use of experienced leaders, who were in short supply after the losses of 1941–2; many commissars and *politruks* were retrained as junior- and medium-level officers.

Equally striking, in this egalitarian socialist state, was the drastic change in the status of the Soviet officer corps, which coincided with the Battle of Stalingrad. The very term '*ofitser*' was only restored in January 1943; before that the more neutral term *komsostav* (command staff) was used.[76] At the same time shoulder straps (*pogoni*) – residual epaulettes, torn off in the egalitarian days of 1917 – were restored. Both officers and other ranks now wore them, but those of the officers were distinctive. The new Soviet officers were given various perquisites, including orderlies. John Erickson aptly used the phrase 'a new glittering Red Army' to describe the force that began to appear in the winter of 1942–3.[77]

The bulk of the 'cadre army' were the rank and file. The USSR's total armed forces grew from 4,800,000 in June 1941 to 11,400,000 in July 1945. Some 29,600,000 personnel were mobilized in the course of the war, beyond those already in service. The ration (*spisochnaia*) strength of the front-line (*deistvuiushchaia*) army recovered from 2,800,000 in the fourth quarter of 1941 and rose to 5,900,000 in the first quarter of 1943. Then it levelled out to the end of the war, fluctuating between 6,300,000 and 6,800,000.[78] Despite the USSR's greater population compared to Germany, the Russian military faced growing personnel problems. The huge loss of men of military age in 1941 and 1942 could never be made up, and in the first two years the territory from which the Red Army could raise conscripts was limited by the Nazi occupation. In 1942 Stalin had rightly emphasized in Order No. 227 that Russia no longer had the luxury of numbers.

The rank and file of the Red Army became more experienced as the war progressed. Former General A. A. Svechin, a senior staff officer in the First World War and the early Red Army's most prominent theorist, described the nature of wars and armies. Writing in the 1920s, he noted that 'over the course of a prolonged war the combat value of the combatants had a tendency to even out, because inferior troops gradually become battle-hardened and learn the enemy's tricks, while the better troops are gradually diluted with increasingly inferior replacements'.[79] A process like this certainly did take place in 1941–2; on the German side dilution included growing reliance on inferior troops provided by the Axis allies. On the Russian side, improving leadership at all levels and more abundant equipment were important factors in raising troop performance. The atrocious behaviour of the invaders, the effective propaganda of the Soviet government and the harsh discipline imposed by its political organs furthered the development. The experience of victory, once it had been achieved, also had a profound effect on morale.

However, the USSR also had to find new human resources.[80] As in Germany, there were 'comb-outs' of the rear echelons to secure combat troops. For example, the 'Workers Columns' (*rabochie kolonny*), those men of military age who, on political, ethnic or other grounds, had been ineligible to bear arms, were ended in April 1942. This yielded 170,000 men.[81] Mass recruitment of women into the Red Army began in the early spring of 1942. In March 1942, some 100,000 young women from the Komsomol were called up to form the crews of anti-aircraft guns. In April 1942, NKO orders were issued to give women tens of thousands of posts in the signals organization and in the rear echelons in general. A total of 490,235 women served in the ranks of the Soviet armed forces and another 500,000 in civilian support staff. Some 86 women won the medal Hero of the Soviet Union.[82] An emergency GKO decree of 26 July 1942 was issued immediately after the fall of Rostov and just before Stalin's Order No. 227 ('Not one step backwards!'). The decree ordered the transfer to combat units of 400,000 personnel from Red Army training and reserve units; this was to be completed by 1 September. At the same time the navy was to be cut by a fifth and 100,000 sailors sent to the front. The industrial commissariats were to give up 150,000 personnel from their work force, and the NKVD was to provide 35,000 of its personnel, plus 30,000 camp inmates.[83]

Greater use was made of Central Asian conscripts, although these were harder to integrate into the Red Army. In the First World War conscription had led to a rebellion in Turkestan. In 1941–2, the formation of military units from these non-Slav national minorities – Uzbeks, Kazakhs, Turkmeny – progressed with difficulty. At first, too many formations were created, and in March 1942, these were reduced to five independent 'national rifle brigades'. In May 1942, rear Military Districts were told that 11,000 Central Asians were on their way, and special efforts had to be made to win them over using the slogan of the 'Friendship of Peoples'.[84]

Another important source of Red Army personnel was the 'liberated' regions of the western USSR. It may seem surprising that there were many males of military age left in these areas, given pre-war Soviet conscription, Soviet evacuation, wartime losses, German recruitment for forced labour and German forced evacuation. But the occupied territories, even up to the time of Stalingrad, had had a population of about sixty-five million. In February 1942, as the Red Army began a first tentative advance back into ethnic Russian regions west of Moscow, army groups were allowed directly to call up men from liberated territories. This was important, as transport difficulties were holding up the arrival of replacements from the rear.[85] In the summer of 1943, as the tide of battle fully turned, these western regions of the USSR became even more important.

The new recruits from liberated territory were a mixed blessing. Having spent up to two years behind enemy lines, they were less amenable to discipline. They were also mostly not ethnic Russians. Initially, they were Belorussians and Ukrainians from the 'old' USSR. When the Red Army got to the 'new' territories annexed in 1939–40, especially western Belorussia, the western Ukraine and the Baltic states, the problems increased. Unlike most pre-1939 Soviet males, these people had had no military training. More importantly, they had questionable loyalty to either the Soviet system or the 'Russian' cause. One Political Administration directive of March 1944 mentioned the particular problems of personnel from the western Ukraine, who had lived for only a year and a half under Soviet power before the war, and who since then had been subject to hostile propaganda from the Germans and 'bourgeois-nationalist elements in a spirit of hatred and hostility to the Soviet Union and to the Red Army'. The centre was also eager to organize enlistment in a systematic way. In October and November 1943, as the Red Army swept across the Ukraine, the military authorities had to issue warning orders. Armies, formations, and in some cases even individual units gathered the male population in the course of the advance and enlisted them in the forces, not even compiling lists of names. This had all kinds of dangers, from the medical to the political. 'There have been cases where completely untrained men, without uniforms, have been used in battle.' Call-ups in liberated areas were to be carried out only by the army military councils, and not by divisions or regiments, and this recruitment had to be carefully regulated.[86]

Harsh internal discipline was still the rule in the Red Army, although in 1943–5 it was geared towards spurring soldiers on to the offensive, rather than combating defeatism or arresting deserters in a period of retreat.[87] During the war – according to published statistics – a total of 990,000 Soviet soldiers were condemned to punishment (*osuzhdeno*) by military tribunals. Some 420,000 of these were sent to punitive units and 440,000 to imprisonment; no fewer than 158,000 were sentenced to be shot. The number of German servicemen executed – some 13,000 to 15,000 – was considerably lower.[88]

Soviet division-level punitive battalions were disbanded in September 1943, although they were retained at army level. Surprisingly, the size of the Soviet punitive units was at its greatest in the years of victory, although this may just reflect better record-keeping and more formal punishments. There were some 25,000 *shtrafniki* (soldiers in punitive units) in 1942. In 1943 the number who served in such units soared to 178,000, and even in 1944 it was 143,000. The punitive units were given dangerous assignments and they took heavy losses; in 1944 the monthly casualty rates (killed, wounded and sick) in punitive units were from three to six times greater than those in regular ones. The 'blocking detachments' (*zagraditel'nye otriady*), tasked to prevent desertion, were disbanded in October 1944. At that time their strength was about 24,000 personnel.[89]

The so-called Special Section (OO) had been organized under the NKVD – the secret police – rather than the People's Commissariat of Defence (NKO) in July 1941. It played a sinister but important role for nearly the first two years of the war. Personnel of the OO, known as *osobitsy*, enforced front-line discipline and carried out counter-intelligence work. In April 1943, the OO was replaced by GUKR SMERSH; it was transferred to the NKO as the Main Directorate of Counter-Intelligence (GUKR) but was still headed by the NKVD official Abakumov. The famous acronym SMERSH came from the *Smert' shpionam* – 'Death to spies' – but as well as combating German intelligence the organization undertook many other activities, including overseeing the 'filtration' of former Soviet POWs and prosecuting German war crimes. SMERSH was very important in the recaptured territory of the USSR and in foreign countries that Soviet troops entered in 1944–5. Like the OO it enforced fulfilment of duties and ideological orthodoxy among the officers and enlisted men of the Red Army. A famous victim of SMERSH was Aleksandr Solzhenitsyn; the future author, then an artillery captain serving in East Prussia, was arrested in February 1945 for writing a letter critical of Stalin.

Despite this system of supervision and harsh discipline, the behaviour of the advancing Soviet troops left much to be desired. In his speech of May 1942, preparing the Reich population for the Stalingrad offensive, Hitler had warned of impending danger: 'If this enemy were to be victorious, then our German people would be exterminated. Asiatic barbarism would be implanted in Europe. The German woman would become fair game for these animals. The intelligentsia would be slaughtered.'[90] In reality, the slaughter would be less than what the SS and Wehrmacht inflicted on the USSR and other parts of Europe, but looting and rape by Soviet troops were still widespread.

Marshal Zhukov maintained that from the time the Red Army entered Poland, there was a serious effort to educate the troops in proper conduct. In late July 1944, very soon after the Red Army first began to advance into 'foreign' territory, army-level military councils were instructed to install 'military commandants' in the frontal belt. A major role of these officials was to prevent excesses by Soviet troops. At the same time, prompted by the Red Army's entry into northern Romania, the NKO had complained about the growth of venereal disease and had insisted on monthly medical checks for all personnel. When elements of the 2nd and the 3rd Ukrainian Army Groups entered central Romania two months later, the Stavka ordered their commander to 'pay attention to the order and discipline of the forces passing through Bucharest'. Despite this, a few days later the General Staff complained to Marshal Malinovskii about 'massive facts of unworthy behaviour by our servicemen in the town of Bucharest', with widespread drunkenness and indiscipline. In September 1944 the General Staff passed on to Marshal Tolbukhin a complaint from the Bulgarian Communist Party on cases of

> looting and even rape on the part of military personnel of our units (mainly rear echelon), which have entered the territory of Bulgaria: I *ask you* immediately to take measures to end occurrences of banditry [*maroderstvo*], looting, and rape, strictly punishing guilty persons.

In Yugoslavia, Antonov, the Deputy Chief of the General Staff, personally intervened in the case of the attempted rape of two women partisans by Soviet officers. In October 1944 each 'warrior' of the 3rd Ukrainian Army Group was given a detailed order about correct behaviour in Yugoslavia: 'At all times and places be disciplined, well-behaved [*kul'turnyi*], and smart, as a representative of the world's most advanced [*peredovaia*] army. ... Be merciless with looters and rapists, and those who break order and discipline!' When it entered Czechoslovakia in early May 1945, Konev's 1st Ukrainian Army Group was ordered to punish indiscipline strictly, as it acted against the interests of Soviet–Czechoslovak relations.[91]

Despite these measures, a certain Soviet tolerance of looting and rape extended to the very top, judging by Stalin's words at a reception for a Czechoslovak delegation in late March 1945:

> Everyone heaps praise on our Red Army. Yes, it has deserved it. But I do not want our guests, who now find the Red Army attractive, to be disappointed later on. The fact is that there are now 12 million people in the Red Army. They are far from being angels. They have been coarsened by war. Many of them have gone 2000 kilometres: from Stalingrad to the middle of Czechoslovakia. On their way they have seen much sorrow and many terrible things. So do not be surprised if some of our people do not behave as they should in your country. We know that some of our soldiers who have a low level of political consciousness [*malosoznatel'nye*] are pestering and abusing girls and women, are behaving badly [*bezobraznichaiut*].

Let our Czechoslovak friends know that now, so that the attraction of our Red Army does not turn into disappointment.[92]

Soviet ground force organization

The Russians had to do more than assemble a large and reasonably disciplined mass of personnel. They had also to create a war-winning army.[93] As we have seen, it had gradually become possible to put together larger and larger Soviet armoured formations, tank armies, and tank and mechanized corps. Unlike the mechanized corps of 1941, these now represented an effective force. Tank corps had begun to reappear in March 1942, and 24 of them were formed or forming by September 1942. With a strength of 270 tanks and SP guns, each tank 'corps' was roughly comparable to a 1941 German panzer division. The mechanized (*mekhanizirovanyi*) corps was similar, the first of a new generation being formed in September 1942; there were 13 by the end of 1943. The Soviet tank and mechanized corps either operated independently, within army groups, or they made up the building blocks of a larger formation, the tank army. Four tank armies had been created in 1942, and two more would follow in 1943–4. Each tank 'army' was comparable to a German panzer corps of 1941. The tank armies varied in size, but on average they had about 800 tanks and SP guns.

The tank forces were seen as the elite of the Red Army. An early order, in August 1941, had stressed that tank crews were to be chosen from 'people with good ability to speak Russian (Russians, Ukrainians, Belorussians)'; they were not to include inhabitants of the new borders, escaped POWs or people whose relatives had been 'repressed', that is sent to the GULAG.[94] The 3rd and 5th Tank Armies became 'Guards Tank Armies' in the spring of 1943, and by the end of the war all six tank armies had Guards status. As John Erickson put it, two different armies were appearing, an 'army of quantity' and an 'army of quality'. In the second army the tank forces played the most prominent role.[95]

Soviet mobile forces still included a substantial amount of cavalry, more than in the wartime armies of other countries. It helped that the Red Army had a strong cavalry tradition, with the memory of the Civil War 1st Cavalry Army, and perhaps also that Zhukov had been a cavalryman. The broken country and the limited transport infrastructure of western Russia and much of Eastern Europe suited the use of cavalry, especially after the weakening of air and mobile forces on the German side. Cavalry were very valuable forces for the exploitation of attacks. In September 1943, there were still eight Soviet cavalry corps, equipped with traditional horse cavalry and light tanks. In May 1944 the Stavka issued an order stressing the great effect of cavalry if used properly, that is on a mass scale at army-group (rather than army) level, supported by armour and aviation, and operating on the enemy's open flanks. The spearhead of the Soviet cavalry, developed before the war and used in the offensives of 1943–5, was the 'Cavalry-Mechanized Group' (*Konno-mekhanizirovannaia gruppa*, or *KMG*).[96] The most successful of the new generation of cavalry leaders was General I. A. Pliev, who commanded cavalry-mechanized groups in the Ukraine and Hungary (and Manchuria); he would later be the commander of the Soviet forces deployed to Cuba in 1962.

The basic formation of the Red Army was what was called a 'combined arms' (*obshchevoiskovaia*) army and what is referred to in this book as an 'infantry army'. The corps echelon was restored in the spring of 1943, and by 1944–5, the standard composition of an infantry army was 3 infantry ('rifle') corps, each with 3 rifle divisions, 3–4 artillery regiments, an independent tank regiment of 40 AFVs, and altogether about 100,000 personnel. Elite units, part of Erickson's 'army of quality', were formed within this mass of infantry. As we have seen, in 1942, elite formations identified as 'shock' (*udarnye*) armies appeared; the 'shock' concept had existed before 1941. Five 'Shock Armies' existed through to the end of war, although they were superseded as an elite by Guards formations.

From early 1943 numbers of larger Soviet Guards formations, both armour and infantry, were put into the field. The 1st and the 2nd Guards Rifle Corps were formed in December 1941 and put at the disposal of the army group commander (rather than the army commander). The 1st Guards Army was originally created (from the 2nd Reserve Army) in August 1942, under General Golikov; it fought at Stalingrad, although it took its final form in December 1942. The 2nd and the 3rd Guards Armies appeared at the end of 1942. By the consolidation of the following spring, the experiment had clearly justified itself, and in mid-April 1943 orders were issued to form no fewer than seven additional Guards infantry armies (along with the 3rd and the 5th Guards Tank Armies). The 4th, 5th, 6th, 7th and 8th Guards Armies were formed from, respectively, the 24th, 66th, 21st, 64th and 62nd Armies, all of which had distinguished themselves at Stalingrad. The 10th and 11th Guards Armies were created from armies in the central sector of the front, the 30th and the 16th. This establishment then essentially continued unchanged to the end of the war, with the most important army groups being assigned one or two Guards Armies.

The role of Guards formations was clarified in the consolidation period after Stalingrad. It was ordered that Guards armies and corps, 'made up of the most experienced and steady troops' should be held in reserve or in the second echelon and used for the decisive attacks and for counter-attacks. They were to be an example by their conduct to all other units. In the winter of 1943–4, the General Staff complained that men from the liberated western regions were being sent to Guards units without proper vetting. Guards units were to be recruited predominantly from the interior districts of the USSR and from wounded men (preferably guardsmen) who were being returned to active service. Wounded guardsmen (*gvardeitsy*) were to be returned to the Guards, and preferably to their original units. Although not stated in the order, this decree tended to reinforce the ethnic Russian predominance in the Guards. A related development was the attachment of honorific formation titles, identifying formations with particular victories, such as the 1st Don Guards Tank Corps or the 3rd Guards Stalingrad Mechanized Corps, both formed in January 1943.[97]

Given the strong interest in 'deep battle' (see below), the failure of the Soviets to use airborne forces on a large scale was surprising. River crossings on the Dnepr, Vistula,

Narew, Oder and Danube were obvious targets for the parachute troops of the advancing army. The Western Allies made use of airborne forces in Sicily, at Normandy, at Arnhem, and for the March 1945 Rhine crossing. A big Soviet night drop in late September 1943 to secure crossings over the Dnepr near Kiev went badly wrong, and Stalin forbade further night attacks and any drops further than 20 miles ahead of ground troops. Clearly, very serious thought was still given to this form of warfare; there existed, in reserve, an Independent Guards Airborne (*Vozdushno-desantnaia*) Army, with nine Guards rifle divisions; a separate air transport organization existed within the Red Army Air Force.[98] In mid-December 1944, however, the Stavka ordered that the airborne army be given heavy equipment and converted into the 9th Guards Army. This army fought conventionally in Hungary and Austria from February 1945.

Air power

The shift in the balance of air power in 1943–5 between the USSR and Germany was also most important. The role of the Luftwaffe is often underrated in the Wehrmacht's initial successes in Russia; air power made up for the numerical weakness of German ground forces. Stalin expressed his view to Roosevelt in October 1942: 'The experience of war has shown that the bravest forces become powerless if they do not have protection against air strikes.'[99] When the Luftwaffe lost air supremacy over Russia in 1943–4, the balance turned even more in favour of the Red Army. The Luftwaffe was pulled in different strategic directions earlier than the German Army, as the air threat from the West emerged earlier. The Germans were struck by the British night offensive in the spring of 1942, and the beginning of a heavy American day offensive in the summer of 1943. Most of the German fighter strength had to be pulled back from the Eastern Front for the air defence of the Reich; many other air units were required for the Mediterranean.

At the beginning of the second half of the eastern war, Luftwaffe involvement in Russia was broadly similar to what it had been in 1941–2. The air force planners had agreed that the ground war with the Red Army was decisive. The Luftwaffe co-operated closely with the German Army, albeit as an independent service, up to the summer of 1943. The last success of this strategy was the counter-offensive against Khar'kov in March 1943; the attempt to lend weight to the Kursk attack in June and July 1943 ended in failure. Luftwaffe strategists now came to the view that the army-support role in a defensive ground battle in the East was not a war-winner.

Strategic air power was, in theory, another weapon that Germany could deploy against the USSR. A few 'propaganda' attacks had been flown against Moscow in 1941–2. In the summer of 1943, just before the Battle of Kursk, the German 6th Air Fleet (based behind Army Group Centre) mounted isolated but relatively large night raids (100 medium bombers) against the important Russian industrial centres of Gor'kii, Iaroslavl' and Saratov.[100]

But late 1943 was the first time since the Battle of Britain in 1940 that 'independent' bombing operations were actually conceived by the German planners as a main element of

Luftwaffe activity.[101] Leading officials like Albert Speer were behind the programme, and there was a degree of civilian involvement in target selection. The Luftwaffe leadership, from Goering on down, were keen to reassert their service's independence against the Army and Navy. In November 1943, the Luftwaffe began to mass an 'independent' attack force of eight bomber groups – about 300 aircraft – as the 4th Air Corps. The target selected for Operation IRON HAMMER (EISENHAMMER) was Soviet electrical power generating stations near Gor'kii, Moscow and Iaroslavl'.

Nothing, however, came of the Luftwaffe's strategic air offensive, and for significant reasons. The Germans were limited by the number and types of aircraft in their bomber force. There had been talk in the mid-1930s of a *Uralbomber*, a genuine strategic aircraft able to hit distant targets; instead, the Luftwaffe had been equipped with medium (twin-engined) bombers. As we have seen, the German heavy bomber, the He 177, became available only in small numbers in the summer of 1944. There were also relatively few of the shorter-range medium bombers available, in part because Germany was fighting a war on several fronts; another air corps had been deployed on a militarily meaningless propaganda campaign against Britain in January 1944, Operation IBEX (STEINBOCK).

What killed off any chance of launching Operation IRON HAMMER was the success of the Red Army's Leningrad–Novgorod operation in January–February 1944. This deprived the Luftwaffe of the main bases east of Lake Chud from which its available bombers could hit their planned targets. In the end, the assembled German bomber force was used for less ambitious attacks on the Soviet railway system, as the Red Army rolled west across the Ukraine. Ironically, the build-up to IRON HAMMER allowed one of the last Luftwaffe successes of the war. This was the attack on an American shuttle bombing force that had landed at Poltava (east of Kiev). Dozens of B-17s were destroyed on the ground on 21 June 1944 (the night before the Soviet Operation BAGRATION began in Belorussia).[102] Even if IRON HAMMER had been launched, it would have been little more than a pinprick; it is doubtful if the Germans could have found numerous small targets in the dark.

It was not just that Luftwaffe units were withdrawn from Russia. 'Stalin's Hawks' also developed during the second half of the war. Arguably, the Red Army Air Force had the same impact on the ground war in 1943–5 as the Luftwaffe had in 1941–2. What was surprising was that it did not achieve more. In contrast, in the West, the American and British tactical air forces sometimes paralysed German Army movement. Part of the answer is that air superiority had its limits against a determined enemy; the Germans were able to hold their own for a year in Italy, despite the considerable British and American advantage in the air. In the Soviet case, there were also organizational and technical factors. The heads of the Red Army Air Force were relatively junior officers, who were kept under the thumb of the Soviet ground forces. Soviet aircraft were relatively short range, and it was difficult to move their bases forward at the pace of rapidly advancing ground troops. Most of the Soviet air effort, moreover, was devoted to direct support of the ground forces; there was less success in paralysing Axis rear communications and isolating the battlefield (what is sometimes called 'interdiction'). These inadequacies were recognized by the Soviet command. For example, during the German retreat to the Dnepr River in August–September 1943, the Stavka complained that huge columns of German vehicles and numerous trains were heading west with relatively ineffective attacks by Soviet aircraft.[103]

The Red Army Air Force was organized differently after the first year of the war. The first air army was formed in early May 1942, and sixteen more were set up in the course of 1942.[104] This represented a greater massing of ground support air power, with the normal match being one air army to each army group; aircraft were no longer dispersed to the level of the infantry army. The 1st Air Army, for example, comprised two fighter divisions and two 'mixed' divisions (with fighters, strike aircraft and bombers), for a total of ten combat air regiments. Other air armies were held in the Stavka Reserve.

In contrast to its two western allies, the USSR did not develop an effective strategic bomber force for 'independent' operations, and the pattern was similar to the German one. Soviet 'Long Range Aviation' (*ADD*), so named from February 1942, mounted desultory night raids against targets in the rear of the German Army, especially railway junctions. Even more than the Luftwaffe, it was limited by lack of four-engined bombers, navigation aids and suitable targets. The massive Soviet air superiority of the last two years of the war was also not applied effectively to 'sea denial', and the German Navy were able to make continued use of shipping routes in the Black Sea and the Baltic. In general, the Soviet emphasis on ground support – tactical (*frontovaia*) aviation – was a sensible prioritization. By 1944–5, the Red Army Air Force had become part of the formula for war-winning success. The lightning advance of the Soviet Army across the Ukraine, Poland, Romania and in Hungary, and finally into Germany, owed much to the massed support of the air armies.

'Deep battle'

All of this re-equipment and reorganization of mobile ground forces and of tactical aviation came together as the background to the battles of 1943–5. In general, the Red Army was also trained to fight better in the second half of the war. To be sure, the Red Army leadership had been fully aware of the importance of manoeuvre warfare and combined arms operations before the war, but with the improvised and untrained new armies of 1941–2 and the predominance of raw officers, this could only be an ideal for the future.

Certainly, the Soviet high command was aware of the limitations of the new armies assembled in 1942. Some of the reforms were basic, intended to make the Red Army fight better. Problems of command and control, for example, were highlighted in a General Staff order of April 1942. In his February 1943 Red Army Day order, Stalin praised 'tens of thousands of the Red Army commanders' who had 'learned how to lead forces on the battlefield, rejecting stupid and harmful linear tactics and becoming confident in the tactics of manoeuvre warfare'. Co-ordination between the different arms – tanks, infantry, artillery, aviation – was important. In May 1944, Zhukov and Antonov instructed army commanders to order their forces to study the experience of the winter–spring offensives of 1943–4. Because the positive lessons had not been studied, they complained, 'there continue to exist shortcomings in the operational–tactical use of various combat arms, in the organization and conduct of battle, [and] in the administration of forces.'[105]

What had happened by the end of 1943, however, was more than the creation of a 'cadre army'. It was not just that the Red Army had learnt to operate in a competent way on the battlefield and prevent more embarrassing defeats. Goebbels' 'assault from the steppe' did not overwhelm the bulwark of the Wehrmacht simply by weight of numbers. The Red Army was now able to put into practice the concept of 'deep battle'. There have been many analyses of the 'Blitzkrieg', the techniques that made it possible for the Wehrmacht to overrun much of Europe in 1939–42. Less attention has been paid to the remarkable development of Soviet offensive warfare during the war. The defensive battles of the first eighteen months of the war, when the Red Army had to pull back to Leningrad, Moscow and Stalingrad, distort our understanding of Red Army doctrine. There was a strong continuity between pre-war doctrine and the way in which the Red Army operated from the middle of 1943.

The Red Army had a long interest in offensive warfare, going back at least to the 'deep battle' and 'deep operations' concepts of the military theorists of the late 1920s and 1930s, commanders like V. K. Triandafillov and M. N. Tukhachevskii. Those theoretical concepts were inherent in Stalin's apparent view of an offensive Red Army in May 1941, although that view would be badly shaken by the events of the first years of the war. Stalin would endorse the offensive doctrine in his February 1944 Red Army Day order, using words which could have been drafted by Tukhachevskii: 'I order … the whole Red Army by a skilful combination of fire and manoeuvre to break through the enemy defence across its full depth, not giving the enemy time to catch his breath.'[106]

Soviet operations in 1943–5 were different from those of 1941–2. After the Battle of Kursk in the summer of 1943, Soviet operations were no longer hastily improvised responses to German offensives. They were stunning attacks intended to overcome and overrun the resistance of a static enemy attempting to hold ground. The crossing of the Dnepr in the late summer of 1943 did not work precisely as planned, but the Red Army succeeded in keeping the Wehrmacht continuously off balance as it made deep advances across the Ukraine. The Stavka had more time to plan Operation BAGRATION in Belorussia in July 1944, and it was a deep-battle set piece. The same could be said of the Red Army's Iași–Kishenev operation in Moldavia and Romania in August 1944, and the Vistula–Oder operation in Poland and eastern Germany in January and February 1945. Recalling this last operation, Zhukov summed up the concept:

Tank armies and independent tanks corps in close co-operation with the air force shattered the enemy front with swift blows, passed through to the lines of communications of his forces, took river crossings and road junctions, sowing panic and disorganizing the enemy's rear.

The deep penetration of the tank forces into the rear of the enemy did not allow the German-fascist forces to use for defence most of the positions that had been prepared.[107]

CONCLUSION

There are differing views about the military situation in the second part of the war. The German leaders later stressed the Soviet advantage of crude numbers. Hitler and Goebbels have already been quoted. Field Marshal Manstein made a typical comment in his memoirs (bemoaning the situation on the Russian front in early 1944), when he said that the 'enemy hydra grew more heads'. It had, in other words, outgrown the German Army. In contrast, David Glantz, the pre-eminent Western writer on Soviet operations, stressed quality. He argued that 'perhaps the principal cause of the reversal in the East was the revolution in Soviet command, staff, and operational and tactical techniques'. This produced 'an entirely new and far more competent Red Army'. Mark Harrison, an expert on the Soviet war economy, had a rather different interpretation; he stressed production. For Harrison, the course of the war up to 1942 was determined by military factors, while from 1942 it was determined by economic ones.[108] What happened in 1943–5 would actually be a combination of all these things, of mass, of organization, of production. The Germans, as Stalin had been saying over and over at least since May 1941, were not unbeatable. The first half of the war had seemingly been devoted to disproving this. The second half, and here both military organization and production were important, would show that the Red Army could overcome German defences, throw the Wehrmacht back and pursue it home to the Reich.

CHAPTER 8
TOTAL WAR II: OCCUPATION AND DIPLOMACY

In the occupied regions to create intolerable conditions for the enemy and all his henchmen, to pursue and destroy them at every step, to block all their efforts.

Order of Stalin and Molotov, 29 June 1941

In principle we have now to face the task of cutting up the giant cake according to our needs, in order to be able, first, to dominate it, second, to administer it, and third, to exploit it.

Adolf Hitler, 16 July 1941

The military situation of the Soviet Union, as well as that of Great Britain, would be significantly improved, if a front was created against Hitler in the West (Northern France) and in the North (the Arctic).

Joseph Stalin to Winston Churchill, 18 July 1941

'STABILITY OF THE REAR'

In the second half of the war, after Stalingrad, the political situation at home in Germany should have been more dangerous for Hitler. When, back in February 1942, Stalin had spoken of the 'permanently operating factors' which affected the correlation of forces in war, he included 'stability of the rear'. Stalin's claim that the German economy was being worn down in a war of attrition was not unreasonable, but it is noteworthy that the Soviet leader suggested that this would happen sooner rather than later: 'A few months, maybe half a year, perhaps a year, and Hitler's Germany must crack under the weight of its crimes.'[1] Stalin wrote about 'stability of the rear' after the Battle of Moscow. A year later, after the Battle of Stalingrad, things looked even worse for the Third Reich. Hitler himself worried about the collapse of the German home front. The events of October–November 1918, the crisis of the German war effort and the sudden end of the Kaiser's Germany, were perhaps his strongest memories.

Stalin's hopes and Hitler's fears were not realized.[2] In 1942, Soviet propaganda made much of supposed growing hardships suffered by the Germans at home, but this stemmed from a combination of poor information, wishful thinking and a desire to reconcile the Soviet population to its own extreme hardships. In reality, the Nazis paid particular attention to maintaining the standard of living at home. And hardship in the Reich would not happen as long as Hitler's government was able to exploit the output and labour of the occupied territories. Meanwhile, the *Ostheer* was soon back on the offensive, and it kept the initiative until the end of 1942. As for 1943, and even into the summer of 1944, the war in the East was still far away from the German homeland.

The defeat at Stalingrad did, however, make for changes in how the German government portrayed the war. Hitler and Goebbels now emphasized the long-term threat from the East and put an emphasis on 'total war'. Even in the last desperate nine months of the war, the Germans could be kept fighting through fear of a terrible Soviet occupation of their country. Hitler's original promises and predictions were invalid after Stalingrad, and the Führer lost his original 'bond' with a large part of the Reich population. But there were few effective sources of opposition. The German officer corps was less of a challenge to the Nazi regime than the class-conscious Hitler – or Stalin – expected. The Nazis had effective tools in the form of German nationalism, the so-called *Volksgemeinschaft*, and anti-Communism; they also had the Gestapo. (The Nazi *Volksgemeinschaft* or 'People's Community' was a propaganda concept emphasizing solidarity and mutual support among the ethnic Germans.) The Nazi leaders were united in their cause; they were so compromised that no Allied surrender terms would pardon them. The main anti-Nazi resistance really only became active in 1943–4, not so much in response to any wrongs committed by German troops, or to the racial atrocities of the regime, as to lost battles. The 20 July 1944 attempt on Hitler's life, the bomb at Rastenburg, was the one serious attempt at 'regime change'. Its defeat was followed by a further hardening of the totalitarian state. The Nazi Party and the SS were given a greater role.

The internal situation in the Union of Soviet Socialist Republics was both similar to and different from that in Nazi Germany.[3] Acute external danger could be used to build support, although in the Soviet case this was true from the beginning of the war, not just (as for the Germans) from 1944. It greatly helped the consolidation of popular support for the Soviet war effort that much of the country was under the jackboot of a particularly brutal occupation regime – and the Soviet countermarch in the winter of 1941–2 quickly produced evidence of Nazi atrocities. Great German triumphs on the battlefield had increased support for Hitler in the Reich in 1939–42. The same thing happened in the USSR from the time of Stalingrad and certainly from the summer of 1943, with an unbroken string of victories. It was now clear to the population – both in Soviet home territory and in the occupied borderlands – that the USSR was winning the war, and that Germany was eventually going to be defeated.

In the Soviet Union, as in Germany, nationalism was stressed. In the Soviet case, this was in direct contrast to the Marxist–Leninist core ideology of 'internationalism'. The war was the 'Fatherland War' from the beginning.[4] In December 1941 the Main Political Directorate of the Red Army ordered all army newspapers to drop the slogan 'Proletarians of all lands, unite!' from their mastheads. 'In war conditions ...', the Directorate explained, 'when the task is to destroy all the German occupiers, this slogan incorrectly orients several layers of service personnel.' The slogan was to be 'Death to the German occupiers!'[5] The shift from internationalism to nationalism continued after Stalingrad. There was the new national anthem replacing the 'Internationale', the adoption of traditional uniforms and the disbandment of the Comintern.

The emphasis, moreover, was on one particular ethnic group, the Russians, rather than on a broader 'Soviet' nationalism. On 24 May 1945, Stalin would make his famous toast 'to the health of our Soviet people and, above all, of the Russian people'. 'Another people would have said to the government: you have not lived up to our expectations, you must go, we will get another government, which will make peace with Germany and let us rest.' Much is made of Stalin's November 1941 address, when he spoke of heroes of the Tsarist past: 'Let us be inspired in this war by the example of our great forefathers: Aleksandr Nevskii, Dmitrii Donskoi, Kuz'ma Minin, Dmitrii Pozharskii, Aleksandr Suvorov, Mikhail Kutuzov!'[6] But even this had not been the turning point. Stalin's government had begun to play on Russocentrism in the middle of the 1930s, not in order to replace the original Marxist–Leninist programme but to buttress it. This change of emphasis came partly from the regime's focus on 'state building' and partly from a realistic sense that even in peacetime nationalist slogans were more popular among the masses than internationalist ones.

This was not simply cynical leaders deceiving the ignorant masses. The rising new Communist elite of the USSR was more Russian (in ethnic terms) than the elite that had led the 1917 Revolution. This change reflected the nature of the dominant urban population, as well as the 'cultural revolution' and upward social mobility of the end of the 1920s; it also followed from the purge of the revolutionary generation of leaders in the late 1930s. This phenomenon has aptly been described as the rise of 'National Bolshevism' or – compared to the original aims of the Revolution – the 'Great Retreat'.[7] Even the top echelon in Moscow came to see the world in traditional terms. In a secret toast on Revolution Day of 1937, Stalin gave his credo to a small audience of Politburo leaders and others: 'The Russian tsars did a great deal that was bad. ... But they did one thing that was good – they amassed an enormous state, all the way to Kamchatka [on the Pacific coast]. We have inherited that state.'[8]

The power of this approach was something which the German leaders, for their part, could not see. Hitler did not initially think nationalism could be a powerful force in the Bolshevik state, at least not according to a speech he made in November 1941:

There are some doubts whether or not the national tendency will win out in this state [i.e. the USSR]. But you must not forget that the bearers of the national vision no longer exist, and that the man who appears to be the master of this state is nothing but a tool in the hand of all-powerful Jewry.[9]

The attraction of a specifically *Russian* (rather than Soviet) patriotism was that this patriotism had the deepest roots and the strongest military tradition. It was important, too, that the Red Army retreat had drawn the line of defence back to the ethnographic frontier of the Great Russians.[10]

One related development that occurred in the second half of the war was the greater toleration of the Russian Orthodox Church. It had been ravaged by Communist campaigns of 'militant atheism' in the 1920s and 1930s. Although the Church was brought in to support the war from the beginning, no concordat was arranged until victory was on the way. On 4 September 1943, as Soviet troops were moving towards the Dnepr River, Stalin met the leaders of the Church hierarchy. Two aspects to this revival suited Stalin. First of all, his regime was attempting to channel a spontaneous revival of popular religious fervour felt during wartime. And second, it wanted to use the Russian Orthodox Church as a means of reasserting its control over the western borderlands.[11] The revival, in terms of reopening churches, was focused in these liberated western borderlands, rather than in the central – never conquered – areas of Russia.

The Soviet population understood the need, in 1944, to take the offensive beyond the borders of the 'Fatherland' and into foreign territory. The invasion of the enemy's homeland was a logical enough objective, especially when, in the last year of the war, the Red Army was making rapid progress. The slogan was 'liberation', not 'broadening the camp of socialism' as it had been before 1941. The situation was not like that in the First World War, when an offensive strategy, especially towards the Dardanelles, had been politically divisive in Russia. In 1944–5, support for continuing and extending the war was still there, even though the population must in truth have been physically more 'war-weary' in 1944 than the previous generation had been in 1917.

It might seem that Germany and the USSR were reversing their polarities in 1943–5, one becoming more ideological, the other less so. This would be an oversimplification of the affairs of both totalitarian states. The formal institutions of the Communist Party did indeed atrophy in Stalin's later years. There would be no party congress until 1952, and the plenums (general meetings) of the party Central Committee were very infrequent. In Stalin's major wartime speeches the first lengthy reference to the 'party of Lenin, the party of the Bolsheviks' came only in November 1943. Communist slogans continued, however, and there was an unprecedented influx of members and candidates into the Communist Party. On 1 July 1941 there had been 2,600,000 full members and 1,210,000 candidates. Between then and the end of 1945, some 5,320,000 people were admitted as full members and 3,620,000 as candidates. Of these, about three-quarters were accepted through Red Army party organizations. The fact that in July 1945 there were 4,290,000 full members and 1,660,000 candidates testifies both to the overall growth of the party and to the very high rate of losses of party members in wartime combat.[12]

OCCUPIERS, COLLABORATORS AND PARTISANS

German occupation policy

Much has been written about German occupation policy in the USSR.[13] As with other aspects of the Third Reich, competing authorities muddled the occupation of the former Soviet space, and this began at the planning stage. The four 'pillars' of German rule were to be the Army, the SS, the Reich economic organs (under Goering) and the civil administration (under Alfred Rosenberg). The pre-war plan was that Soviet territory would be divided into a civilian administration of four regional *Reichskommissariats*, all under Rosenberg's *Ostministerium* (Reich Ministry for the Occupied Eastern Territories). The *Reichskommissariats* for central Russia and the Caucasus were never actually set up. *Reichskommissariat* Ukraine (based in Rovno in the western Ukraine) took in most of the western Ukraine and southern Belorussia, and *Reichskommissariat Ostland* (based in Riga in Latvia) took in the Baltic states and northern Belorussia. At least a third of the occupied population was under the direct control of the German Army, in the 'rear' areas of the field armies (the so-called *Korücks*) or of the army groups. This confusion came partly from the half-finished nature of Hitler's invasion project. Had the Wehrmacht actually reached the Arkhangel'sk–Astrakhan line in 1941, the organization – at least – of the occupation might have been clearer and simpler.

When the Stalingrad pocket surrendered at the start of 1943, the Axis still controlled 850,000 square miles of former Soviet territory and some sixty-five million people. It would take another eighteen months – until the autumn of 1944 – before the borders of the 1941 USSR were nearly completely cleared of occupying troops (the exception was an isolated pocket in western Latvia – Kurland).

Even in 1942, however, the situation was for the occupiers different from what it had been in the summer of 1941. Immediate victory was no longer to be expected. Soviet partisans were becoming more active. On the one hand, this led to a more organized and ruthless German war of counter-insurgency. Rear-echelon formations carried out cruel anti-partisan sweeps, creating 'dead zones' across part of the Russian countryside. On the other hand, the extended war meant there was a need to attempt an accommodation with the local population. Hitler himself in August 1942 ordered the Wehrmacht to treat the population strictly but fairly, as he recognized that the 'bandit movement' threatened the German position in the East; however, strictly punitive measures were still the main thrust of policy.[14] Some Germans, including leaders of the army, realized the need to fight a more 'political' war, with a more pragmatic policy. Often cited is the memorandum by Otto Bräutigam, a leading official in the *Ostministerium*:

> As the population has become aware of our true attitude towards it, so to the same degree has the resistance of the Red Army and the strength of the partisan movement increased. The feats of our magnificent Army have therefore been neutralised. … Our political policy has forced both Bolshevists and Russian nationals into a common front against us.[15]

Some success was achieved in winning over the population of the North Caucasus in late 1942, but this never affected the majority Slav population, and the tentative German programme was soon cut short when the 'model' zone was reconquered by the Red Army in the winter of 1942–3. In any event, such 'enlightened' views were held by only a minority of German officials. Far too much had happened in the first year of occupation for former Soviet citizens to forgive and forget. Finally, the population of the occupied zone, even potential collaborators, could see, after Stalingrad, that Germany was not going to win the war and that the Wehrmacht's presence would not last forever.

In July 1941 Hitler was optimistic about the riches the occupied territory of the USSR would yield. 'In principle', he said, 'we have now to face the task of cutting up the giant cake according to our needs, in order to be able, first, to dominate it, second, to administer it, and third, to exploit it.' In reality, German *Lebensraum* in the East did not provide what was required. Although the huge *Ostheer* was able to live off the land, the occupation authorities did not ship home minerals and foodstuffs in significant quantities. One authoritative estimate is that the Germans obtained from the occupied USSR only one-seventh of what they obtained from France.[16] In theory, an agricultural reform in the occupied USSR, ending the hated collective farms (*kolkhozy*), might have won support, and a nominal German *kolkhoz* reform was enacted in February 1942. The Nazis, however, needed the *kolkhozy* for the same reason that the Communists had needed them, to ensure in the short term the basic flow of agricultural procurements (mainly food). What the occupiers did obtain – and what had not originally been expected – was a large amount of labour for the Reich proper, plus a significant cohort of auxiliary military forces.

Hitler's policy ruled out any wooing of the population of the occupied USSR, even at a regional level. This was in contrast to German policy in the First World War, where German puppet governments were installed in the Ukraine and elsewhere. On the other hand, a good deal of what could be called collaboration [*kollaboratsionizm*] went on at grass-roots level. Its basis was the need of a large number of Soviet citizens who found themselves under long-term German occupation to survive in one way or another.

In contrast to the other major states occupied by the Germans, a very large number of Soviet citizens fought for the invaders. The 1998–9 Russian official history accepts the Western estimate that some 1,000,000 to 1,500,000 Soviet citizens served in the Wehrmacht, the Waffen-SS and the occupation police.[17] This involved both POWs recruited in the *Stalags* and inhabitants of the occupied regions who took part in security detachments. The largest single group of those involved with the German forces were the *Hilfswillige* (Auxiliaries) or *Hiwis*, who served as labourers, cooks, drivers, and so on, in regular Wehrmacht forces. The official establishment of a 1943 German infantry division included 2,005 *Hiwis*, in addition to the basic 'German' strength of 10,708 – the actual combat troops. The *Hiwis* numbered 220,000–320,000 by mid-1943, and about 500,000 a year later.[18]

Other Soviet citizens were drafted as combatants into a confused array of German military units. By the middle of 1943, the Wehrmacht had 130,000–150,000 personnel in the 157 battalions of the *Osttruppen*, recruited from among POWs captured from the Red Army. Most were non-Slavs. Units of Armenians, Azerbaidzhantsy and Georgians, originally from the Caucasus, were recruited, along with representatives of some of the small nations of the North Caucasus. Other units were made up of Tatars from the Volga and the Crimea, and those whom the Germans called *Turkmenen* – Muslims from Central Asia (Uzbeks, Kazakhs, Tadzhiks, Kirgiz).[19] For political reasons, and to prevent desertion, many of the *Osttruppen* were eventually based in Western Europe to meet the expected Allied landing, including no fewer than 60 *Ostbattalions*. Others were sent to

Italy and employed on anti-Resistance duties. In addition to the Wehrmacht's *Osttruppen*, six of the Waffen-SS divisions were notionally manned by former Soviet citizens.[20]

The best-known military collaborator force had little real impact. This was the army of the notorious and tragic A. A. Vlasov, the senior Soviet general who had been captured in mid-1942. Vlasov, or more accurately his German sponsors, were remarkable for their bad timing. The general was allowed to announce his anti-Stalinist 'programme' at Smolensk on 27 December 1942, just as the tide of the war turned at Stalingrad. Two years later, at almost the exact moment that nearly all German troops were driven from Soviet territory, a Committee for the Liberation of the Peoples of Russia (*KONR*) was formed under Vlasov in a ceremony at the Hradčany Palace in Prague (this was in November 1944). In the second half of 1944, now under Himmler's SS patronage, Vlasov was given nominal control of all collaborator forces. His main contingent, however, was the Russian Liberation Army (*ROA*), which eventually numbered about 45,000 troops in three half-formed and poorly equipped divisions.[21] The ROA 1st Division, with a Russian commander, began formation in November 1944 and appeared briefly at the front on the Oder River against the Red Army. In the end these turncoat forces were rounded up by the Red Army in Bohemia. Vlasov himself was captured in May 1945, nearly three years after the destruction of his 2nd Shock Army on the Volkhov River near Leningrad. He was tried and hanged, along with his senior commanders, in Moscow in August 1946.

Another side of the German occupation of Soviet territory was the conscription of forced labour for the Reich, which was carried out under the general supervision of the Gauleiter Fritz Sauckel as Plenipotentiary-General for Labour Deployment (*Arbeitseinsatz*). According to the Nuremberg indictment, conscription involved nearly 5,000,000 Soviet citizens. This was in addition to some 2,000,000 Soviet POWs who were sent to Germany and were employed as forced labourers there.[22] About 40 per cent of the conscripted civilians were in labour camps (*Arbeitslager*), and 60 per cent were living with employers. One official Russian source in the 1990s estimated that up to a quarter of the deported civilians died abroad. A sense of the make-up of the deportees can be obtained from post-war repatriation figures. Some 40 per cent of the repatriates (and presumably a similar proportion of the original deportees) were listed as Ukrainians and nearly 15 per cent as Belorussians. Of the repatriates, 45 per cent were women and 15 per cent children.[23]

Five million Soviet citizens, including forced labourers and POWs, were repatriated to the USSR from 1944 onwards. The majority were transferred by the British and Americans. (One of the first large parties consisted of 10,000 men sent to Murmansk in November 1944, many of them *Osttruppen* captured serving with the Wehrmacht in Normandy.) The Allies reached a formal agreement about mutual repatriation at the Yalta Conference in February 1945. The British and Americans were eager enough to hand over these people to their ally. The 'Soviet' prisoners were excess mouths to feed, and in 1945 the USSR held, to exchange for them, a considerable number of British and American service personnel. These were men the Red Army had freed from POW camps in eastern Germany. In practice, the British and American authorities showed more flexibility and consideration for POWs and deportees originally from the USSR, as relations with Moscow cooled in the early Cold War. They also came to distinguish between 'easterners' and 'westerners', and were prepared to offer more of a haven for the latter – for people from territories annexed by the USSR in 1939–40, for example, eastern Poland and the Baltic states.

A considerable number of the Soviet citizens who found themselves in Germany or other parts of Western Europe in 1945 did not in the end go home to the USSR. They formed the so-called 'Second Emigration' (following from the 'first' emigration after the 1917 Revolution). The Soviet authorities later calculated the number of non-returnees as about 450,000 people, mostly 'westerners' – half from the Baltic nationalities, a third Ukrainians and only 30,000 ethnic Russians.[24]

Most of the 'displaced' Soviet civilians, however, especially the 'easterners' from within the pre-1939 borders of the USSR, wanted to return to their families. Repatriation in Germany and Austria formally began on 23 May 1945. By the start of August, 1,280,000 people had been transferred into the custody of the Soviet authorities, and by 10 December 1945, 2,030,000. Of these, 40 per cent were POWs and 60 per cent civilians. Other Soviet citizens were found by the Red Army in eastern Europe or in the Soviet zones of Germany and Austria. The bulk of *repatrianty* had moved by March 1946, when their number was reckoned as 2,650,000 civilians and 1,550,000 POWs. Repatriation was compulsory. The only people excused were women who had married foreigners and who had given birth to children from this marriage.[25]

Overall, these people – civilians as well as POWs – were treated badly once they returned to the USSR, and much has been written about their fate in the West. According to recently released Russian figures, of the 2,650,000 repatriated civilians mentioned above (including women and children), about 80 per cent had been sent to their homes, 5 per cent to the army, 10 per cent to NKO labour battalions, and a relatively small 1.8 per cent (50,000) to the GULAG – Beria's prison camp empire. The 1,540,000 former POWs fared worse. Only 18 per cent went home; some 43 per cent were sent to the army, with a further 22 per cent to labour battalions of the NKO (People's Commissariat of Defence); 15 per cent went to the GULAG. One account described being met by guards with machine guns at a camp in central Russia: '*Iz ognia, da v polynia*' ('Out of the fire and into a hole in the ice'). The *repatrianty*, civilians and former POWs alike, were always treated with suspicion in the post-war decades. Amnesties promulgated under Khrushchev in 1955 and 1956 did not normalize their status. It was only in January 1995 that President El'tsin passed a decree restoring their legal rights.[26]

In April 1943 the USSR Supreme Soviet passed a decree ordering punishment of Axis personnel and Soviet collaborators responsible for war crimes against Soviet civilians and POWs. Such persons were to be tried by divisional 'field courts'. Those found guilty were to be subject to public hanging, with their bodies left on the gallows for several days. In May 1944 this was changed to execution by firing squad. Those in the local population who helped such criminals were subject to 15–20 years of imprisonment.[27]

There had been another side to the Soviet reckoning with suspected (or potential) collaboration. That was the forced deportation by the Soviets of entire ethnic groups, on a scale comparable with that of the Nazis.[28] Stalin's regime had a terrible record of such 'social engineering', even in peacetime. The NKVD had carried out what would now be called 'ethnic cleansing' before the war in borderland regions, first of all of the Korean minority in the Far East, and then (before 1939) of the Polish minority in the West. Tens of thousands of people regarded as politically suspect by the Soviet occupiers were deported from the former Baltic states on the eve of the BARBAROSSA. When the war actually came, some 1,500,000 Volga Germans, descendants of settlers invited to Russia by Catherine the Great, were deported to Central Asia (in August–October 1941). Since the Wehrmacht was ripping across the Ukraine at this time, and the Soviet regime was always paranoid about internal enemies, the policy was not entirely illogical. The US government deported 110,000 ethnic Japanese from the West Coast in 1941–2.

Less rational, though consistent with Stalinist policy, was what happened after the tide of German occupation had ebbed. In the summer of 1944, when the Red Army retook the Crimea, the local Tatars were accused of collaborating with the occupiers and were deported, en masse, to Central Asia. They were followed by the Chechen-Ingush and some other people from the North Caucasus. Although these people had not all lived in territory occupied by the Wehrmacht, they had consistently resisted Soviet (and Imperial Russian) power. The cost in human life was great, but it is also noteworthy that this vindictive deportation tied up a considerable number of Soviet armed personnel (NKVD troops) and transport facilities in 1944, at a time when both were badly needed at the main battle fronts on the western borders.

Soviet partisans and German counter-insurgency

Collaboration – voluntary, involuntary or even only latent – was one side of the story. The other was resistance. The USSR was unique among the major European fighting powers in that a vast expanse of its territory was occupied by the enemy for a long period of time. Uniquely, also, it was fighting a two-track war, regular and irregular.[29] The USSR had not prepared for partisan war. Pre-war military doctrine had stressed offensive warfare on the enemy's territory. In any event, in the situation of 1941 the Red Army could hardly have planned to fight a guerrilla war on those territories which had just been annexed by the USSR, in Karelia, the Baltic states, eastern Poland and Moldavia. There was, however, a Russian tradition of guerrilla warfare, going back at least to the *partizany* who harried Napoleon's army as it retreated from Moscow in 1812. 'Partisan' warfare had also played an important part in the Civil War of 1917–20. The Soviet government, after the first days of shock after 22 June, placed great hopes in guerrilla warfare behind Axis lines.

A secret directive, issued over the names of Stalin and Molotov on 29 June 1941, ordered the opening of the resistance battle:

> In the districts occupied by the enemy [there are to be set up] partisan detachments and sabotage [*diversionnye*] groups for the struggle with the units of the enemy armies, to ignite a partisan war everywhere, to blow up bridges, roads, to damage telephone and telegraph links, to burn warehouses, and so on. In the occupied

regions to create intolerable conditions for the enemy and all his henchmen, to pursue and destroy them at every step, to block all their efforts.

Four days later Stalin would make the same call publicly in his famous radio address,[30] but the secret 29 June 1941 directive to party leaders had been more concrete: the local party organizations were to create 'from the best people' reliable underground cells in town and country. Three weeks later, after the fall of the cities of Pskov, Vitebsk and Smolensk, and with the Wehrmacht threatening Leningrad, Kiev and Odessa, the party Central Committee sent out a *secret* decree with damning criticism of progress so far:

> In this battle with the fascist aggressors we have had … many missed opportunities to strike heavy blows against the enemy. … There are not a few cases when the leaders of party and state organizations in the districts which are under threat of occupation by the German fascists shamefully abandon their combat posts, withdraw into the deep rear, to quieter places, and transform themselves into deserters and wretched cowards. Meanwhile the leaders of republic and region party organizations in a number of cases are not taking steps for decisive struggle with such shameful facts.

Leaders of party organizations were now ordered to take direct charge of organizing the partisan struggle in the German rear, sending small teams behind enemy lines, and setting up underground groups in threatened areas.[31]

As it turned out, the Soviet partisans did not have much direct effect on the fighting in 1941. The German Army was stopped in that year (and in 1942) not by acts of sabotage or by 'open rebellion' but by the Red Army and by German logistical problems created by vast Russian spaces. The enemy advance was too rapid, and the western territories produced too few enthusiastic volunteers. Partisan detachments raised in the cities found it hard to blend into the countryside. The core of this early resistance was formed by the NKVD and Communist Party officials. The NKVD was responsible for some of the most spectacular acts of resistance, like the blowing up of the German headquarters in Kiev in September 1941. Nevertheless, even the ineffective partisan movement of 1941 symbolized continuing resistance. As for the Germans, they took the partisans seriously. For the advancing Wehrmacht, Russia was not like Denmark, the Low Countries, or even France. In mid-September the OKW, over Field Marshal Keitel's name, issued a directive: 'Since the beginning of the campaign against Soviet Russia, Communist insurrection movements have broken out everywhere in the areas occupied by Germany. The type of action taken … is growing into open rebellion and wide-spread guerrilla warfare.' The response, in line with the pre-war German directives, had to be drastic, including the execution of 50–100 Communist prisoners for every German soldier killed.[32]

The turn of the New Year, 1942, presented a paradox. On the one hand, the chances of partisan warfare increased, especially in the central and northern parts of the front. The Germans were now in territory inhabited by ethnic Russians, among whom enthusiasm for a war of resistance was greater. The Germans were hard-pressed, and the front line was static, very irregular and easily penetrated. The population had become aware of Germany's brutal occupation policy, especially the terrible treatment of captured Red Army soldiers. The partisans did play an important part in harrying the now scattered forces of German Army Group Centre in the forests west of Moscow. On the other hand, the severe winter was, overall, unfavourable to the partisans. Staying alive in wild country in the depths of a Russian winter was no simple matter, and the bare trees of the forest provided no cover. Partisan numbers evidently fell considerably in this period.

It was only in the spring of 1942 that the partisan movement made progress. Stalin had said little concretely about it in his autumn 1941 speeches. In May 1942, he gave the partisans a prominent place, but with rather narrow objectives. They were not 'to ignite a partisan war everywhere' (as in June 1941) but rather 'to destroy the communications and transport of the enemy, to destroy the staff and equipment of the army'. By November 1942, Stalin was treating the partisan movement as one of the three armed services, with the Red Army and the Navy. Alongside the stubborn defence by the Red Army, it was necessary to 'fan the flames of the people's [*vsenarodnaia*] partisan movement in the rear of the enemy, to destroy the enemy's rear, and to annihilate the German-fascist scoundrels'.[33]

In late May 1942, when it was realized – about the time of the Battle of Khar'kov – that there was going to be no quick Soviet victory, the partisan movement was given more of a structure. A Central Staff of the Partisan Movement (*TsShPD*) was created in Moscow, attached to the Stavka. It had taken eleven months from the start of the war to set up this overall headquarters. The Central Staff was led by P. K. Ponomarenko, the pre-war civilian party leader of Belorussian SSR. Belorussia, behind German Army Group Centre, was the region with the densest and most strategically placed partisan movement. There were six subordinate headquarters under the Central Staff: the Ukrainian, Briansk, Western, Kalinin, Leningrad and Karelo-Finnish 'Staffs of the Partisan Movement'. Like the British Special Operations Executive (SOE), the resistance and sabotage movement was bedevilled by institutional conflict, in the Soviet case between the Army General Staff, the NKVD and different levels and regions of the Communist Party. A sign of the continuing conflict and confusion was the sudden appointment, and equally sudden dismissal, of Marshal Voroshilov as overall Main C-in-C (*Glavkom*) of the partisan movement. In September 1942, Voroshilov, a Politburo member and crony of Stalin, was installed above Ponomarenko's Central Staff, and two and a half months later he was removed and his post abolished. In the spring of 1943 the GKO suddenly abolished the Central Staff (while recognizing its 'serious work'). Only six weeks later, it restored the Central Staff with the significant deletion of the Ukrainian organization, which was put directly under the Stavka.[34]

Ponomarenko claimed in July 1942 'that the enemy rear this summer will be disorganized to a catastrophic degree'. This did not happen. By the summer of 1942, it was clear that partisan activity could be concentrated only in certain regions. One report by Ponomarenko, in early July 1942, showed that of 82,000 partisans, 63,000 were in the centre of the front; there were only 12,000 in the Ukraine, 5,000 south of Leningrad and 1,600 in Karelia. Although the partisans were better organized in 1942, they did not make a real military contribution, either supporting the abortive Soviet counter-offensive of the first half of the year, or harrying the German advance in the south towards Stalingrad and the Caucasus in the summer and autumn. The partisans did control larger areas in Briansk Forest, but they were not putting enough pressure on the German occupiers. In July 1942, in a draft order, Stalin complained of the inactivity of some partisan detachments that were 'sitting it out'. Meanwhile, in the spring of 1942, the Germans carried out their first major anti-partisan operations in what they called the *Bandenkrieg* ('the anti-bandit war'). These operations had the effect of polarizing the situation, and the brutal German conduct pushed the population towards the partisans.[35]

One feature of the Soviet partisan movement, in contrast to that in China or post-1945 'wars of national liberation', was that in the later stages of the war its fighters could make use of what was, for the time, advanced technology. By 1943, the partisans' links to the Soviet 'mainland' were much improved, with better air transport and provision of radios and specialized sabotage equipment.

Thousands of trained specialists were inserted into the partisan detachments. Politically, there could now be little doubt that the war was going in the Soviets' favour, and that the German occupation was going to be temporary. Partisan numbers peaked at 200,000 in summer 1943. Russian sources claim that as of 1943 the partisans held some 75,000 square miles of territory, or about a sixth of German-occupied land, but the effective movement was still confined to limited regions.[36]

In 1943 and 1944, the partisans had a chance to co-operate on a large scale with the Red Army, especially in sabotaging German communications and in providing intelligence. In his important Order of the Day of 23 February 1943, after Stalingrad, Stalin made 'the partisan struggle in the enemy's rear' one of three main elements in the ongoing Soviet successes (the first was training and discipline of the Red Army, the second its unrelenting pursuit of the enemy).[37] In this period, the Soviet partisans fulfilled – in a labour-intensive way – many of the functions filled by long-range aviation and airborne forces in the Western armies. When the Red Army was moving forward in 1943 and 1944, the partisans seized bridges and other key points along the line of advance. The most important episodes involved the advance to and crossing of the Dnepr River in the autumn of 1943, and the great campaign of encirclement in Belorussia in 1944, Operation BAGRATION. They also provided a great deal of intelligence.

Their main military task was interdicting enemy road and rail communications. The first major attempt at co-ordinated operations was Operation LAMP (LAMPA) of November 1942, a widespread strike against German railway communications. More successful was Operation RAIL WAR (REL'SOVAIA VOINA), timed to support the fighting at Kursk. In June 1944 a major operation was mounted to cut the rail lines behind Army Group Centre, which contributed to the rout in Belorussia. However, the Germans did succeed in keeping the rail lines open.

In 1943 and 1944, mounted partisans raided into the steppe country of the Ukraine, either breaking through the front or advancing from the Briansk enclave. This was something the Stavka had considered since 1941, when there was a hare-brained scheme for a Cavalry Partisan Army.[38] The raids were spectacular, and indicative of German weakness, but they were not decisive. The GKO wound up the Central Staff in January 1944, on the grounds that most partisans were in the Ukraine and Belorussia and those areas had their own staffs. Once the Red Army rolled through Belorussia and the western Ukraine, the partisan movement was demobilized and its manpower transferred into regular Red Army units for the march into central Europe.

In September 1942, at a time of terrible military threat, Stalin had declared that 'the defeat of the German armies can be brought about only by the simultaneous military operations of the Red Army at the front and the powerful, unbroken blows of partisan detachments against the enemy in the rear'.[39] In reality, the partisans never had that level of importance. There were no major urban uprisings, nothing like the Warsaw Uprising of 1944. The partisans did not drive the Germans out of Russia, and indeed it is striking that the areas of particular partisan strength were those longest held by the Germans: for example, the southern part of Leningrad Region, the western part of Kalinin, Smolensk and Orel Regions, and the Belorussian SSR. The partisan 'territories', large as some of them were, contained little of value to the Germans. The paradox here was that the rough terrain of forest and marsh, sparsely inhabited, that protected the Soviet partisans was also the terrain that best suited the German defence against the Red Army's tanks.[40]

Some Western sources have dismissed the Soviet partisan movement as a 'phantom war'.[41] The partisans did force the deployment by the Germans of significant forces in the rear areas, particularly along the supply railways, although a fair number of these forces were composed of 'native' collaborators. In 1943 and 1944 the Soviet partisans had an important, although not decisive, impact on the war, especially in worsening German communications. Politically, the partisans probably reduced collaboration with the Germans by the local population. This was not a classic war of national liberation, but in fact the Soviet partisans still probably fought the largest and most successful guerrilla campaign of the Second World War.

Occupation, deportation, collaboration, resistance and Soviet punishment are all connected with one another. As for the larger question of German occupation policy and how it could have engendered less resistance and more collaboration, one of the pioneering works on the subject argues that a less harsh policy *might* have made a difference in 1941.[42] It is, however, inherently unlikely that Nazi Germany or the German Army, given their expectations, ideology and past record, could have pursued a different policy. In November 1943 Stalin argued that the barbaric behaviour of the Germans showed their weakness: 'The evil deeds of the Germans show the weakness of the fascist aggressors, because that is the way temporary people [*vremennye liudi*] behave, who do not themselves believe in their victory'.[43] That was probably true in 1943, but not in 1941. Nazi policies put in place during 1941 were based on the expectation of a German quick victory. They could not be reversed when the Russian war turned out to be protracted in the winter of 1941–2. A serious change of German policy was considered only after Stalingrad. Even had that change been decided upon, the German bureaucracy in the East would have been too rickety to deliver it, and it would have come far too late.

AXIS POWS IN SOVIET CAPTIVITY

The outcome of the Battle of Stalingrad brought about another new development for the war in the East, a very large number of Axis POWs. According to official Soviet figures, only 17,000 enemy POWs had been taken up to the end of June 1942, but no fewer than 537,000 were recorded in the following 12 months. The second half of 1943 was somewhat better for the Axis, with only 78,000 POWs recorded as captured by the Russians. In the first half of 1944, the number increased to 260,000, and in the second half, the months of the Belorussian and the Iaşi–Kishenev operations, the total swelled to 949,000.[44]

The number of Axis soldiers who fell into Soviet hands was similar in its huge scale to the number of captured Soviet soldiers, and the barbarous treatment of POWs was comparable. There were two differences: the Soviets did not murder large numbers of prisoners outright on orders of higher authority, and the Red Army was not fighting a war of aggression. But the scale of deaths bears comparison. The current consensus among German historians is that there were a total of 3,155,000 German POWs in Soviet hands, of whom 38 per cent (1,186,000) died in captivity.[45]

In the initial stages of the war, Red Army desperation and official resolutions about killing the 'German aggressors … to the last man' did not encourage the taking of prisoners. The thrust of the Stavka orders in the winter offensive of 1941–2 was still harsh: to give the Germans a chance to surrender, but if they did not take the offer, to wipe them out. Nevertheless, at about this same time, the Russians began to complain about the German treatment of Soviet POWs, and there was a change of emphasis. In his Order of the Day on Red Army Day, February 1942, Stalin denied foreign press reports that the Red Army did not take prisoners.[46]

Like the Germans in the winter of 1941-2, the Russians a year later were overwhelmed by the number of POWs they took. On 4 February 1943, Beria reported to Stalin about the bad conditions in the Soviet POW camps, and a special commission was created to investigate the extremely high mortality rates. An indication of the terrible situation in the middle of the war is the fate of the captured Italian soldiers, nearly all of whom fell into Soviet hands in the winter of 1942–3; 28,000 died among the 49,000 who actually reached NKVD camps (56 per cent).[47]

Figures for German POWs worked out by the Russians are lower, however. In calculations made for internal purposes in 1956, the number of those people of German and other nationalities who had served in the Wehrmacht, and who had reached NKVD camps, was calculated as 2,730,000. Of these, only 380,000 – 14 per cent – were reckoned as having died in captivity.[48] These figures are clearly too low. Large numbers of German POWs died before they reached the NKVD camps, or even while being transferred between the battlefield and army group transit camps (*frontovye punkty sbora*). And many more German prisoners than 2,730,000 were captured, certainly if those taken at the very end of the war or immediately after the capitulation are included. Some 1,760,000 German POWs had been taken between June 1941 and the end of January 1945. The Red Army then captured many more, during and after the final collapse of

FIGURE 9 German prisoners at Stalingrad.

the Third Reich. According to one set of Russian figures, nearly two-thirds of German POWs were taken *after* 1 February 1945. This was after the date the Red Army reached the Oder River in front of Berlin. In the next three months – February, March and April 1945 – 790,000 prisoners were captured; this was half again as many as had been taken in the first three years of the war. A further 630,000 were counted as taken between 1 and 9 May (when the ceasefire went into effect), and 1,590,000 after 9 May.[49]

Two other features of Soviet policy deserve mention. The Russians tried to use their high-ranking senior prisoners for political purposes, just as the Germans tried to use General Vlasov. A National Committee for Free Germany (*NKFD*) was formed in Moscow in July 1943, and a Union of German Officers (*BDO*) in September 1943. The figurehead of this was a general with a famous name, General Walter Seydlitz-Kurzbach; Seydlitz was the hero of the siege of Demiansk who had commanded the 51st Corps at Stalingrad. After the July 1944 bomb plot, even the captured Field Marshal Paulus made propaganda statements against Hitler.[50] These prisoners might have been important if the Hitler regime had collapsed under its own weight, but in fact they had little impact on the course of the war and even on the post-war East German regime. Another little-discussed feature is the treatment of ethnic German civilians captured in Eastern Europe in 1944–5. In mid-December 1944, the GKO ordered the Red Army to collaborate with the NKVD in the deportation of able-bodied Germans from the Balkans and central Europe to the USSR as forced labour.[51]

Overall, Soviet treatment of Germans, military and civilian, was severe, and had elements in common with the policy of the Third Reich. A million Germans and three million Soviets died in captivity; in both cases the loss rate was much higher than among prisoners held by the British and Americans. One might observe that it was a war between totalitarian states, and these things were to be expected. The Soviet government behaved brutally to many of its own people. On the other hand, the European part of USSR had suffered three years of wanton damage on the part of the Axis occupiers, a problem not faced by either of the Western Allies. The Russians had a plausible claim to the use of Axis labour in the slow process of reconstruction; they certainly held hundreds of thousands POWs until the end of the 1940s.

DIPLOMACY AND GRAND STRATEGY

The Alliance and the Second Front

In this war between mortal enemies, the room for diplomatic manoeuvre was limited. The work of diplomats, moreover, would have little impact on who won.[52] Nazi Germany's diplomatic relations with its smaller European allies, the states which had signed up to the September 1940 Tripartite Pact – Finland, Hungary and Romania – were ultimately relations between master and servants.[53] As far as the Russian front was concerned, the issue for Berlin was at first one of how best to extract troops and resources from the smaller states for the battle. From 1943 onwards, the aim was to keep the increasingly frightened allies in the war. The position of Fascist Italy was not by 1942–3 so very different from the others. Mussolini was only indirectly concerned with the Russian campaign, and even before BARBAROSSA Fascist Italy's military weaknesses had shown themselves in Greece and North Africa. Japan, Germany's original partner in the 1936 Anti-Comintern Pact, was not a Nazi dependency, but geography and culture ruled out real co-operation. After Stalingrad the leaders of Japan and (in its last days) Fascist Italy urged Hitler to make a separate peace with the USSR, but their strategic motives were transparent and their advice was unrealistic; from his perverse strategic point of view, Hitler rightly ignored it.

Relations within the anti-German alliance were more complicated and more interesting.[54] During the Cold War (and later), historians on both sides of the Iron Curtain sometimes suggested that 'the Allies' meant, essentially, Britain and America, and that the USSR was in a different category. This is logically and legally a false distinction. Although relations between Britain and America were very different from those between Russia and either of her two great capitalist partners, the three countries were still in an alliance. Three weeks after the German invasion, on 12 July, Britain and the USSR signed in Moscow an agreement pledging mutual military support and declaring that neither would seek a separate peace. The USSR took part in the London Conference of September 1941 (along with Britain and Commonwealth governments, and the various governments-in-exile). On New Year's Day of 1942, the USSR signed in Washington the 'Declaration of the United Nations'. A Soviet–British alliance treaty was finally concluded in London in late May 1942; this was meant to run for twenty years. A looser agreement existed with Washington, but the United States and the USSR were still allies.

As for Stalin, his statements about his allies varied with the course of the war. In the desperate months of 1941, notably in his July and November speeches, the Soviet dictator stressed the help of foreign capitalist powers. In the second speech he even listed the neutral United States as part of a 'coalition' with Britain and the USSR, 'united in one camp'. Early in 1942 Stalin fell back on a line of self-sufficiency. The Red Army had triumphed in front of Moscow in December 1941; the collapse of the Third Reich seemed to be imminent; the British and Americans had meanwhile suffered defeats in Asia, the Pacific and North Africa. Stalin's first public pronouncement after Pearl Harbor, in February 1942, made no reference to the Allies or Allied aid. By May Day 1942, however, the Soviet counter-offensive had stalled, and the Germans seemed ready for a new onslaught; Stalin once again mentioned his allies. The alliance was also a main theme of his 6 November 1942 speech to the Moscow Soviet, on the eve of Stalingrad, and he included a rousing slogan: 'Long live the victory of the Anglo-Soviet-American military alliance!'[55]

The two Western leaders and Stalin began a prolonged correspondence. Despite the cordial tone of many of the messages (including exchanges of birthday wishes), very deep mutual suspicions continued. Various attempts were made to organize face-to-face meetings, partly from a Western belief that direct involvement with Stalin was the only way to get decisions from the Soviet side. There were frequent delays. Churchill went to Moscow twice, in August 1942 and October 1944. Roosevelt and Stalin were less prepared to travel. Roosevelt believed he could make a unique contribution, or so he told Churchill in March 1942: 'I think I can personally handle Stalin better than either your Foreign Office or my State Department. Stalin hates the guts of all your top people. He thinks he likes me better, and I hope he will continue to do so.' If Molotov can be believed, however, Stalin had a greater respect for Churchill than he did for the American president.[56]

Despite mutual mistrust, even the disagreements took the alliance as a starting point. The central themes of Russia's diplomatic discussions with her allies, at least in the first two and a half years after June 1941, were Lend-Lease aid and grand strategy. Lend-Lease has already been discussed. There was little detailed co-ordination of strategy, much less than between the British and the Americans. No practical military planning body existed which took in both the Russians and their partners and, as we have seen, there was little exchange of intelligence. The discussion about grand strategy concerned the opening of the so-called 'Second Front'. Stalin had been preoccupied with the strategy of Germany's two-front war at least since his May 1941 speech. Just four weeks into the war, in one of his first letters to Churchill, Stalin made his position clear. 'The military situation of the Soviet Union', he said, 'as well as that of Great Britain, would be significantly improved, if a front was created against Hitler in the West (Northern France) and in the North (the Arctic).' In a November 1941 speech, with the Germans at the gates of Moscow after the Viaz'ma–Briansk battle, Stalin tried to raise the spirits of the Soviet population by declaring that the 'second front on the continent of Europe' would come in 'the very near future' (*blizhaishee vremia*). From his correspondence with Churchill, he knew this to be untrue.[57]

Later Stalin used his allies as an excuse for Soviet defeats. Stalin spoke publicly about the imbalance between the contributions made by Russia and its partners. In his speech of 6 November 1942, Stalin reported that of 256 German divisions, 179 were on the Eastern Front, and only 4 were fighting the British in North Africa (he also added 61 Axis-satellite divisions in the East). His figures for German forces, at least, roughly corresponded to reality. On 1 July 1942, there were 183 German divisions in 'the East' and in Finland, compared with 3 in Africa. Stalin publicly blamed the German advance into southern Russia on British and American inactivity: 'Making use of the lack of a second front in Europe, they [the Germans] gathered all their free reserves.'[58]

In 1941, the Americans were neutral; the British, for their part, had committed what effective ground forces they had to the Middle East. Things might have been different had Japan not entered the war. Before December 1941 Churchill had hoped to be able to complete the campaign in North Africa and then to send forces to the Caucasus. The war with Japan meant that the Middle East could not be reinforced, and it was the German–Italian forces which took the offensive there. Even in the first half of 1942, when the Red Army was scrambling to keep the initiative in front to Moscow and then in South Russia, there was no chance of a successful operation across the Channel and back into France. America had just entered the war, and its ground forces were still small and inexperienced. Despite a British–American 'Germany first' strategy, the Japanese offensive successes demanded a forceful response.

Nevertheless, Stalin had some reason to feel aggrieved. When Foreign Commissar Molotov flew to Britain and America in May–June 1942, he was given to believe there that some British–American action would be taken to cross the Channel in 1942. An Allied communiqué of 11 June 1942 stated publicly that there was agreement on the urgency of the launching of the 'Second Front'. In reality, strategic planning was bedevilled by disagreements between the British and the Americans. The US Army planners, notably Generals Marshall and Eisenhower, aimed for the earliest possible operation in northwest Europe. As Marshall put it:

> Western Europe is favoured as the theatre in which to stage the first major offensive by the United States and Great Britain. By every applicable basis of comparison, it is definitely superior to any other. In point of time required to produce effective results, its selection will save many months. Through France passes our shortest route to the heart of Germany. … A British–American attack through Western Europe provides the only feasible method for employing the bulk of the combat power of the United States, the United Kingdom, and Russia in a concerted effort against a single enemy.[59]

For the American planners the Russian front was important, because a cross-Channel operation would be possible only if the Red Army was still pinning down the bulk of the Wehrmacht. The American plans, alas, were unrealistic. They could be compared to Stalin's own expectation of victory in 1942. The British, for their part, wanted to avoid repeating the huge losses of 1914–18, and they had committed what available forces they had to the Middle East. As the British would have to provide the bulk of the forces for any early invasion of Western Europe, they effectively had a veto.

The chances of a successful cross-Channel landing in 1942 were still slight. The Americans themselves did not anticipate being able to mount a full-scale invasion until 1943. An attempt to seize even a foothold in France (such as the

Cotentin – Cherbourg – peninsula) might well have led to a disaster like that suffered by the Red Army on the Kerch' Peninsula in the Crimea in early 1942 (and again in 1943–4). In June 1942, almost at the moment of the Molotov communiqué, Churchill convinced President Roosevelt to agree to use available troops and shipping for a landing in Morocco and Algeria in northwest Africa at the end of the year, originally code-named Operation GYMNAST, but later given the more inspiring name of TORCH. From the point of view of the military practicalities, the choice was between GYMNAST/ TORCH and nothing. For the Russians, 'nothing' might in the long run have been better. Operation TORCH was not just a one-off assault. It drew the British and Americans into a Mediterranean strategy; it diverted forces from a possible '1943 cross-Channel invasion and shipping from Lend-Lease supply routes. In the high summer of 1942 it was clear that the cross-Channel attack was off; in August 1942 Churchill took it upon himself to fly to Moscow to explain the TORCH strategy – and the decision to postpone the Arctic convoys – to Stalin.[60]

Operation TORCH, following the British victory over Rommel at El Alamein, did finally clear the Axis out of the south coast of the Mediterranean. The whole final Allied campaign took four or five months longer than expected, but that was partly because Hitler reinforced a hopeless position. By his May Day speech of 1943, Stalin was able to speak much more favourably about the 'victorious forces of our allies' (who were then within a week of their final goal in Africa, Tunis). Stalin referred to an anticipated 'second front in Europe against the Italian–German fascists'. He also spoke for the first time about the American–British strategic bomber campaign which 'delivers crushing blows against the war industries of Germany [and] Italy'.[61] The Mediterranean campaign, Churchill's baby, did yield significant results. Alongside the British–American strategic bombing campaign, the threat in the south meant that a large part of the Luftwaffe and some German elite troops had to be pulled out of Russia. In particular, Hitler's attack at Kursk in July 1943 was called off, partly because it was believed key panzer forces would be needed to cope with the consequences of the invasion of Sicily.

In private, Stalin, however, was much more critical of his allies. Roosevelt had to inform Stalin (in June 1943) that the cross-Channel invasion would not be mounted until 1 May 1944. This was a low point in relations within the alliance. Stalin wrote to Churchill and Roosevelt on 24 June 1943 – ten days before the Battle of Kursk began – to express his feelings:

> I must say to you that what is at stake is not simply the disappointment of the Soviet Government, but of the preservation of its confidence in the Allies, which is being severely tested. It cannot be forgotten that we are talking about the preservation of millions of lives in the occupied regions of Western Europe and in Russia and of reducing the colossal sacrifice of the Soviet armies, in comparison with which the sacrifices of the Anglo-American forces are on a small scale.

A British–American landing in Italy had not been in the strategic calculations of any of the Allies in 1941 or 1942. In November 1943 Stalin declared, 'The present actions of the allied armies in the south of Europe do not count as a second front. But they are something like a second front.' Italy was, like France, in continental Europe. But the campaign drew off relatively few German ground forces, partly thanks to the geography of the narrow and hilly Italian 'boot'. Even after reinforcements were rushed into action, there were only 17 German divisions in Italy in August 1943. Some 27 were in place in May 1944; at about the latter time, there were 156 German divisions on the Eastern Front.[62]

Stalin, Roosevelt and Churchill finally all met together at Tehran in Iran in November 1943.[63] There was now a final debate on the Western side between Churchill, who favoured the development of further operations in Italy and the Balkans, and Roosevelt and the American commanders, who wanted finally to give full priority to a cross-Channel invasion, now code-named OVERLORD. It was at this moment that Stalin made his most significant contribution to Grand Alliance strategy, supporting the Americans in their desire for a final drive across the Channel, with no further delays. This time the Americans won. The strategy of a May 1944 cross-Channel invasion was confirmed, and Stalin undertook to launch a supporting offensive to prevent the transfer of German forces from Russia to the West. In his Revolution Day address in November 1943, Stalin noted, wearily no doubt, that a genuine Second Front was not 'beyond the hills [*ne za gorami*]'.[64]

The Second Front, in the Soviet sense, was opened on D-Day, 6 June 1944. Stalin was fulsome in his praise, and he may genuinely have realized how much had been achieved:

My colleagues and I cannot but recognize that the history of war has never seen a comparable undertaking from the point of view of its scale, its ambitious scale, and its masterly execution. As is known, Napoleon in his time failed in his plan to force the Channel. The hysterical Hitler, who for two years boasted that he would cross the Channel, never made an attempt to carry out his threat. Only our allies succeeded with honour in carrying out the grandiose plan of crossing the Channel.

In November 1944, Stalin told the Soviet people that the 'masterfully carried out major operations in western Europe of the armies of our allies led to the destruction of German forces in France and Belgium'.[65] If anything, Stalin gave more praise to American and British operations than Soviet historians would give them later, during the Cold War.

Overall, the Russians were right to claim that they were paying a much higher cost in lives and were fighting the bulk of German ground forces. They were right, too, to accuse Roosevelt and Churchill of bad faith. The Western Allies made strategic promises that they knew they could not keep. In June 1942, they promised a cross-Channel attack in the next few months; in August 1942 Churchill promised decisive action in April 1943; and then in February 1943, he told Stalin that the cross-Channel attack would come in August 1943.[66] That said, there are significant qualifications to be made. Stalin stood by and let Britain and France be defeated in 1940; there was no Second Front then. Churchill rarely alluded to this after 22 June, but he did so in August 1942 during difficult negotiations in Moscow: 'We had been left entirely alone for a year against Germany and Italy.'[67] Second, the Soviets themselves took a roundabout line of advance in the summer of 1944, through Romania, into Bulgaria, and up the Danube valley to Hungary – rather than by the direct route across Poland to Berlin. Then again, Soviet criticisms were mostly about the German *Army*, that is, the number of ground force formations on the different fronts. They tended to see the Western Allied force structures as a mirror image of their own, giving little importance to the huge resources the Americans and British devoted to their sea and air forces. The first of the 'thousand bomber' raids (on Cologne and Essen in May 1942) did, however, impress Moscow. The Comintern leadership noted that this was a major new development, 'the extension of the war onto Germany's own territory as a result of mass bombing by the English'.[68] The successes of the bombing campaign were also, it must be said, a major theme of Churchill's wartime correspondence with Stalin.

In addition, there was no reason why the Western Allies should have pursued a strategy of high losses just to match the Red Army, casualty for casualty. The Red Army suffered high losses partly because of mistakes made by Stalin's government in the purges, in pre-war deployment, and in being caught by surprise in June 1941. The British–American Mediterranean strategy did in the end draw off substantial German ground and air forces. It also provided an opportunity for American ground forces to obtain combat experience. A cross-Channel operation was qualitatively different from a Soviet ground offensive; it could be thrown back into the sea, with catastrophic military and political consequences.

By 1943, some leaders in the West feared that the Soviets for their part would pause when they reached their pre-war border and would then let the Americans and British fight it out with the Germans (and Japanese), that is that Moscow would return to its policy of 1939–41. The Red Army could rebuild its strength and the capitalists could weaken themselves. Such a strategy may have been hinted at by the Russians as a ploy to speed the Second Front and encourage the flow of Lend-Lease. There is no evidence that it was ever considered in Moscow. It was not in the interests of the USSR, nor did it correspond to the mood of the Soviet population.[69]

Soviet expansion and the Comintern

With D-Day and the steady flow of Lend-Lease, major early points of diplomatic contention between Russia and her allies had been resolved. In 1941, 1942, and most of 1943, given Germany's predominance, there was little point in inter-Allied disagreements about how liberated territory should be administered. The first major cases were in French North Africa and southern Italy, and neither directly involved the Russians. The problem of Eastern Europe and Germany was potentially much more complex, but it only emerged in the spring of 1944, and did not become an issue for some months after that. The implications of these debates, especially for joint strategy in the final months of the war, will be discussed in Chapters 12 and 13. In September 1941 Moscow accepted the Atlantic Charter, which had been drafted by Roosevelt and

Churchill in the previous month. The principles of the Charter, especially the rejection of territorial aggrandizement and the pledge to return self-government to those people who had been deprived of it, fitted awkwardly with Soviet annexations over the previous two years. As early as 1941, notably during Foreign Minister Eden's visit to Moscow in December, the Russians tried and failed to get British acceptance of the 1939–41 border changes, especially the Soviet annexation of the Baltic states, and the final treaty did not guarantee the borders. The situation at the front now, however, seemed to have turned in the Russians' favour. As Stalin wrote to Molotov in May 1942, apropos of the failure to get guarantees of Russia's new border: 'The question of borders … in one or other part of our country will be decided by force.'[70]

A notable development of the middle part of the war, in May 1943, was the dissolution of Moscow's Communist International (Comintern), led at the time by the Bulgarian Georgi Dimitrov.[71] This was not just a concession to the British and Americans. Stalin had never been a great enthusiast for the Comintern. We now know the decision dated back at least to April 1941 when Stalin, eager to improve relations with the Nazis, had spoken within his inner circle about winding down the Comintern. The 'great benefit' to be reaped, Dimitrov noted in his diary, was that 'All anti-Comintern pacts [e.g. between Germany, Japan, and Italy] immediately lose all grounds.' The outbreak of war in June 1941 actually gave the Comintern a new lease of life. Its links with foreign Communist parties and its propaganda and communications resources could be used to develop anti-Nazi resistance. Even here it became an embarrassment, as Stalin explained to Dimitrov: 'The Com[munist] Parties making up the KI [Comintern] are being falsely accused of supposedly being agents of a foreign state, and that is impeding their work in the broad masses. Dissolving the KI knocks this trump card out of the enemy's hands.'[72] The dissolution of the Comintern was partly window dressing. The various Communist parties were in reality 'agents of a foreign state', and they remained so, but they were controlled by Moscow in more discreet ways. Other organizations, the secret police, the foreign commissariat and the Red Army, played a part. A large covert international apparatus (the 'shadow Comintern') survived within the machinery of the Soviet Communist Party's Central Committee. The leaders of the Communist parties during and after the war would be comrades nurtured by the Comintern: Thorez in France, Togliatti in Italy, Tito in Yugoslavia, Gottwald in Czechoslovakia, Pieck and Ulbricht in Germany, even Dimitrov in Bulgaria.

CONCLUSION

There was little interaction between the two warring camps. The British and American statesmen could not, however, forget the First World War, when a battered Russia had made peace with Imperial Germany. Then, in early 1918, Berlin allowed Lenin's government to survive, at the cost of the Bolsheviks giving up Finland, the Baltic states, Poland, Belorussia and the Ukraine. Stalin's government, to be sure, had shown extreme 'flexibility' in dealing with an ideological opponent in 1939–41. However, there was in reality little chance of the anti-German alliance breaking up and none of a separate peace in the East. Stalin thought of approaching the Germans in August 1941, using the good offices of the Bulgarian ambassador, but this was probably no more than a tactical probe.[73] The eminent American historian Gerhard Weinberg took the Soviet–German talks more seriously, but there seems little justification for this interpretation.[74]

Contacts between low-level Soviet and German intermediaries took place in neutral Sweden in 1943. After the Battle of Stalingrad, however, there was even less chance of a compromise peace with Hitler. Before Stalingrad, the Germans had been fighting their war of annihilation with no quarter given. Hitler did not envisage anything less than total victory. The atrocities committed by the Nazis meant – and were probably intended by Hitler to mean – that there could be no going back. There was, moreover, no geographical basis for compromise. In 1943 Russia was not going to accept a peace based on existing lines of occupation. Nor was it conceivable or strategically sensible from the German point of view to pull the Wehrmacht back to the 1941 starting point. Given Hitler's bedrock assumption of Aryan-Slav hostility, a separate peace could be no more than a breathing space for Germany's implacable enemies. Insofar as these feelers had any Soviet purpose, it was to keep pressure on the Western Allies for the launching of the Second Front and the timely delivery of Lend-Lease supplies. In his 1943 May Day speech, Stalin mentioned the possibility that the Germans would try to win over one or other part of the Grand Alliance.[75] This clumsy hinting, like the abolition of the Comintern, had little real effect, as it was just at this time that the British and Americans went ahead with their decision to invade Italy rather than mount the cross-Channel invasion in 1943.

Stalin may have envisaged negotiations with a post-Nazi government, especially during the crisis winter of 1941–2. The Red Army was surging forward, and Stalin imagined Hitler's position to be shaky.[76] Judging from Stalin's speech of February 1942, the Soviet leader was trying to make peace with Germany over the heads of the Nazis: 'The Hitlers come and go, but the German people, and the German state, they remain.' The assumption may well have been that the adventurist nature of the 'Hitler clique' had been made obvious by the defeat at Moscow. Stalin toned down his propaganda, and after November 1941 he did not call for a Soviet 'war of annihilation'. The formation of the Free Germany Committee in 1943, after Stalingrad, was perhaps partly an attempt to find an alternative German government.[77] As for Russia's western partners, once America entered the war in December 1941, no serious faction in Britain was about to seek a separate peace. After Stalingrad (and after the successful end to the British–American North African campaign), when the war was going militarily well for the Allies, there was no reason why they should fall out. There was nothing to be gained from a separate peace, and in any event no one would negotiate with Hitler.

Hitler's preferred outcome was an outright Axis military victory. By early 1943, however, it became clear even to him that this was not likely. The Nazi and Wehrmacht leaders came to see a split in the anti-German coalition, on the lines of Frederick the Great's experience in the Seven Years War, as the route to survival. This was a major thrust of Goebbels' propaganda in the later period of the war. It was not a completely unrealistic hope. Ultimately, however, the two wings of the alliance held together.

The argument is sometimes made that the Western Allies should have used their strength to put pressure on the Soviet government to live up to the Atlantic Charter; this seems far-fetched. It was the Red Army that would take Eastern Europe from German control, and the Russians would be able to do what they liked there once the war was won. It was also greatly in the interests of the Americans and British in wartime to make maximum use of Soviet human resources. Relations would change as the two sides began to think more clearly about the post-war world, and as the Red Army extended Soviet influence into Central Europe. Even then, however, there was overwhelming agreement on the need to defeat Nazi Germany.

CHAPTER 9
THE RED ARMY TAKES THE INITIATIVE, JANUARY TO SEPTEMBER 1943

Besides, in the coming summer the enemy will get to know our old offensive power again!

Josef Goebbels, 18 February 1943

The enemy has lost a battle, but he has not yet been defeated.

Joseph Stalin, 23 February 1943

The victory at Kursk must have the effect of a beacon seen around the world.

Adolf Hitler, 15 April 1943

THE SOVIET WINTER OFFENSIVE AND THE THIRD BATTLE OF KHAR'KOV

The Soviet advance on Rostov

The surrender of the German 6th Army at Stalingrad on 31 January 1943 was an event of the greatest importance, but it did not lead to the immediate collapse of Hitler's forces in Russia. Indeed, the period from February to July 1943 was a time of limited successes and missed opportunities for the Red Army.

The first Soviet operations in 1943 developed at the southern end of the line, near the Sea of Azov.[1] Operation DON, launched on 1 January 1943 and continuing until 4 February, was an attempt by the Soviet Southern, Transcaucasus and North Caucasus Army Groups to get to Rostov and prevent the withdrawal of enemy forces from the Kuban'. But south of the Don, General Kleist effected a fighting retreat of his German Army Group 'A' faster than the Red Army could advance. The 1st Panzer Army was withdrawn to the northwest through Rostov into the Donbass, and the 17th Army was pulled back to the southwest towards the Kerch' Strait (covering the approaches to the Crimea). Hitler promoted Kleist to the rank of Field Marshal on 1 February 1943, a few days after the unfortunate Paulus.

North of the Don, General Eremenko's Southern Army Group crushed in the German Rostov–Voroshilovgrad bulge, the dwarf survivor of the Stalingrad salient (see Map 7). Progress was, however, slower than had been hoped for. Eremenko, the hero of the siege of Stalingrad, was never a great 'offensive' general. The Stavka replaced

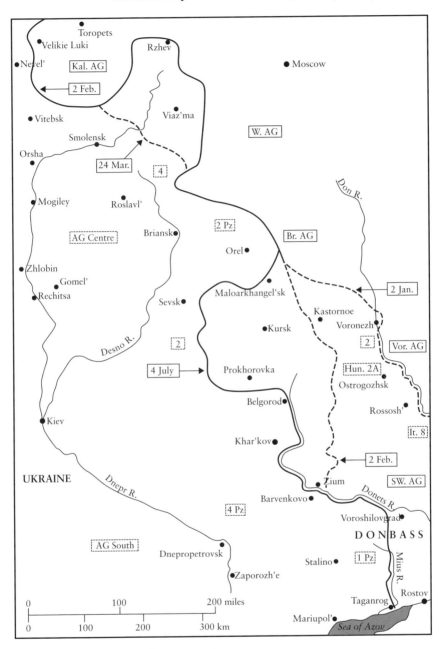

MAP 7 The Soviet winter offensive, 1942–3.

him with General Malinovskii at the start of February. Malinovskii was now fully back in Stalin's favour, after his success with the 2nd Guards Army at Stalingrad, and he would lead the southern wing of the great Soviet offensive all the way to Budapest, Vienna and Prague.

In the meantime, however, Field Marshal Manstein, the commander of Army Group Don, had flown to Rastenburg and asked Hitler's permission to withdraw from Rostov and the eastern Donbass. After lengthy discussions the Führer agreed. Manstein had argued successfully that the Reich could do without the coal of the eastern Donbass and that Rostov had lost its strategic value after the withdrawals from the North Caucasus. He was allowed to pull his line of defence back to the Mius River, which flows into the Sea of Azov west of Rostov, dividing the Donbass in half; here the German Army had stood in the winter of 1941–2. The Red Army entered both Rostov and Voroshilovgrad on 14 February 1943 and then advanced to the Mius line, finally bringing to an end Operation DON.

West from the Don

Further north, the Red Army had also been pushing forwards, and with earlier success – even as the siege of Stalingrad continued. In the second half of January, the Russians had mounted a vitally important but little-known attack, the Rossosh'–Ostrogozhsk operation. It was their third drive over the Don; the first (in November) had been Operation URANUS, the second (in December) LITTLE SATURN. This time the direction of the attack – which did not have a code name – was due west. Under the watchful eyes of Zhukov and Vasilevskii, part of Vatutin's Southwestern Army Group and part of Golikov's Voronezh Army Group pushed across the Don and on to the Oskol River. They hit the Hungarian 2nd Army and the Italian 8th Army around the small towns of Ostrogozhsk and Rossosh' on the eastern edge of Kursk Region. Golikov had been sent reinforcements from the Stavka reserve in the form of Rybalko's new 3rd Tank Army. The Soviet concentration was cleverly masked, and the operation caught the enemy by surprise. The Hungarian and Italian formations broke immediately, in the same way that the Romanian divisions further east had broken in November and December.[2] Supporting German formations could not hold the line; Army Group 'B' was shattered. From the Oskol River line (west of Ostrogozhsk and Rossosh') the Red Army could now threaten the Donets River and Khar'kov with follow-on attacks.

A week later (24 January), and about 75 miles further north up the Don, the rest of Voronezh Army Group and one army of Reiter's Briansk Army Group began another offensive, against the large city of Voronezh on the Don and the important rail junction at Kastornoe behind it (between Voronezh and Kursk). Voronezh was the place from which Paulus's 6th Army had begun its part of Operation BLUE against Stalingrad in June 1942. Now the Russians in short order captured Voronezh (on 25 January) and Kastornoe (three days later), pushing the German 2nd Army well to the west of the Don. Another of the satellite formations was fatally shattered, this time the Hungarian 2nd Army. These twin attacks, the Soviet Ostrogozhsk–Rossosh' and Voronezh–Kastornoe operations, tore a huge breach in the Axis lines.

Operation POLAR STAR

These events coincided with further victories at the northern end of the Soviet–German front. On 19 January 1943, Operation SPARK achieved its main objective and cut through a land supply route to Leningrad. This released forces for other tasks in the northern theatre (see Maps 3 and 4). The day before (18 January), and 250 miles to the south, the Kalinin Army Group finally broke through to the town of Velikie Luki, threatening the communications of both Army Group North and Army Group Centre. (Both these operations were described in Chapter 6.)

All of this success led to some very serious thinking at the Stavka, in the last week of January and the first week of February, about where else on the long front line the enemy could now be hit to achieve decisive results. To understand this, it is useful to start with a panegyric about Stalin's military 'genius' in the Second World War, which appeared in the late 1940s over the name of Voroshilov. The article stressed, before anything else, two things: the overall co-ordination of the various Soviet army groups and the mastery of battles of encirclement. These had a direct relevance to the strategic perspective and intentions of Stalin – and probably that of his military advisers – immediately after Stalingrad.

> The offensive of the Soviet Army in the winter of 1942–3 ... was carried out with remarkable clarity of purpose by the co-ordinated operations of numerous army groups, united across a theatre of military operations extending for a thousand kilometres, according to a single [*edinyi*] strategic plan and a single strategic will, that of the Supreme C-in-C, that of the great Stalin.

The same article laid out another supposed 'form of battle' that was highly relevant to these operations:

> In the Great Fatherland War under the leadership of Stalin one of the most complicated and difficult problems of military art – manoeuvres for the encirclement and annihilation [*okruzhenie i unichtozhenie*] of large masses of the enemy's forces – was also fully realized in practice. ... In the offensive operations of the Soviet Army this strategic movement of encirclement became the leading form of its military operations.

The Germans, Voroshilov continued, had thought they had a monopoly of such operations, modelled on Hannibal's encirclement battle at Cannae. In reality, it was the German forces at Stalingrad which were the object of 'the grandiose Cannae of the 20th Century', and which was executed by the Soviet Army under the supreme command of the great Stalin'.[3] Stalingrad was indeed a brilliant battle of encirclement, and Paulus's 6th Army had been annihilated.

Stalin and the Stavka certainly entertained hopes of repeating the Stalingrad encirclement on other parts of the front in the near future.[4] The first of the co-ordinated operations of 1943, the first attempted post-Stalingrad battle of 'encirclement and annihilation', was Operation POLAR STAR (POLIARNAIA ZVEZDA).[5] This offensive involved the Soviet Northwestern, Volkhov and Leningrad Army Groups, and very serious weight was attached to it, at least for three or four weeks. Marshal Zhukov himself was charged with co-ordinating the three army groups. The overall concept was that the Leningrad Army Group would now drive for Narva on the Estonian border, while – repeating the operation planned for the 1st Shock Army in February 1942 – the left wing of the Northwestern Army Group would strike out for Pskov. The distance to Pskov was some 110 miles. Operation POLAR STAR had much in common with Operation URANUS at Stalingrad and Operation LITTLE SATURN/SATURN on the middle Don, both carried out just two months before. Just as Rostov had been the strategic rail choke point for Hitler's southern army groups, so Pskov was the choke point for his northern one.

Under the plan for Operation POLAR STAR, an inner encirclement would close the narrow exit from the Demiansk salient at the village of Ramushevo and create a small version of Stalingrad. In the outer encirclement, echoing the attacks on Rostov, Soviet forces would drive west towards Pskov and cut off an entire German theatre. Lindemann and the German 18th Army near Leningrad would reprise the part of Paulus and the 6th Army at Stalingrad. On the attacking side the counterpart of Vatutin and the Southwestern Army Group (at Stalingrad) were General M. S. Khozin and a 'special group of forces' set up on 30 January. Khozin had attended a meeting with Stalin, Zhukov and a General Staff officer on the previous night.[6] His 'Special Group' comprised the re-formed 1st Tank Army under General Katukov and the new 68th Army under General Tolbukhin, both commanders being very effective soldiers.

Khozin's directive was issued at 1.00 am on 6 February 1943, the same moment that Timoshenko was ordered to cut off Demiansk with his Northwestern Army Group and – as we will see – the same moment that ambitious instructions were sent to the Soviet army groups in the central part of the front. The Stavka ordered Khozin to be ready for action by the middle of the month:

> The basic task of the group of forces is to cut the communications of the enemy's Leningrad–Volkhov group [i.e. the German 18th Army] by advancing to Luga, Strugi Krasnye, Porkhov, and Dno and not to allow enemy units to get through to help their Demiansk [i.e. the German 16th Army] and Leningrad–Volkhov groupings. A group of forces [sic] composed of two rifle divisions, two ski brigades, two tank regiments, two air regiments of the Stavka reserve, and one engineer brigade are to take and hold the town of Pskov.
>
> After the capture of Luga [and] Strugi Krasnye, part of the forces are to take the area of Kingisepp [and] Narva, cutting off the enemy's retreat into Estonia. The major part of the forces are, in cooperation with the Volkhov and Leningrad Army Groups, to surround and destroy the Volkhov and Leningrad groupings of the enemy.[7]

Hitler, however, had learnt at least some lessons from Stalingrad, and this was a major factor that prevented the success of POLAR STAR. We have seen how in the south he eventually allowed Army Group 'A' to pull back out of the North Caucasus and permitted Manstein to give up Rostov and the eastern Donbass. At the urging of his military advisers and in the face of the Stalingrad crisis, the Führer finally accepted the need for some corrective action in the north as well. Here the main territorial concession was to be Demiansk. The elements of the German 16th Army in the Demiansk salient began their withdrawal on 20 February 1943, and they completed its final stage on 18 March. Becoming aware of German intentions, on 20 February Stalin urged Zhukov to launch POLAR STAR in the next three or four days, blocking off the neck of the Demiansk salient to stop the enemy escaping.[8] This did not succeed. The Germans pulled back, shifted to the west of the Lovat' River, and shortened their total front line by some 175 miles. The manpower saved allowed a robust defence of their new position.

Zhukov had been closely involved with the planning in Moscow for Operation POLAR STAR, but he could see that the situation had changed for the worse. There was apparently a heated telephone conversation between Zhukov and Stalin, and it was only with difficulty that Zhukov was able to convince Stalin that the German evacuation of Demiansk made the operation impossible. In a signal sent a week later (28 February), Zhukov put the blame on the rains and warmer weather of the past two weeks, which hampered movement: 'Considering the rapidly changed situation and the weather I am very much afraid that we will have to sit in our present deployment in a swampy and impassable location, unable to achieve the goals of POLAR STAR.' The best thing to do was to make a limited advance to Staraia Russa (50 miles northwest of Demiansk and south of Lake Il'men) and then to wait until after the *rasputitsa*. Zhukov proposed reinforcing Khozin with two more infantry armies for a spring offensive: 'I think that in the spring such a group of forces could play a very big [*krupnyi*] role.'[9]

In the meantime, however, larger events overshadowed the fighting in the north. Field Marshal Manstein's counter-offensive in the southern theatre began, as we will see, on 19 February 1943. In the course of March, the Wehrmacht rolled several Soviet army groups back northeast past Khar'kov and Belgorod (which the Germans retook on 15 and 18 March, respectively). Just before the loss of Khar'kov, Stalin recalled Zhukov from the futile northern battles and sent him to deal with the crisis. Like Manstein in 1942, Zhukov would not come back to the northern theatre. Timoshenko, whom Stalin had finally lost confidence in as a front-line commander, was also removed from the Northwestern Army Group and replaced by General Konev. Konev pursued the costly Staraia Russa operation in the first three weeks of March 1943; it cost 32,000 Soviet troops and did not achieve its objective.[10] (Staraia Russa would only be liberated in mid-February 1944.) The opportunity for a 'battle of encirclement and annihilation' in the north, comparable to Stalingrad, had passed.

A 'grandiose' plan to destroy Army Group Centre

As the southern Soviet armies pressed towards Rostov and Voroshilovgrad and as Operation POLAR STAR was being set up, the Stavka had laid out further Soviet lines of advance in the central sector of the front (see Map 7). Stalin and the Stavka were still as interested in Field Marshal Kluge's German Army Group Centre as they were in the Axis armies reeling back from Stalingrad and in Army Group North.

The great prize remained the exposed position of Kluge's armies in the Rzhev–Viaz'ma salient west of Moscow. The big Soviet-held Toropets salient still hung north and west of Rzhev and Viaz'ma and threatened the German supply line back to Smolensk. Great Soviet resources of manpower and equipment had been thrown against the Rzhev–Viaz'ma area, notably in Operation MARS of November 1942, but with high losses and little success. Now, at the end of January 1943, there were two new factors: a Soviet advance west into Kursk Region after the Rossosh'–Ostrogozhsk breakthrough, and the surrender of the Stalingrad garrison. The first event opened the long southern flank of the 2nd Panzer Army at Briansk and Orel, which in turn covered the southern flank of the Rzhev–Viaz'ma salient. The second event freed up the Soviet manpower required for an attack.

Stalin and Zhukov issued the key order early on 6 February 1943 (a week after the surrender of Stalingrad and at the same moment as the directive for POLAR STAR). Soviet armies from north and south of what was now called the Orel 'balcony' were to effect a double encirclement of the 2nd Panzer Army. Again, the operation had much in common with Operations URANUS and SATURN against the Stalingrad bulge – and with Operation POLAR STAR. Three armies of General Reiter's Briansk Army Group were to encircle and capture Orel, and they were ordered to complete this task by 15–17 February. Meanwhile, the 13th Army of the Briansk Army Group (advancing from the south) and the 16th Army of the Western Army Group (coming down from the north) would make a second and deeper encirclement behind Briansk (40 miles to the west of Orel). They were ordered to take this city by 23–25 February.[11]

There was more. The Stavka also planned that a new Soviet force was to exploit the Hungarian–Italian collapse at Rossosh' and Ostrogozhsk and the Voronezh–Kastornoe breakthrough. This new force was Rokossovskii's Don Army Group, the formation that had just taken the surrender of the German 6th Army at Stalingrad. Rokossovskii's command was renamed Central Army Group, and he was told to move rapidly to his start position in the western part of the Kursk sector (underneath the Orel 'balcony'), which was in the process of being liberated. The transfer was supposed to be effected by 15 February (nine days after the original 6 February order); from that time, Rokossovskii was to begin a rapid drive to the northwest through the little town of Sevsk, for a third and even deeper thrust against German Army Group Centre. 'On reaching the Briansk–Gomel' line [the railway line running southwest from Briansk and 60 miles northwest of Sevsk] the main blow of the army is to be directed … towards Smolensk with the object of occupying the Smolensk area and cutting off the line of the retreat of the enemy's Viaz'ma–Rzhev grouping.' The 'Viaz'ma–Rzhev grouping' was the German 9th Army and the 3rd Panzer Army of Army Group Centre. Smolensk was to be the cork in the bottle, like Rostov in the south and Pskov in the north. As if Rokossovskii's task were not enough, his orders envisaged a *fourth* and wider encirclement: he was to detach two rifle divisions further west to secure Gomel' and the upper Dnepr crossings between the towns of Rechitsa and Zhlobin (175 miles west of Sevsk).[12]

According to the master plan, at the moment Rokossovskii reached the Briansk–Gomel' railway line, the Soviet Western and Kalinin Army Groups would launch their own pincer movement on either side of the Rzhev–Viaz'ma pocket. The Western Army group would march towards Smolensk via Roslavl', while the Kalinin Army Group would take up where it had left off in early 1942, pushing southwest from the Toropets salient to Vitebsk and Orsha, and cutting the rail lines west of Smolensk and with them the main line of retreat of Army Group Centre.[13]

In mid-February Stalin despatched Vasilevskii, newly promoted to the rank of Marshal, to co-ordinate all this – the actions of the Voronezh, Central, Briansk and Western Army Groups – in what could be called the 'central offensive'. As Vasilevskii, the Chief of the General Staff, later described it, the aim was 'to execute a series of major offensive operations, linked by one strategic conception and plan, with the objective of the defeat of the main forces of German Army Group Centre'.[14] Compared to all this, Operation URANUS at Stalingrad had been simplicity itself.

This complex central offensive might all be seen to be a hare-brained scheme, dreamt up by Stalin while Zhukov and Vasilevskii were away at the front, but that was not the case. Vasilevskii, in his own recollections, stressed that the orders for operations in the central theatre were issued 'after a number of discussions of the Supreme C-in-C with leaders in the centre [i.e. at the Stavka] and at army group level'. Zhukov was strangely silent about the whole episode of the central offensive in his memoirs. It is now known, however, that Zhukov (also just promoted to Marshal) attended meetings with Stalin every evening from 24 January to 5 February. On the critical night of 5–6 February, in the hours before the directives for POLAR STAR and the even bigger central operation were issued, Stalin met with Zhukov, two senior planners from the General Staff, and Red Army chief commissar Shcherbakov; also present, significantly, was General Rokossovskii, who was supposed to lead the striking force through Sevsk and deep into the rear of German Army Group Centre.[15] The directives were issued over the names of Stalin and Zhukov.

Again, the Wehrmacht was able to take preventative action. At nearly the very moment that the Stavka issued its orders, Hitler was conferring with his own hard-pressed Eastern Front commanders at Rastenburg. The Führer had finally been prevailed upon to pull back from the Rzhev–Viaz'ma salient, as he had from other exposed positions. As elsewhere, withdrawal would shorten the German defensive line, free up reserves and put planned Soviet attacks off balance. The pulling back of the front line, as we have already seen, was code-named Operation BUFFALO. It began on 1 March. Skilfully completed within the month, it was preceded by a secret redeployment of German forces. Meanwhile, Rokossovskii, with his new Central Army Group, was delayed by weather and transport problems; he had to cover a distance of over 500 miles from Stalingrad, and he had to rely on one single-track railway. Rokossovskii began attacks with the limited forces that had reached their assembly area, but they ran out of momentum in early March. Meanwhile, the big crisis developing further south near Khar'kov from late February forced the diversion of Soviet forces there.

The overall result of the proposed central offensive was another bloody Soviet failure. Konev (the Western Army Group) and Reiter (the Briansk Army Group), for their part, made little progress against the German 2nd Panzer Army in the Briansk–Orel area, partly because the Germans were already beginning to transfer divisions back there from the Rzhev–Viaz'ma salient. As a result of this setback, General Konev suffered another twist in his winding career path leading to Berlin and Prague in 1945. On 27 February 1943, Stalin declared him 'not up to the task of the command of the army group', removed him from the Western Army Group command, and replaced him with his deputy, General Sokolovskii. After a few days stewing in Moscow, Konev was assigned – as previously noted – to take over the less important Northwestern Army Group. The immediate cause of Stalin's displeasure was the costly failure of a local offensive into the Rzhev–Viaz'ma salient by one of Konev's armies (Cherevichenko's 5th). (As fate would have it, only a week later the Germans began to pull back with Operation BUFFALO.) Konev himself later spoke of long-running intrigues against him (Konev) by his commissar, Bulganin. The real reasons were probably Stalin's annoyance at the lack of progress of the Western Army Group, Konev's general lack of enthusiasm for foolhardy offensives, and perhaps a general simmering frustration on Stalin's part over reverses in the south and slow progress in the centre and north.[16]

Marshal Rokossovskii later recalled that the Stavka had committed a 'crude error' when it ordered a 'grandiose operation' (the central offensive) in early February. 'Appetites', he complained, 'prevailed over possibilities'. He noted in particular the lack of information about the enemy: 'Our deep operational and strategic intelligence turned out to be completely unsatisfactory.'[17] The offensive did not destroy Army Group Centre. It did not even dent the German position in the Briansk–Orel area; the 2nd Panzer Army held firm. Soviet losses were heavy.[18] From the point of view of the whole campaign, the most damaging thing about the central offensive was that considerable Soviet resources were devoted to it in February and March 1943, resources that could have been used better elsewhere.

Unsuccessful dashes to the Dnepr

Operation POLAR STAR and the central offensive had little success. Their objectives were too ambitious, the forces available too weak; the Germans were able to stonewall them. More actual movement took place in the southern part of the front, although part of the Soviet advance was followed by precipitate retreat.

Two other Soviet roads to the west had been opened by the destruction of the Axis armies west of the upper Don in the parallel Rossosh'–Ostrogozhsk and Voronezh–Kastornoe operations (see Map 7). It looked for a time as though the Red Army might drive westwards as far as 150 miles to the great Dnepr River, liberating en route the whole Donbass region and, further north, one of the most important cities in the USSR,

Khar'kov. The two advances, in February 1943, took the form of Operation STAR, by General Golikov's Voronezh Army Group (towards Khar'kov and Kursk), and Operation GALLOP, by General Vatutin's Southwestern Army Group (into the Donbass).[19]

Operation STAR (ZVEZDA) was a continuation of the offensive of Golikov's Voronezh Army Group, and now overseen by General Vasilevskii, the Chief of the General Staff. The original plan for Operation STAR had been submitted to the Stavka on 21 January 1943; the actual attack began on 2 February, the day of the final surrender of Stalingrad, and four days before the Stavka issued directives for POLAR STAR and the central offensive. The northern wing of this offensive pushed beyond the Kastornoe railway junction towards the city of Kursk, and was ultimately the most successful Soviet advance of the late winter campaign. On 8 February the northernmost of Golikov's right-flank armies, General I. D. Cherniakhovskii's 60th, took Kursk. With the victory, this young army commander began a rapid ascent within the ranks of Stalin's generals; in 1944 he would lead an army group. Kursk would, four months later, provide the setting for the best-known battle of 1943.

Golikov's armies took Belgorod on the Donets River, 80 miles south of Kursk, on the same day. Most spectacularly, the major industrial centre of Khar'kov, 50 miles to the southwest of Belgorod, was captured by his forces on 16 February. Turning the German weak defences in front of Khar'kov from north and south, Moskalenko's 40th Army and Rybalko's 3rd Tank Army advanced into the city. The city had been abandoned despite Hitler's express orders that it be held at all costs. Golikov now assumed that the *Ostheer* was going to pull all the way back to the Dnepr River – which would indeed have been the sensible German course of action. In the last week of February he was allowed to give his Voronezh Army Group very ambitious – and incautious – new tasks in the west, fanning his forces out to approach the middle course of the great river[20]; the nearest point on the Dnepr was about 130 miles southwest of Khar'kov.

What eventually became Operation GALLOP (SKACHOK) was proposed by General Vatutin in the Southwestern Army Group. Vatutin took it for granted that the enemy was going to retreat to the Dnepr, and in mid-February he received permission from the Stavka to anticipate this move.[21] This operation envisaged a 'gallop' forward to establish a bridgehead on the western side of the Dnepr River at Dnepropetrovsk, while part of the advancing forces turned south to the Sea of Azov. Three main elements were involved: Group 'Popov', the 1st Guards Army and the 6th Army. Group 'Popov' was an armoured spearhead of several mobile corps under General M. M. Popov, Vatutin's deputy commander.[22] It was supposed to cut German communications 50 miles behind the Mius line and then to push as far south as the Sea of Azov. In the best case this could have trapped the German 1st Panzer Army and Army Detachment 'Hollidt'. Meanwhile, the Soviet 1st Guards Army and the 6th Army were to race west for the strategic Dnepr crossings at Dnepropetrovsk and Zaporozhe.

The problem with both STAR and GALLOP was that the Soviet formations involved were increasingly worn down, had not been sufficiently reinforced, and were being pulled further and further from their supply bases. The Russians tried to supply their spearhead units by air, but with only limited success. The Stavka had other concerns; it was simultaneously mounting POLAR STAR and the big central offensive, and it also had to think about its Southern Army Group, at the left end of the line, which had just taken Rostov. In addition, there had been an important Soviet intelligence failure. The Germans were believed to be without reserves and intending to retreat behind the Dnepr. With his surprise countermarch of 19 February, Field Marshal Manstein once again achieved German operational ascendency.

Manstein counter-attacks

Even more than in the north and the centre of the Soviet–German front, the Wehrmacht had in the south been staring disaster in the face. On 17 February, Hitler himself flew into Zaporozh'e on the Dnepr River, with Generals Jodl and Zeitzler. Two days later, and two months after his unsuccessful attempt to relieve Stalingrad in Operation WINTER STORM, Field Marshal Manstein began to counter-attack.[23] Manstein had finally been able to complete the leapfrogging of his forces out of the North Caucasus and the Rostov area, and into a manoeuvre zone in the Donbass. In late February his own mobile forces, now better supported by the Luftwaffe, were able to pinch off Vatutin's spearheads approaching the Dnepr, hitting them on their flanks. Mackensen's 1st Panzer Army (formerly in Army Group 'A' in the Caucasus) was in place north of Stalino. Hoth's 4th Panzer Army, after its long trip from south of Rostov, was assembling west of Khar'kov. The 1st Panzer Army was able to encircle and disperse much of the overextended Soviet Group 'Popov' (General Popov himself escaped), while further north, the 4th Panzer Army dealt with the Soviet 6th Army and the 1st Guards Army and the approaches to the Dnepr crossings.

There was another new factor. The German reinforcements summoned from France and the Reich at the time of the initial Stalingrad emergency were now arriving on the scene. Best known were the forces from the Waffen-SS. The first SS division to arrive had been unable to save Khar'kov in February, but by March a whole SS Panzer Corps had assembled. This had been set up in September 1942 and now comprised three freshly equipped SS armoured divisions, 'Das Reich', 'Adolf Hitler' ('*Leibstandarte*') and 'Totenkopf'. The corps was now given pride of place. It retook Khar'kov on 15 March, after the city had been in Soviet hands for five weeks. Golikov's Voronezh Army Group was then pursued back east to Belgorod (its headquarters).

In response, the Stavka rushed any fresh forces it could muster into what had become the Kursk 'bulge' and to the line of the Donets River. These reinforcements included Katukov's new 1st Tank Army from the Stavka reserve, where it had originally been designated to take part in POLAR STAR. Stalin, as we have seen, recalled Zhukov from the northern theatre and sent him to oversee the situation. For a time, there seemed a danger that the Germans might advance north to effect a link with the 2nd Panzer Army in the Briansk–Orel area. By doing this, they could have cut off Rokossovskii's Central Army Group in what had become the Kursk 'bulge'. Such an action would have repeated the Wehrmacht's victory in the first Battle of Khar'kov in May 1942; it anticipated, too, the intention of German Operation CITADEL of July 1943.

Fortunately for the Russians, stability was restored in the second half of March. But the setback at Khar'kov had shattered their post-Stalingrad illusions of early victory, and the southern sector of the Soviet front had required reinforcements at the expense of the planned offensives against German Army Groups North and Centre. Golikov's performance as the commander of the Voronezh Army Group was judged to be inadequate, and he was dismissed from his post; he would not be given another major front-line command. Vatutin, commander of the Southwestern Army Group and Golikov's neighbour to the south, escaped Stalin's wrath for being too daring with Operation GALLOP. He was in fact shifted north to take over Golikov's command.[24]

Explaining the German recovery

The fighting on the Nazi–Soviet front in the first three months of 1943 is a neglected subject. It is sandwiched between the Battles of Stalingrad and Kursk, and remembered mainly for Manstein's recapture of Khar'kov and perhaps for the Red Army's breaking of the Leningrad blockade in Operation SPARK. In this period the Russians achieved no battle 'of encirclement and annihilation' comparable to the destruction of the 6th Army at Stalingrad. They had not even chased the Germans back to the Dnepr line. For the Germans, and for Hitler personally, another great crisis of morale had been overcome.[25] The headlong retreat from the Don and the North Caucasus had ended, and a major prize had been retaken by German forces in the form of Khar'kov. The 'assault from the steppe', as Goebbels had put it, had temporarily been brought to a halt.

Historians give Erich von Manstein great personal credit for turning the military situation around in the first three months of 1943. In his widely read memoirs, the German General Mellenthin lavished unreserved praise: 'It may be questioned whether any achievement of generalship in World War II can approach the successful extrication of the Caucasus armies and the subsequent riposte to Kharkov.'[26] Manstein's 'mobile defence' operations in the Donbass became a model for NATO's planning in the 1960s. David Glantz has even argued that by driving off the Soviet GALLOP and STAR offensives, and by recapturing Khar'kov, Manstein thwarted the Soviet intent to collapse the entire Soviet–German front.[27] In any event, this was Manstein's finest hour on the Russian front. He was a gifted operational commander of Army Group South; he kept his nerve and, for the moment, his Führer's confidence. However, there are other reasons for the German Army being able to hold the line in south Russia.

Having given up their Caucasus adventure, the Germans were able to pull their mobile forces back and concentrate them in the Donbass area; indeed, the worst of the German January–February 1943 crisis might have been avoided if this withdrawal had been effected earlier. It was also important that well-motivated and equipped German reinforcements arrived from the West. Paulus's prolonged defence of Stalingrad, meanwhile, tied down Soviet forces. The Luftwaffe's 4th Air Fleet was brought up to greater strength and played a major role over the open steppe; at the same time, the Stavka found it technically difficult to rebase the Red Army Air Force forward to meet it. Overall, the Russians had had to face the problem of advancing rapidly in mid-winter after several months of combat. It was 300 miles from Stalingrad even to the Mius River line west of Rostov, and another 200 miles further on to the Dnepr. Forward units were now very far from their railheads, and Soviet logistic resources were still limited.

But above all, the Stavka had dispersed its efforts up and down the huge front and left the Red Army open to Manstein's thrust against Khar'kov. Some histories of the war contrast Stalin's rashness and over-optimism in early 1942 with his patience in waiting for the German attack on Kursk in mid-1943. In truth, he was overambitious also at the start of 1943, contemplating attacks at too many points on the line. These attacks aimed for decisive results: nothing less than the encirclement and annihilation of the German army groups on the southern, central and northern parts of the front. The spirit of the campaign, after Stalingrad, had been summed up in Stalin's Red Army Day Order of 23 February 1943:

> Increase the blows against enemy forces, tirelessly and persistently pursue the enemy, do not give him time to dig in on some line of defence, give him no rest, either during the day or at night, cut the enemy's communications, surround the enemy forces and destroy them if they refuse to lay down their arms.[28]

As Stalin wrote these words, Zhukov was preparing Operation POLAR STAR, Rokossovskii was frantically deploying with Central Army Group from Stalingrad to the western part of Kursk Region to take part in the central offensive, Golikov was looking towards the Dnepr, and Vatutin was racing for the Dnepr crossings. Stalin could not have Pskov *and* Smolensk *and* Khar'kov *and* Dnepropetrovsk, and in the end, he took none of them.[29]

The Soviets would reach and cross the Dnepr line in 1943, but it would take another six months. Even then, the *Ostheer* would be able to pull back behind the river in a more or less orderly fashion. The Red Army would regain the ground in front of Moscow and even take Smolensk, but only after a German pre-planned evacuation and an orderly German fighting withdrawal. Army Group Centre would live to fight again – for fifteen months. The Red Army would take Orel and Briansk, and recapture Belgorod, Khar'kov and the western Donbass, but that would not now happen until the late summer.

The setbacks of the Red Army at Khar'kov and elsewhere did not make the Battle of Stalingrad any less important. The early months of 1943 were not a period of German victory, despite the recapture of Khar'kov. Manstein had only made the best of a very bad situation. The destruction of a German army at Stalingrad continued to have deep and terrible reverberations. The whole German line was creaking, as the OKH and OKW scavenged for reserves to throw into the southern gaps. The North Caucasus had been abandoned and much of the Donbass, the close blockade of Leningrad had been broken, the long-fought-for Demiansk and Rzhev–Viaz'ma salients given up, and the Russians now held the Kursk bulge in the middle of the front. Worse was to come.

THE BATTLE OF KURSK

Operation CITADEL

The Battle of Kursk is among the best-known episodes of the Second World War, and is sometimes even treated as the turning point of the conflict. The battle had its origins in Operation CITADEL (ZITADELLE), which was a German attempt to encircle and destroy the big salient or 'bulge' created during the February 1943 Soviet offensive.[30] This salient extended across the steppe some 115 miles from north to south, and 80 miles from east to west; it took in a large agricultural region, centred on the medium-sized Russian city of Kursk (120,000 inhabitants in 1939). The Germans eventually concentrated an unprecedented mass of mobile forces above and below the Kursk bulge, built up from divisions that had been cleared out of the Rzhev–Viaz'ma salient and the Kuban'. To the north was the 9th Army (General Model) from Field Marshal Kluge's Army Group Centre. To the south, from Field Marshal Manstein's Army Group South, were the 4th Panzer Army (General Hoth) and Army Detachment 'Kempf'.

First conceived in mid-March 1943, Operation CITADEL began three and a half months later, on 5 July. The German advances ground to a halt within a week. The attacking panzers were stalled by the Red Army's field defences, and then the thrust from the south was countered by massed Soviet armoured counter-attacks. Although Hitler called off CITADEL on 13 July, the second phase of the battle, a full-scale Soviet counter-offensive, ran on from mid-July until 23 August. Not only did the German Army fail to achieve the objective of its summer offensive – the destruction of the Kursk bulge – but it was driven from the flanking positions north and south of Kursk (the Orel and Belgorod–Khar'kov regions, respectively). By late August 1943 the Red Army was positioned on a line from which it could at last drive rapidly forward west to the Dnepr River.

The reasons for the German failure

Planning at Hitler's headquarters for Operation CITADEL in 1943 had been much more hesitant than planning for the 1941 or 1942 German offensives. This was a result of the Wehrmacht's fragile position after defeats at Stalingrad and in North Africa. Zeitzler, the Chief of the Army General Staff, wanted an early offensive to catch the Red Army off balance and blunt any major attack it might attempt. Hitler was enthusiastic; he had been encouraged by the Soviet reverse at Khar'kov in March 1943. On the other hand, the professionals of the Wehrmacht High Command, especially Jodl, were reluctant to commit more forces to Russia. The OKW had to consider the disastrous situation in Tunisia and the imminent danger of a British–American landing somewhere on the north side of the Mediterranean. General Guderian, appointed Inspector of Armoured Troops in January 1943, evidently also opposed the attack. Guderian reported his Führer's own doubts, from a conversation in mid-May: 'Whenever I think of this attack', Hitler said, 'I also always feel sick to my stomach'. Possibly decisions were forced on Hitler by events.

Tippelskirch, a senior German general turned historian, suggested that Hitler wanted a victory to inspire Mussolini in the politically critical summer of 1943. In the original CITADEL directive, back in April, Hitler had declared that 'the victory at Kursk must have the effect of a beacon seen around the world'.[31] The Führer, in short, needed a success.

The projected CITADEL offensive was greatly delayed, which forfeited any element of surprise. The original plan, ordered on 13 March 1943 (as Khar'kov was being recaptured by the Germans), had been for an attack in the middle of April. Hitler's 15 April order then set 3 May as the start date, but this was unrealistic given the ongoing *rasputitsa* and the need to refit his forces. The two main field commanders, General Model (under Field Marshal Kluge) and Field Marshal Manstein, disagreed about timing. Model wanted to assemble more forces. On 4 May, after discussing preparations with his senior generals, Hitler moved the date further back, to mid-June. On 21 June, he reset the date again to early July, which was when the attack actually began.

The major technical cause of the delay at Kursk was a desire allow time to bring up new equipment; this was especially felt necessary by Zeitzler and Model, and their view was supported by Hitler. Since the autumn of 1942, the quality of the best tanks coming from German factories had begun to surpass that of the best Russian ones. The up-gunned version of the (1937) Pz Kpfw IV tank was technically superior to the current version of the T-34 (the T-34-76), and it completely outclassed the 9-ton T-70 light tank, which made up about a quarter of the Soviet tank force. Production had begun of two powerful new tanks, the Tiger heavy with an 88mm gun and the Panther medium with a 'long' 76mm gun. Produced in smaller numbers was the 'Ferdinand', which was effectively an assault gun version of the Tiger, heavily armoured and fitted with an 88mm gun. A pause was also required to refit and strengthen the Luftwaffe formations with tactical aircraft that could support the offensive.[32]

In the end, this pause before Kursk was to be one of the longest in the ground war on the Nazi–Soviet front. From April to June 1943, both the Germans and the Russians suffered their lowest losses for any quarterly period of the war. The best figure for German losses in the East gives 48,000 for this quarter, half that of any other. Meanwhile, the best Russian figure (not directly comparable with the German one) was 125,000. While great in an absolute sense, these losses were for the Russians a third that of any quarter-year of the war so far.[33] There was, however, an unprecedented amount of air combat in this period. The Red Army Air Force developed many of its operational techniques in big air battles over the Kuban' (east of the Kerch' Strait) from March to June 1943. And in May and June, anticipating the German offensive, Soviet air units mounted heavy attacks on the Luftwaffe bases around the Kursk bulge.

In April 1943 Stalin's army held much the same geographical position it had held twelve months earlier. The fighting of the winter of 1941–2 had been brought to a halt by the *rasputitsa*. In 1942 the Soviet leader had decided to develop offensives against Khar'kov and the Crimea, and in May 1942 these decisions had led to momentous defeats. A year later, Stalin, like Hitler, was undecided about what to do. Weeks extended into months. The Red Army would gain an advantage by letting the Wehrmacht impale itself on the Russian defences at Kursk, but there were two outstanding problems. One was a lingering doubt, at least in Stalin's mind, as to whether the Red Army could afford to give the Germans the initiative. Would it stand up to another Blitzkrieg offensive – where the enemy chose the place and the time to concentrate his forces? Would the Red Army not then crumble as it had in June and July 1942? The other problem was whether the Germans planned to attack at all. Excessive delay would give the enemy time to dig in; it would also limit the Soviet campaigning season before the autumn 1943 *rasputitsa*. Stalin and some of his military advisers were doubtless influenced by the recent setbacks suffered in the multiple Soviet offensives of February and March 1943. Opinions were divided in the Soviet army group commands. Vatutin in the Voronezh Army Group, on the south side of the bulge, was eager for a pre-emptive attack. Zhukov, Vasilevskii and Antonov (Vasilevskii's deputy at the General Staff) wanted to wait. Zhukov maintained that Stalin wavered at least until the middle of May.[34]

In his appraisal of early April, three weeks after the loss of Khar'kov, Zhukov wrongly thought there was still a threat to Moscow. Nevertheless, he correctly argued that the Germans would initially attack on a limited front and put the stress on panzers and aircraft:

> I consider it would be unsound to go over to an offensive with our forces in the very near future with the aim of pre-empting the enemy. It would be better if we were to wear down the enemy on our defences, destroy his tanks, and then, throwing in fresh reserves, we can go over to a general offensive [and] decisively defeat the basic concentration of the enemy.[35]

The Russians now had enough strength to prepare both defensive and offensive options. They set up elaborate defences with a depth of 175 miles in case of another catastrophe like that of 1942. These included a 'State Defence Line' (*GRO*), dug by civilians along the Don River. As General Shtemenko, head of the Operations Section of the General Staff, later recalled, preparations for Kursk were very deliberately thought out: 'Measure seven times, cut once.'[36]

On the other hand, on 25 April, two weeks after Zhukov's memorandum, the Stavka did approve a plan by Vatutin for a major attack to the south, out of the Kursk bulge. This would be mounted against Khar'kov and Belgorod, and had the aim of cutting German Army Group Centre off from Army Group South. Deep defences were to be prepared, and it was suggested that the attack might come *after* the defeat of an initial German advance. All the same, this Soviet plan still envisaged an offensive lasting up to 15 days and rolling the Germans back 120 miles. Katukov's 1st Tank Army was, as requested, transferred to the Voronezh Army Group. Vatutin was told to be ready for defensive operations by 10 May, and for an offensive no later than 1 June. Nikita Khrushchev, who was then commissar of the Voronezh Army Group, also recalled that there were plans for the Red Army to take the initiative, but he said that it was Rokossovskii's Central Army Group which was intended to deliver the main blow, and to the north; this was why the forces in the northern part of the bulge were stronger than those in the southern part.[37] In the end, however, the Germans moved first.

At Kursk, Soviet intelligence was an unusually important factor, compared to battles before and after. For nearly two years, before the spring of 1943, the Red Army high command had had only a limited knowledge of German intentions; the invaders had as a result gained a huge advantage of operational and tactical surprise. The worst examples – beyond Operation BARBAROSSA itself – were in September 1941, before the Battle of Viaz'ma–Briansk, and in May–June 1942, in south Russia. In contrast, intelligence was less important in later battles (after Kursk) when the Red Army possessed both the initiative and overwhelming strength, and rarely had to worry about German surprise attacks. Marshal Vasilevskii maintained that, compared with 1941 and 1942, few reproaches could be made against Soviet intelligence in 1943.

> Our intelligence was able to determine not only the general intention of the enemy in the period of the summer of 1943, the [intended] direction of his attacks, the composition of the striking groups and of the reserves, but also to establish the time of the beginning of the fascist offensive.

There has been some debate about who provided the most valuable information. Among the sources were the so-called 'Red Orchestra' in Central Europe and the British traitor John Cairncross, who was supplying ULTRA information (from Bletchley Park's radio intercepts). British Intelligence itself supplied general and accurate information about Hitler's intentions in late April.[38] The Russians also had information from partisans operating behind German lines and a rapidly improving radio intelligence system. Probably no one source was uniquely valuable.

Even with all this intelligence, advance warning about the timing of CITADEL was less clear, partly because Hitler repeatedly changed his mind. Russian air strikes intended to forestall the Luftwaffe were launched on 6–8 May, some eight weeks before the actual attack. On 2 July, however, the Stavka could give three days' warning. The Russians were able to execute a pre-emptive artillery bombardment and to carry out dawn raids on German airfields. Soviet expectations were, however, incorrect about where the heaviest attack would fall, assuming the north face of the bulge rather than the south, and this was the reason General Zhukov was sent there in late June.[39]

Kursk is well known partly because of the amount of armoured strength that the two sides were able to pack into a limited area. The Germans, for their part, would never again have this accumulation of forces. Model in the 9th Army (subordinate to Kluge's Army Group Centre) disposed of the 47th and 51st Panzer Corps with six panzer divisions. In the south the German armies were even stronger. Hoth in the 4th Panzer Army (subordinate to Manstein's Army Group South) commanded the 48th Panzer Corps, with three panzer divisions, and the SS panzer corps (now called the 2nd SS Panzer Corps), with three SS *panzergrenadier* (armoured) divisions. An Army Detachment under General Werner Kempf (also part of Army Group South) was deployed to Hoth's right; it included the 3rd Panzer Corps, with three more panzer divisions. By comparison, the armoured strength of Field Marshal Bock's German Army Group Centre on 22 June 1941, spread out over a roughly comparable area in western Belorussia, had consisted of only nine panzer divisions; the tanks in those 1941 divisions were also smaller and less capable than those of 1943.

Ultimately, the Russians were victorious at Kursk because they had had time to lay out their field defences and to assemble powerful front-line forces and operational reserves. General Rokossovskii, commanding the Central Army Group on the north face of the bulge, had four infantry armies. As a mobile force, he had Rodin's 2nd Tank Army. In the south, in the Voronezh Army Group, Vatutin commanded five infantry armies, with Katukov's 1st Tank Army as a reserve. As a strategic reserve, the Stavka had assembled to the east of the Kursk bulge another very large formation, the Steppe Military District, renamed the Steppe Army Group on 9 July. Its role was to bolster the Kursk defence if necessary and to provide the 'fist' of the counter-attack. At nearly the last minute, on 23 June, General Konev was brought in to take command of these forces; Konev was back at the centre of operations, and he would stay there until the end of the war.[40] Konev's Steppe Army Group comprised two Guards armies, three regular infantry armies and General P. A. Rotmistrov's 5th Guards Tank Army. Zhukov later pointed out that at Stalingrad the Red Army had employed fourteen infantry armies, one tank army and several mechanized corps; at Kursk (including the counter-attacks), it made use of twenty-two infantry armies and five tank armies.[41]

The exact balance of numbers between the Wehrmacht and the Red Army is still debated, but the advantage was clearly on the side of the defenders. Soviet Central and Voronezh Army groups disposed between them 1,340,000 men and 3,440 tanks and SP guns, 19,100 guns and mortars, and 2,170 aircraft. If Konev's Steppe Army Group is taken into account, another 500,000 troops, 1,400 tanks and SP guns, and 2,800 guns and mortars can be added. On the German side, the 1998–9 Russian official history assessed the strength of the 2nd and 9th Armies of German Army Group Centre, and the 4th Panzer Army and Army Detachment 'Kempf' of Army Group South as 'over 900,000' troops, 2,730 tanks and SP guns, 'about 10,000' guns and mortars, and 'about 2,050' aircraft. The historians Zetterling and Frankson, using German sources, came up with lower figures of 777,000 German troops (including non-combat troops), 2,450 tanks and SP guns, 7,420 guns and mortars, and 1,830 aircraft.[42]

The Battle of Kursk and its consequences

The nature of the Battle of Kursk and its impact on the war are often misunderstood. First of all, it is necessary to get beyond the myth of Prokhorovka. Marshal Vasilevskii, who witnessed this battle from the headquarters of the 5th Tank Army, later described it as a 'genuinely titanic duel of two steel armadas'. Some Soviet sources claimed this 'duel' involved 1,500 tanks; more generally, it was argued that the Germans suffered devastating losses at Prokhorovka and were forced to abandon Operation CITADEL.[43]

A major battle was indeed fought southwest of the small railway station at Prokhorovka. The 2nd SS Panzer Corps (commanded by General Paul Hausser, subordinate to Hoth's 4th Panzer Army, and in turn to Manstein's Army Group South) had approached this point, seven days into CITADEL and only about 25 miles from its start line on the south face of the bulge. Hausser's panzer corps was counter-attacked on a narrow front on 12 July by Rotmistrov's 5th Guards Tank Army, rushed forward from the Steppe Army Group, the Soviet strategic reserve. The numbers of tanks and SP guns involved, however, was well under 1,500. The panzer corps consisted of three armoured divisions, and Rotmistrov's tank army was made up of three tank corps and a mechanized corps; the Germans had about 300 tanks and SP guns, the Russians about 700. Rotmistrov's counter-attack, originally intended to envelop the panzer spearhead, actually took the form of a poorly prepared head-on attack. The 5th Guards Tank Army lost about 400 tanks in the fighting on that one terrible day, in the face of better-organized and better-equipped German armour and anti-tank guns. (The Soviet tank army's 29th Tank Corps, most heavily hit, lost 153 out of 199 tanks.) Permanent German losses from the SS panzer corps in this particular battle were evidently very light, fewer than two dozen tanks and SP guns.[44]

Far from being a Soviet triumph, Prokhorovka was a tactical victory for the Germans, as they inflicted much heavier losses and drove off the main Soviet counter-attack. Prokhorovka was also not the reason for the abandonment of CITADEL; the Germans (including the 2nd SS Panzer Corps) only began their withdrawal on 16 July, four days later. On the other hand, Manstein and Hoth did not achieve their objective at Prokhorovka, which was to break into the 'open' operational space behind the Soviet defences. Here, the – costly – actions of 5th Guards Tank Army, and defensive fighting of the flanking 5th Guards Army and 69th Army, could be regarded as successful.

More broadly, it was undoubtedly the case that in the wider fighting in the first half of July, on both the northern and southern faces of the Kursk bulge, the robust Soviet defences effectively held off the attacks of Operation CITADEL. In the north, General Model's 9th Army made little progress against Rokossovskii's Central Army Group. On the south face, the 48th Panzer Corps and 3rd Panzer Corps (flanking the Prokhorovka thrust of the SS panzer corps) were also unable to advance any further.

Hitler informed his army group commanders of his decision to abandon the CITADEL at a conference in East Prussia on 13 July. His main stated explanation for this decision was the invasion of Sicily by the British and Americans three days earlier, and the possibility of Italy's withdrawal from the war. Field Marshal Kluge, for Army Group Centre, agreed with the termination of CITADEL, based on the overall situation; his subordinate, Model, had made only slight progress and on the previous day had come under full-scale attack from the east and north. Manstein, for Army Group South, pushed for a continuation of operations in his part of the Kursk bulge (including Prokhorovka), aimed to bring about a local encirclement. Abandoning the offensive at the critical point, he argued, would mean to 'give away victory'. This judgement was almost certainly wrong, in view of the overall correlation of Soviet and German forces. As for Hitler, while the news of the invasion of Sicily no doubt contributed to his decision to call off CITADEL, he was also influenced by the lack of progress against the Kursk bulge, and a growing and justified concern regarding the threat to his own forces in the Orel and Belgorod–Khar'kov salients.[45]

In terms of the Battle of Kursk in its fullest form (5 July to 23 August), there is no doubt that the result was a Russian victory, albeit one bought at heavy cost. The two arms of the German attack had achieved their limited success only by throwing in nearly all operational reserves, leaving little to deal with the Soviet counter-attacks, north and south of the Kursk bulge, when they came in mid-July. In the north was the German Orel salient which contained the 2nd Panzer Army and the 9th Army, both now subordinated to General Model; the 9th Army had been engaged in CITADEL, and the so-called 2nd Panzer Army (a formation with very few panzers) was covering the salient against attacks from the north and east.

The Russians had in fact massed their largest forces around the Orel salient. Rokossovskii's Central Army Group was to the south, within the Kursk bulge. M. M. Popov's Briansk Army Group (three infantry armies) was deployed at the east end of the salient, and two armies (50th and 11th Guards) of Sokolovskii's big Western Army Group hung over its rear. Behind the Briansk and Western Army Groups was another big Soviet operational reserve, comprising Rybalko's 3rd Guards Tank Army, the new 4th Tank Army and the 11th Army. On 12 July, the seventh day of Operation CITADEL, the Russians launched their own attack here, Operation KUTUZOV, also called the Orel operation.[46] (The desire for a co-ordinated blow on 12 July was also probably a cause of Rotmistrov's overhasty offensive at Prokhorovka.)

This concentric Soviet attack had much in common with the unsuccessful offensive ordered by the Stavka back in February 1943. An important part was assigned to the 11th Guards Army (Briansk Army Group), under General Bagramian, attacking from the north. The Russians broke gaps in the German line, allowing the penetration of Rybalko's 3rd Guards Tank Army and, further north, of two independent tank corps. Eventually, three Soviet tank armies (2nd Tank, 4th Tank and 3rd Guards Tank) were engaged, but this strength was not effectively used, the weather was very wet and there was no encirclement of German forces. At the end of July, Hitler allowed the defenders to withdraw. On 5 August, Rybalko's tanks entered Orel, but General Model had

FIGURE 10 Soviet infantry advances across the steppe of southern Russia in 1943.

successfully pulled the German 2nd Panzer Army and 9th Army back to the HAGEN defensive line. This line covered, among other points, the vital rail junction at Briansk. Rokossovskii could not immediately fulfil Stalin's order to break across the Desna River and cut German communications from Briansk to Gomel'.

At the end of August, the Red Army's Central and Briansk Army Groups would be able to resume their advance. They only halted in early October, and by that time they were 130 miles to the west and on the edge of Belorussia – at the defensive line which Hitler called the *Ostwall*. (The *Ostwall* is described in the following chapter.) Briansk itself had been recaptured by General Popov on 17 September.

Meanwhile, on the *southern* side of the Kursk bulge, the German forces had been weakened by the fighting in their initial Operation CITADEL attack. Some troops, including the 2nd SS Panzer Corps, had been transferred further south to deal with a Russian offensive developing in the Donbass. The planned Soviet drive from the Kursk bulge to the south was delayed for over a week, to Stalin's considerable annoyance. Hoth's 4th Panzer Army and Army Detachment 'Kempf' were hit on 3 August – a month after the start of CITADEL – by the Soviet Steppe and Voronezh Army Groups. This was the so-called Belgorod–Khar'kov operation, code-named Operation RUMIANTSEV (POLKOVODETS RUMIANTSEV) and co-ordinated by Marshal Zhukov himself.[47] Operation RUMIANTSEV went over the ground gained (and lost) by Operation STAR in March 1943. Within two days, the attackers had occupied the ruins of Belgorod. This was the same day (5 August) on which the offensive north of the Kursk bulge took Orel, and the dual victory prompted the first massed artillery *saliut* of celebration in Moscow. Katukov's 1st Tank Army and Rotmistrov's 5th Guards Tank Army then broke out, held off German counter-attacks in the middle of August, and covered the capture of Khar'kov, on 23 August (the date, in Soviet historiography, which marked the end of the Battle of Kursk). The great Ukrainian industrial centre changed hands for the fourth and final time in the war. General Kempf, who had disobeyed Hitler's demand that Khar'kov be held at all costs, was dismissed.

The Germans *did* escape encirclement, both north and south of the Kursk bulge. Some of the Soviet generals favoured attempting to trap Army Group South in the Donbass, but Stalin rightly decided to forgo encirclement and annihilation in favour of pushing the enemy back to the Dnepr as soon as possible. This would secure the river crossings and limit damage to the mines and factories of the region.[48]

Soviet personnel losses (killed, died of wounds and missing) in the whole defensive phase of the Battle of Kursk (5–23 July 1943) were 70,000, with the greater part (54,000) suffered on the southern face of the bulge. Some 1,600 Soviet tanks were lost in the fighting, and 460 aircraft. The human and material costs were considerably higher than those of the Germans. Zetterling and Frankson, using archival sources, came up with a figure of 57,000 German casualties for the 'offensive' period of the battle (5–11 July in the north and 4–20 July in the south), which would suggest about 15,000 fatalities. German tank and SP gun losses in the northern sector at Kursk, as listed by Zetterling and Frankson, were 88 vehicles, and those in the south 190, making a 'total loss' figure of rather less than 300. Luftwaffe losses were 193 aircraft. Heavier Soviet losses were suffered in the 'offensive' stage of the Battle of Kursk, the Orel and Belgorod–Khar'kov operations. The cost of the Orel operation was for the Russians 113,000 personnel and 2,600 tanks, and that of the Belgorod–Khar'kov operation was 72,000 and 1,900, respectively. Another estimate of German personnel losses, by Overmans, gave a figure for the *whole* Eastern Front of 71,000 deaths in July 1943, and of 59,000 in August.[49]

Strategically, the battles of July–August 1943 were less significant than they are often made out to have been. The decision to abandon Operation CITADEL was partly the result of the British–American invasion of Sicily. More important, Hitler never intended CITADEL to be a war-winning operation like BARBAROSSA or his Stalingrad campaign. It was a grandiose spoiling attack, with a secondary role as a propaganda 'beacon'. The Battle of Kursk could not be 'decisive' in a way that the Battle of Moscow or the Battle of Stalingrad were; the stakes were much lower. Hitler wanted to regain the initiative and recover lost prestige; he wanted to expunge the memory of Stalingrad. That really shows how decisive the great battle on the Volga had been.

On the other hand, Kursk had for the Russians a great moral importance: the Red Army held its own for the first time in a summer campaign; its success could not be put down to the role of 'General Winter'.[50] The Wehrmacht was unable to break through the Soviet defences, and the halting of CITADEL was followed by the collapse – by the end of August – of the whole position in the south-central part of the Soviet–German front. It is irrelevant that the Russians suffered heavier losses, and that the Germans were not trapped in another big encirclement like Stalingrad. For the rest of the war, from the middle of July 1943 until May 1945, the Red Army would hold the initiative.

The southern flank

Further south, in the Donbass and down to the Sea of Azov, Malinovskii's Southwestern Army Group and Tolbukhin's Southern Army Group had mounted their own attacks in mid-July. These were the Izium–Barvenkovo operation and the Mius operation, and they were intended mainly to prevent the Germans shifting reserves to the Kursk fighting. Neither Soviet formation was able to make significant initial progress against German Army Group South. A much more ambitious attack, co-ordinated by Marshal Vasilevskii, was mounted in mid-August, with the objective of driving the German forces from the western Donbass. Stalin was edgy about the lack of progress in the south. He actually threatened to sack Vasilevskii for not making prompt reports, and he accused Vatutin of 'repeating old mistakes' – a reference to the Southwestern Army Group's abortive gallop to the Dnepr in February 1943.[51]

Fortunately for the Russians, this time German resistance cracked. At a conference at Vinnitsa on 27 August, four days after the loss of Khar'kov, Manstein confronted Hitler with another of his weighty 'choices': either send German Army Group South twelve new divisions or give up the Donbass. In any event, the new German 6th Army (formerly Army Detachment 'Hollidt') could not resist. Taganrog, the southern anchor of the Mius River defensive line, was abandoned on 30 August. The Red Army advanced rapidly to the west, allowing the German 1st Panzer Army and 6th Army no time to form a new line of resistance. On 8 September, the Soviet Southern Army Group took Stalino (later Donetsk), the main town of the western Donbass. The German defence had now clearly been thrown off balance on the southern part of the front and – as in February 1943 – the various Soviet army groups raced to the Dnepr River, hoping to take the crossings off the march before the Germans could put together any serious resistance. The Russians failed in February 1943 in Operation GALLOP; in September 1943 they succeeded. After flying again to Zaporozh'e in early September, Hitler gave Manstein permission to pull the 1st Panzer Army and 6th Army back to another part of his *Ostwall*, to the so-called WOTAN position. By 22 September, the Red Army finally reached the Dnepr south of Dnepropetrovsk, after an advance of 190 miles.

OTHER FRONTS

More distant sectors of the Nazi–Soviet front were less active in the summer of 1943. Hitler had hoped to mount an operation against Leningrad following the success of CITADEL, but happily that came to nothing. Soviet offensive operations in the northern part of the main front also had little success.[52] The Leningrad and Volkhov Army Groups mounted an attack towards the village of Mga, south of Lake Ladoga, in July–August 1943, but this made virtually no progress for the loss of 21,000 men. The operation was evidently mainly intended to keep the German high command from shifting troops south. The rest of German Army Group North's position held firm, although in early October 1943, two shock armies from Eremenko's Kalinin Army Group would finally overrun the important defended rail junction at Nevel', on the demarcation line between Army Group North and Army Group Centre, and the next step west after Velikie Luki.

The northern flank of German Army Group Centre had come under increasing pressure, starting with a series of attacks by Eremenko's left flank and by Sokolovskii's Western Army Group. The advance was given the name Operation SUVOROV, after the famous Tsarist commander of 150 years before. Stalin actually visited Sokolovskii's headquarters at Khoroshevo on 1 August – a unique appearance of the Soviet dictator at the front. This was at a time when Stalin was developing a strong taste for gold braid and military tradition. In July 1943, People's Commissar Malyshev first saw the dictator wearing his marshal's uniform. Behind Stalin's desk were portraits of Suvorov and Kutuzov. At a display of new armoured vehicles at the Kremlin in September, Stalin climbed, for the first time in his life and reasonably nimbly, into a tank.[53] In any event, a week later, on 7 August, the attack began. The two army groups pushed haltingly forward during August and September, but Smolensk itself was finally taken on 25 September. Hitler had permitted Field Marshal Kluge to pull German Army Group Centre back to the PANTHER position, which was still to the east of the important natural defensive line of the upper Dnepr. The whole 'Smolensk strategic operation', between early August and early October, advanced up to 150 miles on a 250-mile-wide front, but at this rate it would take three or four years to reach the western frontier. It was also an operation that was very expensive in human terms, costing the lives of 108,000 Soviet troops.[54]

In the extreme south, the Germans were pushed out of their GOTH'S HEAD foothold in the Kuban' between mid-September and the start of October 1943, abandoning the ingenious new cable-car system across the Kerch' Strait. The city of Novorossiisk itself was finally captured on 16 September 1943. Leonid Brezhnev, the future President of the USSR, was involved in the operation as commissar of the Soviet 18th Army. At the very end of the month, two Soviet armies were ferried west across the 8-mile strait to the Kerch' Peninsula of the Crimea, beginning a prolonged and costly operation there.

CONCLUSION

On balance, looking at the Eastern Front as a whole in September 1943, the Wehrmacht was still deep in Russia. The supreme German leadership could argue that there was no immediate threat to the Reich compared to the imminent danger in the West. Nevertheless, after the late start to the 1943 summer campaign, the Red Army took and held the initiative in the south. The Soviet offensive attempts of February 1943 were repeated, this time with much greater success. As for the Germans, the contrast with the comparable summer campaigning seasons in 1941 and 1942 was striking. Manstein's brilliant counterstrokes of February and March 1943 would not be repeated, let alone the big German offensive operations in south Russia during the summer of 1942. The Russians had not dissipated their strength as much as they had early in 1942, and there was in any event much more strength to go around. Stalin's objective of the co-ordinated action of several fronts came closer to reality in the Soviet counter-attacks which followed CITADEL, notably Operation KUTUZOV and Operation RUMIANTSEV, but that may have been because the attacks were concentrated in the south-central part of the front. He still did not achieve his goal of encirclement and annihilation.

The battles for Kursk, Orel, Belgorod and Khar'kov cracked open the whole German position in southern Russia. In early August 1943, in private conversation with People's Commissar Malyshev, Stalin implied that the war might be over soon. The discussion was about the new Stalin (IS) tank. "'We don't need this tank for the end of the war [said Stalin]. The tank has to be in combat before the winter.' It was the first time I heard com. Stalin talk about the end of the war. In essence he was saying it might be two months away.'[55] The Red Army was now poised in the central Ukraine; in military terms, there was little but empty space between it and the Soviet western border. Very dramatic events were to follow, as the whole German position in the southern USSR crumbled away.

CHAPTER 10
THE UKRAINE AND LENINGRAD,
AUGUST 1943 TO APRIL 1944

I order ... the whole Red Army by a skilful combination of fire and manoeuvre to break through the enemy defence across its full depth, not giving the enemy time to catch his breath.

Joseph Stalin, 23 February 1944

The Wehrmacht had suffered critical defeats in its abortive attack on the Kursk bulge and the vigorous Soviet counter-attacks which followed it to the north and south of the bulge. In the aftermath, Hitler rethought his strategy. On 12 August he put forward the idea of an *Ostwall* ('East Wall') running over 1,000 miles from the Sea of Azov north to Narva on the Gulf of Finland. From Melitopol' the *Ostwall* would run about 100 miles north across the steppe to Zaporozh'e. From Zaporozh'e, it would follow the course of the Dnepr, and then run in front of the river up to the Orsha–Vitebsk 'land bridge'. From there the defensive line would lead due north to Lake Chud (Lake Peipus), and then on to the sea. The southern part was given the code name WOTAN, the northern part PANTHER (*Pantherstellung*). On 15 September Hitler agreed in principle to a withdrawal to the WOTAN and PANTHER positions. It was to this line that Himmler was evidently referring in his infamous speech to SS leaders in Poznań on 4 October: 'Whether 10,000 Russian females fall down from exhaustion while digging an anti-tank ditch interests me only in so far as the anti-tank ditch for Germany is finished.'[1]

The *Ostwall* as a defensive structure was largely a figment of Nazi imagination. The geographical position chosen, however, with supporting river lines and shorter length, made more sense than trying to hold on at the high-water mark of conquest. The German situation was very varied. Army Group North, still besieging Leningrad, was well to the east of the proposed *Ostwall*; it would remain there for four or five more months. In contrast, in the far south, German Army Group South and the southern part of Army Group Centre were in August–September 1943 already on the brink of falling back behind the 'wall', as the Red Army raced to the Dnepr. The main Red Army successes after Kursk, in the autumn of 1943 and in the following winter, were at either end of the long front. In the south, in the Ukraine, the Soviets won striking victories. A tsunami of tanks and infantry swept away the whole rickety dike, and flooded west right across the Ukraine to the old border of the USSR. In the north, the Russians in January and February 1944 moved up to the 1940 border with Estonia, in effect to the *Ostwall*. Only in the north-central part of Hitler's front was the position, for the moment, relatively stable, although here too Army Group Centre had to pull back some distance to the *Ostwall* line.[2] The fighting was still nearly entirely within the Soviet frontiers of 1941, but the Red Army had grasped the initiative.

THE SECOND BATTLE OF THE UKRAINE

From the Dnepr to the Carpathians

The Second Battle of the Ukraine has been overshadowed in histories of the war by other campaigns.[3] Before it, in mid-1943, there had been the huge tank battle at Kursk. After it, in June–July 1944, German Army Group Centre was destroyed in Belorussia in the sudden, spectacular, Operation BAGRATION. The period between Kursk and BAGRATION has rightfully been called the 'forgotten year'.[4] But the Second Battle of the Ukraine, the most important event of this 'forgotten year', was extraordinary in its scope. It was the longest campaign of the war, fought out over eight months, across the winter, between August 1943 and April 1944. And it took in a vast territory, as the Wehrmacht retreated first to the *Ostwall* of the Dnepr River, and then far beyond it to the Carpathian Mountains and the pre-1939 border with Poland. Unlike the months after Stalingrad, the Red Army kept the initiative throughout, despite temporary setbacks, changing seasons and high losses.[5] What these operations had in common was that they were fought out in the territory of the Ukrainian Soviet Socialist Republic, which stretched 850 miles east to west (from the Donbass to the Carpathian Mountains) and 400 miles north to south (from the latitude of the upper Dnepr River and the Poles'e south to the Black Sea). The Ukraine had been the greatest territorial loss the USSR suffered in 1941, with a population of over 40,000,000 and a vast expanse of rich steppe land covering some 205,000 square miles, with a remarkable combination of agriculture and industry. In terms of size and population, the Ukraine was very similar to France.

The Red Army now had enormous offensive forces available for use in the Ukraine. Five army groups were thrown into the attack. As they advanced, they were re-designated, with famous names that they would keep from the autumn of 1943 (20 October) to the fall of Berlin and Vienna. General Tolbukhin's Southern Army Group became the 4th Ukrainian Army Group, the Southwestern Army Group (Malinovskii) became the 3rd Ukrainian, the Steppe Army Group (Konev) became the 2nd Ukrainian, and the Voronezh Army Group (Vatutin) became the 1st Ukrainian. At the right end of the line, Rokossovskii's Central Army Group became the Belorussian Army Group in October 1943, and then the 1st Belorussian Army Group in February 1944. The Germans, perversely, only renamed Army Groups South (Manstein) and 'A' (Kleist) as Army Groups 'North Ukraine' and 'South Ukraine' in April 1944, after the Wehrmacht had been driven out of all but the northwestern tip of the Ukraine.[6]

In the first phase, the five Russian army groups in the south pressed forward to the wide Dnepr River, along which Hitler had belatedly decided to create the defensive barrier of the *Ostwall*. They advanced through four Ukrainian regions along the east bank of

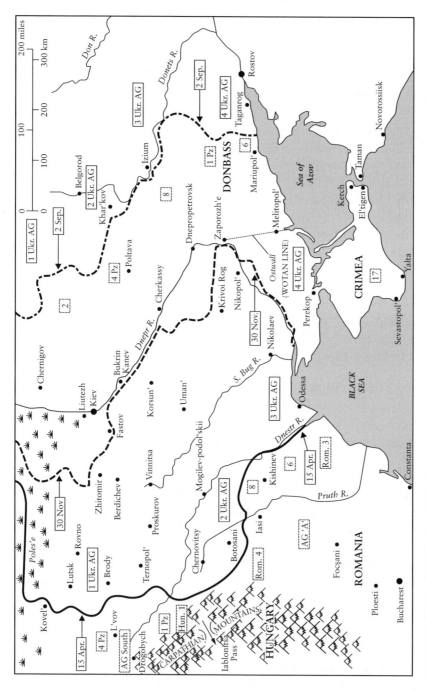

MAP 8 The Battle of the Ukraine, 1943–4.

the river: Chernigov, Poltava, Dnepropetrovsk and Zaporozh'e. The retreating Germans were unable to establish solid lines of resistance east of the river. The Belgorod–Khar'kov operation, starting on 3 August and discussed in the previous chapter, was really the first body blow in the Second Battle of the Ukraine. Manstein pulled his forces out of the Khar'kov salient, which had been just south of the Kursk 'bulge'. These became a new German 8th Army under Wöhler. The Soviet Donbass operation, launched in mid-August 1943, was the next strike. Malinovskii's Southwestern and Tolbukhin's Southern Army Group finally completed the Soviet conquest of the Donbass. This coal-mining region east of the Dnepr, which had changed sides so many times in the previous two years, was back in Soviet hands for good. Manstein's southern flank, the 1st Panzer Army (Mackensen) and the 6th Army (Hollidt) were driven back. As we have seen, by late September 1943 the Russians had even thrown small bridgeheads across the Dnepr.

In late August and September, the Stavka mounted the Chernigov–Poltava operation. Konev's Steppe Army Group, Vatutin's Voronezh Army Group and Rokossovskii's Central Army Group took the northern part of the 'left-bank' of the Ukraine, east of Kiev; this is where Kirponos's armies had been annihilated in 1941. Under the force of the 1943 advance, Manstein's other two armies, the 4th Panzer (Hoth) and the 8th (Wöhler), had to be pulled back to the Dnepr and the *Ostwall*. This was a complex manoeuvre that was completed by the end of September.

The next phase of the campaign now began, as the Stavka ordered a very rapid advance to the Dnepr and beyond. The aim was to keep up the pressure on the retreating Germans, to stop them from building up defences, and to prevent their carrying out a 'scorched earth' policy. The Southwestern Army Group and Steppe Army Group expanded the bridgeheads they held on the west bank of the Dnepr along a 175-mile stretch of the river running south from Cherkassy (opposite Kremenchug) to the Dnepr bend at Zaporozh'e. Meanwhile, south of the Dnepr bend, Tolbukhin's Southern Army Group broke through the main German WOTAN defensive line – the southern section of the *Ostwall* – which ran across the steppe from Zaporozh'e on the Dnepr to the Sea of Azov. By late December 1943, Tolbukhin's forces (now called the 4th Ukrainian Army Group) had reached the lower Dnepr, where the river ran southwest into the Black Sea. With this, Tolbukhin had bypassed the Perekop Isthmus to the south and isolated the Crimea. Hitler demanded that the easternmost bend of the Dnepr, north of Tolbukhin's advance, be held as a redoubt. A powerful centre of resistance was to be formed by the 1st Panzer Army at Nikopol', just downstream from Zaporozh'e. These German forces covered the iron and manganese mines of Krivoi Rog and Nikopol'.

The Soviet advance, inevitably, did not go according to plan everywhere. In early September 1943, Zhukov (serving as the Stavka representative) and Vatutin (Voronezh Army Group) received Stavka approval for a daring main blow. This was to be struck at the end of the month. A 'deep operation' using massed armour and airborne forces would crash across the Dnepr at its strategically and politically most important point, just south of Kiev. Rybalko's 3rd Guards Tank Army and several independent mobile corps were aimed at a small loop in the river, containing on the west bank the village of Bukrin. The crossing was supported by a night landing of two airborne brigades at nearby Kanev.

This was the first significant Soviet airborne operation since the Battle of Moscow, and much more in the spirit of 'deep battle' than the 1941 episode. Lead elements from the mobile units got across the Dnepr on 22 September, but the night parachute drop on the 25th was a fiasco. The ground was difficult, and the enemy counter-attacked from the west with strong forces. Several weeks were needed to ferry Soviet armour in any strength into the bridgehead, and the element of surprise was lost. Two bloody Soviet attempts to break out in the course of October were unsuccessful.[7] In the end, however, the situation was saved, through a remarkable example of Soviet command skill. Vatutin secretly shifted powerful forces, including the 3rd Guards Tank Army, into another bridgehead at Liutezh, just north of Kiev. From here, he burst out on 3 November. The attackers overwhelmed the German forces covering the Ukrainian capital and took the city on 6 November.[8] Kiev was a major prize, a centre of Russian culture and the capital of the Ukraine. The timing of the Red Army's success was perfect, on the eve of the anniversary of the Bolshevik Revolution.

Vatutin, with Zhukov looking over his shoulder, was at first able to expand his bridgehead west and southwest of Kiev. Hoth's defending 4th Panzer Army was thinly spread. The commitments in the Dnepr bend 250 miles to the southeast, forced on Manstein by Hitler, left few German forces immediately available to deploy around Kiev. It was only after some weeks, and on the far side of Kiev, that Manstein and Army Group South were able to put up some resistance. Vatutin had driven his forces by the middle of November as far as Zhitomir, 90 miles west of Kiev. Now he was pushed halfway back to the Dnepr by Wehrmacht counter-attacks. Hoth and Vatutin came in for severe criticism from their respective supreme commanders, Hoth for the loss of Kiev and Vatutin for the failure fully to exploit the Soviet success. Hitler dismissed Hoth; it was the end of the career of one of the three or four most outstanding Eastern Front panzer commanders. Vatutin, despite an uneasy relationship with Stalin, was able to retake the initiative in December 1943 and keep his post.

Vatutin's 1st Ukrainian Army Group greatly expanded the bridgeheads west of Kiev in the Zhitomir–Berdichev operation (through mid-January 1944), although Vatutin was faced with continuing German counter-attacks. In the middle of the Soviet attacking line in the Ukraine, between Tolbukhin and Vatutin, was Konev's Steppe (2nd Ukrainian) Army Group, which was also supervised by Zhukov. Konev's armies were opposed by a very thinly spread German 8th Army; they were able to establish a shallow but very long bridgehead on the western side of the Dnepr. Some 150 miles to the southeast, Konev extended his Dnepr bridgehead to Kirovograd. Then, in an operation not unlike that at Stalingrad in November 1942, Vatutin and Konev trapped between them – at the end of January 1944 – two German corps (the 11th and the 42nd, comprising 6 divisions and including SS 'Wiking') near Korsun'. This was 15 miles west of the Dnepr and not far from the city of Cherkassy.[9] As at Stalingrad 12 months before, the weather was severe, with alternating blizzards and mud. Manstein's attempts to break through to relieve the pocket with what armour he could scrape together were unsuccessful – as they had been at Stalingrad. This time, however, many of the trapped and desperate soldiers of the two Germans corps were able to break out across the steppe. According to German sources, some 30,000 troops were extracted, though the wounded and heavy equipment had to be left behind; the Soviets claimed 18,000 prisoners. Stalin sharply criticized Zhukov for delaying the destruction of the pocket by not properly planning for joint action between Vatutin and Konev. On 12 February 1944, he unified authority for the encirclement under Konev – repeating what had happened with Rokossovskii at Stalingrad. The 2nd Ukrainian Army Group was, rather unjustly, given all the credit for the victory. Konev was awarded the rank of Marshal of the Soviet Union.[10]

The newly promoted Marshal Konev, with his 2nd Ukrainian Army Group, now exploited the success of the Korsun' victory to drive 150 miles across the Ukraine. Three large rivers flow southeast across the Ukrainian steppe into the Black Sea, west of the Dnepr and parallel to its middle course; these are the Southern Bug, the Dnestr and the Pruth (listed from east to west). Konev now in mid-March 1944 pushed southwest, at right angles to the river lines, past Uman' (scene of a terrible Red Army *Kessel* in 1941). He now had under his command three tank armies, two guards armies and four other infantry armies. The Southern Bug was crossed just after the middle of March, and beyond it the main railway from Odessa to L'vov and central Europe. German divisions scuttled westwards to escape the trap. Konev reached the Dnestr River and the border with Moldavia. Here was the town of Mogilev-Podol'skii (captured on 19 March) and the last major rail line out of the Ukraine. His final bound took him over the Pruth River and into the northeast tip of Romanian territory around the town of Botoşani (7 April). This was the first time, thirty-four months after the war started, that the Red Army had entered 'foreign' territory. It prompted the first Stavka directives on how 'liberated' territories should be treated.

Hitler, latterly against Manstein's better judgement, had ordered fierce resistance by Hube's 1st Panzer Army and Hollidt's 6th Army inside the Dnepr bend and on the lower course of the river. A successful German defence had been mounted against Konev's initial advances from the north in October 1943. General Ferdinand Schörner, who enjoyed Hitler's personal favour and who would have a meteoric rise in the next year and a half, was brought from northern Finland to take command of three corps in the Dnepr bend. Nikopol' and Krivoi Rog were finally taken (8 and 22 February 1944) from the Germans by the 3rd and 4th Ukrainian Army Groups. This time it was possible for the German command to extract Hollidt's 6th Army to the west (unlike what had happened to Paulus's 6th Army at Stalingrad), but great losses were suffered in the process. The seven infantry armies of Malinovskii's 3rd Ukrainian Army Group then advanced, roughly in parallel with Konev and on his left flank, from Krivoi Rog towards the river lines. Hollidt attempted to make a stand on the Southern Bug River in mid-March, but he then had to fall back another 100 miles to behind the Dnestr (the pre-1940 border with Romania). Here in mid-April his retreat, and that of the whole German eastern front, finally came to a halt. On the Dnestr River line the front would stabilize for four months. In passing, the Russians liberated the third great city of the Ukraine, Odessa, on 10 April 1944.

While Konev and Malinovskii were taking control of the southwestern Ukraine, Zhukov and Vatutin were achieving an even more spectacular success in the north of the republic. If they had been paying too little attention to the situation around the Korsun' pocket in early February 1944, it was because the spearheads of the 1st Ukrainian Army Group were already 250 miles to the northwest. The northern armies of Vatutin's army group, covered to their north by the swamps and forests of the Poles'e, dashed far to the west of Kiev. Manstein had positioned only a weak corps in this area, and he himself was preoccupied with the most immediate danger of a Soviet attack from the Korsun' area into the rear of his 8th and 6th Armies. On 2 February, Vatutin's spearheads – Pukhov's 13th Army, Cherniakhovskii's 60th Army, and two guards' cavalry corps – captured Rovno and Lutsk in the northwestern corner of the Ukraine. (Rovno had been the capital of Nazi *Reichskommissariat Ukraine*.) For the first time in the war, the Red Army had broken into the new territories annexed in 1939–40.

Vatutin and Zhukov were in mid-February 1944 ordered to prepare another phase of the huge battle in the Ukraine, this time a turn south towards the towns of Proskurov and Chernovitsy; the aim was to cut the route of retreat of the entire German Army Group South.[11] Konev at this time was far behind, some 250 miles to the southeast, in the aftermath of the Korsun' battle. As Vatutin was preparing this operation he was mortally injured. His command convoy, with an escort of only eight men, ran into a band of several hundred Ukrainian nationalist guerrillas in a village a few miles south of Rovno on the evening of 29 February. Rovno Region was a turbulent place, formerly part of Poland, and with a three-sided battle going on involving the newly arrived Soviet forces and Ukrainian and Polish partisans. After the incident, the Stavka ordered decisive measures against the 'bands' and a regime of robust security for commanders. Evacuated to Kiev, Vatutin had a leg amputated and then succumbed in April. Vatutin had shown extraordinary abilities as a planner and an operational commander. He had been Deputy Chief of the General Staff before the war, but his greatest triumphs came with leading the secret Southwestern Army Group in the Stalingrad counter-offensive and with the capture of Kiev.[12]

Marshal Zhukov himself now took over command of the 1st Ukrainian Army Group and implemented the planned drive to the south, the Proskurov–Chernovitsy operation. This began in early March 1944, four days after the mortal wounding of Vatutin, and continued through to mid-April. Driving ahead with the 3rd Guards Tank Army, the 60th Army and the 4th Tank Army, Zhukov captured on 29 March the town of Chernovitsy (Cernăuţi). With this, he cut the last direct railway connection from the Ukraine to the Reich (via L'vov). Fifty miles west of Chernovitsy, Russian units faced the Carpathian Mountains and the Iablonitsa Pass leading into Hungary. The Red Army had reached the natural western frontier of the Ukraine and of the USSR.

In early March 1944, Hitler tried to create 'fortified places' (*feste Plätze*) as strong points, a wholesale extension of his Alcázar strategy at Sukhinichi in January 1942. In the Ukraine, these 'fortified places' were Nikolaev, Voznesensk, Novoukrainka, Pervomaisk, Vinnitsa, Zhmerinka, Proskurov, Ternopol', Brody and Kovel'. Most of them were quickly abandoned without a fight. The exception was Ternopol', which was lost with its garrison on 14 April 1944. Only Brody and Kovel', on the extreme western edge of the Ukraine, held out. Manstein had been able to pull the 4th Panzer Army out to the west into

Poland in the course of March, but Hube's 1st Panzer Army was temporarily trapped by the Red Army advance. The Soviet armoured spearheads were thin, and Hube was ordered to direct the remains of his army group to the northwest and the temporary safety of southeastern Poland. Hube was becoming the Wehrmacht's expert on this kind of delicate operation. In August 1943 he had extracted German forces from Sicily; he succeeded with the 1st Panzer Army as well. Hube was killed in a plane crash a month following the March 1944 breakout, flying out of Hitler's headquarters immediately after having been promoted to the rank of Colonel-General and awarded the Knight's Cross. The German 8th Army (General Wöhler) was pushed back south into Romania, where it was passed from Manstein's command to Kleist's Army Group 'A'. With this, the German forces defending the southern part of the great front were also cut in two. Army Group South under Manstein (the 4th Panzer Army and the survivors of the 1st Panzer Army) in the eastern Ukraine now had no direct link with Kleist's Army Group 'A' (the Romanian 4th and the German 8th and 6th Armies).

Even in April 1944, despite the long advance and the continuing *rasputitsa*, the Soviet Army Group staffs still pondered further operations. In late March, Zhukov had proposed an advance west to Poland and the line of Vladimir-Volynskii, L'vov and Drogobych, to begin on 8–10 April. Konev, for his part, proposed in early April an advance against Kishenev and on to the Focşani gap in Romania.[13] Neither of these were practical propositions at the time. The L'vov advance would begin only in July, and the drive into Romania only in August. Now, after the middle of April 1944, began the first prolonged pause since July 1943 in the Red Army's march across the Ukraine. This final advance of all three army groups from the Bug to the Dnestr River, the pre-1940 border with Romania, was the second of what Stalin would call the 'ten crushing blows' of 1944 (the first was at Leningrad and Novgorod in January).[14]

On 30 March 1944, Field Marshal Manstein, the commander of Army Group South, was wakened at his new headquarters at L'vov and informed that he was being summoned to the Obersalzberg in Bavaria with Field Marshal Kleist (Army Group 'A'). On their arrival, Hitler told the two Field Marshals, with some politeness, that they were to be replaced.[15] Both Kleist and Manstein went into retirement, and neither played any further part in the war. Kleist was captured in April 1945 and imprisoned in Yugoslavia, for war crimes committed by his forces during the Balkan campaign. He was then moved to the USSR, and he died in a Soviet prison in 1954 at the age of seventy-three; Kleist was the only one of Hitler's field marshals to perish in Soviet captivity.

Manstein was more fortunate, although he served several years of imprisonment in the West. He lived to 1973 and wrote influential memoirs. Manstein's gifts as a commander can be overstated. He had a high opinion of his own abilities, and both Hitler and the German Army possessed confidence in him as an operational leader. His decisive moment of impact or insight had been the revised war plan in France. This had allowed the German Army and Hitler to win a striking victory in 1940 and fundamentally to shift the balance of power in Europe. Manstein's siege of Sevastopol' was prolonged, and he was not without blame in the Stalingrad catastrophe of the German 6th Army. However, Manstein did hold the southern front together in the late winter of 1942–3 and prevented an even worse catastrophe than Stalingrad. His conception of the 1943 Kursk offensive was unrealistic, and he was certainly incorrect to see the operation as a potential war-winner. His 1943–4 campaign in the Ukraine was a disaster for the Wehrmacht, and one for which he must take a good share of the blame. Like most commanders, Manstein focused on his own command and did not fully consider whether divisions could really be spared from Army Group Centre or from the German forces in the West. At least from September 1943, he was simply lurching clumsily from one crisis to another.

Manstein was right, however, that Hitler's priorities in the Ukraine were fundamentally flawed. It was foolish to try to defend the indefensible. By attempting to hold out in the south of the Ukraine, first in the western Donbass (on the Mius River line) and then inside the Dnepr bulge and the Crimea, German Army Group South lost any chance to assemble reserves, especially in the vital northern part of the Ukraine. In 1944, Hitler made precisely the same mistake Stalin had made in 1941, and tried to hold the Dnepr River line for political, economic and diplomatic reasons, rather than for military ones.

The campaign in the Ukraine more generally showed a pattern in Hitler's strategy which appeared first at Moscow in December 1941 but which now became the dominant theme. Early in the war he had committed himself to foolhardy offensives, the last of which was Kursk. Now the policy had become one of holding on to all the territories seized, even when such a strategy prevented building up strong forces anywhere. At Moscow in 1941–2 and at Stalingrad in 1942–3, he had stressed holding fast, but in those cases there was the realistic prospect of using the seized areas as a springboard for renewed offensives to the east. Now territory was being held for its own sake, as an expression only of the Führer's will. The pattern of defending Nikopol' and the Dnepr bend would be repeated in the Crimea, in the Baltic states, in Kurland, in northern Scandinavia, even in East Prussia. Even if Nazi Germany's grand strategy was now one of hanging on until new 'miracle' weapons became available or the Grand Alliance split, the generals were probably right that greater flexibility would have gained more time.

Hitler's conduct was a symptom of the problem rather than the source of it. The fact was that the Wehrmacht was desperately overstretched. It became more overstretched by the month, as Soviet strength built up and the German Army and the Luftwaffe faced increased attacks in the West. Manstein's 'solution', the abandonment of the southern end of the Dnepr line and concentration in the northern flank of Army Group South, would have ameliorated the particular crisis that occurred in the winter of 1943–4, but it would have made no difference in the long term. The Reich did not have the reserves to spare. The considerable defensive barrier of the lower Dnepr would have been lost, and Malinovskii and Tolbukhin would have reached Odessa, Moldavia and Romania that much sooner. Manstein entertained hopes of a decisive battle, won by his massed forces and his self-perceived unique operational abilities, in the northern Ukraine, but this was a pipe dream. As for General Zeitzler and the Army General Staff, they were now totally in Hitler's power. Manstein suggests that Zeitzler agreed with most of his (Manstein's) opinions, but he (Zeitzler) lacked the authority to argue with Hitler. Zeitzler was increasingly irrelevant, and would disappear a few months after the fall of the Ukraine, after an even more sudden disaster in Belorussia.

If the Second Battle of the Ukraine foreshadowed Hitler's approach for the rest of the war, it can also be seen as a watershed in Soviet strategy. The victories at Stalingrad and even Kursk had been rather different from the victory in the Ukraine, and despite their scale and importance, more limited. Stalingrad and Kursk had been successful efforts to stop German advances and regain ground. The Second Battle of the Ukraine was something that had happened only once before in the Second World War on the Russian Front, a continuous advance. The German armies committed to Operation BARBAROSSA rolled east from June to November 1941. The Red Army did something very similar, but for an even longer period, from August 1943 to April 1944. Moreover, the autumn *rasputitsa* and the winter snows which had so disrupted German movements in 1941–2 had much less effect on the Red Army in the Ukraine in 1943–4. This can be explained partly by the natural conditions of the southern USSR, a somewhat warmer climate and the more open steppe terrain.

Technical improvements in the equipment of the Red Army also affected its ability to sustain an advance. The T-34-76 was still the main tank of the Red Army; the first of the much improved T-34-85s began to enter service only towards the end of the campaign in the Ukraine. Nevertheless, a larger proportion of the Soviet tank force was now made up of the powerful, mobile, long-ranged T-34-76, rather than the light T-70 or other old tanks. Self-propelled (tracked) artillery became an important element for the first time, able to support Soviet rapid advances. As important was the arrival of larger American trucks and other vehicles, which could bring up reinforcements and supplies to rapidly advancing formations; they could also tow conventional artillery forward.[16] There was qualitative change in the Red Army Air Force, with a higher proportion of new fighters – Yak-9s, La-5s and American Airacobras – and larger numbers of two-seater Il-2 attack planes and American A-20 bombers. These only brought the Red Army Air Force to the qualitative standard of the battlefield Luftwaffe, but the point was that Soviet aircraft were available in much larger quantities than German ones. This factor was especially important in the open steppe of the Ukraine.

The Russians were now able to commit huge forces to this complex operation. At the start of the Dnepr-Carpathian operation at the end of 1943, the four Ukrainian Army Groups had, between them, 2,400,000 personnel in 19 tank or mechanized corps and 171 rifle divisions. What was also new was how these forces were organized, on lines that would continue until the end of the war. Particularly striking in the second phase of the Soviet offensive in the Ukraine was the use of concentrated armoured forces. For the Stalingrad counter-offensive, the Red Army deployed 5 tank corps and 2 mechanized corps. For the Orel and Belgorod–Khar'kov offensives in August 1943, after Kursk, the 5 army groups used 16 tank corps and 3 mechanized corps. During the advance to the Dnepr, Vatutin was assigned in mid-September Rybalko's 3rd Guards Tank Army from the Stavka reserve. Vatutin received Katukov's 1st Guards Tank Army from the Stavka reserve at the end of November 1943. In February 1944, he was assigned Leliushenko's 4th Tank Army, which had been refitted after the Orel operation. Konev, meanwhile, received Bogdanov's 2nd Guards Tank Army and Kravchenko's new 6th Tank Army, both in January 1944. Malinovskii was given Rotmistrov's 5th Guards Tank Army in August 1943, and 6th Tank Army in February 1944, transferred from Konev.

The Crimea once more

The Russians approached the Crimea again in October 1943, after a year and a half. The northern entrance to the big peninsula, at the Perekop, isthmus was about to be cut off by a Soviet army group storming along the north coast of the Sea of Azov and the Black Sea. The Stavka believed that the Germans were planning to evacuate the whole of the Crimea, and took steps to move into it from the east, across the Kerch' Strait. Although the general situation for the Germans was by this time poor, the initial outcome in the Crimea was to be a Russian setback.

Hitler had insisted on holding on to the eastern side of the Kerch' Strait – the Taman' Peninsula in the Kuban' – throughout the battles and retreats at Kursk and on the Dnepr in the summer of 1943. Novorossiisk, near the eastern side of the strait, was finally retaken by the Soviet North Caucasus Army Group commanded by General Petrov – the defender of Sevastopol' – in mid-September 1943. At the very end of October 1943 – after a delay of several weeks – Petrov put forces across the Kerch' Strait in another large Russian amphibious operation; eventually, 150,000 troops were involved. At one time, the Soviet planners discussed an ambitious operation against Yalta – on the southern tip of the peninsula – or even against Sevastopol' itself, but the more cautious option was taken.[17] Significantly, there was little attempt to use the larger surviving units of the Black Sea Fleet to block the German evacuation of Taman' or to support the Russian landings at Kerch'. The loss in one incident of three modern destroyers, the *Khar'kov*, *Sposobnyi* and *Besposhchadnyi*, to a Stuka attack off the Crimea in early October 1943 – the worst loss suffered by the Soviet Navy after 1941 – further put off the use of the bigger Russian ships. They were forbidden to operate without the authority of the Stavka, and effectively they played no further part in the war.[18]

Meanwhile, Petrov's overall forces were reduced; his North Caucasus Army Group was renamed the Independent Coastal Army, and he had to give up his 18th Army to the main front to the north, in the Ukraine. There were prolonged battles around the Kerch' bridgeheads, which were actively defended by the Germans – against the better judgement of the commander in the Crimea, General Jänecke of the 17th Army. This tenacious German defence bore similarities to the fighting around the Allied landing at Anzio, which took place at about the same time in Italy. A Soviet toehold was kept at the northern bridgehead near Kerch' (although the Germans kept control of the city itself), but the southern landing site at the village of El'tigen was effectively cut off by German small craft and destroyed in December 1943; Soviet losses were 7,000.[19]

The Crimea was finally recaptured only in the spring of 1944. This was the third of what were later called the 'ten Stalinist crushing blows' of 1944. At the time, the Crimean operation was overshadowed by further Russian victories in the Ukraine. The Red Army had sealed off the peninsula by the end of November 1943, when the 4th Ukrainian

Army Group reached the lower Dnepr, well west of Perekop isthmus. An initial Soviet attempt to take the defences off the march had failed. Marshal Vasilevskii proposed an attack for mid-February 1944, but it was delayed. By April 1944, when the attack on the Crimea actually began, Russian armies were west of Odessa and on the Romanian border. Hitler still saw the Crimea as strategically and diplomatically important (with respect to Turkey). He actually reinforced the German–Romanian 17th Army, at a time when his other armies were falling back in the Ukraine. By an irony of history, one of the victims of this strategy would be Field Marshal Manstein, the 1942 conqueror of the Crimea who had become commander of Army Group South. Manstein desperately needed the forces that were tied down in the Crimea and the lower Dnepr River (protecting the approaches to the Crimea). The five German divisions (four newly arrived) and seven Romanian divisions were in the Crimea against the advice of the German high command and the Romanians – and against the expectations of the Russian high command.

The Soviet attack was co-ordinated by Marshal Vasilevskii, who was with General Tolbukhin's 4th Ukrainian Army Group at Perekop. (He was to have a lucky escape when his staff vehicle hit a mine outside Sevastopol' after the city had been recaptured. He was sufficiently badly injured to require evacuation to Moscow.) The plan was that two armies of the 4th Ukrainian Army Group, Zakharov's 2nd Guards Army and Kreizer's 51st Army, would break into the Crimea through Perekop. Meanwhile, the Independent Coastal Army was to advance west out of the Kerch' bridgehead; this army was now commanded by the Stalingrad veteran General Eremenko. The Axis defending force, Jänecke's 17th Army, was on paper as large as Manstein's 11th Army in 1941–2: 11 Romanian and German divisions and initially a total of about 200,000 personnel. Russian forces, however, were more numerous than in 1942, and much better equipped and led. The Red Army now deployed the equivalent of 31 rifle divisions, as well as a tank corps and over 1,250 aircraft – a total of 470,000 personnel.[20] The Russian operation was delayed for over a month by the weather, but on 10 April 1944, after two days of fighting, Tolbukhin's two northern armies broke through Perekop; within three more days Simferopol' had been recaptured and the German GNEISENAU defensive line broken.

Within the Crimea, the assault on Sevastopol' developed more slowly than expected. The Russians' initial hope to take the city off the march was unsuccessful, and then a two-week postponement roused the ire of the Stavka. Stalin no doubt wanted to achieve the victory by May Day 1944 – but he was probably more concerned about releasing the 2nd Guards Army and the 51st Army for the main attack in Belorussia (Operation BAGRATION), which was scheduled for late June. The Axis forces had a reasonably well-prepared position and 65,000 remaining personnel. The Russian attack finally began with a diversionary attack from the north on 5 May 1944, followed two days later by the main blow through the Sapun Heights to the southeast of the city. Sevastopol' was retaken. Two days later (12 May 1944), those Axis survivors who had not been able to evacuate by sea or air to Romania were taken prisoner at Cape Khersones – where the Soviet garrison had made its last stand in July 1942.

Hitler had finally permitted an evacuation by sea and air to Constanţa in Romania, 240 miles to the west, initially of those troop not required for the defence of Sevastopol' itself. Some movement had been going on despite Hitler's orders, and in the end about 130,000 personnel were evacuated by sea and 21,000 by air. This was more successful than the final Russian operations in June–July 1942, but some 21,000 German and Romanian troops were still captured at Khersones. Russian recorded losses were relatively light, 18,000 out of 462,000 personnel committed, a fraction of the 400,000 men lost in the battles of 1941-2 in the Kerch' Peninsula and Sevastopol'.[21]

Almost as soon as the Crimea had been captured by the Red Army, the mass deportation of the Crimean Tatars began. The Tatars were a Turkic people who had inhabited the peninsula before it was conquered by Catherine the Great in the eighteenth century; they still made up about a quarter of the pre-war population. They were held collectively responsible for collaboration with the enemy during the two and a half years of German–Romanian presence. They were now deported under NKVD guard to Uzbekistan in Central Asia, no fewer than 180,000 men, women and children.[22] The loss of the Crimea in 1944 did not in itself have the military or diplomatic repercussions that Hitler had feared. The Red Army was on the verge of entering the Balkans in any event, and the Axis oil production centres around Ploesti in Romania had been destroyed by bombers flown not from the Crimea but from American airfields in Italy. Turkey did not enter the war against Germany until February 1945. The last episode in the history of the Crimea was one that the German dictator cannot have imagined. In February 1945, Roosevelt, Churchill and Stalin would meet at Yalta, 30 miles southeast of Sevastopol', to decide the fate of Hitler's Europe.

BREAKOUT IN THE NORTH: LIBERATING LENINGRAD REGION

The Leningrad–Novgorod operation of January and February 1944 was a major Russian offensive across a front about 300 miles in length (see Map 3).[23] It would be the first of Stalin's 'ten crushing blows' of 1944, and it involved the 2nd Baltic, Volkhov and Leningrad Army Groups (Generals Popov, Meretskov and Govorov). Altogether, the Russians had 1,250,000 personnel, as well as 1,580 tanks and SP guns. They also deployed 1,390 aircraft, including four bomber corps of 'long-range aviation', the first time such a concentration of aircraft had been assembled. Field Marshal Küchler's German Army Group North was now massively outnumbered. He had had to release experienced divisions to the more active parts of the German–Russian front, in the centre and south. His German 18th and 16th Armies – north and south of Lake Il'men – had 400,000 men, and limited equipment – only 16 tanks and 109 SP guns, and 381 aircraft.[24] Some of his formations were of low quality, including several Luftwaffe field divisions and three newly raised Waffen-SS divisions made up of volunteers from the Baltic and Scandinavia.

Following Hitler's *Ostwall* concept, Küchler had from the autumn of 1943 begun preparing a rear line of defence, the PANTHER position. For Army Group North, the PANTHER position ran from Narva on the Gulf of Finland behind Lake Chud (Lake Peipus) to Pskov. Part of the planning for this strategic retreat involved the forced movement west of much of the remaining adult population of the villages and small towns of the occupied Leningrad Region, some 250,000 people. Küchler was not in the end able to carry out the orderly removal of his troops to the PANTHER position in advance of the Soviet attack. Hitler would not give up the ground, and he was supported in his obstinacy by General Lindemann, Küchler's subordinate; Lindemann commanded the 18th Army in front of Leningrad.

The Stavka's preparation for a conclusive offensive in the north dated from October and November 1943, but that had been based on an assumption that Army Group North would begin a phased withdrawal on the lines of that of Army Group South and Army Group Centre. In the event, the Germans stayed put and the proposed autumn offensive came to nothing.[25] By the new year, Soviet forces were stronger. The most southerly of the three Soviet army groups, south of Lake Il'men, was General M. M. Popov's 2nd Baltic Army Group. Popov controlled in January 1944 the 22nd Army and 1st Shock Army.[26] Meretskov's Volkhov Army Group, with three infantry armies, had a front that was now set well west of the Volkhov River, at least in the north; it ran from Lake Il'men to just east of the Neva. The Leningrad Army Group, under Govorov, included the 67th and 42nd Armies just west and south of the city.

What was proposed was a complicated operation involving the three army groups. Unusually, there was no Stavka representative to co-ordinate the breakout; the most experienced co-ordinators, Zhukov and Vasilevskii, concentrated their efforts on the Ukraine. These three Soviet army groups also did not include any major tank formation; all six of Stalin's tank armies were also deployed in the south. Indeed, there was not even any independent tank or mechanized corps. The ground was not suited to tank warfare, and the distances involved were relatively short; independent tank operations were more valuable on other fronts.

The first Russian attack (the Krasnoe Selo–Ropsha operation) achieved tactical surprise. The previous three major Russian offensives in the Leningrad Region, in 1942 and 1943, had come mainly from the Volkhov River side of the Shlissel'burg corridor. There had been only supporting attacks from the Leningrad side, across the middle and upper Neva River, to the east of the city.[27] The more ambitious 1st Shock Army plan of early 1942 and the POLAR STAR plan of early 1943 (right after Stalingrad) had proposed a deep sweep from the south of Lake Il'men northwest in front of Pskov and Narva to cut off all of Army Group North. In the end, neither plan had been put into practice. This time, in January 1944, the Soviet attack started from *southwest* of Leningrad. When the Germans had rushed towards Leningrad back in September 1941, some of the Soviet defenders had held on to a strip of the coast of the Gulf of Finland. This was cut off from Leningrad proper by enemy troops who had reached the Gulf near Peterhof (Petrodvorets) and Strel'na. The pocket was some 20 miles long and 5–10 miles deep, and centred on the town of Oranienbaum (a place name later Russianized to Lomonosov); this was the site of one of the old capital's outlying Imperial palaces. Supported by the heavy guns of the island naval base at Kronshtadt (6 miles to the north, out in the Gulf), the defenders held on for twenty-eight months, sharing all the hardships of the Leningrad blockade.

On 14 January 1944, the Soviet 2nd Shock Army under General Fediuninskii burst out of the Oranienbaum pocket; some 44,000 Red Army troops had been secretly ferried there across the Gulf of Finland. A second attack was mounted from the southwestern part of Leningrad itself, by the 42nd Army, and the two wings of the attack joined together on the evening of the 19th near the Leningrad suburban towns of Ropsha and Krasnoe Selo. The surviving German troops were able to pull out, but many of the heavy guns which had been bombarding Leningrad for two years were captured.

German forces were now hurriedly pulled out of the Mga salient (the remains of the Shlissel'burg corridor) – against Hitler's better judgement. Mga had become a very exposed position, lying as it did 40 miles *east* of Ropsha. With this withdrawal, the Germans lost their very last chance to throttle Leningrad's supply lines. As they pulled back from Mga, the Germans were pursued by the Russian 67th Army, advancing from the middle Neva River. By the end of January 1944, the Russian offensive had covered 50 miles to reach the Luga River, which flows northwest across Leningrad Region; the Luga was the line the defenders of Leningrad had tried in vain to hold in the summer of 1941. By the middle of the following month, the Red Army had covered another 50–100 miles to the Narva River and to Lake Chud, which had made up the 1940 Soviet border with Estonia.

The southern part of the German 18th Army was attacked at the same time, by Popov's 2nd Baltic Army Group. Some 100 miles up the Volkhov River, the 59th Army of Popov's army group encircled the ancient and now ruined city of Novgorod, after bitter battles in severe winter weather. The German garrison was able to break out, but the town was taken on 20 January 1944. Staraia Russa, to the south of Lake Il'men, finally fell on 18 February 1944. This was the strategic railway town that had been a major Red Army objective since January 1942.

The German defenders in Army Group North were soon tightly stretched and had few reserves. Hitler, who was preoccupied with the simultaneous Anzio landing west of Rome (22 January 1944), still would not give the Army Group North commander, Küchler, permission to pull back to the PANTHER position. Küchler now joined the ranks of Hitler's sacked field marshals. His replacement, two weeks after the start of the Russian offensive, was General Model, Hitler's 'fire-fighter'. This was a further promotion for Model, to army group command. His first major action on the Eastern Front was when he was brought in to save the 9th Army of Army Group Centre after the December 1941 Russian counter-offensive in front of Moscow. In 1942 Model had vigorously led the 9th Army in the defence of the Rzhev–Viaz'ma pocket, and in 1943, he had played a prominent part at the Battle of Kursk.

German Army Group North was fighting a very confused battle without clear front lines. The considerable Russian partisan force in the southern and western part of Leningrad Region was now brought into play. The advancing Russians took the important rail junction at Luga on 12 February 1944. Hitler now, in mid-February, became more keen on a retreat to the PANTHER line, and in the end, Model fell back there. The Russians turned to the southwest, reaching the outskirts of Pskov and Ostrov by 1 March 1944, as the 2nd Baltic Front finally began an advance to the west. Pskov had been the main communications hub of Army Group North throughout war. After approaching the outskirts of Narva and Pskov, the Russians, however, were able to make little further progress due to German resistance and the very early *rasputitsa*.

There was disappointment for the Soviets, too, in the northern sector of this front. In mid-February 1944 the Stavka ordered Govorov to take Narva – the gateway into Estonia – by 17 February. The Stavka stressed the political side: 'This is demanded both by the military and the political situation.'[28] The 'political situation' was evidently a reference to hopes that Finland would seek a negotiated peace if the Red Army made impressive advances on the south shore of the Gulf of Finland. Govorov's forces were, however, weakened as a result of their long advance from Leningrad. Meanwhile, the Germans threw a number of strong formations into the narrow 50-mile gap between Lake Chud and the Gulf. Shortly afterwards, Govorov was ordered to break around both ends of Lake Chud. The northern group would head across Estonia for Piarnu on the Gulf of Riga (cutting off the Tallin garrison), while the southern group was to bypass Pskov and hurl itself towards Riga. Neither operation was successful. The Narva gap held firm. Attacks against Pskov from 9 March to 15 April 1944 involved 173,000 Soviet troops but cost 10,000 in personnel losses and could not break through the German defences.[29] The withdrawal to the *Ostwall* shortened the Wehrmacht's front, but it also shortened that of the Red Army. Meretskov's Volkhov Army Group was wound up, after two years of the most bitter trench fighting in the swamps and forests along the Volkhov. Its forces were transferred to the Leningrad Army Group.

The Soviet Leningrad–Novgorod operation was not the overwhelming success the Stavka had hoped for. Despite Russian numerical superiority in personnel and equipment, most of the German 18th Army was able to escape, and the Red Army could not break through into Estonia. The advance was brought to a stop at Narva and Pskov, blocked for the moment by Hitler's PANTHER position. The Soviets would not break through this line until July 1944. The Germans, meanwhile, were fortunate that Hitler's dithering had not led to disaster. The difficult mid-winter weather, the swamps, rivers and woods of the region, and the deep German defences built up over two years of static warfare had slowed down the attack. The tactics of some of the Russian corps commanders were awkward, and only a relatively limited amount of men and matériel could be made available to the Stavka for this northern theatre, given the offensive taking place at the same time in the Ukraine. At least the operation was less expensive in troops and equipment lost than others, including those fought earlier around Leningrad. The Soviet offensive had, after twenty-seven months, completely transformed the position around Leningrad. The opening of the main Moscow–Leningrad rail line on 26 January 1944 marked the final end of the terrible siege of Leningrad.[30]

CONCLUSION

The fighting around Leningrad won much less territory for the Russians than the fighting in the Ukraine. In the late winter of 1943–4, German Army Group North fell 100–150 miles back to the *Ostwall* line and then held firm. Army Group South had been thrown back 200–250 miles *west* of the *Ostwall*. There were good reasons for this discrepancy. The Stavka had concentrated much stronger forces and command talent in the south. The north was better defensive ground for the *Ostheer*. Nevertheless, the two theatres had much in common. Hitler's policy of holding on to everything that had been seized in the East left exposed German outposts – around Leningrad, in the Dnepr bend and in the Crimea. On the positive side, the Germans – Manstein in the Ukraine, Model in the north – were able to conduct a withdrawal without full-scale Wehrmacht catastrophes and mass surrenders like those at Stalingrad in 1943 or in Belorussia in mid-1944.

CHAPTER 11
TO THE SOVIET FRONTIERS,
JUNE TO OCTOBER 1944

The 'Fortified Places' will fulfil the functions of fortresses in earlier times. They will prevent the enemy from occupying these places of decisive operational importance. They are to allow themselves to be surrounded, thereby tying down the largest possible number of enemy forces. They are by this means to establish the preconditions for successful counter-operations.

Adolf Hitler, 8 March 1944

The Red Army has admirably fulfilled its patriotic duty and freed our Fatherland from the enemy. From now on and forever our land will be free of the Hitlerite filth.

Joseph Stalin, 6 November 1944

The offensive of the Soviet Army ... was carried out with remarkable clarity of purpose by the co-ordinated operations of numerous army groups, united across a theatre of military operations extending for a thousand kilometres, according to a single [edinyi] strategic plan and a single strategic will, that of the Supreme C-in-C, that of the great Stalin.

K. E. Voroshilov, *Stalin and the Armed Forces of the USSR*

Germany's overall military situation was perilous. The British and American strategic bombing campaign was now having a serious impact on German industry and on the dispositions of the Luftwaffe. The Western Allies had been fighting in Italy since the summer of 1943. Although the invasion of northwest Europe was delayed, Germany had to prepare for it. The German grand strategy – if it can be called that – was to hold on in the East until the expected cross-Channel landing had been repelled. In reality, the invasion of Normandy would coincide with the Soviet summer offensive.

In 1941, the course of the fighting was set by Hitler's Operation BARBAROSSA. In 1942, the German BLUE plan determined that the main fighting would be in south Russia. In 1943, CITADEL led both sides to concentrate forces in south-central Russia and especially around the Kursk salient. In April 1944, however, as the Red Army's long drive across the Ukraine paused at the pre-1939 Soviet–Polish frontier, it was the Soviet Stavka, not the German high command, which began to work out how an offensive summer campaign would develop. This plan took in the entire front; in scope it had more in common with BARBAROSSA than it did with Operation BLUE or Operation CITADEL.

Stalin and the Stavka had aspired to the overall coordination of strategic operations since the momentum of Operation BARBAROSSA slowed. In the spring of 1942 and again in the winter of 1942–3, they had attempted wide-ranging operations taking in the whole front, but they had achieved at best local successes; often their overconfidence had led to defeat. The summer of 1943 took Soviet co-ordination to a higher and more successful level, but events were still driven by German initiatives, and victories came only on parts of the long front. In 1944 the Stavka finally achieved its goal. In his Revolution Day speech of November 1944, Stalin would speak of the 'ten crushing blows [*sokrushitel'nye udary*]', which later became the 'ten Stalinist crushing blows':

> The decisive successes of the Red Army in this year and the expulsion of the Germans beyond the borders of the Soviet land were brought about by a series of crushing blows by our forces against the German forces, which began as early as January of the this year [1944] and developed in the course of the whole year.[1]

As we have already seen, the important assessment of Stalin's wartime achievements which appeared over Voroshilov's name in 1951 had made the first feature 'the co-ordinated operations of numerous army groups, united across a theatre of military operations extending for a thousand kilometres according to a single strategic plan and a single strategic will'. The supreme example of this was held to be the Soviet offensives of 1944–5 'when in the huge space from the Barents Sea to the Black Sea the sequential and simultaneous crushing blows of the Soviet forces completely finished off the armies of fascist Germany and her allies'. The operations in 1944 were 'conducted in the style of classic Stalinist *offensive strategy* [and] on a gigantic scale'.[2] This was not an exaggeration.

FINLAND: THE SECOND BATTLE OF KARELIA

Finland leaves the war

The first three of Stalin's 'crushing blows', on the northern and southern flanks, were dictated by the winter campaign of 1943–4. The Stavka had more freedom to decide where the blows would fall in the summer campaign of 1944. The main offensive was to be in Belorussia, but there was discussion among the General Staff planners as to where it would be best to start the campaign. One possibility was to continue the advance in the northwestern Ukraine (with the 1st Ukrainian Army Group). General Antonov, Deputy Chief of the General Staff and currently Stalin's closest military adviser, preferred to begin with the Finns, and his arguments won the day.[3]

The Soviet attack on the Karelian Isthmus, the neck of land some 40–50 miles wide, between the sea and Lake Ladoga, began on 10 June; this was four days after the Normandy landings. The Finns were taken by surprise. General Govorov's Leningrad Army Group deployed two infantry armies, one fresh from the Stavka reserve. Less than two weeks later, on 21 June (two days before the start of the main Operation BAGRATION in Belorussia) Govorov had reached his main objectives, the town of Vyborg (Viipuri) and the Vuoksi River line on the far side of the Karelian Isthmus. Southern Finland was open to invasion. Govorov – also the defender of Leningrad in 1941–4 – was promoted to the rank of Marshal. After this Vyborg operation, a second phase began. In the Svir'–Petrozavodsk operation, beginning on 21 June, the Soviet 7th Army, the left flank of General Meretskov's Karelian Army Group, pushed through the forests between Lakes Ladoga and Onega; Meretskov's 32nd Army turned around the north end of Lake Onega. The Finns abandoned the Svir' River line that they had reached in September 1941 and, on 28 June 1944, the Karelian capital of Petrozavodsk.

The 1944 Soviet campaign in Karelia was in sharp contrast to the bungled campaign the Red Army had fought three and a half years earlier, in the Winter War. General Meretskov, the 1944 commander of Karelian Army Group, had also been a senior leader in the Winter War. The 1939–40 campaign had hung up for four months in the Karelian Isthmus, faced by mid-winter conditions, difficult terrain and the defences of the Finnish Mannerheim Line. Other Soviet thrusts had been savaged by Finnish ski troops in the frozen forests and lakes north of Lake Ladoga. In 1944 the Russians achieved their primary objective of Vyborg in a couple of weeks. Much better weather conditions were important, but the Red armed forces were also far superior to those of 1941. In the three-and-a-half-month campaign in 1939–40, the Soviets lost 127,000 men; in the whole two-month Red Army campaign of 1944 (10 June to 9 August), Soviet losses were still very significant, but at 67,000 they were only half the earlier figure.

Soviet operations in Finland in 1944 are especially interesting, in that they had limited objectives. The Finns had put out peace-feelers in February 1944, but these failed, partly because of the extent of Russian demands, and partly because of German counter-pressure. Even the Soviet Vyborg and Svir'–Petrozavodsk operations did not immediately knock Finland out of the war; indeed, the Finns requested Berlin to provide more ground troops and aircraft. The Red Army, however, stopped when it had achieved the basic border objectives of Vyborg and Petrozavodsk. The Soviet Karelian Army Group did have plans for an advance into central Finland, and there were contingency plans for the occupation of the whole country, but the stress was on diplomatic pressure.[4]

If one of the Stavka's aims in the 1944 Karelia campaign was to draw German ground and air reinforcements to the north, away from the central part of the front, then this was not successful. The attacks did, however, have the effect at least of fixing the attention of Hitler and the German high command on Finland, and more generally, on the Army Group North area (i.e. Estonia and Latvia). They made the Germans unwilling to make withdrawals from what, in any logical strategy, was an untenable position. When the great crisis of the Eastern Front came in July 1944, Hitler would use the wavering Finns to rationalize his refusal to give up ground; any retreat would lessen their resolve to fight on.

To some extent Hitler was right. The beginning of the collapse of German Army Group North in Estonia and northern Latvia *would* actually precipitate Finland's withdrawal from the war. The anchor points, at Pskov and Narva, finally broke on 23 and 26 July 1944, respectively. Far to the west – and deeply outflanking Army Group

North – a Soviet mechanized corps reached the Gulf of Riga on 31 July. Within days, there were drastic changes in the Finnish government. Marshal Mannerheim replaced the pro-German President Ryti as head of state. On 24 August, the Finnish government, despite a desperate visit by Field Marshal Keitel, finally decided to leave the war. On 29 August, the Soviet armies facing the Finns were ordered to 'strict defence'. Four days later, the Finns broke off relations with Germany, and on 4–5 September, fighting – after nearly three years – ceased.

In the armistice agreement the Finns confirmed the loss of territory handed over in 1940, and in addition gave up their access to the Barents Sea at Petsamo (Pechenga). They had to pay large reparations and provide the Red Army with a base outside Helsinki (at Porkkala). In one respect in particular, the treatment of Finland was very different from that of the other Soviet borderlands: Moscow did not send the Red Army into southern Finland, and the Finns were required to eject the Wehrmacht themselves.[5] There was an Allied Control Commission presided over by Stalin's ideological deputy Andrei Zhdanov, but it did not put extreme political pressure on Finland. The Finnish Communist Party was weak at the end of the war, and the government of President Mannerheim and Prime Minister Paasikivi acceded promptly to Stalin's demands.

Victory in the far north

The tenth and last of Stalin's 'crushing blows' of 1944 would also take place in Finland, the Petsamo–Kirkenes operation. It came in the Arctic, a month after the Soviet–Finnish armistice, and was also delivered by Meretskov's Karelian Army Group. Finland might have left the war, but the German 20th Mountain Army, 200,000 strong, still held three sectors in the Finnish Arctic. In mid-September Stalin emphatically told Meretskov that it was the Finns who should drive the Germans out of northern Finland and not the Red Army. He ended his signal with a remarkable threat: 'non-fulfilment of the Stavka's instruction and any attempt by you to race ahead will entail your dismissal from command of the army group'.[6] V. I. Shcherbakov's 14th Army, the right flank of Meretskov's Karelian Army Group, attacked on 7 October 1944. A German mountain corps was pushed out of the positions it had held before Murmansk since 1941. Petsamo, the little port on the Barents Sea which Finland was now ceding to the USSR, was taken on 15 October (D + 8). A few days later, the nickel mines so prized by Hitler were captured by the Red Army. The Norwegian port of Kirkenes, the forward base for the three-year campaign against Murmansk, fell on 25 October (D + 18). Further south the Soviet 26th and 19th Armies struck at the two German corps facing the Murmansk–Vologda railway, chased them back to the Soviet–Finnish border, and then stopped.

Although at first the Germans had hoped for a tidy withdrawal from Finland, real fighting with their former comrades in arms began north of the Gulf of Bothnia at the end of September. The Finnish Army fought its third war in five years. The Wehrmacht's Murmansk corps, and two mountain corps facing the railway to the south, were pulled back 350–400 miles in operations which the Germans code-named BIRCH TREE (BIRKE) and NORTHERN LIGHTS (NORDLICHT). By January 1945, German forces had withdrawn to a narrow segment of Norway, between the Swedish border and the port of Tromsö. It was at Tromsö in mid-November 1944 that RAF long-range bombers finally picked off the *Tirpitz*, the battleship which had threatened the northern convoys for so many months. The withdrawal of the German 20th Mountain Army had been an epic, carried out along the crude roads of Lapland during an Arctic winter. As they withdrew, the Germans devastated this sparsely settled part of Finland. The campaign in the North was over.

The Soviet 14th Army was left to defend the new Arctic border of the USSR, but in November 1944, the other northern armies were available for combat use elsewhere. The 26th Army was sent to Hungary, while the 19th and the 32nd were ordered to prepare for an even longer transfer. They were among the first formations to be readied for the attack against the Japanese Army in Manchuria. In the previous month Meretskov had finally been awarded the rank of Marshal of the Soviet Union. The commander who had been Chief of the General Staff in 1940, and a leading commander in Finland and Leningrad, had now acquitted himself well enough in Stalin's eyes. He and his staff were ordered to take up command of the 1st Far Eastern Army Group for the war against Japan.[7]

OPERATION BAGRATION: THE SECOND BATTLE OF BELORUSSIA

Stalemate on the central front

Field Marshal Ernst Busch's German Army Group Centre occupied the Belorussian SSR. The front line of Army Group Centre was located roughly where it had been at the end of the first Nazi jump into Belorussia in mid-July 1941 (see Map 9). At stake, as in 1941, was a vital element of strategic geography, the line of the Dvina and upper Dnepr Rivers, and the narrow 50-mile Orsha 'land bridge' in between them. This time, however, the attack on the Dvina–Dnepr line was coming from the east rather than the west; it was the Red Army that was attacking. German Army Group Centre's eastern face along the line measured about 180 miles.

In addition, German Army Group Centre had a 250-mile-long right (southern) flank. Another geographical parallel with the late summer of 1941 was that the front line did not simply run from north to south. Both in 1941 and in 1944, the difficult terrain of the Poles'e (the Pripiat' Marshes) divided the Nazi–Soviet front into two parts, Belorussia and the Ukraine. In the first months of 1941, the panzers had driven through Belorussia faster than through the Ukraine (pushing some 200 miles further into the USSR). German-conquered Belorussia became a huge salient thrust into Soviet territory, from which the Wehrmacht could break out to turn the flank of the Red Army's defences in the Ukraine and win their huge victory at Kiev. In 1944 just the opposite had happened. The Red Army had made faster progress in the Ukraine than in Belorussia; the 1st and 2nd Ukrainian Army Groups, driving against German Army Group North Ukraine, had pushed some 300 miles further west, and presented a similar threat to the rear of

German Army Group Centre. The Germans called this strategic position jutting out in Belorussia the 'balcony' (*Balkon*), and the Soviets called it the 'step' (*vystup*).

As late as the spring of 1944, German Army Group Centre had successfully withstood major Soviet offensives into Belorussia, operations until recently left out of Russian histories.[8] In 1943 Army Group Centre, originally under Field Marshal Kluge, had been forced to give ground, although it did so in a fairly orderly way. This happened at the beginning of 1943 in the Rzhev–Viaz'ma salient in front of Moscow, then in the summer in the Orel salient north of Kursk. The next stages of the Soviet Western Army Group advance, the Smolensk operation (Operation SUVOROV) from August to October 1943, had brought Soviet troops as much as 200 miles further west. The withdrawal was furthest in the south, by the German 9th Army; the 4th Army and the 3rd Panzer Army had to make smaller steps back. The original fallback position was the *Ostwall* line, which in this sector of the front was 30–40 miles to the east of the Dnepr River. Vatutin's breakout at Kiev in November 1943 shook the southern part of this line, which had to pull further back beyond the town of Gomel', and beyond the Dnepr River. Meanwhile, north of Vitebsk, the Soviet capture of Nevel' in early October 1943 represented a major victory, creating a significant bulge in the enemy line at the boundary between German Army Groups North and Centre; the advance cut the Dno–Nevel'–Vitebsk–Orsha lateral (north–south) railway. The Germans were, however, able for the moment to establish a position further west, anchored on the towns of Vitebsk, Orsha, Mogilev and Bobruisk, with the swamps of Poles'e covering their flank to the south. This was at the western edge of the Kalinin, Smolensk and Orel regions of the Russian republic (the RSFSR), on the border with the Belorussian SSR.

In the autumn of 1943, the Stavka had had hopes for more rapid progress across Belorussia, and in early October, it assigned ambitious objectives to the four army groups in the central theatre.[9] On the left flank, the Stavka aimed Rokossovskii's Central Army Group, now significantly renamed the Belorussian Army Group, towards Minsk from the southeast, via Zhlobin and Bobruisk. Sokolovskii's Western Army Group was aimed towards Vil'nius in Lithuania west via Orsha, Borisov and Molodechno (north of Minsk). These two army groups were ordered, at the very least, to break the Dvina–Dnepr line (and the *Ostwall*) at Vitebsk, Orsha and Mogilev. Eremenko's Kalinin (later the 1st Baltic) Army Group was aimed towards Riga, the capital of Latvia; it was to go there from north of Velikie Luki via Vitebsk, Polotsk and Daugavpils. To the north, Kurochkin's Northwestern (later the 2nd Baltic) Army Group was aimed west towards Ostrov, a town south of Lake Chud on the Estonian border.

The German line held. In the early spring of 1944, Timoshenko could only with difficulty explain the very slow progress of the 1st and 2nd Baltic Army Groups. Eremenko's Kalinin (later 1st Baltic) Army Group, after taking Nevel' in October, had pushed south to effect a close investment of the fortified town of Vitebsk. But it could not take Vitebsk, let alone threaten Riga. Here, and probably elsewhere, effective German radio intelligence seems to have provided warning of the strength and timing of Soviet attacks.[10] In any event, the career of General Eremenko, the hero of Stalingrad, went again into eclipse; he was removed from his command in November 1943. Eremenko's

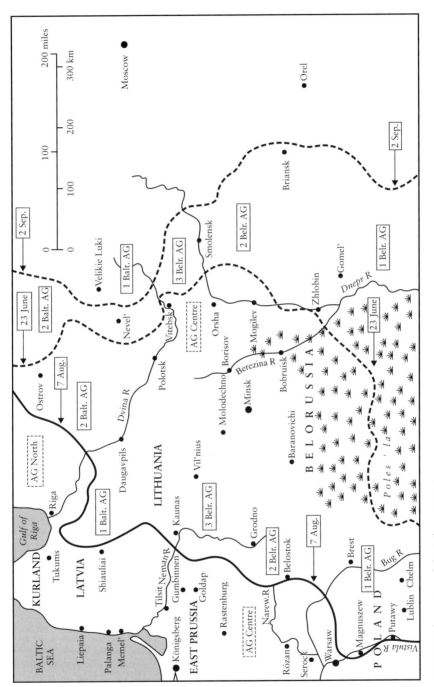

MAP 9 Belorussia and the Baltic, 1943–4.

neighbour to the south, Sokolovskii's Western Army Group, mounted no fewer than eleven major attacks between mid-October 1943 and the end of March 1944, but made little headway. The fierce commissar Mekhlis was moved into the Western Army Group in mid-December 1943. When no further progress was made there, a high-powered 'Extraordinary Commission' was sent out to investigate in April 1944, led by Politburo member Malenkov, with Shcherbakov, General Shtemenko and others. Sokolovskii was demoted and commissars Bulganin and Mekhlis censured.[11] The Western Army Group was divided into the more manageable 2nd and 3rd Belorussian Army Groups.

These Soviet offensives in the central theatre had not been altogether in vain. They pinned down German Army Group Centre and made it impossible to send troops from there to reinforce Manstein in Army Group South as its front collapsed during the winter. Nevertheless, the Soviet attacks had been intended to do more than that. Part of the reason for the continuing failure of the Soviet army groups in the central part of the front was that there was a vicious circle at work. The Stavka reinforced success and starved failure. Other sectors – especially the Ukraine – had had more successes over the winter of 1943–4 and consequently they received more reinforcements from the centre. The Ukraine was also where the most powerful Stavka 'representatives', Zhukov and Vasilevskii, were operating. Stalin in the late period of the war economized on men and equipment in his reserves. As Zhukov put it, 'He gave them now in the first instance only to those army groups that were really carrying out decisive operations. Other army groups received forces and supplies on a considerably more limited scale.'[12]

The destruction of Army Group Centre

In June 1944, it suddenly became very clear that Stalin and the Stavka had turned their attention back to Belorussia, as a huge Soviet offensive opened up there. In the course of it, German Army Group Centre was virtually destroyed.[13] This was the fifth, and most important, of Stalin's 'crushing blows' of 1944. A series of large attacks by the 1st, 2nd and 3rd Belorussian Army Groups, and the 1st Baltic Army Group, broke through the German front and achieved a pace of advance matching that of the Wehrmacht three years earlier. By the close of the main part of operation, in the last days of July 1944, the Red Army had moved the front line forward over 300 miles to the west, taking all of the Belorussian SSR and the southern part of the Baltic states (Lithuania and southern Latvia). The Red Army was within a few miles of the East Prussian border – and indeed it was less than 60 miles from Hitler's WOLFSSCHANZE headquarters near Rastenburg. The final phase of the operation, moreover, coincided with the start of another full-scale Soviet campaign, in southwestern Poland.

Stalin himself thought up the operational code name for the Belorussian offensive, BAGRATION. This was based on Prince Petr Ivanovich Bagration, a Tsarist army commander who was mortally wounded at the Battle of Borodino in front of Moscow in 1812.[14] Russian military historians formally call this the 'Belorussian operation'. Western sources sometimes called it 'the destruction of Army Group

Centre'. To give the battle a clear location and sequence, it could be called the Second Battle of Belorussia.

The preliminary actions of the BAGRATION offensive were mounted on 22 June 1944. Although this date was the third anniversary of Operation BARBAROSSA, the coincidence was accidental. The operation was initially planned for the 19th and was postponed – like BARBAROSSA itself had been – by transport hold-ups. In any event, Soviet operations on 22 June 1944 took the form of a reconnaissance in force, and the full-scale offensive began on 23 and 24 June.

Russian military historians divide the first phase of the Belorussian offensive into three parallel breakthrough battles: the Bobruisk operation, the Mogilev operation and the Vitebsk–Orsha operation. Bobruisk, Mogilev, Orsha and Vitebsk were the four towns on the Dvina–Dnepr line, with 40–60 miles between them. There German Army Group Centre had formed its new strategic line of resistance, roughly Hitler's *Ostwall* line, in late 1943. Bobruisk, on the lower Berezina River (a tributary of the upper Dnepr), was the southern German anchor. Mogilev was on the rail line to Baranovichi; it had been the Tsar's Supreme Headquarters in 1915–17. Further north on the Dnepr was Orsha, on the south side of the 'Orsha land bridge', and astride the Smolensk–Minsk railway; it was at a staff conference at Orsha in November 1941 that General Halder of the German General Staff had argued for the final drive on Moscow. Vitebsk, on the Dvina, was the second biggest city in the Belorussian SSR, with a pre-war population of 167,000. All four were among the borderland towns that Hitler in March had specially designated as 'fortified places' (*festen Plätze*).

In each sector, the outcome of the early operations against the crust of the German defence was successful. Soviet breakthroughs quickly threatened to envelop the towns. The local German commanders requested permission to withdraw the garrisons, which the high command refused, on the basis of the 'fortified places' strategy. There was no effective German mobile defence. The Soviets then completed the encirclement and quickly took the line of towns – Vitebsk on 26 June, Orsha on the 27th, Mogilev on the 28th and Bobruisk on the 29th (D + 6 of Operation BAGRATION). Meanwhile, Soviet mobile corps advanced rapidly through the gaps between the 'fortified places'.

Once the forward German line had been penetrated, the Soviet armour raced for the next major obstacle, some 100 miles to the west, the upper Berezina River.[15] The Berezina is famous for the episode in November 1812 when Napoleon's retreating Grande Armée had had to fight its way west across the bridges at Borisov. Minsk itself was taken on 3 July (D + 10). Much of the city lay in ruins, but the rapid advance in the last hours prevented the demolition of some buildings, including the huge Government House (*Dom pravitel'stva*). Minsk was of much symbolic value to Stalin, as the first large city lost in June 1941. The German 4th Army under General Vincenz Müller was trapped after the fall of Minsk in a *kotel* ('cauldron') to the east of the city, between Minsk and the Berezina. (In November and December 1941, the 4th Army, then commanded by General Kluge, had been the main infantry force advancing on Moscow.)

The actual 'destruction of Army Group Centre', the encirclement and surrender of Field Marshal Busch's command, took place in this first phase of BAGRATION. The second phase, in contrast, was the Soviet pursuit of shattered German formations – rather than the completion of further encirclements. This successful Soviet deep pursuit was as surprising for the Germans as the success of the initial attack. They had expected the Red Army to lose momentum, as it had in the past, once the spearheads had thrust forward 125 miles or so. The Soviet advance did not stop, however, just beyond the line of the Dvina–Dnepr line, nor even at Minsk.

South of Minsk, the right wing of Rokossovskii's 1st Belorussian Army Group moved on to Baranovichi (8 July, D + 15) and to Brest (28 July, D + 36) on the 1941 state border.[16] Cherniakhovskii's 3rd Belorussian Army Group raced on to the important rail junction of Molodechno and then to Vil'nius (13 July), and Kaunas (1 August, D + 40) in Lithuania. Between Rokossovskii and Cherniakhovskii, Zakharov's 2nd Belorussian Army Group continued due west to Grodno (16 July) and Belostok (27 July, D + 35), where the first terrible *Kesselschlacht* (battle of encirclement) had been fought out in June 1941. Bagramian's 1st Baltic Army Group continued without pause past Daugavpils (Dvinsk), on the lower Dvina River, and to Shiauliai. Daugavpils, 135 miles to the east of Shiauliai, was briefly encircled, and then also taken by the Red Army, on the 27th (D + 35). Advanced Red Army units, as we will see later in this chapter, would in a few days break through to the Gulf of Riga, temporarily cutting German Army Group North off from Army Group Centre. This forward line of conquests – Brest, Kaunas, Shiauliai – was no less than 300 miles west of the 22 June 1944 start line. With this advance, the Red Army has also taken three-quarters of the Lithuanian SSR, with its capital Vil'nius (Wilno), and two major towns, Kaunas and Shiauliai.

Causes and consequences

Operation BAGRATION was unprecedented for the speed of its advance: 300 miles in five weeks.[17] The only comparable campaign, on the Soviet side, would be the Vistula–Oder operation of January–February 1945, but there the deepest Soviet penetration was initially achieved only on a fairly narrow front, along 120 miles of the Vistula River, and against a broken-backed enemy. The most dramatic part of the fighting, in central and eastern Belorussia in 1944, had ended about three weeks after it began, in the middle of July.

However inevitable the course of the Soviet summer offensive in Belorussia may seem with hindsight, the success of Operation BAGRATION was not altogether a foregone conclusion. Hitler's high command turned out to have been grossly overconfident, but this overconfidence was not completely inexplicable, in view of the strength of German Army Group Centre and the defensive successes it had achieved over the past two years. On the eve of the battle, Field Marshal Busch's Army Group Centre was on paper the largest of the four German army groups in Russia. It numbered 792,000 men, as opposed to 541,000 in Lindemann's Army Group North, 401,000 in Model's Army Group North Ukraine and 509,000 in Schörner's Army Group South Ukraine. Busch's army group in Belorussia consisted of 51 divisions. Army Group North Ukraine, in contrast, had only 45.[18] Army Group Centre had also had the advantage of three years to prepare its defences. The terrain – wooded, with many small rivers and swamps – should have been less favourable to a rapid advance by the Red Army than the Ukrainian steppe.

The 1944 offensive in Belorussia had much in common with the 'deep operations' proposed by Soviet military theorists in the 1930s. The Red Army pincers closed *behind* Minsk, and at the same time Soviet spearheads continued to make rapid progress into the western part of Belorussia. The advance continued to Shiauliai, Vil'nius, Kaunas, Grodno and Belostok, and across the Berezina, the Neman and the Western Bug Rivers. The distance the four Soviet army groups advanced was further than the distance from Moscow to their starting points. The Stalingrad counter-offensive (Operation URANUS) in the winter of 1942–3 had achieved surprise, but it was essentially a counter-attack against a recklessly exposed German salient. Dramatic Red Army successes elsewhere in later 1943 and 1944 – especially in the Ukraine – took the form of a pursuit of German forces that were already reeling back. Operation BAGRATION started from a static position with surprise breakthroughs. Previous Soviet operations in the centre had been equally ambitious in their objectives but had not been as well prepared or resourced, and they had not involved the successful co-ordination of four army groups.

The decision to mount the main blow of 1944 in Belorussia may well have been Zhukov's, made at a Stavka conference at the end of April. That, at least, is what he claimed in his memoirs. On the other hand, he also stated that a decision had been made by the Stavka for a series of offensives on 12 April. The detailed planning was undertaken by General Antonov, the Deputy Chief of the General Staff, since Marshal Vasilevskii was still tied up with the Crimean offensive. The initial proposal for a 45–50-day campaign was made by Antonov in mid-May. Operation BAGRATION was part of a most impressive strategic plan, and this was another reason for its success. Before BAGRATION the Germans were distracted by the Karelian operation, and in the later stages of BAGRATION the Germans were suddenly hit by attacks to the south, the big so-called L'vov–Sandomierz operation, south of the Poles'e (the Pripiat' Marshes), which began on 13 July (D + 21 of BAGRATION).

Operation BAGRATION could also be pursued successfully because of the growing experience and skill of Soviet leaders. Stalin had developed into an effective military co-ordinator. Vasilevskii thought that in 1944 he was at the height of his powers.[19] Stalin committed his most able commanders to BAGRATION. In June Marshal Zhukov, the Deputy Supreme C-in-C, co-ordinated the two southern army groups (the 1st and 2nd Belorussian), and Marshal Vasilevskii, the Chief of the General Staff, the two northern ones (the 3rd Belorussian and the 1st Baltic). Three of the army group commanders – Bagramian, Zakharov and Rokossovskii – were experienced and proven commanders, and the fourth was General I. D. Cherniakhovskii, an energetic and highly talented young general. Only a colonel in June 1941, Cherniakhovskii became, at thirty-eight, the Red Army's youngest army group commander. He had distinguished himself as commander of the 60th Army at the Battle of Kursk in 1943 and in the northern Ukraine, and in June 1944 his talents were committed to the 3rd Belorussian Army Group and the key breakthrough zone south of Vitebsk. His command style involved leading from the front; it would contribute to his early death in February 1945.

The Soviets also achieved success because they concentrated overwhelming strength at a critical point – and because the Germans were ignorant of the scale of their concentration. German Army Group Centre was surprised by the initial onslaught on the Vitebsk–Orsha–Mogilev–Bobruisk line. The German attempts at static resistance were based on false assumptions – that the Soviet concentration of forces was less than it was and that the Soviet powers of mobility were still limited. Very large fresh Soviet forces had been concentrated in the central part of the front with a high degree of successful *maskirovka* (strategic deception). Operation BAGRATION involved a huge logistical operation. Some 440,000 freight cars were required to build up the attack force, 65 per cent of the total rolling stock available. Despite this, overall knowledge of the plan was confined to Stalin and five others. All movement was to be carefully concealed, and there was strict prohibition on use of radios; in contrast to earlier battles, the Germans received less help from the '*elektronische-Orakel*' of intercepted Soviet signals.[20]

Rokossovskii's immense 1st Belorussian Army Group comprised four infantry armies, with two independent armoured mobile corps and a cavalry corps. Zakharov, in the 2nd Belorussian Army Group, commanded three armies. Cherniakhovskii, in the 3rd Belorussian, had four infantry armies, plus a powerful mobile element comprising the 5th Guards Tank Army, two independent armoured corps and a cavalry corps. Finally, on the right flank of the advance was Bagramian's 1st Baltic Army Group. Bagramian had three infantry armies and an independent tank corps. Altogether, the four Soviet army groups involved in BAGRATION, plus the left flank of the 1st Ukrainian Army Group (not directly involved in the initial fighting), had available 12 tank or mechanized corps and 166 rifle divisions. There were 2,400,000 personnel, 36,000 guns and mortars, and 5,200 tanks and SP guns. Air support in the four air armies comprised 5,300 combat aircraft. By contrast, the Soviet army groups engaged at Kursk in 1943 had numbered 1,270,000 personnel (9 tank or mechanized corps and 76 rifle divisions). (And in June–July 1941, in the *First* Battle of Belorussia, the Soviet Western Army Group – under the unfortunate General Pavlov – had comprised only 625,000 personnel.)[21]

As with the 1941 campaign in Belorussia, the defending army made fundamental and fatal mistakes in its intelligence assessments. In 1944, the German high command, which had just been steamrollered by six tank armies in the central and western Ukraine, believed that the bulk of Soviet armour was still deployed in the south. For the German high command, the failure to predict where the Soviet offensive in the East would come was one of two crucial strategic-intelligence mistakes made in the summer of 1944. The other mistake was being taken in by the British–American FORTITUDE deception plan. This led the Germans to believe after D-Day in Normandy that another landing was imminent in the Pas de Calais area (northwest of Normandy); it prevented German reserves being employed fully against the actual landing area. Another shortcoming of the German assessment was that they did not believe the Red Army would be capable of such deep operations.[22]

An important factor in the German defeat was Hitler's over-reliance on static defence, the so-called 'fortified places'. In early March 1944, his Order No. 11 made these a central part of his 'strategy' in the East:

The 'Fortified Places' [*Die festen Plätze*] will fulfil the functions of fortresses in earlier times. They will prevent the enemy from occupying these places of decisive operational importance. They are to allow themselves to be surrounded, thereby tying down the largest possible number of enemy forces. They are by this means to establish the preconditions for successful counter-operations.[23]

As we have seen, this concept had been unsuccessful in the Ukraine, where the fortified places were quickly overrun. Three months later, the doctrine was still in place in Belorussia. To be sure, these places were not simply points on the map, but road and railway junctions, usually on river lines, which, if held, might be expected to slow the Soviet onslaught. However, this strategy depended on the Red Army being unable to move rapidly off the few major roads, something which in fact became easier with the improvement of Red Army transport, notably the availability of the big American trucks. Even more important, the fortified places strategy depended on the Germans having sufficient mobile forces available both to fight the main battle and to mount a counter-attack. The strategy had had some success in France and the Low Countries, where the Germans held on to key ports to prevent their use for Allied supply ships, although this slowed only marginally the American and British advance.

Another explanation for the German defeat in Belorussia involves Hitler, the German high command and a mediocre local commander. As elsewhere, the *Ostheer* suffered from the lack of an overall professional commander. Hitler attempted to direct the battle from his headquarters on the Obersalzberg in Bavaria, where he was also overseeing operations in Normandy. Zeitzler, the Chief of the Army General Staff, had been increasingly marginalized and he was dismissed during the battle, after suffering a nervous breakdown. Field Marshal Ernst Busch had been commander of Army Group Centre since November 1943, when Field Marshal Kluge was injured in a car accident. Busch's subordinates were highly experienced. Hans Reinhardt, still commanding the 3rd Panzer Army on the left wing, had been a very successful tank commander. His panzer corps, which had taken part in the French campaign, was in September 1941 the spearhead formation that thrust closest to Leningrad. In October 1941 Reinhardt took over the 3rd Panzer Group (later the 3rd Panzer Army) for the drive on Moscow. In the centre the 4th Army had General Tippelskirch as acting commander. Tippelskirch had been head of intelligence in the Army General Staff during the planning of BARBAROSSA, and was one of the first post-war German historians of the Second World War.[24] The 9th Army, which had fought the defensive battles in the Rzhev–Viaz'ma pocket in front of Moscow under Model, was now commanded by General Jordan. (The German 2nd Army under General Weiss, covering the southern flank of Army Group Centre, was not part of the initial battle.) The commander of the German 6th Air Fleet, supporting Army Group Centre, was General Greim, who had led Luftwaffe formations in Russia since

June 1941. Nine months after BAGRATION, in the dying days of the Reich, Greim would very briefly replace Goering as head of the Luftwaffe.

The problem lay partly with the overall German leadership in Belorussia. Busch, a close personal friend of Field Marshal Manstein, was an experienced front-line commander. He had led a corps in the Polish campaign and the 16th Army (on the right wing of Army Group North) in 1941. From his headquarters in Minsk, Busch had overseen the blunting of the series of Soviet attacks in late 1943 and early 1944. But he failed to detect Soviet preparations, he lacked the political weight to demand armoured reinforcements, and he accepted Hitler's 'fortified places' strategy.

Busch, for all his supine adherence to Hitler's strategy, was replaced in the second phase of the Battle of Belorussia (at the very end of June 1944) by the ubiquitous Field Marshal Model, a more energetic commander. Model simultaneously kept command of Army Group North Ukraine. He was, as we have seen, a specialist in vigorous defensive battles, first of all as commander of the 9th Army in the desperate actions in front of Moscow in January 1942 and then in July and August 1942. (The 9th Army had just been largely destroyed around Bobruisk by the time Model took command of Army Group Centre.) Model, an enthusiast for the Nazi cause and not of a *Junker* background, was more politically acceptable to Hitler than other senior generals. From the summer of 1943, he had been shifted around the Eastern Front to deal with one crisis after another. Hitler would award Model the Diamond Clasp to the Knight's Cross in mid-August 1944 for preventing a total disaster in the Army Group Centre area. While Model's efforts seemed more successful than those of Busch, this was partly because by the time he took over, the Soviet drive had lost the element of surprise. Moreover, like Manstein at Stalingrad, another 'saviour' of a difficult situation, Model must bear some responsibility for the whole debacle. Prior to the Soviet offensive in Belorussia, Model, as commander of Army Group North Ukraine, had demanded and received armoured reinforcements at the expense of Busch. Model, for his part, departed in mid-August from Army Group Centre to deal with the crisis in Western Europe. (His replacement was Hans Reinhardt, commander of the 3rd Panzer Army.)

Even if Model had been in Busch's place on 22 June 1944, and even if Hitler and the High Command had allowed him more operational flexibility, the resources available to German Army Group Centre would have been limited. On paper, things did not look all that different from the days of BARBAROSSA. In June 1941, Field Marshal Bock as commander of Army Group Centre had had available fifty divisions; in 1944, Busch had fifty-one. However, the quality and size of divisions in 1944 were lower, and the order of battle included some Luftwaffe field divisions and four Hungarian divisions (in 1941 all the divisions had been German). Most important was Busch's relative weakness in armour. Bock had commanded eight panzer divisions and four motorized divisions in 1941, while Busch possessed only three mobile divisions. Reinhardt's 1944 3rd Panzer Army was a 'panzer army' in name only. He had no panzer divisions, and his infantry divisions contained very few tanks. (Model's Army Group North Ukraine, in contrast, contained eight panzer divisions.) German Army Group Centre possessed only 570 tracked armoured vehicles, of which 452 were turretless 'assault guns' (StuG IIIs). In

1941, Bock's air support, Kesselring's 2nd Air Fleet, had been the largest air formation in the BARBAROSSA campaign, with 1,370 front-line aircraft; Greim in 1944 commanded 602 operational aircraft, including only 61 fighters.[25]

Partisans had been important for the Soviet side in earlier campaigns (see Chapter 8), but Belorussia was a special case. The front line here had been relatively static for a long period, so it had been possible for the partisans to establish links across the front line. The woods and swamps of Belorussia favoured partisan operations. As already mentioned, the importance of the region within the partisan movement as a whole was emphasized by the fact that the head of the Central Staff of the Partisan Movement (i.e. for all the occupied territories) was a Belorussian. This was P. K. Ponomarenko, post-purge 1st Secretary of the Belorussian party. This would also be the last opportunity for major partisan involvement by Soviet citizens. After BAGRATION the Red Army was fighting beyond the pre-1939 USSR borders. As we have seen, there is disagreement among historians over how widespread and how effective the Soviet partisan movement was. It is also not clear how effective German anti-partisan sweeps were in 1943–4. Certainly, a concerted campaign of railway sabotage was carried out on the eve of the Soviet offensive. The partisans also helped guide Red Army units through difficult territory, and after the successful advance, partisans (and other civilians) were drafted en masse into the Red Army to reinforce conventional units.

Victory in Belorussia and most of Lithuania was followed, as in the Ukraine, by the arrival of the NKVD to seek out collaborators. Lithuania had been an independent state before 1940, the most populous of the three Baltic republics. Western Belorussia had been part of Poland. Events here were complicated for the 'liberators' by the presence of Polish nationalist groups, who claimed influence, especially in some of the towns of the region. NKVD General Serov, based in Vil'nius, was tasked to eliminate anti-Soviet 'bandit formations'. In addition, a considerable amount of forced population transfer would take place in 1944–5; ethnic Poles were moved to Poland from the Belorussian and Lithuanian SSRs, and ethnic Belorussians and Poles to the USSR from Poland.[26]

The unprecedented success of Operation BAGRATION needs to be linked with British and American operations in Western Europe. The Russians were told on 10 April 1944 that the cross-Channel operation was set for 31 May 1944. Soviet historians maintained that the Belorussian operation was a clear fulfilment of obligations made at the Tehran Conference, but Stalin had his own reasons for launching it. It is debatable whether BAGRATION was essential for the success of Operation OVERLORD, the Normandy invasion, as Marshal Vasilevskii and others have suggested.[27] If anything, the opposite was true. The lack of German reserves in Belorussia, and the surprising extent of Soviet success, resulted from Hitler's pre-Normandy grand-strategic preparations for the expected Anglo-American landing. Hitler and his generals thought that only after the defeat of such a landing could a change be brought about in the East.

Following the initial OVERLORD landings on 6 June 1944, the American–British expeditionary force was pinned down by the German 7th Army in Normandy for the better part of two months – in effect for the whole time of the Belorussian campaign. But neither the 7th Army, nor the German 15th Army covering the Pas de Calais, could release forces for the crisis (or rather *crises*) in Russia. (The 7th and the 15th Armies together made up Rommel's 1944 Army Group 'B'.) The American breakout (Operation COBRA) began in Brittany at the end of July. The Americans and British then made very rapid progress against the threadbare German Army Group 'B', reaching the line of the Seine River by the end of August (Paris fell on 23–25 August). Two further German armies, the 1st and the 19th, were tied down in the south of France and then engaged after the American–British ANVIL landings there in mid-August 1944. The Western Allies were also finally making progress in Italy, and so the Germans could not withdraw reserves from that theatre either. The Allies attacked the German 10th and 14th Armies in May 1944, took Rome in early June, and pushed north 150 miles to the Arno River by the start of August.

Likewise, the air campaign of the Americans and British over France and Germany aided the rapid defeat of Army Group Centre in Belorussia. The Luftwaffe units in Belorussia were not able to defend German ground forces against Soviet air attacks, let alone slow down the enemy drive by air strikes of their own. The Germans could not even carry out effective air reconnaissance. By the summer of 1944, the American daylight strategic bombing operations – formerly concentrated on northwestern Germany – were striking the greater part of the Reich. This development came as a result of the arrival of more and more American bombers, the deployment of long-range escort fighters and the opening of new bases in Italy. In May 1944, the German 6th Air Fleet, covering Army Group Centre, had only two groups (*Geschwadern*) of fighters (104 aircraft). In contrast, some twenty-nine groups of German day fighters were deployed in the home-defence Air Fleet 'Reich', and another thirteen in the 2nd and 3rd Air Fleets (in Italy and France, respectively). Reflecting the success of the Soviet strategic deception, the Luftwaffe's 4th Air Fleet in southern Russia (famous under Richtofen in 1941–2) was substantially stronger than the 6th Air Fleet in Belorussia: the 4th Air Fleet contained seven groups of day fighters and eleven of strike aircraft. The four Soviet army groups in Belorussia were supported in late June by five air armies, with a total of 5,300 combat aircraft.[28]

Evaluating the victory

How can we evaluate the importance of Operation BAGRATION as one of the great battles of the Eastern Front? It was not decisive, as the Soviet war was clearly already being won. It was not a 'turning point', more a sudden steepening of the Wehrmacht's angle of descent. The extended campaign in the Ukraine in 1943–4 was more important strategically, although it extended over a much greater time and space. Nevertheless, BAGRATION broke German resistance in the sector where it had always been stiffest. It also inflicted extremely heavy casualties on the *Ostheer*, more even than Stalingrad, and much more than Moscow or Kursk, as whole formations were trapped. Field Marshal Busch suffered the most crushing single defeat in the history of the German Army. In May 1944 – a relatively quiet period – German losses in the East had been only 48,000. In June 1944 they have been calculated as 142,000. In July they were 170,000 and in August they soared to 277,000. The July and August 1944 figures also need to be compared to the 180,000 counted as lost in the month of Stalingrad's agony, January 1943. (The high August 1944 figure includes major campaigns that were taking place elsewhere on the Eastern front, notably in the Baltic, Moldavia and northeastern Romania.) The total German losses in the East for June, July and August 1944, then, were 589,000. In contrast, the estimate for German losses on *all other* fronts – mainly in France – in the months June, July and August 1944 taken together was only 157,000. A remarkable number of the Axis losses in the East were POWs, which Russian sources give as 200,000.[29]

The Red Army had been victorious, but the human cost was high. The available Russian figures indicate that the Red Army suffered some 179,000 permanent losses in the 'Belorussian strategic offensive operation', but the number lost in Belorussia proper in July and early August was probably rather less, perhaps 125,000–150,000 in the course of July and August. The Soviets also lost 3,000 tanks and SP guns, and 820 combat aircraft. In contrast, the British and Americans lost (killed) in Normandy up to the breakout, some 30,000 personnel.[30] Red Army losses had, however, been higher in previous battles, when German resistance had been stiffer, or when the enemy had had greater initiative. In the various operations fought around Kursk in south central Russia in the previous summer, over a comparable period (the defence of the Kursk bulge, and in the Orel and Belgorod–Khar'kov counter-offensives, July to August 1943), personnel losses had been 254,000, as well as 6,050 tanks and 1,630 aircraft. And earlier Soviet battles had been even more costly: 479,000 personnel in the Stalingrad campaign (July 1942 to February 1943), 654,000 in the Moscow campaign (September 1941 to January 1942), and 486,000 in the 1941 Battle of Smolensk.

One event symbolic of the changing course of the Soviet–German front in the early summer of 1944 was the parade of 57,000 German POWs from Army Group Centre, including 19 generals, through the streets of Moscow on 17 July.[31] Some 16 of the German generals captured in the previous month in Belorussia signed an appeal against Hitler. A second event was the attempt on Hitler's life three days later, on 20 July. Hitler had moved back from his residence in the Bavarian Tyrol to his eastern headquarters at Rastenburg on 9 July. By coincidence, a group of officers on the staff of Army Group Centre had been among the leaders of the plot against Hitler.

REOCCUPYING THE BALTIC STATES

The Baltic states under German occupation

The Finns had been defeated in Karelia. The German Army had collapsed in Belorussia, and then in the Baltic republic of Lithuania. The next step in the reconquest of pre-war Soviet territory was the Red Army's entry into the other two Baltic republics, Estonia and Latvia. This was the Soviet Baltic operation, the eighth of the Stalinist 'crushing blows' of 1944.[32]

Thunder in the East

In the summer of 1940, the small independent states of Estonia, Latvia and Lithuania had been forcibly incorporated into the USSR as 'Soviet Socialist Republics' (SSRs). They had been subjected to a cruel Sovietization, including the forced deportation of tens of thousands of inhabitants. The Lithuanian SSR, the Latvian SSR and the Estonian SSR were then quickly overrun by the Wehrmacht in the summer of 1941. The 1940 annexation was a contradiction to the Atlantic Charter that the Soviets would sign in 1942. Even in the most difficult time of the war, the Russians demanded of the British and their other allies the recognition of their new borders, including the incorporation of the Baltic states. Unlike the situation with respect to Poland and its eastern border, Moscow's stand did not in the end cause great diplomatic ructions within the Alliance. Poland was a large state with a long history, a government in exile, and large forces fighting with the Allies. The populations of the Baltic states were small, and they appeared to have done little to protect their independence or to resist Nazi occupation. The largely non-Russian (and non-Slav) region had occupied an anomalous position in the Nazi system in the East as part of the *Reichskommissariat Ostland*. Many Balts regarded the Germans as the lesser of two evils, and a number of them undertook active collaboration. Some were enlisted in security detachments and police battalions, others in auxiliary military forces that were sent to the front against the Russians, as the Germans attempted to enlarge their manpower pool. The German Army and Himmler's SS competed for the Baltic manpower, and Himmler won. In 1942 Estonia provided the first unit of the 'eastern' SS, first an Estonian Legion, then a brigade. Latvia followed suit, and in the end three Waffen-SS divisions (one Estonian, two Latvian) were established.[33] In 1943 and 1944 compulsory conscription for these formations was decreed for men in a range of age groups. In the first half of 1944, with the Red Army now aligned along the eastern border of Latvia and Estonia (the *Ostwall*), there was some support for national defence against the Russians.[34]

In grand strategic terms, the region of the Baltic states was a secondary theatre for both sides. Unlike other areas, the region possessed no key raw materials to attract Hitler, and after Finland left the war in September 1944, it had little immediate strategic importance for the Wehrmacht. Its value to Hitler was the narrow technical one of covering the Baltic Sea U-boat training areas (west of Kurland). For the Russians, also, it did not have the highest priority. It was a detour from the main route to the Reich, and there was no danger of the British and Americans getting there first. But the Baltic was of historic and long-term strategic value, and Moscow wished to confirm its hold over this area.

The Soviet offensive in the Baltic

The Soviet operations against the Baltic involved, among other forces, General Bagramian's 1st Baltic Army Group. Bagramian was an Armenian, one of the few non-Russian (indeed, non-Slav) senior commanders in the Red Army. He was still only a colonel in June 1941, but held senior staff posts in the years of defeat. He narrowly escaped from the Kiev encirclement in 1941, and he was involved in the planning of the 1942 Khar'kov fiasco. Stalin did not hold him personally responsible, and Bagramian had successfully led infantry armies since the middle of 1942, and army groups since November 1943.[35] His 1st Baltic Army Group formed the right flank of the BAGRATION offensive. By mid-September 1944, Bagramian commanded five infantry armies; his mobile forces included two tank corps. Also taking part were the three northern Red Army formations that had not been involved in BAGRATION: Eremenko's 2nd Baltic Army Group (four infantry armies), Maslennikov's 3rd Baltic Army Group (three infantry armies), and the two infantry armies of Marshal Govorov's Leningrad Army Group that were operating south of Leningrad. Marshal Vasilevskii, who had co-ordinated the northern flank of Operation BAGRATION, was in overall control as Stavka representative.

Facing the Russians were the veterans of German Army Group North, the 18th and the 16th Armies. Generals Lindemann and Friessner had been removed as commanders of Army Group North in rapid succession in July 1944 for their failure to fulfil Hitler's orders to counter-attack during the Battle of Belorussia or to hold the line in the Baltic. Replacing Friessner on 23 July – three days after the assassination attempt at Rastenburg – was Ferdinand Schörner, one of Hitler's most fanatical generals. Schörner would be Hitler's penultimate – and youngest – field marshal (promoted on 5 April 1945). He had made his name as an energetic commander of mountain troops, especially in the Russian Arctic in 1942. In March 1944 he had replaced Field Marshal Kleist in Army Group 'A' (later renamed Army Group South Ukraine). At the same time, he was the head of the army's newly formed National Socialist Leadership Staff. In his new post in Army Group North, Schörner was given the 3rd Panzer Army from the left flank of Army Group Centre. The 3rd Panzer was now backing up into East Prussia, and elements of this formation were rushed into western Latvia to block the Red Army's advance towards the eastern frontier of the Reich proper. Although politically odious and a harsh disciplinarian, Schörner was skilful; the Soviet General Shtemenko described him as 'one of the most able of the German commanders'.[36]

The Baltic states had been insulated from the fighting from the autumn of 1941. First of all, there had been Army Group North's control of the Narva–Pskov–Leningrad triangle. Even after January 1944, the line of Lake Chud (Lake Peipus) and Lake Pskov, the northern part of Hitler's *Ostwall*, created a strong defensive position. Also important was German occupation of Belorussia, to the south, and German and Finnish naval control of the Gulf of Finland, to the north. A Soviet attempt to storm Narva in February 1944, partly to put pressure on the Finns, failed, and there had been other failures against Pskov and Ostrov. With the collapse of Army Group Centre, however, the German defensive position significantly worsened. The successful Soviet Pskov–Ostrov operation in July 1944 and the Tartu operation in August set up a starting point for the attack on the main part of Estonia and Latvia. (Pskov, Ostrov and Tartu had been counted among Hitler's 'fortified places'.) Maslennikov's 3rd Baltic Army Group had finally broken through and taken most of southeastern Estonia. Further north, the Leningrad Army Group had strengthened its position north of Lake Chud by finally taking Narva (26 July).[37]

The final Soviet Blitzkrieg into Estonia, part of the Baltic strategic operation, began on 14 September 1944. This was a week after the Finns left the war. The Leningrad Army

Group had now been given responsibility for the whole attack on the republic. The Soviet 8th Army attacked west from Narva; the 2nd Shock Army (a name famous from the battles of 1942 and 1943 on the Volkhov River) drove north from Tartu. Tallin, the capital of Estonia, fell on 23 September (D + 10), abandoned by the Germans. The main force of the attackers pushed on to the west coast of Estonia. Amphibious operations, carried out by small craft, overran the Baltic islands. A German garrison held out on the southern tip of the largest island, Saaremaa, where coastal guns on the Siaere peninsula commanded the deep-water entrance into the Gulf of Riga. The 'pocket battleships' *Admiral Scheer* and *Lützow* took turns to bombard the Soviet force besieging the narrow neck of the peninsula. The Germans finally abandoned the position at the end of November.

The fighting in Latvia and western Lithuania was much heavier than in Estonia. Riga, at the mouth of the Dvina, was the key position. It was a large city, with a population of 350,000 on the eve of the war. Riga saw mass deportation in the first Soviet takeover, then an even worse experience under the Nazis with the Riga ghetto and improvised death camps for the Jews. Bypassed in 1941, Riga was in 1944 the centre of the German military position in the Baltic. German Army Group North came very near catastrophe at the end of July 1944, when forward elements of Bagramian's 1st Baltic Army Group, approaching from the southeast, reached the Gulf of Riga just west of Riga, cutting Army Group North off from Army Group Centre. The Stavka on 28 July ordered the Soviet 2nd Baltic Army Group to take the city itself by no later than 10 August.[38] Fortunately for the Germans the Soviet force was reaching the physical limits of its advance. The Red Army had just stalled before the East Prussian border, and on 1 August they would be forced on to the defensive in front of Warsaw. The Soviet toehold on the Gulf was broken by German counter-attacks in mid-August supported by the heavy cruiser *Prinz Eugen*. In the glory days of Hitler's navy, *Prinz Eugen* had accompanied the *Bismarck* out into the Atlantic, and then returned to Germany in the 'Channel Dash'. For the Red Army, the early August battle near Riga was a tragic lost opportunity. Vasilevskii was unable to obtain the reinforcements needed to expand or even hold the window on the Gulf of Riga. Had Army Group North been cut off, many German troops could still have been evacuated by sea, but the campaign in the Baltic would have come to a close much earlier, and Soviet forces would have been freed for operations elsewhere.[39]

It would be a month before the Red Army was able to mount another attack on the Riga area. The attacking Soviet forces were now heavily reinforced at the expense of the 'inactive' army groups in the central theatre, primarily in Poland. A concentric attack on Riga by no fewer than three Soviet army groups (the 3rd, 2nd and 1st Baltic) was mounted in mid-September 1944. Unfortunately, the Germans had also been able to concentrate forces in the area. Dense defensive lines had been created, making full use of the lakes, swamps and woods. On 24 September, the Stavka took the important decision to change the main line of the attack. German Army Group North would be cut off, not at Riga, but 150 miles to the southwest, around Memel (Klaipeda). The axis of Bagramian's 1st Baltic Army Group was changed from north (towards Riga) to west (towards Memel) on the Baltic coast.

The biggest operation was Bagramian's drive 75 miles from Shiauliai to the Baltic coast near Memel. The 1st Baltic Army Group now comprised five infantry armies, as well as the 5th Guards Tank Army and two independent mobile corps. On the German side was the 3rd Panzer Army (now under General Raus); recuperating from a hammering in BAGRATION, it had been rushed into western Latvia when Riga was first threatened. The Soviet advance, which began on 5 October, was very rapid. Within five days, Bagramian's lead units had reached Palanga, 20 miles up the Baltic coast from Memel, cutting again – and finally – the land route of German Army Group North to the Reich. Memel itself was closely invested, and the Germans finally evacuated it by sea, after a three-month siege, in late January 1945. Meanwhile, Bagramian's southern army (the 2nd Guards), with the 39th Army from the 3rd Belorussian Army Group, had reached the Neman River and the old East Prussian border in the region of Tilsit.

The Soviet advance on Palanga and the threat to Saaremaa Island cut the land and sea approaches to Riga and meant that by early October, that city had lost its strategic significance. General Schörner – with Hitler's grudging permission – pulled the remains of German Army Group North out of Riga into the region of Kurland (Kurzeme, Courland), which had good natural defences and a seaborne supply line though Liepaia (Libau) and smaller ports. The Red Army fought its way through the suburbs of Riga and stormed the centre of the city on the following day, 13 October. West of Riga, at the defensive line at Tukums, the defenders of Kurland held off a series of attacks over the winter of 1944–5.

The final seven months of the war saw no further change. The Kurland pocket, some 90 miles across, was not much smaller than the Stalingrad pocket. The Stavka originally expected a quick victory. Noting the 'exceptional importance of the most rapid liquidation' of the Kurland pocket, the Stavka in mid-October 1944 ordered Marshal Vasilevskii to carry this out using the 1st and 2nd Baltic Army Groups and massed artillery and air power.[40] Quick victory there was not to be, and Kurland held out until the end of the war. It originally contained about 400,000 troops, the remains of the whole of German Army Group North. As at Stalingrad, the defenders fought bitter defensive battles. Unlike Stalingrad, Kurland could be supplied and evacuated by sea, despite harassing attacks by the submarines and aircraft of the Soviet Baltic Fleet, the former now based in ports in western Finland. In mid-January 1945 German Army Group North was given the more accurate name of Army Group Kurland. A new Army Group North was formed by renaming Army Group Centre in East Prussia. As the German military situation worsened in East Prussia and Pomerania in January and February 1945, German divisions had to be shipped there from Kurland. Schörner himself was flown out to take command of Army Group 'A' (later renamed Army Group Centre) in Poland, when the Soviet Vistula–Oder operation began in January 1945. He was replaced in turn by Generals Rendulic and Vietinghoff. When Germany finally capitulated, there were still 200,000 German troops in Kurland. A week after Hitler's death, on 10 May 1945, the remnants of Army Group Kurland laid down their arms and became Soviet POWs. The Leningrad Army Group would take 274,000 POWs in Kurland after 9 May.[41]

Estonia, Latvia and Lithuania were now part of the USSR again. Many people from these nationalities had compromised themselves in Soviet eyes during the German occupation, a considerable number having served in German uniform, notably that of the Waffen-SS. The anti-German partisan movement in the region had been half-hearted. Tens of thousands of Baltic nationals left with the Germans; some fled to the forests to continue a fitful guerrilla resistance, many were deported to the GULAG. 'Chekist-military operations' were carried out. Deputy Commissar of the NKVD Kruglov was sent with five internal security regiments to Lithuania.[42] The Balts were at least too large in numbers, and too close to western European (and especially Scandinavian) sensibilities, to be deported wholesale, as happened to other regions where the Kremlin saw collaboration, for example in the Crimea or the North Caucasus. Nevertheless, the Baltic peoples were brought back into the USSR, where they would stay until 1991.

CONCLUSION

The summer campaign had been a catastrophe for German strategy. The Germans' resources were limited in terms of manpower, equipment and fuel. By the time the Ukrainian campaign finished in the spring of 1944, Poland and East Prussia should have been the centres of German attention, not any region further east. The Wehrmacht's position in Belorussia and the Baltic was completely untenable. Once Belorussia had fallen, and once the government in Helsinki had surrendered, there was certainly no point in holding on to the Baltic states, or even Kurland. At the same time, the maintenance of a large German army in northern Finland and then in Norway made no sense. Given the collapse of Army Group Centre, it would have been better to pull back into the 'funnel' of central Europe, shortening the front line and freeing reserves.

Hitler's decisions possessed, as before, a kind of twisted logic. Just as the Crimea was needed by the Wehrmacht for a renewed thrust to the Caucasus, so the Baltic states were needed for a future attack against Leningrad. Withdrawal of the Wehrmacht, however skilfully executed, made strategic sense only if there was somewhere to withdraw to. From Hitler's 'all-or-nothing' point of view, there was no point in tactical withdrawals that prolonged the war for just a few more months.

For the Red Army, the 'crushing blows' in Karelia and Belorussia in 1944 counterbalanced two of its most crushing defeats, the Winter War of 1939–40 and the massacre of the Western Army Group in 1941. By September 1944 and the recapture of three more Soviet 'republics' in the Baltic, nearly all the territory of the USSR as of June 1941 had been brought back under Moscow's control. In his Revolution Day speech of 6 November, Stalin could boast of liberation: 'The Red Army has admirably fulfilled its patriotic duty and freed our Fatherland from the enemy. From now on and forever our land will be free of the Hitlerite filth.'[43] Facing the Red Army now was the prospect of fighting in central Europe, and in the Reich itself.

CHAPTER 12
THE MARCH INTO EASTERN EUROPE, JULY 1944 TO MAY 1945

But our tasks cannot be limited to expulsion of enemy forces from the borders of our Motherland.

Joseph Stalin, May 1944

This war is not as in the past; whoever occupies a territory also imposes on it his own social system. Everyone imposes his own system as far as his army has power to do so. It cannot be otherwise.

Joseph Stalin, April 1945

From Stettin in the Baltic to Trieste in the Adriatic, an iron curtain had descended across the Continent. Behind that line lie all the capitals of the ancient states of Central and Eastern Europe. Warsaw, Berlin, Prague, Vienna, Budapest, Belgrade, Bucharest and Sofia, all the famous cities and the populations around them lie in what I must call the Soviet sphere.

Winston Churchill, March 1946

EASTERN EUROPE: CONQUEST, LIBERATION, REVOLUTION

As far back as his radio speech of 3 July 1941, Stalin had emphasized that the struggle was not just a 'fatherland war' but also a 'war of liberation', a war of 'help to all the peoples of Europe who was suffering under the yoke of German fascism'. Previous chapters have been about fighting on Russian territory, or at least the fighting in regions that had been part of the USSR on 22 June 1941. These included the large western zone gained by Moscow as a result of the Nazi–Soviet Pact and the Winter War with Finland. The Red Army now had to fight campaigns on the *other* side of the 1941 border. As Stalin declared in his 1944 May Day speech: 'Our tasks cannot be limited to expulsion of enemy forces from the borders of our Motherland.'[1] For the next ten months, the Soviets would unleash one offensive after another, right across eastern Europe, in what was in military terms the most complex period of the war.

One background element was the common Allied interest in breaking up the enemy coalition in Europe. After the overthrow of Mussolini in July–August 1943, and the Italian surrender, the Allies appealed to the other Axis partners, especially Bulgaria,

Finland, Hungary and Romania, to take similar action. In the early spring of 1944, these smaller states became more anxious, as the Russians approached their pre-war frontiers. On the other hand, the Italian events, where Mussolini was overthrown but the Germans occupied two-thirds of the country, showed the risk of trying to change sides. On 13 May 1944 the Allies had sent notes to the governments of Romania, Hungary, Bulgaria (and Finland), warning them that the time had come to leave the collapsing Axis. Operations against the outer defences of the Third Reich began in the East and in the West at about the same time – June and July 1944. The Russian advance to the Reich through the belt of East European states coincided with the American and British advance through northern Italy, France and the Low Countries. The Red Army breakthrough into the Balkans from mid-August 1944 coincided with the extremely rapid advance of the American and British armies beyond the Seine River and a second landing in the south of France. By the end of September 1944, the western Allies had liberated most of France and Belgium.

At one time, an Allied victory seemed possible before the end of 1944, but then the advance slowed. Alsace-Lorraine and the Rhineland remained in German hands, as the enemy settled in behind the fixed defences of the *Westwall*. With the failure of the Arnhem airborne operation in the Netherlands (mid-September 1944), the Western Allies could not immediately establish a bridgehead over the lower Rhine River. The stiffening resistance of the German forces against the Red Army in Hungary in October–November 1944 was matched by continuing resistance along the Rhine. In mid-December 1944 Hitler used forces that had been accumulated, partly at the expense of the Nazi–Soviet front, to launch an offensive with four armies in the West. This came out of the Ardennes Forest in the direction of the Belgian port of Antwerp and is known as the 'Battle of the Bulge'.

The relative state of the Wehrmacht and the Red Army resembled the situation during the Battle of Belorussia. The German forces were shattered and dispersed; they lacked reserves and a rational command structure. The Russians had made great strides in their ability to conduct operations. The same Soviet commanders were in charge, although the role of Vasilevskii and Zhukov changed from co-ordination to the actual command of several army groups.[2] There were, however, three major potential changes from the situation in Belorussia. First, the Red Army was now operating over very long supply lines, just as the Wehrmacht had been in 1941, 1942 and 1943. The extreme case was that of the Soviet formations that advanced across the ravaged Ukraine, through Romania, and into Hungary. The logistic problems were nearly as great for those army groups that crossed Poland to the Oder. Especially important was the need to transfer goods from 'Union' (i.e. Soviet Union) gauge railways (5ft) to 'Western European' gauge (4ft 8.5in). This led to much conflict even with 'friendly' civil authorities, for example when branch lines were torn up to prepare the right of way for the east–west trunk lines needed to supply the Red Army. The Wehrmacht, for its part, now had shorter and more secure supply lines behind it, and in the eastern part of the Reich those railways and road systems had not been badly damaged by air attacks. The second and related change was that it was now the *Germans* rather than the Russians who were operating on what the military call 'interior lines'. They could move large forces from theatre to theatre with relative ease. Finally, the essence of Soviet actions in 1941–4 had been the defence of the Motherland. It was now the Germans who were defending the distant approaches to their homeland.

There were, as was suggested in the beginning of this book, two aspects to Stalinist Russia's relations with eastern Europe and the outside world more generally. This relationship involved what has aptly been called the 'revolutionary-imperial paradigm'.[3] The first aspect of the paradigm was political transformation through revolution; the second was territorial gain. How this was all thought of within the People's Commissariat of Foreign Affairs (NKID or *Narkomindel*) is still not fully clear; even less clear is the real thinking of Stalin and Molotov. Some sense of Soviet perspectives and war aims in eastern Europe, however, is given in papers on future policy which were drafted by two 'elder statesmen' early in 1944. Ivan Maiskii is best known as the Ambassador to Britain in 1932–43. Maksim Litvinov had served from 1930 to 1939 as People's Commissar of Foreign Affairs; in 1941–3, he was Ambassador to the United States. Both men were rare survivors of a revolutionary generation of NKID staff that had been slaughtered in Stalin's purges; both now held the rank of Deputy People's Commissar, under Molotov. Litvinov was in charge of the NKID commission formed in late 1943 to consider the peace treaties, and Maiskii of another commission charged with considering reparations.[4]

The basis of policy for Maiskii, writing at the start of 1944 as the Red Army assembled on the borders of eastern Europe, was safeguarding the Soviet Union: 'It is necessary to secure for the USSR peace in Europe and Asia for a period of 30–50 years. … With this in view, the USSR must come out of the present war with advantageous strategic borders, which must be based on the borders of 1941.' He also wrote, 'This does not exclude, of course, the possibility of partial modification of the borders (for example with Poland, with Romania, with Finland, etc.) depending on our gains or the necessity to take into account the policies of the USA and Britain.' The way People's Commissar Molotov put it, much later, was simpler: 'My task as minister of foreign affairs was to expand the borders of our fatherland. And it seems that Stalin and I coped with this task quite well.'[5] Perhaps here an old man was speaking for effect, but his words fitted well with his crude world view and his rough tactics.

The territorial (imperial) side of Soviet policy was more straightforward than the political side. It certainly had nothing to do with the Atlantic Charter, which Roosevelt and Churchill had put forward in August 1941, and which the Soviets had accepted. The signatories to the Charter espoused 'certain common principles'; they sought 'no aggrandizement, territorial or other', and 'no territorial changes that do not accord with the freely expressed wishes of the peoples concerned'; 'they respect the right of all peoples to choose the form of government under which they will live; and they wish to see sovereign rights and self-government restored to those who have been forcibly deprived of them'. Although the signatories were applying these principles against Germany, Italy and Japan, they could equally be applied to Soviet policy in 1939–40, or from 1944 onwards. For historical, ethnographical and strategic reasons, the USSR claimed territories from neighbouring states: all of the Baltic republics and parts of Czechoslovakia, Finland, Romania and Poland. Moscow had already made its demands ruthlessly clear with the annexations of 1939–40; hence the importance of 'the borders of 1941'. This meant that there could be no negotiation about annexations made at the expense of Finland, Poland and Romania. It meant, too, that the fate of three of the ten East European states was resolved in advance. There was no reference to Lithuania, Latvia or Estonia in Maiskii's paper; they had already ceased to exist as states from the Soviet point of view.

Traditional strategic diplomacy also affected Maiskii's view of two other East European states, Finland and Romania. These two countries were given a special place in the Soviet security scheme. We have already seen how Finland had negotiated with the USSR from the beginning of 1944 and had finally made terms. While these involved loss of territory by the Finns, and even the granting of a Soviet base near Helsinki, the concessions could have been greater. Maiskii had proposed

> a long-term pact of mutual support [*vzaimopomoshch'*] between the USSR, on one side, and Finland and Romania on the other, with the USSR being granted a sufficient number of bases – army, air force, and naval – on the territories of the countries named. Besides this the USSR must be linked with Finland and Romania by a system of railways and highways [which are] important both strategically and economically.

This was imperial, rather than revolutionary, but the Finns were probably fortunate to get off as lightly as they did; the Romanians lost more. Stalin had been brutally frank in discussion about Finland at the time of the Winter War: 'There should be nothing left but the bare bones of a state.' 'We have no desire for Finland's territory,' he said. 'But Finland should be a state that is friendly to the Soviet Union.'[6]

In their search to build 'conventional' influence in eastern Europe, the Russians also attempted to play the Slav card. This had an effect in Slav Bulgaria, Czechoslovakia, Poland and Yugoslavia; it did not win support in non-Slav Finland, Hungary and Romania, or in the former Baltic states. This had something in common with the pan-Slav ideology of Imperial Russia, and it was a means of building cohesion between Russians, Ukrainians and Belorussians at home. It was also a response to the racist ideology of Hitler's Germany. The first All-Slav Anti-Fascist Meeting (*miting*) was held in Moscow in August 1941, and half a dozen followed to April 1944. After the first meeting, an All-Slavic Committee was set up in October 1941, which eventually had Russian, Ukrainian, Belorussian, Polish, Czech and South Slav sections. Stalin himself embraced the notion, despite the fact that he was a (non-Slav) Georgian by birth and a Marxist–Leninist internationalist by conviction. In early 1945, speaking to a visiting Czechoslovak delegation, Stalin actually described himself as a 'new Slavophil-Leninist'.[7]

The political or revolutionary side of the Soviet 'revolutionary-imperial paradigm' was more complex. It lies at the heart of debates about the nature of the Cold War. The USSR wanted 'friendly' governments, governments with which it would conclude treaties of mutual assistance, but it is still not clear whether from the start these were intended to be Communist governments. Maiskii's early 1944 view was that as far as the states occupied by Germany were concerned, 'the state structure … should be based on the principles of wide (*shirokaia*) democracy in the spirit of the ideas of the popular front'. Maiskii was speaking from the point of view of the People's Commissariat of Foreign Affairs rather than that of the Comintern, let alone that of Stalin. Nevertheless, it was relevant that he pointed out that the nature of the post-war states could lead to conflict with the British, and especially the Americans who, he maintained, supported more conservative political forces.[8]

The USSR was, after all, a revolutionary state, and the Communist International (Comintern) had been created in 1919 to further the cause of world revolution.[9] People's Commissar Molotov was a revolutionary. His statement at the 15th Party Conference in 1926 is well known: 'The policy of our party is and remains the policy of the victory of socialism in our country and together with that the policy of the final triumph of socialism on an international scale.' He cited this in the recollections of his retirement years, and he stood by it.[10] The latest evidence does seem to confirm the 'traditional' view among Cold War historians that Stalin had no illusions about long-term co-operation with the capitalist West. He made the following remark to Soviet and East European Communist leaders in 1945 on the eve of the Yalta Conference:

> The crisis of capitalism had manifested itself in the division of the capitalists into two factions – one *fascist*, the other *democratic*. The alliance between ourselves and the democratic faction of the capitalists came about because the latter had a stake in preventing Hitler's domination. … We are currently allied with one faction against the other, but in the future we will be against the first faction of capitalists too.

In April 1945 he told the Yugoslav Communist Milovan Djilas that the imminent victory would involve expanding the Soviet system. 'This war is not as in the past; whoever occupies a territory also imposes on it his own social system. Everyone imposes his own system as far as his army has power to do so. It cannot be otherwise.'[11]

In the late 1930s, the Soviets had groomed a new generation of apparently 'reliable' East European Communist leaders in Moscow. These people returned home, and in the late 1940s emerged as the leaders of Communist states. Examples were Bierut in Poland, Tito in Yugoslavia, Pauker in Romania, Rákosi in Hungary. The numbers involved were relatively small. The External Policy Department (OVP) of the CC reported in 1947 that 2,000 political émigrés had been returned from the USSR to their home countries.[12]

On the other hand, proletarian revolution seemed a long way away. Whatever Stalin's real sentiments about the other great powers, especially the United States and Britain, those states were very powerful militarily and economically, and politically they showed no signs of imminent conversion to Bolshevism.[13] Close co-operation with the 'bourgeois' great powers would prevent – as a worst case – their rapprochement with Germany, and help bring about a post-war settlement favourable to the USSR. There is an oft-cited passage from Djilas's memoirs which is indicative of Stalin's caution: he warned the Yugoslav Partisans against wearing red stars on their caps, as this would alarm the British and Americans. The same point was made in the official record of Molotov's (earlier) talks with Djilas. 'At the present time the situation at the battle fronts with Germany is one in which the Allies will be more active, and for us it is important to have good relations with them during this period.'[14] The most striking manifestation of this was the disbanding of the Comintern in the spring of 1943. The question is whether this moderation was a long-term policy, linked to positive relations with the West, or whether it was a short-term tactical manoeuvre, designed to mislead the West – while building up an impregnable position in the states liberated from Nazi rule. The Comintern centre lived on through other Soviet agencies, especially the International Information Department (OMI) of the Central Committee (CC) of the Soviet Communist Party.

Not only did the Kremlin have ambivalent policies, it also had to deal with independently minded local Communists outside the borders of the USSR. There were rivalries between the comrades who fought at home in the wartime resistance and those who had been in exile in the USSR before the war, and stayed there after 1941 to become Moscow's 'cadres'. It was not that the Communist resistance leaders were necessarily any more moderate than the 'Muscovites'; if anything, the problem for Stalin was that they were too radical, wanting to push ahead too rapidly, 'sectarian' in relation to other parties, insensitive to the worries of the British and the Americans. The extreme example was Tito in Yugoslavia.[15]

Up until the summer and autumn of 1944 and the ejection of the Nazis, the fate of eastern Europe was hypothetical. After that the Russians did come into conflict with the British and Americans about post-war eastern Europe, both the new borders and the nature of the governments. Maiskii was right to detect a greater interest and flexibility on the part of the British as opposed to the Americans. Prime Minister Churchill, both a realist and an imperialist, hoped to use traditional policies of spheres of influence to resolve the competition over parts of eastern Europe (beyond Poland). As a realist he knew he could have little influence in territories occupied by the Red Army, and he feared Communist-supported guerrillas in areas taken over by the British. In May 1944 he proposed to Stalin that the Soviet government should 'take the lead in Romanian affairs', while the British would do the same in Greece.[16] His view was not that of Roosevelt; the American president did not like the British making separate deals with the Russians. Churchill, however, attempted to push his own concept further, when he visited Moscow in October 1944 for the British–Soviet TOLSTOY conference. This was right in the middle of the big eastern European battles discussed in this chapter. The best-known outcome was the so-called 'percentages agreement', which attempted to establish levels of influence (expressed in percentage terms) across all of southern central Europe, that is, in the Danube basin and the Balkans. Churchill conceded the Russians 90 per cent influence in Romania and 75 per cent in Bulgaria (both just occupied by the Red Army), in exchange for British 90 per cent predominance in Greece (still nominally under German control). In Hungary and Yugoslavia, under the initial version of the 'agreement', Soviet and non-Soviet influence was supposed to be equal; each would have 50 per cent.[17]

Whatever agreement Churchill and Stalin came to, the fact was that real power in most of eastern Europe was held by the Red Army. This put the local Communists in a position of relative strength and weakened non-Communist elements. Behind the Red Army lurked the secret police, the NKVD-NKGB. Originally called the Cheka, it was an organization even older and more powerful than the Red Army. Its leader, Beria, was a member of the GKO. Each Soviet army group had a powerful police office attached to it (latterly as 'plenipotentiary of the NKVD'); in the case of the 1st Belorussian and the 1st Ukrainian Army Groups, these were I. A. Serov and L. F. Tsanava. What were called 'operational-Chekist methods' were applied against the best organized nationalist groups (the term *Cheka* was commonly used for the Soviet secret police). This was especially important in Poland, where there existed an extensive nationalist and anti-Communist underground in the form of the Home Army (*Armia Krajowa* or AK). In mid-December 1944, on the eve of the great offensive, the GKO issued instructions to the NKVD on the defence of the rear area of the Soviet army in East Prussia and Central Europe.[18]

Above all, however, the instrument for spreading Soviet control over eastern Europe was the Red Army. It incorporated the two parts of the 'revolutionary-imperial paradigm'. Its revolutionary potential dated back well before Stalin's time, when Lenin in 1920 had hoped to use the Red Army to crush the resistance of counter-revolutionary forces and allow a breakthrough to the German proletariat. Another of Stalin's remarks to Dimitrov, although made in connection with the Winter War against Finland, is also indicative of his attitude on this issue. Military conquest and international revolution were welded together in Stalin's mind: 'World revolution as a single act is nonsense. It transpires at different times in different countries. The Red Army activities are also a matter of world revolution.'[19] The same sentiments probably existed in 1944. But first it was necessary to defeat the Wehrmacht.

TO THE VISTULA AND BEYOND: THE CAMPAIGNS FOR POLAND

Poland and the USSR

The Red Army fought two hard campaigns in Poland in 1944–5; nearly half a year elapsed between them. The Soviet offensive in eastern Poland began in mid-July 1944, with the L'vov–Sandomierz and Lublin–Brest operations. By the second half of the following month, the Red Army had closed up to the line of the Vistula River and its northern tributary, the Narew. Soviet engineers threw bridgeheads across both rivers. The Germans, for their part, had been driven from about a quarter of ethnic Poland.[20] Then the front line in Poland locked into immobility for five months. The main action on the Nazi–Soviet front shifted to other theatres – to the Baltic, East Prussia and the Balkans. The second round in Poland, the Vistula–Oder operation, began only in January 1945. Soviet tanks and troops poured out of the Vistula–Narew bridgeheads, and across central and western Poland. In early February, after a four-week campaign, Red Army spearheads reached the Oder River in Germany.

It was a paradox, but just as the Red Army advanced to deliver Poland from a particularly cruel Nazi occupation, the Kremlin had virtually severed relations with the Polish government-in-exile in London. Despite common Slavic roots, antipathy ran deep between the Catholic Poles and the Orthodox Russians. When Poland was partitioned between its big neighbours at the end of the eighteenth century, the larger part of the country had been swallowed up by the Russian Empire. Two bloody Polish uprisings were fought against Russian domination, in 1830 and 1863.

At the end of the First World War, a new independent Poland was reassembled from territories of the defeated European empires. Territorial and political conflict between the new Poland and Soviet Russia escalated to all-out war in 1920. The Poles briefly held Kiev and Minsk; the Red Army in its counter-offensive nearly took L'vov (Lwów) and Warsaw. The British Foreign Minister, Lord Curzon, acting as an intermediary of sorts, tried to lay down an ethnographical border between Poles and non-Poles. The Soviet–Polish War of 1920, however, left Poland holding extensive territories in the east beyond the 'Curzon Line' including the 'historic' Polish cities of Wilno (Vil'nius) and Lwów. The government in Warsaw, from the mid-1920s dominated by the Army, made little attempt to come to terms with the 'Muscovites' (i.e. the USSR). The Soviet Communists, for their part, saw Poland as an aggressive puppet of French and British imperialism. In 1939 Stalin accepted Hitler's proposals for the extinction of Poland as a state. The Red Army took by force the territories to the east of the Curzon Line; this left, as Stalin privately put it in September 1939, 'one fewer bourgeois fascist state to contend with'. Of the population of thirteen million in the lands annexed by the USSR, most were Ukrainians or Belorussians, but as many as five million were ethnic Poles.[21]

Even when the USSR became de facto an ally of Poland on 22 June 1941, there remained fundamental misunderstandings. Maiskii's confidential notes of the winter of January 1944 are probably an accurate summary of feelings in Moscow:

> In the past Poland was almost always an enemy of Russia, and whether a future Poland will in reality be a friend of the USSR (at least in the lifetime of the present generation) no one can say with certainty. ... In view of the above, post-war Poland is to be formed with caution with the minimum size, strictly following the principle of the ethnographic border. Put concretely, the eastern border of Poland must follow the border of 1941 or something close to it (for example the 'Curzon Line'), and [the cities] of L'vov and Vil'no must in any event remain within the borders of the USSR.[22]

The eastern frontier of Poland remained an irreconcilable problem. On top of this was the very bitter taste for the Poles of the recent Soviet collusion with Hitler and the deportation deep into the USSR of over a million ethnic Poles from the Soviet-annexed regions. In April 1943 the Germans revealed their discovery of mass graves at Katyn in Smolensk Region; here the Soviet NKVD had executed several thousand imprisoned Polish officers in early 1940. Shortly afterwards, relations between the Polish government-in-exile in London and the USSR were broken off. At the Tehran Conference in late 1943, the Big Three provisionally agreed – in the absence of the Poles – to accept the Curzon Line, compensating Poland with former German territory to the west and north. The London-based Polish government-in-exile was never reconciled to the loss of territory to the Soviet Union, and neither were many of the Poles who joined the main anti-Nazi underground in Poland, the Home Army.

The summer 1944 campaign

Meanwhile, in early July 1944 the possibilities of a Polish campaign were being discussed in the Soviet high command. Marshal Zhukov assured Stalin that the Red Army was capable of going to the Vistula River and establishing large bridgeheads on the western side. The Polish campaign of July and early August 1944 was the first major Russian strategic offensive after the stunning success of Operation BAGRATION in Belorussia. In many respects, it was equally successful. Essentially, the advance took the Red Army 150–200 miles across one German defensive river line and on to another. The first line was the Western Bug (effectively the 1941 border of the USSR – also the Curzon Line), which it had reached at the end of July 1944; the second was the Vistula–Narew line. The breadth of the front from north to south was some 350–400 miles. The offensive had two wings: in the north, the Lublin–Brest operation of Rokossovskii's 1st Belorussian Army Group, and in the south, the L'vov–Sandomierz operation of Marshal Konev's 1st Ukrainian Army Group.[23]

The L'vov–Sandomierz operation was carried out by Konev against Field Marshal Model's German Army Group North Ukraine, the former Army Group South. The 1st Ukrainian Army Group was the largest single formation in the Red Army. Konev commanded seven infantry armies. The main mobile forces were the 1st and 3rd Guards Tank Armies (under Gordov and Rybalko), and the 4th Tank Army (Leliushenko), plus four independent mobile corps. Konev's operation began on 13 July 1944, just three weeks after the opening of Operation BAGRATION. Starting from a position in the western central Ukraine, Konev's armies drove to the natural lines of the Carpathian Mountains (to the south) and to the Vistula River (to the west). They occupied all of the territory of the western Ukraine (Galicia) – so fought over in the First World War.

Galicia, centred on the city of L'vov, had been held by Austria after the eighteenth-century Partitions and regained by an independent Poland in 1918. It had then been invaded twice by the Russians. The first attempt in 1920 was unsuccessful; a Soviet army group spearheaded by Budennyi's Red Cavalry – with Stalin as its commissar – had been stopped by the Poles in front of L'vov. In 1939 another Red Army, this time with Nikita Khrushchev as commissar, successfully occupied the region.[24] By the fourth day of the 1944 penetration, the lead Soviet tank units were over the Bug and racing for the next river line, 60 miles to the west, the San. The major objective reached by Konev's armies was a bridgehead over the upper Vistula River, near the little town of Sandomierz. The first Soviet units forced the Vistula in this sector on 29 July, and Sandomierz itself was finally captured on 18 August. There would be fierce battles in the following weeks for the

FIGURE 11 Red Army forces cross a river in the western Ukraine, near L'vov.

Sandomierz bridgehead. (The Germans called this battlefield the Baranow bridgehead, after another nearby Polish town.)

As the tank columns on Konev's right wing were racing west to the San and the Vistula, other forces on his left wing encircled a concentration of 40–50,000 German troops near Brody. Rybalko's tanks did not succeed in taking L'vov off the march, but the city was encircled and fell on D + 14 of the L'vov–Sandomierz operation (27 July 1944). L'vov had a pre-war population of 340,000, mainly ethnic Poles, and it was an important transport hub, the junction of the east–west and north–south rail lines. As we have seen, the city was one of the main territorial issues at stake between the Kremlin and the London Poles, but it was situated on the 'Russian' side of the Curzon Line.

On 18 July, five days after Konev's attack and twenty-six days after the start of Operation BAGRATION, the offensive of the 1st Belorussian Army Group began. The dash to the Vistula was to be the finest moment of its commander, Marshal Konstantin Konstantinovich Rokossovskii.[25] Rokossovskii had won his marshal's baton in late June 1944, and he had played an important part in the campaigns of the past three years. When the war began, he was in command of a mechanized corps in the Ukraine, but in July 1941 he was quickly shifted to command forces on the Smolensk sector under Timoshenko. In the autumn he commanded an army in the western theatre, and after surviving the Battle of Viaz'ma–Briansk his forces stood directly in front of Moscow and then helped push German Army Group Centre back to the west. During the German 1942 summer offensive, Rokossovskii held a number of army-group-level posts before being given command of the Don Army Group to the north of Stalingrad in September. He led the Don Army Group in the great battle for the city, and most memorably in Operation RING, the final destruction of Paulus and the Stalingrad pocket. In 1943 Rokossovskii commanded the Central Army Group, defending the northern side of the Kursk bulge; in 1944 he led this army group, now designated the 1st Belorussian, in the drive to the west. The Marshal's personal background was now of particular interest: Rokossovskii (the Polish version of his name was Rokossowski) was an ethnic Pole.[26] His father and mother were Polish, and he had attended secondary school in Warsaw when it was part of the Russian Empire. He had suffered greatly for his ethnicity in Stalin's purges; he was arrested in August 1937 and spent two and a half years in prison. In 1949, he would take Polish citizenship and be made by Stalin Minister of Defence of the Polish People's Republic, as Cold War forces were built up.

The main axis of Rokossovskii's advance was about 100 miles to the north of Konev's. In this Lublin–Brest operation, the forces of Rokossovskii's 1st Belorussian Army Group were initially divided by the marshes of the Poleśe (roughly at the latitude of Brest). Rokossovskii had available for this operation five infantry armies to the south of Brest and three to the north. His mobile force was Bogdanov's 2nd Tank Army, along with three other tank or cavalry corps organized as a 'mobile group'. Within two days, Rokossovskii's lead elements were over the Bug River. Then Bogdanov's tanks raced ahead to take Chełm and Lublin, something that was achieved on 22 July and 24 July, respectively (D + 4 and D + 6 of Rokossovskii's operation).

Chełm and Lublin were the first major Polish towns which the Red Army had captured beyond the pre-war borders of the USSR.[27] Both towns would play an important role in Polish politics. A Russian-sponsored authority, the Polish Committee of National Liberation (PKWN), was immediately established in Chełm, and shortly afterwards the PKWN was moved to the larger town of Lublin. Stalin on 21 July had ordered Zhukov and Rokossovskii to take Lublin with their tank formations no later than 26–7 July, adding an unusual political explanation: 'The political situation and the interests of an independent democratic Poland urgently demand this.'[28] (Marshal Zhukov, as already mentioned, was in overall charge of the 1st and 2nd Belorussian and the 1st Ukrainian Army Groups.) A very senior party official, Nikolai Bulganin, was attached to the PKWN. In January 1945 the PKWN would be transformed into a Communist-dominated Provisional Government, and shortly afterwards transferred to Warsaw. There was a second extraordinary non-military side to this particular Soviet advance. West of Lublin, Soviet troops uncovered the first of the German death camps, at Majdanek. The Nazis had sited three other extermination camps in this part of eastern Poland: Treblinka, Sobibor and Belzec. Altogether, well over a million Jews had been systematically murdered here. (The largest of the Nazi death camps, Auschwitz-Birkenau, was in south central Poland, west of Kraków. It would be taken by the Red Army only in late January 1945, during the West Carpathian operation.)

Meanwhile, the headlong advance of Rokossovskii's 1st Belorussian Army Group continued. Bogdanov was seriously injured in the outskirts of Lublin, but General Radzievskii took over his 2nd Tank Army. The tank army reached the central Vistula River, some 120 miles from its starting point, on 26 July (D + 7). The mobile columns then turned north up the east bank of the river towards Warsaw. The main part of the former Polish capital was on the west bank of the Vistula, but forward Soviet elements on 31 July were aimed towards the fortified suburb of Praga, on the east bank. Chuikov's 8th Guards Army had on its own initiative established a bridgehead over the Vistula at Magnuszew, about 50 miles south of Warsaw, on 1 August. By this time, Rokossovskii's other northern armies had encircled and captured Brest (28 July, D + 9). Marshal Rokossovskii himself was awarded the Hero of the Soviet Union medal.

The success of the first weeks of the Soviet campaign in eastern Poland is easy enough to explain. The Wehrmacht had been thrown completely off balance after the late June catastrophe in Belorussia. It had few reserves. General Josef Harpe's Army Group North Ukraine totalled only forty divisions.[29] Harpe had had to send several divisions to fill the gap left by the destruction of his neighbour to the north, German Army Group Centre. At this moment, too, the German forces had an extraordinary command problem. The bomb under Hitler's table at Rastenburg exploded on 20 July, a week after the Soviet offensive into Poland. General Heinz Guderian took over as Chief of the Army General Staff (vacant since Zeitzler's departure, following a nervous breakdown, at the end of June). The pioneer of German armoured warfare and the 'panzer leader' in campaigns in France and Russia had been removed from operational command since the Moscow crisis of December 1941. He was not, either then or later, to be the saviour of the situation. His proposed solution to the immediate crisis was a large-scale counter-attack between the Vistula and the Bug, which was an entirely unrealistic course of action.[30]

Despite their setbacks and weaknesses, the Germans won a major battle, arguably a vitally important one, in the first days of August; this was fought out some 12 miles northeast of Warsaw. Radzievskii's 2nd Tank Army, subordinate to Rokossovskii's 1st Belorussian Army Group, had been driving rapidly to the northwest up the right bank of the Vistula, in front of German-occupied Warsaw. The spearhead was the Soviet 3rd Tank Corps (effectively an armoured division), which on 31 July was less than 5 miles from the strategic crossing of the Narew River at Serock. (The Narew is a tributary of the Vistula, and runs into it from the northeast, a few miles downstream from Warsaw.) Over the next four days, Field Marshal Model – who had just taken over direct control of Army Group North Ukraine – organized a brilliant operational counter-attack, employing elements of four German armoured divisions. The Soviet 3rd Tank Corps was cut off and heavily damaged, and the rest of the tank army was halted well south of the Narew.

Model's battle has no name. In the official German history, Karl-Heinz Frieser simply used the term '*die Panzerschlacht vor Warschau*' ('the tank battle in front of Warsaw'). Russian historians sometimes call it the Battle of Radzymin or the Battle of Wołomin, from nearby Polish towns. Soviet historians mostly ignored it. Frieser, in contrast, suggests that the battle should be seen as a repeat of the August 1914 Battle of Tannenberg, based on the possible Soviet intention to cross the Narew River and drive north across East Prussia to the Baltic (see Maps 9 and 10); this repeated the operations of the Tsarist General Samsonov at the start of the First World War. Had this operation been successfully carried out in 1944, it would indeed have cut German Army Group Centre and Army Group North off from the Reich, collapsed the entire German eastern front and possibly ended the war.[31]

Marshal Zhukov certainly envisaged such an operation. On 19 July – the same day he was appointed Stavka co-ordinator of the 1st and 2nd Belorussian, and 1st Ukrainian

Army Groups – he proposed to Stalin that the immediate next step of the 1st, 2nd and 3rd Belorussian Army Groups should be an advance from the Vistula to Danzig Bay, with the aim of occupying all of East Prussia, or at least cutting it off from central Germany. And on the 28th the Stavka gave orders for Rokossovskii to establish a major bridgehead north of the Narew, which would have been the starting point for such an advance.[32]

With his vision of a war-winning Soviet drive across East Prussia, Frieser may have may have taken too seriously the fears of German intelligence in 1944. It is worth recalling that Operation BAGRATION in Belorussia has succeeded well beyond the expectations of Stalin and the Stavka, and planning for the next stage of the war was probably only just beginning. The leading Soviet army groups had advanced several hundred miles, and it was not realistic to expect a continued attack into the difficult and well-defended territory of East Prussia – unless the whole German Army or the government of the Third Reich collapsed. The situation was, to be sure, complicated both by the attempted assassination of Hitler on 20 July and by the beginning of the uprising in Warsaw on 1 August. In any event, Model had certainly effected one of the last striking operational victories of the German Army. Zhukov in his memoirs praised the German field marshal for his successful mobile defence.[33]

At about the same time (23 July 1944), Marshal Zhukov had made an ambitious suggestion for the future operations in southern Poland of Konev's 1st Ukrainian Army Group, then in the tenth day of its own L'vov–Sandomierz offensive (see Map 11). He proposed that after breaking across the upper Vistula, Katukov's 1st Guards Tank Army should continue northwest towards Kielce, while Rybalko's 3rd Guards Tank Army drove west 100 miles, bypassing Kraków to the north – an operation uncannily like the Soviet pre-war plan of 1941 (see Chapter 2). The Stavka thought this too ambitious, and it also rejected Konev's own proposal to dash forward to Częstochowa (halfway to the Oder) by mid-August.[34] In the end Częstochowa would not be taken until 17 January 1945.

The front in Poland now became static for six months, and 29 August 1944 was to be an important turning point. On that day the Stavka ordered the 1st, 2nd and 3rd Belorussian Army Groups to shift to 'strict defence'. Similar orders were also sent to the 4th and the 1st Ukrainian Army Groups facing the northern Carpathians.[35] Attention and offensive activity were now to be centred on the flanks of the great advance. The 3rd (Tolbukhin) and the 2nd Ukrainian (Malinovskii) Army Groups were now advancing rapidly into Romania. The orders their commanders were sent on 29 August instructed them to go, respectively, to the borders with Bulgaria and Hungary. On the same day, in the north, the 2nd Baltic Army Group was ordered to launch its offensive against Riga, with a scheduled date of 5–7 September; the Germans were believed to be sending strong reinforcements to this sector. The 3rd Baltic Army Group continued a more limited attack into eastern Estonia, the Tartu operation. Also on the 29 August, Vasilevskii was ordered to concentrate his personal attention on the three Baltic army groups, giving up the 3rd Belorussian Army Group facing East Prussia.[36]

The Red Army stood still at the line of the Vistula and Narew rivers. The Russians could not break out of their Vistula bridgeheads at Sandomierz, at Magnuszew and Puławy south of Warsaw, or out of their Narew River bridgeheads at Serock and Rózan, northeast of the city. In a speech on Stalin's military abilities written in 1956 (but not delivered), Zhukov singled out the Narew offensives for criticism:

> The operations north of Warsaw were carried out in an exceptionally incompetent manner [*iskliuchitel'no bezgramotno*], as a result of which many tens of thousands of our people were killed. It was repeatedly reported to Stalin that the conditions of the locality made it impossible to carry out the operation there, but such conclusions were rejected as 'half-baked', and the operation was repeated several times with one and the same result.[37]

About three-quarters of Poland remained under German occupation for six more months, including Warsaw and the other major cities. A broad explanation for this, aside from the demands of the other fronts on which the Red Army was fighting, would include the shorter and more easily defended German front, with closer communications to the Reich, and interior lines. The front line was about 250 miles long and held by German Army Group Centre and Army Group 'A' (formerly Army Group North Ukraine). This front, moreover, was anchored in East Prussia to the north and the Carpathian Mountains to the south. The Warsaw area, particularly the Narew River line, was important to the Germans for defending the approaches to East Prussia, and the Germans concentrated their forces there.

The Warsaw uprising

Most of Warsaw lies on the western side of the Vistula, but the suburb of Praga is on the eastern bank. On 31 July Soviet forward elements from the 2nd Tank Army, from Rokossovskii's army group, approached Praga, which had suddenly become a *German* bridgehead. The thunder of the distant artillery could be heard by people in central Warsaw. On the afternoon of 1 August, the Polish nationalist Home Army rose in revolt. The city would then be the scene of violent street fighting for over two months; only on 2 October did the surviving insurgents surrender.[38] Although the resistance fighters originally numbered several tens of thousands, there were arms and ammunition for only a fraction of these. The battle in the city was a police action fought by notorious SS elements, including the Kaminski Brigade (composed of former Soviet citizens) and the Dirlewanger Brigade (formed from German common criminals). Warsaw was also subjected to bombing and artillery bombardment by the regular Wehrmacht. Altogether about 200,000 civilians were killed in this tragedy. In Hitler's reprisals, many of the town's surviving buildings were intentionally demolished.

Bitter controversy still surrounds the Warsaw Uprising. Some historians accuse Stalin of leaving the insurgents to their fate, and even of provoking the uprising to bring about the destruction of the nationalist underground by the Germans. What happened has no simple explanation. It is undeniable that on 29 July the wireless stations of the Moscow-based Union of Polish Patriots (ZPP) called for 'active struggle' against the German occupiers, and similar appeals were made by the Soviet 'Radio

Kosciuszko [Kostiushko]'.[39] This was not, however, why the Home Army acted. General Bór-Komorowski and the other Home Army leaders fatally mistimed their rising, which for them had political as much as military goals. Their aim was not to help the Red Army to take Warsaw, but to take the city *before* the Red Army. They wanted to present Stalin with a fait accompli. The Home Army did not have a realistic plan for an uprising in Warsaw, and a fatal problem was the lack of liaison with the approaching Soviet forces.[40] The Home Army's leaders exaggerated the effect on the Wehrmacht of its recent catastrophe in Belorussia (from 22 June) and of the attempt on Hitler's life (20 July). The exiled Polish leaders in London saw the danger of isolated action, but they gave Bor and the Home Army freedom of action. Marshal Rokossovskii was very dismissive in an interview he gave the British journalist Alexander Werth in August 1944: '*We* [the Red Army] are responsible for the conduct of the war in Poland ... and Bór-Komorowski and the people round him have butted in *kak ryzhy v tsirke* – like the clown in the circus who pops up at the wrong moment and gets rolled up in the carpet.'[41]

The Home Army leaders were not the only ones to misread the situation. Although Stalin would later excuse the inaction of the Red Army by military problems which resulted from the 300-mile advance from Belorussia and the Ukraine, he and the Stavka had also hoped to achieve quick results in the Warsaw area. The Stavka directive to Zhukov and Rokossovskii on 28 July (D + 10 of the Lublin–Brest operation) did not tell them to take the Polish capital off the march, but did instruct them to take the western suburb of Praga by 5 August and bridgeheads over the Narew and Vistula rivers, some miles north and south of the city. The next objectives set out in this directive were to be Toruń and Łódź, towns well to the west of Warsaw in central Poland. The directive was consistent with what Stalin told the head of the London government, Stanisław Mikołajczyk, during talks in Moscow, which was that he had expected Warsaw to fall by 6 August but that the Red Army had been thwarted by unexpected German resistance. Stalin was not, however, lying when he told a later Polish delegation that the Red Army did not favour head-on attacks against major cities, giving as another example the avoidance of a direct attack on Kiev in 1943.[42]

Rokossovskii's 1st Belorussian Army Group, the main Soviet command in north central Poland, had – as already mentioned – encountered unexpectedly stiff German resistance in the first part of August. Rokossovskii held only limited bridgeheads over the Vistula, and his forces were under great pressure from Field Marshal Model, one of Hitler's most able commanders, and an expert in flexible defence. The Red Army was also weakened by a long advance and exposed at the end of overstretched lines of communication. It would have been impossible for Rokossovskii to have taken Warsaw in the first three weeks of August, the period before the backbone of the Home Army's very limited powers of resistance were effectively broken.

While the Soviet failure to take Warsaw in the first two-thirds of August 1944 can be explained by military factors, it is less clear why more forces of the Red Army could not have been concentrated against Warsaw at the *end* of the month, or in September. Stalin and the Stavka could have made a strategic decision to break the central Vistula–Narew line, committing there some of the troops that were eventually used in the Baltic or the Balkans. At the very least, the Red Army Air Force might have achieved air superiority over Warsaw, and supply drops to the insurgents could have begun earlier. A week after the uprising began, Zhukov and Rokossovskii, at Stalin's request, put forward a plan for a 'Warsaw operation' by (Rokossovskii's) 1st Belorussian Army Group. It was proposed that this would begin on 25 August. The attack involved throwing bridgeheads over the Narew River north of Warsaw, and expanding the bridgeheads over the Vistula south of the city. It would also require transferring the 1st Guards Tank Army to Rokossovskii from Marshal Konev in southern Poland, and transferring another army from Rokossovskii's right flank to his left.[43] The intended end result would be an arc about 50 miles west and north of Warsaw.

Leaving aside any political calculations being made in the Kremlin, the problem was that German resistance against both of Rokossovskii's bridgeheads was strong, while the Sandomierz bridgehead in Konev's sector had also come under heavy German attack. Zhukov's proposal for a 'Warsaw operation' was not taken up. On 21 August, Stalin stressed to Zhukov and the commanders of the 1st and 2nd Belorussian Army Groups the importance of getting across the Narew River, promising their men various medals. The bridgeheads were not for relieving Warsaw (which lay to the southwest) but to have 'the possibility to develop large-scale offensive operations [northwest] beyond the Narew *against East Prussia*' (my emphasis). As late as 29 August, it was intended that the right flank of the 1st Belorussian Army Group and the left flank of the 2nd Belorussian should seize the Narew bridgeheads by 4–5 September, although the two groups were then to shift to 'strict defence'.[44]

The Red Army Air Force began to drop supplies into Warsaw in a systematic way only on 13 September, and Rokossovskii reported to Stalin that over the following two and a half weeks the Red Army Air Force mounted nearly 5,000 sorties in support of the insurgents, half of them supply missions. This may have been Stalin's cynical way of prolonging the agony of the Home Army and causing it maximum casualties, but it was also a Soviet means of tying down German forces and responding to appeals from their 'own' Poles of the PKWN and the pro-Communist resistance, the People's Army (the AL). In mid-September the Soviet 47th Army finally drove the Germans out of Praga and forced them to blow up the Vistula bridges. The 1st Polish Army, apparently on the initiative of its own commander, put some small units across the river at this time.

The Russians attached little military importance to the rising, certainly in its final period. On 21 September Rokossovskii reported to Stalin that although supplies would continue to be dropped to the insurgents, they would do little to help the Red Army's advance:

Considering the number of insurgents, their extremely weak armaments, their isolated strongholds, and also the lack of unified military leadership and of political unity, the insurgents do not represent any real force in the battle for Warsaw, and they cannot be counted on for any kind of substantial assistance.[45]

Politically the Russians had no compelling reason to take Warsaw. It is true that the 'liberation' of Warsaw by the Red Army might have had the same positive 'historical–political' value that the 'liberation' of Prague in May 1945 had in Czechoslovakia. On the other hand, there was in Warsaw a concentration of several tens of thousands of resistance fighters loyal to the London government-in-exile and hostile to the USSR and the Red Army. Moreover, it was in Stalin's interest to consolidate his hold on eastern Poland, where he could build up an authority friendly to him, the Committee of National Liberation (PKWN) in Lublin, before attempting to establish a pro-Soviet government in the other three-quarters of the country. Stalin was aware of the difficulties the 'Lublin' leaders were having with local Home Army bands. 'What will happen', he asked them in October 1944, 'if the Red Army moves westwards together with the [Berling] Polish Army? Who will you be left with?'[46] For Stalin, delaying an advance to Warsaw and into western and central Poland also postponed a conflict with America and Britain. The intentions – and limitations – of Soviet policy in occupied Poland were indicated in a directive of mid-October from Rokossovskii's chief commissar (General K. R. Telegin). Telegin noted that the Stavka and the Military Council of the 1st Belorussian Army Group had ordered the disarming of the Home Army and the population in general, but little had been accomplished: 'The measures thus far taken by the Military Councils of the army and the punitive organs of the Red Army ... have been completely unsatisfactory.'[47]

Military factors were probably as important as political ones in explaining the extended delay in front of Warsaw. The Red Army had little to gain from a head-on attack against central Poland. As early as the beginning of July 1944, Marshal Zhukov had been reluctant to commit excessive forces here. He preferred a concentration of strength on northern Poland and East Prussia. According to Zhukov, in early October (after the Germans had crushed the rising), he and Rokossovskii had to convince a reluctant Stalin and other Politburo leaders to *halt* operations in the Warsaw area.[48] This may be true but, if so, Stalin's change of heart came before 9 October. On that day Stalin told a visiting delegation from the PKWN that preparations were being made to take Warsaw from the flank but that these would take *two to three months*.[49] Although this prediction was evidently made before the Stavka worked out its definitive plans for the Red Army's winter 1944–5 offensive, it was generally accurate – Warsaw would be taken three and a half months after this meeting.

The Red Army was not simply pausing in front of Warsaw; it was forgoing the decisive offensive in the central part of the front (Poland) for six months. Much more was involved than the Polish Home Army and its uprising. One broad strategic explanation for the pause is that unexpected opportunities for the Red Army opened up on the strategic flanks. As we will see in the following sections, at this time the Soviet armies were taking part in the Iaşi–Kishenev operation in Romania (20–29 August 1944), and then advancing into Bulgaria, Serbia and Hungary in September and October. They were also involved in the Baltic operation in Estonia and Latvia (14 September to 24 November 1944). Finally, there was a new element of longer-term planning: Antonov and the General Staff were by October 1944 developing plans for the ultimate 'deep operation', a rapid advance towards Berlin. Such an operation would in the short term demand a pause to create adequate logistical bases behind the bridgeheads on the Vistula and the Narew rivers. All these developments carried weight, and the final moment of decision was evidently the conference at the Stavka with members of the GKO at the end of October. It was agreed that the Red Army would go over to the defensive in central and northern Poland, pending a build-up of forces for the final attack towards Germany.[50]

The Vistula–Oder operation, January 1945

Only on 12 January 1945, seven months after Operation BAGRATION and five months after the halt before Warsaw, did the Soviet march into Poland resume.[51] The main forces involved were still the 1st Belorussian Army Group and 1st Ukrainian Army Group, with the 2nd and 3rd Belorussian Fronts making flanking attacks into East Prussia. This was part of a general Soviet offensive, which included operations in Hungary in November and December to draw off German reserves. The plan was confirmed in late November 1944.[52]

The Red Army's victorious battles of 1942–4 had seen the evolution of a two-stage command structure. 'Stavka representatives' – most successfully Zhukov and Vasilevskii – co-ordinated several army groups on behalf of the Moscow Stavka. In early October 1944, however, Stalin proposed a change: he, as Supreme Commander-in-Chief, should take over direct command of the whole central theatre. This change may well have come from a desire to take full credit for victory and to fulfil the boast of Soviet propaganda that Marshal Stalin was a military genius. He may have wanted to avoid any single general building up too much prestige. The new structure also made military sense, as the main front had narrowed geographically and the span of command there was reduced to three army groups.[53] The disadvantage of this arrangement was that important decisions had to be made far away, in Moscow.

Early in October 1944 Stalin told Marshal Zhukov that he wanted him to command the spearhead formation, the 1st Belorussian Army Group, and the appointment was formally made in mid-November.[54] This might be seen as a demotion for Zhukov. He was, after all, Deputy Supreme Commander-in-Chief of the Red Army. Since the autumn of 1942 Zhukov had controlled several army groups at a time; the exception was for a few months in the spring of 1944, when he stepped in to take over the 1st Ukrainian Army Group, after General Vatutin was mortally wounded. In the huge campaigns of the summer of 1944, Zhukov had effectively been in charge of both the 1st Belorussian Army Group (Rokossovskii) and the 1st Ukrainian Army Group (Konev). Now he was being reduced to their command level. On the other hand, the post that Zhukov was being given was the most important of the war, that of director of the 'main blow' against Berlin. If Stalin feared Zhukov's popularity, moreover, it was hardly logical to give him the key appointment on the 'Berlin axis'. It may be that Zhukov wanted to take on the post, and that Stalin felt that it was Zhukov who could carry out these operations most successfully. In addition, each army group was now so large that it was no dishonour to command just one. The 1st Belorussian Army Group contained as many armies as the whole Red Army had deployed on the western border in 1941.

FIGURE 12 Marshals Rokossovskii and Zhukov with Field Marshal Montgomery in Berlin, July 1945.

Zhukov's assumption of command took place on 16 November 1944, which was some ten weeks before the projected start of major operations (15–20 January), and nine weeks before they actually began (12 January). Zhukov took the place of Marshal Rokossovskii, who had led the 1st Belorussian Army Group (and its predecessor, the Central Army Group) from February 1943, in the march across the Ukraine to the Vistula. Rokossovskii was transferred to the formation on his right flank, replacing General Zakharov as commander of the 2nd Belorussian Army Group, the army group facing East Prussia.[55] Rokossovskii's new command was also certainly a major one, but the Marshal resented his being removed from the *glavnyi udar* (main effort, *Schwerpunkt*), and his long personal friendship with Zhukov suffered.

Zhukov's 1st Belorussian Army Group was deployed in northeast Poland, on the line of the Narew and Vistula which had been seized in the later summer (see Map 11). The other force engaged in the offensive into Poland was the 1st Ukrainian Army Group, under Marshal Konev. Konev still held the large bridgehead on the upper Vistula at Sandomierz and was readying his forces for the invasion of southern Poland. Opposed to the main Soviet forces were German Army Group Centre and Army Group 'A' (formerly Army Group North Ukraine), with their fronts divided just north of Warsaw. Army Group Centre was commanded by General Hans Reinhardt, and Army Group 'A' by General Harpe. Total German strength has been given by modern Russian sources as about 400,000 troops, 5,000 artillery pieces, 1,220 AFVs and 630 aircraft, but even this low figure is probably an exaggeration. Hitler's forces had now been ground down by fruitless campaigns in the Ardennes, the Rhineland and Hungary. Meanwhile, the Soviet 1st Belorussian Army Group and 1st Ukrainian Army Group had been massively reinforced. Their strength was some 2,200,000 troops, 33,000 guns and mortars, 7,000 tanks and SP guns, and 5,000 aircraft.[56] Their logistical situation was now greatly improved from the summer of 1944. The 1st Belorussian now had seven infantry armies, plus one in reserve. Massive mobile forces available to Zhukov now comprised two Guards tank armies (Bogdanov's 2nd and Katukov's 1st) and four independent mobile corps (Bogdanov's tank army had been awarded Guards status in November 1944). Konev's 1st Ukrainian Army Group also had eight infantry armies (two of them in reserve). His main mobile forces were Rybalko's 3rd Guards Tank Army and Leliushenko's 4th Tank Army, plus five independent mobile corps.

The Vistula–Oder operation unfolded at breakneck speed in January 1945, even more rapidly than the German campaign in Poland at the start of the war. Then, Hitler's armies, advancing on 1 September 1939 from Silesia and East Prussia, had swept across Poland to envelop Warsaw. The Polish capital capitulated on D + 26. By that date, most of the other Polish towns had been occupied for some days, and the Polish field army had been destroyed.

In 1945, Konev's 1st Ukrainian Army Group began to move on 12 January, with a breakout from the Sandomierz bridgehead. The leading element was Rybalko's 3rd Guards Tank Army. The German 4th Panzer Army was largely overrun near Kielce. To the north, Zhukov attacked two days after Konev. The 1st Belorussian Army Group moved out of its Vistula and Narew bridgeheads either side of Warsaw, driving back the German 9th Army. Simultaneously with Konev and Zhukov, and in accordance with the Stavka's co-ordinated offensive plan, two other army groups lurched into devastating action. Cherniakhovskii's 3rd Belorussian Army Group (five infantry armies) and Rokossovskii's 2nd Belorussian Army Group (six infantry armies) attacked the Wehrmacht in, respectively, East Prussia (the Insterburg–Königsberg operation) and Pomerania (the Mława–Elbing operation). By 25 January – D + 13 of the whole Vistula–Oder operation – the 2nd Belorussian Army Group had overrun northeastern Poland and West Prussia. Having broken out of the Serock and Rózan bridgeheads on the Narew, it had reached the Bay of Danzig. The rump of German Army Group Centre was now isolated in the Königsberg area of East Prussia. This was essentially the advance Zhukov had had in mind in July–August 1944, before it was stopped by Model's *Panzerschlacht* in front of Warsaw (the Battle of Radzymin/Wołomin).

Stalin's confidence in Marshal Zhukov in January 1945 had not been misplaced. Zhukov's part of the Vistula–Oder operation is called the Vistula–Poznań operation. The 1st Belorussian Army Group bypassed the Poznań (Posen) area. The big industrial city and key railway junction, held by 60,000 defenders, fell only after a lengthy siege, on 23 February. On the German side, the arrival of some reserves and the appointment of one of Hitler's favourite 'last-ditch' commanders, General Schörner, to Army Group Centre made no difference. The Stavka itself had expected Zhukov to halt at the Poznań–Bydgoszcz line, but in fact he pushed his forces another 100 miles on to the Oder River in front of Berlin. Zhukov was eager at least to get through the old German defensive line around Meseritz (Międzyrzecz), but this position turned out to be largely unmanned. On 31 January (D + 19) the 1st Belorussian Army Group had completed a breathtaking advance. Zhukov had reached the Oder River just north of the historic Prussian fortress town of Küstrin, and actually thrown shallow bridgeheads onto the western side of the frozen river. It was one of his finest moments as a commander.

Meanwhile, in southern Poland, Konev's Sandomierz–Silesia operation was rolling on; it was also part of the larger Vistula–Oder operation. The 1st Ukrainian Army Group drove ahead due west in the general direction of Breslau on the Oder River in Silesia. His right wing advanced through central Poland, crossed the pre-war German–Polish border and reached the Oder River downstream from Breslau in front of Glogau (Głogów). Meanwhile, Konev's left-flank forces moved through Kraków towards Katowice and Upper Silesia.[57]

Further north, a new German formation, Army Group Vistula ('Weichsel' in German), held on for the moment to an expanse of the pre-war Polish 'corridor' leading to Danzig. All the rest of pre-war Poland – and some German territory – was now in the hands of the Red Army. It was the most rapid of any of the Red Army's major offensives and had unfolded twice as fast as even the Stavka expected.[58] The Red Army could advance in January 1945, but not in August 1944, because it had been massively reinforced, and because the Wehrmacht was even more threadbare. Above all, the supply base of this massive Red Army had been consolidated. Once again Hitler and the German high command had underestimated Russian potential. Hitler did not take seriously December 1944 intelligence reports on the Soviet build-up in Poland. What reserves the Wehrmacht was able to accumulate after the double summer debacle in Normandy and Belorussia had been used in Hitler's 'decisive' December 1944 Ardennes offensive against the Americans in Belgium. After the Battle of the Bulge stalled, surviving German mobile reserves (especially the 6th SS Panzer Army) were moved not to Poland but to Hungary.

As in previous German fiascos, a bad situation was made worse by command shake-ups. Four days after the January Russian attack in Poland (16 January), General Schörner, still Hitler's favourite general, was called in from Army Group North in Kurland to take over Army Group 'A' in central Poland from Harpe. On arrival, Schörner in turn sacked the commander of his 9th Army, Lüttwitz. Meanwhile, Hitler imposed even more rigid control over his field commanders down to corps and division level. This was a consequence of what the Führer regarded as the treasonable abandonment of Warsaw. The measures taken included the arrest of the head of the Operations Department of the Army General Staff and his subordinate.

The Red Army captured some of the largest Polish towns relatively intact, as the Germans reeled back, but Warsaw lay in ruins. Just as the British and Americans allowed the Free French to liberate Paris, so the honour of entering Warsaw fell to the 1st Polish Army. Zhukov reported the situation to Stalin: 'The largest factories have been razed from the face of the earth. Houses have been blown up or burned. … Tens of thousands of inhabitants have been destroyed, the rest have been driven away. The city is dead.'[59]

The Russians claimed to have completely destroyed some thirty-five German divisions in the Vistula–Oder operation. Total Soviet losses in 'Poland' were taken to be 600,000, although this probably takes into account all battles fought within the borders of the post-war Polish state, including (German) Pomerania, (German) Silesia, and part of East Prussia. The combined Soviet losses in the L'vov–Sandomierz, Lublin–Brest and Vistula–Oder operations were less than this, perhaps about 150,000 all told.[60] This was still a figure equal to half of American or British total deaths in the Second World War.

At this cost, the USSR had extended its control over its eastern neighbour. The Warsaw Uprising broke the back of the Home Army and weakened the London Poles. Mikołajczyk, the prime minister of the London government-in-exile, was received in Moscow in August 1944 but failed to convince his colleagues back in London to make territorial concessions; in November 1944 he resigned. Despite the great contribution of Polish formations fighting alongside the British in western and southern Europe, the London-Polish government-in-exile had few assets left in Poland itself. The Communist-dominated PKWN extended its control west over the whole country, following the Red Army. At the time of the Yalta Conference in February 1945, the exiles had no influence; Mikołajczyk, making the best of a bad situation, joined three other 'London' ministers in the Soviet-sponsored Warsaw government.

Poland ceased to be a military problem in early February 1945 and became a political one. The Lublin PKWN administration became a Provisional Government and was installed in Warsaw. The president was a previously little-known Comintern functionary, Bolesław Bierut, and the prime minister a pro-Communist leader of the Socialist Party (PPS), Edward Osóbka-Morawski. In February the Allied Big Three tacitly accepted the authority of this Provisional Government. The NKVD was busy eliminating the remnants of the Home Army, first in eastern Poland, and then in the centre and the west. Several hundred Soviet soldiers were killed by the Home Army. In January 1945, at the time of the Vistula–Oder offensive, the Home Army dissolved itself. At Yalta, Stalin made much of the need to secure Red Army lines of communication. 'We want tranquility in our rear. We will support the government which gives us peace in the rear, and as a military man [*sic*] I could not do otherwise.' In late February–March 1945, Serov, the NKVD plenipotentiary in the 1st Belorussian Army Group, arrested sixteen leaders of the Polish underground, including the 'delegate' of the London government, Jankowski, and the head of the Home Army, Okulicki. The Soviet authorities had lured them together under the guise of negotiation. The arrests were kept secret until VE Day, but in June 1945 the Polish leaders were tried and sentenced in Moscow. Nearly 30,000 Polish prisoners were held in Soviet camps by October 1945.[61]

FROM THE CARPATHIANS TO BUDAPEST: ROMANIA, BULGARIA, YUGOSLAVIA AND HUNGARY

Romania

The offensive in the northern half of the Nazi–Soviet front was not a complete success in the second half of 1944, despite the great victories of Operation BAGRATION in Belorussia. German Army Group North held on to Riga until October 1944, and in Kurland (in Latvia) until the end of the war. There was little movement in Poland, from early August 1944 to January 1945. The main advances of the Red Army in the autumn of 1944 and early winter of 1944–5 came in the southern half of the front, in the Balkans and the Danube basin. If Soviet strategic attention had returned to the central theatre in the high summer of 1944 (after a two-year gap) with the Belorussian offensive and the drive into Poland, in the early autumn it shifted back to the south. A new geographical feature imposed itself on overall strategy: the arc of the Carpathian Mountains now divided one set of advancing Russian army groups from the other (see Map 10). To the north was Poland, with central Germany beyond it (the Warsaw–Berlin axis); to the south were Romania, Bulgaria, Yugoslavia, Hungary and Austria.

The first stage of the Soviet campaign south of the Carpathians was fought across the territory of Romania, which extends about 450 miles west from the Black Sea coast, and 200–250 miles north from the Danube. Within Romania's borders of 1940–41, the Carpathians and the Transylvanian Alps stretched across the northern part of the country. They represented a formidable defensive barrier against the Russians but, unfortunately for the Axis, Bucharest, and the vital oil wells and refineries at Ploesti, were south or east of the mountains.

Deputy Foreign Commissar Maiskii's report of the winter of 1943–4 gave Romania, alongside Finland, a special place in post-war Europe. According to Maiskii, after the defeat of the Axis and the establishment of a 'democratic' government, Romania was to become a major buttress of the Soviet security system. Long-term pacts of mutual support were to be signed, and the Soviet forces were to be given adequate air, land and sea bases, with good lines of communication back into the USSR. Romania was to be receive preference in any territorial dispute with Hungary (there had been bitter disputes between the countries, mainly over Transylvania). Whereas mutual security pacts with Bulgaria and Yugoslavia might be tripartite, with British participation, that with Romania had to be bilateral; Romania would be an exclusive partner of the USSR.[62]

The original Soviet military intention in the late spring of 1944 had probably been to inflict enough of a defeat in Romania to divert German forces from the central front, on the Warsaw–Berlin axis. The Stavka on 3 May 1944 ordered the 3rd and the 2nd Ukrainian Army Groups (then under Malinovskii and Konev, respectively) to attack to the south and to start by 15–17 May. The 3rd Ukrainian was to drive southwest from the Dnestr on the Bîrlad–Focşani axis, bypassing the important city of Kishenev (Chişinău). This attack was put off by the Stavka, however, presumably to concentrate Soviet forces for the big operation in Belorussia. Meanwhile, some of the largest German–Soviet air battles of the whole war took place over the Iaşi (Jassy) area of northern Romania in May and June.[63]

The German–Romanian defensive line in northeastern Romania now ran about 250 miles east from the Carpathians, in front of the towns of Iaşi and Kishenev, and then down the Dnestr River to the sea. The German high command had grossly underestimated the danger from the Red Army, and the weight of the Soviet attack, when it came, caught them by surprise. This was partly because they were preoccupied by the crisis in Poland and the Baltic, and partly because the Russians were known to be pulling important formations out of the 2nd and the 3rd Ukrainian Army Groups facing Romania. The German army group, however, had for its part to give up twelve divisions to help deal with the June–July crisis in Poland and the Baltic, including six (out of eight) panzer divisions and a motorized division.

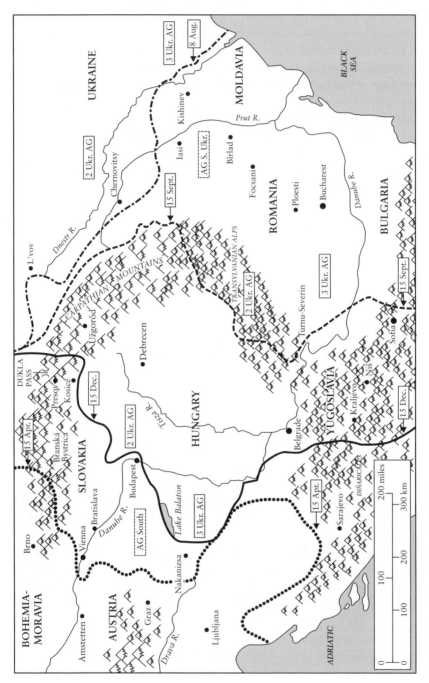

MAP 10 Southeastern Europe, 1944–5.

The astute military decision for the German high command would have been to pull back from northeastern Romania to the defensible Carpathians and the lower Danube, with the Focşani (Fokshani) gap between them. The Germans were loath to do this prior to a Soviet attack. Such a withdrawal would probably have been unacceptable to Hitler and, politically, to the Romanian Marshal Antonescu. It would have meant giving up 'Greater Romania' in Moldavia and would have brought the Red Army closer to Bucharest and the oil facilities around Ploesti.

There was, in any event, little command continuity on the German side. The attempted assassination of Hitler had just taken place (20 July), and Guderian had replaced Zeitzler as Chief of the General Staff. In a counterproductive German command reshuffle, General Johannes Friessner had been 'parachuted' into command of Army Group South Ukraine (in Romania) about four weeks before the attack. After commanding an infantry division and then a corps in Army Group Centre in 1942–4, Friessner had led the defence of Narva (west of Leningrad) from February 1944. He then served for a few weeks as commander of Army Group North (replacing General Lindemann) before exchanging posts with General Schörner of Army Group South Ukraine, who was being sent to the Baltic to deal with the crisis there. The upshot of this game of musical chairs was that General Friessner would rank with Field Marshal Busch as the least successful Wehrmacht commander of the war.[64]

The Russians, for their part, had a numerical advantage, and were now proficient in the use of mobile forces. Interestingly, Stalin assigned a figure from earlier years to co-ordinate the two army groups, Marshal Timoshenko. But both army group commanders were competent and experienced.[65] General Tolbukhin, fresh from his victory in the Crimea, had taken over the 3rd Ukrainian Army Group in May 1944. The 3rd Ukrainian Army Group was deployed on the line of the Dnestr and had four infantry armies and two mobile corps. On Tolbukhin's right, on a line west from the middle Dnestr to the Carpathians, was Malinovskii's 2nd Ukrainian Army Group. General Malinovskii had been shifted from the 3rd to the 2nd Ukrainian Army Group (replacing Konev). In June 1941 Malinovskii had commanded a corps of the old Soviet 6th Army, not far to the north of his present position. In 1944 he had charge of a larger force than Tolbukhin, with six infantry armies. His mobile striking force consisted of Kravchenko's 6th Tank Army and three mobile corps, two of them concentrated in a cavalry-mechanized group.

Tolbukhin and Malinovskii began the six-month march of the Red Army across southern central Europe on 20 August 1944. This was the seventh of Stalin's 'crushing blows' of 1944, and was later called the Iaşi–Kishenev operation.[66] Together with the Stavka, a new plan had been worked out to advance from two sides, from northwest of Iaşi and from a Dnestr bridgehead southeast of Kishenev; the pincers would trap the main German–Romanian field forces around Kishenev. The offensive proceeded according to plan. Iaşi fell on 21 August, and Kishenev, the once and future capital of the Moldavian SSR, on the 24th, having first been encircled by mobile corps from the two fronts. Some eighteen German divisions, and numerous Romanian formations, were destroyed or captured here, including the whole of the German 6th Army – repeating the experience of Stalingrad. Worse still for the Germans, Kravchenko's 6th Tank Army raced ahead and on through the Focşani Gap on 27 August. In the first week the pro-German government of Marshal Antonescu was overthrown in a Romanian military coup (on 23 August), and the Red Army entered Bucharest on 31 August (D + 11). Within another week, Soviet troops had overrun most of the country, even crossing north through the passes of the Transylvanian Alps and onto the edge of the Hungarian plain.

The Iaşi–Kishenev operation was one of the most successful offensives of the Red Army in the whole war. For their victory, Malinovskii and Tolbukhin were in September 1944 promoted to the rank of Marshal of the Soviet Union. Kravchenko's 6th Tank Army was awarded Guards status. Curiously, Marshal Timoshenko, the Stavka co-ordinator, has not received much credit for this remarkably successful operation from historians, but he was awarded the Order of Suvorov by Stalin.

Neither the Russians nor the Germans had anticipated the political developments that occurred in Romania. If that upheaval did not alone lead to the defeat of German Army Group South Ukraine, it certainly contributed to its complete rout. The campaign was very unlike the ones against Finland or Hungary, or the fighting in Poland, thanks to the abrupt desertion of the Romanian Army. Romanian politicians had been seeking a way out of the war for months, with secret approaches to the Allies in Cairo and Stockholm. A complex Ruritanian political scene involved Marshal Antonescu (the 'Conductor'), King Michael and the court, the army, the Communists, and hard-line Fascists. There had been some fantastic hopes about the arrival of British and American airborne forces. Illusions about the Western Allies were also shattered by the beginning of their heavy air attacks against Bucharest in April 1944. After the Soviet August offensive began, the twenty-year-old king grasped the nettle and ordered Antonescu arrested. The Marshal was overthrown in a palace coup in Bucharest in the name of King Michael on the afternoon of 23 August (D + 3 of the Soviet operation). A new government was created under General Sănătescu. The plotters were fortunate that the Romanian Army was unanimous in supporting the new government; it prevented the entry of German punitive forces into Bucharest.

General Friessner commanded Army Group South Ukraine, but he had no authority in the Romanian hinterland. Although the Germans had several hundreds of thousands of men under arms in Romania, their attempted counter-coup was unsuccessful. Hitler ordered the Luftwaffe to bomb parts of Bucharest, but this only inflamed the crisis, allowing the new Romanian government to pass from 'neutrality' to armed resistance against their former allies. It seems extraordinary that Hitler was caught by surprise, in view of his experience of the Italian desertion in 1943 and his knowledge of Romanian peace-feelers. He counted on the anti-Communism of most Romanian politicians and was evidently misled by the complacent local German representatives. Soviet spearheads entered Bucharest, 100 miles to the south of the initial attack, on 31 August (D + 11), a week after the coup. There was a demonstrative Red Army march through the capital, and a flyover by every available Soviet aircraft. The oil centre at Ploesti had been taken on 30 August.

The Royal Romanian Army and Air Force, still a considerable force on paper, now supported the Red Army in its campaign against the old enemy, Hungary, although mainly on secondary sectors. Rather more use was made of the 'Tudor Vladimirescu' Division, which had been raised by the Soviets from Romanian POWs captured earlier in the war. In exchange for fighting the Germans, Romania won scaled-down reparations; it also received back northern Transylvania, which had been lost to Hungary in 1940. On the other hand, the formation of a stable Romanian government proved difficult, with a wavering king and a conflict of forces that the Soviet ambassador described in October 1944 as 'having the character of a comedy'.[67] Soviet promises of political non-intervention were not honoured. Communist pressure, in the form of the so-called National Democratic Bloc, led to the replacement in early December of Sănătescu by a more amenable general, Radescu. Then at the end of February and the beginning of March 1945, a confrontation between the Communist-led National Democratic Front and the Radescu government brought the intervention of Soviet Deputy Foreign Commissar Vyshinskii. The prosecutor at the Moscow trials of 1937–8, Vyshinskii, was chairman of the Allied Control Commission. He confronted the king and forced the appointment of a new cabinet under Petru Groza, leader of a left-wing agrarian party whom Moscow regarded as reliable. To back up the Soviet demand, the tanks of the 7th Mechanized Corps were sent back from the front to occupy Bucharest. As Churchill grumbled to Roosevelt: 'The Russians have succeeded in establishing the rule of a Communist minority by force and misrepresentation.'[68]

The loss of Romania would have been a greater economic blow to Germany earlier in the war. In fact, American bombing had virtually ended the production of the Ploesti refineries before the Red Army arrived. The unexpectedly easy capture of Romania was strategically very important, however, as it opened the way to what Churchill had called the 'underbelly of Europe'. The cost to the Red Army of the Romanian campaign was re-markably light, given the great strategic advantage gained. Some 13,000 Soviet person-nel were lost in the Iaşi–Kishenev operation (i.e. 20–29 August), and a total of 69,000 in all the fighting in Romania – about half the losses in Hungary or Czechoslovakia.[69]

Bulgaria

The sudden collapse of Romania opened the Red Army's road to its neighbour south of the Danube, Bulgaria. The position here was even odder than in Romania. The government in Sofia had involved itself in the Second World War by allowing the Wehrmacht to pass through its territory in the invasions of Greece and Yugoslavia in 1941. The Bulgarian Army took part in occupation duties in Macedonia, the mountainous region between Yugoslavia and Greece. Luftwaffe and German naval units were based on Bulgarian territory, operating on the Black Sea. The Bulgarians were at war with the British and Americans, but had never gone to war with the USSR. King Boris had refused to send forces to Russia. Slav Bulgaria had also fought on the opposite side from Russia in the First World War, but there remained considerable mutual goodwill. The language and culture of the two countries had strong similarities. Russia had helped in the liberation of the country from the Turks in the nineteenth century. The death of King Boris in 1943 left a vacuum, as the Regency Council had little authority. On top of all that, the head of the Comintern and its shadowy successor was a Bulgarian, Georgi Dimitrov.

The Soviet view on Bulgaria was less clear than that on Romania. Maiskii's overview of the winter of 1943–4 had not considered a Soviet declaration of war on Bulgaria. He assumed that after the end of the war, there would be change from the existing right-wing government and a mutual support pact with the USSR, both emerging from popular pressure. Bearing in mind the dangers of Balkan politics and the sensitivities of the British, this pact might be a tripartite one involving the USSR, Britain and Bulgaria.[70] In reality, the Bulgarian Regency Council was desperate to extract itself from the war. There was an important insurgent movement in the form of the 'Fatherland Front', formed by the small Bulgarian Communist Party and factions of other parties. The sudden appearance of Russian troops on the Danube in Romania precipitated a revolution in Sofia. Moscow declared war on Bulgaria on 5 September (D + 15 of the Iaşi–Kishenev operation); three days later three of Tolbukhin's infantry armies (with two mobile corps) invaded.[71]

There is an extraordinary feature to this little conflict that historians have largely ignored. Stalin attached great importance to the occupation of Bulgaria, and he sent his best commander, Marshal Zhukov, to oversee it. Zhukov was recalled to Moscow from the now static front in Poland as early as 22 August.[72] This date must have coincided with Stalin's realization that the Romanian advance would be much faster than anticipated. In any event, there was no Bulgarian military opposition, because the Fatherland Front seized power in Sofia on the morning of the 9th; Sofia lay 200 miles to the west of the leading Red Army units. The Soviet troops paused after entering the country, and then sent advance units ahead. A mixed air corps and a bomber division were flown into the airfields around Sofia, and a Soviet rifle corps entered the city on 16 September. This initial thrust was followed by the redeployment of elements of Tolbukhin's 3rd Ukrainian Army Group into the western and southern part of the country. The Soviet 57th Army moved rapidly across Bulgaria and threatened the German rail line of communications from Greece, the Salonika–Belgrade railway. The Soviet 37th Army was left behind to garrison Bulgaria.

According to current Russian figures, the Red Army lost about a thousand personnel in operations in Bulgaria.[73] Bulgaria, like Romania, now contributed troops to the Soviet effort. Militarily, the country had advantages for the USSR over Yugoslavia and Romania. Bulgaria possessed an intact regular army (unlike Yugoslavia), one that had received some modern equipment from the Germans but had not been battered in previous campaigns (i.e. unlike the Romanian Army). Acting in uneasy collaboration with very different Yugoslav partisan forces, one Bulgarian army briefly supported the attack against the Germans around Niš in western Serbia, and another pushed west between the Sava and Drava rivers, covering the left flank of the 3rd Ukrainian Army Group in Hungary.

The Bulgarian Communists used their control of the Ministry of the Interior and the People's Militia to dominate the country; they were helped by the presence of the Red Army. The political struggle in Bulgaria had been particularly bloody and polarized in the interwar years, and this was reflected in the bloodiest beginnings of any of the

Communist regimes in eastern Europe. Bulgarian authorities were early off the mark with trials of the leaders of the old government, which began in December 1944. Severe punishments were doled out, including execution of the wartime leaders. Meanwhile, the Communists marginalized their opponents, abolishing the monarchy and securing final power through rigged elections in 1947.

Yugoslavia

Yugoslavia was different from anywhere else in eastern Europe. One factor here was the strength and success of Tito's Communist Partisan (guerrilla) movement, which came to style itself the People's Liberation Army of Yugoslavia (NOAJ or Yugoslav PLA). The Axis invasion of April 1941 had begun a cruel period of occupation, alongside a parallel civil war among the 'South Slavs'. Although nationalist and Communist resistance movements were formed, the major cities and the main transport routes stayed in the hands of the Axis occupiers or one of the pro-German local authorities. All the same, the prospects of Tito's partisans improved greatly when Mussolini fell in the summer of 1943. The Italian part of the occupation force crumbled, leaving much military equipment in partisan hands. Yugoslavia also came within range of Allied supply aircraft operating from southern Italy.

For the Germans, Yugoslavia was especially important from the late summer of 1944. Through its territory ran the only route that could be used to extract the big Wehrmacht garrisons in Greece and the Mediterranean islands (German Army Group 'E'). This protracted evacuation began on 10 October 1944 and ended on 31 December. The Russians too had an interest in Yugoslavia, but it was not an area of the greatest strategic importance to them, either for the current war with the Axis or for some future conflict with the capitalists. (Bulgaria, which provided an access to Turkey and the straits between the Black Sea and the Mediterranean, had greater strategic value.) Yugoslavia had not had a common border with the USSR, nor was it likely to do so.

In Maiskii's East European overview, Yugoslavia was important, but less so than Romania. He believed that if Tito maintained his influence, it would be possible to sign a treaty of mutual support with him; this would not be the case if the Royalist (émigré) government of King Peter won the power struggle. With Yugoslavia, as with Bulgaria, Maiskii's view was that British sensitivities had to be kept in mind; a cautious policy was advocated, possibly involving a tripartite pact with Britain and Yugoslavia.[74] To be sure, Yugoslavia had been one of the most successful areas of anti-Axis resistance, and this resistance was led by Communists. But there had been little the USSR could do to help the partisans until late in the war. Supply drops from Russian territory began in late February 1944 but on a small scale; until August 1944 the distance from the Red Army's front line was beyond the practical range of Soviet transport aircraft. What little the Russians could do was, as it happened, made possible by the British and Americans; after prolonged negotiations, the Red Army Air Force was allowed use of an air base in southern Italy.

The direct role of the Red Army in Yugoslavia was limited.[75] The unexpected collapse of Romania opened up a route to Belgrade via the town of Turnu-Severin and the north side of the Danube. The two-day war with Bulgaria provided access south of the river, through western Bulgaria. The Bulgarian Army, which had occupied Macedonia for the Germans, was also available, although this time on the Allied side. (The Yugoslavs reluctantly agreed to allow Bulgarian troops to support an attack on Niš in eastern Serbia, but the Stavka had to get directly involved.) The Red Army's 'Belgrade operation' lasted from 28 September (D + 38 of the Iaşi–Kishenev operation) to 20 October. It was put forward three or four weeks by General Tolbukhin. Yugoslav partisans attacked from the south and west, and the Soviet 46th and 57th Armies and a mechanized corps from the north and east. In a symbolic finale, the battle for Belgrade was fought by Yugoslav partisans riding on the tanks of the Soviet 4th Guards Mechanized Corps.

The German front in Yugoslavia then stabilized about 50 miles west of Belgrade and, further south, around Kraljevo. The railway had been cut, but the Germans were able to continue pulling their troops out of Greece along the Skopje–Kraljevo–Sarajevo road. At the November 1944 planning conferences, Tolbukhin proposed a direct advance on Vienna northwest via Croatia, bypassing Hungary. Antonov and the General Staff, however, preferred the route up the Danube through Budapest, and their view prevailed.[76] Soviet attention was concentrated on operations further north in Hungary, leaving only some air force units to help the Yugoslav PLA. The Russians also began to supply equipment to Tito's forces in large quantities. Until the very last days of the war, however, German Army Group 'F' kept control of northwestern Yugoslavia, with Croatia, Bosnia, Herzegovina and Montenegro.

Yugoslavia was more important politically than militarily. A key factor was the radical programme of the partisans. This was a resistance movement very unlike that of the Home Army in Poland; 'Tito' (the Croat Josip Broz) was a Communist and former Comintern operative. The partisans were able to secure a large region of rugged country away from the main transport route, and in 1942 they created a prototype for successful resistance in the form of the Anti-Fascist Assembly for the Popular Liberation of Yugoslavia (AVNOJ). An executive National Committee for the Liberation of Yugoslavia (NKOJ) was set up under Tito at the end of 1943 to become the 'government' of the liberated zone and the heir apparent to power once Germany was defeated.

Remarkably, given their policy elsewhere, the Soviets even made some effort at the beginning of 1945 to encourage the British and Americans to establish themselves in western Yugoslavia. At Yalta, General Antonov was reported to have said that 'it seemed to him expedient that Allied [i.e. British and French] land offensives should be directed toward the Ljubljana Gap and Graz [in Austria]'.[77] Military considerations presumably overcame political ones here; an American or British presence would tie more German troops down, presumably as a means of easing the Soviet advance further north in central Europe. All Soviet forces were ordered to be withdrawn from Yugoslavia on 15 May 1945. Soviet losses in Yugoslavia are counted as 8,000, about half in the Belgrade operation. Among those lost was General G. P. Kotov, killed by 'friendly fire' on 7 November 1944. Kotov's 6th Guards Rifle Corps was redeploying towards Hungary via Niš when its headquarters vehicles, mistaken for fleeing Germans, were strafed by American fighter-bombers on a narrow mountain road.[78]

Hungary

The Red Army's campaign in Hungary turned out to be a much more drawn-out affair than the fighting in Romania, Bulgaria or Yugoslavia. It lasted from October 1944 to March 1945.[79] This happened partly because the Germans attached a high priority to the country. Hitler made much of the Nagykanizsa oil fields southwest of Lake Balaton, which became important with the loss of the Romanian oil and the damage by air bombing of the German synthetic fuel plants. More generally, Hitler, as an Austrian, took a greater interest in the south of Germany than the north. The other factor was that more careful measures were taken to ensure Hungarian loyalty, especially after the defection of Italy in 1943. The Germans sent occupation troops into the country in March 1944 (Operation MARGARETHE), as the Red Army, racing across the Ukraine, reached the other side of the Carpathians. Admiral Horthy, the Hungarian head of state, was forced to install a government that would obey all the demands of the Reich. One infamous consequence of this was the deportation of 400,000 Hungarian Jews to their deaths in Auschwitz.

Rather little thought seems to have been given to Hungary in Soviet planning for the post-war period. In Maiskii's paper of early 1944, he envisaged an isolated Hungary, cut down to its barest ethnographical frontiers and subject to heavy reparations; it was Romania on which Russia would base its defence.[80] It is probable, too, that Moscow did not expect that Red Army troops would reach Hungary as quickly as they did. The Soviet forces were led by Generals Tolbukhin and Malinovskii, who had stormed into Romania in August with two army groups. By October 1944 Malinovskii's 2nd Ukrainian Army Group comprised seven infantry armies. As a mobile force, he commanded the 6th Guards Tank Army and a Cavalry-Mechanized Group. Malinovskii's southern flank was still covered by Tolbukhin's 3rd Ukrainian Army Group, two of whose infantry armies operated in southern Hungary.[81] New 'allies' fought alongside the Russians: Malinovskii commanded two Romanian armies, and Tolbukhin had under his command Bulgarian and Yugoslav formations.

Having broken north through the passes of the Transylvanian Alps (the southern face of the Carpathians), Malinovskii had rapidly taken up a starting position in northwestern Romania. Much of Hungary is a great plain, the *Pustyna*, bounded on the north by the Carpathians and bisected by the bend of the Danube. The Stavka originally hoped in October 1944 to advance without pause to Budapest. The first Russian offensive, the Debrecen operation, opened on 6 October 1944. In the ninth of Stalin's ten 'crushing blows' of 1944, the Red Army quickly pushed 75 miles into Hungary across open country to the cities of Szeged and Debrecen (20 October, D + 14), taking most of the Hungarian territory east and south of the Tisza (Theiss) River. The Russian high command was optimistic that events in Romania could be repeated in Hungary, and there was a serious attempt by Malinovskii's 2nd Ukrainian Army Group to take Budapest off the march.

Debrecen had fallen, and behind the back of the Germans, Hungarian negotiators were trying to arrange a separate peace. On 18 October (D + 12), the Soviet 46th Army was ordered to create a striking group.[82]

Much depended on politics and chance. Admiral Horthy, the septuagenarian Hungarian regent, had sent a delegation to Moscow to negotiate, and in fact a preliminary armistice was signed. On 15 October (D + 9), Horthy announced over the radio that he was seeking peace. Hitler, however, had also taken steps. After the fiasco in Romania in August 1944, he had ordered the SS commando leader, Otto Skorzeny, to prepare for the removal of Horthy. Skorzeny was the man who a year earlier had freed Mussolini, when the new Italian government interned him. He achieved another remarkable success in Hungary, taking Horthy's headquarters in the Budapest citadel by a *coup de main*, and opening the way for the creation of a full-blown fascist government under the Arrow Cross movement.

The attitude of the Hungarian armed forces was of critical importance; there were only half a dozen Wehrmacht divisions in the country and twenty-five Hungarian ones. The chief of the Hungarian General Staff, General János Vörös, ordered his forces to cease fire on the Red Army. One of his commanders, General Miklos, commanding the 1st Hungarian Army in the northeast, went over to the Russians, which dislocated the defence of the Carpathians. But Miklos's subordinate commanders did not follow him, and meanwhile the 2nd and the 3rd Hungarian Armies also proved more loyal to the Axis cause. In the end, much of the Hungarian Army fought alongside the Germans, in marked contrast to what had happened in Romania. As General Vörös told Marshal Malinovskii, 'The Germans learned a great deal from the experience of Romania and Bulgaria, and especially of Romania.' One of the senior Hungarian officers who went over to the Russians explained that the reason some of the population and the army sided with the Germans was 'fear of the expected atrocities of the Soviet Army. The intelligentsia and officers are convinced of their total destruction. The people fear that they will be deprived of their property and sent to Siberia. They expect that all women will be raped.'[83] It was very important, too, that local rivals, the Romanians, were now fighting on the Allied side and threatening to gain territory from 'greater Hungary'.

By 24 October (D + 22), Soviet patience with the wavering Hungarian forces was exhausted, and the Stavka ordered the 2nd and 3rd Ukrainian Army Groups to treat the Hungarian Army like the German one.[84] It was a missed opportunity for the Russians and probably for the Hungarians. Had Regent Horthy acted more decisively, and had his army followed him, the Red Army might have established itself on the approaches to Vienna and Bohemia–Moravia (the Czech lands) by the middle of November. Budapest would not have been devastated by a long siege, and the human cost on all sides would have been much less, not least among the Hungarian Jews in the final throes of the Nazi Holocaust.

The bitter campaign in Hungary, fought from October 1944 to March 1945, is one of the least known of the European war. Axis resistance was bolstered by the presence – at the start of the campaign – of substantial forces under the command of General Friessner (from December, General Otto Wöhler) at German Army Group

South. These comprised (from west to east) the Hungarian 2nd Army, the 2nd Panzer Army, the German 6th Army (*again* reconstituted after its second destruction in Moldavia), the German 8th Army and the Hungarian 1st Army. Hungary was still a front to which Hitler attached great importance, and he favoured it with whatever reinforcements could be raised. Indeed, in Moscow the Stavka, after the initial hopes of quick victory were dashed, evidently saw Hungary (the 'Vienna axis') as a means of drawing off German reserves, for what was expected to be the main effort further north (the 'Warsaw–Berlin axis').

Surprisingly, no Stavka co-ordinator was initially assigned to oversee the operations of Malinovskii and Tolbukhin in Hungary; Marshal Timoshenko only took this role on after the German counter-attack in January 1945.[85] A major Budapest operation was launched by Malinovskii from his left flank (the 46th Army) on 29 October 1944, but this could not break through to the Hungarian capital. Two further attempts failed in the period through the beginning of December. Meanwhile, in December and further south off on the left flank, the armies of Tolbukhin's 3rd Ukrainian Army Group finally broke across the Danube. They were able to advance as far as the large Lake Balaton southwest of Budapest. This operation coincided with Hitler's Ardennes offensive (the Battle of the Bulge). Budapest was finally encircled by Malinovskii only on the day after Christmas, 1944. Malinovskii had on 17 December hoped to take Budapest off the march and reach a line well west of the city by 25–28 December, but it was not to be.[86]

Hitler, as might be expected, had forbidden the abandonment of the Hungarian capital. Budapest lay athwart the main entry route to Austria and Bohemia. It was the main railway hub of the region and also the largest Danubian port. The Red Army could not bypass it. This was the first time in the war that the Red Army had to lay siege to a major city.[87] The situation was complicated by the fact that Budapest was a large European city with a normal civilian population of about a million; one senior Soviet visitor reported that few inhabitants had been evacuated and the population had swollen to about two million. The large buildings provided good cover for the defenders; the citadel on the western bank of the Danube (Buda) was a fortress. The Stavka ordered the use of 'artillery of all calibres, including the most powerful, as well as air bombardment and demolition groups'. The defenders were led by an SS police officer, General Pfeffer-Wildenbruch, commander of the 9th SS Mountain Corps, with four German and two Hungarian divisions. A Soviet ultimatum to surrender, issued by Malinovskii at the end of December, was rejected. On 1 January 1945 a German attempt to relieve the city began, code-named Operation KONRAD. The main striking force was the 4th SS Panzer Corps, transferred from Army Group Centre; this was a transfer which would have dire consequences for the Wehrmacht when the Soviet Vistula–Oder offensive began in Poland, eleven days later. Operation KONRAD failed to break the encircling ring of Soviet troops. As at Stalingrad, Hitler forbade a breakout by the garrison. A senior Soviet political officer reported the situation at the end of January: 'The town of Budapest, especially its central area, is heavily damaged, hardly one building has been preserved intact. The western part of the town, Buda, where fighting is still going on, has literally been transformed into a ruin, the bridges across the Danube have been blown up.'[88] Pest, on the east bank, was secured by mid-January, but Buda and the citadel held out for another month, until 13 February. In the end, the fanatical Pfeffer-Wildenbruch ordered a breakout of the garrison, which was a bloody failure. Altogether, the Russians claimed to have captured 110,000 prisoners during the siege of the city, and killed 49,000 enemy troops.

Hitler mounted his last offensive of the Second World War in Hungary, an attempt to push the Russians back to the Danube and to retake Budapest. Operation SPRING AWAKENING (FRÜHLINGSERWACHEN) began on 6 March 1945. The main new force was Sepp Dietrich's 6th SS Panzer Army, which had recently spearheaded the December 1944 Ardennes offensive. The 6th SS Panzer Army and the German 6th Army advanced from between Lake Balaton and Lake Velencze, heading towards the Danube south of Budapest and driving slowly back the 26th Army of Tolbukhin's 3rd Ukrainian Army Group. The German force was a considerable one, including on paper ten panzer divisions, among them the still formidable 'Adolf Hitler', 'Das Reich' and 'Hitlerjugend' divisions.

The Soviets resisted bitterly, and effectively. Tolbukhin had had time to make some defensive preparations. German fuel supplies were limited; the muddy ground bogged down the panzers. The Germans also attacked from several other directions. The (tankless) 2nd Panzer Army advanced east from below Lake Balaton. There was even a co-ordinated attack north from the Drava River by surviving elements of Army Group 'E' in Croatia, attacking against the 1st Bulgarian and 3rd Yugoslav Armies. These were essentially diversionary operations, and neither had much effect. After ten days of heavy initial fighting, much of the 6th SS Panzer Army was shattered. Operation SPRING AWAKENING ended in failure on 15 March. Essentially it was a repetition of Kursk in 1943, but for the Germans much nearer home. The operation did not seriously distract the Russians from preparing their own offensive across western Hungary towards Vienna. In view of the fact that Soviet forces stood on the Oder, only 40 miles from Berlin, it had been a most foolhardy deployment of German elite forces.

The next Soviet bound, the Vienna operation, began with the capture of western Hungary. Tolbukhin's 3rd Ukrainian Army Group was now the centre of gravity, and Kravchenko's 6th Guards Tank Army was transferred to him, to support the 4th Guards Army and the new 9th Guards Army in the drive towards Vienna. (Malinovskii, with the 2nd Ukrainian Army Group, was turning north into Bohemia.) Tolbukhin's forces broke out across western Hungary and by 30 March 1945 had reached the Hungarian–German (Austrian) border. The way was clear for an operation against Vienna. As had happened in Poland in January 1945, and would happen east of the Rhine in late March, the German front now collapsed. This was the absolute end of Germany's mobile reserves. Hitler's prized Nagykanizsa oil fields were lost too, by the end of March.

The Russians had also gone some way to installing a friendly government in Hungary, although the situation was less clear-cut than it had been in the other Axis satellites, Romania and Bulgaria. The authority established by the Soviets in the central and eastern part of Hungary, the Provisional National Government, signed a peace agreement on 20 January 1945; Marshal Voroshilov, Stalin's old crony, signed for the Allies. This authority was made up of figures from the Hungarian establishment and had very little in the way of armed forces, but about three-quarters of pre-1939 Hungary was now notionally under its control. The elections that took place in 1945 in Hungary were relatively fair by eastern European standards, and the Smallholders Party, an agrarian group, emerged as head of the post-war coalition. Nevertheless, the Communists held the key posts in the government and were gradually able to increase their influence; there was also still a vital Red Army presence. After rigged elections in 1947, the moderates were forced out and a Communist-led government installed.

In the autumn of 1944, after the collapse in Romania, the Soviet planners assumed a fairly rapid march up the Danube, with the Red Army reaching the outskirts of Vienna by the end of December. In reality, the advance through Hungary was relatively slow, and the campaign very costly; losses suffered in five months of fighting were 140,000. In the Red Army's 'mission of liberation' in eastern Europe, only the fighting in Poland claimed the lives of more of its troops. The Debrecen and Budapest operations, from October 1944 to February 1945, cost 100,000 Soviet soldiers. Equipment losses were also high; in the Budapest operation alone numbering 1,760 Soviet tanks and 290 aircraft.[89]

THE RED ARMY IN THE SLOVAK AND CZECH LANDS

Between Poland in the north and Hungary in the south, stretching 550 miles from east to west, was the territory of the pre-war Czechoslovak state. Bohemia–Moravia, the western part of the country, was incorporated as a 'protectorate' within the Reich. In the east was rural Slovakia, with a collaborationist government installed in the southern city of Bratislava on the Danube. Slovakia was a member of the Axis, and it sent small ground and air forces against the USSR. Meanwhile, the pre-annexation prime minister of Czechoslovakia, Beneš, headed a Czechoslovak government-in-exile in London. Moscow and the Comintern had in 1942 placed considerable hopes on 'a nat[ional] liberation war by the Czech people', but little had come of this.[90] 'Free Czechoslovak' personnel had fought in the West, most famously in the RAF. A token Czechoslovak force was formed in Russia in early 1942 under Ludvik Svoboda, a future President of Czechoslovakia (1968–75). The Czechoslovak independent brigade fought alongside the Red Army at Kiev in 1943. By 1944, partly thanks to an influx of Slovak deserters and POWs, this had become a Czechoslovak Corps with four brigades, and there were also Czechoslovak air units in the Red Army Air Force.[91]

The Czechoslovak situation had much in common with that in Poland. Both states were major victims of Nazi aggression, both had governments-in-exile in London, both had significant numbers of volunteers fighting with the Allies. The Czechoslovak government-in-exile, however, had much better relations with Moscow than did that of the Poles. Neither the Czech lands nor Slovakia had ever been part of the Tsarist Empire, there was a strong spirit of Slavic kinship with the Russians, and the Moscow government was seen as a protector against the Germans. As with Poland, Romania and Finland, there was an element of territorial conflict with the USSR. In this case, it concerned the eastern tip of the country ('Sub-Carpatho Ruthenia'), from the town of Užgorod to the east. 'Sub-Carpatho Ruthenia', however, had none of the emotional significance for the Czechs and Slovaks that the historic lands beyond the Curzon Line had for the Poles. The region had a largely Ukrainian (Ruthene) population, and Beneš was prepared to cede it to the USSR.[92] Maiskii's summary of January 1944 saw Czechoslovakia as a real ally:

> In contrast to Poland the USSR is successfully striving to create a strong Czechoslovakia, which in view of the political mood of its population, and also in connection with the recently signed Soviet–Czechoslovak Twenty-Year Pact of Mutual Support, is able to be an important conduit [*provodnik*] of our influence in central and southeastern Europe. In concrete terms, Czechoslovakia must as a minimum be restored to its present borders with the addition of Teschen. If in the final carve-up of the map of Europe it is possible to cut off something more for Czechoslovakia, so much the better. In accord with the wishes of the Czechoslovaks the [Sudeten] Germans must be resettled beyond the borders of their country. Between the USSR and Czechoslovakia … a common border of sufficient length must be established. The two countries must be joined by good transport routes.[93]

Here, Maiskii called Czechoslovakia a 'conduit'; elsewhere in his paper he described it as an 'outpost [*vorpost*] of our influence'.

The USSR was soon able to put this Czechoslovak policy into practice. The Red Army had now reached the western edge of the great Eurasian plain. The deep advance into southern Poland, with the establishment in mid-August 1944 of the bridgehead over the lower Vistula River at Sandomierz, left the Red Army with a long left flank on the Carpathian Mountains. In the mountains and beyond them lay the territory of Slovakia. The front line further east (in the part of Czechoslovakia annexed by Hungary in 1938) was held by General Gotthard Heinrici's – tankless – 1st Panzer Army, now under German Army Group North Ukraine. Slovakia itself, until very recently a place of little strategic importance, was not yet occupied by the Germans. On the other hand, the Carpathians comprised a very serious obstacle to a Soviet military advance into the main part of Czechoslovakia. They were a mountain chain 70 miles wide, with high passes, few roads, wild mountain streams and some fixed defences. Offensive warfare in mountain conditions was another new combat setting for the Red Army.[94]

The main Red Army formations involved in eastern and central Czechoslovakia were Konev's 1st Ukrainian Army Group, and a new army group created in August 1944 from Konev's left-flank forces, the 4th Ukrainian.[95] The commander of the new army group was General I. E. Petrov, the defender of Sevastopol'. He had recently been pulled out of Belorussia because of disagreements with commissar Mekhlis. The initial components under Petrov's command were the 1st Guards Army and the 18th Army; the latter is of interest because its commissar was General Leonid Brezhnev, the future Soviet President. Petrov had ambitious plans in mid-August 1944 to break through the mountain passes into the eastern Hungarian plain, but his advance met repeated delays. At the end of August, in light of the unexpected success at the other end of the Carpathians in Romania, Petrov was ordered to 'strict defence'.[96]

Then the Slovak National Uprising broke out. It began at the very end of August 1944 and was ruthlessly put down by German punitive units in late October.[97] This tragic episode had features in common with the Home Army uprising in Warsaw, which preceded it by four weeks; it also had similarities with events that autumn in Romania. Basically it was another variation on the difficult theme of leaving the doomed Axis. There was a nationalist conspiracy among the leaders of the (Axis) Slovak Army. The conspirators hoped to wait until the Red Army arrived, and then quickly to take control or change sides, keeping their political and social order intact. (Something like this had been attempted in Poland and, more successfully, in Romania.) The Soviets, however, wanted more decisive action. As the Red Army approached within air range, it began to drop partisan organizers into the mountains. Guerrilla attacks, plus the advance of the Red Army and the experience of what had just happened in Romania, caused the Germans to send troops into Slovakia at the end of August 1944. This in turn triggered off prematurely, on 29 August, the uprising that was being planned in the Slovak Army.

The conspirators were not supported by other parts of the Slovak Army. Bratislava and the south of Slovakia were not seriously affected by the uprising. Most important of all was the failure to win control over the so-called Slovak Corps, the Slovak formation which could most easily have linked up with the Red Army. The corps was stationed around the towns Prešov and Košice, south of the vital Dukla Pass over the Carpathians. In the confusion, the Germans were able quickly to disarm the Slovak Corps; they avoided a repetition of their Romanian fiasco, which had occurred a few days previously. What the Slovak rebels did succeed in taking was the town of Banská Bystrica in the Tatra mountains of north central Slovakia. They were, however, 125 miles to the west of the Prešov–Košice area and the Dukla Pass. When Marshal Konev's forces did try to storm through the Dukla Pass at the beginning of September (the Carpathian–Dukla operation), there was no surviving Slovak support from the south, and they met stiff German resistance.

The object of the Slovak uprising became one of holding on to the island of liberated territory around Banská Bystrica. The nearest Russian ground forces were 125 miles away to the northeast, across rugged country. General Moskalenko's 38th Army, including Svoboda's 1st Czechoslovak Corps, finally took the Dukla Pass in October but made little progress beyond it. In September and early October 1944, men and munitions were flown in by the Red Army Air Force into a small airfield near Banská Bystrica. The Soviet-organized 2nd Czechoslovak Parachute Brigade arrived, and the region was protected by a Czechoslovak air regiment flying Soviet-built fighters. Unfortunately, the Wehrmacht were gradually able to regain control, even of this very difficult territory and even in the terrible strategic situation in which the Germans found themselves. The change of government in Hungary in October (rabid fascists replacing conservatives) opened up southern Slovakia to German punitive units, including the infamous Dirlewanger Brigade from Warsaw. On 27 October 1944 the Germans finally took Banská Bystrica, and the Allied forces that had not been evacuated by air had to flee into the mountains. Red Army ground forces only reached Banská Bystrica in March 1945, as the German front to the south, in Hungary, crumbled. The Slovak National Uprising was a missed opportunity.

If the uprising had been successful, it might have had a significant impact on the war, outflanking Hungary.[98] There were mutual recriminations later about the competence of the Slovak rebel officers and the London government, and about whether the Soviets gave less help than they might have done. Ultimately, the cause of the fiasco was the difficulty of changing sides at the right moment, a problem not confined to Slovakia.

Petrov's 4th Ukrainian Army Group was grinding slowly down from the north. On the other side of the Carpathians, the right flank of Malinovskii's 2nd Ukrainian Army Group was now moving north from the Hungarian plain, as the Axis front in eastern Hungary collapsed. The two army groups were co-ordinated by Marshal Timoshenko, representing the Stavka. The Soviet 18th Army was able to get through the passes into Sub-Carpatho Ruthenia and Transylvania at the end of October, as the Slovak uprising was being crushed 150 miles to the west. In this 'East Carpathian operation', three Soviet infantry armies were able to snip off what had been the extreme eastern part of pre-1938 Czechoslovakia (but most recently part of Hungary). The town of Užgorod was taken by the Red Army, and with it the route across the Carpathians from L'vov in the Ukraine to Debrecen in Hungary (which had been captured from the south on 20 October). Užgorod was captured on 27 October, the same day the Germans took Banská Bystrica. Heinrici's 1st Panzer Army and Wöhler's 8th Army now held a north–south front line straddling the Carpathians just west of Užgorod.[99]

After a delay of over two months, the Carpathian theatre became active again (see Map 11). On 12 January 1945, the Vistula–Oder operation began to the north, in Poland. A general Soviet attack across Slovakia, the 'West Carpathian operation', was launched by the Soviet 4th Ukrainian Army Group from the east and the 2nd Ukrainian Army Group from the south (from Hungary). The right flank rapidly reached Kraków on 19 January, fortunately with little damage to the beautiful ancient town. Beyond Kraków were found the horrors of Auschwitz. The main drive, however, was held up in the difficult country of central Slovakia by mid-February. Petrov, commander of the 4th Ukrainian Army Group, in mid-February proposed another ambitious offensive. This was to advance from the lower Vistula (in southwestern Poland) through Ostrava, Olomouc and Pardubice (all in northern Moravia) to Prague and the Vltava River. The attack was to begin on about 10 March and reach its objective by mid-April. Petrov was an experienced and talented officer, but the offensive by the 38th Army (Moskalenko) and the 1st Guards Army (Grechko) made poor progress. The terrain was difficult, it was mid-winter and Schörner's German Army Group Centre conducted a stubborn defence. Stalin was so angry that General Petrov and his chief of staff were removed from their posts. Petrov was no stranger to controversy; he had been involved in another controversy at the start of BAGRATION. He was nevertheless considered an able officer and was made Konev's chief of staff on the eve of the Berlin operation.[100] Mekhlis, who had still been serving as Petrov's commissar, was also criticized, but he was not dismissed.

Petrov's replacement at the end of March 1945 was none other than General Eremenko, the defender of Stalingrad. Eremenko was transferring from command of the 2nd Baltic Army Group facing Kurland; the responsibilities of the 2nd Baltic had just been taken over by the Leningrad Army Group. Eremenko, who had never distinguished himself as an offensive commander, was also unable to make much progress here, even with the transfer to him of a fourth infantry army from Konev. Eremenko's offensive began in mid-April, at a time when decisive battles were already being fought around Berlin and Vienna. The Czech towns of Ostrava and Žilina were finally taken on 30 April. A month had gone by, and the advance represented only a local success for Eremenko's army. One indirect reflection of Stalin's frustration here was in his last letter to Roosevelt. He complained that the Germans were giving up major towns in western Germany to the Americans and British; meanwhile, 'they continue to fight like fury with the Russians for some little known station like Zemlianitsa in Czechoslovakia, which they need as much as a dead man needs a poultice'.[101]

History unfolds in unexpected ways. Czechoslovakia, which had been at the epicentre of the pre-war crisis in 1938–9, was the last major holdout of Nazi forces in 1945, a seemingly impenetrable fortress. Of the various Wehrmacht commands surviving when the German surrender documents signed at Reims and Karlhorst went into effect at the end of 8 May, the largest by far was Field Marshal Schörner's Army Group Centre, with 600,000 troops.[102] The liberation of western Czechoslovakia was finally to come from quite a different direction than that which the Stavka had planned. In the end the Red Army outflanked the mountains to the south and north of Bohemia–Moravia. The main thrust of the 2nd and the 3rd Ukrainian Army Groups up the Danube valley had allowed the 7th Guards Army to capture the river city of Bratislava (capital of Slovakia) on 4 April, and the 53rd Army and 6th Guards Tank Army to take the important industrial town of Brno in Moravia on 28 April. At the beginning of May, Malinovskii's 2nd Ukrainian Army Group was ready to send spearheads – the 6th Guards Tank Army and 7th Guards Army – northwest towards Prague. The final liberation of the capital, however, was mounted earlier – a matter of hours – by forces that followed a roundabout route through Saxony around the north of Bohemia–Moravia. These were the left-flank forces of Konev's 1st Ukrainian Army Group. The 4th and the 3rd Guards Tank Armies, which had taken a direct part in the Battle for Berlin, now swivelled their front by 90 degrees, raced south to the Czechoslovak border, and then southeast towards the Czechoslovak capital.

In Prague, spontaneous street demonstrations broke out on 4 May, which pre-empted the plans of the more organized Czechoslovak underground. A National Council was formed on 5 May. German forces from Army Group Centre attempted to regain control of the city, not least because it stood athwart the army group's line of retreat to the Reich. Prague was finally taken by the Red Army on 9 May. By another extraordinary twist of fate, the 1st Division of General Vlasov's Russian Liberation Army (ROA), based near Prague, became involved in the fighting, although its role is often exaggerated.[103] Vlasov himself was captured near Plzeň (Pilsen) on 12 May.

There would be historical controversies about whether the Americans should have tried to be the ones to liberate Prague and western Czechoslovakia, and thus to extend Western influence in central Europe. Churchill strongly urged this to the new President Truman at the very end of April. The US forces had been having an easier time of it on the other side of Bohemia–Moravia. Since the second half of April, the US 7th and 3rd Armies (under Generals Patch and Patton) had been racing through Bavaria against

FIGURE 13 The Red Army enters Prague on 9 May 1945. The Soviet soldiers ride in Lend-Lease American M3 half-tracks.

crumbling resistance. They reached the pre-war Czechoslovak border on 25 April. The previous day General Antonov, now Chief of the Soviet General Staff, had informed Eisenhower that the Red Army planned to take the Vltava valley, with Prague, and that the Americans should not advance further; this was confirmed on 5 May. Although American scouts were sent as far east as Plzeň, there was no American advance to take Prague. The military defeat of the Third Reich was only a matter of days away. Neither Marshall nor Eisenhower could see the need for a purely 'political' operation, and Eisenhower was given no guidance by Washington.[104]

The Reims/Karlhorst ceasefire went into effect at 11.01 pm (Central European Time) on the evening of 8 May. At that hour, however, Konev's forces opened a huge artillery bombardment against German forces in Bohemia. The local Wehrmacht had failed to respond to a ceasefire ultimatum made three hours earlier. Konev's vanguard raced into Prague on the morning of the 9th, followed a few hours later by columns from Malinovskii's army group in the south. With hindsight, the liberation of Prague by an American column would have been of undoubted political value. Whether it would have headed off the Communist coup in the city three years later is impossible to say. In any case, the Soviet capture of Prague rewarded the Red Army's nine-month slog through the

Czech and Slovak territory since September 1944. The current Russian estimate is that the Red Army lost 140,000 men in the fighting for Czechoslovakia, almost the same number as it lost in Hungary. Even the Prague operation was costly, with Russians losses reaching the remarkable level of 11,000 for a six-day campaign which took place after Hitler's death.[105]

East of Prague, around Poděbrady on the Elbe (Labe) River, the last remnants of a German force with an historic name were compacted into a black hole 50 miles across. This was *Heeresgruppe 'Mitte'*, Army Group Centre.[106] The remnants of the 17th Army and 1st Panzer Army were encircled on three sides by Soviet forces. They surrendered on 11 May 1945. Much of the largest post-war Soviet haul of POWs came from Czechoslovakia. The 2nd Ukrainian Army Group took 86,000 POWs between 1 and 9 May, and no fewer than 470,000 after 9 May. The 4th Ukrainian Army Group took 33,000 and 130,000 POWs in the same periods.[107] Among those captured, with the headquarters of the famous JG 52 fighter wing, was the leading Luftwaffe ace, Erich Hartmann. He had claimed his 352nd enemy plane over Brno on 8 May and was to spend over ten years in Russian prison camps. The commander of Army Group Centre, the newly minted Field Marshal Schörner, did not initially share the fate of his men or – like Model in the Ruhr – commit suicide. Dressed in civilian clothes, Schörner escaped to the Tyrol in a light aircraft. He was arrested and eventually tried for war crimes in Russia. He served 9 years of a 25-year sentence, and was then tried and imprisoned again in West Germany.

The fate of post-war Czechoslovakia is well known. The Red Army withdrew from the country, and Czechoslovakia did indeed seem to serve its role of a 'conduit' or 'outpost' of Soviet influence. The Czechoslovak Communists were successful in the polls. A left-wing Czechoslovak government had been formed at Košice in the east of the country on 4 April 1945. A Communist, Klement Gottwald, served as prime minister under President Beneš. But the USSR had meanwhile secured its influence over the whole East European region by other means. Hungary and Poland, perhaps contrary to initial Soviet expectations in early 1944, were now largely under Communist control. In the end, when East–West relations worsened in 1947–8, Moscow ordered the Czechoslovak Communists to seize power. The Prague coup took place in February 1948. All of eastern Europe was now under Soviet control, and it would remain so for forty years.

CONCLUSION

The military campaign of 1944 in eastern Europe demonstrated the emergence of the USSR as a superpower. In the summer of that year, the Red Army carried out a remarkable range of operations from the Balkans to northern Norway. It was also, arguably, an extreme example of the importance of Lend-Lease. The Red Army was able to sustain huge operations over great distances – deep into Bulgaria, across the Hungarian plain, across eastern Poland, because of fleets of Studebaker and GM trucks.[108] Given the distances involved and the damages to the railway infrastructure, there was no other way the pace of advance could have been kept up.

How did operations in eastern Europe compare to those in Germany's western borderlands? The losses suffered in the 'liberation march' of 1944–5, beyond the 1941 borders of the USSR, were high. Taking Poland, Romania, Bulgaria, Hungary and Czechoslovakia was reckoned by the Russians to have cost about 1,100,000 men. In comparison, the Americans lost about 60,000 men in the fighting in France, Belgium and the Netherlands, and the British about 40,000.[109] As for the German Army, this period of the war, like June 1944, was exceedingly costly. As we have seen, in July 1944 German losses in the East were 170,000, and in August they soared to an astonishing 277,000. In contrast, the estimate for German losses on other fronts in June, July and August 1944 was 198,000, an average of 66,000 a month.[110] The Battle of the Bulge in the Ardennes was small in scale compared to what had been happening in the East. The German attacker employed 500,000 troops and lost 100,000 as casualties (killed and wounded).[111]

The 'liberation' of eastern Europe by the Red Army was an important chapter in the history of the war. It was distinct from the battles within Russia; it was distinct, too, from the final destruction of the Third Reich on 'German' territory. For the Soviet Union, in 1944, eastern Europe represented a strategic danger zone, dangerous partly because of the unpredictable behaviour of its American and British allies. To be sure, the Wehrmacht would fight as effectively in eastern Europe as it did in Russia. It resisted determinedly in front of the Vistula in Poland, in the mountains of Czechoslovakia, in the Finnish Arctic and in central Hungary. But states and armies could now change sides in a matter of weeks, as the Axis alliance crumbled. Germany's satellites could see that the Allies were going to win the war. The Third Reich had failed to create genuinely binding forces in the region. Berlin could not even play on the local elites' fear of Bolshevism and the 'assault from the steppe' – once it became clear that in reality the Wehrmacht did not have the power to protect the region.

The Romanian defection at the end of August 1944, in particular, was not expected in the form it took, either by the Germans or the Russians. With it the whole balance of the front shifted, and Hitler's southern theatre was only stabilized on the outskirts of Budapest four months later. Other defections forced the Germans to give up their hold on the vast swathes of European territory, from Lapland to the southern Balkans. The situation was actually more stable and predictable for the Germans in the 'occupied' territories like Poland and Bohemia–Moravia, where the Reich had no allies.

Deputy People's Commissar Maiskii's glimpse into the future of eastern Europe in January 1944 was too pessimistic. In Maiskii's view, the USSR should base itself on the 1941 borders of the USSR. It should strengthen its position by deploying Soviet forces on the northern and southern flanks in Finland and Romania, and make use of a genuine ally in the centre in the form of Czechoslovakia. The rest of eastern Europe would be held at arm's length.[112] In fact, the Red Army's victories assured Soviet dominance over the entire region. Two years after Maiskii's secret paper, Churchill could make his own famous public declaration about an 'iron curtain' behind which lay 'all the capitals of the ancient states of Central and Eastern Europe': 'All are subject in one form or another to a very high and, in many cases, increasing measure of control from Moscow.'[113] By 1948, all the states Churchill mentioned (except Austria) had Communist governments.

CHAPTER 13
THE DESTRUCTION OF NAZI GERMANY, OCTOBER 1944 TO MAY 1945

[W]ar is the continuation of political intercourse, with the addition of other means.

Carl von Clausewitz, *On War*

Now for the Red Army there remains one last and conclusive mission: to complete, together with the armies of our allies, the destruction of the German-fascist army, to kill the fascist beast in its own den, and to hoist over Berlin the banner of victory.

Joseph Stalin, 6 November 1944

I always stop only at five past twelve!

Adolf Hitler, 8 November 1942

The last chapter was about the battle for eastern Europe; this one is about the final struggle on German territory.[1] Greater Germany still possessed considerable military potential. Germany was a technically advanced state producing weapons that in terms of quality still compared well with those of the Allies. Hitler's propaganda made much of the *Wunderwaffen* – missiles, advanced submarines and jet aircraft – but even at a more basic level, excellent army equipment was still available. Military production had increased during 1944, though with no prospect for further expansion. An army of several millions was still in the field. It had been badly mauled, but it still contained highly experienced men. Auxiliary units, the *Volkssturm* (created on 18 October 1944), were being raised under the auspices of the Nazi Party. The German forces, like those of Frederick the Great in the eighteenth century, could now in theory be moved from front to front on interior lines. Meanwhile, the enemy armies on Germany's western and eastern borders were now fighting at the end of long supply lines, either transoceanic or transcontinental.

Fear of what the Russians would do was an important factor in German last-ditch resistance. The Bolshevik peril had been a central feature of propaganda aimed at the German people since June 1941, and certainly since Stalingrad. In what was, even for him, an extraordinary piece of hypocrisy, Goebbels had said: 'Behind the advancing Soviet divisions we see the Jewish death squads [*Liquidations-kommandos*], behind these rise the Terror, the ghost of the starvation of millions, and complete European anarchy.' Churchill sensed this German fear. When President Roosevelt suggested an appeal to the German people in late November 1944, the prime minister rejected the idea:

> I do not think that the Germans are very much afraid of the treatment they will get from the British and American armies or Governments. What they are afraid of is a Russian occupation, and a large proportion of their people being taken off to toil to death in Russia, or as they say, Siberia. Nothing that we say will eradicate that deep-seated fear. Moreover, U.J. ['Uncle Joe', i.e. Stalin] certainly contemplates demanding two or three million Nazi youth, Gestapo men, etc., doing prolonged reparation work, and it is hard to say that he is wrong.[2]

Hitler had his own motives. A defining moment for Hitler and many Germans of his generation had been the sudden collapse of Imperial Germany in 1918. He fought the Second World War with that memory near the centre of his thoughts. This was shown in his words to the Reichstag on the day he invaded Poland in 1939: '*A November 1918 shall never occur again in Germany.*' He returned to this in his last major public speech, at a turning point of the war, in early November 1942. The German 6th Army had stalled at Stalingrad; Hitler contrasted Imperial Germany in 1918 with the Third Reich. 'Germany at that time laid down its arms at quarter to twelve – in principle I always stop only at five past twelve!' In 1944–5 Hitler and the Nazi leadership were ready to fight to the last, and so were the generals who had ended up in charge of the Wehrmacht. The term 'catastrophic nationalism', coined by the historian Michael Geyer, aptly sums up their state of mind. Such chances as there had been for 'regime change' died with the army conspirators of 20 July 1944.[3] Most Germans were sick of the war, but for others defeat and surrender were still unthinkable. Some men had committed such crimes that they had nothing to lose by fighting on. The younger generation were strongly influenced by ten years of Nazi political indoctrination. Everyone was now affected by propaganda which stressed over and over again the imminent national peril. Fears of atrocity were fuelled by pre-war cultural biases and wartime realities.

Natural barriers protected Germany from invasion. In the south rose the Alps, and the high country of the Austrian Tyrol had been nearly untouched by the war. There were fears, both in Washington and in Moscow, that the Nazis might set up a final 'national redoubt' here. The north was protected by the closed Baltic, which the German Navy and the Luftwaffe still controlled. Command of this sea also allowed the Germans to supply isolated armies in Kurland and East Prussia, and to move forces along the coast. In the west, the Rhine and its fixed defences served as a stout barrier, although beyond that, in central Germany, the terrain was relatively open and a developed road network could be used by the invaders. In the east two main avenues, north and south of the Carpathians, led to the heart of the Reich. The southern approach, up the Danube and through Hungary to Lower Austria and Bavaria, was relatively easy for the Wehrmacht to defend and presented the Red Army with especially difficult logistical problems. The northern approach, however, was across the north German plain with open country up to beyond the Elbe River, and it led to a vulnerable objective, the national capital. From the point of view of strategic geography, Berlin was one of the more exposed places in Germany. It was protected from the east mainly by the river line of the Oder. The exposed 'balcony' of East Prussia overhanging Poland raised particular problems for German defenders, just as it had in 1914. Although this region had good natural defences and developed fortifications, it was relatively easy to cut off from the rest of the Reich. Also vulnerable was the eastern German industrial region of Silesia, on the upper Oder.

Allied leaders and diplomats, meanwhile, had discussed – if not entirely settled – the fate of Germany's territory. How far the Reich would be broken up was not clear, even at the inter-Allied Yalta Conference in February 1945. Ivan Maiskii's January 1944 paper on post-war planning, which probably related closely to thinking in the Commissariat of Foreign Affairs, argued that Germany had to be 'rendered harmless' for a period of 30–50 years. Maiskii assumed Germany would be occupied for ten years and divided into 'more or less' independent states. It was to be subject to 'triple disarmament' – military, industrial and ideological. Germany was to pay heavy reparations for at least ten years, especially in the form of forced labour. Its war criminals, who included the upper echelons of the civil service, were to be subject to severe punishment. A more detailed paper was produced two months later by Maksim Litvinov, who strongly argued for the partition of Germany.[4]

The Allies had agreed on the creation for the immediate post-war period of three roughly equal occupation zones. These had originally been worked out by a British Cabinet committee in the late summer of 1943 – when the Red Army were still far away in the eastern Ukraine and the British and Americans had just landed in southern Italy. The British would occupy the northwest of Germany, the Americans the southwest and the Russians the east.[5] The line between the Russian and Western zones would in the Cold War become the border of East and West Germany.

Even less clear was the political state of post-war Germany. The fighting powers all had an eye to the post-war world, although how far this affected their conduct in early 1945 is still much debated by historians. Stalin certainly desired to install a 'friendly' popular front and perhaps Communist governments in eastern Europe.[6] Whether he also seriously intended this as a near-term objective in the 'grand prize' of Germany is open to question. For Stalin there was a dilemma of choice. One option was firm, long-term, Soviet control over part of Germany. The other was getting a say over all of Germany and a share of all German resources – in partnership with the Western powers. An important 'accidental' factor here was the location of the larger part of the industrial resources of Germany in the western part of the country, notably in the Ruhr. These would be under the immediate control of the British and Americans. Likewise, Moscow could have a say in the disarmament, 'denazification' and economic control of Germany as a whole only if it co-operated with London and Washington. Related to this was the incompatibility between, on the one hand, taking revenge and exploiting German resources as reparations, and on the other hand, winning the support of the vanquished population.

GERMANY IN SOVIET STRATEGY

The operations of the Red Army in East Prussia, Pomerania, Silesia, Austria and Berlin – and in Hungary, Czechoslovakia and western Poland – were closely interconnected in time and space. They were another genuine example of what was called in Soviet military theory 'the co-ordinated operations of numerous army groups, united across a theatre of military operations extending for a thousand kilometres, according to a single strategic plan and a single strategic will.'[7] Everything, however, would not go as smoothly as Stalin and his advisers intended.

The Stavka had a general plan for the offensive aimed against eastern and central Germany.[8] Worked out in October and November 1944 by General Antonov and the planners at the General Staff, this envisaged several months of preparation followed by a two-stage 'deep operation'. The first stage (*etap*) was to take the Soviet spearheads – Zhukov's 1st Belorussian and Konev's 1st Ukrainian Army Groups – to the Bydgoszcz– Poznań–Breslau line in northwestern Poland and Silesia. This first stage was to last fifteen days. Based on the original proposed start date of 20 January 1945, this stage would run to 3 February.[9] In the second stage, which was to follow without a pause, the 1st Ukrainian Army Group was to move to the upper Elbe and the 1st Belorussian Army Group to Berlin. This stage was to last thirty days, and according to the original plan it would have run from 4 February to 5 March. As we will see, by the end of the year the start date had been moved forward two weeks to 8 January. Mapping the operation forward to that date, the expectation would have been to have the first stage completed by 22 January and the second by 21 February. (The Soviet planners also assumed that by the end of December 1944, the Red Army would be on the outskirts of Vienna; in fact at that date Russian forces were still enmeshed 125 miles to the east of Vienna, around Budapest.[10])

When the Stavka conceived this extraordinary Berlin operation in October and November 1944, it was probably influenced by the rapid advance of the Western Allies into France and the Low Countries. The plan was also affected by the weather, if what Stalin and Antonov (later) said at Yalta can be accepted. The Russians assumed that operations would come to a halt in late March and April 1945 with the spring *rasputitsa*. Their intention was evidently to take Berlin before this.[11]

The Soviet offensive – which we now know as the Vistula–Oder operation – began on 12 January 1945.[12] In the first week of February, however, the plan was drastically changed. In effect, the second stage was cancelled. Zhukov and Konev had reached the middle Oder, but they did not plunge on to Berlin. Instead, the Stavka ordered them to secure their flanks. Zhukov in particular was drawn into a two-month campaign on the Baltic coast in Pomerania (between the Vistula and the Oder). Stalin's decision to advance across the Oder to Berlin was only taken at the end of March and the start of April, and it was only implemented on 16 April. When this advance did begin – in effect, the second stage of the October 1944 plan – Berlin was encircled by D + 9, and the garrison surrendered on D + 16.

Why did the original plan for the two-stage 45-day final campaign go awry? The most authoritative account is by General S. M. Shtemenko, Chief of the Operations Directorate

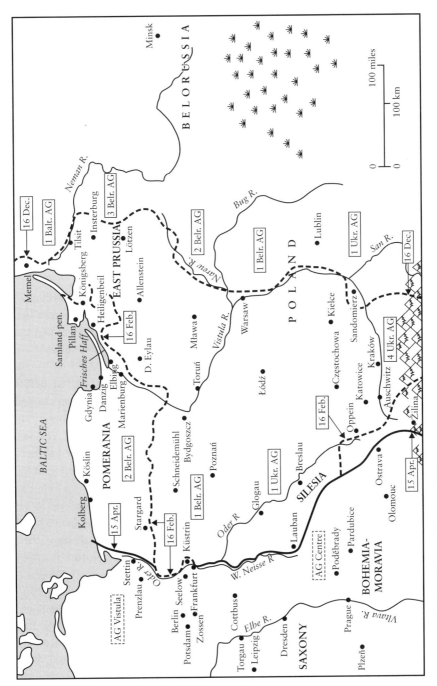

MAP 11 Poland and Eastern Germany, 1945.

FIGURE 14 A column of 'Stalin' heavy tanks in Germany. Alongside, French liberated forced labourers make their way home from Germany.

of the Soviet General Staff; he was Antonov's immediate subordinate. According to Shtemenko, powerful German threats appeared on the flanks, the Soviet forces had severe supply problems and difficult weather conditions (a sudden thaw) blunted the advance.[13] This is not a fully convincing explanation, as such factors surely should have been built into any military plan.

Another explanation might be that the January 1945 operation started before preparations were complete. For many years Russian historians, following Stalin, claimed that the Soviet offensive had been moved *forward* over a week (from 20 to 12 January) in response to American and British pleas for help during the Battle of the Bulge. This was Hitler's offensive in the Ardennes that began on 16 December. At Yalta, on 4 February 1945, Antonov said that the Soviet winter offensive had been due to commence 'at the end of January', but 'in view of the difficult circumstances on the Western Front in connection with the German attack in the Ardennes, the high command of the Soviet Army gave an order to commence the attack not later than the middle of January, not waiting for improvement in weather'. Stalin added that the Russians 'had staged their winter offensive because they felt it was their duty as Allies to do it'.[14] Neither Antonov nor Stalin was speaking the truth.

Rather than the Soviet winter offensive having been moved forward from 20 to 12 January, it had actually been *delayed*, due to bad weather, from 8 to 12 January. The point of the Soviet diplomatic lie was presumably to demonstrate the Red Army's great willingness to co-operate.[15] In any event, the Americans and British had stopped the desperate German offensive in the West by about 24 December. Why the planned start date had earlier been moved up from 20 to 8 January is not clear. Paradoxically, Stalin and the Stavka would have suddenly discovered in early January that the Germans had committed major forces to the Ardennes offensives, and they may have wished to take advantage of this. The intention may also have been to improve their negotiating position at the forthcoming inter-Allied conference, which was now set to take place in Yalta at the start of February. In any event, one can also speculate that the premature start may have contributed to problems later in the operation.

The Soviet armies certainly had extraordinary short-term success at the opening of the Vistula–Oder offensive. We have already seen how Zhukov and Konev were able to drive very rapidly across Poland. Zhukov in particular had reached the Bydgoszcz–Poznań line by 25 January (D + 13 of the whole offensive), several days before the planners had expected. He then pushed on another hundred miles to the Oder. The problem was that he had achieved this by bypassing centres of German resistance. The most important such place was the city of Poznań (Posen), which controlled the rail routes to the west. Poznań, with nineteenth-century fortifications, would hold out for a month, and the German garrison only surrendered on 23 February.

At the end of January, Zhukov did not want to stop. For Stalin's leading marshal, neither supply problems nor the German threat from the flanks seem to have presented insurmountable problems. On 22 January, Zhukov instructed his tank army commanders to plough through the fixed defences in front of the Oder. Zhukov evidently wanted to keep to the original plan. On 26 January (D + 14), in response to a query from the Stavka, Zhukov proposed to Stalin that the 1st Belorussian Army Group continue to the Oder *and beyond it*. His 2nd Guards Tank Army was 'to force the Oder off the march and envelop Berlin from the northwest and west', while the 1st Guards Tank Army attacked the German capital from the north and northeast. His other armies would cross the Oder further south.[16] This plan was approved by the Stavka on the evening of 27 January. Shortly after that (probably on 3 February – which is also the 'official' end date of the Vistula–Oder operation), Zhukov issued an order for the 1st Belorussian Army Group to take Berlin by 15–16 February, 'with a swift rush [*stremitel'nym broskom*]', before the Wehrmacht could move in reserves. On 10 February he sent Stalin at Yalta a detailed proposal for a continuing advance which would take the 1st Belorussian Army Group to Berlin by 18–19 February.[17]

Even after he had had to send forces to cover his right flank, in Pomerania, Zhukov hoped this would be only a temporary diversion. On 16 February he grudgingly signalled Stalin that 'in execution of your personal instructions I am reporting my considerations on the carrying out of a limited offensive operation by the forces of the right wing of my army group'. The aim was to help Rokossovskii's 2nd Belorussian Army Group advance towards Stettin at the mouth of the Oder. But that did not necessarily affect the offensive by the main forces of the 1st Belorussian Army Group across the Oder towards Berlin. On 16 February Zhukov also asked Stalin to confirm that this Berlin offensive would be scheduled for 1–2 March. Only on 20 February did Zhukov put his army group onto the defensive. In his 1974 memoirs, Zhukov would devote considerable space to denying the claim of General Chuikov (of the 8th Guards Army), that a Berlin attack could have been mounted in February. Thirty years earlier, Zhukov himself had thought that such a blow was possible.[18]

On Zhukov's left, Marshal Konev also favoured a continued drive to the west. On 28 January Konev proposed resuming the advance on 5–6 February and reaching the Elbe by 25–8 February.[19] As we will see, Konev – unlike Zhukov – was able to continue to push 75 miles further west in mid-February, but he finally stopped on the Western Neisse River, which forms a north–south line with the Oder. Beyond that line, he could not advance deeper into Germany without the support of Zhukov on his right flank.

No one can know what would have happened had Zhukov and Konev pressed on. It is doubtful that a February assault on Berlin would have been less bloody than the actual operation in April 1945. By April German forces were weaker, and they were being hard-pressed by the Americans from west of the Elbe, not west of the Rhine. But a February attack on Berlin might have brought the European war to a close two months earlier and saved hundreds of thousands of Russian lives in East Prussia and Pomerania.

It has been suggested that the fundamental reason for the halt on the Oder was that Stalin did not want to take Berlin during the Yalta Conference (4–11 February).[20] That explanation is not confirmed by the documents nor by common sense. Zhukov was still pressing for an advance during and after the Yalta meetings, but Berlin would in any event not have fallen until after the Yalta Conference had ended. If Stalin was concerned about not frightening the Western Allies, he would not have overrun the remaining three-quarters of Poland. An alternative explanation which has been suggested, and a more narrow one, is based on an event that occurred after the close of the Yalta Conference. This was the German counter-offensive south from Stargard in Pomerania into Zhukov's right flank, Operation SOLSTICE (SONNENWENDE) of Army Group Vistula, which began on 16 February.[21] However, while SOLSTICE was perhaps a contributing factor, the Soviet offensive was already running into trouble before this.

More practical problems must have had an effect. As had been the case on the Vistula–Narew line in mid 1944, the Red Army had advanced beyond its supplies. Soviet engineers had to build bridges across the Vistula, and repair damaged railways and road bridges across Poland. The Germans clung on to communications hubs at Schneidemühl (Pila), Poznań, Glogau and Breslau. There was a sudden thaw at the start of February 1945 which clogged the roads, thinned river ice and closed the improvised forward airstrips of the Soviet air armies. From the beginning of February, the Oder bridgeheads were pounded by what was left of the Luftwaffe, operating off hard runways in central Germany.

Poor Soviet intelligence may well also have played a part, exaggerating the perceived danger to the flanks. Zhukov himself commented on the greater difficulty of obtaining information about the enemy once the Red Army had passed the limits of Soviet partisan activity. The Soviet General Staff apparently had only limited sources of information, and it was only from mid-February that the provision of intelligence information from the Western Allies to the Russians increased – based on ULTRA decrypts. At Yalta, General

FIGURE 15 Stalin and Molotov at the Yalta Conference, February 1945. In the background is A. Ia. Vyshinskii, the Deputy Foreign Commissar.

Antonov had to ask the western commanders where they thought Hitler's key striking force, the 6th SS Panzer Army, had been moved to, and two months later Stalin grumbled about the poor information that had been supplied.[22]

Another explanation is more speculative. Stalin may have had in mind what had happened to the Red Army twenty years earlier in the Soviet–Polish War. Then, in 1920, the Red Army under Mikhail Tukhachevskii had been poised in front of the Vistula, ready for the capture of Warsaw, a breakthrough to revolutionary Germany and the achievement of a European Revolution by the bayonets of the Red Army. In his haste, Tukhachevskii had left open his flanks. His overextended forces were hit by a Polish counter-attack, and his forces were driven back in disorder. Meanwhile, in 1945, the most optimistic military prognosis for the collapse of the Wehrmacht had been proven wrong, and the enemy had surviving forces in Pomerania and Silesia. The Western Allies were still behind the Rhine, and there was then no question yet that the USSR had to worry about a race with the British and Americans for Berlin. The Soviet dictator's political reckoning may have been that there was no great advantage in a Blitzkrieg on Berlin and much to be lost by an expensive failure.

EAST PRUSSIA, POMERANIA AND SILESIA

Northeastern Germany

The best simple explanation for the Red Army's failure to take Berlin in February or March, following the late 1944 plans of the Soviet General Staff, was a chain of events in the Baltic 'balcony' overhanging the Soviet armies advancing across Poland.[23] Difficulties in middle and late January in taking East Prussia led to a change in the line of Marshal Rokossovskii's advance into Pomerania. This in turn opened up a gap between Zhukov and Rokossovskii. By February this weakness on the Russian right flank allowed a concrete German threat to emerge near Stargard (in western Pomerania). After that, the Stavka decided to eliminate any danger to the right and left flanks before advancing on to Berlin. That process took the better part of two months.

East Prussia stretched 150 miles from east to west, and 120 miles from north to south. It was a relatively poor farming region of Germany, with a pre-war population of 2,500,000. The most important centre was the ancient city of Königsberg (now Kaliningrad in the Russian Federation). Between 1919 and 1939, East Prussia had been divided from the rest of Germany by a corridor of Polish territory about 50 miles wide (part of West Prussia).[24] West Prussia and Pomerania lacked such a clear political and historical identity as East Prussia, but they were about the same size, running west from Danzig to beyond Stettin at the mouth of the Oder. The population here was about 1,200,000, and like that of East Prussia it was predominantly German.

West Prussia and Pomerania were important politically for the revised Polish border and for resolution of the 'Danzig question'. East Prussia was of even greater strategic importance to the Russians. Stalin was to make much of Königsberg as a 'warm-water' port, but the real importance of the province was for land and air warfare. In both 1914–15 and 1941, East Prussia had been a forward German base for operations against Russia. The region was also a critical part of the defences of eastern Germany, threatening the flank of any Russian attack on Berlin. If the USSR held East Prussia, any future state in central Germany, whoever governed it, would be much more vulnerable. The Allied leaders had already informally agreed among themselves that Germany would lose East Prussia and most of Pomerania. Stalin's own position seems to have been clear from the beginning of the war. Comintern leader Georgi Dimitrov heard him thinking out loud about East Prussia in September 1941, while waiting out a German air raid on Moscow: 'If we win, we'll give East Prussia back to Slavdom, where it belongs. We'll settle the whole place with Slavs.'[25]

The initial beneficiary was to be Poland. Such a step would require the forced migration of several million Germans, but the complications of the Polish corridor and Danzig had, after all, been the immediate cause of the European war in 1939. At the Tehran Conference in December 1943 – at a time when German Army Group North was still closely investing Leningrad, and German Army Group Centre was still holding its own in Belorussia – Stalin had proposed an exchange of territories. The USSR would cede to the revived Polish state some territory east of the June 1941 Soviet–Polish border. In exchange, Moscow would be granted the northern part of what was now presumably 'Polish' East Prussia, including the towns of Königsberg, Insterburg (now Cherniakhovsk) and Tilsit (Sovetsk). Churchill saw nothing wrong with this, as he told the Polish government-in-exile in February 1944: 'The Russians had an historical and well-founded claim to this territory.' He based this claim, however, on the very far-fetched argument that as part of a 'thirty-year war' against German aggression, the Russians had shed their blood there in the campaigns of 1914–15.[26]

Pomerania

Pomerania was the coastal region closest to Berlin and the Oder front, and most directly linked to events there. We will begin with it, although this means approaching events in a roundabout way. Rokossovskii's 2nd Belorussian Army Group, north of Zhukov, was logically the force that should have taken East Pomerania (Hinterpommern).[27] The 2nd Belorussian Army Group still had seven infantry armies. Its mobile forces were the 5th Guards Tank Army and three mobile corps. After breaking out of the Narew bridgeheads, however, Rokossovskii developed his main axis of advance not to the northwest but to the north. A drive to the northwest would have taken him across the upper Vistula and into Pomerania, advancing towards Stettin; it would also have enabled the 2nd Belorussian Army Group to cover Zhukov's right flank.

Rokossovskii's actual movement took his army group in a more northerly direction, on the shortest route to the Baltic and through the town of Mława towards Deutsch Eylau (Iława) and Marienburg (Malbork).[28] This orientation followed from a Stavka directive issued early on 21 January (D + 9 of the Vistula-Oder operation); with this, Rokossovskii had been ordered to move his three central armies (the 2nd Shock, the 48th and the 3rd) and his mobile striking force (the 5th Guards Tank Army) north and northeast to support operations in East Prussia. As we have already seen, the results of the order were valuable enough. The tank army reached the Frisches Haff, the lagoon between Königsberg and the Vistula, on 25 January (D + 13). Rokossovskii had effectively cut East Prussia off from Pomerania and from the rest of the Reich.

The Stavka's order of 21 January had, however, come as a complete surprise for Rokossovskii. All previous discussion had involved close co-operation with his left-flank neighbour, Zhukov's 1st Belorussian Army Group.[29] Rokossovskii's 70th and 65th Armies did indeed continue northwest beyond the Vistula, but his army group's centre of gravity was now on the eastern side of the river. Rokossovskii was supposed to be reinforced with the 19th Army, which was to operate on his left flank. Unfortunately, the erstwhile defenders of the Murmansk railway took some time to make the long transfer to their new position. Meanwhile, aside from opening up a gap with Zhukov, Rokossovskii's change of direction also allowed part of the damaged German 2nd Army (General Weiss) to pull back and fight again in the Vistula estuary, and around Danzig and Gdynia.

The overall problem for the Soviet forces was made more challenging by the unexpected pace and depth of the advance of Zhukov and the 1st Belorussian Army

Group. With Rokossovskii diverted to East Prussia, Zhukov now had to cover his right
flank with his own forces. He had pushed six armies (the 33rd, 1st Guards Tank, 69th, 8th
Guards, 5th Shock and 2nd Guards Tank Armies) to the Oder by the start of February,
but he now had a long 150-mile right flank thinly covered by his 47th Army, 61st Army
and 3rd Shock Army. By the middle of February, Zhukov had had to reorient the face
of the 1st and the 2nd Guards Tank Armies from west to north, and he had been made
responsible for ensuring the link with Rokossovskii.[30]

The big question was whether the Wehrmacht would be able to exploit the Red
Army's confusion. The German high command had within a few days of the start of
the Soviet Vistula–Oder operation (12 January) realized that a huge hole was being
blown in its position in the east. One of the backup measures adopted was the creation
of a new formation to cover the northern region – West Prussia, Pomerania and
Brandenburg – between Army Group Centre and Army Group 'A' (soon to be renamed
Army Groups 'North' and 'Centre', respectively). This new formation was Army
Group Vistula (Weichsel). In Hitler's most extraordinary front-line appointment,
'Reichsführer SS' Heinrich Himmler was put in command of this formation in late
January.[31] Himmler's headquarters were supposed to control two shattered armies,
the 2nd (Weiss) in West Prussia and the 9th (Busse) to the southwest of Weiss, behind
the Oder. Between them a new formation was established called – for a couple of
weeks – the 11th SS Panzer Army under SS General Felix Steiner. Army Group Vistula
was reinforced to a paper strength of over thirty divisions.

From this situation came Operation SOLSTICE, the German Stargard offensive.[32]
Within three or four weeks of the start of the Vistula–Oder operation, Guderian, the
Chief of the Army General Staff, had begun to consider the possibility of a counter-attack.
He had already done this, equally unrealistically, in the region between the Bug and the
Vistula rivers back in July 1944. A plan was now prepared for a limited attack from the
north. After a famous row with the Führer, Guderian was able to have an able staff officer,
General Walter Wenck, put in effective charge of operations. Wenck had been Guderian's
right-hand man at the OKH since July 1944. The German attack began on 16 February
1945, but in the end SOLSTICE was a damp squib. The advance of the scratch force of three
corps, including SS divisions manned by Western European volunteers, was contained
by the 1st Belorussian Army Group after about 10 miles. Any coherence was lost when
Wenck injured himself in a traffic accident on the *Autobahn* at the end of the second
day. Operation SOLSTICE in Pomerania does not bear comparison in scale or impact even
with December's Operation WATCH ON THE RHINE (WACHT AM RHEIN) in the Ardennes,
January's NORTHWIND (NORDWIND) in Alsace, or SPRING AWAKENING in March in
Hungary. Also, coming as it did at least two weeks *after* Zhukov halted on the Oder,
SOLSTICE was not the cause of that pause, although it may have reinforced the caution
now felt back in Moscow, and it may have added to the length of the break in the advance.

The pressure was very soon going in the opposite direction, as the Red Army counter-
attacked as part of the East Pomeranian operation. Zhukov, with the 47th, 61st, 2nd
Guards Tank, 3rd Shock and 1st Polish Armies, advanced from 1 March to the east of the
lower Oder, taking Stargard on the 4th and fighting through the outskirts of the port city

of Stettin (Szczecin). Zhukov had turned 90 degrees (south–north), away from the Berlin axis (east–west). By 21 March, the 1st Belorussian Army Group controlled the entire region on the right (east) bank of the lower Oder. Meanwhile, Zhukov's right flank, now working closely with Rokossovskii's left, had by the first days of March reached the Baltic near Köslin (Koszalin) and Kolberg (Kołobrzeg). Between the two Soviet army groups was trapped the eastern wing of the defending German army, now called the 3rd Panzer Army (formerly the 11th SS Panzer Army) and led by General Raus.[33] Further east, in West Prussia, the German 2nd Army was now cut off from the Reich.

Any thoughts Zhukov and other commanders might have had of immediately pressing on to Berlin had now passed. Rokossovskii had given up four armies to Cherniakhovskii (the 3rd Belorussian Army Group) in East Prussia in early February but had been reinforced in turn by Zhukov's 1st Guards Tank Army. He now drove *east* some 80 miles with five infantry armies back towards the cities at the top of the Polish corridor in West Prussia: Gdynia (Gotenhafen) and Danzig. Meanwhile, in giving up Marienburg and Elbing (Elbląg) on 9 and 10 March, the Germans completed the process of isolating Pomerania and East Prussia from one another, one to the west of the Vistula mouth, the other to the east. The German 2nd Army, now under General Saucken, was driven back in the last two weeks of March to the coastal cities. Gdynia and Danzig fell on 28 and 30 March, respectively. The long sandspit of the Hela Peninsula, northwest of Gdynia, had been shelled on 1 September 1939 in the opening shots of the war; the last Polish soldiers had surrendered there. Now it was the turn of the surviving German soldiers and civilians to find some miserable shelter on the sandspit for the five weeks until the total Nazi defeat. Other Germans, numbering in the tens of thousands, took desperate refuge on the Danziger Werder and the nearby Nehrung sandspit, protected by the flooded Vistula delta.

East Prussia

East Prussia, meanwhile, was also an important part of the Stavka's problem. The Soviet General Staff had considered offensive operations here before the war in 1940–1. At that time, the General Staff had been unenthusiastic about this axis of attack, believing that it compared unfavourably with southern Poland. The terrain was difficult, there were elaborate German fortifications, and it was believed the Germans would fiercely defend an historic part of their country. (The experience of the spring of 1945 would show this caution to have been fully justified.) The Russians also had the memory of the disastrous Tannenberg campaign of 1914. Then, the Russian army of General Rennenkampf had attacked from the east, through the Insterburg corridor; General Samsonov had made a separate attack from the south, towards Allenstein (now Olsztyn). The Russian thrusts were poorly co-ordinated; a brilliant defence by Generals Hindenburg and Ludendorff defeated the Tsarist armies in detail and drove them back to the frontier.

As we have already seen, as early as July 1944 – in the aftermath of Operation BAGRATION – Zhukov had put forward to Stalin a proposal to give priority to a campaign to take East Prussia.[34] The objective was to cut off both German Army Groups Centre (in East Prussia) and North (in Kurland). However, in the end, priority was given – as in the 1940–1 planning – to southern and central Poland, and then to the Balkans. Nevertheless, the first strictly 'German' territory to come under Russian attack was in East Prussia. The Red Army approached the historical border of East Prussia at the end of July 1944, at the time Kaunas in Lithuania fell and in the aftermath of the great victory in Belorussia (Operation BAGRATION). A Soviet patrol breached the territory of pre-war Germany near Stallupoenen (now Nesterov) on 17 August 1944; this was D + 55 of Operation BAGRATION.

The first major Soviet attack on East Prussia, however, came only in October 1944.[35] This was mounted from the east by Cherniakhovskii's 3rd Belorussian Army Group. Although the operation prevented the transfer of German reserves north into Latvia against General Bagramian's Memel operation, this was not the main intention. It was also not just a probe of the German defences. In early October the Stavka ordered Cherniakhovskii with the 3rd Belorussian Army Group to destroy the German formations concentrated around Insterburg and Tilsit and to take Königsberg.

The operation was launched into the Insterburg corridor towards the towns of Gumbinnen (now Gusev) and Goldap (Gołdap) on 16 October 1944 and halted after two weeks. It is known as the Gumbinnen–Goldap operation, and it cost the Red Army 17,000 personnel. Cherniakhovskii's attack was related to unsuccessful and costly attempts to broaden and consolidate two bridgeheads on the Narew River northeast of Warsaw. From there, attacks could have been launched by the 1st and the 2nd Belorussian Army Groups (under Rokossovskii and Zakharov) towards the towns of Mława and Allenstein, and towards the Baltic (i.e. attacking East Prussia from the south). The Stavka finally called these off at the start of November 1944 after heavy losses. Zakharov, the commander of the 2nd Belorussian Army Group, was removed and demoted to an army-level command.[36]

In any event, the German 4th Army under General Hossbach mounted a successful counter-attack east from Gumbinnen. At the beginning of November, the Soviet 3rd Belorussian Army Group was ordered onto the defensive, and Vasilevskii was relieved of his overall responsibility for the army group. Goebbels' propaganda organization gave huge coverage to Soviet atrocities apparently committed during the brief Red Army occupation, especially in the small town of Nemmersdorf (now Maiakovskoe).[37] There was one other development relating to these attacks. On 20 November 1944 Hitler left for the last time his eastern headquarters at Rastenburg in East Prussia. Rastenburg was just 60 miles from the Red Army's front line.

The main attack on East Prussia was actually mounted three months after the unsuccessful Gumbinnen–Goldap operation, in mid-January 1945. It coincided with the beginning of the Vistula–Oder operation. The main attacking force, again, was Cherniakhovskii's 3rd Belorussian Army Group. Cherniakhovskii now commanded the 11th Guards Army and six other infantry armies, with two mobile corps. Initially the northern part of East Prussia was attacked by the 43rd Army, controlled by Bagramian's 1st Baltic Army Group, but at the end of February, command in this theatre was consolidated under the 3rd Belorussian Army Group.[38] To the southwest, as we have seen, Rokossovskii was to deploy his centre and right-flank forces, the 2nd Shock, 48th, 3rd, 49th and 50th Armies, as well as the 5th Guards Tank Army. On 9 February 1945 the tank army and the 48th, 3rd and 50th Armies would be transferred from Rokossovskii to Cherniakhovskii.

Cherniakhovskii's initial offensive was the Insterburg–Königsberg operation, which began on 13 January. Attacking head-on the German 3rd Panzer Army and the fortifications blocking the Insterburg 'corridor' (Rennenkampf's line of advance in 1914), Cherniakhovskii made only limited progress for over a week. His forces suffered heavy losses. This delay contributed to the Stavka's decision (on 20–21 January) to shift the centre of gravity of Rokossovskii's operation east of the Vistula mouth. This gave Rokossovskii the part of Tsarist General Samsonov in 1914 at Tannenberg, in what became the Mława–Elbing operation. With a little more patience in Moscow, the diversion of effort might have been avoided. Cherniakhovskii, one of the most effective army group commanders, shifted the 11th Guards Army to his right flank, wheeled it around the now strained German defences, and punched deep. The enemy front caved in, Insterburg fell on 22 January (D + 9), and by the 27th (D + 14) the Russians had advanced 75 miles to Königsberg's nineteenth-century city defences. Soviet troops even broke in for two weeks behind Königsberg; they took most of the Samland (Zemland) Peninsula, and temporarily cut the vital link from Königsberg to the sea at Pillau (now Baltiisk).

Even more dramatic successes were achieved by Rokossovskii and the 2nd Ukrainian Army Group in the south. Allenstein fell on the same day as Insterburg (22 January). Whatever negative effect Rokossovskii's change of direction had on the Berlin operation, it certainly speeded up the advance from the south into East Prussia. As we have already seen, west of Allenstein the 5th Guards Tank Army drove to the Baltic on 25 January. It reached the frozen lagoon of the Frisches Haff, just east of Elbing. The Germans blew up the huge Tannenberg memorial to prevent it falling into Russian hands, and evacuated Field Marshal Hindenburg's coffin to the Reich.

Hit from the left and right, the commander of the German 4th Army, General Hossbach, abandoned the (southeast) corner post of the East Prussian defences at Lötzen, with its formidable fixed defences. He pulled back, partly in the hope of hitting Rokossovskii's right flank, partly to get near the relative safety of the sea. Hossbach was to achieve notoriety after the war; as Hitler's military adjutant, he had taken the minutes of Hitler's November 1937 meeting with German leaders; the 'Hossbach memorandum' was later used to show Hitler's premeditated campaign of aggression. In 1945, with the abandonment of Lötzen, Hossbach was in disgrace with Hitler himself, and he was sacked. Also dismissed was Hans Reinhardt, Hossbach's superior as commander of Army Group North (renamed from Army Group Centre the week before); Reinhardt was a very experienced Eastern Front panzer commander.[39] Reinhardt's replacement was General Rendulic, who lasted until mid-March, and was then replaced by General Weiss. Reinhardt and Hossbach had failed where Hindenburg and Ludendorff had succeeded. Where Samsonov and Rennenkampf had met disaster at Tannenberg in 1914,

Cherniakhovskii and Rokossovskii, respectively, on the same lines of advance, won a great victory.

The investment of German Army Group North in and around Königsberg did not, however, guarantee immediate and total Soviet success.[40] After giving up most of East Prussia, the Germans held on grimly to the coastal pockets, not least because they were protecting hundreds of thousands of German civilian refugees. The Nazi government had made little provision to evacuate East Prussia. The arrival at Pillau of two German divisions withdrawn from the Memel (further north up the Baltic coast) allowed Rendulic to re-establish rail communications across southern Samland between Königsberg and Pillau in mid-February, and to evacuate as many as 100,000 civilians from the city. Meanwhile, the bulk of the German 4th Army, and some elements of the 2nd Army, fifteen divisions in all, retreated to a perimeter backing on the Frisches Haff, southwest of Königsberg and centred on the town of Heiligenbeil (now Mamonovo). The Stavka ordered that this pocket be eliminated by 20–25 February, but the effort was to take over a month longer. Cherniakhovskii was killed trying to achieve this goal, fatally injured on 18 February outside Mehlsack (now Pieniężno), on the south side of the Heiligenbeil pocket. He was on the way to a forward army headquarters when a shell exploded near his jeep. Cherniakhovskii was unlucky; none of the other four men in the vehicle were harmed.[41] The youngest of Stalin's army group commanders, he was only thirty-nine when he died. He was one of three Soviet army group commanders to be killed in action (along with Kirponos in 1941 and Vatutin in 1944). Insterburg was renamed Cherniakhovsk in his honour.

Marshal Vasilevskii now stepped in to take overall command of what had become a slow-moving push into East Prussia. Here was a very senior officer, the man who had served from 1942 as the Chief of the Red Army General Staff. Vasilevskii had been in the field more than he had been in Moscow. Matters may have been brought to a head in early February 1945 when Vasilevskii temporarily 'replaced' Antonov during the latter's trip south with Stalin to the Yalta Conference. In fact, during the summer of 1944 Stalin had chosen Vasilevskii for a quite different role, overall command of operations in the coming war in the Far East against Japan. In any event, in the middle of February 1945 Stalin sent Vasilevskii back to the front to sort out the operations of the 1st Baltic and 3rd Belorussian Army Groups. His appointment coincided by chance with the death of Cherniakhovskii, and – unexpectedly – Vasilevskii was made commander of the 3rd Belorussian Army Group. This was, as it happened, the first time the marshal had ever directly commanded an army group. Like Zhukov – who in November 1944 had been made commander of the 1st Belorussian Army Group – this could be seen as a demotion. In Vasilevskii's case, there was compensation in his appointment for the first time to membership of the small committee of the Stavka.

Vasilevskii took three weeks to regroup his forces. The final Soviet operations in the Königsberg area fell into several methodical phases, beginning on 12 March 1945. First the considerable field forces of the German 4th Army and fixed defences around Heiligenbeil had to be crushed. This was achieved, after two and a half weeks of heavy fighting, on 29 March. Some German survivors escaped by boat across the Frisches Haff. The second phase, the attack on Königsberg itself, began on 6 April. The city fell on the 9th (four days before Vienna fell), yielding over 90,000 prisoners. Hitler ordered General Otto Lasch, the commander of Königsberg, hanged in absentia; Lasch outlived his Führer and got to write his memoirs. Holding onto the East Prussian city for two and a half months (since late January) actually amounted to a remarkable German military achievement, although this was bought at the price of tens of thousands of needless civilian deaths. The Soviet operations around Königsberg made heavy use of artillery and air bombardment, and the logistical requirements were very high. Artillery included siege guns with a bore as large as 305mm. Air operations were co-ordinated directly by Marshal Novikov, commander of the whole Red Army Air Force; 2,500 aircraft took part, grouped into five large air formations – the Baltic Fleet Air Force and four air armies. Finally, in the last days of the war, Vasilevskii eliminated the pocket to the west of Königsberg, on the Samland Peninsula. This held nine German divisions. The Samland operation began on 13 April – about the time Zhukov and Konev began their move to Berlin. It ended with the capture of Pillau on 25 April. Those German soldiers and civilians who could escape crossed to the overcrowded misery of the Nehrung sandspit on the sea side of the Frisches Haff.

The whole Baltic campaign had an important naval element. The spring of 1945 was the last gasp of the German *Kriegsmarine*. German cruisers and destroyers provided artillery support. Some 35–40 German ships of over 5,000 tons, and many smaller vessels, were involved in the evacuation of East and West Prussia. The fighting also showed one of the limitations of Soviet power. The Soviet Baltic Fleet had been a serious force on paper in 1941, but it was severely worn down during the war by bombing, lack of maintenance and training, and transfer of personal to the Red Army. The Gulf of Finland was still heavily mined. No major Soviet surface ships, not a single destroyer, would be deployed into the open Baltic in the spring of 1945.

A flotilla of Soviet submarines was based in southwestern Finland, and motor torpedo boats operated down the coast. One submarine, *S-13*, was involved in the fatal sinkings of two evacuation ships. On 30 January, during the first week of the evacuation, it torpedoed the liner *Wilhelm Gustloff* (25,500 tons) off Gdynia, with the loss of over 4,000 civilians. Two weeks later, the same submarine sank the liner *General Steuben* (14,700 tons) off Pillau with 2,000 wounded German troops on board. The heaviest single loss for the Germans – and possibly the worst disaster in the history of seafaring – was the sinking by the submarine *L-3* of the small German freighter, *Goya* (5,200 tons). Torpedoed in a convoy from the Hela Peninsula on the night of 16– 17 April, the *Goya* went down with over 6,000 people on board. Despite these horrors, the evacuation of civilians and soldiers across the Baltic to northern Germany and Denmark was extraordinary in its scale.

The fighting in East Pomerania and West Prussia cost the Red Army 53,000 lives, 1,000 tanks and 1,100 aircraft. East Prussia was much worse. The offensive there took three months to complete. Operations from mid-January to late April 1945 cost 126,000 Soviet lives (mostly in the 3rd Belorussian Army Group), 3,500 tanks and 1,500 aircraft. The losses in East Prussia alone were three times those of the Vistula–Oder operation, and 40 per cent higher than the Berlin operation – although, to be sure, the fighting in East Prussia lasted much longer.[42] The wisdom of this expenditure of human lives is certainly not obvious. By early February, at least, the German pockets on the Baltic might have been allowed to 'wither on the vine'. There are evidently no available figures for German military and civilian deaths in the fighting in this theatre from January to May, but they must have been extremely high.

Silesia

On the southern edge of the Soviet tsunami, was Silesia, a region extending up the Oder River to the northern edge of Czechoslovakia. Lower (northern) Silesia, the main city of which was Breslau (Wrocław), had been part of the pre-war Reich. The population had been almost completely German. Upper Silesia, further south, had a mixed population and had been argued over between Weimar Germany and Poland after 1919. Roughly three million Germans inhabited the two parts of Silesia. Upper Silesia was one of Europe's richest coal-mining regions. In addition, unlike the Ruhr, Silesia was distant from Allied bomber bases in Britain and Italy. Silesia was a kind of German Urals, a region to which the war factories and population of the Reich had been evacuated. The population of Breslau, the main town, had risen to over a million people by 1945. Stalin, a veteran industrializer, was keenly aware of the region's resources. He described them as 'gold' to Marshal Konev, and he ordered him to encircle manufacturing and mining districts and capture them intact, rather than plough through them.[43]

Diplomatically, Silesia, or at least that part of the region south and west of the Oder, was more complicated than Pomerania or East Prussia. At Yalta, Stalin claimed to Roosevelt and Churchill that all the German civilians had been driven out of Silesia, but it was not until the Potsdam Conference in June 1945 that the Americans conceded that the territory beyond the Western Neisse River (i.e. Upper Silesia) would be under Polish rather than German control.

South of Frankfurt-on-Oder, the line of the Oder River turns sharply east and then southeast. The Red Army's Sandomierz–Silesia operation had by 3 February 1945 taken Konev's 1st Ukrainian Army Group to this part of the river. It held bridgeheads north of Breslau, at Ohlau (Oława), and south of it, at Steinau (Ścinawa).[44] Konev had eight infantry armies; his mobile forces were the 3rd Guards Tank Army, 4th Tank Army and five independent mobile corps. While Zhukov in the first weeks of February had been ordered north to deal with Pomerania, Konev was able to resume his advance to the west, in the Lower Silesian operation (8–24 February 1945). North of Breslau, three of his armies moved forward another 70–80 miles to the Western Neisse River, which forms a north–south line with the upper Oder. As we have seen, in late January, Konev had proposed driving another 75 miles beyond the Western Neisse to the upper Elbe. In fact, he only established a small bridgehead on the Western Neisse. Then he, like Zhukov, was ordered by the Stavka to deal with complications in the rear of his army group.

Konev had a German strongpoint astride his rail communications at Breslau, presenting a problem similar to the one Zhukov had with Poznań. Rather than sending all his forces west, Konev had to use the 6th Army and the 5th Guards Army in his centre, supported by the 3rd Guards Tank Army, to encircle Breslau. From its bridgehead on the Oder, the 6th Army turned east, while the 5th Guards thrust forward to the west, and the two linked up behind Breslau on 15 February. Much of the population of Breslau had been hastily evacuated by the local Nazi leaders as the Russian offensive developed – in the last days, women and children were simply driven out into the snow.[45] (Many refugees from Silesia soon found themselves in another calamity, the bombing of Dresden on 13–15 February.) Some 100,000 civilians remained in Breslau when the Russian pincers closed behind it, and the blockade of the city was to last three months. It was another siege like Königsberg and Danzig, difficult for the Red Army, deadly for the Wehrmacht defenders, and terrible for the trapped civilians. For the Nazis, Breslau was a symbol of last-ditch resistance. In the last hours of his life, Hitler chose the local Gauleiter, Karl Hanke, to replace Himmler as head of the SS.

Further south, Konev had advanced into Upper Silesia in the last weeks of January 1945. This had been a complex and rapidly successful operation, but it had tied down one of his tank armies. Three infantry armies, which had just taken Kraków, attacked west frontally. Meanwhile, Rybalko's 3rd Guards Tank Army, having approached the Oder near Breslau, now turned back southeast up the river to threaten from the rear Schulz's 17th Army in Upper Silesia. Konev had provided an exit route for the German defenders out of the salient around Katowice and west across the Oder; he evidently did this intentionally to avoid the damage that might be caused by a last-ditch defence.[46] Unusually, Hitler sanctioned the withdrawal, as it was supported by the newly arrived army group commander, the ubiquitous General Schörner. Katowice, the main town of the Upper Silesian industrial district, was taken by the Red Army on 28 January 1945.

Schörner's German Army Group Centre (until late January known as Army Group 'A') remained for Konev and the Stavka a distant threat and a distraction, south and west of Silesia. Its elements included the 4th Panzer Army (General Gräser) in Saxony, and the bulk of the 17th Army (General Schulz) in Bohemia. For Marshal Konev, the danger continued of a German attempt to relieve Breslau. At the beginning of March, Schörner mounted nearly the last German wartime offensive which achieved any success, against the small Silesian town of Lauban (Lubań), in the southwestern corner of Konev's front.[47] Goebbels himself travelled down from Berlin to inspect the scene of the victory with Schörner.

In the end, Konev dealt with this region in the second half of March, in the Upper Silesian operation. Four Soviet armies (one of them the 4th Tank Army) were devoted to reducing the minor city and rail junction at Oppeln (Opole), encircling it with two armies on either side. This may have been a Soviet strategic feint, to threaten northern Bohemia and keep the Germans for transferring troops to the defence of Berlin. More likely the Stavka connected it with the abortive advance of Petrov's 4th Ukrainian Army Group to the Vltava River and Prague, which began on 10 March.[48] In any event, when the Stavka's sudden reconsideration of strategy came at the end of March, and Stalin decided to resume the drive on Berlin, Konev was caught off balance. A significant part of his strength was 190 miles from the Western Neisse River, its allocated start-point.

The bloody fighting in East Prussia, Pomerania and Silesia from January to April 1945 was for the Russians a strategic distraction. Given the initial success of Zhukov and Konev, and the massive resources available to them, the campaign here was excessively drawn out. The German forces were weak and poorly equipped; many of them were *Volkssturm* divisions. Such forces might be capable of the last-ditch defence of cities like Königsberg, Danzig, Poznań or Breslau, but they were not capable of any sustained offensive manoeuvre which could seriously threaten the flanks and rear of the Red Army. Although the Soviet commitment of forces to these flanks did limit the German ability to reinforce the immediate defences of Berlin, these battles probably tied up even larger Red Army forces. The capture of Berlin would inevitably have led to the surrender of the armies on the Baltic coast and in Upper Silesia. There was no danger of the Western Allies approaching any of these regions first. It may be, however, that the Russians were marking time as they built up supplies in the centre and awaited better weather.

VIENNA

On the other side of Greater Germany, the Red Army was pressing into Austria. The Soviet Union had agreed to the independence of the Austrian state, cancelling the *Anschluss* of 1938. As already mentioned, the Stavka had originally expected the Red Army to get to the outskirts of Vienna by the end of December 1944. In fact, the Russians were held up by the fighting in Hungary, with the stubborn defence of Budapest and Hitler's commitment of reserves for a final offensive there. On 17 February 1945, the Stavka issued a series of directives to the various army groups. The 2nd and 3rd Ukrainian Army Groups (commanded by Marshals Malinovskii and Tolbukhin) were to complete the capture of western Hungary and to drive northwest into the Czech lands and west up the Danube to Vienna. Budapest had fallen four days earlier, and this was a time of considerable optimism in the Stavka, at least as far as the southern theatre was concerned. The operation was scheduled to start on 15 March and to be completed within twenty days.[49] Preparation for this major assault was disrupted first by the German elimination of the bridgehead held by Soviet 7th Guards Army on the Hron (Gran) River northwest of Budapest, and then by the 6 March offensive of German Army Group South, Operation SPRING AWAKENING. The 6th SS Panzer Army ploughed deep into Marshal Tolbukhin's lines between Lake Balaton and Budapest.[50]

The Soviet commanders were, however, able to keep to the Stavka's original schedule, attacking on 16 March.[51] The weight, however, was now more south of the Danube, rather than north of it, and the main responsibility for the attack passed from Malinovskii to Tolbukhin. The spearhead was the newly formed 9th Guards Army, under Tolbukhin's army group. The last of the Guards Armies, the 9th Guards, had been held back from the big defensive battle at Lake Balaton. It had been created from elite divisions of the disbanded (and never used) Independent Guards Airborne Army.

Vienna was now under direct threat. In one of Hitler's last spasms of command appointment, General Rendulic was ordered back from Kurland at the end of March to replace Wöhler in German Army Group South; he arrived on 7 April. Rendulic had only been sent to Kurland on 13 March. In April Rendulic's command was very briefly renamed Army Group *Ostmark* (the *Ostmark* being the Nazi term for Austria). His forces comprised the German 8th Army in southern Moravia, the 6th SS Panzer Army around Vienna and the 6th Army in southeastern Austria.[52] The 6th SS Panzer Army, which had spearheaded the Ardennes offensive and was still commanded by Sepp Dietrich, included the remnants of three Waffen-SS formations, the 'Adolf Hitler', 'Das Reich' and 'Hitlerjugend' divisions, old foes of the Red Army.

The Soviet 46th Army enveloped Vienna from the north, and the 6th Guards Tank Army moved in from the south. A fierce battle within the big city began on 5 April (some two weeks before the fighting in Berlin). The vanguard formation in the direct attack on the city was the 4th Guards Army, which was moving in from the southwest. Defended by the remnants of Sepp Dietrich's 6th SS Panzer Army, with a paper strength of seven panzer divisions, Vienna finally fell on 13 April, just before the offensive against Berlin began. Hitler ordered Dietrich's divisions to be stripped of special insignia, and Heinrich Himmler, ultimately responsible for the Waffen-SS, suffered a fatal loss of face.

The Russians and the western Allies had only captured a small part of Austria before the Nazi capitulation. The Red Army held the northeast part of the country. The main part of Austria was not taken by any of the Allied armies until the war ended. After capturing Vienna, the 3rd Ukrainian Army Group moved on to Graz and Amstetten. Had the war lasted a few more days, Tolbukhin's forces would have met American troops advancing from Bavaria.

The Red Army's operations in Austria were not an historical footnote or a minor mopping-up operation. Hitler's heart was here rather than in the north, and he had been generous with what reinforcements he had available. There was fanatical resistance for the homeland. The 3rd Ukrainian Army Group claimed that in the battles from mid-March to mid-April 1945, it destroyed no fewer than eleven Axis armoured divisions, including the Waffen-SS panzer divisions 'Adolf Hitler', 'Das Reich', 'Totenkopf', 'Hitlerjugend' and 'Wiking'. In terms of troops committed, the Soviet Vienna operation was only about a third the size of the Berlin operation. As a proportion of the forces involved, however, losses were heavier, at 39,000 troops.[53]

BERLIN

The defences of Berlin

Many books have been written about the Battle of Berlin and the fall of the Third Reich.[54] The outcome was inevitable. All the same, the battle tells much about the capabilities of the Red Army at the end of the war, and about the mentality of the German high command. It provides insights, too, about the relations between the Allies, as they stood on the brink of victory, and as politics and strategy intersected.

At Berlin the German high command suffered from the same shortcomings as it had during the past three years. Now these shortcomings were compounded by an impossible strategic, logistic and even communications situation. Hitler continued to attempt to micro-manage operations and to forbid withdrawals, although he was physically drained, aware that the war was lost, and fighting a bizarre political endgame. His strategic vision had always been fatally flawed, but now it had parted company from any military rationality and descended into pure fanaticism. Most striking here was the 'scorched earth' order of 19 March 1945, ordering Germans to destroy the economic infrastructure around themselves. On 13 March, Hitler made one final visit to the front, to Wriezen on the Oder River. The Russian enemy were now just a short car journey away from central Berlin.

The behaviour of the German military in the last months was little better than that of Hitler, as the generals allowed themselves to administer his bizarre finale. Keitel and Jodl remained at their Führer's side until the last few days of the war. They then left Berlin and became directly involved in the fantasy plans to relieve the city. Guderian, the Chief of the Army General Staff since July 1944, was unable to cope politically or militarily with the situation. In his memoirs, he made much of his attempts to find rational solutions to military problems, but in truth he remained an ambitious supporter of the Nazi cause. Attempting to find any type of military solution was completely irrational. And the headship of the Army General Staff was not the mighty post it had been in the time of Halder, or even of Zeitzler. Guderian was sent on 'health leave' after the failure of a scheme to relieve the Küstrin fortress on the Oder at the end of March 1945. His replacement at the General Staff in the last six weeks of the war was General Hans Krebs.

FIGURE 16 A Soviet self-propelled gun firing in a Berlin street, 1945.

A youthful forty-seven, Krebs was a veteran of the Russian Front. He had been chief of staff of the 9th Army in Army Group Centre from January 1942 to September 1944. Before that, he had been acting military attaché in Moscow on the eve of Operation BARBAROSSA. Krebs played little part in the events of April 1945, and he killed himself at the end of war.

The German defences were a ragtag by mid-April, confused by a very rapidly changing situation. For the first time, German field commands had to face both to the west and to the east. Two German Army Groups were now in play in the fighting around Berlin: Army Group Vistula and Army Group Centre.[55] These were directly controlled by the high command in Berlin.

The area from the Baltic to south of Berlin was covered by Army Group Vistula. SS leader Himmler was replaced here in late March by General Heinrici, former commander of the 4th Army in Russia, and more recently of German forces south of Silesia. Heinrici eventually fell out with Keitel and Jodl over operational priorities. Conflict was sharpened by the evacuation of the Wehrmacht headquarters from Berlin to the rear area of one of Heinrici's armies. On the night of 28–29 April, as his Army Group Vistula collapsed around him, Heinrici was sacked. General Manteuffel (the 3rd Panzer Army commander) was ordered to replace him, but refused, and late on the 29th, General Tippelskirch formally took over the ruins.

Heinrici had had four armies. Two were the 21st and 12th Armies, newly minted to cover the Elbe River front in the west against the advancing Americans and British. They were originally commanded by Generals Tippelskirch and Wenck; hurriedly formed from military cadets and other scratch elements, they possessed little real substance. The other two armies, covering the Oder River front in the east, were the 3rd Panzer Army and the 9th Army, under Generals Manteuffel and Busse. Both commanders were

FIGURE 17 Soviet T-34s fight their way into Berlin in April 1945.

highly experienced; Manteuffel had commanded the 5th Panzer Army in December's Ardennes offensive.

Army Group Centre held the southern part of the defensive line, on the Neisse River. It was under General Schörner, who in early April became Hitler's penultimate Field Marshal. (The very last would be Robert von Greim, the new Luftwaffe C-in-C, promoted when he flew into Berlin on the night of 26–7 April.) Schörner would even, very briefly and in the true vacuum after the suicides in the Berlin bunker, nominally replace Hitler as C-in-C of the German Army; Hitler had named Schörner in his political testament. As commander of Army Group Centre, Schörner controlled four armies, the 4th Panzer Army (in Saxony), the 17th Army (Upper Silesia and Bohemia–Moravia), the 1st Panzer Army (central Bohemia) and the 7th Army (Danube/Alps).[56]

Meanwhile, the Soviet command was gathering its forces for the final operations of the European war. As we have already seen, the first Soviet plan to take Berlin in February or March had miscarried. The Soviet dash to Berlin in late April contrasted sharply with the inactivity on the Oder–Neisse front in the two months which preceded it. According to Zhukov, serious thought was given to the Berlin axis in early March, when he and Antonov put their heads together in Moscow and submitted a plan, based on earlier ones, to the GKO.[57] However, given the missions currently assigned to the three Soviet army groups on the deep flanks – in Pomerania, East Prussia and Silesia – this plan would not seem to have involved an offensive beginning before the end of April or the beginning of May.

It is still not clear that Stalin and the Stavka had a clear vision of what was going to happen in the last stages of the war against Hitler. In strategic discussions at Yalta in early February 1945, the British and American planners favoured 1 July 1945 as the earliest date for the defeat of Germany, and 31 December 1945 as the latest. Antonov, after some hesitation, agreed that 'he regarded the summer [of 1945] as the earliest date [for the defeat of Germany] and the winter [of 1945–46] as the latest. The first of July [1945] should be a reasonably certain date for the defeat of Germany if all our efforts were applied to this end.' The Stavka may have originally wanted to wait until after the end of April 1945 for the main blow against Berlin, because they believed that was when the weather would have improved. Antonov, it will be recalled, had said at Yalta that operations would be resumed after 'the most difficult season' of late March and April.[58] In the meantime, available Soviet forces could usefully be employed on secondary fronts.

There seems to be little doubt, however, that Stalin and the Stavka attached great importance to Berlin. To be sure, at the start of April 1945, Stalin told Eisenhower that Berlin had lost its former significance and was now only a secondary objective. Although this was certainly 'disinformation' (i.e. a lie), it was not evident even to the Russians that – in military terms – the *final* battle would be fought, as in fact it was fought, in and around Berlin. The battle would take place where Hitler was, and from the German point of view Berlin was more vulnerable than other places. The Nazis might move their centre of resistance into Bavaria and the Tyrol. Like the Western Allies, the Russians had also heard reports of an '*al'pinskaia krepost*', an Alpine fortress.[59] This made no long-term sense, but it was no more irrational than the rest of German grand strategy.

Hitler had indeed chosen to devote many of his remaining military assets to the south, to Hungary, Bohemia–Moravia and Austria.

However, Stalin undoubtedly saw the psychological importance of the capture of Berlin for Soviet domination over Germany, and over central Europe. Internally, the conquest of Berlin would cement his bond with the Russian people. Throughout the war, Stalin's rhetoric had centred on the Reich capital. In his Revolution Anniversary speech of 1944, for example, he made the point again: 'Now for the Red Army there remains one last and conclusive mission: to complete, together with the armies of our allies, the destruction of the German-fascist army, to kill the fascist beast in its own den, *and to hoist over Berlin* the banner of victory' (my emphasis).[60]

Stalin changes gear

Stalin made a decision at the very end of March 1945 to accelerate Soviet operations against Berlin. This was surely brought about by the sudden progress of the British and the Americans. In the course of February and March, as the Red Army fought extensive battles in East Prussia, Pomerania and Silesia, the British and Americans (and the Canadians and French) were fighting a large campaign in the Rhineland, overcoming difficult terrain and the fixed defences of the German *Westwall*. The bulk of the German field army in the West was concentrated for a 'forward defence', west of the Rhine. The Western Allies were only drawing up to the line of the river. In the middle of March, however, the situation on Germany's western front began to change radically, and the pace of this change was unexpected for the Russians. The surprise capture of the Ludendorff railway bridge at Remagen on the Rhine (south of the Ruhr) on 7 March 1945 allowed the Americans to establish themselves on the far side of the river. A more thoroughly prepared Rhine crossing, further north, was carried out under the British General Montgomery on 24 March.[61] Hitler had decided to deploy most of his western military forces on the far side of the Rhine, and when those forces were destroyed in February and March, the Wehrmacht's cupboard was bare. The remaining defenders of the Rhine line, Model's Army Group 'B', were trapped on 1 April in the penultimate and biggest *Kessel* of the war, in the Ruhr. This pocket finally capitulated on 18 April, with some 317,000 German troops surrendering to the Allies.

The British and the Americans then implemented a charge into the Reich. The three American–British army groups (the 21st, the 12th and the 6th) pushed east across Germany, reaching the Weser River on 9 April and the Elbe River on the 11th. The spectacular breakout was comparable to the Soviet Vistula–Oder operation of January and February in its speed. It was accompanied by the disintegration of the Wehrmacht in western and central Germany. It should be noted, however, that when Stalin made his decision on Berlin – at the end of March – the British and Americans held only four small bridgeheads 10–20 miles deep on the far side of the Rhine. It may well be, however, that Antonov and other advisers provided Stalin with an accurate prediction of what would happen to the German Army in the next weeks; this would have shocked the Soviet dictator into a clearer sense that the final days of the Third Reich were now at hand.

Stalin also could not rule out a sudden German separate surrender in the West, whatever prior understandings the USSR had made with the Americans and British. To Stalin, hidden negotiations between the Germans and the Western Allies might explain the rapid western Allied progress since the middle of March. Stalin reacted very sharply to news about negotiations that the American OSS (Office of Strategic Services, the precursor of the CIA) was conducting in Switzerland with German leaders from northern Italy. At the end of March, he told a visiting Czechoslovak delegation:

> We are whipping the Germans, and it's almost over. But keep in mind that the allies [i.e. the British and Americans] will try to save the Germans and come to terms with them. We will be merciless with the Germans, but the allies will try to settle things in a gentler way.

In a top-level exchange, Stalin suggested to Roosevelt on 3 April that the Germans in the West had effectively ceased fighting America and Britain, in exchange for better peace terms. This was something which Roosevelt, a week before his death, described in his reply as a 'vile misrepresentation'.[62] The impact on the Kremlin of either the Remagen breakthrough or the Swiss negotiations should not be exaggerated. The Red Army was going to assault Berlin that spring, no matter what happened. The Stavka was probably only putting forward the start of its already planned Berlin operation by two or three weeks. Given the scale of the operation, however, even a small advance of the timetable could involve serious consequences.

At the end of March 1945 the Stavka suddenly began concrete planning for an operation across the Oder directly towards Berlin. *Maskirovka* (military deception) was again put into action, but this time directed against the Western Allies. A message arrived on 31 March from General Eisenhower, the C-in-C of the Western Allies in the northern European theatre. Eisenhower proposed two meeting areas for the Allied armies. One was on the upper Elbe, the Erfurt–Leipzig–Dresden area, *east* of the agreed inter-Allied zonal division; the other was in the Danube valley. In his response of 1 April (April Fool's Day), Stalin spoke of a Russian operation against Berlin which would take place at the *end* of May (rather than when it would actually happen, in the middle of April). Even after the Berlin operation began, on 14 April, Antonov told Eisenhower that it was a secondary operation. Not until the 24th, when Berlin was encircled, did he impart the information that this was the main blow.[63]

Armchair generals continue to speculate whether the Western Allies, specifically the Americans, could have taken Berlin before the Russians. There were critical unknown factors: these are *still* imponderables which can only be speculated about today. The most important unknown is how much German military resistance an American thrust would have met. It is in any event unfair to blame Eisenhower for the decision not to go for Berlin; he was only a theatre commander. A political decision would have had to come from above, at the end of March, from President Roosevelt or the American Joint Chiefs of Staff, especially General Marshall. Roosevelt was possibly too ill to make a decision (he died on 12 April), and the Chiefs were preoccupied with preparations for the Pacific War. Churchill and the British Chiefs of Staff took a more 'political' point of view, but the capture of Berlin would need to have been an American effort, given the preponderance of American strength and the location of the various armies (the British armies were further north in Germany). The force sent to Berlin would have been from General Bradley's American 12th Army Group.[64]

The thinking of both the British and the American planners from January to early March 1945 was influenced by the sensible consideration that the Russians, being only 40 miles east of Berlin, were bound to reach the city first. Eisenhower, like others before him, also placed rather too much confidence in Nazi rationality. He worried about protracted fighting for a German 'National Redoubt' in southern Bavaria and the Tyrol. Eisenhower did make a decision on 15 April to halt a further advance across the Elbe by Simpson's 9th Army (of Bradley's 12th Army Group), but by that time the Soviet Berlin operation was already beginning. From the time of his message to Stalin on 31 March, Eisenhower had effectively committed himself to an advance to the southeast (to Erfurt, Dresden and Leipzig, etc.) rather than to the east (Berlin).

Arguably Stalin, more than Eisenhower (or General Marshall), saw the big picture and could look beyond the military campaign. (The same was true of Churchill.) With the capture of Berlin – and later of Prague – Stalin was operating under the principles of the great Prussian military thinker Carl von Clausewitz:

> It is, of course, well known that the only source of war is politics – the intercourse of government and peoples; but it is apt to be assumed that war suspends that intercourse and replaces it by a wholly different condition, ruled by no law but its own.
>
> We maintain, on the contrary, that war is simply a continuation of political intercourse, with the addition of other means. … The main lines along which military events progress, and to which they are restricted, are political lines that continue throughout the war into the subsequent peace. How could it be otherwise?[65]

Another insight emerged during the battle itself. Zhukov sent Stalin a report with information from a German POW; the prisoner said that the Germans were going to fight to the last man in their defensive positions on the Oder, facing the Red Army. They would do this even if the Americans attacked their lines from the west (i.e. passing through Berlin). Stalin told Zhukov to ignore this:

> Hitler is spinning a web in the Berlin area, in order to stir up a disagreement between the Russians and the Allies. This web must be swept aside by the capture of Berlin by Soviet forces. We can do this and we must do this. Hit the Germans without mercy and you will soon be in Berlin.[66]

It was at this moment that Stalin turned both Konev's and Rokossovskii's army groups towards Berlin.

Whatever Stalin's ultimate motives, whatever events most influenced him, we know that on the evenings of 2 and 3 April, he and the other Soviet civilian leaders discussed the shape of the Berlin operation with Zhukov, Konev and Rokossovskii. The general aim was to be the capture of the Nazi capital and the establishment of a front along the Elbe River.[67] (Even this advance, it should be noted, would not have taken the Russians to the full depth of their occupation zone that had been agreed among the Allies.) Preparing an operation against the heart of Germany, at unexpectedly short notice and on a broad front, was not an easy matter. When these discussions were taking place (in early April), Rokossovskii's army group was still concentrated around Danzig, and Konev was still finishing off the Upper Silesian operation. Despite the shattered Polish and eastern German railway networks, the Red Army was to carry out one of the fastest redeployments of the war.

Of the three army groups, Rokossovskii's 2nd Belorussian attacked after the others (on 18 April, rather than 16 April); it had the furthest to redeploy, from Pomerania and West Prussia. It attacked in line with the other army groups, but into relatively open space. Rokossovskii's advance was technically part of what the Russians call the 'Berlin operation', but he was really covering the distant flanks and overrunning north-central Germany. Rokossovskii now commanded five rifle armies and three independent mobile corps. After breaking through the Oder defences north and south of Stettin, Rokossovskii's mobile forces advanced to Prenzlau on the 27th, broke out, and then raced northwest across Brandenburg, West Pomerania (Vorpommern) and Mecklenburg. The remnants of Manteuffel's 3rd Panzer Army were destroyed on the spot or fled west in hopes of surrendering to the British and Americans. Rokossovksii cleared the Baltic coast, and his Army Group met the British 2nd Army at a line running from Wismar on the Baltic, south through Schwerin, to the Elbe. Rokossovskii's losses of about 13,000 troops were relatively light, about 15 per cent of the Russian losses of the whole 'Berlin operation'.[68]

The heavier fighting for Berlin involved the 1st Belorussian and the 1st Ukrainian Army Groups. The attack began on 16 April. Zhukov's 1st Belorussian Army Group was the greatest concentration of ground forces ever assembled. With 908,000 men, it was nearly twice the size of Rokossovskii's command. Zhukov's main forces consisted of no fewer than eight infantry armies, the 33rd, 69th, 8th Guards, 5th Shock, 3rd Shock, 47th, 1st Polish and 61st, ranged along a 135-mile front from Gubin on the Neisse north to Schwedt on the Oder. Waiting behind was a mass of mobile forces: the 2nd and the 1st Guards Tank Armies and three independent mobile corps. Two air armies supported the ground forces.

Konev's 2nd Belorussian Army Group, to the southwest, had 551,000 men. Konev covered a line along the Western Neisse River from Gorlitz (essentially on the pre-1938 Czechoslovak border) north to Gubin. The centre of his concentration was near Forst, about 75 miles southeast of Berlin. Konev had five infantry armies, the 52nd, 2nd Polish, 5th Guards, 13th and 3rd Guards. Another army, the 28th, was arriving from reserve.

Konev had abundant second-echelon mobile forces: the 3rd and 4th Guards Tank Armies, and five mobile corps. Air support came from an air army.

Overwhelming force meant that the outcome of the battle was never in doubt. The three Russian army groups in the 'Berlin' operation included 2,500,000 men, 6,250 tanks, 7,500 aircraft, and 41,600 guns and mortars. The formations involved numbered 171 divisions and 21 mobile corps. This could be compared with 5,200 tanks in Operation BAGRATION in the previous year. In April 1945, Zhukov's 1st Belorussian Army Group alone comprised 72 divisions and 7 mobile corps, with 3,200 tanks and 17,000 artillery pieces. Facing it, the German 9th Army had 14 divisions, with 512 tanks, 344 field guns plus 300–400 AA guns. The 3rd Panzer Army had 11 divisions and 242 tanks. The new 12th Army, on which Hitler put considerable hopes on 21 April, had 7 divisions.[69]

Zhukov and Konev attack

Zhukov and Konev attacked simultaneously in the last great battle of the Second World War in Europe. The first stage was a preliminary 'reconnaissance in force' on the morning of Saturday, 14 April 1945. The main attack began before dawn on Monday, the 16th. Zhukov used searchlights – taken from the now redundant Soviet air defences – to show the way forward and blind the defenders. This was a clever tactical innovation that seems to have had little real effect. The direct road to Berlin went through the small town of Seelow. The country between Küstrin and Berlin was relatively open, but the Germans had now had time to prepare defensive lines and flood the low ground. Zhukov's first attack wave became entangled in the defences. Under pressure from Stalin, Zhukov released his main mobile force that morning; this added to the confusion. Bogdanov's 2nd Tank Army and Katukov's 1st Tank Army were not able to break clear of the mess. It was not until Wednesday morning that the central combined armies smashed their way through the defences.

Military historians have accused Marshal Zhukov of botching this operation, or going at it in a blunderbuss manner. Zhukov was in fact given orders from above to proceed down the direct route to the German capital. On 2 April a directive from Stalin and Antonov included clear instructions: 'The main blow is to be struck from the Oder bridgehead west of Küstrin with the forces of four infantry armies and two tank armies.'[70] The extent of the confusion at Seelow can also be exaggerated, both in terms of losses and of the delay. The Soviet losses were certainly much less than the figure of 30,000 killed which has been cited by one historian, and the delay amounted to only forty-eight hours.[71] Fortunately, Zhukov's flanking armies did rather better, especially on the right, once Rokossovskii began his attack on Wednesday. Eventually the resistance of the Germans was broken by greatly superior forces, and the survivors of Weidling's German 56th Corps (of the 9th Army) withdrew towards Berlin.

Konev's original objective, meanwhile, was rather general. He was to advance with the 1st Ukrainian Army Group south of Berlin – through Cottbus to the west and to the

Elbe – with the possibility of a turn deeper south into Saxony or Bohemia. His attack, also on Monday, 16 April, allowed for a quicker breakout. He had few bridgeheads, but the river barrier in front of him was narrower. By Tuesday evening (17 April), with Zhukov's advance apparently hung up on the Seelow Heights, Stalin famously set up a race of the two army groups by not marking clear demarcation lines between them. On Thursday and Friday (19–20 April), Konev's two tank armies (Leliushenko's 4th Guards and Rybalko's 3rd Guards) were able to move ahead 60 miles and wheel north towards Berlin and its western suburbs. On Saturday they overran the German Army's headquarters at Zossen and pushed into the outskirts of the Reich capital. Stalin has been accused of more bloody cynicism here, but evidently the view of the General Staff was also that Konev's army should be given the opportunity to take part in the operation, to make more practical the great encirclement. It is not often noted that when Zhukov ran into difficulties on 16–17 April, it was not just Konev whom the Stavka ordered to turn towards Berlin. Rokossovskii was also, on 18 April, told to move on the Reich capital; the 2nd Belorussian Army Group was told to turn southwest towards Birkenwerder in the northwestern suburbs of Berlin. This order was only countermanded on the 25th, when Rokossovskii was told to aim once more for his original objectives to the west.[72]

On Tuesday, 24 April, elements of the Soviet 1st Ukrainian and the 1st Belorussian Army Groups made their initial link-up. This was southeast of Berlin, at Bohnsdorf, and they isolated between them much of the main German field force in the region, Busse's 9th Army. The remains of this formation had been concentrated between Berlin and the Oder, thanks to another of Hitler's stand-fast orders. The main outer encirclement, west of Berlin, was effected on Wednesday (25th) when the 4th Guards Tank Army and the 2nd Guards Tank Army met up west of Potsdam. The last great *Kessel* of the Second World War had been created, this time not around Minsk, or Kiev, or Stalingrad, but around Hitler's capital.

The main street fighting for central Berlin was fought out over a very long weekend, from Thursday, 26 April, to Wednesday, 2 May. It was carried out by the 3rd Guards Tank Army, the 3rd and 5th Shock Armies, and the 8th Guards Army (Chuikov) from Zhukov's army group, and Rybalko's 3rd Guards Tank Army from Konev's army group. On Monday afternoon (30 April) the Soviet flag was raised over the ruins of the Reichstag. Some 750 metres to the southeast, in the bunker behind the Reich Chancellery, Hitler committed suicide. The Russians may have wanted to complete their victory on Tuesday, which was May Day, but the first ceasefire talks between General Weidling and Chuikov came to nothing. Broken-backed resistance continued through Wednesday, 2 May. The formal surrender of the German garrison by Weidling took place early on Wednesday morning, and the Red Army ceased fire in the city at 3.00 pm.

The battle was costly. Russian losses – in the army groups of Rokossovskii, Zhukov and Konev – totalled 78,000 troops over a three-week period. It can be compared to the American attack on the large Japanese island of Okinawa, which occurred at the same time as the Berlin operation. Okinawa was a battle that the Americans rightly perceived as an especially costly one for their forces, but total American losses were 7,600 personnel from the Army and Marines. In the Berlin operation, Soviet equipment

FIGURE 18 Soviet soldiers in Berlin, May 1945. The men who destroyed the German Army.

losses included 2,000 tanks, 2,108 guns and mortars, and 917 combat aircraft. On the other hand, this 'operation' was more extensive than just the fighting in the city. As the American historian Earl Ziemke put it:

> The battle for Berlin was fought outside the city; what went on in the capital was hardly more than a contested mop-up. ... The fighting in Berlin lasted as long as it did because a great metropolis ... cannot be quickly taken even against a lame defence, particularly by troops who know the war is over and intend to see their homes again.[73]

The final drama in the streets of Berlin in the last days of April 1945 was symbolically and politically of the highest importance; in narrow military terms the fighting was limited. The Wehrmacht and Waffen-SS garrison of Berlin proper was comparable to only four or five full-strength divisions (45,000 personnel); there were also 40,000 *Volkssturm*. Few steps had been taken to prepare defences. The real battle was fought outside the city limits, and this was evidently where the Russians suffered most of their casualties. The 'Berlin operation' was in reality a much bigger campaign for most of central and eastern Germany between the Elbe and the Oder, a large region about 100 miles deep and 200 miles from north to south. Well before the Red Army got in sight of Berlin, it had had to carry out a number of difficult river crossings, over the Oder by Rokossovskii and Zhukov, and over the Western Neisse by Konev.

Losses in this larger battle demonstrate the extent of last-ditch German resistance. The 2,000 Soviet tanks put out of action could be compared to 6,100 tanks lost in the 1943 Kursk battles, 3,000 in the Belorussian operation and 1,300 in the Vistula–Oder operation.[74] It was very expensive for the Germans, whose overall losses (troops killed) have been estimated to be 300,000 to 400,000 men a month in 1945. Western historians of the Battle of Berlin have generally been more favourable about Konev than about Zhukov. In the end, Zhukov's army group suffered higher losses than Konev's – 38,000 troops versus 28,000 – but that was at least partly because the 1st Belorussian was a much larger formation. Despite the crisis on the Seelow Heights, and despite carrying the larger share of the street fighting in Berlin itself, Zhukov's forces had a lower per capita loss rate than those of Konev.[75] Konev's armies were involved in heavy fighting outside Berlin, to the south, as the German 9th Army fought desperately to pull back from the Oder through the wooded country south of the capital.

At Torgau on the Elbe, about 70 miles southwest of Berlin, lead elements from one of Konev's infantry formations, the 5th Guards Army, met American troops for the first time on Wednesday, 25 April. This event was celebrated with a huge artillery salute in Moscow. Meanwhile the Soviet 52nd Army, on the far left of Konev's flank, was advancing into Saxony, bypassing the ashes of Dresden on 8 May. The war was not completely over. As we have already seen in Chapter 12, Konev now turned south to destroy the main active enemy grouping in central Europe, in Bohemia (the western part of Czechoslovakia).

Meanwhile, the lustre of the Soviet victory was tarnished by the conduct of some Soviet troops in Germany. One aspect was massive looting. As the Red Army approached Germany, more systematic thought was given to how the Soviet state could exploit the economic resources of Germany and its satellites. In January 1945 'departments of captured economic resources' were created at army group and army level. Even Zhukov was touched by this; when he fell from favour in 1947, one of the charges was that he had sent railway cars full of booty home to Russia. Even worse was the widespread rape of German – and non-German – women.[76]

Problems with the discipline of the Red Army have already been discussed.[77] Events in Germany were an extreme version of what happened elsewhere in eastern Europe. It has been suggested that Soviet 'revenge' propaganda played an important part in leading to the gross excesses. What seems extraordinary was the failure of the highly politicized Red Army leadership to see that this behaviour ran counter to attempts to win over the German population. Only towards the end of April 1945 was there a perceptible change of the top-level 'line', a recognition that in the post-war world Russia would need friends in Germany. On 20 April, the fourth day of the Berlin offensive, the three army groups involved were sent an order to implement a new policy of 'humane behaviour':

> You are to demand of the troops to change [*izmenit'*] their behaviour toward the Germans, both POWs and the civilian population, and treat them better. Harsh treatment of the Germans makes them fearful and forces them into determined resistance, and not giving themselves up. The civilian population, fearing being swept away, organizes itself into bands. Such a situation is not convenient to us.

'Familiarity' [*paniobratstvo*] was to be avoided, but west of the Oder–Neisse line, German civil administration was to be left in place and even rank-and-file Nazis left unharmed.[78]

Surrender

Broken-backed resistance continued for a week after Hitler's suicide and the surrender of Berlin. The Russians did not necessarily expect a total collapse of the Wehrmacht, even after the death of the German dictator had been announced. On the evening of 2 May, Marshal Malinovskii was ordered to continue the advance of his 2nd Ukrainian Army Group northeast into the centre of Czechoslovakia; he was to reach Jihlava, 70 miles southeast of Prague, no later than 12–14 May, and after that to move on the Vltava River and Prague.[79] In fact events moved much faster. Wehrmacht forces in northwest Germany surrendered at Lüneburg on Friday, 4 May; those in Bavaria followed on Saturday.

The overall surrender arrangements were confused, an omen of East–West tension to come. The Germans had to capitulate twice, although there was some satisfaction to be gained from the opportunity to put both Jodl and Keitel, Hitler's closest military collaborators, through the ordeal. Field Marshal Jodl was flown on Sunday afternoon (6 May) to Reims, northeast of Paris. Reims was the 'Supreme Headquarters' of the American and British forces (SHAEF) – General Eisenhower's command centre. Jodl signed an 'Act of Military Surrender' early (1.41 am) on Monday morning, 7 May. Eisenhower signed for the Allies. The Soviet representative at SHAEF, General Susloparov, initialled the surrender document. The Stavka even cited this document, without qualification, in an order issued late on Monday evening; all Soviet army group commanders were informed that the Germans had signed an act of military capitulation at Reims earlier in the day, and fighting was to end at 11.01 pm on Tuesday. Nevertheless, the Reims surrender was not formally accepted by Stalin.[80]

The 'official' surrender of the German armed forces, as far as the Russians were concerned, took place at Karlshorst in the eastern suburbs of Berlin at 10.43 pm on the evening of Tuesday, 8 May – 44 hours after the Reims surrender. Effectively, the Karlshorst ceremony gave the German forces 18 minutes to surrender (from 10.43 pm to 11.01 pm). This document was signed on the German side by Jodl's superior, Field Marshal Keitel. Zhukov signed for the Russians in his capacity as Deputy Supreme C-in-C of the Red Army. Deputy Foreign Minister Vyshinskii had flown to Berlin to oversee the ceremony. The surrender instrument was then flown to Moscow.

In his 'victory day' speech on Wednesday, 9 May, Stalin described the Reims document as a 'preliminary protocol of capitulation' and the Karlshorst document as the 'definitive' (okonchatel'nyi) one. Western sources, in contrast, tend to describe Karlshorst as just a formality. A defeated army can only surrender once, and the terms were effectively the same, with German forces on all fronts to cease fighting at 11.01 pm, Central European Time, on 8 May.[81]

Looked at from hindsight, this two-act drama was the only way the surrender could have been signed, at short notice, by senior commanders from both sides of the 'Grand Alliance'. The Reims surrender had been signed far from Soviet forces, although it was initialled by a Soviet representative. The Karlshorst surrender was a mirror image, signed by the most senior Soviet field officer, Zhukov, and in the presence of relatively junior generals on the Western side, Air Marshal Tedder and General Spaatz. There was no easy safe neutral ground – Zhukov could not come to Reims, and Eisenhower could not quickly go to Berlin.

There were loose ends in the East. The garrison of Breslau finally surrendered on 6 May, after a three-month siege. As we saw in Chapter 12, lead units of the Red Army only entered Prague later on Wednesday morning, 9 May. There was one last big evacuation convoy in the Baltic. German troops made desperate attempts to get over the Elbe in order to surrender to the Americans or British, rather than the Russians. Only a third of 10 million Wehrmacht POWs fell into Soviet hands. Nevertheless, the Red Army took over 2 million prisoners after 1 May: the 1st Belorussian Army Group counted 230,000 POWs, and the 1st Ukrainian 540,000. Rokossovskii's 2nd Belorussian in Mecklenburg took 200,000, and the 3rd Ukrainian, mainly in Austria, counted 234,000. Some 280,000 POWs were recorded as taken in Kurland. The biggest bag, mentioned in the previous chapter, was in Czechoslovakia. German troops here, from Schörner's Army Group Centre, were unable to break through to the west; the Soviet 2nd and 4th Ukrainian Army Groups between them took 720,000 German POWs, 85 per cent after 9 May.[82] Hitler's Wehrmacht was no more.

CHAPTER 14
CONCLUSION

I na vrazh'ei zemle my vraga razgromim/Maloi krov'iu, moguchim udarom!
[We smash the foe on his own soil/At little cost but with mighty blows.]

Soviet popular song, 1938

Our cause is just. The enemy will be defeated. Victory will be ours.

Molotov, radio address, 22 June 1941

The tragedy of the Germans is that we never have enough time. We will always be pushed on by circumstances.

Hitler's Testament, 14 February 1945

EXPLAINING VICTORY AND DEFEAT

'Our cause is just. The enemy will be defeated. Victory will be ours.' Molotov's prediction, in his radio address of 22 June 1941, turned out to be correct. At the risk of seeming overly deterministic, I would agree with the American military historian Williamson Murray that even in 1939 the Germans had 'only the slightest chance of victory'.[1] This is certainly not a view that all historians hold, nor is it the most suspenseful one, and it requires explanation. Why did the Russians win and the Germans lose? There are other questions that need to be asked as well. Why did it take three years to clear the German Army out of the USSR? As John Armstrong, one of the most astute writers about the war, observed: 'Rarely, if ever, has an invading force maintained itself on enemy territory for so long a period of time when it was so enormously inferior in manpower and military equipment.'[2] And there is a third question. Why was this struggle against a weaker enemy so extraordinarily costly to the Soviet Union?

In an early wartime speech, Stalin outlined five 'permanently operating factors' (*postoianno deistvuiushchie faktory*) which decided the outcome of modern wars. These can be brought to bear on the big questions about the Nazi–Soviet war. This is not because Stalin's factors were breathtakingly original or even wholly correct. They do, however, provide a useful framework, and they do show the perceptions of a supreme leader at a critical moment. Stalin said that 'the fate of the war' would be decided by these factors and not by the 'temporary' German advantage of surprise (*neozhidannost' i vnezapnost'*).[3] Although they became post-war orthodoxy, Stalin did not lay out the 'permanent factors' from the hindsight of 1945, but rather from February 1942, a point only a fifth of the way through the war. The 'factors' can also help us understand why the Red Army did not win the quick victory Stalin expected at this time, after the Battle of Moscow.

As Stalin saw it, the initial events of the war, in the first six months, were important but not decisive. In his interpretation the Red Army was forced to retreat, but in retreating it wore down the enemy and gained time to gather strength. The Germans lost the 'momentum of surprise'. In reality, the first period of the war was truly important, because the initial German attack on 22 June 1941 inflicted so much damage on the Red Army and drove it so far back into the depths of Russia; this military catastrophe meant the war would last as long as it did. There was more than simple German trickery involved here. In his explanation, Stalin placed an exaggerated importance on the supposed lack of mobilization of the Red Army, and ignored his own ineptitude and that of his senior advisers. The Red Army was also not ready for the kind of war that it had to fight, and at the Battle of Viaz'ma–Briansk – in the fourth month of the war – it suffered a devastating defeat that owed little to grand-strategic surprise. But it is true that early defeats, whatever their basic cause, became part of a vicious cycle for the Red Army. The huge early losses and the forced evacuation of war industry could not be made good quickly. The raw new Soviet formations of late 1941 and early 1942 would be easy meat for the veterans of the Wehrmacht when Hitler's 'second campaign' began in May 1942.

After the initial shock of the surprise attack, Stalin's 'permanently operating factors' were supposed to take effect. The first of these was 'stability of the rear' (*prochnost' tyla*). The USSR would win because the enemy's rear, at home in the Reich and especially in the occupied territories, was unstable. The Soviet rear, in contrast, was supposed to be stable. From hindsight we know that the first assumption was false. Nazi Germany did not crumble internally, in the way the Kaiser's Germany did in 1918. The Nazi rear was stable to the extent that Germany fought on, as Hitler promised, until 'five past twelve'. It fought on after the point that he himself was dead and the Red Army held the centre of Berlin.[4] Fear of Bolshevism kept Germans fighting, especially from 1944 onwards. There was much more instability in the rear of some of the Axis satellites, but only in the case of Romania did this greatly help the Red Army. The Russians (and the British and Americans) expected revolt among the oppressed peoples of Europe, but Nazi terror and local self-interest made armed resistance the exception rather than the rule.

It was the *Soviet* 'rear' that was not stable in 1941, especially on the western, non-Russian, fringes of the Soviet Union, perhaps even in the Ukraine. This was a factor that contributed much to early Red Army retreats. Hitler's Operation BARBAROSSA had itself been premised on the instability of the Soviet system: the colossus with feet of clay. Nevertheless, the survival of the USSR in the face of the Nazi Blitzkrieg in the summer of 1941 was due to the *overall* stability of the Stalinist political and economic system. By February 1942, when Stalin wrote his order, the Soviet rear had recovered its equilibrium. Both nationalism and socialism were vital to the stability and survival of the Stalinist system. Russian nationalism was not, as is often suggested, something Stalin discovered on 22 June 1941; it played a big part in the propaganda of the 1930s. Nevertheless, the Soviet rear became more stable after the Red Army's forced retreat into ethnic Russian territory in the autumn of 1941. The Georgian Stalin explicitly recognized the ethnic Russian contribution in his famous May 1945 victory toast. He also pointed out that it was non-Russian areas that had been given up.[5]

Stalin also argued that victory came from the superiority of the Soviet socialist system, for which the war was a supreme test. He made this point at greatest length in his post-war 'election speech' of February 1946, but he said the same thing in November 1943, when he first used the metaphor of the war as a 'test [*ispytanie*] of all the material and spiritual strength of our people'.[6] On the other hand, because both totalitarian states were stable, geared up for total war and highly nationalistic, their strengths to some extent cancelled each other out. 'Stability of the rear' was more a factor explaining the prolonged war than one explaining Soviet victory.

Stalin's other four 'permanently operating factors' concerned the front rather than the rear, and they overlapped. 'Morale of the army' (*moral'nyi dukh armii*), Stalin's second factor, was also not obviously a reason for Soviet victory. Stalin assumed in February 1942 that the morale of the German Army would crumble after the battering of the past winter, while the victory before Moscow would give the Red Army a renewed will to fight. The morale of the German Army turned out to be the one thing that kept the battle going so long. It is true that the morale of some of Hitler's satellite armies cracked in the winter of 1942–3, and that the Germans were not able to create a high-quality coalition army, but this was still a marginal factor. Stalin laid weight in his analysis on the fact that 'not one German soldier can say that he is fighting a just war', but for a number of reasons this did not affect the fighting ability of the Wehrmacht. From 1943 onwards, the Germans could make the same general argument: that they were defending the approaches to the homeland against an enemy that wanted to destroy it totally. It was the morale of *Stalin's* army that was badly shaken in the autumn of 1941, despite the fact that Soviet citizens were defending their own country. Even in February 1942, the Red Army had probably not plumbed the depths of its demoralization, at least not in the southern theatre. The morale of the Russian forces certainly improved from the time of the Stalingrad counter-offensive (November 1942) onwards, but there is little evidence that morale was higher in the Soviet Army than in the German one.

The USSR, with nearly double the population, put many more troops into the field than did Germany. Stalin's third factor of the 'number and quality of divisions' was certainly telling. Everyone agrees about the Red Army's numerical advantage. *Quality* arouses more debate, but the Soviet divisions of 1943 were certainly better than those of 1941. The quality of German forces became much more varied from 1942 onwards, and that of the satellite armies (except the Finns) was always low. The rapid Soviet advance across the Ukraine in 1943, the Belorussian and Iaşi–Kishenev operations of 1944, and the Vistula–Oder operation of 1945 had much to do with the deteriorating quality of German divisions. In order to meet the manpower demands of the long front, the Wehrmacht had to accept personnel of lower quality. But it was the net quality (alongside the morale) of German forces that allowed them to fight on for as long as they did.

Stalin cited 'armaments' (*vooruzhenie armii*) as a fourth factor, which overlapped with the 'number and quality of divisions'. Throughout the war, Stalin claimed that Soviet weapons were qualitatively superior and available in sufficient numbers. Again, there is no doubt about the *quantity* of Soviet matériel, and Lend-Lease added to the Russians' relative advantage. The Grand Alliance as a whole certainly had an overwhelming superiority in this 'war of motors'. German war production was not well organized, even after 1942. As for quality, there can be technical arguments about the relative merits of this or that tank or aircraft. What was important was the mix of quality and quantity, and here the Russians undoubtedly had a great advantage.

The 'organizational ability of army leaders' is a more complex factor in Stalin's scheme. The Wehrmacht was well led at an operational and tactical level. It was better than the Red Army here, at least until the middle of the war. *Strategic* leadership was different. Stalin could argue even in February 1942 that poor leadership had led the German Army to the failure at Moscow. It was not only Stalin who would maintain that Hitler, and the structural and personal weakness of the German high command, were to blame for the defeat of the Third Reich. In retirement, the German generals blamed the 'amateur' Hitler. Historians now blame the generals as well and criticize their lack of strategic perspective. On the other hand, Nazi Germany followed a high-risk strategy *because* it began the war in a position of strategic and economic weakness. As Hitler noted in his 1945 *Testament*, 'The tragedy of the Germans is that we never have enough time. We will always be pushed on by circumstances.'[7]

In contrast, the leadership of the Red Army improved, to a limited extent by February 1942, and even more clearly by the end of that year. The claim that the 1937–8 purges had destroyed the leadership cadres of the Red Army was shown by experience not to be true. After an extremely wasteful process of natural selection, effective leaders like Marshals Zhukov and Vasilevskii came to occupy the top posts. Stalin's role as a military leader is contentious here, especially in light of his overall place in Soviet history and his responsibility for the sufferings of the people of Russia. Khrushchev tried to portray Stalin as a blunderer and military ignoramus. Earl Ziemke argued that Stalin had 'a largely counterfeit military image'. Both views seem wide of the mark. John Erickson summed up the reality: Stalin's 'regulation of his command was minute, strict, and all-pervading'.[8] Stalin proved to be an effective military executive who was right at the centre of the running of the war.

In sum, one might agree with a modified version of Stalin's 'permanently operating factors'. Given an equally stable rear and comparable army morale, the Russians (and the Allies as a whole) won because they had larger armies, more efficient war production and better strategic leadership. Stalin's five factors are, however, simplistic. First of all, the USSR emerged victorious from the Second World War because it was part of a superior coalition.[9] Stalin, to be fair, had commented on this as a potential factor as far back as his secret May 1941 speech to military academy graduates, when he dealt at length with the danger for Germany of a two-front war. Indeed, in his 6 November 1941 speech, Stalin had put forward three rather different 'basic factors' (*osnovnye faktory*) which made inevitable the defeat of Hitler; one of them was the 'coalition of the USSR, Great Britain, and the United States of America against the German-fascist imperialists'.[10] The reality was that the Allied coalition had access to the economic and human resources of the Americas, of Africa, of the Middle East and of South Asia. It had great advantages in population, raw materials, farms and factories. Part of the Allies' resources was diverted to a parallel war with Japan, but that conflict always had a lower priority than the war in Europe. The Germans, for their part, had to make do with the resources of western and central continental Europe. Germany's European allies were secondary powers, with politically weak governments, backward economies and limited military strength.

Had Britain made peace in the summer of 1940, the Germans might actually have been able to conquer European Russia, as they almost did in 1917–18. Britain, fortunately for Stalin, did not make peace. After June 1941 Germany had two further possible opportunities for real victory, for dominating Russia and with it all of continental Europe. The first was the attempt to destroy the USSR in one blow (in 1941); the second was the attempt to seize a dominant part of Soviet resources (in 1942). These attempts failed, and with them Germany's chance for decisive success. Hitler's only hope was now a stalemate, but from the time the United States became an active participant in the war, even that was unlikely. A stalemate, and German survival, could now only come through a split in the Allied coalition. The nature of Hitler's government, and the nature of Nazi conduct early in the war, meant that it was hardly conceivable that the Allies would break up. This was true even though there were extreme differences between the liberal capitalist systems of Britain and the United States and the totalitarian socialist system of the USSR. Hitler was the greater and immediate threat. A German strategy for prolonging the war would have made some sense, but Hitler did not trust his generals to do this. And for him a stalemate was not a victory. As Hitler said in January 1943: 'In this war there will be not the victors and the defeated, only the survivors and the destroyed.'[11]

What was the relative importance of the Nazi–Soviet campaign within the Second World War? Was Soviet Russia Germany's 'main enemy', as Stalin alleged as late as November 1944? Voroshilov was even bolder in a post-war article: 'The Hitlerite army suffered a catastrophic defeat in single combat [*edinoborstvo*] with the Soviet Army led by the Communist military genius Stalin.'[12] The argument about who made the greatest contribution to the victory over Nazi Germany is one of the longest running ones in the history of the Second World War, even after the end of the Cold War. During the conflict, Stalin repeatedly contrasted the great number of German divisions on the Russian Front with the smaller number elsewhere. From the perspective of the history of the Eastern Front, the invasion of Normandy comes very late in the drama, towards the end of Act III. On the other hand, the Russians did not get back to their own state border until the summer of 1944. The Germans, for their part, rated the threats from West and East as about equal.[13] Despite their propaganda about defending European civilization against the 'assault from the steppe', the Germans faced closer threats and more direct and immediate attacks from their Western opponents. It was an interconnected war. Stalin's judgement of November 1944 was a remarkably balanced one:

> There can be no doubt that without the organization of a second front in Europe, drawing in up to 75 German divisions, our forces would not have been able in such a short space of time to break the resistance of the German forces and to kick them out of the territory of the Soviet Union. But it is also undoubted that without the powerful offensive operations of the Red Army in the summer of this year, drawing to itself up to 200 German divisions, the forces of our allies would not have been able so quickly to deal with the German forces and to kick them out of Italy, France, and Belgium.[14]

One of the saddest ironies was the Soviet pre-war perception of what the fighting would be like. As a Soviet popular song of the 1930s put it, 'We smash the foe on his own soil/At little cost but with mighty blows.' This strategy made a great deal of sense, especially for a state that had suffered so much in the First World War. But in the end it was the British and Americans who were able to smash Hitler 'on his own soil ... at little cost'.[15]

Stalin's five factors and the alliance are still not the whole story. Other interpretations of the Nazi–Soviet war have made much of the weather and geography. 'General Winter' was a factor, which Stalin himself from time to time alluded to. The Red Army changed the course of the defensive war in two winter campaigns, at Moscow in 1941–2 and at Stalingrad in 1942–3. On the other hand, the weather affected both sides, and it was readily overcome by the Red Army in its winter offensives of 1943–4 and 1944–5.

As for geography, one of the most influential overviews of the Soviet experience stated:

> When ... the test [of war] did come, the Soviet Union survived, yet not through a win on the merits of the system, at least in the first phase. Rather survival came because the country was so huge it could afford ... to lose space long enough to permit Hitler to make mistakes enough to set himself up for defeat.[16]

It is true that the leaders of Nazi Germany were handicapped by the extensive nature of the task that they set themselves in the Second World War. The shallowness of the Wehrmacht's preparations for the battle in 1939 was obvious enough. The forces of the Third Reich were not, in the foreseeable future, going to be able to cross the narrow seas, let alone the broad oceans, to threaten Germany's Western enemies. Indeed, the possession of superior sea and air power enabled the British and Americans directly to threaten the Reich, by air in the first half of 1942, and by sea from the middle of 1943. More relevant to this study, the Wehrmacht was also unable to project its power by land (and air) very far into the Eurasian 'heartland'. Even the European part of the USSR had a vast territory, with a sparsely settled population, a correspondingly thin transport network and a difficult climate. The German task was enormous, and one which was initially planned to be achieved in one campaigning season in 1941. What was remarkable was the ability of the *Soviet* forces to overcome the factors of space and climate, to take the war across the breadth of western Russia in 1943–4, to the Balkans and northern Finland, and deep into the heart of Central Europe in 1944–5. For this, Western-supplied motor transport, as well as the skill, courage and mass of the Red Army, were responsible.

Finally, it is a mistake to concentrate solely on strategy and 'operational art' or to think of the war as a conventional one. It was a 'total war' in more than just the breadth of industrial mobilization or the direct involvement of civilians. The Third Reich suffered a catastrophe in Russia, and in the European war more generally, for reasons that were essentially *political*. Only a certain kind of super-nationalist government, structured on narrow leadership grounds, with a monopoly of political power, would have embarked on the adventures the Nazis did in 1938, 1939, 1940, 1941 and 1942. Germany did not stumble into war, as it did in 1914. It was not a rational government; it did not have rational objectives. The Third Reich invaded the Soviet Union for reasons which, on the part of the Nazi leadership at least, were political. The leaders of Germany (including the leaders of the Wehrmacht) fatally underestimated Russian war potential, and they did so for reasons that were largely ideological and racial. For political reasons, the invaders – including many of the rank and file of the German Army – treated the people of the USSR with a cruelty and contempt that alienated them and ruled out anything more than ground-level collaboration. For political reasons it was impossible for the government in Berlin to split the anti-Nazi coalition, and for political reasons it was impossible to bring the war to an end when it was clearly lost (in 1943).

THE COST OF WAR

If Stalin's system deserves more credit for the eventual victory than it is sometimes given, still that system deserves the most severe criticism for the enormous cost paid in achieving victory. Why was the burden of the war so great for the Soviet Union? Soviet losses, like so much else, were cloaked in secrecy and confusion for many years. Originally a figure of 8,000,000 military and civilian deaths was used; then under Khrushchev, the toll rose to 20,000,000. In the 1980s, the currently accepted total of about 27,000,000 'excess deaths' was published. Soviet military deaths were about 10,000,000, of which 3,000,000 were POWs.[17] British military losses in the whole Second World War were 350,000, and those of the Americans even lower, at 300,000. Looking at the figures another way, Soviet losses in every three-month period of the war (except April–June 1943) were greater than the number suffered by the Americans for the whole war. German fatalities were much heavier in Russia than on the other fronts, as is clear from Table 14.1. If this is how we weigh up 'relative contribution', then undoubtedly the Russians killed many more German soldiers than the British or Americans did. It was only in one period of the war, in the fourth quarter of 1944, that German losses against the Russians were lower than those on all other fronts combined.

Table 14.1 German and Russian military personnel losses in the Second World War (1,000s)

Quarter	German losses			Soviet losses
	East	All fronts	Other fronts	
To II/41	–	–	147	–
III/41	185	–	15	2,130
IV/41	117	–	7	1,008
I/42	136	–	15	675
II/42	90	–	12	843
III/42	145	–	21	1,224
IV/42	135	–	17	516
I/43	295	–	24	727
II/43	48	–	25	192
III/43	188	–	27	804
IV/43	170	–	35	590
I/44	228	–	57	571
II/44	264	–	89	344
III/44	518	–	198	511
IV/44	223	–	224	338
I–II/45	–	1,230	–	801

Source: Overmans, *Verluste*, pp. 239, 266, 278–9; *Poteri*, pp. 252–3.

Note: German loss figures for 1945 (from Overmans) were not divided into East and West, but rather listed together as 'final battles' (*Endkämpfe*); they were also not broken down by quarter. *The Soviet column should certainly not be seen as directly comparable to the German ones.* Leaving aside fundamental problems of methodology and statistical accuracy, the Russian figures include POWs, while the German figures are just deaths (although including deaths among POWs). For comparison, see the quarterly overview of German losses through November 1944 in Müller-Hillebrand, *Das Heer*, vol. 3, p. 171.

The German and Russian loss figures in Table 14.1 are not directly comparable, as they come from very different sources. Nevertheless, according to those figures (and probably in reality), the third quarter of 1944 was the only period when German losses in the East exceeded those of the Russians. Much greater losses were suffered by the Russians across nearly the whole war and despite their advantages in terms of Stalin's 'permanently operating factors'.[18] This was an indictment of the Stalinist system and of the 'Stalinist' Red Army. It would be an oversimplification, however, to say that heavy losses were incurred simply because the Red Army fought crudely and because its leaders were unconcerned about human life.[19] One partial explanation is that a third of Soviet military losses are accounted for by the capture and murder by neglect of three million POWs, mostly taken in 1941. Another partial explanation is that offensive warfare is inherently expensive. The Wehrmacht took advantage of the fragmentation of the Red Army to win easy victories during its offensives in 1941–2; the Russians were not able to do this in their own attacks in 1942–5.

Civilian losses were a different matter. Like the military loss figures they were asymmetrical, but much more so; in the war the Germans occupied far more Soviet territory and for a much longer period. Civilian deaths in the Third Reich (including those in Austria) were about 2,150,000, which was less than half those of the Wehrmacht. Of these civilian deaths, more were caused by American and British air raids than Soviet operations or occupation policy. The Soviet figure of 17,000,000 for civilian deaths is much greater than those for the Red Army.[20] These civilian deaths were not all caused by direct enemy action. Some were the result of the relative poverty of the USSR, the shortages and priorities of wartime, and the brutalities of the Stalinist system (including the GULAG and deportations). But most of them would not have happened without the German invasion.

Economically, Germany recovered with remarkable speed from the Second World War. Some of Stalin's fears of 1944–5 about German revival turned out to be accurate. The defeated powers in the Second World War – Germany, Japan and Italy – paid no lasting economic penalty. Wartime reorganization and rationalization of production would actually help Germany post-war. The war immediately damaged the USSR more than it damaged Germany. The recent Russian estimate that the war cost some ten years' development seems a reasonable one. It is probably also true that the Soviet economy never recovered from the war.[21]

The ultimate paradox was that the Russian victory over Nazi Germany in 1945 was a factor which contributed to the eventual collapse of the Soviet system. Moscow's fear of the outside world was increased by the war. The growth of ethnic Russian nationalism (or Russocentrism) in the long term encouraged a reaction among that half of the Soviet population who were not Russians. Post-war possession of a security zone in eastern Europe, conquered by the Red Army in 1944–5, would turn out to be a liability, perpetuating hostility with the West and putting a brake on the reform of the Soviet system. The next time the Red Army was in action would be eleven years later in 1956, in Hungary (when the invasion forces were commanded by Marshal Konev). The role of the 'military-industrial complex', crucial in the victory over Nazism, would in the long term be malignant. It drained off resources that were needed for economic and social modernization. Germany lost the Second World War, partly because of the war fought in Russia. Yet the Federal Republic emerged within twenty years as an economic great power and achieved reunification in 1989. The USSR won its 'Great Fatherland War' yet lost the peace, as the system collapsed, economically in the 1980s and politically in 1991. Defeat made possible the transformation of Germany; victory perpetuated the most harmful features of the Soviet system.

Nazi and Communist propagandists portrayed one another in very similar terms. Almost from the start, the Russians stressed the horrors of German racist policy against the Slavs and the barbarity of their attackers. Later in the war, Moscow's propaganda portrayed the USSR as the real defender of Western values. In November 1944 Stalin claimed that 'the Soviet people by their selfless struggle saved European civilisation from the [atrocity-committing] fascist *pogromshchiki*'.[22] The Germans, too, spoke of a barbaric Bolshevik threat to Germany and then to Europe and the West as a whole. They used this first of all to justify their 'preventative' attack, and then in attempts to rally support at home and in the occupied and neutral countries against the Soviet counter-attack. This war of words does not mean that one opponent was just as bad as the other. A very able historian maintained that it was 'profitless' to debate 'whether the misery and destruction the Germans visited on half of European Russia ... exceeded the rape, arson, pillage and wanton murder that accompanied the Russian march into Eastern Germany'.[23] Without trying to whitewash the conduct of some Soviet troops in 1944–5, the two things are not worthy of comparison. After all, the Red Army won its war. There is no doubt that the alternative outcome, the victory of the Wehrmacht and of National Socialism, would have been far worse, for the Russians and for the rest of Europe and the world.

CHRONOLOGY OF EVENTS, 1939–45

AG = Army Group (Russian *front*); FM = Field Marshal; MD = Military District; MSU = Marshal of the Soviet Union; PC = People's Commissar; aka = also known as.

1939

23 August	German–Soviet Non-Aggression Pact.
1 September	German invasion of Poland.
3 September	Britain and France declare war on Germany.
17 September	Soviet invasion of Poland.
28 September	German–Soviet Treaty (with secret protocols).
30 November	USSR invades Finland; 'Winter War' begins.

1940

12 March	Soviet–Finnish peace treaty; end of Winter War.
April–May	Soviet NKVD mass murder of Polish POWs at three sites ('Katyn massacre').
7 May	Gen. Timoshenko replaces MSU Voroshilov as PC of Defence; promoted to MSU.
10 May	German invasion of Low Countries and France begins.
16–17 June	Soviet occupation of Lithuania, Latvia and Estonia.
22 June	French sign armistice with Germany.
22 June	Gen. Halder memorandum; first German consideration of invasion of USSR.
28–30 June	Red Army occupies Bessarabia and Northern Bukovina (Romania).
22 July	German planning for invasion of USSR begins.
27 September	Tripartite Pact signed by Germany, Italy and Japan.

October	Luftwaffe begins spy flights over USSR. First Soviet protest on 26th.
October	German training mission arrives in Romania; followed by combat forces.
4–5 October	Moscow: conference with Stalin on the Red Army strategic plan; counter-offensive to be directed against South Poland and not East Prussia.
12–14 November	Molotov, PC for Foreign Affairs, visits Berlin; unsuccessful attempt to improve German–Soviet relations.
20 November	Hungary joins Tripartite Pact.
20 November	Romania joins Tripartite Pact.
18 December	Hitler signs Directive No. 21; Operation BARBAROSSA set for 15 May 1941.

1941

2–11 January	Red Army war games.
14 January	Gen. Zhukov replaces Gen. Meretskov as Chief of the Red Army General Staff.
12 February	Soviet draft mobilization plan, MP-41, confirmed.
28 February	Soviet agent Stöbe ('*Al'te*') reports from Berlin on 20 May attack plan.
1 March	USA warns Soviet ambassador about German plans to invade USSR.
11 March	Red Army deployment plan; confirms counter-offensive into Poland.
27 March	Coup in Yugoslavia; pro-German government overthrown.
27 March	Operation BARBAROSSA postponed from mid-May to mid-June.
30 March	Hitler outlines 'war of annihilation' at Wehrmacht planning conference.
3 April	Churchill warns Stalin of German invasion plans (received on 16th).
6 April	Germany, Italy and Bulgaria invade Yugoslavia and Greece.
13 April	Soviet–Japanese Neutrality Pact.
30 April	Operation BARBAROSSA set for 22 June.
May	800,000 reservists mobilized into Red Army.
5 May	Stalin's Kremlin speech to military cadets on offensive strategy.

Chronology of Events (1941)

6 May	Stalin becomes Premier (Chairman of Council of People's Commissars), replacing Molotov.
13 May	Red Army General Staff orders movement of three armies to border.
15 May	Timoshenko and Zhukov present pre-emptive attack plan to Stalin.
20 May	German airborne invasion of Crete.
24 May	Stalin meets with Timoshenko, Zhukov and border MD commanders.
1 June	Soviet agent Sorge warns of German attack in the second part of June.
6 June	Wehrmacht 'Commissar Order' issued. Red Army political officers to be shot and not taken prisoner.
11 June	Stalin receives warning of imminent attack from agent Schulze-Boysen ('*Starshina*') in Berlin.
11 June	Stalin forbids Red Army occupation of border security zone (*predpol'e*).
14 June	TASS (Soviet news agency) bulletin minimizing German threat.
14 June	Red Army Air Force leaders Shtern and Smushkevich arrested.
14 June	Soviet NKVD begins mass deportations from the Baltic states.
16 June	Final British warning of German invasion given to Ambassador Maiskii.
22 June	(3.15 am) Beginning of Operation BARBAROSSA by German Army Groups North (FM Leeb), Centre (FM Bock) and South (FM Rundstedt). Italy and Romania also declare war on the USSR. Red Army ordered to counter-attack.
23 June	Soviet border MDs converted into army groups (*fronty*): Northwestern (Kuznetsov), Western (Pavlov) and Southwestern (Kirponos) AGs.
23 June	Creation of Stavka (Soviet GHQ) under Timoshenko.
24–29 June	Big tank battle in Lutsk, Brody, Rovno area (northwestern Ukraine) between German AG South and Soviet Southwestern AG.
26 June	Minsk pocket closed; Western AG (Pavlov) trapped by Army Group Centre; 28th, Minsk captured.
29 June	Secret Soviet decree on use of partisans.
29–30 June	Stalin's crisis; Stalin leaves the Kremlin for his *dacha*.
30 June	GKO (State Defence Committee) created under Stalin.

Chronology of Events (1941)

30 June	Soviet Southwestern and Southern AGs ordered back to the 'Stalin Line' (1939 border).
30 June	Mobilization of the People's Militia (*Narodnoe opolchenie*) in Leningrad.
30 June	MSU Timoshenko replaces Pavlov as commander of Western AG.
3 July	Stalin's 'Brothers and sisters!' radio speech.
9 July	Pskov captured by German AG North.
10 July	Stalin replaces Timoshenko as head of the Red Army and of the Stavka.
10 July	Soviet Northern (MSU Voroshilov), Western (MSU Timoshenko) and Southwestern (MSU Budennyi) Theatres (*Napravlenii*) set up.
10 July	Battle of Smolensk begins, continues till 10 September.
10 July	AG North (FM Leeb) advance to Leningrad begins, aka Leningrad defensive operation, continuing to 30 September.
14 July	Hitler Directive No. 32b on post-BARBAROSSA national armaments priorities; stresses Luftwaffe.
16 July	Smolensk captured by German AG Centre (Bock).
16 July	Commissars reintroduced in Red Army.
16 July	Soviet secret order against 'panic-mongers'.
17 July	Ministry for Occupied Eastern Territories (*Ostministerium*) under Rosenberg.
22 July	Trial and execution of Gen. Pavlov and other senior officers.
23 July	First major Soviet counter-offensive at Smolensk by forces of Western Theatre (Timoshenko).
29 July	MSU Shaposhnikov replaces Zhukov as Chief of the General Staff.
30 July	Hitler's Directive No. 34: AG Centre to go over to defensive.
5 August	Defence of Odessa by Soviet Coastal Army, continues till 16 October.
6 August	First British Arctic convoy arrives at Arkhangel'sk.
8 August	Soviet Uman' pocket in western Ukraine destroyed with the Soviet 6th (Muzychenko) and the 12th (Ponedelin) Armies.
12 August	Hitler Directive No. 34a; orders northern and southern flanks cleared.
16 August	Stalin Order No. 270 on punishments for cowardice and desertion.
17 August	Narva, Novgorod, Dnepropetrovsk, Nikolaev captured by Germans.

Chronology of Events (1941)

25 August	USSR and Britain begin occupation of Iran.
27–30 August	Evacuation by sea of Tallin (Estonia); disaster of evacuation convoy.
28 August	Soviet government orders deportation of Volga Germans.
29 August–12 September	General counter-offensive by Soviet Western Theatre (Timoshenko).
30 August	Successful El'nia counter-offensive of Reserve AG (Zhukov), continues till 8 September.
1 September	German *Reichskommissariats* for Ukraine (Koch) and *Ostland* (Lohse).
6 September	Hitler Directive No. 35: for attack towards Moscow by end of month.
6 September	Smolensk pocket finally eliminated.
8 September	Shlissel'burg captured by Germans. Blockade of Leningrad begins, continues till 27 January 1944.
10 September	End of the Battle of Smolensk.
10 September	Siniavino offensive operation of Soviet Leningrad AG, continues till 28 October.
11 September	Zhukov takes over Soviet Leningrad AG.
11 September	Konev replaces Timoshenko as commander of Soviet Western AG.
11 September	Timoshenko replaces Budennyi as commander of Southwestern Theatre.
12 September	Soviet Stavka directive on 'blocking detachments'.
18 September	First Soviet Guards divisions established (after El'nia victory).
19 September	Kiev captured by the German 6th Army (Reichenau).
20 September	Death in battle of Gen. Kirponos, commander of Soviet Southwestern AG.
27 September	Germans capture Perekop at the entrance to the Crimea.
28 September–1 October	Babii Iar massacre of Jews in Kiev by Germans.
30 September	Guderian begins attack towards Moscow, aka Moscow strategic defensive operation, continues till 5 December.
2 October	Operation TYPHOON launched towards Moscow by German AG Centre (Bock) against Soviet Briansk (Eremenko), Reserve (Budennyi) and Western (Konev) AGs; 'twin battle' of Viaz'ma–Briansk begins, aka Viaz'ma defensive operation, continues till 13 October.

Chronology of Events (1941)

5 October	Soviet GKO orders establishment of ten reserve armies and creation of rear defensive line covering the Volga.
5 October	Briansk taken by the 2nd Panzer Group (Guderian).
5–10 October	'Battle on the Sea of Azov'; big encirclement of Soviet forces east of Melitopol' by AG South.
7 October	Orel captured by the 2nd Panzer Group.
7 October	Viaz'ma taken by the 3rd Panzer Group (Hoth).
8 October	Gen. Zhukov replaces MSU Budennyi as commander of Soviet Reserve AG; on 11th he replaces Konev as commander of Western AG.
14 October	Kalinin taken by the German 3rd Panzer Group.
15 October	Evacuation of many government institutions from Moscow ordered by Stalin.
16 October	Offensive by AG North, aka Tikhvin defensive operation, continues till 18 November.
16 October	Odessa captured by Germans and Romanians; massacre of Jews from 22nd.
16–18 October	Moscow evacuation panic.
18 October	German offensive in Crimea by 11th Army (Manstein), aka Crimean defensive operation (till 16 November) of Soviet Coastal Army.
25 October	Khar'kov taken by German 6th Army (Reichenau).
30 October	Soviet Defence of Sevastopol' in Crimea, continues till 4 July 1942.
7 November	Revolution Day military parade in Red Square; speech by Stalin.
7 November	American Lend-Lease aid extended to USSR.
8 November	Tikhvin (east of Leningrad) captured by Germans; furthest advance of German AG North.
13 November	German command conference at Orsha; Gen. Halder wins agreement for continued advance towards Moscow.
15 November	Kerch' (eastern Crimea) captured by the German 11th Army (Manstein).
15 November	German advance on Moscow, aka Klin–Sol'nechnogorsk defensive operation, resumes after *rasputitsa*, continues till 5 December.
17 November	Stalin's 'scorched earth' Order No. 428.

18 November	British CRUSADER offensive in North Africa.
20 November	Rostov captured by German AG South (FM Rundstedt).
28 November	Furthest advance east of 3rd Panzer Army (Hoth), to Iakhroma on Moscow Canal.
29 November	Taganrog, Rostov recaptured by Soviet Southern AG (Cherevichenko).
30 November	Hitler removes Rundstedt from AG South; replaces him with Reichenau.
5 December	Moscow offensive operation by Western (Zhukov) and Kalinin (Konev) AGs, and part of Southwestern AG (Timoshenko), continues till 7 January.
5 December	Soviet–Polish Declaration of Friendship and Mutual Assistance signed in Moscow.
7 December	Japanese attack on Pearl Harbor.
8 December	Hitler Directive No. 39; Wehrmacht goes over to the defensive.
9 December	Tikhvin recaptured by Soviet 4th Army.
11 December	Hitler declares war on the USA.
16 December	Kalinin recaptured by Kalinin AG.
16 December	Hitler refuses withdrawal of German AG Centre; on 18 December orders 'fanatical resistance'.
17 December	Soviet Volkhov AG created under Meretskov.
18 December	Bock (commander of German AG Centre) sent on leave; (permanently) replaced by Gen. Kluge.
19 December	Hitler takes place of FM Brauchitsch as C-in-C of German Army.
25 December	Guderian dismissed as commander of 2nd Panzer Army.
25 December	Soviet Kerch'–Feodosiia amphibious operation in the Crimea, continues till 2 January.

1942

1 January	Declaration of the United Nations issued in Washington by USSR, Britain, US, China and others.
7 January	Demiansk operation of Soviet Northwestern AG (Kurochkin). Till 20 May.

Chronology of Events (1942)

7 January	Liuban' offensive of Soviet Volkhov AG (Meretskov). Till 30 April.
8 January	Rzhev–Viaz'ma strategic operation of Kalinin (Konev) and Western (Zhukov) AGs. Till 20 April.
9 January	Toropets–Kholm operation of the Soviet 3rd and 4th Shock Armies, till 6 February.
17 January	FM Leeb (AG North) dismissed.
18 January	Death of FM Reichenau (AG South); FM Bock takes over.
20 January	Wannsee Conference in Berlin on murder of Western European Jews.
9 February	Speer becomes Minister for Weapons and Munitions; Todt killed in air crash on 8th.
12 February	German Demiansk airlift starts (town encircled from 15 February to 7 April).
17 March	Soviet 2nd Shock Army cut off in Volkhov pocket; German Operation BEAST OF PREY (RAUBTIER).
5 April	Hitler Directive No. 41 for offensive in southern theatre.
17 April	Trapped Soviet 33rd Army near Viaz'ma ceases resistance.
20 April	Instructions by Sauckel (Reich Plenipotentiary for Labour Mobilization) on Eastern forced labourers.
24 April	MSU Shaposhnikov ill; Gen. Vasilevskii takes over as acting Chief of General Staff.
5 May	Soviet 1st Air Army created (first of seventeen eventually formed).
8 May	Operation BUSTARD HUNT (TRAPPENJAGD) attack on Kerch' Peninsula by the German 11th Army (Manstein); aka Kerch' defensive operation of Soviet Crimean AG (Kozlov), continues till 19 May.
12–29 May	Battle of Khar'kov; unsuccessful offensive by Soviet Southwestern (Timoshenko) and Southern (Malinovskii) AGs.
22 May	Molotov visits London and Washington, till 1 June.
26 May	British–Soviet Treaty of Alliance signed in London.
30 May	Central Partisan Staff (*TsShPD*) created in Moscow (under Ponomarenko).
30 May	RAF 'thousand bomber' raid on Cologne.

7 June	Final attack of the German 11th Army against Sevastopol', till 4 July, Operation STURGEON CATCH (STÖRFANG).
12 June	US–USSR communiqué (after Molotov visit) notes 'full agreement' on 1942 'second front'.
26 June	Vasilevskii officially replaces Shaposhnikov as Chief of the General Staff.
28 June	Summer offensive of German Army Group South (Bock) begins against Southern (Malinovskii), Southwestern (Timoshenko) and Briansk (Golikov) AGs; aka Soviet Voronezh–Voroshilovgrad strategic defensive operation (to 24 July).
2–12 July	Operation SEYDLITZ: destruction of Soviet 39th Army (Maslennikov), trapped west of Viaz'ma.
4 July	Sevastopol' captured by the German 11th Army (Manstein).
4 July	Day of heaviest damage to British–American convoy PQ17 en route to North Russia; convoy ordered to scatter.
6 July	Voronezh captured by the German 6th Army (Paulus).
7 July	Donbass defensive operation of Southwestern (Timoshenko) and Southern (Malinovskii) AGs, till 24 July.
9 July	German Army Group South (Bock) divided into Army Group 'A' (List) and Army Group 'B' (Bock).
12 July	Gen. Vlasov captured after destruction of the 2nd Shock Army on the Volkhov.
16 July	FM Weichs replaces FM Bock as commander of German Army Group 'B'.
17 July	Beginning of Stalingrad strategic defensive operation, continues till 18 November.
17 July	Voroshilovgrad captured by German Army Group 'A'.
23 July	Rostov captured by German Army Group 'A'.
23 July	Hitler's Directive No. 45 on the further offensive in the southern Russian theatre, Operation BRUNSWICK (BRAUNSCHWEIG).
25 July	Beginning of North Caucasus strategic defensive operation, till 31 December.
28 July	Stalin Order No. 227: 'Not one step backwards!'

Chronology of Events (1942)

30 July	Rzhev–Sychevka operation of Western (Zhukov) and Kalinin (Konev) AGs against German AG Centre, till 23 August.
5 August	The Soviet 1st Guards Army established; first of eleven guards infantry armies formed during war.
9 August	Maikop in North Caucasus captured by German Army Group 'A'(List).
12–15 August	1st Moscow Conference; Churchill in Moscow.
19 August	British and Canadian raid on Dieppe.
19 August	Siniavino operation of Volkhov (Meretskov) and Leningrad (Govorov) AGs against AG North (Küchler), till 10 October.
23 August	The German 14th Panzer Corps of 6th Army (Paulus) reaches the Volga River north of Stalingrad.
26 August	Gen. Zhukov becomes Deputy Supreme C-in-C under Stalin.
1 September	The German 6th Army (Paulus) reaches the suburbs of Stalingrad.
7 September	Novorossiisk on Black Sea captured by the German 17th Army (Ruoff).
10 September	Hitler puts himself in charge of Army Group 'A', replacing FM List.
12 September	Stavka begins to plan for a Stalingrad counter-attack.
24 September	Gen. Halder replaced by Gen. Zeitzler as Chief of the Army General Staff.
30 September	Hitler's Sportpalast speech: Germany will not be driven from Stalingrad.
9 October	End of dual command in Red Army.
14 October	German offensive; most critical day in Stalingrad street fighting.
23 October	German defeat at El Alamein in North Africa, till 4 November.
7 November	Hitler leaves his eastern HQ at Vinnitsa for Germany (returns on 23rd).
8 November	Operation TORCH: British–American landings in northwest Africa.
8 November	Hitler's radio speech: claims German Army holds 'nearly all' of Stalingrad.
11 November	German occupation of Vichy France.
19 November	Operation URANUS: Southwestern (Vatutin), Don (Rokossovskii) and Stalingrad (Eremenko) AGs against 3rd Romanian Army, German

	6th Army (Paulus), German 4th Panzer Army (Kleist/Mackensen) and 4th Romanian Army. Beginning of Stalingrad strategic offensive operation, till 2 February.
24 November	Soviet spearheads link up at Kalach on the Don; the German 6th Army cut off.
25 November	Operation MARS: Rzhev–Sychevka operation of Western (Konev) and Kalinin (Purkaev) AGs against AG Centre (Kluge), till 20 December.
12 December	Operation WINTER STORM (WINTERGEWITTER): Army Group Don (Manstein) attempts to relieve Stalingrad from the southwest, aka Kotel'nikovo operation of Stalingrad AG (Eremenko), till 30 December.
16–30 December	Middle Don (*Srednedonskaia*) operation of Soviet Southwestern (Vatutin) and Voronezh (Golikov) AGs, aka Operation LITTLE SATURN.
27 December	'Smolensk Appeal' of collaborator Gen. Vlasov and the 'Russian Liberation Army'.
27 December	Hitler allows withdrawal of Army Group 'A' from North Caucasus.

1943

1 January	Millerovo–Voroshilovgrad offensive of Southwestern AG (Vatutin), till 22 February.
1 January	Operation DON, aka North Caucasus strategic offensive operation of Transcaucasus (Tiulenev), Southern (Eremenko) and North Caucasus (Maslennikov) AGs against German AG 'A' (Kleist), till 4 February.
10 January	Operation RING of Don AG (Rokossovskii) against Stalingrad, till 2 February.
12–30 January	Operation SPARK of Leningrad (Govorov) and Volkhov (Meretskov) AGs to break Leningrad blockade.
13 January	Voronezh–Khar'kov strategic offensive operation of Soviet Southwestern (Vatutin), Voronezh (Golikov) and Briansk (Reiter) AGs, till 3 March.
13 January	Ostrogozhsk–Rossoshan' operation of Voronezh AG against the Hungarian 2nd and the Italian 8th Armies, till 27 February.
13 January	Hitler's 'Total War' decree.

14–24 January	American–British Casablanca Conference. Demand for Axis 'unconditional surrender'.
18 January	Velikie Luki recaptured by Kalinin AG.
18 January	Leningrad Blockade broken; Shlissel'burg recaptured by Leningrad AG.
18 January	Zhukov promoted to MSU.
24 January	Voronezh–Kastornoe operation of Voronezh and Briansk AGs, till 2 February.
25 January	Voronezh recaptured by Soviet Voronezh AG.
27 January	First US bombing raid on Germany.
29 January	Voroshilovgrad operation of Soviet Southwestern AG (Vatutin), till 18 February.
30 January	Goebbels' 'Total War' speech.
31 January	Surrender of German 6th Army (FM Paulus) at Stalingrad.
2 February	Khar'kov offensive operation of Southwestern (Vatutin), Voronezh (Golikov) and Briansk (Reiter) AGs, aka Operation STAR, till 3 March.
4 February	Novorossiisk landing operation of Soviet North Caucasus AG (Maslennikov), till 6 April.
5–18 February	Rostov operation of Southern AG (Eremenko/Malinovskii).
5 February	Maloarkhangel'sk operation of Soviet Briansk AG, till 2 March: failed Soviet advance towards Orel.
6 February	Stavka issues directives for major offensives in the northern (Operation POLAR STAR) and central sectors (Orel–Briansk, Sevsk).
8 February	Kursk recaptured by Soviet Voronezh AG.
9 February	Krasnodar operation of North Caucasus AG (Maslennikov) against Army Group 'A' (Kleist, till 24 May); Krasnodar recaptured on 12 February.
13 February	German AG Don (Manstein) becomes AG South; AG 'B' headquarters (Weichs) disbanded.
14 February	Rostov recaptured by Soviet North Caucasus AG and Southern AG.
15–28 February	Demiansk offensive of Soviet Northwestern AG (Timoshenko) against German AG North (Küchler).
16 February	Khar'kov recaptured by Soviet Voronezh AG.

16 February	Vasilevskii promoted to MSU.
17 February	Stalin approves plan for Operation GALLOP by Southwestern AG (Vatutin), to the Dnepr crossings.
19 February	German counter-attack by FM Manstein begins in south.
20 February	German phased withdrawal from Demiansk pocket, till 18 March.
1–24 March	German Operation BUFFALO (BÜFFEL): evacuation of Rzhev–Viaz'ma salient.
3 March	Rzhev recaptured by Soviet Western AG.
6 March	Stalin awarded rank of MSU.
12 March	Viaz'ma recaptured by Soviet Western AG.
15 March	German AG South (Manstein) recaptures Khar'kov.
13 April	Germans reveal Katyn mass execution of Polish officers by NKVD.
19 April	Supreme Soviet decree on war crimes.
26 April	USSR breaks with London-based Polish government-in-exile after revelation of Katyn massacre.
13 May	Axis capitulation in North Africa.
11–25 May	American–British TRIDENT conference in Washington, DC, decides on invasion of Italy, sets cross-Channel invasion for 1 May 1944.
14 May	Formation of Polish units in Red Army begins.
22 May	Dissolution of Comintern announced.
4 July	German Operation CITADEL (ZITADELLE) begins, by the German 9th (Model) and the 4th Panzer (Hoth) Armies, aka Kursk defensive operation of Voronezh AG (Vatutin) and Central AG (Rokossovskii) (5–23 July).
10 July	British–American invasion of Sicily.
12 July	Soviet Operation KUTUZOV aka Orel operation by Western (Sokolovskii), Briansk (Popov) and Central (Rokossovskii) AGs, north of the Kursk bulge, till 18 August.
12–13 July	Free Germany (*Freies Deutschland*) Committee set up at Soviet Krasnogorsk POW camp.
11–12 July	Tank battle at Prokhorovka on south side of Kursk bulge.
13 July	Hitler calls off Kursk offensive.

1 August	Stalin visits Soviet Western AG (Sokolovskii) headquarters.
3–23 August	Operation POLKOVODETS RUMIANTSEV, aka Belgorod–Khar'kov operation, by Southwestern (Malinovskii), Steppe (Konev) and Voronezh (Vatutin) AGs, south of the Kursk bulge, against AG South (Manstein).
5 August	Orel recaptured by Soviet Briansk AG (Popov). Belgorod recaptured by Steppe and Voronezh AGs. First artillery 'salute' in Moscow.
7 August	Smolensk operation (Operation SUVOROV) of Soviet Western (Sokolovskii) and Kalinin (Eremenko) AGs against the German 3rd Panzer (Reinhardt) and the 4th (Heinrici) Armies, till 2 October.
12 August	Hitler decides to create *Ostwall* defensive line on Dnepr.
13 August	Donbass operation of Southern (Tolbukhin) and Southwestern (Malinovskii) AGs against the German 8th (Wöhler), the 1st Panzer (Mackensen) and the 6th (Hollidt) Armies, till 22 September.
23 August	Khar'kov recaptured by Soviet Steppe AG.
26 August	Chernigov–Poltava operation of Soviet Steppe, Voronezh and Central (Rokossovskii) AGs against German AG South, till 30 September.
1 September	Briansk operation of Soviet Briansk AG (Popov), till 3 October.
4 September	Metropolitans of Russian Orthodox Church received at the Kremlin.
9 September	British–American landings on mainland Italy at Salerno.
12 September	Russian Orthodox Church Patriarchate re-established under Sergius.
15 September	Smolensk–Roslavl' operation of Soviet Western AG (Sokolovskii), till 2 October.
15 September	German AG South (Manstein) ordered to withdraw behind the *Ostwall*.
16 September	Novorossiisk recaptured by Soviet North Caucasus AG (Petrov).
17 September	Briansk recaptured by Briansk AG (Popov).
22 September	Abortive Bukrin operation by Voronezh AG (Vatutin); Dnepr crossed by Voronezh AG spearheads; failed Dnepr airborne operation at Kanev on 24th.
25 September	Smolensk recaptured by Soviet Western AG (Sokolovskii).
26 September	Lower Dnepr operation of Southern (Tolbukhin), Southwestern (Malinovskii) and Steppe (Konev) AGs, against right wing of German Army Group South (Manstein), till 20 December.

Chronology of Events (1943)

1 October	Liutezh operation of Voronezh/1st Ukrainian AG (Vatutin), till 2 November.
9 October	Litvinov paper in PC of Foreign Affairs on post-war planning.
12 October	Failed attacks by Western AG (Sokolovskii) against Orsha, till 2 December.
14 October	Zaporozhe on Dnepr recaptured by Soviet Southwestern AG (Malinovskii).
19–30 October	Moscow Conference of American, British and Soviet foreign ministers.
20 October	Soviet army groups renamed: Southern, Southwestern, Steppe and Voronezh AGs become, respectively, the 4th (Tolbukhin), the 3rd (Malinovskii), the 2nd (Konev) and the 1st (Vatutin) Ukrainian AGs; Central Army Group becomes Belorussian AG (Rokossovskii); Kalinin AG becomes the 1st Baltic AG (Eremenko); Baltic AG (Popov) becomes the 2nd Baltic AG.
25 October	Dnepropetrovsk on Dnepr recaptured by the Soviet 3rd Ukrainian AG.
28 October	AG Centre: FM Kluge injured in car accident, replaced by FM Busch.
31 October	Kerch'–El'tigen operation; failed amphibious landing in eastern Crimea by North Caucasus AG (later Coastal Army) (Gen. Petrov), till 11 December.
31 October	Perekop recaptured by the Soviet 4th Ukrainian AG; Axis-held Crimea cut off.
3 November	Führer directive. Priority shifted from East front to West.
3–13 November	Kiev offensive operation of the 1st Ukrainian AG (Vatutin) against German AG South (Manstein); breakout from Liutezh bridgehead near Kiev.
6 November	Kiev recaptured by the 1st Ukrainian AG.
13 November	Kiev defensive operation, of the Soviet 1st Ukrainian AG against counter-attacks by the 4th Panzer Army (Raus), till 22 December.
28 November	Tehran Conference of Stalin, Churchill and Roosevelt, till 1 December.
14 December	Cherkassy on Dnepr recaptured by 2nd Ukrainian AG (Konev).
15–18 December	First Soviet war crimes trial held at Khar'kov.
20 December	Supreme Soviet decree on new national anthem replacing 'Internationale'; played on radio on 1 January 1944.

22 December	Führer Order. National Socialist Leadership Officers installed in German Army.
24 December	Beginning of Soviet general winter offensive across the Ukraine, aka Dnepr–Carpathian operation, till 17 April 1944.
24 December	Zhitomir–Berdichev operation west of Kiev by the Soviet 1st Ukrainian AG (Vatutin), till 14 January.
29 December	Failed attack by Western AG (Sokolovskii) against Vitebsk, till 6 January.
31 December	Zhitomir recaptured by the Soviet 1st Ukrainian AG (Vatutin).

1944

1 January	Formation of Polish National Council of the Homeland (*KRN*) in Moscow.
4 January	Leningrad–Novgorod operation of the Soviet Leningrad (Govorov), Volkhov (Meretskov) and the 2nd Baltic (Popov) AGs, till 1 March.
10 January	Maiskii paper in PC of Foreign Affairs on post-war planning.
20 January	Novgorod recaptured by Volkhov AG.
24 January	Korsun'–Shevchenkovskii operation of the 2nd (Konev) and the 1st (Vatutin) AGs against German AG South (Manstein) west of Dnepr, till 17 February.
27 January	Rovno–Lutsk operation of 1st Ukrainian AG (Vatutin) in northwest Ukraine, till 11 February.
27 January	Leningrad Blockade lifted; end of the '900 days'.
29 January	Model replaces FM Küchler as commander of German AG North.
30 January	Nikopol'–Krivoi Rog operation of the 4th (Tolbukhin) and the 3rd (Malinovskii) AGs against German AG South, till 29 February.
3 February	Failed Vitebsk operation of the 1st Baltic (Bagramian) and Western AGs (Sokolovskii), till 13 March.
8 February	Nikopol' recaptured by the 3rd (Malinovskii) and 4th (Tolbukhin) Ukrainian AGs.
16 February	Breakout of German forces from Korsun'/Cherkassy pocket.
22 February	Krivoi Rog recaptured by the 3rd Ukrainian AG (Malinovskii).

23 February	Soviet NKVD begins deportation of Chechen (310,000) and Ingush (80,000) minorities from North Caucasus to Central Asia.
29 February	Gen. Vatutin, commander of the 1st Ukrainian AG, mortally injured in skirmish with Ukrainian nationalist guerrillas (dies 15 April); replaced by MSU Zhukov.
4 March	Proskurov–Chernovitsy operation of the Soviet 1st Ukrainian AG (Zhukov) in northwestern Ukraine, till 17 April.
5 March	Uman'–Botoşani operation of the Soviet 2nd Ukrainian AG (Konev), till 17 April.
8 March	Hitler Order No. 11 on 'Fortified Places'.
9 March	Pskov operation of Soviet Leningrad AG (Govorov), till 15 April.
19 March	Germans occupy Hungary (Operation MARGARETHE); more compliant government installed.
30 March	FM Manstein replaced by Model in AG South; FM Kleist replaced by Schörner in AG 'A'; Lindemann takes over AG North.
4 April	German AG South becomes AG North Ukraine, AG 'A' become AG South Ukraine.
7 April	Botoşani (Romania) captured by the 2nd Ukrainian AG (Konev); first foreign town taken by Red Army.
8 April	Crimea operation of the 4th Ukrainian AG (Tolbukhin), till 12 May.
10 April	Odessa recaptured by the Soviet 3rd Ukrainian AG (Malinovskii).
10 May	Sevastopol' recaptured by the Soviet 4th Ukrainian AG (Tolbukhin).
18 May	Soviet NKVD begins deportation of 150,000 Crimean Tatars.
6 June	D-Day landings in Normandy.
10 June	Vyborg–Petrozavodsk strategic operation against Finns by Leningrad (Govorov) and Karelian (Meretskov) AGs, till 9 August.
20 June	Vyborg recaptured by Soviet Leningrad AG (Govorov).
21–22 June	Luftwaffe attack on American 'shuttle' bomber base at Poltava.
23 June	Belorussian strategic operation of the 1st (Rokossovskii), 2nd (Zakharov), 3rd (Cherniakhovskii) Belorussian and 1st Baltic (Bagramian) AGs against Army Group Centre (FM Busch), aka Operation BAGRATION.
28 June	FM Model replaces Gen. Busch as commander of German AG Centre.

Chronology of Events (1944)

3 July	Minsk recaptured by the 2nd and 3rd Belorussian AGs.
11–31 July	Pskov–Ostrov operation of the 3rd Baltic AG (Maslennikov).
13 July	L'vov–Sandomierz strategic operation of the Soviet 1st Ukrainian AG (Konev) against German AG North Ukraine (Model), till 29 August.
18 July	Lublin–Brest operation of Soviet 1st Belorussian AG (Rokossovskii), till 2 August.
20 July	Stauffenberg's attempt to assassinate Hitler; abortive military coup in Berlin.
21 July	Gen. Guderian becomes Chief of German Army General Staff.
22 July	Chełm (Poland) captured by the 1st Belorussian AG. Polish Committee of National Liberation (PKWN) established; later moved to Lublin.
23 July	Pskov recaptured by the 3rd Baltic AG.
24 July	Lublin (Poland) captured by the Soviet 1st Belorussian AG.
25 July	Hitler decree on Total War Mobilization.
24–30 July	Narva operation of Leningrad AG (Govorov); Narva recaptured on 26th.
31 July	The Soviet 1st Baltic AG reaches the Gulf of Riga west of Riga, cutting off German AG North (Schörner) until 21 August.
31 July	Battle of Radzymin/Wołomyn (near Warsaw), defeat of Soviet 2nd Tank Army by forces of AG Centre (Model), till 8 August.
1 August	Warsaw Uprising of Polish Home Army; insurgents surrender on 2 October.
1 August	Bridgehead thrown over Vistula at Magnuszew (Poland) by the 1st Belorussian AG (Rokossovskii).
10 August	Tartu operation (eastern Estonia) of the 3rd Baltic AG (Maslennikov), till 6 September.
16 August	FM Model transferred to West; replaced in AG Centre by H. Reinhardt.
17 August	The 3rd Belorussian AG (Cherniakhovskii) reaches East Prussian border.
20–29 August	Iaşi–Kishenev (Romania/Moldavia) operation of the 2nd (Malinovskii) and 3rd (Tolbukhin) AGs against German Army Group South Ukraine (Friessner).

Chronology of Events (1944)

23 August	Palace coup in Bucharest; FM Antonescu arrested.
25 August	Paris liberated by Americans and Free French.
29 August	The Soviet 1st, the 4th Ukrainian, the 1st, the 2nd, the 3rd Belorussian, Leningrad and Karelian AGs ordered onto 'strict defensive'.
29 August	Slovak Uprising begins (defeated 27 October).
30 August	Łomza–Rózan operation of 2nd Belorussian AG (Zakharov) against German AG Centre (Reinhardt) northeast of Warsaw, till 2 November.
31 August	The 2nd Ukrainian AG enters Bucharest.
5 September	Soviet–Finnish ceasefire.
5 September	USSR declares war on Bulgaria.
8 September	East Carpathian strategic operation by the 1st (Konev) and 4th (Petrov) Ukrainian AGs against German AG 'A' (Harpe), till 28 October.
9 September	Soviet–Bulgarian ceasefire. Pro-Soviet Fatherland Front takes power.
14 September	Baltic strategic operation of the 1st (Bagramian), 2nd (Eremenko) and 3rd (Maslennikov) Baltic and Leningrad (Govorov) AGs against German Army Group North (Schörner), till 24 November.
16 September	The 3rd Ukrainian AG enters Sofia (Bulgaria).
17–26 September	Tallin (Estonia) operation of Leningrad AG (Govorov) against German AG North (Schörner).
25 September	German *Volkssturm* emergency militia established by Nazi Party.
28 September	Belgrade operation of the 2nd and 3rd Ukrainian AGs, till 20 October.
5–22 October	Memel operation of the 1st Baltic AG (Bagramian) against AG North (Schörner).
6–28 October	Debrecen (Hungary) operation of the Soviet 2nd (Malinovskii) and the 3rd (Tolbukhin) Ukrainian AGs against German AG South (Friessner).
6 October	4th Ukrainian AG (Petrov) takes Dukla Pass into eastern Slovakia.
7–29 October	Petsamo–Kirkenes operation of Karelian AG (Meretskov); Germans defeated in the Arctic.
9–18 October	British–Soviet TOLSTOY conference: Churchill meets with Stalin; informal 'percentages agreement' about Balkan spheres of influence.

10 October	The 1st Baltic AG reaches the Baltic Sea at Palanga. German AG North (Schörner) cut off in Kurland. Port of Memel (Klaipeda) held by Germans until 28 January.
13 October	Riga recaptured by the 2nd and 3rd Baltic AGs.
16 October	German coup in Hungary. Regent Horthy deposed; fascist Szalasi government installed.
16–30 October	Gumbinnen–Goldap operation of 3rd Belorussian AG (Cherniakhovskii) against German AG Centre (Reinhardt); failed Soviet attack on East Prussia.
18 October	Formation of the *Volkssturm* (people's militia).
20 October	Belgrade captured by 3rd Ukrainian AG and Yugoslav partisans.
21 October	Massacre of German civilians by Soviet troops at Nemmersdorf in East Prussia.
27 October	Banská Bystrica (central Slovakia) captured by Germans; defeat of Slovak Uprising.
29 October	Budapest strategic operation of the 2nd and 3rd Ukrainian AGs, till 13 February.
16 November	Zhukov takes over 1st Ukrainian AG, Rokossovskii transferred to 2nd Ukrainian AG.
20 November	Hitler leaves Rastenburg (East Prussia) headquarters for the last time.
16 December	German Ardennes offensive in West, stopped by 24 December.
21 December	Hungarian National Government under Gen. Miklos created at Debrecen in Soviet-occupied territory.
26 December	Budapest cut off by the 3rd (Tolbukhin) and the 2nd (Malinovskii) Ukrainian AGs.
31 December	PKWN in Lublin becomes Soviet-backed Polish Provisional Government.

1945

1 January	Operation KONRAD: counter-attack in Hungary by AG South (Wöhler).
12 January	Vistula–Oder strategic operation by 1st Ukrainian (Konev) and 1st Belorussian (Zhukov) AGs against German AG Centre/North (Reinhardt) and AG 'A'/Centre (Harpe/Schörner), till 3 February.

Chronology of Events (1945)

12 January	Western Carpathian strategic operation of the 2nd (Malinovskii) and the 4th (Petrov) Ukrainian AGs against AG 'A'/Centre and AG South (Wöhler), till 18 February.
13 January	East Prussian strategic operation by 3rd Belorussian AG (Cherniakhovskii/Vasilevskii) against German AG Centre/North (Reinhardt/Rendulic/Weiss), till 25 April.
14 January	The 1st Belorussian AG (Zhukov) joins in the Vistula–Oder offensive against AG Centre; Soviet Warsaw–Poznań operation runs to 3 February.
14 January	Mława–Elbing operation of the 2nd Belorussian AG (Rokossovskii) against German AG Centre/North (Reinhardt), till 26 January.
17 January	Warsaw captured by Red Army.
19 January	The 4th Ukrainian AG (Petrov) begins advance into central Slovakia; Košice taken.
19 January	Kraków (Poland) taken by the 1st Ukrainian AG. Łodž taken by the 1st Belorussian AG.
21 January	The 2nd Belorussian AG (Rokossovskii) ordered to redirect offensive, with the main thrust to northeast (East Prussia) rather than northwest (Pomerania).
22 January	Zhukov orders the 1st Belorussian AG to drive on to Berlin.
22 January	German position in East Prussia crumbles; the 3rd Belorussian AG takes Insterburg, the 2nd Belorussian AG takes Allenstein.
24 January	German army groups in East renamed: AG North (Rendulic), Centre (Reinhardt) and 'A' (Schörner) become AG Kurland, North and Centre.
25 January	German evacuation by sea of East and West Prussia begins.
25 January	The 2nd Belorussian AG reaches Baltic near Elbing; East Prussia and AG North cut off.
27 January	The 1st Ukrainian AG reaches Auschwitz.
31 January	The 1st Belorussian AG crosses the Oder River near Küstrin.
4–11 February	Yalta Conference of Churchill, Roosevelt and Stalin.
8–24 February	Lower Silesia operation of the 1st Ukrainian AG (Konev).
10 February	East Pomerania operation of the 1st (Zhukov) and the 2nd (Rokossovskii) Belorussian AGs, till 4 April.

13 February	Budapest taken by the 2nd Ukrainian AG.
13–15 February	British and American air raids against Dresden.
16–20 February	Unsuccessful German Operation SOLSTICE (SONNENWENDE) counter-offensive at Stargard in Pomerania.
16 February	Hitler arrives in Berlin; he remains there until his death.
18 February	Gen. Cherniakhovskii killed in East Prussia; MSU Vasilevskii takes over the 3rd Belorussian AG.
24 February	Political crisis in Romania, till 6 March. Soviet emissary Vyshinskii installs more compliant Groza government.
3–5 March	Lauban offensive in Upper Silesia by AG Centre (Schörner) against the 1st Ukrainian AG (Konev).
4 March	The Soviet 1st (Zhukov) and 2nd (Rokossovskii) Belorussian AGs reach the Baltic coast in Pomerania; East Pomerania (Gdynia and Danzig) and the German 2nd Army (Gen. Saucken) cut off.
6–15 March	Operation SPRING AWAKENING (FRÜHLINGSERWACHEN): offensive in Hungary by the German 6th SS Panzer Army (Dietrich) against the 3rd Ukrainian AG (Tolbukhin); last major German offensive of the war, aka Balaton defensive operation.
7 March	Americans capture Rhine bridge at Remagen.
10 March	Failed offensive by the 4th Ukrainian AG (Petrov/Eremenko) in central Czechoslovakia (Ostrava operation or Morava–Ostrava operation) against German AG Centre, till 5 May.
15–31 March	Upper Silesia operation of the 1st Ukrainian AG (Konev).
16 March	Vienna operation of the 3rd (Tolbukhin) and 2nd (Malinovskii) Ukrainian AGs against German AG South/Ostmark (Rendulic), till 15 April.
19 March	Hitler's 'Scorched Earth' directive.
25 March	Bratislava–Brno operation of the 2nd Ukrainian AG (Malinovskii) against AG Centre and AG South/Ostmark, till 5 May.
27 March	Representatives of Polish (London) government-in-exile arrested by NKGB.
28 March	Eisenhower decides on southern German orientation of his armies.
30 March	Danzig captured by the 2nd Belorussian AG.
2–3 April	Stavka conference on Berlin operation.

9 April	Königsberg captured by the 3rd Belorussian AG (Vasilevskii).
12 April	Death of President Roosevelt.
13 April	Vienna taken by the 3rd (Tolbukhin) and 2nd (Malinovskii) Ukrainian AGs.
16 April	Eastern Germany: Soviet Berlin operation. The 1st Ukrainian (Konev) and the 1st Belorussian (Zhukov) AGs attack, till 8 May.
18 April	The 2nd Belorussian AG (Rokossovskii) attacks.
20 April	Stavka order on humane behaviour to Germans.
21 April	Soviet–Polish Friendship Treaty.
25 April	US Army and the 1st Ukrainian AG meet on the Elbe River at Torgau.
30 April	(afternoon) Hitler commits suicide; Red flag raised over Reichstag.
2 May	Berlin garrison surrenders.
6 May	Breslau surrenders.
6–11 May	Prague operation of the 1st (Konev) and the 2nd (Malinovskii) Ukrainian AGs.
7 May	(1.41 am) Gen. Jodl signs surrender document before Eisenhower at Reims (France).
8 May	(10.43 pm) FM Keitel signs surrender document before Zhukov at Karlshorst (Berlin).
8 May	(11.01 pm, Central European Time) Formal end of fighting in Europe.
9 May	The 1st and the 2nd Ukrainian AGs enter Prague.
10 May	AG Kurland surrenders.

GLOSSARY

The Soviet and German military forces were organized on similar lines. Army groups contained several armies, armies contained two or three corps, corps contained two or more divisions. Full-strength infantry divisions numbered rather more than 10,000 personnel, but it was not unusual to have divisions with strength reduced to 2,000 or 3,000. Infantry divisions contained several regiments, and, typically, 6–8 infantry battalions (2–3 to a regiment); full-strength infantry battalions numbered about 750–1,000 personnel.

However, the two armies used different strengths for some formations, and these strengths changed over time. For example, a Soviet 'tank army' of 1944 was roughly equivalent in tank strength to a German 'motorized corps' or 'panzer corps' of 1941. Meanwhile, a German 'panzer army' of 1944 might well have contained very few tanks. The largest tank formations of the war were the four German panzer groups of 1941. These were made up of two or three panzer corps, each with two or three panzer divisions and motorized divisions. Soviet tank and mechanized corps typically were made up of two or three tank brigades (each with 50–60 tanks) and/or two or three mechanized brigades. German panzer divisions normally had two panzer regiments; each regiment normally had two battalions, each with 60–70 tanks.

The term 'Red Army Air Force' is used to describe the main air combat organization on the Soviet side. The obvious alternative, the Russian abbreviation 'VVS' (*Voenno-vozdushnye sily*), misleadingly suggests the existence of an independent air arm like the Luftwaffe. Soviet air defence forces (interceptor squadrons and AA guns) were under a separate organization, the PVO (Air Defence Forces). Soviet front-line 'air armies' were more rigidly linked to army formations than Luftwaffe air fleets were, although some Soviet air armies were held in the High Command Reserve. Within a Luftwaffe air fleet or a Soviet air army, the air corps was the next echelon.

air army (*vozdushnaia armiia*) The largest Soviet air formation.
air corps *Fliegerkorps* (German) or *aviatsionnaia korpus* (Russian).
air fleet (*Luftflotte*) The largest Luftwaffe formation, typically supporting one army group (qv). No Soviet equivalent.
army detachment (*Armeeabteilung*) Term used by the Germans for a relatively small army-level formation, often of an ad hoc nature and named after its commander (e.g. Army Detachment 'Hollidt' in the Donbass in early 1943). The Russians called this an 'operational group'.
army group A large formation incorporating several field armies; a German army group was larger than a Soviet one. Many books use the word 'front' for a Soviet army group, the Russian-language word being *front*.
attack aircraft Category of specialized aircraft used in support, direct or indirect, of ground troops. The generic names in Russian and German, *shturmovik* and *Stuka*, came to be attached to particular aircraft types, the Il'iushin Il-2 and the Junkers Ju 87.
blocking detachment (*zagraditel'nyi otriad*) Soviet unit positioned behind the front line to enforce discipline and prevent desertion.
Comintern Communist (Third) International. Body set up by Lenin in 1919 to co-ordinate international Communist movement; disbanded in May 1943.
commissar A Communist Party political officer assigned to supervise a Soviet unit. Although 'commissars' were formerly abolished in the Red Army in 1942, the term is also used here

generally for Soviet political personnel in 1943–5 rather than the opaque 'member of military council' (qv) or, at lower level, *politruk* (political leader).

district Normally this is used here for a low-level Soviet civilian territorial-administrative unit, roughly equivalent to an American county, known as a *raion*. Usually part of a 'region' (*oblast'*) (qv).

Einsatzgruppe Battalion-sized SS force tasked with destroying enemies of Nazi order in occupied zone; four existed in 1941. Notorious for mass murders of Jews in western USSR.

formation A relatively large military organization made up of units (qv). In the Red Army a formation (*soedinenie*) was a brigade or larger.

front Russian word for 'army group' (qv).

Hero of the Soviet Union (*Geroi Sovetskogo soiuza*) A title or award, the highest possible, given for service to the Soviet state. Established in 1934. Some 11,000 awards were made in 1941–5, many posthumously.

High Command Reserve (*Rezerv Verkhovnogo Glavnokomandovaniia* or RVGK) Soviet ground and air formations under the direct control of the Stavka (qv) which were committed to individual army groups for operations.

infantry army A term used in this book for a Soviet general purpose or 'combined-arms' (*obshchevoiskovaia*) army, to distinguish it from a tank army.

Katiusha Soviet multiple rocket launcher, usually truck-mounted. Also called an RS unit, 'Guards mortar' unit (for deception purposes) or a 'Stalin organ' (by the Germans).

Korück Rear area of a German field army.

Luftwaffe German Air Force.

mechanized corps (*mekhanizirovannyi korpus*) At the start of the war, the 'mechanized corps' was the main Soviet type of armoured formation, with two 'tank divisions' and a 'motorized rifle division'; these corps were unwieldy and were destroyed or disbanded in 1941. A smaller 'mechanized corps' reappeared in autumn 1942, with three mechanized brigades and one tank brigade; it was less 'tank-heavy' than a contemporary 'tank corps'.

military council (*Voennyi sovet*) Collegial body attached from July 1941 to Soviet theatres, army groups and some other military organizations. The key figures were the commander, his chief of staff and the political 'member' (a senior party official or commissar) (qv).

military district A large rear-echelon territory for the raising and administration of military forces, abbreviated in English as MD. The Russian version was a *voennyi okrug*, the German one a *Wehrkreis*. In the Soviet case, usually made up of several civilian administrative regions. In 1941 the Soviet border MDs were immediately converted into army groups (qv).

motorized division Infantry division with a large number of organic motor vehicles. Motorized divisions were converted to rifle divisions (qv) in the Red Army in 1941, and in the German Army they were renamed as panzer grenadier divisions (qv) in 1942.

Narodnoe opolchenie People's Militia. Emergency defensive units formed from civilians. Comparable to German *Volkssturm* (qv).

NSDAP National Socialist German Workers Party, 'Nazi' Party.

Operation A sequence of military actions having one objective (e.g. the 'Vistula–Oder operation'). Code names were often assigned to individual operations (e.g. Operation CITADEL).

Operational Level of war below military 'strategy' but above 'tactics'. Also used to describe events with long-term consequences, an 'operational breakthrough' (as opposed to a mere 'tactical breakthrough').

Ostheer Literally 'Eastern Army'. General term used for German ground forces on the Russian front.

People's Commissar (*Narodnyi kommissar*, abbreviated to *Narkom*) Term used for a Soviet government 'minister' in the 1917–46 period.

Glossary

People's Commissariat (*Narodnyi komissariat*) Term used for a Soviet government 'ministry' in the 1917–46 period (e.g. People's Commissariat of Internal Affairs, or NKVD).

Politburo Executive body of the Central Committee of the Soviet Communist Party.

political member A senior Communist Party official attached to the military council (qv) of a Soviet military formation, effectively as a commissar (qv). His role was to ensure obedience, facilitate supply, etc.

rasputitsa Spring and autumn seasons in Russia when roads are made very muddy by thaw or rain.

Region Normally this term is used for a medium-level Soviet administrative unit called an '*oblast*', comparable to an American state (e.g. Smolensk Region or Leningrad Region). A region was made up of several 'districts' (*raiony*).

rifle division (*strelkovaia diviziia*) Soviet name for an infantry division.

Schwerpunkt Literally 'centre of gravity'. Term used in German strategic thought, in which concentration was very important, as the point of 'main effort'. The Russians used the roughly comparable term *glavnoe napravlenie*, the 'main direction'.

shock army (*udarnaia armiia*) A Soviet infantry army (qv) with extra artillery and assault units; five of these existed.

SMERSH (*Smert' shpionam*, 'Death to Spies') Red Army directorate of counter-intelligence (GUKR), set up in April 1943 under V. S. Abakumov and superseding the OO (qv).

SS Originally a paramilitary organization with the Nazi Party (*Schutzstaffel*), later becoming under Himmler a huge organization charged with implementing Nazi policy.

Stavka Soviet wartime general headquarters (GHQ) in Moscow, headed from July 1941 by Stalin. Officially from August 1941, this headquarters was the 'Stavka VGK', the 'Stavka of the Supreme Main Commander-in-Chief'. In theory, the Stavka was a committee made up of Stalin and senior generals, but it never met as a collective body.

Stavka representative (*predstavitel' Stavki*) Senior officers assigned by the Soviet Stavka (qv) to co-ordinate major operations. Zhukov and Vasilevskii were the most successful 'Stavka representatives'.

theatre Large region of military operations. Used here also as translation of the Russian word *napravlenie*, the three large Soviet (theatre) headquarters that operated in 1941–2.

unit A basic military organization, smaller than a formation (qv). In the Red Army, a unit (*chast'*) was a regiment or smaller.

Volksgrenadier Name used for German infantry divisions in 1944–5.

Volkssturm Last-ditch German militia with over-age and under-age personnel set up in October 1944 and under the control of the Nazi Party.

Waffen-SS Armed units of the Nazi SS (qv), which in the later part of the war included some formations comparable in strength to those of the German Army.

Wehrmacht The German armed forces, taken together (i.e. including the Army, Navy and the Luftwaffe). Technically speaking, this did not include the Waffen-SS (qv).

NOTES

Preface

1. Hereafter, *GSWW*. The German original was *Das Deutsche Reich und der Zweite Weltkrieg* (hereafter, *DRZW*), 10 vols (Stuttgart: Deutsche Verlags-Anstalt, 1979–2008). The English translation published by Clarendon Press does not yet include vols 8 and 10.

2. This would include some of the most important 'full-length' accounts in English: E. Ziemke and M. E. Bauer, *Moscow to Stalingrad: Decision in the East* (Washington, DC: Center of Military History, [1985] 1987); E. Ziemke, *Stalingrad to Berlin: The German Defeat in the East* (Washington, DC: Center of Military History, [1968] 1987); and A. Seaton, *The Russo-German War 1941–45* (London: Arthur Barker, 1971). None of the preceding sources are uncritical of the German cause. R. Smelser and E. Davies, *The Myth of the Eastern Front: The Nazi-Soviet War in American Popular Culture* (Cambridge: Cambridge University Press, 2007), discusses a more unthinking 'German' orientation.

3. Major general works based largely on Soviet sources are J. Erickson, *The Road to Stalingrad* (New York: Harper & Row, 1975); J. Erickson, *The Road to Berlin* (London: Weidenfeld & Nicolson, 1983); and D. Glantz and J. House, *When Titans Clashed: How the Red Army Stopped Hitler* (Lawrence, KS: University Press of Kansas, 1995).

4. *The Russian Civil War* (Edinburgh: Birlinn, [1987] 2008); *The Stalin Years: The Soviet Union 1929-1953* (Manchester: Manchester University Press, [1998] 2003); and *World War II: A New History* (Cambridge: Cambridge University Press, 2009).

5. The main available published sources on Germany are listed in the notes or bibliography. At the top command level, these include Hitler's speeches, M. Domarus (ed.), *Hitler: Reden und Proklamationen* [Hitler: Speeches and Proclamations], *1932–1945*, 4 vols (Wiesbaden: R. Löwit, 1973), and his war directives, W. Hubatsch (ed.), *Hitlers Weisungen für die Kriegführung 1939–1945: Dokumente des Oberkommandos der Wehrmacht* [Hitler's Directives for the Conduct of the War: Documents from the Supreme Command of the Wehrmacht] (Frankfurt: Bernard & Graefe, 1962). Also important is the war diary of Franz Halder, *Kriegstagebuch: Tägliche Aufzeichnungen des Chefs des Generalstabes des Heeres, 1939–1942* [War Diary: Daily Notes of the Chief of the Army General Staff], 3 vols (Stuttgart: Kohlhammer, 1965).

6. The works of Ziemke (see n. 2), based on extensive use of captured German military archives, are especially important here. Among more recent books, the second volume of Ian Kershaw's biography, *Hitler 1936–45: Nemesis* (London: Allen Lane, 2000), G. Megargee, *Inside Hitler's High Command* (Lawrence, KS: University Press of Kansas, 2000), and S. Fritz, *Ostkrieg: Hitler's War of Extermination in the East* (Lexington: U of Kentucky, 2011), stand out. The German 'official' history (*GSWW*, see n. 1) is largely based on these archives (after they were repatriated to Germany).

7. For details of the historical discussion, see W. Wette, *The Wehrmacht: History, Myth, Reality* (Cambridge, MA: Harvard University Press, [2002] 2007), pp.195–291, and K. Naumann, 'The "Unblemished" "Wehrmacht": The Social History of a Myth', in Heer and Naumann, *War of Extermination*, pp. 417–29. The term 'Wehrmacht' is often used, incorrectly, as

shorthand for 'Nazi-era German Army'. The Wehrmacht was actually all three armed services – Army (*Heer*), Navy (*Kriegsmarine*) and Air Force (*Luftwaffe*).

8. S. V. Borisnev, 'Organizatsiia i sostoianie voenno-istoricheskikh issledovanii v SSSR' [The Organisation and State of Military-Historical Research in the USSR], *Voprosy istorii* (hereafter, *VI*), 2005, no. 4, pp. 156–65, provides a short survey.

9. The Soviet dictator's own wartime writings and speeches, collected in I. Stalin, *O Velikoi Otechestvennoi voine Sovetskogo Soiuza* [On the Great Fatherland War of the Soviet Union], 5th edn (Moscow: GIPL, 1951), are remarkably interesting and underused. Hereafter, Stalin, *OVOVSS*. (There is at least one recent reprint of this book, published in Moscow by Kraft + (*sic*) in 2002.) The newly published 15th volume [*tom*] of the collected works, I. V. Stalin, *Sochineniia* [Works], vol. 15, 3 parts (Moscow: ITPK, 2010), includes in its three sub-volumes all the *OVOVSS* documents, as well as other wartime material.

10. D. Glantz, 'Forgotten Battles of the German-Soviet War (1941-1945)', *Journal of Slavic Military Studies* (hereafter, *JSMS*) 8:4 (1995), pp. 768–808.

11. *Russkii arkhiv. Velikaia Otechestvennaia* (Moscow: Terra, 1993–2001), was published under the general editorship of General V. A. Zolotarev. *Velikaia Otechestvennaia* is a sub-series of a document publication entitled *Russkii arkhiv*. Hereafter, *RA/VO*. The content largely overlaps that of an older collection not available to Western writers before the 1990s, *Sbornik dokumentov Verkhovnogo glavnokomandovaniia za period Velikoi Otechestvennoi voiny* [Collection of Documents of the Supreme High Command in the Period of the Great Fatherland War], 4 vols (Moscow: VIMO, 1968). Hereafter, *SDVG*.

12. V. P. Naumov et al. (eds) *1941 god*, 2 vols (Moscow: Demokratiia, 1998). Hereafter, *1941 god*.

13. R. Aldrich, *The Hidden Hand: Britain, America and Cold War Secret Intelligence* (London: John Murray, 2001), p. 5.

14. G. K. Zhukov, *Vospominaniia i razmyshleniia* [Memoirs and Reflections], 10th edn, 3 vols (Moscow: APN, 1990). The interviews which Konstantin Simonov and G. A. Kumanev conducted with Zhukov, Marshal Vasilevskii and other senior leaders also provide many new insights: K. Simonov, *Glazami cheloveka moego pokoleniia: Razmyshleniia o I. V. Staline* [Through the Eyes of a Person of My Generation: Reflections on I. V. Stalin] (Moscow: Kniga, 1990), and G. A. Kumanev, *Riadom so Stalinym: Otkrovennye svidetel'stva* [Alongside Stalin: Candid Testimony] (Moscow: Bylina, 1999). The 1997 edition of Marshal Rokossovskii's memoirs contained much that was left out of the 1968 original: K. K. Rokossovskii, *Soldatskii Dolg* [A Soldier's Duty] (Moscow: Voennoe izdatel'stvo, 1997).

15. N. S. Khrushchev, 'Memuary' [Memoirs], *VI*, 1990, nos 9–12, 1991, nos 1–8; A. I. Mikoian, *Tak bylo: Razmyshleniia o minuvshem* [The Way it Was: Reflections on the Past] (Moscow: Bagrius, 1999); F. Chuev (ed.), *Sto sorok besed s Molotovym: Iz dnevnika F. Chueva* [140 Conversations with Molotov: From the Diary of F. Chuev] (Moscow: Terra, 1991); G. Dimitrov, *The Diary of Georgi Dimitrov, 1933–1949* (New Haven, CT: Yale University Press, 2003); V. A. Malyshev, 'Dnevnik narkoma' [Diary of a People's Commissar], *Istochnik*, 1997, no. 5, pp. 103–47.

16. *Velikaia Otechestvennaia voina, 1941-1945: Voenno-istoricheskie ocherki*, 4 vols (Moscow: Nauka, 1998–9). Hereafter, *VOV/VIO*. The final version of Krivosheev's work on casualties is G. F. Krivosheev et al. (eds), *Rossiia i SSSR v voinakh XX veka. Poteri vooruzhennykh sil: Statisticheskoe issledovanie* [Russia and the USSR in the Wars of the Twentieth Century. Losses of the Armed Forces: A Statistical Survey] (Moscow: OLMA-Press, 2001). Hereafter, *Poteri*. An English translation of an earlier edition is G. F. Krivosheev (ed.), *Soviet Casualties and Combat Losses in the Twentieth Century* (London: Greenhill Books, 1997). A. N. Grylev,

Boevoi sostav Sovetskoi armii [Order of Battle of the Soviet Army], 5 vols (Moscow: VNU GSh, 1963–90), was only declassified after the collapse of the USSR.

17. S. Kudriashov (ed.), *Voina: 1941-1945* [The War: 1941-1945] (Moscow: APRF, 2010), for example, is a large collection of documents from the Presidential Archive. For a fairly recent discussion of historiography, see N. V. Ilievskii, 'Problemy i zadachi sovremennoi istoriografii Velikoi Otechestvennoi voiny' [Problems and Tasks of the Contemporary Historiography of the Great Fatherland War], *Voenno-istorichskii zhurnal* (hereafter, *VIZh*), 2010, no. 5, pp. 3–9. Three valuable works by 'private' historians are V. N. Zamulin, *Prokhorovka: Neizvestnoe srazhenie velikoi voiny* [Prokhorovka: An Unknown Engagement of the Great War] (Moscow: Tranzitkniga, 2005), L. Lopukhovskii, *Viazemskaia katastrofa 41-go goda* [The Viaz'ma Catastrophe of '41] (Moskva: Iauza/Eksmo, 2007), and S. A. Gerasimova, *Rzhevskaia boinia: Poteriannaia pobeda Zhukova* [The Rzhev Slaughterhouse: Zhukov's Lost Victory] (Moscow: Eksmo, 2009). These deal candidly and in detail with the Battle of Kursk (1943), the Battle of Viaz'ma–Briansk (1941) and Operation MARS (1942). For an old-school criticism of current writing, in textbooks and elsewhere, see V. I. Mikriukov, 'O fal'sifikatsii istorii Velikoi Otechestvennoi voiny' [On the Falsification of the History of the Great Fatherland War], *VI*, 2010, no. 12, pp. 74–81.

18. Since my first edition, Catherine Merridale's *Ivan's War: The Red Army, 1939-1945* (London: Faber and Faber, 2005) has appeared. This account of the Russian soldier's war experience is based on published recollections, archival sources and interviews. On the German experience, see S. Fritz, *Frontsoldaten: The German Soldier in World War II* (Lexington, KY: University Press of Kentucky, 1995).

19. Sources on this topic, as well as those on war crimes, POWs, the home front and diplomacy, are discussed in the relevant parts of the main text.

20. The best work on German losses, based on sampling of personnel records, is R. Overmans, *Deutsche militärische Verluste im Zweiten Weltkrieg* [German Military Losses in the Second World War] (Munich: R. Oldenbourg, 1999); for Krivosheev's work on Russian losses, see n. 17.

21. R.-D. Muller, *The Unknown Eastern Front: The Wehrmacht and Hitler's Foreign Soldiers* (London: I. B. Tauris, 2012), p. 255.

22. A. A. Svechin, *Strategy* (Minneapolis: East View, [1927] 1992), p. 269; A. Philippi and F. Heim, *Der Feldzug gegen Sowjetrußland 1941 bis 1945: Ein operativer Überblick* (Stuttgart: Kohlhammer, 1962).

Chapter 1

1. This discussion of the structural problems of the German high command follows Megargee, *Inside Hitler's High Command*. See also W. Deist in *GSWW*, vol. 1, pp. 505–40. Kershaw, *Hitler: Nemesis* provides an overall view of the dictator and the Nazi system.

2. See W. Gorlitz, 'Keitel, Jodl and Warlimont', in C. Barnett (ed.) *Hitler's Generals* (London: Phoenix, [1989] 1995), pp. 139–71.

3. See B. Bond, 'Brauchitsch', in Barnett, *Hitler's Generals*, pp. 75–99.

4. See B. Leach, 'Halder', in Barnett, *Hitler's Generals*, pp. 101–26.

5. A. Hitler, *Hitlers Politisches Testament: Die Bormann Diktate vom Februar und April 1945* (Hamburg: Albrecht Knaus, 1981), pp. 78–9 [15 February]. Hitler's 'Testament' was dictated to Martin Bormann, his deputy, in February and April 1945. It was rambling, self-serving

and written from hindsight. Hitler was also inconsistent about when he made his decision to attack Russia. But this account of his thinking about grand strategy fits in with other evidence.

6. Hitler, *Testament*, p. 79 [15 February 1945]; *Documents on German Foreign Policy*, Ser. D, vol. 12, p. 1065 [22 June 1941]; Domarus, *Hitler: Reden*, vol. 2, p. 1731 [22 June 1941]; J. Goebbels, *Goebbels Reden 1932–1945* (Düsseldorf: Droste Verlag, 1972), p. 176 [18 February 1943].

7. Rezun-Suvorov's best-known book is V. Suvorov, *Icebreaker: Who Started the Second World War?* (London: Hamish Hamilton, 1989). The latest version is *The Chief Culprit: Stalin's Grand Design to Start World War II* (Annapolis: Naval Institute Press, 2008). For a discussion of the controversy, see E. Mawdsley, 'Crossing the Rubicon: Soviet Plans for Offensive War in 1940–1941', *International History Review*, vol. 25, 2003, no. 4, pp. 818–65.

8. *Die Tagebücher von Joseph Goebbels* (Munich: K. G. Saur, 1998), Teil 1, Band 9, p. 295 [7 May].

9. On this, see R. Citino, *The German Way of War: From the Thirty Years' War to the Third Reich* (Lawrence, KS: University Press of Kansas, 2005).

10. *Hitlers Weisungen*, pp. 84–8 [18 December 1940].

11. For the early war plans, see G. Ueberschär and I. Bezymenskij (eds), *Der deutsche Angriff auf die Sowjetunion 1941: Die Kontroversie um die Präventivkriegsthese* (Darmstadt: Wissenschaftliche Buchgesellschaft, 1998), pp. 223–38 [5 August 1940], 240–7 [15 September 1940]. The planning process is described in detail by E. Klink in *GSWW*, vol. 4, pp. 240–325.

12. A. Kay, *Exploitation, Resettlement, Mass Murder: Political and Economic Planning for German Occupation Policy in the Soviet Union, 1940-1941* (Oxford: Berghahn Books, 2006), and Tooze, *Wages of Destruction*, pp. 461–80, provide a pre-war overview. S. Fritz, *Ostkrieg: Hitler's War of Extermination in the East* (Lexington, KY: University Press of Kentucky, 2011), and G. Megargee, *War of Annihilation: Combat and Genocide on the Eastern Front, 1941* (Lanham, MD: Rowman & Littlefield, 2007), achieve an effective integration of 'conventional' German Army operations and the ideologically motivated crimes committed against Soviet civilians.

13. Tooze, *Wages of Destruction*, p. 462.

14. The Nazi plans for exploiting the food resources of the USSR and denying them to the local inhabitants are covered in L. Collingham, *The Taste of War: World War Two and the Battle for Food* (London: Allen Lane, 2011), pp. 32–9, 180–218, and Tooze, *Wages of Destruction*, pp. 476–80.

15. Tooze, *Wages*, pp. 466–76.

16. Halder, *Kriegstagebuch*, vol. 2, p. 337. It is from this quotation that Christian Streit's book on the mass murder of Soviet POWs takes its title: *Keine Kameraden* [No Comrades]: *Die Wehrmacht und die sowjetischen Kriegsgefangenen 1941–1945*, 3rd edn (Bonn: J. H. W. Dietz, [1978] 1997). On the speech, see also J. Förster and E. Mawdsley, 'Hitler and Stalin in Perspective: Secret Speeches on the Eve of Barbarossa', *War in History* (hereafter *WH*), vol. 11 (2004), no. 1, pp. 62–78.

17. For the development of Nazi policy, see Y. Arad, *The Holocaust in the Soviet Union* (Lincoln, NE: University of Nebraska Press, 2009), pp. 51–62, and T. Jersak in *GSWW*, vol. 9.1, pp. 289–312. The Holocaust is discussed more fully in Chapter 4.

18. These measures are discussed by J. Förster in *GSWW*, vol. 4, pp. 481–521. Wette, *Wehrmacht*, pp. 1–24, outlines the views of Russia and Communism held by the Wehrmacht leaders, which were similar to those of the Nazis.

19. The best description of the pre-war 'system' is given in O. V. Khlevniuk, *Master of the House: Stalin and His Inner Circle* (New Haven: Yale University Press, 2009).

20. D. C. Watt, *How War Came: The Immediate Origins of the Second World War, 1938–1939* (London: Mandarin, 1989), p. 113.

21. The concept of 'revolutionary imperialism' is developed in V. Zubok and C. Pleshakov, *Inside the Kremlin's Cold War: Soviet Leaders from Stalin to Khrushchev* (Cambridge, MA: Harvard University Press, 1996), pp. 4–5, 13–16. See also D. Brandenberger, *National Bolshevism: Stalinist Mass Culture and the Formation of Modern Russian National Identity, 1931-1956* (Cambridge, MA: Harvard University Press, 2002), and E. van Ree, *The Political Thought of Joseph Stalin: A Study in Twentieth-Century Revolutionary Patriotism* (London: RoutledgeCurzon, 2002). For two recent but rather different interpretations of Soviet policy: R. Gellately, *Stalin's Curse: Battling for Communism in War and Cold War* (Oxford: Oxford University Press, 2013), and G. Roberts, *Stalin's Wars: From World War to Cold War, 1939-1953* (New Haven: Yale University Press, 2006).

22. Mawdsley, *Stalin Years*, pp. 76–80.

23. See H. Ragsdale, *The Soviets, the Munich Crisis, and the Coming of World War II* (Cambridge: Cambridge University Press, 2003).

24. S. Pons, *Stalin and the Inevitable War, 1936–1941* (London: Frank Cass, 2002), p. 179. As Stalin put it, in private conversation: 'In Germany, the petty-bourgeois nationalists [i.e. the Nazis] are capable of a sharp turn – they are flexible – not tied to capitalist traditions, unlike bourgeois leaders like Chamberlain and his ilk' (Dimitrov, *Diary*, p. 121 [7 November 1939]). See also G. Roberts, *The Soviet Union and the Origins of the Second World War: Russo-German Relations and the Road to War, 1933–1941* (Basingstoke: Macmillan, 1995).

25. Suvorov, *Icebreaker*, pp. xvi–xvii. The most insightful discussion of pre-war policy is given in Pons, *Stalin*.

26. Dimitrov, *Diary*, p. 115 [7 September 1939]. This makes a companion to the better-known press comment by Senator Harry Truman in June 1941: 'If we see that Germany is winning, we should help Russia, and if Russia is winning we ought to help Germany and that way kill as many as possible' (A. L. Hamby, *Man of the People: A Life of Harry S. Truman* (New York: Oxford University Press, 1995), p. 270).

27. For Soviet policy in 1939–41, see G. Gorodetsky, *Grand Delusion: Stalin and the German Invasion of Russia* (New Haven, CT: Yale University Press, 1999).

28. Dimitrov, *Diary*, p. 116 [7 September].

29. T. Hiio et al. (eds), *Estonia 1940-1945: Reports of the Estonian International Commission for the Investigation of Crimes against Humanity* (Tallin: Estonian Foundation for the Investigation of Crimes against Humanity, 2006), pp. 1–410, is a very extensive account, well documented and well illustrated, of Soviet occupation of one of the borderland regions in 1939–41.

30. A. Coox, 'The Pacific War', in P. Duus (ed.), *The Cambridge History of Japan* (Cambridge: Cambridge University Press, 1988), vol. 6, pp. 326–8; *Hitlers Politisches Testament*, pp. 92–3 [18 February 1945].

Chapter 2

1 *GSWW*, vol. 4, p. 318; *VOV/VIO*, vol. 1, pp. 113, 340; Glantz and House, *When Titans Clashed*, p. 301; Ziemke, *Stalingrad to Berlin*, p. 9.

2 Dimitrov, *Diary*, p. 195 [3 October].

3   R. Citino, *The German Way of War: From the Thirty Years' War to the Third Reich*, presents
      an historical overview; see also his *The Path to Blitzkrieg: Doctrine and Training in the
      German Army* (Boulder, CO: Lynne Rienner, 1999). On the overall effectiveness of the
      Wehrmacht, see J. Förster, 'The Dynamics of Volksgemeinschaft: The Effectiveness of the
      German Military Establishment in the Second World War', in R. Millett and W. Murray
      (eds), *Military Effectiveness*, 3 vols (Boston: Unwin Hyman, 1987), vol. 3, pp. 180–220, and
      M. van Creveld, *Fighting Power: German and U.S. Army Performance, 1939-1945* (Westport,
      CT: Greenwood Press, 1982). M. Habeck, *Storm of Steel: The Development of Armor Doctrine
      in Germany and the Soviet Union, 1919-1939* (Ithaca, NY: Cornell University Press, 2003), is
      a valuable comparative study.

4   D. Glantz, *Stumbling Colossus: The Red Army on the Eve of World War* (Lawrence, KS:
      University Press of Kansas, 1998), provides extensive details. There is now a whole shelf
      of English-language works about Soviet doctrine in the 1930s, including: J. Erickson,
      The Soviet High Command: A Military-Political History, 1918-1941 (London: Macmillan,
      1962); Habeck, *Storm;* R. Harrison, *The Russian Way of War: Operational Art, 1904-1940*
      (Lawrence, KS: University Press of Kansas, 2001); C. Roberts, 'Planning for War: The Red
      Army and the Catastrophe of 1941', *EAS*, 1995, vol. 48, no. 8, pp. 1293–326, and E. Ziemke;
      The Red Army, 1918-1941: From Vanguard of World Revolution to America's Ally (London:
      Frank Cass, 2004).

5   O. F. Suvenirov, *Tragediia RKKA 1937-1938* (Moscow: Terra, 1998), p. 306; Dimitrov, *Diary,*
      p. 146 [4 February 1941]. Suvenirov is the best account of the Red Army purge, along with
      A. A. Pechenkin, *Voennaia elita SSSR v 1935-1939 gg.: Repressii i obnovlenie* (Moscow:
      VZFEI, 2003). R. Reese, *Stalin's Reluctant Soldiers: A Social History of the Red Army,
      1918-1941* (Lawrence, KS: University Press of Kansas, 1996), pp. 132–44, corrected earlier
      Western exaggerations of the impact of the army purges.

6   Suvenirov, *Tragediia*, p. 304. Ranks were abolished in the 'egalitarian' Red Army of 1918;
      functional but 'politically correct' titles like 'army commander' (*komandarm*) were
      reintroduced in 1935 and used until 1940, when they were replaced by traditional ranks.
      (The rank of Marshal of the Soviet Union was also introduced in 1935.) The numbers are
      confused by promotions between 1937 and 1941; a few commanders promoted after 1936
      also fell victim to the purge.

7   See D. Volkogonov, 'Kliment Yefremovich Voroshilov', in Shukman, *Stalin's Generals,*
      pp. 313–24.

8   Naumov, *1941 god*, vol. 2, p. 507.

9   On this neglected subject, see N. Short, *The Stalin and Molotov Lines: Soviet Western
      Defences 1926-41* (Oxford: Osprey, 2008).

10   Convenient introductory English-language guides, with tables of organization, are J. Lucas,
      German Army Handbook 1939-1945 (Stroud: Sutton, 1998), and S. Zaloga and L. Ness, *Red
      Army Handbook 1939-1945* (Stroud: Sutton, 1998).

11   *Poteri*, p. 404; *GSWW*, vol. 4, Item No. 2.

12   *1941 god*, vol. 2, pp. 471–2 [15 July].

13   *Hitlers Weisungen*, p. 87 [18 December]; *RA/VO*, vol. 5(1), p. 61 [10 July]. The Germans
      were able to seize bridgeheads in Russia in 1941 using fast-moving ground forces. It is
      interesting that in the middle of the 1941 crisis, the Soviet Defence Commissariat ordered
      the formation of ten (division-sized) airborne 'corps'. These were supposed to be ready
      for operations by early 1942; see *RA/VO*, vol. 2(2), pp. 80–2 [4 September 1941], and
      V. A. Zolotarev (ed.), *Velikaia Otechestvennaia voina 1941-1945 gg.: Deistvuiushchaia armiia*

(Moscow: Animi Fortitudo/Kuchkovo pole, 2005), p. 424. See also D. Glantz, *The Soviet Airborne Experience* (Fort Leavenworth, KS: Combat Studies Institute, USA CGSC, 1985).

14 R. Muller, *The German Air War in Russia* (Baltimore, MD: Nautical and Aviation, 1992); J. Corum, *The Luftwaffe: Creating the Operational Air War, 1918–1940* (Lawrence, KS: University Press of Kansas, 1997); J. Sterrett, *Soviet Air Force Theory, 1918–1945* (London: Routledge, 2007); V. Hardesty and I. Grinberg, *Red Phoenix Rising: The Soviet Air Force in World War II* (Lawrence, KS: University Press of Kansas, 2012); J. Corum, *Lothar von Richtofen: Master of the German Air War* (Lawrence, KS: University Press of Kansas, 2008).

15 Bookshop shelves sag under the weight of books about the military technology of the Second World War. The equipment side is also outlined in the two 'handbooks' by Lucas and Zaloga and Ness (see n. 10).

16 *GSWW*, vol. 4, p. 318; Malyshev, 'Dnevnik', p. 118 [10 January 1942]. Artillery figures here refer to proper artillery pieces mounted on wheeled carriages, rather than to the simpler mortars. For numbers, see Table 2.6. See also C. Bellamy, *Red God of War: Soviet Artillery and Rocket Forces* (London: Brassey's, 1986), pp. 1–80.

17 See R. DiNardo, *Mechanized Juggernaut or Military Anachronism? Horses and the German Army in World War II* (New York: Greenwood, 1991).

18 The best source for specifications and production details of German armoured vehicles is still P. Chamberlain and H. Doyle, *Encyclopedia of German Tanks of World War Two: The Complete Illustrated Directory of German Battle Tanks, Armoured Cars, Self-propelled Guns and Semi-tracked Vehicles, 1933–45* (London: Weidenfeld & Nicolson, [1978] 1999). A useful technical introduction to 'softskins', especially for the German side, is G. Georgano, *World War Two Military Vehicles* (London: Osprey Automotive, 1994).

19 The German term for 'tank' is *Panzerkampfwagen*, abbreviated to *Pz Kpfw*. The Allies used simplified terminology, and this is still met in the sources. The British, for example, called the *Pz Kpfw* III the 'Panzer III' or the 'Mark III', and the Russians called it the 'T-III'. A breakdown of numbers available by type as of June 1941 is given in *GSWW*, vol. 4, p. 219.

20 For Soviet tanks, see S. Zaloga and J. Grandsen, *Soviet Tanks and Combat Vehicles of World War II* (London: Arms and Armour Press, 1984). Since the early 1990s, there have been numerous Russian publications about wartime weapons. An important example is the archivally based I. Zheltov et al., *Neizvestnyi T-34* (Moscow: Ilksprint, 2001); this looks at both the operational and the technical side of the famous medium tank. For 1940–5 production figures, see A. V. Lobanov, 'Tankostroitel'naia promyshlennost' SSSR v 1941-1945 gg.', *VIZh*, 2010, no. 6, pp. 30–4, and A. V. Lobanov, 'Proizvodstvo tankov i SAU [etc]', *VIZh*, 2012, no. 5, pp. 33–7. V. Beshanov, *Tankovyi pogrom 1941 goda (Kuda ischezli 28 tysiach sovetskikh tankov?)* (Moscow: AST, 2001), discusses the catastrophe of the Soviet tank force in 1941.

21 *1941 god*, vol. 2, p. 469 [7 July].

22 The best technical source for the Russian side is Ye. Gordon and D. Khazanov, *Soviet Combat Aircraft of the Second World War*, 2 vols (Hinckley: Midland, 1998–9). For the Germans, see D. Donald, *Warplanes of the Luftwaffe* (London: Aerospace Publishing, 1994).

23 On the arrests in the Red Army Air Force, see V. Birstein, *Smersh, Stalin's Secret Weapon: Soviet Military Counterintelligence in World War II* (London: Biteback Publishing, 2011), pp. 84–5, and M. Parrish, *Sacrifice of the Generals: Soviet Senior Officer Loses, 1939-1953* (Lanham, MD: Scarecrow, 2004), pp. 331–4, 359–61, 370–2.

24 On distortions of Soviet war production, see J. Sapir, 'The Economics of War in the Soviet Union during World War II', in I. Kershaw and M. Lewin (eds), *Stalinism and Nazism: Dictatorships in Comparison* (Cambridge: Cambridge University Press, 1997), pp. 208–36.

25 *1941 god*, vol. 2, pp. 54–5 [9 April 1941]. Accidental aircraft losses continued at a high rate after the war began. In the second half of 1941, some 750 were lost due to accidents in the internal military districts (*RA/VO*, vol. 2(2), pp. 132–4 [4 January 1942]).

26 *RA/VO*, vol. 2(2), pp. 34–5 [23 July 1941]. More material on this sensitive but highly important subject has been published in the last decade. On the national communications system, see A. P. Zharskii, 'Obshchegosudarstvennaia set' sviazi … ', *VIZh*, 2010, no. 12, pp. 3–6. A. P. Zharskii (ed.), 'Nel'zia pod vidom bor'by s edokami … ', *VIZh*, 2007, no. 3, pp. 40–4, reprints a memorandum written by Grigor'ev to Gapich a year before the war, describing in detail the shortcomings of the Red Army signals service. On the arrests, see Parish, *Sacrifice*, pp. 113, 126–7. The problems were also discussed by Marshal P. M. Kurochkin (1941 chief of signals troops in the Baltic MD): 'Osnovnye prichiny nedostatochnoi ustoichivoi raboty sviazi v nachal'nyi period voiny', *VIZh*, 2008, no. 1, pp. 58–63, no. 4, pp. 58–61, no. 5, pp. 57–61, no. 7, pp. 44–9; this material was censored from Kurochkin's 1969 memoirs.

27 The operational/tactical successes of German radio intelligence in Russia, especially the use of direction finding (DF) and traffic analysis to ascertain the Red Army order of battle in the western regions, was brought out in post-war interrogation of German personnel. A source that became available in the 1980s is the account by General A. Praun and others: 'German Radio Intelligence', in J. Mendelsohn (ed.), *Covert Warfare*, 8 vols (New York, Garland, 1984), vol. 6, pp. 86–128, 130–5, 147–94, 229–39.

   More detailed revelations from the 1945 TICOM (Target Intelligence Committee) programme have recently been released by the National Security Agency in the United States. *European Axis Signal Intelligence in World War II as Revealed in 'TICOM' Investigations*, 9 vols (Washington: Army Security Agency, 1946), especially vols 1, 4 and 9, provides an overview, http://www.nsa.gov/public_info/declass/european_axis_sigint. shtml. On German cryptanalytic activities against the Russians, another available TICOM document is report DF-112 by A. Dettmann, 'Survey of Russian Military Systems' (Army Security Agency, 1948), http://www.scribd.com/paspartoo/d/85583814-DF-112-Dettmann. R. Rezabek, 'TICOM: The Last Great Secret of World War II', *Intelligence and National Security*, vol. 27, 2012, no. 4, pp. 513–30, provides background.

28 B. Müller-Hillebrand, *Das Heer, 1933–1945: Entwicklung des organisatorischen Aufbaues*, 3 vols (Darmstadt: E. S. Mittler, 1954–69), vol. 3, p. 251. On military manpower in 1939–41, see B. Kroener in *GSWW*, vol. 5.1, pp. 787–1001.

29 The indoctrination and wartime character of the German Army are discussed in Fritz, *Frontsoldaten*, and by J. Förster in *GSWW*, vol. 9.1, pp. 479–558. See also S. Neitzel and H. Welzer, *Soldaten: On Fighting, Killing and Dying: The Secret Second World War Tapes of German POWs* (London: Simon and Schuster, 2012). M. van Creveld, *Fighting Power* (Westport, CT: Greenwood Press, 1982), concentrates on the high military effectiveness of German troops. For motivation in the later stages of the war, see also Chapter 7.

   C. Rass provides a social profile of a typical Eastern front division, the 253rd Infantry, in *GSWW*, vol. 9.1, pp. 671–770. The case study approach is also used, for other formations involved in occupation and counter-insurgency duties, in B. Shepherd, *War in the Wild East: The German Army and Soviet Partisans* (Cambridge, MA, Harvard University Press, 2004), and J. Rutherford, *Combat and Genocide on the Eastern Front: The German Infantry's War, 1941–1944* (Cambridge: Cambridge University Press, 2014).

30 There is a huge literature on Nazi Germany and its people. R. Evans, *The Third Reich in Power, 1933-1939* (London: Allen Lane, 2005), and *The Third Reich at War: How the Nazis Led Germany from Conquest to Disaster* (London: Allen Lane, 2008), provide an excellent

starting point. See also M. Geyer and S. Fitzpatrick (eds), *Beyond Totalitarianism: Stalinism and Nazism Compared* (Cambridge: Cambridge University Press, 2009).

31 Fritz, *Frontsoldaten*, p. 10.

32 V. A. Zolotarev (ed.), *Istoriia voennoi strategii Rossii* (Moscow: Kuchkovo pole/ Poligrafresursy, 2000), p. 216. These are figures for the entire Soviet armed forces, not just those deployed in western European Russia, which explains the discrepancy with the figures cited previously.

33 Glantz, *Stumbling Colossus*, pp. 56–81; D. Glantz, *Colossus Reborn: The Red Army at War, 1941-1943* (Lawrence, KS: University Press of Kansas, 2005), pp. 536–607; Merridale, *Ivan's War*; and R. Reese, *Why Stalin's Soldiers Fought: The Red Army's Military Effectiveness in World War II* (Lawrence, KS: University Press of Kansas, 2011).

34 Reese, *Why Stalin's Soldiers Fought*, pp. 28–54, argues that the Soviet–Finnish War demonstrated the considerable military effectiveness of the pre-war Red Army.

35 N. M. Ramanichev in *VOV/VIO*, vol. 1, p. 88; Reese, *Why Stalin's Soldiers Fought*, p. 310.

36 *RA/VO*, vol. 12(1), p. 90 [17 July].

37 A. M. Sokolov and E. I. Ziuzin in *VOV/VIO*, vol. 1, pp. 146, 174.

38 Brandenberger, *National Bolshevism*, and *Propaganda State in Crisis: Soviet Ideology, Indoctrination, and Terror under Stalin, 1927-1941* (New Haven: Yale University Press, 2011).

39 Thurston, *Life and Terror*, pp. 199–226.

40 M. Harrison (ed.), *The Economics of World War II: Six Powers in International Comparison* (Cambridge: Cambridge University Press, 1998), pp. 3–4, 7, 9, 268.

41 S. Fitzpatrick, *Stalin's Peasants: Resistance and Survival in the Russian Village after Collectivization* (Oxford: Oxford University Press, 1995), and L. Viola, *Peasant Rebels under Stalin: Collectivization and the Culture of Peasant Resistance* (New York: Oxford University Press, 1996).

42 *VOV/VIO*, vol. 1, pp. 146, 161, 174, 193; *RA/VO*, vol. 2(2), pp. 108–9 [4 October], vol. 12(1), p. 101 [26 July]. See also Merridale, *Ivan's War*, pp. 72–100.

43 This is discussed more fully in Chapter 7.

44 On the German planning and build-up, see the chapter by E. Klink and H. Boog in *GSWW*, vol. 4, pp. 225–385.

45 *1941 god*, vol. 2, p. 629 [7 December 1940]. Both *1941 god*, and V. A. Gavrilov (ed.), *Voennaia razvedka informiruet: Dokumenty Razvedupravleniia Krasnoi Armii. Ianvar' 1939 – iun' 1941 g.* (Moscow, MF 'Demokratiia', 2008), provide substantial intelligence reports from 1939 to 1941. On the intelligence organizations in general, see C. Andrew and O. Gordievsky, *KGB: The Inside Story of its Foreign Operations* (London: Sceptre, 1991). A secret Soviet in-house history, now available, is V. M. Chebrikov et al. (eds), *Istoriia sovetskikh organov gosudarstvennoi bezopasnosti: Uchebnik* (Moscow: Tipografiia RIO VKSh KGB, 1977), pp. 292–445.

46 *1941 god*, vol. 2, pp. 17–8 [3 April], F. H. Hinsley, *British Intelligence in the Second World War: Its Influence on Strategy and Operations*, 5 vols (London: HMSO, 1979–90), vol. 1, p. 451. The failure to heed this particular warning was stressed by Khrushchev in his 1956 speech denouncing Stalin: N. S. Khrushchev, 'O kul'te lichnosti i ego posledstviiakh. Doklad Pervogo sekretaria TsK KPSS tov. Khrushcheva N. S. XX s'ezdu Kommunisticheskoi partii Sovetskogo soiuza', *Izvestiia Tsentral'nogo Komitet KPSS* (hereafter *ITsK*), 1989, no. 3, pp. 146–7.

47 *1941 god*, vol. 1, p. 747 [11 March], vol. 2, p. 289 [31 May]; Hinsley, *British Intelligence*, vol. 1, p. 451; Müller-Hillebrand, *Das Heer*, vol. 2, p. 111. Golikov's assessment was confirmed in

a much-delayed memoir-article about pre-war Soviet military intelligence: F. I. Golikov, 'Sovetskaia voennaia razvedka pered gitlerovskim nashestviem na SSSR', *VIZh*, 2007, no. 12, pp. 5–11, 2008, no. 1, pp. 27–32; this manuscript was evidently refused publication when originally written in the late 1960s.

48 *1941 god*, vol. 1, p. 122 [July 1940], 181 [19 August 1940 or earlier], 237 [18 September 1940); Müller-Hillebrand, *Das Heer*, vol. 2, p. 110. Of particular interest is the map reproduced in L. Dvoinykh and N. Tarkhova, 'O chem dokladyvala voennaia razvedka', *Nauka i zhizn'*, 1995, no. 3, pp. 3–11.

49 Zhukov, *ViR*, vol. 1, pp. 324, 366–7.

50 *1941 god*, vol. 1, pp. 7, 683 [28 February], 779 [20 March]. The fullest treatments are Gorodetsky, *Grand Delusion*, and B. Whaley, *Codeword Barbarossa* (Cambridge, MA: MIT Press, 1973). Important new documents have been published in S. V. Stepashin et al. (eds), *Organy gosudarstvennoi bezopasnosti SSSR v Velikoi Otechestvennoi voine: Sbornik dokumentov*, 5 vols (Moscow: Kniga v biznes/Rus', 1995–2007), vols 1–2, and V. A. Gavrilov (ed.), *Voennaia razvedka informiruet: Dokumenty razvedupravleniia Krasnoii Armii, ianvar' 1939 - iiun' 1941 g.* (Moscow: MF 'Demokratiia', 2008).

51 Zhukov, *ViR*, vol. 1, p. 365; Chuev, *Sto sorok besed s Molotovym*, p. 42. For an insight into Stalin's foolhardy domination of intelligence analysis, see C. Andrew and J. Elkner, 'Stalin and Foreign Intelligence', in H. Shukman (ed.), *Redefining Stalinism* (London: Frank Cass, 2003), pp. 69–94, and J. Erickson, 'Threat Identification and Strategic Appraisal by the Soviet Union, 1930-1941', in E. May (ed.), *Knowing One's Enemies: Intelligence Assessment Before the Two World Wars* (Princeton: Princeton University Press, 1986), pp. 375–423.

52 *1941 god*, vol. 1, pp. 695 [1 March], 780 [20 March]; Zhukov, *ViR*, vol. 1, p. 366. The source of the American warning was the German diplomat von Bittenfeld, via the US commercial attaché in Berlin.

53 *1941 god*, vol. 2, pp. 180–1 [9 May], 252 [21 May], 303 [1 June], 349–50 [12 June], 382–3 [17 June].

54 *1941 god*, vol. 2, p. 423 [22 June]; Zhukov, *ViR*, vol. 1, pp. 370–1.

55 Cynthia Roberts was the first historian to stress the negative consequences of Soviet war plans, in Roberts, 'Planning'. See also E. Mawdsley, 'Crossing the Rubicon', *International History Review*, vol. 24 (2003), no. 4, pp. 818–65.

56 *1941 god*, vol. 2, p. 219 [c. 15 May]. B. Menning and J. House, 'Soviet Strategy', in J. Ferris and E. Mawdsley (eds), *Cambridge History of the Second World War*, 3 vols (Cambridge: Cambridge University Press, 2015), vol. I, pp. 213–31, provides the most recent western discussion of this question. See also E. V. Zhukunov (ed.), *1941g. – Uroki i vyvody* (Moscow: Voennoe izdatel'stvo, 1992), and P. N. Bobylev, 'Tochku v diskussii stavit' rano: K voprosu o planirovanii v General'nom shtabe RKKA vozmozhnoi voiny s Germaniei v 1940-1941 godakh', *Otechestvennaia istoriia* (hereafter *OI*), 2000, no. 1, pp. 41–63.

57 '"Sovremennaia armiia armiia nastupatel'naia". Vystupleniia I. V. Stalina na prieme v Kremle pered vypusknikami voennykh akademii. Mai 1941 g.', A. A. Pechenkin (ed.), *Istoricheskii arkhiv* (hereafter *IA*), 1995, no. 2, p. 30.

58 Some of the covering plans and responses were published in several numbers of the *Voenno-istoricheskii zhurnal* in 1996 (Iu. A. Gor'kov and Iu. N. Semin, 'Konets global'noi lzhi', *VIZh*, 1996, nos 2, 3, 4, 5, 6).

59 V. A. Nevezhin (ed.), 'Dve direktivy 1941 g. o propagandistskoi podgotovke SSSR k voine', *Arkheograficheskii ezhegodnik za 1995 god*, 1997, p. 200. For a careful analysis of these documents and others, see V. A. Nevezhin, *Sindrom nastupatel'noi vomy* (Moscow: AIRO-XX, 1997).

60 *1941 god*, vol. 2, p. 361 [13 June]; *GSWW*, vol. 4, pp. 288, 315.

61 This division of the Soviet European border leaves out two other theatres, facing Romania and Finland. Neither was practical as the main axis of attack for either the Red Army or the Wehrmacht.

62 *1941 god*, vol. 1, p. 743 [11 March]; *GSWW*, vol. 4, pp. 288, 315.

63 For details of the war plans, see Mawdsley, 'Rubicon'.

64 *Hitlers Weisungen*, p. 84 [18 December].

65 *GSWW*, vol. 4, pp. 323–4, 338, 351; *VOV/VIO*, vol. 1, pp. 89–90. Halder, *Kriegstagebuch*, vol. 2, p. 267; *Poteri*, p. 475.

66 Stalin, *OVOVSS*, p. 26; N. Khrushchev, 'O kul'te lichnosti', p. 147.

67 J. Schneider, *The Structure of Strategic Revolution* (Novato, CA: Presidio, 1994), p. 3 ['Soviet warfare state']. See also M. von Hagen, *Soldiers of the Proletarian Dictatorship* (Ithaca, NY: Cornell University Press, 1995) ['proletarian Sparta']; W. Dunn, *The Soviet Economy and the Red Army* (Westport, CT: Praeger, 1995); N. Simonov, *Voenno-promyshlennyi kompleks SSSR v 1920-1950-e gody: Tempy ekonomicheskogo rosta, struktura, organizatsiia proizvodstva i upravelenie* (Moscow: Rosspen, 1996); Sapir, 'Economics of War'; S. Stoecker, *Forging Stalin's Army: Marshal Tukhachevskii and the Politics of Military Innovation* (Boulder, CO: Westview, 1998); L. Samuelson, *Plans for Stalin's War Machine: Tukhachevskii and Military-Economic Planning, 1925–1941* (Basingstoke: Palgrave, 2000); D. Stone, *Hammer and Rifle: The Militarization of the Soviet Union, 1926–1933* (Lawrence, KS: University Press of Kansas, 2000).

68 Malyshev, 'Dnevnik', pp. 114–5 [4 February]. For the version by another comrade who was present, see Dimitrov, *Diary*, p. 147 [4 February]: 'We now have an army of four million men on their feet and ready for anything. The Tsar used to dream of a standing army of 1,200,000 men.'

69 Stalin, *OVOVSS*, p. 22 [6 November].

70 The population figures come from I. Dear and M. Foot (eds), *The Oxford Companion to the Second World War* (Oxford: Oxford University Press, 1995), p. 1207, and Harrison, *The Economics of World War II*, p. 7. The 1939 figures could be considered the 'core' populations for purposes of strategic comparison. By June 1941 annexations had raised the Reich population to 116 million (with Alsace-Lorraine, the Czech lands and part of Poland) and that of the USSR to nearly 200 million (with parts of Poland and Romania, and the Baltic states).

71 A. Dallin, *German Rule in Russia, 1941–1945: A Study of Occupation Policies*, 2nd edn (London: Macmillan, [1957] 1981), p. 365.

72 *Narodnoe khoziaistvo SSSR v Velikoi Otechestvennoi voine, 1941–1945: Statisticheskii sbornik* (Moscow: Informatsionno-izdatel'skii tsentr, 1990), p. 20. In the winter of 1941–2 the Germans had to retreat a few hundred miles in the north and centre of the front, but in the following summer they gained much more territory in the south.

73 The figure for the *occupied* zone of the USSR is used, because it was typical of where the fighting was going on. The average population density of the European part of the USSR as a whole was actually only seventy-eight inhabitants per square mile, but this takes into account the very thinly settled northern regions.

74 For the most part, Tables 2.5 and 2.6 give comparable figures for Russian procurement, but there are discrepancies. For example, Table 2.5 gives Soviet production of machine guns as 356,000 in 1942, while Table 2.6 gives 238,200 machine guns entering Red Army

service. The two tables come from different sources (although both ultimately derive from the Russian archives). Also, Table 2.5 is about *production* of equipment in the USSR, while Table 2.6 is about equipment *entering service* from USSR production, from the USSR civilian sector and from foreign supply (Lend-Lease).

75 Chuev, *140 besed s Molotovym*, p. 35.

76 *VOV/VIO*, vol. 4, p. 75.

77 J. Barber and M. Harrison, *The Soviet Home Front, 1941–1945: A Social and Economic History of the USSR in World War II* (Harlow: Longman, 1991), p. 130.

78 V. K. Triandafillov, *The Nature of the Operations of Modern Armies* (London: Frank Cass, [1929] 1994), pp. 66–7.

79 Stalin, *OVOVSS*, p. 120 [6 November 1943].

80 *VOV/VIO*, vol. 4, p. 89.

81 *VOV/VIO*, vol. 4, p. 397; E. Bacon, *The Gulag at War: Stalin's Forced Labour System in the Light of the Archives* (Basingstoke: Macmillan, 1994); 'Gulag v gody voiny. Doklad nachal'nika GULAGa NKVD SSSR V. G. Nasedkina. Avgust 1944', *IA*, 1994, no. 3. pp. 60–86.

82 *VOV/VIO*, vol. 4, p. 75. The figures given are 63 per cent for coal and 65 per cent for iron ore.

83 *Narodnoe khoziaistvo*, p. 54; Dear and Foot, *Oxford Companion to the Second World War*, p. 1061.

84 *VOV/VIO*, vol. 4, p. 88. The more exact figure given for cultivated land occupied by the enemy is 47 per cent; the source did not specify a time period but presumably it took into account the deepest German advance, that is to the end of 1942. For the Nazi food-resource plans, see Chapter 1.

85 *VOV/VIO*, vol. 4, pp. 75, 88; the figure given is 31 per cent. On this vital element, see W. Moskoff, *The Bread of Affliction: The Food Supply in the USSR during World War II* (Cambridge: Cambridge University Press, 1990), and Collingham, *Taste of War*, pp. 317–46.

86 *VOV/VIO*, vol. 4, p. 88.

87 The significant weaknesses of the economy of the Third Reich in the 1930s and the fractured nature of its strategic mobilization prior to the summer of 1941 are detailed in Tooze, *Wages*. On the specific requirements of the war with Russia, see R.-D. Müller in *GSWW*, vol. 4, pp. 187–224. Broader aspects of German economic mobilization in the first half of the war are dealt with by Müller in *GSWW*, vol. 4, pp. 1081–188, and vol. 5.1, pp. 405–721.

88 *VOV/VIO*, vol. 1, p. 73, vol. 4, p. 85.

89 I am following here the interpretation of R. Overy, *War and Economy in the Third Reich* (Oxford: Clarendon Press, 1994).

90 *Hitlers Weisungen*, pp. 136–9 [14 July].

91 J. Barber and M. Harrison (eds), *The Soviet Defence-Industry Complex from Stalin to Khrushchev* (Basingstoke: Macmillan, 2000), p. 100. For the late-war German economic developments, see Chapter 7.

92 G. Megargee, *Inside Hitler's High Command* (Lawrence, KS: University Press of Kansas, 2000), deals at length with systemic German shortcomings including intelligence work; see also Citino, *German Way of War*, pp. xiv–xv, 297–8, and M. Geyer, 'National Socialist Germany: The Politics of Information', in May, *Knowing One's Enemies*, pp. 310–46. For the incorrect assessment of Russia, see J. Förster, 'Zum Rußlandbild der Militärs 1941–1945', in H.-E. Volkmann (ed.). *Das Rußlandbild im Dritten Reich* (Cologne: Böhlau, 1994), pp. 141–63. On the underestimation by British and American intelligence, see B. Smith,

Sharing Secrets with Stalin: How the Allies Traded Intelligence, 1941–1945 (Lawrence, KS: University Press of Kansas, 1996), pp. 30–4.

93 *GSWW*, vol. 4, pp. 283–4; Beck is cited in Förster, 'Dynamics', p. 191. In his famous postwar 'election speech', Stalin cited ironically the suggestion that the Red Army had been a 'colossus with feet of clay'; see I. V. Stalin, *Sochineniia* (Stanford, CA: Hoover Institution, 1967), vol. 3(16), p. 9 [10 February 1946].

Chapter 3

1. Erickson, *Road to Stalingrad*, pp. 101–35, provides an excellent treatment of the events of 22 June. For the summer 1941 campaign as a whole, see: V. A. Anfilov, *Groznoe leto 41 goda* (Moscow: Izdatel'skii tsentr Ankil-Voin, 1995); D. Glantz, *Barbarossa: Hitler's Invasion of Russia 1941* (Stroud: Tempus, 2001); and M. Iu. Miagkov, 'Groznoe leto 1941 goda', *NNI*, 2011, no. 2, pp. 143–65, 2011, no. 3, pp. 130–50. The 'official histories', *GSWW*, vol. 4, and *VOV/VIO*, vol. 1, also provide much material.

2. For Luftwaffe operations in 1941, see R. Muller, *The German Air War in Russia* (Baltimore: Nautical and Aviation Publications, 1992), pp. 27–64, and H. Boog in *GSWW*, vol. 4, pp. 763–814. Hardesty and Grinberg, *Red Phoenix*, pp. 5–47, deal with the early air battles from the Russian perspective.

3. *VOV/VIO*, vol. 1, pp. 136–7, 155, 158; *Poteri*, p. 484; *GSWW*, vol. 4, p. 764.

4. *Poteri*, pp. 474–5, 484; *GSWW*, vol. 4, pp. 764, 817–18; I. Dear and M. R. D. Foot (eds), *The Oxford Companion to the Second World War* (Oxford: Oxford University Press, 1995), p. 163. As with personnel losses, figures for equipment must be treated with great caution. Transnational comparisons demand special care.

5. For the border battles in the central sector of the front in late June and early July, see E. Klink in *GSWW*, vol. 4, pp. 525–37, and A. M. Sokolov in *VOV/VIO*, vol. 1, pp. 129–47. C. Luther, *Barbarossa Unleashed: The German Blitzkrieg Through Central Russia to the Gates of Moscow: June-December 1941* (Atglen, PA: Schiffer, 2013), provides abundant detail from the German side.

6. On Bock, see A. Turney, *Disaster at Moscow: Von Bock's Campaigns 1941–1942* (London: Cassell, 1970), and K. Gerbet and D. Johnston, *Generalfeldmarschall Fedor von Bock: The War Diary 1939-1945* (Atglen, PA: Schiffer Publishing, 2000).

7. Guderian wrote one of the best-known memoirs of the Second World War, *Erinnerungen eines Soldaten* (Heidelberg: Kurt Vowinckel, 1951), translated as *Panzer Leader* (New York: Dutton, 1952). See also K. Macksey, 'Guderian', in Barnett, *Hitler's Generals*, pp. 440–60, and J. Strawson, 'General Heinz Guderian', in M. Carver (ed.), *The War Lords* (London: Weidenfeld & Nicolson, 1976), pp. 298–315, neither of which overemphasizes its subject's personal commitment to the Nazi cause.

8. *Poteri*, pp. 267–8, 484; *GSWW*, vol. 4, p. 536; *VOV/VIO*, vol. 1, p. 136. German POW figures were probably somewhat exaggerated by the inclusion of civilians; see Chapter 4.

9. *1941 god*, vol. 2, pp. 455, 468, 472–3. For the Pavlov case, see I. A. Basiuk, 'General Armii D. G. Pavlov i tragediia 1941 g', *VI*, 2010, no. 5, pp. 41–50, and Birstein, *Smersh*, pp. 90–95.

10. *1941 god*, vol. 2, pp. 467–8.

11. Chuev, *Sto sorok besed s Molotovym*, p. 36. 'General of the Army' (*General armii*) was a rank second only to that of Marshal. For Pavlov's 1938 service autobiography, see 'Dmitrii Grigor'evich Pavlov', *VIZh*, 1990, no. 2, pp. 53–5.

12. Zhukov, *ViR*, vol. 2, p. 8.

13. *VOV/VIO*, vol. 1, pp. 136, 139.

14. *1941 god*, vol. 2, p. 455.

15. R. Aliev, *The Siege of Brest 1941: A Legend of Red Army Resistance on the Eastern Front* (Barnsley: Pen and Sword, 2013). C. Ganzer used German casualty records to argue that Soviet resistance has been exaggerated and only lasted for two or three days: 'German and Soviet Losses as an Indicator of the Length and Intensity of the Battle for the Brest Fortress (1941)', *JSMS*, 27:3 (2014), pp. 449–66.

16. *RA/VO*, vol. 12(1), pp. 252–3 [24 November].

17. Halder, *Kriegstagebuch*, vol. 3, p. 38 [3 July]. To be fair to Halder, he followed this assessment with two more cautious and less often quoted, sentences: 'Naturally, that does not mean it is all over. The territorial expanse and the stubborn and fierce resistance will keep us busy for many more weeks.'

18. The fullest account of this episode is that of Politburo member Mikoian, *Tak bylo*, pp. 389–91. For Stalin's appointments diary, see A. V. Korotkov et al. (eds), 'Posetiteli kremlevskogo kabineta I. V. Stalin', *IA*, 1996, no. 2, pp. 51–4. Hereafter cited as 'Posetiteli'.

19. There is much information on the committee's activities in Iu. A. Gor'kov, *Gosudarstvennyi komitet oborony postanovliaet (1941–1945): Tsifry, dokumenty* (Moscow: Olma-Press, 2002). Hereafter cited as Gor'kov, *GKO*.

20. The word 'theatre' (or *TVD*) can have a broader meaning in both Russian and Western technical military usage, but as a loose translation of the Russian word *napravlenie*, it is clearer than other translations, like 'direction' or 'axis'. The three theatre headquarters were disbanded in 1941–2, but later in this book the word 'theatre' will still be used informally (in lower case) for a large part of the front, e.g. the central theatre.

21. *1941 god*, vol. 2, pp. 448–52. Stalin's 3 July speech was based closely on a secret Party/State decree of 29 June, see *RA/VO*, vol. 9, p. 17.

22. *1941 god*, vol. 2, pp. 471–2 [15 July].

23. *1941 god*, vol. 2, pp. 467, 472–3; *RA/VO*, 2(2), 37–8 [16 July].

24. For General Trubetskoi's report on the shortcomings of the railway system in the new western territories of the USSR, see *RA/VO*, vol. 14, pp. 54–60 [26 May 1941]. Trubetskoi had meetings with Stalin on 27 May and 1 July; M. Parrish, *Sacrifice of the Generals: Soviet Senior Officer Loses, 1939-1953* (Westport, CT: Greenwood, 2001), pp. 399–400, provides details. On the Meretskov case, see Birstein, *Smersh*, pp. 89–90.

25. *RA/VO*, vol. 5(1), p. 77 [16 July]; *1941 god*, vol. 2, pp. 473–4 [17 July]; V. N. Khaustov et al. (eds), *Lubianka: Stalin i NKVD-NKGB-GUKR "Smersh", 1939-mart 1946* (Moscow: MF 'Demokratiia', 2006), pp. 317–8 [31 October 1941]. Birstein, *Smersh*, pp. 96–142, provides in-depth coverage of Abakumov and the OO.

26. See O. Rzheshevsky, 'Boris Mikhailovich Shaposhnikov', in Shukman, *Stalin's Generals*, pp. 217–30. There is no full biography tracing the extraordinary career of this Tsarist colonel. Shaposhnikov was also implicated heavily in the 1937–8 Army purge, as he sat on the courts which tried the purged commanders.

27. According to the 'official' Russian version, the Battle of Smolensk began on 10 July and ended on 10 September. Two detailed studies have recently been published, both of which assign great importance to the resistance put up by the Red Army: D. Glantz, *Barbarossa Derailed: The Battle for Smolensk, 10 July – 10 September 1941*, 2 vols. (Solihull: Helion, 2010), and D. Stahel, *Operation Barbarossa and Germany's Defeat in the East* (Cambridge:

Cambridge University Press, 2009). See also Klink in *GSWW*, vol. 4, pp. 525–37, and E. I. Ziuzin in *VOV/VIO*, vol. 1, pp. 169–84. Smolensk, like the provincial town of Kursk in 1943, was only the cartographical centre of a widespread series of battles. Party-line Soviet military historians added to the confusion by writing about a Smolensk *srazhenie* ('engagement') but about a Moscow *bitva* ('battle'), a Stalingrad *bitva* and a Kursk *bitva*; they also called the unsuccessful Soviet Khar'kov offensive of 1942 a *srazhenie*.

28. Gor'kov, *GKO*, p. 503–4 [16 July]; *RA/VO*, vol. 5(1), p. 77 [18 July 1941].

29. See V. Anfilov, 'Semen Konstantinovich Timoshenko', in Shukman, *Stalin's Generals*, pp. 239–53. Unusually, Timoshenko did not leave extensive memoirs. The post-Soviet book-length biography, R. M. Portugal'skii, *Marshal S. K. Timoshenko* (Moscow: MOF- Pobeda, 1994), is of limited value.

30. '"My raspolagaem samymi luchshimi kadrami": Zapiski o poslevoennom ustroistve armii', *Istochnik*, 1996, no. 2, p. 137 [22 August 1944]; V. A. Anfilov, '"… [*sic*] Razgovor zakonchilsia ugrozoi Stalina": Desiat' besed s marshalom G. K. Zhukovym v mae-iiune 1965 goda', *VIZh*, 1995, no. 2, p. 42.

31. Iu. G. Murin (ed.), *Iosif Stalin v ob"itiiakh sem'i* (Moscow: Edition q [*sic*], 1993), p. 74; Anfilov, 'Razgovor', p. 43. For details of the abortive Soviet attack in which Dzhugashvili was involved, see Glantz, *Barbarossa Derailed*, vol. 1, pp. 70–8.

32. *VOV/VIO*, vol. 1, p. 171.

33. *RA/VO*, vol. 5(2), p. 85 [20 July]; Zhukov, *ViR*, vol. 2, pp. 62, 64–5; Gor'kov, *GKO*, p. 82; Dimitrov, *Diary*, pp. 187–8 [5 August].

34. *Hitlers Weisungen*, pp. 150–3 [6 September].

35. *Hitlers Weisungen*, pp. 140–2 [19 July], 142–4 [23 July]. On this important debate in the German Army, see Klink in *GSWW*, vol. 4, pp. 569–73.

36. *Hitlers Weisungen*, pp. 148–50 [12 August], 150 [6 September]. David Glantz argued that Hitler's decision to protect the flanks of Army Group Centre was indeed correct; otherwise an advance towards Moscow, not to mention a German defence of the capital (were Moscow to have been captured), would have been very risky (*Barbarossa Derailed*, vol. 2, p. 515).

37. The supply problem is central to the argument of M. van Creveld, *Supplying War: Logistics from Wallenstein to Patton* (Cambridge: Cambridge University Press, 1977), pp. 166–71, 175–6, that a successful German advance was impossible. For the opposite view, giving the Germans a much better chance of success, see R. Stolfi, *Hitler's Panzers East: World War II Reinterpreted* (Norman, OK: University of Oklahoma Press, 1991), pp. 166–77.

38. *Hitlers Weisungen*, pp. 145 [30 July], 149 [12 August]. The leading Western expert on the campaign stresses the crucial role of 'fierce Soviet resistance around Smolensk' in Hitler's decision to move to the flanks: Glantz, *Barbarossa*, pp. 83, 96.

39. *VOV/VIO*, vol. 1, pp. 182–3.

40. Zhukov, *ViR*, vol. 2, pp. 132–3. See also Glantz, *Barbarossa Derailed*, vol. 1, 532–75, vol. 2, pp. 322–63, and G. Roberts, *Stalin's General: The Life of Georgy Zhukov* (London: Icon Books, 2012), pp. 112, 114–7. Glantz argued, however, that the offensive mounted by Timoshenko's Western Army Group against Dukhovshchina (northeast of Smolensk) was more important than Zhukov's El'nia battle; the first Soviet success, he maintained, came when General Konev's 19th Army (subordinate to Timoshenko) forced the Vop River on 18 August (*Barbarossa Derailed*, vol. 1, 406–80, vol. 2, pp. 162–321, 511).

41. *RA/VO*, vol. 2(2), p. 86 [18 September].

42. Glantz, *Barbarossa Derailed*, vol. 2, p. 547; Stahel, *Barbarossa*, p. 348.

43. S. Hayashi, *Kōgun: The Japanese Army in the Pacific War* (Westport, CT: Greenwood Press, 1978 [1959]), pp. 19–23; A. Coox, 'The Pacific War', in P. Duus (ed.), *Cambridge History of Japan*, 6 vols (Cambridge: Cambridge University Press, 1988), pp. 326–9; A. Coox, *Nomonhan*, 2 vols (Stanford: Stanford University Press, 1985), vol. 2, pp. 1033–53. Arguably, the Japanese were only postponing their attack on the USSR to the spring of 1942, but by then, the global situation was quite different.

44. Glantz, *Barbarossa*, pp. 87,135, rightly highlights the negative consequences of Stalin's and Timoshenko's offensives.

45. *RA/VO*, vol. 5(1), p. 210 [29 September]; *Poteri*, pp. 271–2, 484; K. von Tippelskirch, *Geschichte des zweiten Weltkriegs* (Bonn, Athenäum-Verlag, 1951), p. 222.

46. B. H. Liddell Hart, *The German Generals Talk* (New York: Berkeley, 1958), p. 139. An August 1941 offensive against Moscow is a favourite subject for 'counter-factual' historians. The argument has been made most recently and most baldly in Stolfi, *Hitler's Panzers*, pp. 139–49. It is implicit in many of the German memoirs, including Guderian, *Erinnerungen eines Soldaten*, pp. 180–3.

47. On the crucial changes in the situation, see also Glantz, *Barbarossa Derailed*, vol. 2, pp. 514–5.

48. The German side of the fighting in the Ukraine in the first four months of the war is covered in D. Stahel, *Kiev 1941: Hitler's Battle for Supremacy in the East* (Cambridge: Cambridge University Press, 2012), and Klink in *GSWW*, vol. 4, pp. 546–68, 594–603. For the Soviets, see: Glantz, *Barbarossa*, pp. 46–53, 117–36; A. M. Sokolov in *VOV/VIO*, vol. 1, pp. 155–64; and N. M. Ramanichev in *VOV/VIO*, vol. 1, pp. 184–97.

49. *VOV/VIO*, vol. 1, p. 155.

50. *VOV/VIO*, vol. 1, p. 155.

51. *1941 god*, vol. 2, p. 439 [22 June].

52. *RA/VO*, vol. 5(1), p. 34 [30 June].

53. See V. Anfilov, 'Semen Mikhailovich Budenny', in Shukman, *Stalin's Generals*, pp. 57–65.

54. *GSWW*, vol. 4, p. 568.

55. *1941 god*, vol. 2, pp. 476–8 [16 August]; A. A. Maslov, *Fallen Soviet Generals: Soviet General Officers Killed in Battle 1941–1945* (London: Frank Cass, 1998), p. 17; *RA/VO*, vol. 5(1), p. 361 [19 August].

56. Zhukov, *ViR*, vol. 2, pp. 119–22; *RA/VO*, vol. 5(1), p. 361 [19 August]. This account has been questioned by Geoffrey Roberts, who suggests that Zhukov resigned from the General Staff post because he thought he would function better as an operational commander, that is at El'nia (*Stalin's General*, pp. 111–14).

57. *RA/VO*, vol. 5(1), pp. 182 [13 September], 380 [13 September].

58. *GSWW*, vol. 4, p. 604; *VOV/VIO*, vol. 1, p. 195; *Poteri*, p. 270.

59. For the fighting in the northern part of the front from June through September, see: D. Glantz, *The Battle for Leningrad, 1941-1944* (Lawrence: University Press of Kansas, 2002), pp. 24–86; Klink in *GSWW*, vol. 4, pp. 537–46, 631–54; A. M. Sokolov in *VOV/VIO*, vol. 1, pp. 147–55; and N. M. Ramanichev in *VOV/VIO*, vol. 1, pp. 197–206.

60. *Poteri*, pp. 267, 484. Stolfi, *Hitler's Panzers East*, pp. 41–55, argues that more energetic panzer commanders – more energetic even than Manstein – might have converted the Dvina River coup into a quick capture of Leningrad. This is far-fetched.

61. V. D. Dotsenko, *Mify i legendy russkoi morskoi istorii* (St Petersburg: Ivan Fedorov, 1997), pp. 143–60.

62. H. Picker (ed.), *Hitlers Tischgespräche im Führerhauptquartier* (Stuttgart: Seewald, 1977), cited in R.-D. Müller and G. Ueberschär (eds), *Hitler's War in the East, 1941–1945: A Critical Assessment* (Oxford: Berghahn, 1997), p. 106 [16 September].

63. Iu. V. Rubtsov, 'Vinovnykh nashli na peredovoi', *VIZh*, 1994, no. 9, pp. 8–11; *RA/VO*, vol. 5(1), p. 154 [1 September].

64. For new details on the fall of Voroshilov, see R. Bidlack and N. Lomagin, *The Leningrad Blockade, 1941-1944: A New Documentary History from the Soviet Archives* (New Haven: Yale University Press, 2012), pp. 105–9.

65. *GSWW*, vol. 4, p. 640; Roberts, *Stalin's General*, pp. 128–34. In mid-September the Stavka gave orders to prepare the destruction of the ships and bases of the Baltic Fleet, and the blocking of channels into Leningrad; fortunately, these measures did not have to be carried out (*RA/VO*, vol. 5(1), pp. 378–9 [13 September]). The harsh disciplinary regime imposed by Zhukov during his short stay in Leningrad is detailed in Bidlack and Lomagin, *Leningrad Blockade*, pp. 118–27.

66. L. Goure, *The Siege of Leningrad* (Stanford, CA: Stanford University Press, 1962), pp. 89, 300.

67. Stalin, *OVOVSS*, pp. 9–10 [3 July]; Overmans, *Verluste*, pp. 238, 277. Only 15,000 further German service personnel were lost on other fronts during the June–September 1941 period, a reminder of how much of the Allied burden the Red Army was now bearing.

68. Halder, *Kriegstagebuch*, vol. 3, p. 170 [11 August].

69. *Poteri*, p. 422.

70. *Poteri*, pp. 261, 422; H. Greiner and P. Schramm (eds), *Kriegstagebuch des Oberkommandos der Wehrmacht (Wehrmachtführungsstab) 1940-1945*, 4 vols (Frankfurt: Bernard & Graefe, 1961–79), vol. 1, p. 1106. Hereafter, *KTB OKW*. The figure for prisoners taken by the Germans is only an approximation; there will be a fuller discussion of these POWs in Chapter 4.

71. *Poteri*, p. 252; A. A. Shabaev, 'Poteri ofitserskogo sostava Krasnoi armii v Velikoi Otechestvennoi voine', *Voenno-istoricheskii arkhiv* (hereafter, *VIA*), 1998, *vypusk* 3, p. 173; Maslov, *Fallen Soviet Generals*, pp. 2–38, 44; A. A. Maslov, *Captured Soviet Generals: The Fate of Soviet Generals Captured in Combat 1941–45* (London: Frank Cass, 2001), pp. 3–19, 46–65, 113–19, 124–79, 307–16.

72. Stalin, *OVOVSS*, p. 23 [6 November].

Chapter 4

1. For operations in southern Russia in the late autumn of 1941, see Klink in *GSWW*, vol. 4, pp. 604–31, and Nevzorov in *VOV/VIO*, vol. 1, pp. 236–7.

2. A. A. Maslov, *Fallen Soviet Generals* (London: Frank Cass, 1998), p. 44; K. von Tippelskirch, *Geschichte des zweiten Weltkriegs* (Bonn: Athenäum-Verlag, 1951), p. 235.

3. *SDVG*, vol. 1, p. 345 [29 November.].

4. The operations from October through December 1941 are covered in Glantz, *Battle for Leningrad*, pp. 87–116. See also Klink in *GSWW*, vol. 4, pp. 643–54, and B. I. Nevzorov in *VOV/VIO*, vol.1, p. 235.

5. *Hitlers Weisungen*, pp. 150–2 [6 September]; Domarus, *Hitler: Reden*, p. 1757 [2 October].

6. On the Battle of Viaz'ma–Briansk and its immediate consequences, see: N. Zetterling, and A. Frankson, *The Drive on Moscow, 1941: Operation Taifun and Germany's First Great Crisis*

in World War II (Havertown, PA: Casemate, 2012), pp. 19–172; L. Lopukhovsky, *The Viazma Catastrophe, 1941: The Red Army's Disastrous Stand against Operation Typhoon* (Solihull: Helion, 2013); D. Stahel, *Operation Typhoon: Hitler's March on Moscow, October 1941* (Cambridge: Cambridge University Press, 2013); and M. Iu. Miagkov, 'Bitva pod Moskvoi: Ot oborony k kontrnastupleniiu', *Novaia i noveishaia istoriia* (hereafter, *NNI*), 2010, no. 3, pp. 22–38. Earlier sources include Klink in *GSWW*, vol. 4, pp. 664–84, and B. I. Nevzorov in *VOV/VIO*, vol. 1, pp. 212–34.

7. Iu. A. Gor'kov, 'Gotovil li Stalin uprezhdaiushchii udar protiv Gitlera v 1941 g', *NNI*, 1993, no. 3, pp. 44–5 [15 May]; *VOV/VIO*, vol. 1, p. 176.

8. 'Ivan Stepanovich Konev', *VIZh*, 1991, no. 2, pp. 18–20; Zhukov, *ViR*, vol. 1, p. 228, vol. 2, p. 144; O. F. Suvenirov, *Tragediia RKKA 1937–1938* (Moscow: Terra, 1998), pp. 105, 108. For general biographies, see J. Erickson, 'Marshal Ivan Koniev', in Carver, *The War Lords*, pp. 285–97, and O. Rzheshevsky, 'Ivan Stepanovich Konev', in Shukman, *Stalin's Generals*, pp. 91–107.

9. *VOV/VIO*, vol. 1, p. 226; *Poteri*, p. 455.

10. *RA/VO*, vol. 5(1), p. 224 [5 October 1941].

11. A. M. Vasilevskii, *Delo vsei zhizni*, 2 vols, 6th edn (Moscow: IPL, [1975] 1989), vol. 1, p. 159; *Hitlers Weisungen*, p. 85 [18 December 1940]. The order creating Engineer Armies was issued by the GKO on 13 October. By January 1942 there were ten Engineer Armies. Once the most immediate threat had passed, these big formations were disbanded. See G. V. Malinovskii, 'Sapernye armii i ikh rol' v pervyi period Velikoi Otechestvennoi voiny', *VIA*, vol. 2(17), 2001, pp. 146–88, and Zolotarev, *Deistvuiushchaia armiia*, pp. 222–4, 414.

12. V. A. Anfilov, 'Stolitsa vystoiala pod natiskom gitlerovskogo "taifuna"', *VIZh*, 2001, no. 12, pp. 19–21.

13. Dimitrov, *Diary*, p. 197 [15 October]. Documents on the 'Moscow panic' can be found in *Moskva voennaia. 1941–1945: Memuary i arkhivnye dokumenty* (Moscow: Mosgorarkhiv, 1995), pp. 100–25.

14. Klink in *GSWW*, vol. 4, p. 671, and K. Reinhardt, *Moscow: The Turning Point* (Oxford: Berg, 1992), p. 63, accept a strength of 1,900,000 for Army Group Centre. Zetterling and Grandson, *Drive on Moscow*, pp. 123, 251–3, question this and suggest a figure for early October of only 1,200,000. The view of the American military historian Earl Ziemke was that, in view of the large number of auxiliary troops, the combat strength of Army German Group Centre 'would hardly have given it more than numerical equality' (Ziemke and Bauer, *Moscow to Stalingrad*, p. 36). Ziemke accepted a figure of 1,700,000 in Army Group Centre, including a very large rear-echelon element. Moving forward, he reckoned that only some 800,000 German troops would have been available for combat in December 1941 (p. 66).

15. *VOV/VIO*, vol. 1, p. 213; *GSWW*, vol. 4, p. 671. At Stalingrad, the Germans had more air support relative to their ground forces, some 1,200 aircraft. At Kursk in 1943, there was an even heavier concentration of German armour and air power: 2,400 tanks and assault guns, and 1,800 planes.

16. W. Dunn, *Stalin's Keys to Victory: The Rebirth of the Red Army* (Westport, CT: Praeger Security International, 2006), p. 71–4.

17. 'Iz istorii Velikoi Otechestvennoi voiny', *ITsK*, 1990, no. 12, p. 204 [1 October 1941]; I. S. Konev, 'Nachalo Moskovskoi bitvy', *VIZh*, 1966, no. 10, p. 63. Another recent source, however, suggests the local air strength was about equal for the two sides, and that the Red Army Air Force played an important role in slowing the Germans' advance after their initial breakthrough (Hardesty and Grinberg, *Red Phoenix*, pp. 67–78).

18. For Konev's attempt at self-justification, see his 'Nachalo Moskovskoi bitvy', *VIZh*, 1966, no. 10, pp. 56–67. His defence plan was printed in *RA/VO*, vol. 4(1), p. 77 [28 September 1941].

19. Anfilov, 'Razgovor', p. 44; Simonov, *Glazami cheloveka moego pokoleniia*, pp. 350–1.

20. Konev, 'Nachalo', p. 59; 'Iz istorii', *ITsK*, 1990, no. 12, p. 204 [1 October]; Anfilov, 'Razgovor', p. 43.

21. Vasilevskii, *Delo*, vol. 1, pp. 149, 151.

22. Anfilov, 'Razgovor', p. 44.

23. *RA/VO*, vol. 5(1), pp. 236–7. Very soon, however, the northern wing was hived off as Kalinin Army Group, under Konev.

24. Halder, *Kriegstagebuch*, vol. 3, p. 287 [4 October]. See the Stavka withdrawal order issued late on 5 October: *RA/VO*, vol. 5(1), p. 222.

25. Y. Arad, *The Holocaust in the Soviet Union* (Lincoln, NE: University of Nebraska Press, 2009); Domarus, *Hitler: Reden*, pp. 1772–3, 1779. Lazar' Kaganovich held leading posts in the Soviet economic bureaucracy and was one of a small number of officials of Jewish origin in Stalin's inner circle in 1941; many other Jews in the Soviet leadership had perished during the Purges. On anti-Semitism as a central German wartime propaganda theme, see J. Herf in *GSWW*, vol. 9.2, pp. 163–204.

26. The fullest account is Arad, *Holocaust*; see also T. Jersak in *GSWW*, vol. 9.1, pp. 312–32. R. Hilberg, *The Destruction of the European Jews*, 3 vols, 3rd edn (New Haven, CT: Yale University Press, 2003), deals with the Holocaust in general. For the Ukraine, see K. Berkhoff, *Harvest of Despair: Life and Death in Ukraine under Nazi Rule* (Cambridge, MA: Belknap Press, 2004), pp. 59–88. W. Lower, *Nazi Empire-Building and the Holocaust in Ukraine* (Chapel Hill, NC: University of North Carolina Press, 2005), is a detailed case study of German actions in the Zhitomir Region of the western Ukraine.

27. M. V. Koval', 'Tragediia Bab'ego Iara: istoriia i sovremennost', *NNI*, 1998, no. 4, pp. 14–28.

28. Hilberg, *Destruction*, vol. 1, pp. 304, 327, 353; Arad, *Holocaust*, pp. 125–40; P. Desbois, *The Holocaust by Bullets: A Priest's Journey to Uncover the Truth Behind the Murder of 1.5 Million Jews* (New York: Palgrave Macmillan, 2008).

29. For an insightful discussion on differing German attitudes, see J. Steinberg, 'The Third Reich Reflected: German Civil Administration in the Occupied Soviet Union, 1941-4', *English Historical Review*, vol. 110 (1995), June, pp. 620–51.

30. Arad, *Holocaust*, pp. 521, 524; Hilberg, *Destruction*, vol. 1, p. 295, vol. 3, pp. 1313–19. Hilberg counted 700,000 victims from the pre-1939 USSR, and added an estimated 200,000 in the Baltic, most of the 550,000 million Jews in eastern Poland and several hundred thousand in Romanian-occupied territory. His total death toll for the European Holocaust was 5,100,000.

31. On the active collaboration of the German Army in 1941 and later, see: Arad, *Holocaust*, pp. 212–22; Fritz, *Ostkrieg*; W. Wette, *The Wehrmacht: History, Myth, Reality* (Cambridge, MA: Harvard University Press, 2007), pp. 92–138; and W. Beorn, *Marching into Darkness: The Wehrmacht and the Holocaust in Belarus* (Cambridge, MA: Harvard University Press, 2014). J. P. Reemtsma et al. (eds), *Verbrechen der Wehrmacht: Dimensionen des Vernichtungskrieges 1941-1944: Ausstellungskatalog* (Hamburg: Hamburger Edition, 2002), pp. 77–185, contains documentation on Wehrmacht involvement.

32. The standard account of Russian POWs in German hands is Streit, *Keine Kameraden*; for a summary, see his 'Soviet Prisoners of War in the Hands of the Germans', in Heer and Nauman, *War of Extermination*, pp. 80–91. Also important is the discussion by R. Overmans

in *GSWW*, vol. 9.2, pp. 804–29, and Reemtsma, *Verbrechen der Wehrmacht*, pp. 187–298. There were relatively few Axis POWs in Soviet hands in the first year of the war; the Russian official total is only 17,000 (*Poteri*, p. 511). The fate of such prisoners will be discussed more fully in Chapter 8.

33. Domarus, *Hitler: Reden*, p. 1775 [8 November 1941]; Streit, *Keine Kameraden*, p. 83. Four smaller encirclements by Army Group North yielded only 84,000 POWs in 1941.

34. *VOV/VIO*, vol. 4, p. 172. The Russians admitted that 2,835,000 of their soldiers became POWs in 1941, which was 500,000 less than the highest German claim for that year. The overall total admitted for the period 1941–5 was 5,254,000. This can be compared with 'year of capture' given in Russian sources for some 1,370,000 POW survivors who had been repatriated by October 1945: 49 per cent said they had been captured in 1941, and 33 per cent in 1942 (*Poteri*, p. 463). See also N. F. Kovalevskii, 'Voennoplennye: Voenno-istoricheskii i statisticheskii obzor (po opytu Rossii)', *VIZh*, 2010, no. 8, pp. 42–6, and V. N. Zemskov, '"Statisticheskii labirint": Obshchaia chislennost' sovetskikh voennoplennykh i masshtaby ikh smertnosti', *Rossiiskaia istoriia* (hereafter, *RI*), 2011, no. 3, pp. 22–32.

35. A. Philippi and F. Heim, *Der Feldzug gegen Sowjetrußland* (Stuttgart: Kohlhammer, 1962), pp. 122–5, 137, 157; V. P. Naumov, 'Sud'ba voennoplennykh i deportirovannykh grazhdan SSSR: Materialy Komissii po reabilitatsii zhertv politicheskikh repressii', *NNI*, 1996, no. 2, p. 92.

36. It is extraordinary that so little has been published in Britain and America on this subject, and that Christian Streit's book has never been translated into English.

37. The Russians argue that the German wartime statistics included as POWs many people who were not actually serving in the Red Army, that is other individuals in uniformed service, partisans or even civilians of military age (*Poteri*, p. 462). A Russian report published in 1996 gave a considerably lower figure for POW deaths in captivity: 1,230,000 to 2,000,000; see Naumov, 'Sud'ba', p. 95.

38. Streit, *Keine Kameraden*, p. 105. On the murder of Jewish POWs, see Arad, *Holocaust*, pp. 376–81.

39. *VOV/VIO*, vol. 4, p. 155. Military 'collaboration' by Soviet POWs is discussed more fully in Chapter 8.

40. Reemtsma, *Verbrechen der Wehrmacht*, p. 188,

41. Reinhardt, *Moscow*, p. 102.

42. *RA/VO*, vol. 2(5), pp. 130–1 [19 April 1943], vol. 6, p. 86 [25 November 1941]. The Soviet November 1941 note may have been a response to Hitler's speech of 8 November claiming 3,600,000 POWs.

43. *1941 god*, vol. 2, pp. 479–80 [27 December].

44. *RA/VO*, vol. 5(4), 236–7 [11 May 1945].

45. V. N. Zemskov, 'K voprosu o repatriatsii sovetskikh grazhdan. 1944–1951 gody', *ISSSR*, 1990, no. 4, pp. 33–5.

46. G. K. Zhukov, 'Chego stoiat polkovodcheskie kachestva Stalina: Neproiznesennaia rech' marshala G. K. Zhukova', *Istochnik*, 1995, no. 2, p. 159; *VOV/VIO*, vol. 4, p. 194.

47. Anfilov, 'Razgovor', pp. 45–6; Zhukov, *ViR*, vol. 1, p. 208.

48. *RA/VO*, vol. 5(1), pp. 249, 388–9 [19 October].

49. Sources for the crucial late November–early December phase of the Battle of Moscow include Reinhardt, *Moscow*; Miagkov, 'Bitva pod Moskvoi', pp. 38–61; E. Mawdsley, *December 1941: Twelve Days that Began a World War* (New Haven: Yale University Press,

2011); and Zetterling and Frankson, *Drive on Moscow*, pp. 199–246. See also Klink in *GSWW*, vol. 4, pp. 685–707, and B. I. Nevzorov in *VOV/VIO*, vol. 1, pp. 238–83.

50. This memorable phrase was actually invented by the party propaganda organs after the fact. It was based on another famous saying from the Crimean War of 1854–56: K. Dushenko, *Russkie politicheskie tsitaty ot Lenina do El'tsina: Chto, kem i kogda bylo skazano* (Moscow: Iurist', 1996), p. 31. For the reality of the event, see A. Statiev, '"La Garde meurt mais ne se rend pas!": Once Again on the 28 Panfilov Heroes', *Kritika*, vol. 13, 2012, no. 4, pp. 769–98.

51. General Hans Reinhardt had replaced Hoth as commander of the 3rd Panzer Group in October. At the end of 1941 the four panzer groups were re-designated as 'panzer armies'. To avoid confusion, the old term is used throughout this chapter.

52. The formation, re-formation and renaming of Soviet formations cause confusion for any historian of the Eastern Front. The first Soviet 20th Army was badly weakened at the Battle of Smolensk, and then trapped and destroyed at the Battle of Viaz'ma–Briansk in early October; a replacement 20th Army was created in the following month. The Soviet 1st Shock Army, meanwhile, was formed from the remnants of the 19th Army (Konev's old army), much of which was also destroyed at Viaz'ma–Briansk; a new 19th Army would be created in the Karelian Army Group in 1942.

   The concept of shock armies (*udarnye armii*) had been developed in Soviet doctrine in the interwar years, as heavily equipped forces for breaking through enemy lines. Shock armies were first actually formed in November 1941. Although they existed throughout the war, the winter of 1941–2 was their high point. The ill-fated 2nd Shock Army was created on the Leningrad front. The 3rd and the 4th Shock Armies were formed in the Northwestern Army Group. See Zolotarev, *Deistvuiushchaia armiia*, pp. 89–93.

53. *Hitlers Weisungen*, p. 171 [8 December]; *Pravda*, p. 1 [13 December 1941].

54. *RA/VO*, vol. 5(1), pp. 333–4 [13 December].

55. Domarus, *Hitler: Reden*, pp. 1843–4 [15 February 1942], 1871 [26 April 1942].

56. *Hitlers Politisches Testament*, pp. 87–8 [17 February 1945]. For the fullest discussion of this question, see M. van Creveld, *Hitler's Strategy: The Balkan Clue* (Cambridge: Cambridge University Press, 1973).

57. *Hitlers Weisungen*, p. 171 [8 December]; Stalin, *OVOVSS*, p. 20 [6 November]; Dimitrov, *Diary*, p. 128 [28 March 1940]. A detailed treatment of the weather was given in R. H. Stolfi, 'Chance in History: The Russian Winter of 1941–1942', *History*, vol. 65, June 1980, no. 214, pp. 214–28. The Russians had winter problems too. See Western Army Group's complaints about lack of warm clothes in *RA/VO*, vol. 14, p. 168 [9 November].

58. G. Blumentritt, 'Moscow', in W. Kreipe (ed.), *The Fatal Decisions* (London: Michael Joseph, 1956), pp. 55–6.

59. Zhukov, *ViR*, vol. 2, p. 240; Reinhardt, *Moscow*, pp. 92–3. German and Russian historians differ widely on the effect of the *rasputitsa*. Russian writers often do not mention it at all, stressing the bravery of the defenders. In contrast, there is a whole section on the *Schlammperiode* ('mud season') in Philippi and Heim, *Feldzug*, pp. 90–3. Klink said little about the *rasputitsa* as a factor in his account; he did note that '[t]he weather conditions cannot have come as a surprise' (*GSWW*, vol. 4, pp. 677–9).

60. Müller and Ueberschär, *Hitler's War in the East*, pp. 93–9; Reinhardt, *Moscow*, p. 255. For another point of view, arguing this was perhaps the coldest winter in 250 years, see Stolfi, 'Chance', pp. 214–28; this is not, however, convincing. See also M. Cherniavsky, 'Corporal Hitler, General Winter and the Russian Peasant', *Yale Review* (Summer 1962), pp. 547–58.

61. Domarus, *Hitler: Reden*, p. 1767.

62. Zhukov, *ViR*, vol. 2, p. 219. One early western account regarded Bock's decision to give priority to finishing off the pockets around Viaz'ma and Briansk as the crucial German blunder: A. Turney, *Disaster at Moscow: Von Bock's Campaigns 1941-1942* (London: Cassell, 1970), pp. xiv, 101–2. This seems too simplistic.

63. Klink in *GSWW*, vol. 4, pp. 687–8; Reinhardt, *Moscow*, p. 191. Criticism of Halder's strategic decision-making is a general feature of the account of the 1941–2 campaigns in GSWW.

64. Reinhardt, *Moscow*, pp. 187–9, n. 19, 299.

65. Cited in Ziemke, *Moscow to Stalingrad*, p. 296.

66. Domarus, *Hitler: Reden*, p. 1775 [8 November 1941]. Hitler actually believed this; see Halder's account of the Führer's private citation of the same figures in early December (Halder, *KTB*, vol. 3, pp. 328–9 [6 December]).

67. Halder, *KTB*, vol. 3, p. 303 [22 November]

68. *GSWW*, vol. 4, p. 704, n. 571. On the 'Marne Complex' see also Mawdsley, *December 1941*, pp. 41–2, 88, 111, 148.

69. Stalin, *OVOVSS*, p. 53. Stalin commented on the German military: 'Its senior experienced generals, the likes of Reichenau, Brauchitsch, Todt and others have either been killed by the Red Army or thrown out by the German-fascist leadership.' Some details were wrong: no senior officers had been killed by the Red Army, Reichenau had had a stroke and Todt's death in an air crash was probably an accident.

70. A. A. Pechenkin, 'V osazhdennoi Moskve', *VIZh*, 2001, no. 12, pp. 26–7.

71. *RA/VO*, vol. 5(1), pp. 299–300 [17 November], 407 [29 November].

72. See M. M. Gorinov, 'Zoia Kosmodem'ianskaia (1923–1941)', *OI*, 2003, no. 1, pp. 77–92, for an unvarnished account.

73. Vasilevskii, *Delo*, vol. 1, pp. 150, 159–60, 171.

74. Dunn, *Stalin's Keys*, pp. 63–4; Kudriashov, *Voina*, pp. 55–57 [11 August], 76–8 [13 October], 79 [14 October], 84 [18 October].

75. Dunn, *Stalin's Keys*, pp. 79–80. A full-strength rifle division contained nine rifle battalions (each of about 1,000 men) and included light artillery. An independent rifle brigade comprised only three or four rifle battalions, with mortars rather than field guns. See also *VOVE*, p. 690 ('*strelkovaia brigada*') and p. 705 ('*tankovaia brigada*').

76. *VOV/VIO*, vol. 1, p. 244. Rebuilding the Red Army is discussed at length in Dunn, *Stalin's Keys*. See also: Zetterling and Grandson, *Drive on Moscow*, pp. 264–5; Glantz, *Colossus Reborn*, pp. 537–9.

77. *RA/VO*, vol. 12(1), p. 234 [5 November]. The eight new armies set up on 5 November were the 10th, 26th, 28th, 39th, 58th, 59th, 60th and 61st.

78. *RA/VO*, vol. 5(1), pp. 242–3 [12 October].

79. Mawdsley, *December 1941*, pp. 150–1, 311, n. 48; Zetterling and Grandson, *Drive on Moscow*, pp. 242–3, 266–71; Dunn, *Stalin's Keys*, p. 81; Grylev, *Boevoi sostav*, vol. 1 [1941]; V. M. Petrenko, 'Dal'nevostochnyi front nakanune i v period Velikoi Otechestvennoi voiny 1941-1945 gg', *VIZh*, 2010, no. 11, pp. 20–25.

80. H. Hunter, *Soviet Transportation Policy* (Cambridge, MA: Harvard University Press, 1957), pp. 41–109, 365–6.

81. *VOV/VIO*, vol. 1, p. 229; *Skrytaia pravda voiny: 1941 goda: Neizvestnye dokumenty* (Moscow: Russkaia kniga, 1992), pp. 313–4.

82. The fullest biography of Zhukov is Roberts, *Stalin's General*. See also J. Erickson, 'Marshal Georgii Zhukov', in Carver, *War Lords*, pp. 244–59, and V. Anfilov, 'Georgy Konstantinovich Zhukov', in Shukman, *Stalin's Generals*, pp. 343–60. Colonel Anfilov had the opportunity to interview Zhukov in the 1960s, as did N. A. Svetlishin, who much later published *Krutye stupeni sud'by: Zhizn' i ratnye podvigi marshala G. K. Zhukova* (Khabarovsk: Khabarovskoe knizhnoe izdatel'stvo, 1992). For a typically iconoclastic treatment, see V. Suvorov, *Ten' pobedy* (Donetsk: Stalker, 2003). Zhukov's memoirs, *Vospominaniia i razmyshleniia*, are very useful; the three-volume edition published in 1990 during the Gorbachev era and showing earlier censorship cuts is the most important; the lengthy but less complete English-language version is G. Zhukov, *The Memoirs of Marshal Zhukov* (London: Jonathan Cape, 1971).

83. The smaller pictures in *Pravda* did not include Konev or his Kalinin Army Group commanders. They did include the future traitor General A. A. Vlasov, who commanded Zhukov's 20th Army.

84. Chuev, *Sto sorok besed s Molotovym*, p. 58.

85. *RA/VO*, vol. 5(1), p. 408.

86. M. Gallagher, *The Soviet History of World War II: Myths, Memories, Realities* (New York: Praeger, 1963), pp. 42, 527. This stress on counter-offensive was based on a bizarre 1946 letter of Stalin to a military theoretician, 'Otvet tov. Stalina na pis'mo tov. Razina', *Voprosy istoriii*, 1947, no. 2, pp. 3–7. One American historian attempted to explain the events of 1941 as an essentially defensive Russian strategy of this type, but his argument is not convincing: B. Fugate, *Operation Barbarossa: Strategy and Tactics on the Eastern Front, 1941* (Novato: Presidio, 1984).

87. Zhukov, *ViR*, vol. 2, pp. 230–2; Vasilevskii, *Delo*, vol. 1, p. 161. For a discussion of the development of the Moscow counter-offensive, see N. G. Andronikov, 'Rozhdenia zamysla', *VIA*, 2002, no. 1(25), pp. 22–60.

88. *RA/VO*, vol. 12(1), p. 234 [5 November].

89. On 24 November Golikov's 10th Army was ordered to Riazan', southwest of Moscow, where it would confront Guderian's 2nd Panzer Group (*RA/VO*, vol. 5(1), pp. 308–9). On 29 November Kuznetsov's 1st Shock Army was transferred to Zhukov from the Stavka reserve, and Vlasov's 20th Army was formed and put under Zhukov (*RA/VO*, vol. 5(1), pp. 312–13).

90. Zhukov, *ViR*, vol. 2, pp. 233–4; Svetlishin, *Krutye stupeni sud'by*, pp. 101–2. In another interview with Zhukov, this conversation was taken to refer to the October crisis (after the Battle of Viaz'ma–Briansk) rather than the November one; see Anfilov, 'Razgovor', p. 45. Perhaps Zhukov and Stalin had the same conversation twice. There is a different pro-Stalin account (*versiia*) which comes from a post-war conversation between Molotov and Marshal of Aviation Golovanov. According to this, Zhukov wanted to pull the headquarters of Western Army Group back to the safety of the town of Arzamas, well west of Moscow. Stalin told him to stand fast and die on the spot: 'Dig your graves' (Chuev, *140 besed*, p. 430f). Another version of this story has Stalin saying the same thing to an air force commissar; see Pechenkin, 'V osazhdennoi Moskve', p. 27

91. *RA/VO*, vol. 5(1), pp. 316–18 [1 December]; Vasilevskii, *Delo*, vol. 2, pp. 163–4.

92. *RA/VO*, vol. 4(1), p. 160; Zhukov, *ViR*, vol. 2, p. 245; Vasilevskii, *Delo*, vol. 1, p. 161. Zhukov maintained that the overall plan had been already agreed in person with Stalin and Shaposhnikov. In Moscow the central direction of the campaign was confused by the health of Marshal Shaposhnikov; at the end of November he had temporarily to be replaced by his deputy, Vasilevskii.

93. *Poteri*, p. 261; Stalin publicly admitted losses of 350,000 killed and 378,000 missing from 22 June to 6 November; see *OVOVSS*, p. 20 [6 November 1941].

94. Overmans, *Verluste*, p. 239; Halder, *Kriegstagebuch*, vol. 3, p. 306 [23 November 1941]. On 11 December Hitler publicly stated that Wehrmacht losses had been 162,000 killed, 563,000 wounded and 33,000 missing (Domarus, *Hitler: Reden*, p. 1800). Stalin had claimed on 6 November that 4,500,000 Germans had been killed, wounded and captured (*OVOVSS*, pp. 20, 39).

95. Domarus, *Hitler: Reden*, p. 1776.

96. Robert Citino rightly described the Battle of Moscow as a fundamental failure of the German 'way of war', committing the Third Reich to an unwinnable war of attrition: *German Way of War*, pp. 268–70, 290–305.

97. The relationship between the Battle of Moscow and the Japanese raid on Pearl Harbor is discussed in Mawdsley, *December 1941*.

Chapter 5

1. Stalin alluded to Napoleon in his Revolution Day speech of 1941, although he made the point that Hitler was a kitten compared to Napoleon's lion. Napoleon, Stalin pointed out, had fought against 'reaction' and based himself on 'progressive forces'; see Stalin, *OVOVSS*, pp. 31–2 [6 November].

2. In his 7 November 1941 speech, Stalin had argued that the cost of the war to Germany meant that Hitler's war effort would collapse after half a year or a year, perhaps in only a few months (Stalin, *OVOVSS*, p. 39); Stalin probably believed this.

3. Although issued over the names of Stalin and Vasilevskii (the Chief of the Operations Directorate of the General Staff), the style suggests it was mainly Stalin's work. An 'artillery offensive' involved massed artillery and close co-operation between artillery and infantry; for an April 1942 post-mortem by the head of artillery of Western Army Group, see *RA/VO*, vol. 4(1), pp. 348–56 [22 April].

4. *RA/VO*, vol. 5(2), pp. 33–5 [10 January 1941]; Zhukov, *ViR*, vol. 2, pp. 253–5; Vasilevskii, *Delo vsei zhizni*, vol. 1, pp. 167–8, 199–200. In January 1942 Zhukov seems to have been especially concerned about a diversion of forces to the Leningrad theatre.

5. The Briansk Army Group was disbanded after the battering it received in Operation TYPHOON. It was re-formed on 24 December 1941 from the three armies of the Western Army Group's left flank.

6. German accounts of the complex battles in front of Moscow, from early January 1942 up to the destruction of isolated Soviet pockets in April–June, are Ziemke and Bauer, *Moscow to Stalingrad*, pp. 88–104, 118–98; Klink in *GSWW*, vol. 4, pp. 725–34; and B. Wegner in *GSWW*, vol. 6, pp. 954–7. The Russian side is now covered in depth in S. Gerasimova, *The Rzhev Slaughterhouse: The Red Army's Forgotten 15-Month Campaign against Army Group Center, 1942-1943* (Solihull: Helion, 2013), pp. 26–73; see also B. I. Nevzorov in *VOV/VIO*, vol. 1, pp. 285–303.

7. *KTB OKW*, vol. 1, pp. 1084–5 [18 December].

8. *RA/VO*, vol. 5(2), p. 32 [7 January], 54–5 [19 January]. The 3rd and the 4th Shock Armies were led by commanders in whom Stalin and Shaposhnikov had confidence, Generals Purkaev and Eremenko.

9. Ziemke and Bauer, *Moscow to Stalingrad*, pp. 122–3. The Alcázar was a fortified palace in Toledo, southwest of Madrid. Having failed to take the city of Toledo at the start of the uprising in July 1936, the pro-Franco troops withdrew into the fortress. They were besieged by Republican forces and relieved by a Nationalist column in late September.

10. For planning details, see *RA/VO*, vol. 5(1), pp. 196–9 [29 December 1941].

11. C. D'Este, 'Model', in Barnett, *Hitler's Generals*, pp. 319–33.

12. War diary of Army Group North, cited in Ziemke and Bauer, *Moscow to Stalingrad*, p. 172.

13. This order to shift to defence has evidently not been published as a document. See, however, *Velikaia Otechestvennaia voina, 1941–1945: Entsiklopediia* (Moscow: Sovetskaia entsiklopediia, 1985), p. 612.

14. For the saga of Demiansk, see Ziemke and Bauer, *Moscow to Stalingrad*, pp. 153–5, 186–98, 254–5, and Klink in *GSWW*, vol.4, pp. 734–51. R. Forczyk, *Demyansk 1942-43: The Frozen Fortress* (Oxford: Osprey, 2012), outlines events with good maps and illustrations.

15. The others were awarded for Narvik (1940), the Crimea (1942) and the Kuban' bridgehead (1943). An arm shield was designed for Stalingrad, but never awarded.

16. *Poteri*, p. 311.

17. For details of the ambitious Soviet plan, see *SDVG*, vol. 2, p. 33 [19 January]; *RA/VO*, vol. 5(2), pp. 75 [28 January], 91 [10 February 1942], 114 [2 March 1942], 495–6 [26 January], 496–8 [31 January], 501–2 [8 February].

18. V. A. Zolotarev et al. (eds), *G. K. Zhukov v bitve pod Moskvoi: Sbornik dokumentov* (Moscow: Mosgorarkhiv, 1994), p. 189; *Poteri*, p. 277.

19. *RA/VO*, vol. 4(1), p. 280; Zhukov, *ViR*, vol. 2, p. 267.

20. When this big central encirclement was considered again in early 1943, an overall Stavka co-ordinator was put in place, in the person of Vasilevskii. Even this did not guarantee success, and the operation misfired; see Chapter 9.

21. *RA/VO*, vol. 4(1), p. 275 [29 January 1942]. Losses cited here by Zhukov would include troops who were wounded and sick, not just 'permanent' losses.

22. *Poteri*, pp. 276, 311.

23. Army Group Centre received only 180,000 reinforcements from 1 December 1941 to 31 March 1942 (Reinhardt, *Moscow*, p. 317). By the spring, Axis replacements and reinforcement were being concentrated in the southern theatre, ready for the 1942 offensive.

24. See R. Lamb, 'Kluge', in Barnett, *Hitler's Generals*, pp. 395–409.

25. For military operations around Leningrad in the winter of 1941–2, see Glantz, *Battle of Leningrad*, pp. 87–198, and B. I. Nevzorov in *VOV/VIO*, vol. 1, pp. 304–6. On the German side there are Klink in *GSWW*, vol. 4, pp. 734–51, and Ziemke and Bauer, *Moscow to Stalingrad*, pp. 143–55, 186–98.

26. *RA/VO*, vol. 5(1), p. 259 [23 October].

27. For the fighting in the northern theatre, see Ziemke and Bauer, *Moscow to Stalingrad*, pp. 143–55, 186–98.

28. *VOV/VIO*, vol. 1, p. 304.

29. *VOV/VIO*, vol. 1, p. 304.

30. G. Jukes, 'Meretskov', in H. Shukman (ed.), *Stalin's Generals* (London: Weidenfeld and Nicolson, 1993), pp. 127–34.

31. For the terrible and long-forgotten battles on the Volkhov around Miasnoi Bor and in the so-called 'valley of death', see V. I. Gavrilov, *'Dolina smerti': Tragediia i podvig 2-i udarnoi*

armii (Moscow: IRI RAN, 1999), and V. I. Gavrilov, 'V Miasnom Boru, v "doline smerti"', *OI*, 2004, no. 3, pp. 3–13.

32. *RA/VO*, vol. 9, pp. 111–2 [1 April 1942]. The Stavka representative (*predstavitel'*) was sent out by Stalin to 'supervise' and advise local commanders in major operations. This important institution is discussed in Chapter 7.

33. The previous commander of the 2nd Shock Army, General N. K. Klykov, had been hospitalized due to illness.

34. *Poteri*, p. 311.

35. *VOV/VIO*, vol. 1, p. 328.

36. Details regarding Khozin's dismissal, including his bad relations with his chief commissar, may be found in Bidlack and Lomagin, *Leningrad Blockade*, pp. 144–9. For losses in this operation, see *Poteri*, p. 311. General Vlasov's later collaboration with the Germans is discussed in Chapter 8.

37. The classic account by the journalist Harrison Salisbury remains valuable: *The 900 Days: The Siege of Leningrad* (London: Secker and Warburg, 1969). Glantz, *Battle for Leningrad*, covers military aspects. The new documents in Bidlack and Lomagin, *Leningrad Blockade*, are important, especially regarding the maintenance of state control over the population. C. Merridale, *Night of Stone: Death and Memory in Russia* (London: Granta Books, 2000), provides a moving account of the human losses.

38. A. R. Dzeniskevich (ed.), *Leningrad v osade: Sbornik dokumentov o geroicheskoi oborone Leningrada v gody Velikoi Otechestvennoi voiny, 1941–1944* (St Petersburg: Liki Rossii, 1995), p. 573.

39. Dzeniskevich, *Leningrad*, pp. 316–7, 339, 573–4, 593, n. 77.

40. *Poteri*, pp. 338, 343.

41. Dzeniskevich, *Leningrad*, pp. 277, 301–2, 350–1, 560, n. 59.

42. On this, see *GSWW*, vol. 4, pp. 1169–72.

43. Dzeniskevich, *Leningrad*, pp. 441–3.

44. Dzeniskevich, *Leningrad*, pp. 160–1, 313, 348.

45. For outlines of the campaign in the Crimea in 1941–2 from the German perspective, see: Ziemke and Bauer, *Moscow to Stalingrad*, pp. 105–17, 261–9; Klink in *GSWW*, vol. 4, pp. 627–31, 758–60; and Wegner in *GSWW*, vol. 6, pp. 930–41. The important German air operations are covered in detail in J. Hayward, *Stopped at Stalingrad: The Luftwaffe and Hitler's Defeat in the East, 1942-1943* (Lawrence: University Press of Kansas, 1998), pp. 27–119. For the Russian perspective, see Nevzorov in *VOV/VIO*, vol. 1, pp. 310–14, and P. P. Chevela in *VOV/VIO*, vol. 1, pp. 330–5. R. Forczyk, *Sevastopol 1942: Von Manstein's Triumph* (Oxford: Osprey, 2008), provides maps and other details.

46. A recent biography is M. Melvin, *Manstein: Hitler's Greatest General* (London: Weidenfeld and Nicolson, 2010). Manstein's influential and self-justifying memoirs, *Verlorene Siege* (Bonn: Athenäum-Verlag, [1955] 1958), were translated in an abbreviated form as *Lost Victories* (Novato: Presidio, [1958] 1994).

47. Arad, *Holocaust*, pp. 202–11.

48. *Poteri*, p. 310; *RA/VO*, vol. 2(2), pp. 162–3. Kulik's story is extraordinary. He was destined for an even more spectacular fall: he was arrested in 1947 and secretly executed in 1950. Bitter at his wartime disgrace, Kulik had evidently made foolhardy political comments. He was posthumously exonerated by an army investigation in 1957, on the grounds that no one could have saved Kerch'. He was probably a drunkard and an ignoramus, but at Kerch' he

had been 'parachuted' into an impossible situation not of his making; see the documents in 'Iz istorii Velikoi otechestvennoi voiny', *ITsK*, 1991, no. 8, pp. 197–221.

49. *SDVG*, vol. 1, p. 390; E. Ziemke, *Stalingrad to Berlin*, p. 115, n. 26.

50. *RA/VO*, vol. 5(2), pp. 28–9 [1 January], 481 [1 January].

51. On the role of Mekhlis in the Crimea, see Iu. V. Rubtsov, *Alter ego Stalina (stranitsy politicheskoi biografii L. Z. Mekhlisa)* (Moscow: Zvonnitsa-MG, 1999), pp. 201–28. Mekhlis was unusual in that as a party official he had been given the assignment as a Stavka 'representative'; this post was usually held by a professional Red Army man. It will be recalled that Voroshilov had turned down a similar Stavka 'representative' post in the Leningrad area.

52. Muller, *German Air War in Russia*, pp. 69, 219, argues that the peak use of Luftwaffe ground support for the whole war was in the Crimea in 1942.

53. *RA/VO*, vol. 5(2), p. 205 [15 May].

54. *Poteri*, p. 311; *GSWW*, vol. 6, p. 932; Zhukov, *ViR*, vol. 2, p. 279. General Kozlov survived in Red Army service, but he was assigned to relatively junior posts.

55. *GSWW*, vol. 6, p. 939.

56. This is the view of Wegner in *GSWW*, vol. 6, pp. 940–1.

57. *Poteri*, p. 310–11.

58. Stalin, *OVOVSS*, p. 44 [23 February 1942]; Zhukov, *ViR*, vol. 2, p. 277.

59. Zhukov, *ViR*, vol. 2, p. 255.

60. Zhukov, *ViR*, vol. 2, p. 277; Vasilevskii, *Delo vsei zhizni*, vol. 2, p. 206.

61. On the Battle of Khar'kov, see D. Glantz, *Kharkov 1942: Anatomy of a Military Disaster* (Shepperton: Ian Allan, 1998); this is further developed in D. Glantz and J. House, *To the Gates of Stalingrad: Soviet-German Combat Operations, April-August 1942* (Lawrence, KS: University Press of Kansas, 2009), pp. 33–83. For an extended Russian account, see S. A. Gabov et al., 'Vesnoi sorok vtorogo pod Khar'kovom', *VIA*, 2002, no. 5(29), no. 9(33); P. P. Chevela provides an outline in *VOV/VIO*, vol. 1, pp. 335–8. The German side is covered by B. Wegner in *GSWW*, vol. 6, pp. 942–53, and Ziemke and Bauer, *Moscow to Stalingrad*, pp. 269–82. R. Forczyk, *Kharkov: The Wehrmacht Strikes Back* (Oxford: Osprey, 2013), provides maps and other details.

62. *Poteri*, p. 311; *KTB OKW*, vol. 2(1), pp. 2, 391; *GSWW*, vol. 6, p. 949. As elsewhere, there are discrepancies. Compared to the German claim of 1,200 panzers captured, Russian sources state that only 1,134 tanks were deployed, and not all of them had been in the Barvenkovo pocket.

63. Khrushchev, 'O kul'te lichnostu', pp. 149–50. For the definitive published version of Khrushchev's account, see 'Memuary', *VI*, 1990, no. 11, pp. 68–94

64. Glantz, *Kharkov 1942*, pp. 111–2, 246.

65. Georgi Dimitrov, the Comintern leader, received a high-level briefing from Red Army intelligence in early May 1942. He was told there were three possible directions for a German offensive: '(1) against Moscow; (2) between Moscow and Leningrad; and (3) to the south: Rostov and the Caucasus' (Dimitrov, *Diary*, pp. 215–6 [7 May]). The order in which the directions were listed suggests that Moscow was being assessed as the most likely objective.

British Intelligence, in contrast, expected the main German effort to come in the south. It is not clear whether London communicated this threat assessment to Moscow (Hinsley,

British Intelligence, vol. 2, p. 97). Also unclear is the advance intelligence that the Germans had of the projected Soviet attack towards Khar'kov.

The 1998 Russian official history attaches importance to the German capture of General A. G. Samokhin, commander-designate of the 48th Army, whose courier plane landed by mistake at a German airfield (*VOV/VIO*, vol. 1, p. 336). This is not, however, mentioned as a factor by Glantz in *Kharkov*. Released from a German POW camp, Samokhin was imprisoned in the USSR from 1945 to 1953. He survived and was eventually rehabilitated (Maslov, *Captured Soviet Generals*, pp. 102–4, 111, n. 134).

66. A. Hitler, *Hitler's Table Talk, 1941–1944* (London: Weidenfeld & Nicolson, 1953), p. 257 [27 January 1942]; Stalin, *OVOVSS*, p. 46 [23 February 1942].

67. *Poteri*, pp. 277, 310–11. The Moscow battle was probably more immediately lethal to the Red Army rank and file, as a higher proportion of 'permanent losses' at Khar'kov and in the Crimea were presumably POWs.

68. *Poteri*, p. 261. Soviet losses were also lower than they had been in 1941, and lower than they would be in the second half of 1942. However, by comparison, Soviet losses in the second quarter of 1943 would be relatively low.

69. Overmans, *Verluste*, p. 277.

70. Domarus, *Hitler: Reden*, p. 1850 [15 March 1942]; see also p. 1832 [30 January 1942]. Strictly speaking, a hecatomb was a *place* of great sacrifice.

71. *Poteri*, pp. 474–5. Another figure given for total Soviet tanks on the Soviet–German front in May 1942 is 3,900 (Vasilevskii, *Delo*, vol. 1, p. 206); this may refer to tanks in front-line units.

Chapter 6

1. *Hitlers Weisungen*, pp. 84, 184. Wegner outlines overall German plans for 1942 in *GSWW*, vol. 6, pp. 843–63.

2. For the operations in front of Moscow from late July to the end of December 1942: Gerasimova, *Rzhev Slaughterhouse*, pp. 74–125; Glantz, *Zhukov's Greatest Defeat*; D. Glantz, *After Stalingrad: The Red Army's Winter Offensive 1942-1943* (Solihull: Helion, 2009), pp. 38–91. Wegner in GSWW, vol. 6, pp. 954–7, 1001–5, 1193–5, and Ziemke and Bauer, *Moscow to Stalingrad*, pp. 328–30, 398–407, provide the German perspective.

3. Kudriashov, *Voina*, p. 218 [14 February 1943]. These figures are based on a report to Stalin from General E. A. Shchadenko, head of the Red Army personnel directorate. They exclude reinforcements raised *within* the individual army groups, that is from their own reserve units and hospitals.

4. Stalin, *OVOVSS*, pp. 65–6; A. A. Danilevich and A.S. Kniaz'kov in *VOV/VIO*, vol. 2, p. 27. Stalin, to be sure, would not give away strategic secrets. Arguably, the point of his speech was to justify the activity of the Red Army; whatever the setbacks in the south, the centre had held firm. Zhukov, for his part, maintained that Stalin saw Red Army operations in the central theatre as a diversion, to 'disorient' the Germans (*ViR*, vol. 2, p. 322).

5. Operation MARS is examined in detail in Glantz, *Zhukov's Greatest Defeat*, and Gerasimova, *Rzhev Slaughterhouse*, pp. 104–25. M. A. Gareev, 'Operatsiia "Mars" i sovremennye "marsiane": K 60-letiiu okonchaniia srazhenii na rzhevsko-viazemskoi zemle', *VIZh*, 2003, no. 10, pp. 17–21, criticized Glantz and argued that MARS was a

diversion. There were never sufficient munitions, fuel and supplies, Gareev asserted, to mount full-scale attacks in both the Stalingrad and Moscow sectors. Gareev was both an eminent military historian and a participant in Operation MARS. See also V. V. Gurkin, '"Mars" v orbite "Urana" i "Saturna": O vtoroi Rzhevsko-Sychevskoi nastupatel'noi operatsii 1942 goda', *VIZh*, 2000, no. 4, pp. 14–19.

6. *Poteri*, p. 312; Glantz, *Zhukov's Greatest Defeat*, pp. 20, 24, 383, n. 26. In February 1943, after the Germans surrendered at Stalingrad, the Stavka certainly did have in mind – and did issue directives for – an operation even larger in scale than the speculative Operation JUPITER. This abortive operation will be discussed in Chapter 9.

7. *RA/VO*, vol. 5(3), p. 81 [27 February].

8. On Demiansk, see: Wegner in *GSWW*, vol. 6, pp. 997–8, 1201–5; N. I. Kobrin and V. I. Fesenko in *VOV/VIO*, vol. 2, pp. 224–9; Glantz, *After Stalingrad*, pp. 92–107. The background is provided in Chapter 5.

9. Kobrin and Fesenko in *VOV/VIO*, vol. 2, p. 229.

10. *VOV/VIO*, vol. 2, pp. 212–23.

11. Glantz, *Stalingrad to Berlin*, pp. 115–7; Wegner in *GSWW*, vol. 6, pp. 1199–1200; Gerasimova, *Rzhev Slaughterhouse*, pp. 126–48; Reemtsma, *Verbrechen der Wehrmacht*, pp. 386–7; *VOV/VIO*, vol. 2, p. 336.

12. When plans for Operation BLUE fell into Soviet hands, the Germans renamed the overall operation BRAUNSCHWEIG (BRUNSWICK); they also renamed its components. For simplicity's sake the original code names will be used here.

    For the whole 1942 campaign in the south, from late June, the latest and fullest sources are the monumental volumes of the 'Stalingrad Trilogy', written by David Glantz with Jonathan House, *To the Gates of Stalingrad* (2009), *Armageddon at Stalingrad* (2009), and *Endgame at Stalingrad* (2 parts, 2014). On the German side, see Wegner in *GSWW*, vol. 6, pp. 843–1215, and Glantz and Bauer, *Moscow to Stalingrad*, pp. 309–65, 382–97, 432–502. Russian-language sources include A. M. Samsonov, *Stalingradskaia bitva*, 4th edn (Moscow: Nauka, [1960] 1989); P. P. Chevala in *VOV/VIO*, vol.1, pp. 319–84; and B. P. Frolov in *VOV/VIO*, vol. 2, pp. 46–107.

13. *Hitlers Weisungen*, pp. 196–200 [23 July].

14. Khrushchev maintained that Stalin considered General Vlasov for the post as commander of Stalingrad Army Group ('Memuary', *VI*, 1990, no. 11, p. 91). This seems unlikely, as Vlasov was captured by the Germans on 12 July, and Eremenko was summoned to the Kremlin to be given his appointment only on 1 August.

15. For the campaign in the North Caucasus, see Glantz and House, *To the Gates of Stalingrad*, pp. 396–453, and D. Glantz and J. House, *Armageddon in Stalingrad, September – November 1942* (Lawrence, KS: University Press of Kansas, 2009), pp. 544–607. The German side is covered by Wegner in *GSWW*, vol. 6, pp. 1022–48; Ziemke and Bauer, *Moscow to Stalingrad*, pp. 366–81, 452–4; and W. Tieke, *The Caucasus and the Oil: The German-Soviet War in the Caucasus 1942/3* (Winnipeg: Fedorowicz, 1995).

16. *VOV/VIO*, vol. 2, p. 27.

17. This important command crisis, which included the dismissal of both List (on 10 September) and General Halder, Chief of the Army General Staff (on 24 September), is discussed by Wegner in *GSWW*, vol. 6, pp. 1048–59. List played no further part in the fighting; after the war he would be imprisoned for war crimes committed during his time in the Balkans in 1941.

18. The effect of this raid has been greatly exaggerated. Richard Overy has recently confirmed that deaths were a tenth of the 40,000 commonly given in both Soviet-era and uncritical

Western accounts: *The Bombing War: Europe, 1939-45* (London: Allen Lane, 2013), pp. 210–12. See also the report in A. A. Gurov et al. (eds). *Stalingrad 1942–1943: Stalingradskaia bitva v dokumentakh* (Moscow: Biblioteka, 1995), p. 395.

19. Five of the Stalingrad armies would become the 'guards armies' in 1943: the 21st became 6th Guards, the 24th became the 4th Guards, the 62nd became the 8th Guards, the 64th became the 7th Guards and the 66th became the 5th Guards.

20. For the great encirclement and siege of the German 6th Army in Stalingrad, see D. Glantz and J. House, *Endgame at Stalingrad*, 2 vols (Lawrence, KS: University Press of Kansas, 2014). German accounts include Wegner in GSWW, vol. 6, pp. 1100–172.

21. The Soviet southern offensives in early 1943, leading up to the third Battle of Khar'kov in March, will be dealt with in Chapter 9.

22. For a good discussion of the size of German losses, see A. Beevor, *Stalingrad: The Fateful Siege, 1942–43* (New York: Viking, 1999), pp. 439–40.

23. This Achilles' heel of the German command system is discussed in Megargee, *Inside Hitler's High Command*, p. 189.

24. Wegner in *GSWW*, vol. 6, pp. 977–8.

25. On Hitler's allies in 1941-2, see: R. DiNardo, *Germany and the Axis Powers: From Coalition to Collapse* (Lawrence: University Press of Kansas, 2005); J. Förster in *GSWW*, vol. 4, pp. 386–428, 1021–48; and Wegner in *GSWW*, vol. 6, pp. 904–28.

26. *SDVG*, vol. 2, p. 309 [21 September 1942].

27. *Poteri*, p. 514.

28. From the point of view of strategic planning, Manstein's preliminary campaign in the Crimea was a waste of resources. It delayed the start of Operation BLUE. If Rostov and the North Caucasus were taken, Sevastopol' would 'wither on the vine'. Meanwhile, besieged Sevastopol' was no threat to Army Group South. In another act of Nazi strategic foolhardiness, the forces of the 11th Army which had reduced Sevastopol' were in late July 1942 ordered away from south Russia to the Leningrad front and to France.

29. On the critical decision to split the southern offensive, see Wegner in *GSWW*, vol. 6, pp. 980–91. Glantz and House argue convincingly that the July battles in the Don bend, although they seized much territory, caused heavy attrition to front-line German divisions, and that Hitler and the German High Command did not pay attention to this (*To the Gates of Stalingrad*, pp. 267–8, 485–6).

30. This dispersal of air strength is a major point in Hayward, *Stopped at Stalingrad*, pp. 150–51, 313–5.

31. On the other hand a deep thrust into the Caucasus would always have been exceptionally foolhardy, even for Hitler, if powerful Soviet armies had remained in the southeast around Stalingrad. At the same time, there was little strategic point in taking Stalingrad on its own.

32. *KTB OKW*, vol. 2(2), pp. 1305–7 (6, 12 November 1942); on this crucial issue of faulty German intelligence assessments, see *GSWW*, vol. 6, pp. 882–903, 1118–23.

33. Domarus, *Hitler: Reden*, pp. 1914, 1916 [30 September], 1937–8 [8 November].

34. Glantz and House suggest that Paulus could probably have extracted about half his forces had the attempt been made, at least up until the middle of December (*Endgame*, vol. 2, pp. 386, 596).

35. For a thoughtful discussion of the relative role of Paulus, Manstein and Seydlitz (the commander of 51st Corps) in the final catastrophe – although a discussion that largely ignores the Red Army – see J. Wieder and H. Graf von Einsiedel (eds), *Stalingrad: Memories and Reassessments* (London: Arms and Armour, 1995). Glantz and House

strongly criticize Manstein for opposing the idea of a breakout, at a time when Paulus and his corps commanders were in favour of attempting such an action (*Armageddon*, vol. 3.2, pp. 532–3).

36. On the disastrous Luftwaffe airlift and the 'air blockade' by the Red Army Air Force, see: Hayward, *Stopped at Stalingrad*, pp. 251–310; Muller, *German Air War*, pp. 92–100; and Hardesty and Grinberg, *Red Phoenix*, pp. 134–53.

37. H. Heiber (ed.), *Hitlers Lagebesprechungen: Die Protokollfragmente seiner militärischen Konferenzen 1942–1945* (Stuttgart: Deutsche Verlags-Anstalt, 1962), p. 84 [12 December].

38. *VOV/VIO*, vol. 1, pp. 505–7, gives the Russian text of Order No. 227; it was read to the troops rather than issued as a printed order, and it was not reprinted in Russia until 1988. Hill, *Great Patriotic War*, pp. 100–2, provides an English translation. For discussion, see: M. A. Gareev, *Neodnoznachnye stranitsy voiny* (Moscow: RFM, 1995), p. 157; *RA/VO*, vol. 6, p. 330, n. 40; Vasilevskii, *Delo*, vol. 1, pp. 230–2; Merridale, *Ivan's War*, pp. 134–9; and Reese, *Why Stalin's Soldiers Fought*, pp. 162–5.

39. *Pravda*, 22 June 1942, p. 1; *RA/VO*, vol. 6, pp. 133–4 [2 May], 154–5 [2 August 1942].

40. This is a point stressed by Glantz and House in *To the Gates*, pp. 481, 485–6.

41. Prisoner numbers require a degree of estimation. For the calculations of Glantz and House, see *To the Gates*, pp. 204, 539, n. 59, p. 540, n. 61. On the other hand the Russian government produced a figure in the 1990s of 1,339,000 Soviet POWs in 1942 – compared to 2,000,000 in six months of 1941 (V. K. Luzherenko in *VOV/VIO*, vol. 4, p. 172). In the middle of July the Germans publicly claimed 88,000 POWs captured in the first phase of Operation BLAU (Philippi and Heim, *Feldzug gegen Sowjetrußland*, pp. 137). The German 6th Army alone took another 57,000 prisoners between 23 July and 10 August (*GSWW*, vol. 6, p. 1065). Official Russian figures for the period of the fighting in the south from 28 June to 24 July are 371,000 for killed, missing and captured, compared to 198,000 injured. This suggests a high rate of capture (or desertion), as normally the number of soldiers killed in action would have been considerably less than the number injured. For 17 July to 18 November, the figures are 324,000 killed, missing and captured, and 320,000 injured (*Poteri*, 278–9).

42. Glantz and House, *To the Gates*, p. 485.

43. *Poteri*, pp. 474–5.

44. Dunn, *Stalin's Keys*, provides an analysis of this 'third generation' of mobilization in 1942 (pp. 95–125). For armour, see Glantz and House, *To the Gates*, pp. 33–7, 486.

45. In August the Americans passed information to Stalin that there would be no Japanese operation against the Soviet Far East until 1943 at the earliest: A. A. Gromyko et al. (eds), *Perepiska Predsedatelia Soveta Ministrov SSSR s prezidentami SShA i prem'er-ministrami Velikobritanii vo vremia Velikoi Otechestvennoi voiny, 1941–1945 gg.*, 2 vols (Moscow: Politizdat, 1986), vol. 2, p. 25 [5 August 1942]. It is not yet known whether this had any impact on Soviet force movements.

46. This was a second batch of Soviet reserve armies. The first batch had been set up from October 1941 after the defeat at Viaz'ma–Briansk.

47. Ziemke and Bauer, *Moscow to Stalingrad*, p. 511; Wegner in *GSWW*, vol. 6, pp. 970–1; Samsonov, *Stalingradskaia bitva*, p. 69.
   Marshal Vasilevskii made no claim for introducing a new strategy in his memoirs (*Delo*, vol. 1, pp. 216–28). The fullest biography of Timoshenko also makes no such assertion; it simply notes that 'the forces of the Southwestern Army Group were forced to begin a retreat' and implies that the most important factor was the military situation in the aftermath of the Khar'kov catastrophe (Portugal'skii, *Timoshenko*, pp. 248–9). Erickson was more

non-committal (*The Road to Stalingrad*, p. 360), as are Glantz and House (*When Titans Clashed*, pp. 120, 343, n. 15).

48. Glantz and House, *To the Gates*, p. 485.

49. *Poteri*, p. 278.

50. See J. Erickson, 'Rodion Yakovlevich Malinovsky', in Shukman, *Stalin's Generals*, pp. 117–24. Malinovskii had served as a machine-gunner in the Russian expeditionary forces in France in 1916–17 and returned to Russia via White territory, biographical events which would have aroused suspicion in the 1930s. His survival of the purges and his rise to high command posts may have come from links with Timoshenko and the cavalry; he was chief of staff of Timoshenko's cavalry corps in the mid-1930s. On Stalin's alleged wartime mistrust of Malinovskii, see N. S. Khrushchev, 'Memuary', *VI*, 1990, no. 11, p. 93, 1991, no. 1, pp. 77–8, 90–3.

51. *Poteri*, pp. 278, 484–5.

52. After the fall of Bataisk near Rostov, Budennyi made the strategically reasonable proposal on 27 July to withdraw to the mountains and the Terek and conduct a mobile defence (*RA/VO*, vol. 5(2), pp. 328–30, 530–2 [27 July]). He was not allowed to do this.

53. G. Jukes, 'Alexander Mikhailovich Vasilevsky', in Shukman (ed.), *Stalin's Generals*, pp. 275–85; O. A. Rzheshevskii and V. V. Sukhodeev, 'Marshal A. M. Vasilevskii i delo vsei ego zhizni', *NNI*, 2005, no. 3, pp. 3–16; S. E. Lazaev, 'Sud'ba "marshal'skogo kursa" Akademii General'nogo shtaba', *VI*, 2009, no. 12, pp. 107–114.

    A proper biography of Vasilevskii is badly needed; among Stalin's commanders, he was second in importance only to Zhukov. There is no edition of Vasilevskii's memoirs, *Delo vsei zhizni*, that is as candid as the late editions of Zhukov's memoirs from the Gorbachev era. The interviews with the Marshal conducted in the 1960s and 1970s and printed in Simonov, *Glazami cheloveka moega pokoleniia*, pp. 390–421, and Kumanev, *Riadom so Stalinym*, pp. 223–46, are important.

54. Vasilevskii had broken off all contact with his 'class enemy' father; it was apparently only on Stalin's prompting that he got in touch with him again during the war (Vasilevskii, *Delo*, vol. 1, pp. 104–5).

55. Zhukov, *ViR*, vol. 2, pp. 352–3; Khrushchev, 'Memuary', *VI*, 1991, no. 1, pp. 79–82.

56. The fighting in Stalingrad itself was also highly unusual. Static fronts and trench warfare were a common feature of the Eastern Front, but not prolonged street fighting. The skills of urban warfare developed in the ruins of Stalingrad were later exploited in urban battles two and a half years later, in Budapest and Berlin.

57. Zhukov, *ViR*, vol. 2, pp. 302, 304.

58. Glantz and House, *Endgame*, vol. 1, p. 22 ('patently incorrect'), vol. 2, p. 587. Eremenko's original claim was published in his memoir *Stalingrad: Zapiski komanduiushchego frontom* (Moscow: Voenizdat, 1961), pp. 325–6. The memorandum from Eremenko and Khrushchev to Stalin can be found in *SDVG*, vol. 2, pp. 532–4 [9 October]. No overall planning document of the type mentioned by Zhukov has been found in the archives. What exists are separate documents issued in November for individual army groups (Gurov, *Stalingrad 1942–1943*, pp. 210–16).

    The Zhukov–Eremenko conflict was coloured by the political situation under Nikita Khrushchev, who was the dominant leader of the USSR from 1957 to 1964, and who had sacked Zhukov as Minister of Defence in 1957. Khrushchev had worked with Eremenko – as his political commissar – in the Stalingrad Army Group and shared any credit gained by him. Zhukov and Vasilevskii were only able to publish their memoirs after Khrushchev was removed from power.

59. Vasilevskii, *Delo*, vol. 2, pp. 241–2; S. I. Isaev, 'Vekhi frontovogo puti: Khronika deiatel'nosti Marshala Sovetskogo Soiuza G. K. Zhukova v period Velikoi Otechestvennoi voiny 1941-1945 gg.', *VIZh*, 1991, no. 10, p. 24; *VOV/VIO*, vol. 2, pp. 36, 39, 49–50; Roberts, *Stalin's General*, pp. 167–9. Korotkov, 'Posetiteli', is the source for Stalin's reception register (*zhurnal zapisi*), a notebook kept in his office (*kabinet*) in the Kremlin; the entries for September 1942 were published in *IA*, 1996, no. 3, pp. 35–9. If the diary recorded *all* the Soviet dictator's activities, he would seem have led a remarkably unhectic life. What is listed are meetings with groups of people in his Kremlin office for 3–4 hours a day (usually late in the evening), and there is nothing at all listed for 10–12 (Thursday to Saturday) or 14–16 September (Monday to Wednesday). The meeting with Zhukov and Vasilevskii on the 12th could have gone unrecorded, or Stalin could have met the two generals somewhere other than in his *kabinet*.

   In their account of at least one important meeting between Stalin and his generals, on 28–29 October 1944, Glantz and House accept that the event took place, although there is no record of such a meeting in the reception register (*When Titans Clashed*, p. 237; Korotkov, 'Posetiteli', *IA*, 1996, no. 4, p. 87).

60. Glantz and House, *Endgame*, vol. 2, p. 587.

61. Ziemke, *Stalingrad to Berlin*, p. 53.

62. *Stalingrad 1942–1943*, pp. 210–16 (URANUS) [November 1942]; *RA/VO*, vol. 5(2), pp. 394, 543–4 [19 September 1942] (VENUS); Glantz, *Defeat*, p. 20 (MARS). In 1943 and 1944, different kinds of names were sometimes used, notably those of great Tsarist generals – KUTUZOV, RUMIANTSEV and BAGRATION.

63. An example of this is the major work of Ziemke (*Stalingrad to Berlin*, p. 80). The thrust of Wegner's conclusions about the Battle of Stalingrad in *GSWW*, vol. 6, pp. 1169–72, is similar.

64. For operations around Leningrad in the autumn and winter of 1942, see Glantz, *Battle for Leningrad*, pp. 189–232. The German side is covered by: Wegner in *GSWW*, vol. 6, pp. 991–1001, with developments in Finland on pp. 916–23; Ziemke and Bauer, *Moscow to Stalingrad*, pp. 408–421; and Ziemke, *Stalingrad to Berlin*, pp. 111–2. For the Russians, see Kobrin and Fesenko in *VOV/VIO*, vol. 2, pp. 195–212.

65. *Hitlers Weisungen*, p. 184 [5 April 1942].

66. Iu. A. Siakov, 'Siniavinskaia operatsiia sovetskikh voisk 1942 goda', *VI*, 2008, no. 6, pp. 83–93.

67. *Hitlers Weisungen*, pp. 191–3 [21 July].

68. *Poteri*, pp. 282, 485.

69. Stalin, *OVOVSS*, p. 65. This was, even by Stalin's standards, a repetitive speech. He cited a captured German map which gave objectives for a rapid and very deep advance into the Don–Volga triangle along two parallel axes running east and then north: Voronezh–Borisoglebsk–Penza–Arzamas (i.e. in the general direction of Gor'kii) and Stalingrad–Saratov–Kuibyshev (i.e. up the Volga).

70. Stalin, *OVOVSS*, p. 66 [6 November].

71. Overmans, *Verluste*, p. 277.

Chapter 7

1. Stalin, *OVOVSS*, p. 90 [23 February].

2. Domarus, *Hitler: Reden*, p. 1977 [30 January 1943]; *Goebbels Reden 1932–1945*, vol. 2, pp. 172–208 [18 February 1943]; Stalin, *OVOVSS*, p. 98 [1 May].

3 Stalin, *OVOVSS*, pp. 90–1 [23 February]. Stalin did not mention Lend-Lease supplies from the United States and Britain in this speech.

4 Domarus, *Hitler: Reden*, p. 1977 [30 January 1943]; *Goebbels Reden*, vol. 2, p. 184 (18 February 1943).

5 There was an important debate among economic historians on this. Alan Milward's argument in *The German Economy at War* (London: Athlone Press, 1965), that Germany had a 'Blitzkrieg' (civilian-oriented) economy until 1942, and only really organized for total war in 1944, is not supported by recent interpretations. The German economic war effort in the first part of the war was discussed in Chapter 2. For the later years, see: Overy, *War and Economy*; Tooze, *Wages of Destruction*, pp. 486–676; and R.-D. Müller in *GSWW*, vol. 5.2, pp. 293–831.

6 On the Soviet war economy, see M. Harrison, *Accounting for War: Soviet Production, Employment, and the Defence Burden, 1940-1945* (Cambridge: Cambridge University Press, 1996).

7 M. Harrison (ed.), *The Economics of World War II* (Cambridge: Cambridge University Press, 1998), pp. 273, 283.

8 On the Soviet and German food supply systems, see: Collingham, *Taste of War*, pp. 155–65, 219–27, 317–83. Also Tooze, *Wages of Destruction*, pp. 538–49. Contrary to expectations, the Third Reich received more food imports from occupied western Europe than from occupied Soviet territory.

9 G. A. Kumanev in *VOV/VIO*, vol. 2, p. 364, vol. 3, p. 337; A. S. Iakushevskii in *VOV/VIO*, vol. 4, pp. 88, 100.

10 Harrison, *Economics of World War II*, p. 7. GDP is in international dollars and 1990 prices. These figures were intended by the author to make possible broad comparisons, and there are many caveats to be attached to them. They indicate that the USSR's 1942 share of this Allied (pre-war) GDP, after wartime losses of Soviet territory, was about $225,000,000, an eighth of the total for the Grand Alliance. Elsewhere, Harrison estimated that in 1944, Allied GNP was four times that of the Axis: Harrison, *Accounting for War*, p. 123.

11 There is a large literature on the politics and diplomacy of Lend-Lease: J. Beaumont, *Comrades in Arms: British Aid to Russia, 1941–1945* (London: Davis-Poynter, 1980); G. Herring, *Aid to Russia, 1941–1946: Strategy, Diplomacy, and the Origins of the Cold War* (New York: Columbia University Press, 1973); R. Jones, *The Roads to Russia: United States Lend-Lease to the Soviet Union* (Norman, OK: University of Oklahoma Press, 1969); B. V. Sokolov, 'The Role of Lend-Lease in Soviet Military Efforts, 1941–1945', *JSMS*, vol. 7, 1994, no. 3, pp. 567–86; H. Tuyll, *Feeding the Bear: American Aid to the Soviet Union, 1941-1945* (New York: Greenwood Press, 1989); V. V. Sokolov, 'Lend-liz v gody vtoroi mirovoi voiny', *NNI*, 2010, no. 6, pp. 3–17.

   What is lacking is an analysis of the effect of Lend-Lease on front-line fighting; the best attempt so far is W. Dunn, *Hitler's Nemesis: The Red Army, 1930-1945* (New York: Greenwood Press, 1994), and W. Dunn, *The Soviet Economy and the Red Army, 1930-1945* (Westport, CT: Praeger, 1995). See also http://lend-lease.airforce.ru/index.htm.

12 Tuyll, *Feeding*, p. 164. The decline in the percentage of shipments through North Russia in 1943 was partly from the threat of German action, and partly from the growth of total shipments to other ports. In 1944, with the German threat in the Barents Sea reduced, North Russia accounted for nearly a quarter of shipments.

13 Tuyll, *Feeding*, p. 154; *Hitlers Politisches Testament*, p. 56 [7 February]; *Foreign Relations of the United States, 1945: The Conferences at Malta and Yalta* (Washington, DC: GPO, 1955), p. 768.

14 *RA/VO*, vol. 6, pp. 39–40 [13 July].

15 *VOV/VIO*, vol. 3, pp. 333, 335; Harrison, *Economics*, p. 287.

16 Stalin, *OVOVSS*, p. 33 [6 November]. The United States was still neutral at this time.

17 *Poteri*, p. 471.

18 Artillery losses were higher in 1944 than in 1942, the result either of heavy fighting or the retirement of worn-out guns.

19 *VOVE*, pp. 68, 605–6.

20 The technical difference between an SP gun and a tank was that the former was more lightly armoured and did not have a turret.

21 SP gun and tank details and production figures are given in Zaloga and Grandsen, *Soviet Tanks and Combat Vehicles*, and Chamberlain and Doyle, *Encyclopedia of German Tanks*.

22 A. V. Lobanov, 'Artilleriia rezerva Verkhovnogo Glavnokomandovaniia v gody Velikoi Otechestennoi voiny', *VIZh*, 2006, no. 2, pp. 12–15, outlines the deployment of all types of artillery through the RVGK.

23 *VOVE*, p. 105–6; Iakushevskii in *VOV/VIO*, vol. 4, p. 83; Simonov, *Glazami cheloveka moego pokoleniia*, p. 312. The USSR received from its allies 9,400 artillery pieces and mortars (*Poteri*, p. 471).

24 Stalin, *OVOVSS*, p. 102 [1 May 1943]; V. A. Malyshev, 'Dnevnik narkoma', *Istochnik*, 1997, no. 5, p. 118 [10 January 1942].

25 With hindsight, it is surprising that Soviet tank production was kept so high in 1945. After all, the war was nearly over. In July 1945 the GKO passed a decree on the complete re-equipment of tank forces and the creation of a reserve of 3,000 tanks (Gor'kov, *GKO*, p. 547 [9 July]). Not until September of 1945 was tank production cut, and even then Stalin apparently had to convince the Red Army leadership of the need for this step (Malyshev, 'Dnevnik', p. 130 [8 September]).

26 Some tank losses may have been worn-out vehicles rather than combat casualties, although the editors of the main Russian source on losses state that non-combat losses, other than for aircraft, were 'insignificant' (*Poteri*, p. 481, n. 4).

27 *Poteri*, p. 471.

28 Kudriashov, *Voina*, pp. 173–7 [10 September]. Shchadenko proposed the creation of five new-type shock armies and five tank armies. He had been close to Stalin and Voroshilov in the Civil War, and was in 1941–3 head of the *GU formirovaniia i ukomplektovaniia voisk Krasnoi Armii*.

29 Zolotarev, *Deistvuiushchaia armiia*, pp. 551–2, 567–8, 572–3. There are no available figures for motor vehicle *losses* over this period, so these are net figures. The strength of the Red Army increased from 10,600,000 personnel in November 1942 to 11,408,000 in January 1945.

30 Sokolov, 'Role of Lend-Lease', p. 571 [409,500 vehicles], and V. F. Vorsin, 'Motor Vehicle Transport Deliveries through "Lend-Lease"', *JSMS*, vol. 10, 1997, no. 2, pp. 164 [312,600 vehicles]. Perhaps the difference is partly explained by late 1945 deliveries or inclusion in the higher figure of some combat vehicles.

31 Vorsin, 'Motor Vehicle Transport Deliveries', pp. 153–75, is the most detailed source. Vorsin gives a total of 267,000 imported trucks becoming available in the USSR, 30,000 delivered in 1941–2, 81,000 in 1943, 122,000 in 1944 and 39,000 in 1945. To this were added 41,000 jeeps and about 5,000 special vehicles. At least 30,000 of all these motor vehicles were used in the civilian economy, leaving 285,000 or less available to the NKO. Some 60,000 of the 312,600 imported vehicles were delivered to the Far East, and 181,000 (58 per cent) came via the

Persian Gulf; the latter route worked effectively only from the middle of 1943. Both delivery points were far distant from the battlefields of Eastern Europe. Another source of delay was the requirement to put together vehicles that were supplied in component form to save shipping space; some 120,000 of the imported vehicles (38 per cent) had to be assembled, mainly at Moscow and Gor'kii.

32 Vorsin, 'Motor Vehicle Transport Deliveries', pp. 164, 169.

33 On this, see also I. V. Kovalev, *Transport v Velikoi Otechestvennoi voiny (1941-1945)* (Moscow: Nauka, 1981).

34 Simonov, *Glazami cheloveka moego pokoleniia*, p. 312.

35 Zolotarev, *Deistvuiushchaia armiia*, pp. 552, 557, 563, 573. The total includes the Active Army, the VGK Reserve and rear-echelon organizations.

36 *Poteri*, p. 471. The West also helped with two other aspects of aviation supply. These were aluminium, which had been an important bottleneck in Soviet aircraft construction, and high octane aviation fuel.

37 *Poteri*, pp. 261, 476, 480; *VOVE*, pp. 603–4, 636–7. American Lend-Lease supply was 36,900 radio stations, or well over half the total (Jones, *Roads,* Appendix A). For recent revelations about Red Army signals networks, see A. P. Zharskii, 'Boevye primenie frontovykh i armeiskikh uzlov sviazi v gody Velikoi Otechestvennoi voiny', *VIZh*, 2005, no. 1, pp. 26–32.

38 On this, see J. Sapir, 'The Economics of War in the Soviet Union during World War II', in Kershaw and Lewin, *Stalinism and Nazism*, pp. 208–36, and M. Harrison 'Wartime Mobilization: A German Comparison', in J. Barber and M. Harrison (eds), *The Soviet Defence-Industry Complex from Stalin to Khrushchev* (Basingstoke: Macmillan, 2000), pp. 99–117. The possible exceptions to this point about non-innovation were the mass use of the multiple rocket launcher (the *Katiusha*) and the armoured battlefield aircraft (the Il-2 *Shturmovik*).

39 This perceptive point has been made by my colleague Phillips O'Brien in 'East versus West in the Defeat of Nazi Germany', *Journal of Strategic Studies*, vol. 23, 2000, no. 2, p. 93.

40 Stalin, *OVOVSS*, pp. 57 [1 May 1942], 179 [23 February 1945].

41 *Goebbels Reden*, vol. 2, p. 180 [18 February].

42 Manstein, *Verlorene Siege*, pp. 572–3.

43 B. Wegner, 'Hitler, der Zweite Weltkrieg und die Choreographie des Untergangs', *Geschichte und Gesellschaft*, vol. 26, 2000, no. 3, pp. 493–518.

44 Manstein, *Verlorene Siege*, p. 574.

45 For the background of opposition groups in the Army, see J. Fest, *Plotting Hitler's Death: The German Resistance to Hitler, 1933-1945* (London: Weidenfeld & Nicolson, 1996), pp. 170–291, and W. Heinemann in *GSWW*, vol. 9.1, 780–875.

46 This is discussed further in Chapter 13. Operations in Belorussia and Poland in 1944 were controlled by two 'Stavka representatives'; in eastern Germany in 1945, Stalin took direct command of the three army groups involved.

47 Khrushchev, 'Memuary', *VI*, 1990, no. 11, p. 80; Vasilevskii, *Delo*, vol. 2, pp. 234–5; A. D. Pedosov, 'Vospominaniia A. D. Pedosova o vystuplenii Marshala G. K. Zhukova v Akademii Obshchestvennykh Nauk (1966)', *Arkheograficheskii ezhegodnik*, 1995, pp. 286–8.

48 Zhukov, *ViR*, vol. 2, p. 107; Simonov, *Glazami*, p. 33–3.

49 Glantz, *After Stalingrad*, pp. 449–51.

50 *RA/VO*, vol. 2(3), pp. 3–32 [23 November 1944], 342–3 [23 December 1944].

51 A. A. Pechenkin, 'Narkom oborony SSSR I. V. Stalin i ego zamestiteli', *VIZh*, 2005, no. 6, pp. 3–10, no. 8, 20–29.

52 It is interesting that even at that time Shcherbakov, the head of the Political Administration, was not made a member of the Stavka.

53 Zhukov, *ViR*, vol. 2. p. 111.

54 *General'nyi shtab Rossiiskoi armii: Istoriia i sovremennost'* (Moscow: Akademicheskii Proekt, 2006), pp. 203–37.

55 Vasilevskii, *Delo*, vol. 2, pp. 218–9; Zhukov, *ViR*, vol. 2, p. 88.

56 Vasilevskii, *Delo*, vol. 2, p. 202; Rokossovskii, *Soldatskii dolg*, pp. 253–4.

57 Korotkov, 'Posetiteli', *IA*, 1998, no. 4, pp. 21–2, 40–1, 73–4; Zhukov, *ViR*, vol. 3, p. 76.

58 Vasilevskii, *Delo*, vol. 2, pp. 208, 215–16; *RA/VO*, vol. 5(3), p. 193 [17 August 1943]. On the powers of General Staff representatives, including a direct communications link to the General Staff, see *RA/VO*, vol. 2(3), pp. 184–5 [22 June 1943], vol. 12(2), pp. 63–4 [23 March 1942], vol. 12(3), p. 235 [29 July 1943].

59 D. Glantz, *The Role of Intelligence in Soviet Military Strategy in World War II* (San Francisco: Presidio, 1990), is an insightful introduction to the subject, but it is based mostly on published sources. G. Jukes, 'The Soviets and "Ultra"', *Intelligence and National Security*, vol. 3, 1988, no. 2, pp. 233–47, speculates about the importance of Soviet 'sigint', but even now little new information has been published to support Jukes' argument. David Kahn thought it unlikely that the Russians could decrypt German signals; see his 'Soviet Comint in the Cold War', *Cryptologia*, vol. 22, 1998, no. 1, pp. 11–14.

Many decisions and orders of the Stavka have now been published, but very seldom the intelligence that lay behind them. Exceptionally, the Russians published a British assessment of German intentions as of the end of January 1945, based on 'a very reliable source'. This was evidently published because it was *incorrect*; it warned of a dangerous concentration of German forces in Pomerania and northwest of Breslau (*RA/VO*, vol. 12(4), p. 633 [14 February 1945]). The Russians also told their allies little about the deployments of the Red Army. The British had to rely on decrypts of German signals to learn more about the Soviet order of battle.

60 Zhukov, *ViR*, vol. 2, pp. 107–8; M. A. Bobrov, 'Organizatsiia i vedenie vozdushnoi razvedki v period Velikoi Otechestvennoi voiny 1941-1945 gg.', *VIZh*, 2006, no. 2, pp. 7–11.

61 On wartime intelligence, in addition to Andrew and Gordievsky, *KGB*, pp. 281–348, and Chebrikov, *Istoriia Sovetskikh organov*, pp. 325–410, see B. Smith, *Sharing Secrets with Stalin: How the Allies Traded Intelligence, 1941-1945* (Lawrence, KS: University Press of Kansas, 1996), and R. Stephan, *Stalin's Secret War: Soviet Counterintelligence against the Nazis, 1941-1945* (Lawrence, KS: University Press of Kansas, 2004).

62 D. Thomas, 'Foreign Armies East and Germany Military Intelligence in Russia, 1941–1945', *Journal of Contemporary History* (hereafter *JCH*), vol. 22, 1987, pp. 261–302. On radio intelligence, see Mendolsohn, *Covert Warfare*, vol. 6, pp. 108–109, 131–2, 194, 232, and the TICOM report, *European Axis Signals Intelligence*, vol. 1, pp. 7, 9, appendix, vol. 4, pp. 82–138, vol. 9, pp. 42–3.

63 Domarus, *Hitler: Reden*, p. 1941 [9 November].

64 Förster in *GSWW*, vol. 9.1, pp. 559–659, and Wette, *Wehrmacht*, pp. 139–75.

65 B. Müller-Hillebrand, *Das Heer, 1933–1945* (Darmstadt: E. S. Mittler, 1954–69) vol. 3, p. 251. In 1944 the German Replacement Army numbered 2,510,000. For the acute German manpower problem in the latter half of the war, see B. Kroener in *GSWW*, vol. 5.1, pp. 1001–1140, vol. 5.2, pp. 833–1064.

66   On 'de-modernization', see O. Bartov, *Hitler's Army* (New York: OUP USA, 1991), pp. 12–28.

67   On the rank and file of the German Army, both their indoctrination and response, see J. Echternkamp in *GSWW*, vol. 9.1, pp. 49–60, and Wette, *Wehrmacht*, pp. 175–94. K. Kilian and R. Zagovec in *GSWW*, vol. 9.2, pp. 253–382, discuss, respectively, attitudes as expressed in soldiers' letters and POW interrogation. Information from covert eavesdropping can also be found in S. Neitzel and H. Welzer, *Soldaten: On Fighting, Killing and Dying: The Secret Second World War Tapes of German POWs* (London: Simon and Schuster, 2012). Fritz, *Frontsoldaten*, remains a basic source.

68   Another name change had occurred in May 1943, when motorized divisions became *Panzergrenadier* divisions. *Volksgrenadier* divisions should also not be confused with the *Volkssturm* militia.

69   Collaborator personnel within the Wehrmacht are discussed more fully in Chapter 8.

70   D. Yelton, *Hitler's Volkssturm: The Nazi Militia and the Fall of Germany, 1944–1945* (Lawrence, KS: University Press of Kansas, 2002).

71   B. Wegner, *The Waffen-SS, Hitler's Political Soldiers: Organization, Ideology and Function* (Oxford: Blackwell, 1990).

72   Stalin, *OVOVSS*, pp. 92 [23 February 1943], 189 [1 May 1945]. Stalin made the same point about the cadre army in a private conversation with Malyshev: 'Our infantry [*pekhota*] and its commanders have been a cadre force. They will do well [*derutsia khorosho*].' Malyshev, 'Dnevnik', no. 5, p. 122 [17 August 1943].

73   For excerpts from *The Front*, see J. von Geldern and R. Stites, *Mass Culture in Soviet Russia: Tales, Poems, Songs, Movies, Plays and Folklore, 1917-1953* (Bloomington, IN: Indiana University Press, 1995), pp. 345–71. Most of the Red Army commanders who were purged in 1937–8 were members of this Civil War cohort. If anything, however, Stalin was remarkably tolerant during the war. Commanders like Timoshenko, Malinovskii and Konev could and did suffer catastrophic defeats without severe punishment. See E. I. Malashenko, 'Komandarmy Velikoi Otechestvennoi voiny', *VIZh*, 2005, no. 1, pp. 13–18, no. 2, pp. 9–16, no. 3, pp. 19–26, no. 4, pp. 9–17, no. 5, pp. 15–24, no. 6, pp. 21–5, and no. 7, pp. 9–17, and A. A. Pechenkin, 'Komanduiushchie frontami 1944 goda', *VIZh*, 2005, no. 10, pp. 9–14, no. 11, pp. 17–22.

74   *RA/VO*, vol. 2(2), pp. 200–1 [9 April 1942]. The Voroshilov General Staff Academy became the Voroshilov Higher Military Academy, with a six-month course. The Frunze Military Academy trained infantry regiment commanders in a four-month course. There was also the '*Vystrel*' ['Gunshot'] programme, in which company and battalion commanders were trained in a two-month course (*RA/VO*, vol. 2(2), p. 128 [2 December 1941]).

75   *RA/VO*, vol. 2(2), pp. 326–7 [9 October 1942]. Commissars had been removed and reinstated on several previous occasions.

76   In his speech of May 1942 Stalin referred to *ofitserskie kadry* (Stalin: *OVOVSS*, p. 55 [1 May]). This movement away from revolutionary equality was part of what has been described as the 'Great Retreat' in Soviet society under Stalin. On this, see N. S. Timasheff, *The Great Retreat: The Growth and Decline of Communism in Russia* (New York: Arno Press, [1946] 1972), and V. Dunham, *In Stalin's Time: Middleclass Values in Soviet Fiction* (Cambridge: Cambridge University Press, 1976).

77   Erickson, *Road to Berlin*, p. 38.

78   *Poteri*, pp. 247, 258, 261. The July 1945 figure excludes 1,100,000 personnel in hospital, and 400,000 individuals in the civilian sector who were receiving military rations. The 'active army groups', for which quarterly ration strengths have been published, excludes the personnel of the Stavka Reserve, and the internal Military Districts, as well as of the Navy

and the Air Defence command (*PVO*). An interesting discussion of Soviet manpower, based largely on Wehrmacht sources, can be found in Dunn, *Hitler's Nemesis*, pp. 51–73.

79 Svechin, *Strategy*, p. 181. Svechin did not live to see his prediction come true. He was imprisoned in 1931–2 (after arguing about strategic theory with Tukhacheskii), and although returned to service, he was arrested again in 1937 and executed the following year. On the changing situation in the Red Army in 1942–3, see also Reese, *Why Stalin Soldiers Fought*, and Glantz, *Colossus Reborn*, pp. 536–90.

80 D. Glantz. 'Soviet Use of "Substandard" Manpower in the Red Army, 1941–1945', in S. Marble (ed.), *Scraping the Barrel: The Military Use of Substandard Manpower, 1860-1960* (New York: Fordham University Press, 2012), pp. 151–78.

81 *RA/VO*, vol. 2(2), pp. 197–8 [5 April 1942], p. 395, ns. 36, 37.

82 *RA/VO*, vol. 2(2), pp. 184, 212–14; *Poteri*, p. 453. On the role of women, see also: A. Krylova, *Soviet Women in Combat: A History of Violence on the Eastern Front* (Cambridge: Cambridge University Press, 2010); R. Pennington, 'Offensive Women: Women in Combat in the Red Army', in P. Addison and A. Calder (eds), *Time to Kill: The Soldiers' Experience in the West* (London: Pimlico, 1997), pp. 249–62; R. Pennington, 'Women', in D. Stone (ed.), *The Soviet Union at War, 1941-1945* (Barnsley, UK: Pen and Sword, 2010); and R. Markwick and E. Cardona, *Soviet Women on the Frontline in the Second World War* (Houndmills: Palgrave Macmillan, 2012).

83 Gor'kov, *GKO*, pp. 514–20 [26 July].

84 RA/VO, vol. 5(2), p. 130 [16 March 1942], vol. 6, pp. 139–40 [22 May 1942]. See also J. Smith, 'Non-Russian Nationalities', in D. Stone (ed.), *The Soviet Union at War, 1941-1945*, (Barnsley, UK: Pen and Sword, 2010), pp. 225–9, and *VOVE*, pp. 739–40.

85 *RA/VO*, vol. 5(2), pp. 88–9 [9 February 1942].

86 *RA/VO*, vol. 2(3), p. 219 [16 November 1943], vol. 5(3), p. 223 [15 October 1943]; vol. 6, pp. 263–4 [22 March 1944]; vol. 12(3), pp. 410–11 [5 November 1943]. Under the order of 16 November 1943, each army group was to be given an allotment of such recruits, for example, 30,000 a month for the 1st Ukrainian Army Group, and any excess was to be sent on to the central pool.

87 On Soviet organizations created to maintain control over the personnel of the Red Army, see: D. Glantz, *Colossus Reborn*, pp. 564–82; A. Statiev, 'Penal Units in the Red Army', *EAS*, vol. 62, 2010, no. 5, pp. 721–47; A. Statiev, 'Blocking Units in the Red Army', *JMilH*, vol. 75, 2012, no. 3, pp. 475–95; Birstein, *Smersh*; and V. O. Daines, *Shtrafbaty i zagradotriady Krasnoi Armii* (Moscow: Iauza/Eksmo, 2008).

88 *Poteri*, pp. 436–42; *RA/VO*, vol. 2(3), p. 326 [29 October 1944], 411, n. 61, vol. 12(3), p. 329 [18 September 1943], vol. 12(4), pp. 455–6 [29 September 1944]; Naumov, 'Sud'ba', p. 101; Bartov, *Hitler's Army*, pp. 95–6.

89 *RA/VO*, vol. 2(3), pp. 326 [29 October 1944], 411, n. 61, vol. 12(3), p. 329 [18 September 1943], vol. 12(4), pp. 455–6 [29 September 1944]; *Poteri*, p. 441.

90 Domarus, *Hitler: Reden*, p. 1887 [30 May].

91 Zhukov, *ViR*, vol. 3, p. 182; A. F. Noskova et al. (eds), *Iz Varshavy: Moskva, tovarishchu Beria …: Dokumenty NKVD SSSR o pol'skom podpol'e 1944–1945 gg.* (Moscow: Institut slavianovedeniia RAN/Sibirskii khronograf, 2001), pp. 337–8; *RA/VO*, vol. 2(3), p. 304 [11 July 1944], vol. 3(2), pp. 221–3 [October 1944], 547–8 [6 May 1945), vol. 5(4), p. 138 [30 August 1944], vol. 12(4), pp. 438 [20 September 1944], 472 [5 October 1944], 483–4 [12 October 1944].

92 Malyshev, 'Dnevnik', pp. 127–8 [28 March 1945]. The conduct of Soviet troops in Germany in 1944–5 is discussed in Chapter 13.

93 Zolotarev, *Deistvuiushchaia armiia*, is a valuable outline of the Soviet order of battle.

94 *RA/VO*, vol. 6, pp. 61–2 [12 August].

95 Erickson, *Road to Berlin*, p. 84. There was in November 1943 a GKO directive to form no fewer than ten tank armies. This target was not reached, perhaps from a desire to keep existing formations at full strength (Gor'kov, *GKO*, pp. 120–3, 527).

96 *RA/VO*, vol. 12(3), pp. 357–8 [5 October 1943], vol. 5(4), pp. 80–1 [1 May 1944]; *VOVE*, p. 365.

97 *RA/VO*, vol. 2(3), pp. 41–2 [27 January 1943], vol. 5(3), p. 122 [18 April 1943], vol. 12(4), pp. 65–6 [10 February 1944].

98 *RA/VO*, vol. 5(3), pp. 221–2 [13 October 1943], vol. 9, pp. 426–7 [25 March 1943]. For background, see Glantz, *Soviet Airborne Experience*.

99 *Perepiska*, vol. 2, p. 30 [7 October 1942].

100 On Luftwaffe raids and Soviet defences, see Overy, *Bombing War*, pp. 213–34. Russian archival data cited by Overy suggest that a relatively small number of 52,000 Soviet civilians were killed in German bombing raids in the period 1941–5, about 45 percent in the first half of 1942. A. A. Gordina et al., '… Nemetskie aviatsionnye udary po Gor'kovskomu avtozavodu (1941-1943 gg.)', *VIZh*, 2011, no. 11, pp. 27–33, provides a rare account of raids on one important industrial target. Details in Zolotarev, *Deistvuiushchaia armiia*, pp. 244–8, 500–6, give a sense of the large number of Soviet aircraft and AA guns committed to the Air Defence Force (*PVO*) command.

101 On this, see Muller, *German Air War in Russia*, pp. 149–88.

102 M. Conversino, *Fighting with the Soviets: The Failure of Operation Frantic, 1944–1945* (Lawrence, KS: University Press of Kansas, 1997).

103 *RA/VO*, vol. 12(3), pp. 307–8 [7 September 1943].

104 Guards Air Armies were not created. There were, however, a number of Guards Air Corps: Zolotarev, *Deistvuiushchaia armii*, pp. 226–42, 481–99.

105 RA/VO, vol. 2(2), pp. 221–3 [29 April 1942]; Stalin, *OVOVSS*, pp. 92–3 [23 February 1942]; *SDVG*, vol. 4, p. 95 [29 May 1944].

106 Stalin, *OVOVSS*, p. 140 [23 February 1944].

107 Zhukov, *ViR*, vol. 3, pp. 207–8.

108 Manstein, *Verlorene Siege*, p. 582; Glantz and House, *When Titans Clashed*, p. 176; Harrison, *Economics*, pp. 1–2. One of the leading historians of the Eastern Front, Earl Ziemke, was more grudging with his praise. He said that a new stage of development had been reached after Stalingrad in which 'the Russians demonstrated a command of offensive tactics equal to that of the Germans in conception and sufficiently effective in execution to prevail against an opponent who had passed the peak of his strength' (*Stalingrad to Berlin*, p. 52).

Chapter 8

1. Stalin, *OVOVSS*, pp. 31–2 [6 November 1941], 39 [7 November 1941].

2. From the abundant literature on the 'home front' in Nazi Germany, see: Evans, *The Third Reich at War*, I. Kershaw, *The End: Hitler's Germany, 1944-1945* (London: Allen Lane, 2011), and chapters by various authors in *GSWW*, vol. 9.

3. J. Barber and M. Harrison, *The Soviet Home Front, 1941-1945: A Social and Economic History of the USSR in World War II* (Harlow: Longman, 1991).

4. Up to May 1945 the Soviet propaganda organs called the conflict the 'Fatherland War' (*Otechestvennaia voina*), not the 'Great Fatherland War'. They also made wide use of the word *rodina*, which is usually translated as 'motherland'.

5. *RA/VO*, vol. 6, p. 91 [10 December 1941]. The old slogan was still permissible in propaganda directed towards the Germans.

6. Stalin, *OVOVSS*, p. 40 [7 November 1941]. Aleksandr Nevskii and Dmitrii Donskoi were medieval princes. Minin and Pozharskii, a merchant and a nobleman, fought the Poles in the late 1500s, and Suvorov and Kutuzov were Imperial generals. See also K. Berkhoff, *Motherland in Danger: Soviet Propaganda during World War II* (Cambridge, MA: Harvard University Press, 2012).

7. This is development discussed in Brandenburger, *National Bolshevism*.

8. Dimitrov, *Diary*, p. 65 [7 November 1937].

9. Domarus, *Hitler: Reden*, p. 1773 [8 November 1941].

10. There were scattered minorities – for example, Tatars – in central Russia, between Moscow and the Urals, but their numbers were relatively small. Other non-Russian groups inhabited the Transcaucasus and Central Asia. But the ethnic Russians now made up the largest share of the population of the unoccupied Soviet Union.

11. This is the interpretation in S. M. Miner, *Stalin's Holy War: Religion, Nationalism, and Alliance Politics, 1941–1945* (Chapel Hill, NC: University of North Carolina Press, 2003).

12. Stalin, *OVOVSS*, p. 119 [6 November 1943]; 'Iz istorii Velikoi Otechestvennoi voiny', *ITsK*, 1991, no. 5, pp. 213–17. Many of the candidates would have been promoted to full members. Some party members may have been expelled, but the number of combat deaths was surely much greater.

13. A. Dallin, *German Rule in Russia* (London: Macmillan, 1981); T. Mulligan, *The Politics of Illusion and Empire: German Occupation Policy in the Soviet Union, 1942–1943* (New York: Praeger, 1988); A. Kay, J. Rutherford, and D. Stahel, *Nazi Policy on the Eastern Front, 1941: Total War, Genocide, and Radicalization* (Rochester, NY: University of Rochester Press, 2012); B. Chiari in *GSWW* vol. 9.2, pp. 881–989; and A. S. Kniaz'kov and V. L. Maksimenko in *VOV/VOI*, vol. 2, pp. 328–39.

    M. Mazower, *Hitler's Empire: Nazi Rule in Occupied Europe* (London: Allen Lane, 2008), is a valuable comparative study; see especially pp. 137–78 on the USSR. The survey of occupation policy by H. Umbreit in *GSWW*, vol. 5.1, pp. 9–404, vol. 5.2, pp. 2–291, 138–260, includes developments on Soviet territory. J. Steinberg, 'The Third Reich Reflected: German Civil Administration in the Occupied Soviet Union, 1941–4', *EHR*, vol. 110, 1995, pp. 620–51, is a thought-provoking summary. L. Cohen, *Smolensk under the Nazis: Everyday Life in Occupied Russia* (Rochester: University of Rochester Press, 2013), is a recent case study of a western region that was largely inhabited by ethnic Russians.

14. *Hitlers Weisungen*, pp. 201–6 [18 August 1942].

15. J. Noakes and G. Pridham, *Documents on Nazism, 1919–1945* (New York: Viking, 1975), p. 630 [25 October 1942]. On this, see Mulligan, *Politics*, pp. 47–55.

16. Noakes and Pridham, *Documents*, p. 623 [16 July]; Dallin, *German Rule*, p. 407.

17. N. M. Ramanichev in *VOV/VIO*, vol. 4, p. 154. A Russian Federation special commission which considered the rehabilitation of ex-POWs and repatriated civilians suggested that only 280,000–300,000 people served with the Germans (Naumov, 'Sud'ba', pp. 95–6.). This seems much too low.

18. Müller-Hillebrand, *Das Heer*, vol. 3, p. 135.

19. Ironically, a racist pre-invasion (May 1941) Wehrmacht briefing had observed that 'the Asiatic soldiers of the Red Army in particular are inscrutable, unpredictable, insidious and unfeeling'; cited in *GSWW*, vol. 4, pp. 514–5.

20. The 1996 report (see n. 17) gave a total of 250,000 individuals organized into combat formations over the whole war.

21. See C. Andreyev, *Vlasov and the Russian Liberation Movement: Soviet Reality and Emigré Theories* (Cambridge: Cambridge University Press, 1985). The ROA existed from the spring of 1943 as an ephemeral Nazi propaganda tool and notionally took in the various collaborator units. It only existed as an actual force in the desperate winter of 1944–5.

22. On deportation and repatriation, see two articles by V. N. Zemskov: 'K voprosu o repatriatsii sovetskikh grazhdan. 1944–1951 gody', *ISSSR*, 1990, no. 4, pp. 26–41, and 'Repatriatsiia sovetskikh grazhdan i ikh dalneishaia sud'ba', *Sotsiologicheskie issledovaniia*, 1995, no. 5, pp. 3–13, and no. 6, pp. 3–12. Soviet POWs held by the Germans were discussed in Chapter 4.

23. This 'official' calculation of 23.2 per cent deaths among deportees was not made altogether clear, but it was based on figures of 4,829,000 deportees and 3,582,000 repatriated citizens (Naumov, 'Sud'ba', p. 100). This percentage is probably too high, understating the number of those who stayed abroad or who returned to the USSR before the end of the war. The fact remains, however, that the *Ostarbeiters* were treated very badly in Germany.

   Another interesting point concerns the date of deportation. Sauckel accelerated the deportation programme in 1943, and there were forced evacuations of Soviet civilians as the Wehrmacht withdrew. Nevertheless, of those Soviet citizens repatriated in 1945, the majority (60 per cent) were civilians who had been sent to the Reich before the end of 1942, and only a quarter had been sent in 1943 (Zemskov, 'K voprosu', p. 35).

24. Zemskov, 'K voprosu', pp. 37–9.

25. Zemskov, 'K voprosu', pp. 33, 35, 37, 39.

26. Zemskov, 'K voprosu', and V. N. Zemskov, 'Repatriatsiia sovetskikh grazhdan i ikh dalneishaia sud'ba', *Sotsiologicheskie issledovaniia*, 1995, no. 5, pp. 3–13, no. 6, pp. 3–12; Naumov, 'Sud'ba', pp. 103, 109. N. Tolstoy, *Victims of Yalta* (London: Hodder and Stoughton, 1977), was an important early account, although the stress was on the policy of the Western Allies.

27. *RA/VO*, vol. 2(3), pp. 130–1 [19 April 1943], 282–3 [29 May 1944].

28. For an introduction, see A. M. Nekrich, *The Punished Peoples: The Deportation and Fate of Soviet Minorities at the End of the Second World War* (New York: W. W. Norton, 1978). A useful survey in Russian of the deportations and the role of Beria's NKVD in them is N. F. Bugai, *L. Beriia – I. Stalini: 'Soglasno Vashemu ukazaniiu'* (Moscow: AIRO-XX, 1995).

29. For an overview, see J. Armstrong (ed.), *Soviet Partisans in World War II* (Madison, WI: University of Wisconsin Press, 1964); L. Grenkewich and D. Glantz, *The Soviet Partisan Movement, 1941–1944: A Critical Historiographical Analysis* (London: Frank Cass, 1999); K. Slepyan, *Stalin's Guerrillas: Soviet Partisans in World War II* (Lawrence, KS: University Press of Kansas, 2006); A. S. Kniaz'kov and V. Maksimenko in *VOV/VIO*, vol. 2, pp. 328–54; A. S. Kniaz'kov in *VOV/VIO*, vol. 4, pp. 130–53; and V. I. Piatnitskii, 'Za liniei sovetsko-germanskogo fronta', *NNI*, 2005, no. 3, pp. 16–37. E. Mawdsley, 'Anti-German Insurgency and Allied Grand Strategy', vol. 31, 2008, no. 5, pp. 695–719, compares the organization of Soviet partisans with British and the American support for resistance movements in Western Europe.

30. *RA/VO*, vol. 9, pp. 17–8 [29 June]; Stalin, *OVOVSS*, p. 15 [3 July].

31. *RA/VO*, vol. 9, pp. 19–20 [18 July]. The powerful Russian word *zakhvatchiki* is translated a little imprecisely here as 'aggressors'. (*Aggressory* is also a Russian word.) The word *zakhvatchiki* was much used in propaganda documents and slogans, especially 'Death to the German aggressors!' 'Occupiers' would be an alternative translation of *zakhvatchiki*, but it is more neutral, and there is a direct Russian equivalent, *okkupanty*. A closer but silly translation of *zakhvatchiki* would be 'grabbers'.

32. M. Cooper, *The Phantom War: The German Struggle against Soviet Partisans, 1941-1944* (London: Macdonald & Janes, 1979), pp. 169–70 [16 September 1941].

33. Stalin, *OVOVSS*, p. 81 [7 November 1942].

34. *RA/VO*, vol. 9, pp. 114–5 [30 May 1942], 277–8 [7 March 1943], 281–2 [17 April 1943].

35. *RA/VO*, vol. 9, p. 127 [July 1942]. For recent local studies, see: B. Shepherd, *War in the Wild East: The German Army and Soviet Partisans* (Cambridge, MA: Harvard University Press, 2004); and A. Hill, *The War behind the Eastern Front: The Soviet Partisan Movement in North-West Russia 1941–44* (London: Frank Cass, 2005); B. Shepherd and J. Pattinson (eds), *War in a Twilight World, Partisan and Anti-Partisan Warfare in Eastern Europe 1939-1945* (London: Palgrave Macmillan, 2010); and J. Rutherford, *Combat and Genocide on the Eastern Front: The German Infantry's War, 1941–1944* (Cambridge: Cambridge University Press, 2014). War crimes of the *Bandenkrieg* are illustrated in Reemtsma, *Verbrechen der Wehrmacht*, pp. 429–505.

36. Armstrong, *Soviet Partisans*, p. 151; *VOV/VIO*, vol. 2, p. 345.

37. Stalin, *OVOVSS*, p. 95 [23 February].

38. *RA/VO*, vol. 9, p. 32 [7 December 1941].

39. *RA/VO*, vol. 9, p. 132 [5 September 1942].

40. The corollary is that it was at those points where the front was grid-locked that the partisans could best develop.

41. Cooper, *Phantom War*.

42. Dallin, *German Rule*, p. 680.

43. Stalin, *OVOVSS*, p. 120 [6 November 1943].

44. *Poteri*, p. 511. For a general discussion of Soviet-held POWs, see S. Karner, *Arkhipelag GUPVI: Pleny i internirovanie v Sovetskom Soiuze 1941–1956* (Moscow: RGGU, 2002), and Overmans in *DRZW*, vol. 10.2, pp. 402–13, 429–30, 489–503.

45. *Verbrechen der Wehrmacht*, p. 188.

46. Stalin, *OVOVSS*, pp. 46–7 [23 February].

47. *Poteri*, p. 512.

48. *Poteri*, p. 512.

49. *Poteri*, pp. 511–15.

50. On this, see B. Scheurig, *Free Germany: The National Committee and the League of German Officers* (Middletown: Wesleyan University Press, 1969), and W. Heinemann in *GSWW*, vol. 9.1, pp. 823–6.

51. T. V. Volokitina et al. (eds), *Sovetskii faktor v Vostochnoi Evrope 1944–1953: Dokumenty*, 2 vols (Moscow: Rosspen, 1999), vol. 1, p. 116–8; *RA/VO*, vol. 5(3), p. 183.

52. Soviet policy towards Eastern Europe and Germany, respectively, will be discussed more fully in Chapters 12 and 13. The diplomacy of Lend-Lease and the Arctic convoys was dealt with in Chapter 7.

53. J. Förster and G. Ueberschär in *GSWW*, vol. 4, pp. 386–480, 941–1049; B. Wegner in *GSWW*, vol. 6, pp. 904–23; R. DiNardo, *Germany and the Axis Powers: From Coalition to Collapse* (Lawrence, KS: University Press of Kansas, 2005).

54. Roberts, *Stalin's Wars*, pp. 61–295; V. Mastny, *Russia's Road to the Cold War: Diplomacy, Warfare, and the Politics of Communism, 1941-1945* (New York: Columbia University Press, 1979); M. Stoler, *Allies in War* (London: Arnold, 2005).

55. Stalin, *OVOVSS*, pp. 16 [9 July 1941], 32–3 [6 November 1941], 41–8 [23 February 1942], 54 [1 May 1942], 76 [6 November 1942].

56. F. L. Loewenheim et al. (eds), *Roosevelt and Churchill: Their Secret Wartime Correspondence* (London: Barrie & Jenkins, 1975), p. 196 [18 March 1942]; Chuev, *Sto sorok besed s Molotovym*, p. 65.

57. *Perepiska*, vol. 2, p. 19 [18 July 1941]; Stalin, *OVOVSS*, p. 25 [6 November]. Initially, Stalin displayed a fundamental ignorance of British potential and made a proposal that Churchill send 25–30 divisions to Arkhangel'sk or to southern Russia.

58. Stalin, *OVOVSS*, pp. 25 [6 November 1941], 63, 68–9 [6 November 1942]; Müller-Hillebrand, *Das Heer*, vol. 3, p. 125. There were forty-two German divisions in western Europe and Scandinavia, and five in the Balkans.

59. The memorandum urging an early cross-Channel invasion was printed in J. Butler (ed.), *Grand Strategy*, 6 vols (London: HMSO, 1964), vol. 3, part 2, p. 675.

60. The timing of a cross-Channel invasion would be affected by the weather. Realistically, it had to be fitted into a weather 'window' between May and October. If the Channel were the only option, then American ground-force involvement on the other side of the Atlantic would not begin until May 1943, eighteen months into the war. In this lay the attraction of a landing elsewhere, that is North Africa. Some historians argue that the British and Americans could have mounted a cross-Channel invasion in 1943 had they not carried out Operation TORCH. See, for example, *VOV/VIO*, vol. 4, pp. 223–4, and W. Dunn, *Second Front: Victory 1943* (Tuscaloosa, AL: University of Alabama Press, 1980).

61. Stalin, *OVOVSS*, p. 98 [1 May 1943].

62. *Perepiska*, vol. 1, p. 163 [24 June]; Stalin, *OVOVSS*, p. 122 [6 November 1943]; Müller-Hillebrand, *Das Heer*, vol. 3, pp. 145–6, 148.

63. An early meeting between Roosevelt and Stalin was discussed. In April 1942 Roosevelt proposed getting together somewhere between Alaska and Siberia, see *Perepiska*, vol. 2, pp. 15–16 [c. 12 April 1942].

64. Stalin, *OVOVSS*, p. 122 [6 November 1943]. On Stalin's important intervention at the Tehran Conference, see K. Greenfield (ed.), *Command Decisions* (Washington, DC: OCMH, 1960), pp. 197–202, and Stoler, *Allies*, Chapter 7.

65. *Perepiska*, vol. 1, p. 265 [11 June]; Stalin, *OVOVSS*, pp. 172–3 [7 November].

66. *Perepiska*, vol. 1, p. 110 [9 February 1943].

67. Loewenheim, *Roosevelt and Churchill*, p. 238 [15 August 1942]. Churchill made the same point in correspondence with Stalin in 1943 (*Perepiska*, vol. 1, p. 165 [27 June]).

68. Dimitrov, *Diary*, p. 224 [7 June 1942].

69. In 1944–5, there were similar, unfounded, worries that the USSR would sit out the Pacific War. This led the Americans to make diplomatic compromises at the Yalta Conference in February 1945.

70. Mawdsley, *December 1941*, pp. 273–8; O. Rzheshevskii, *Stalin i Cherchill': Vstrechi, besedy, diskussii* (Moscow: Nauka, 2004), p. 157 [24 May 1942].

71. K. McDermott and J. Agnew, *The Comintern: A History of International Communism from Lenin to Stalin* (Basingstoke: Macmillan, 1996).

72. Dimitrov, *Diary*, pp. 155–6 [20 April 1941], 163 [12 May 1941], 276 [21 May 1943].

73. See the interesting account of these peace feelers in N. Khrushchev, 'Memuary', *VI*, 1990, no. 11, p. 68, and in the memoirs of the senior NKVD official Pavel Sudoplatov: P. Sudoplatov and A. Sudoplatov, *Special Tasks* (London: Little Brown, 1994), pp. 145–8. The NKVD leader Beria would be blamed for these covert negotiations in 1953, without any apparent justification.

74. G. Weinberg, *A World at Arms: A Global History of the World War II* (Cambridge: Cambridge University Press, 1994), pp. 609–11. We should not think only in terms of what actually happened. Unpredictable events, such as the death or removal of key figures (Hitler or Stalin), could not be ruled out at the time. Neither side was sure of how robust (or fragile) the totalitarian political structures of their enemy were.

75. Stalin, *OVOVSS*, p. 99 [1 May].

76. The notion of a vulnerable Hitler fitted in with Stalin's flawed conception of German politics: Hitler as a creature of the large capitalists. It also related to Stalin's (and Hitler's) recollection of October–November 1918, when Germany, defeated on the battlefield, collapsed from within.

77. Stalin, *OVOVSS*, pp. 46–7 [23 February 1942]. There also were American–British contingency plans for a rapid entry into continental Europe in the event of a German political collapse (Operation RANKIN).

Chapter 9

1. For the German withdrawal from the North Caucasus, subsequent regrouping in the western Donbass, and the Soviet attacks across the upper Don, see: Wegner in *GSWW*, vol. 6, pp. 1173–84; A. A. Danilevich, N. N. Kobrin, and V. V. Abamurov in *VOV/VIO*, vol. 2, pp. 116–78; and Glantz and House, *Endgame*, vol. 2, pp. 599–601.

2. On the experience of the Italian troops in Russia, especially the disastrous defeat in early 1943, see H. Hamilton, *Sacrifice on the Steppe: The Italian Alpine Corps in the Stalingrad Campaign, 1942-1943* (Havertown, PA: Casemate, 2011).

3. K. E. Voroshilov, *Stalin i vooruzhennye sily SSSR* (Moscow: GIPL, 1951), p. 124. The two other Stalinist 'forms of struggle', beyond strategic co-ordination and battles of encirclement and annihilation, were the frontal attack and the counter-offensive. Voroshilov was presumably not the actual author of this important and authoritative article, which was written to mark Stalin's 70th birthday.

4. For a general discussion of the numerous Soviet offensives launched in February 1943, see Glantz, *After Stalingrad*, and Kobrin and Fesenko in *VOV/VIO*, vol. 2, pp. 229–39.

5. These unsuccessful attempts to achieve an operational breakthrough against German Army Group North in February–March 1943 are discussed in Glantz, *Battle for Leningrad*, pp. 287–306, and Glantz, *After Stalingrad*, pp. 390–442.

6. *RA/VO*, vol. 5(3), p. 49 [30 January]; Korotkov, 'Posetiteli', *IA*, no. 3, p. 54 [29 January].

7. *RA/VO*, vol. 5(3), pp. 70–1 [6 February]. Luga, Strugi Krasnye, Porkhov and Dno were junctions on the two railway lines running southwest from Leningrad to the German rear. Kingisepp and Narva, between Lake Chud and the Gulf of Finland, blocked the other potential escape route of German Army Group North.

8. *RA/VO*, vol. 5(3), p. 76 [20 February]; Wegner in *GSWW*, vol. 6, p. 1205.

9. N. A. Svetlishin, *Krutie stupeni sud'by* (Khabarovsk: Khabarovskoe knizhnoe izdatel'stvo, 1992), p. 140; *RA/VO*, vol. 5(3), pp. 282–3 [28 February].

10. *Poteri*, p. 313; Glantz, *After Stalingrad*, pp. 428–42.

11. *RA/VO*, vol. 5(3), p. 72 [6 February].

12. *RA/VO*, vol. 5(3), p. 73 [6 February].

13. *RA/VO*, vol. 5(3), p. 74 [6 February]. Altogether, then, at least five major orders were issued by the Stavka over the names of Stalin and Zhukov at 1.00 am on 6 February 1943: the POLIARNAIA ZVEZDA directive, two orders concerning the attack on the Briansk–Orel salient, an order to attack Demiansk, and the order to Rokossovskii to move towards Smolensk.

14. Vasilevskii, *Delo*, vol. 1, p. 308. There was apparently no Soviet code name for this central operation, which resembled the future Operation KUTUZOV of July 1943; it also had elements in common with what David Glantz has named Operation JUPITER.

15. Zhukov, *ViR*, vol. 2, p. 358, vol. 3, pp. 7–9; Vasilevskii, *Delo*, vol. 1, p. 308; Korotkov, 'Posetiteli', *IA*, 1996, no. 3, p. 54. The planners were General F. E. Bokov (Deputy Chief of the General Staff) and General A. N. Bogoliubov (Deputy Chief of the Operations Directorate of the General Staff). General Shtemenko, who at this time headed a section of the General Staff, recalled that Stalin took a strong and direct personal interest in the planning of this Orel–Briansk operation; he thought it might be decisive. See S. M. Shtemenko, *General'nyi shtab v gody voiny* (Moscow: Voenizdat, 1989), p. 97.

16. I. S. Konev, *Zapiski komanduiushchego frontom* (Moscow: Voenizdat, 1991), pp. 581–5; *RA/VO*, vol. 5(3), p. 81 [27 February]; Zhukov, *ViR*, vol. 3, p. 8.

17. Rokossovskii, *Soldatskii dolg*, pp. 250–2. This failure of intelligence presumably was related to the movement of German reinforcements and the redeployment from the salients. Vasilevskii made a much more positive assessment of Soviet intelligence in 1943 in *Delo*, vol. 2, p. 23.

18. Rokossovskii, *Soldatskii Dolg*, pp. 250–1. The offensive by Golikov's Briansk Army group, the Maloarkhangel'sk operation (5 February to 3 March 1943), cost it 20,000 troops. The Sevsk operation (25 February to 28 March) of Rokossovskii's Central Army Group claimed another 30,000 (*Poteri*, p. 313).

19. On Operations GALLOP and STAR, see D. Glantz, *From the Don to the Dnepr: Soviet Offensive Operations, December 1942–August 1943* (London: Frank Cass, 1991), pp. 82–376; on GALLOP see also Glantz, *After Stalingrad*, pp. 110–98. The German perspective on the early operations between the Don and the Dnepr is provided by Wegner in *GSWW*, vol. 6, pp. 1177–84. Kobrin and Abamurov in *VOV/VIO*, vol. 2, pp. 160–78, is an objective Russian treatment.

20. *VOV/VIO*, vol. 2, p. 170. On this operation, see Glantz, *After Stalingrad*, pp. 228–51.

21. *RA/VO*, vol. 5(3), pp. 74 [11 February], 76 [17 February], 277–8 [9 February], 280–2 [11 February]; Vasilevskii, *Delo*, vol. 2, pp. 6–7.

22. General M. M. Popov was an outstanding commander, but a heavy drinker even by the standards of the wartime Soviet Army. This resulted in an extraordinary pattern of promotion and demotion. See Vasilevskii, *Delo*, vol. 2, p. 22, and Khrushchev, 'Memuary', *VI*, 1990, no. 12, pp. 91, 95. In June 1941, at the age of thirty-nine, Popov had held the important post of commander of the Leningrad Military District. In 1955, he became 1st Deputy C-in-C of Ground Forces, but he retired at the relatively young age of sixty in 1962.

23. In addition to Manstein's own widely read memoirs, *Verlorene Siege,* there is D. Sadarananda, *Beyond Stalingrad: Manstein and the Operations of Army Group Don* (New York: Praeger, 1990), a useful summary of operations using archival sources. See also: Wegner's discussion in *GSWW*, vol. 6, pp. 1184–93; R. Citino, *The Wehrmacht Retreats: Fighting a Lost War, 1943* (Lawrence, KS: University Press of Kansas, 2011), pp. 61–74; and Melvin, *Manstein,* pp. 347–81.

24. When Vatutin was transferred to command of the Voronezh Army Group (replacing Golikov), Malinovskii replaced him in the Southwestern Army Group, and Tolbukhin was promoted to army-group commander level, replacing Malinovskii in the Southern Army Group. Golikov was made head of the Red Army Main Personnel Directorate for the rest of the war. Under Khrushchev, he became head of the Red Army's Main Political Directorate and was promoted to the rank of Marshal.

25. For Hitler, human catastrophe came closer than he could have imagined. It was during one of his trips to his army group commanders in March 1943 that a bomb was placed aboard his aircraft by disgruntled army officers from the staff of Kluge's Army Group Centre; it failed to explode (W. Heinemann in *GSWW*, vol. 9.1, p. 861).

26. F. von Mellenthin, *Panzer Battles: A Study of the Employment of Armor in the Second World War* (New York: Ballantine, [1956] 1971), p. 253. At this time, Mellenthin commanded one of Manstein's panzer corps.

27. Glantz, *After Stalingrad*, pp. 228, 387–8.

28. Stalin, *OVOVSS*, p. 95.

29. In *After Stalingrad*, David Glantz vigorously debunks the 'myth' that by the end of 1942, Stalin and the Stavka had finally learnt the value of concentrating their military efforts. Indeed, Glantz's argument is that throughout the war, up to its end, Stalin 'remained convinced the most useful military strategy the Red Army could pursue was to apply maximum pressure against the German strategic defenses by conducting simultaneous offensive operations along as many strategic axes of the front as possible. The dictator did so because, appreciating the numerical superiority of the Red Army over the *Wehrmacht*, he was certain that, if attacked everywhere, the German defense was likely to crack and break somewhere' (pp. 448–9, 505, n. 368).

30. For overall studies, see D. Glantz and J. House, *The Battle of Kursk 1943* (Lawrence, KS: University Press of Kansas, 1999), and N. Zetterling and A. Frankson, *Kursk 1943: A Statistical Analysis* (London: Frank Cass, 2000). See also: Z. A. Shumov and N. M. Ramanichev in *VOV/VIO*, vol. 2, pp. 249–90; K.-H. Frieser, in *DRZW*, vol. 8, pp. 93–208; Citino, *Wehrmacht Retreats*, pp. 110–44, 198–231; and D. Showalter, *Armor and Blood: The Battle of Kursk: The Turning Point of World War II* (New York: Random House, 2013). Aviation aspects are covered in Hardesty and Grinberg, *Red Phoenix Rising*, pp. 223–75.

31. Guderian, *Erinnerungen*, p. 280; Tippelskirch, *Geschichte des Zweiten Weltkneges*, pp. 379, 381; *KTB OKW*, vol. 3(2), pp. 1425 [15 April 1943]. For general background, see Wegner in *DRZW*, vol. 8, pp. 61–79.

32. The Ferdinand (or *Elefant*) was based on a rival to the Tiger, designed by Ferdinand Porsche. Kursk was the Ferdinand's one moment of glory; the Tiger, built in larger numbers, fought on through the rest of the war. On the Luftwaffe, see Muller, *German Air War*, pp. 135–9. Muller argues that a delayed offensive was inevitable, as the air force in the East was too badly weakened in March–April 1943.

33. Overmans, *Verluste*, p. 279; *Poteri*, p. 261. To be sure, these Soviet losses were still huge, over a third of the number of American troops killed in the whole war. Aside from small-scale

fighting right along the front, there was a Soviet offensive around Krymskaia in the Kuban' against the German 17th Army. This was, however, in marked contrast to the second quarter of 1942, when Russia suffered disasters on the Volkhov, in the Crimea and at Khar'kov.

34. Zhukov, *ViR*, vol. 3, p. 31.

35. *SDVG*, vol. 3, p. 353 [8 April 1943].

36. Shtemenko, *General'nyi shtab*, p. 124.

37. *SDVG*, vol. 3, pp. 129–30 [25 April 1943], 365–75 [21 April 1943]; Khrushchev, 'Memuary', *VI*, 1991, no. 2–3, pp. 74f. no. 4–5, p. 59.

38. Vasilevskii, *Delo*, vol. 2, p. 23; Andrew and Gordievsky, *KGB*, pp. 315–20; J. Cairncross, *The Enigma Spy: An Autobiography: The Story of the Man Who Changed the Course of the Second World War* (London: Century, 1997); Hinsley, *British Intelligence*, vol. 2, pp. 616–27, 769f., vol. 3, pp. 18–23; T. Mulligan, 'Spies, Ciphers and "Zitadelle": Intelligence and the Battle of Kursk, 1943', *JCH*, vol. 22, 1987, pp. 235–60; Smith, *Sharing Secrets*, pp. 149–55.

39. Zhukov, *ViR*, vol. 3, p. 37.

40. Konev had been in command of Northwestern Army Group since March 1943 after Stalin sacked him from Western Army Group. With his move to the Steppe Military District, he replaced General M. A. Reiter, whose talents lay more in raising new formations than in leading them into battle.

41. Zhukov, *ViR*, vol. 3, p. 74.

42. *VOV/VIO*, vol. 2, pp. 258; Zetterling and Frankson, *Kursk*, pp. 17–8, 32.

43. Vasilevskii, *Delo*, vol. 2, pp. 27–9; The figure of 1,500 tanks was cited in P. A. Rotmistrov's memoirs, *Tankovoe srazhenie pod Prokhorovkoi* (Moscow: Voenizdat, 1960), p. 7.

44. For an exhaustive study, see V. Zamulin, *Demolishing the Myth: The Tank Battle at Prokhorovka, Kursk, July 1943: An Operational Narrative* (Solihull: Helion, 2011; this is a translation of *Prokhorovka: Neizvestnoe srazhenie velikoi voiny* (Moscow: Tranzitkniga, 2005). The historian Karl-Heinz Frieser maintained that in the 2nd SS Panzer Corps those tanks classified as 'total losses' (*Totalverlusten*) numbered only *three*. This extraordinarily low figure was explained partly by the technical and tactical superiority of the German armour and artillery; in addition, their occupation of the Prokhorovka battlefield for several days after 12 July enabled German troops to salvage their own damaged AFVs and finish off any immobilized or abandoned Soviet ones (*DRZW*, vol. 8, pp. 129–30). Another source based on German archives suggested a maximum of seventeen tanks lost by the SS panzer corps at Prokhorovka (Zetterling and Frankson, *Kursk*, p. 108).

45. For Manstein's assessment, see his *Verlorene Siegen*, p. 502. The invasion of Sicily was mounted by seven British and American infantry divisions; the first stage alone of Kursk involved nine Soviet tank or mechanized corps (comparable to armoured divisions) and seventy-six rifle divisions. On the other hand, for Berlin, the potential collapse of Mussolini's government had enormous implications in Italy and the Balkans.

46. Field Marshal Prince Kutuzov (1745–1813) was C-in-C of the armies that defeated Napoleon in 1812.

47. P. A. Rumiantsev-Zadunaiskii (1725–96) was another of Catherine the Great's Field Marshals, famous for his victories against the Turks. *Polkovodets* is not an actual rank, but a positive term for a senior military leader.

48. Zhukov, *ViR*, vol. 3, pp. 72, 77.

49. *Poteri*, pp. 285–7, 485; Overmans, *Verluste*, p. 277. The question of relative losses is discussed in detail by Frieser, in *DRZW*, vol. 8, pp. 129–35, 150–8, and Zetterling and Frankson, *Kursk*,

pp. 111–31. The latter authors assumed a quarter of German 'casualties' might be fatalities, that is personnel who were killed or died of their wounds. Soviet sources claimed 1,500 German tanks were lost in the Kursk, Briansk–Orel and Belgorod–Khar'kov battles from 5 July to 23 August;VOVE, 394b according to German sources, total German tank and SP gun losses on the whole Eastern Front from 1 July to 31 August 1943 were only 1,331. The greater losses of the Red Army at Kursk are conceded in the 1998–9 Russian official history, see Z. A. Shumov and N. M. Ramanichev in *VOV/VIO*, vol. 2, p. 284.

50. The proven ability of the Red Army to fight in the summer as well as in the winter was a point made by Stalin. See also Khrushchev's colourful account: 'Memuary', *VI*, 1991, no. 4–5, pp. 59–60.

51. General Antonov, deputy chief of the General Staff, told Vasilevskii that he thought Stalin was concerned about the slow pace of the southern offensive, the Belgorod–Khar'kov operation of 3 August and the Donbass operation of 13 August (Vasilevskii, *Delo*, vol. 2, pp. 40–1).

52. For the late summer stalemate, see Glantz, *Battle for Leningrad*, pp. 305–23, and K.-H. Frieser in *DRZW*, vol. 8, pp. 279–84.

53. Malyshev, 'Dnevnik', pp. 121 [2 July], 122–3 [8 September 1943]. Malyshev was impressed that the 63-year-old Stalin was able to climb into a tank without assistance.

54. *Poteri*, p. 288.

55. Malyshev, 'Dnevnik', p. 122 [7 August 1943].

Chapter 10

1. Noakes and Pridham, *Nazism*, vol. 3, pp. 919–21 [4 October 1943]. It was in this same speech that Himmler spoke openly of the mass murder of the Jews. He also put forward an entirely unrealistic assessment of the military situation: 'We shall charge ahead and push our way forward little by little to the Urals, I hope that … every one of our divisions spends a winter in the East every second or third year.'

2. The situation in the central sector of the front, including the period of the autumn and winter of 1943–4, will be discussed in Chapter 11, in connection with the great Soviet offensive in Belorussia in June 1944.

3. The 'Second Battle of the Ukraine' is a term made up for this book. Russian historians use the terms the 'Battle of the Dnepr' (*Bitva za Dnepr*) and the 'Offensive in the Right-bank Ukraine' (*Nastuplenie … na pravoberezhnoi Ukraine*). My term emphasizes the scope, cohesiveness and particularity of this long campaign, which continued over eight months, was conducted by the same forces, and took in most of the territory of the Ukraine. Soviet historians used to divide the war rigidly into periods. For them, the 'third period' (*tretii period*) began in January 1944. This schema is not fully satisfactory, because it plays down the extraordinary nature of the campaign in the Ukraine, which began in August 1943 and ran without pause or change of geographic setting until April 1944.

4. The term '*das "vergessene" Kriegsjahr*' is used in *DRZW*, vol. 8, p. 277, to emphasize this important gap in the historiography of the Nazi–Soviet war.

5. For operations in the Ukraine and the Crimea from August 1943 to April 1944, see: Ziemke, *Stalingrad to Berlin*, pp. 160–89, 218–47, 252–95; V. T. Eliseev and S. N. Mikhalev in *VOV/VIO*, vol. 3, p. 33–53; Frieser in *DRZW*, vol. 8, pp. 339–450; and K. Schönherr in *DRZW*, vol. 8, pp. 451–90.

6. Army Group North Ukraine would mostly be based in Poland, and Army Group South Ukraine would be located in Romania and Soviet Moldavia.

7. The Bukrin operation of September–October 1943 is obscured in Russian histories and memoirs by November's Liutezh breakout and by the overall success of operations around Kiev. Bukrin was an ambitious operation which, like the British MARKET-GARDEN airborne assault at Arnhem in the Netherlands, went badly wrong; see Frieser in *DRZW*, vol. 8, pp. 364–7. Zhukov maintained in his memoirs that the initiative for the Bukrin crossing came from the Stavka, but in fact he and Vatutin drafted the directive. Zhukov, remarkably, made no mention of the unsuccessful airborne side of the operation in his memoirs (*SDVG*, vol. 3, pp. 211–2, 405–7; Zhukov, *ViR*, vol. 3, pp. 80–6). At the time, both Zhukov and Vatutin were sharply criticized by Stalin; Vatutin was compared unfavourably to Konev (*RA/VO*, vol. 5(3), pp. 227–8 [24 October], 321–2 [24 October]).

8. The Stavka seems to have deserved credit for the Liutezh breakout. It had been Zhukov's opinion that, on balance, it was better to keep the main force where it was, in the Bukrin bridgehead (*RA/VO*, vol. 5(3), pp. 227–8 [24 October], 321–2 [24 October 1943]).

9. The Germans called the Korsun' pocket the Cherkassy pocket. To add to the confusion, the Russians normally call this the 'Korsun'-Shevchenkovskii' operation, although the small but ancient town of Korsun' was only renamed in 1944, after the great nineteenth-century Ukrainian poet Taras Shevchenko.

10. Konev was the fourth of the wartime Soviet marshals, after Zhukov, Vasilevskii and Stalin. He had made good his failures of 1941 and 1942 in the centre of the front. Although Konev had distinguished himself in the Kirovograd operation, as well as at Korsun', the latter was not a decisive triumph. Vatutin had not been awarded a Marshal's star for the capture of Kiev in November 1943. Stalin knew Konev well, and he may have wanted to use him as a counterweight to Zhukov. Soviet censors cut from early editions of Zhukov's memoirs his complaints about the lack of credit given to Vatutin (and to himself), and his hints about Konev's alleged backstabbing (*ViR*, vol. 3, pp. 112–15).

11. *RA/VO*, vol. 5(4), pp. 47 [18 February], 51 [25 February], 268–71 [23 February].

12. *RA/VO*, vol. 5(4), pp.47, 51, 56–7, 268–71. Maslov, *Fallen Soviet Generals*, pp. 129–31, and G. I. Rubtsov, 'S Ukrainoi porodnennyi armeiskoi sud'boi: General armii N. F. Vatutin (1901-1944)', *NNI*, 2005, no. 2, pp. 20–40, provide detailed accounts of Vatutin's ambush. Vatutin was only made a Hero of the Soviet Union posthumously, in 1965.

13. *RA/VO*, vol. 5(4), pp. 280–1 [25 March], 281–2 [5 April]; *SDVG*, vol. 4, p. 66 [5 April]. See D. Glantz, *Red Storm over the Balkans: The Failed Soviet Invasion of Romania, Spring 1944* (Lawrence, KS: University Press of Kansas, 2006).

14. Stalin's 'ten crushing blows' are discussed more fully in the following chapter.

15. Frieser in *DRZW*, vol. 8, pp. 447–50.

16. On 1 January 1943 the total Soviet tank park was 7,600 medium tanks (nearly all T-34s) and 11,000 light tanks. A year later, in the middle of the Battle of the Ukraine, the count was 9,200 mediums and only 10,300 light tanks. There were no self-propelled guns in the Red Army in January 1943; by January 1944 there were 3,300 (*Poteri*, pp. 475, 479). The number of trucks in the strategic reserve (*rezerv VGK*) had risen from 5,700 in November 1942, to 30,000 on 1 July 1943 (Zolotarev, *Deistvuiushchaia armiia*, pp. 552, 557), and many of these vehicles would have been made available in the autumn of 1943.

17. *RA/VO*, vol. 5(3), p. 314 [30 September 1943].

18. *RA/VO*, vol. 5(3), p. 222 [11 October 1943].

19. *Poteri*, p. 314.

20. Vasilevskii, *Delo*, vol. 2, p. 115.

21. Vasilevskii, *Delo*, vol. 2, p. 105; Ziemke, *Stalingrad to Berlin*, p. 295; *Poteri*, p. 294.

22. Bugai, *Beriia – Stalinu*, pp. 142–62.

23. On the breakout and its consequences, see: Glantz, *Battle for Leningrad*, pp. 327–66; V. O. Daines in *VOV/VOI*, vol. 3, pp. 20–32; and Frieser in *DRZW*, vol. 8, pp. 284–93.

24. Frieser in *DRZW*, vol. 8, pp. 285–6.

25. *RA/VO*, vol. 5(3), pp. 218–9 [8 October 1943], 246, 371 [12 October 1943], 425–30 [6 October 1943]; *SDVG*, vol. 3, p. 256 [25 October 1943].

26. *RA/VO*, vol. 5(4), p. 44 [14 February].

27. A complex reorganization had taken place in the northern part of the Soviet front in the autumn of 1943. In October the Baltic Army Group was formed under Popov, between Northwestern and Kalinin Army Groups. This used the headquarters and some units of the liquidated Briansk Army Group. On 20 October 1943, Baltic Army Group was renamed the 2nd Baltic Army Group, and on the same day Eremenko's Kalinin Army Group (on Popov's left flank) was renamed the 1st Baltic. The headquarters of Kurochkin's Northwestern Army Group, between the 2nd Baltic and Volkhov Army Groups, was finally disbanded on 20 November 1943.

28. The earlier attempts to break the Leningrad blockade were the Liuban' operation of April 1942, the Siniavino operation of August 1942 and Operation SPARK of January 1943.

29. *RA/VO*, vol. 5(4), p. 50 [22 February]; *Poteri*, p. 315.

30. In Operation SPARK of January 1943, a roundabout land route (with a new railway) had been established for Leningrad, but capacity was limited. The January 1944 success opened all the main transport routes from Leningrad to the centre of the USSR.

Chapter 11

1. Stalin, *OVOVSS*, p. 153 [6 November].

2. Voroshilov, *Stalin i vooruzhennye sily*, pp. 102, 120, 123.

3. Zhukov, *ViR*, vol. 3, pp. 126–7. For the campaign in Karelia, see: Ziemke, *Stalingrad to Berlin*, pp. 296–303; Glantz, *Battle for Leningrad*, pp. 415–45; P. Ia. Tsygankov in *VOV/VIO*, vol. 3, pp. 147–55; and M. Iu. Miagkov, 'Sovetskoe nastuplenie v Karelii letom 1944 goda i peremirie s Finliandiei', *NNI*, 2008, no. 6, pp. 120–45.

4. *SDVG*, vol. 4, pp. 385–7 [30 June 1944]; J. Nevakivi, 'The Soviet Union and Finland after the War, 1945–53', in F. Gori and S. Pons (eds), *The Soviet Union and Europe in the Cold War, 1943–53* (Basingstoke: Macmillan, 1996), p. 91.

5. The Red Army did enter northern Finland, but only into territory that had been ceded by Helsinki. There were also Soviet submarines based in southwestern Finland. For political aspects, see A. Richer, *Zhdanov in Finland*, Carl Beck Papers, No. 1107 (Pittsburgh, PA: University of Pittsburgh, 1996).

6. *RA/VO*, vol. 5(4), p. 143 [12 September].

7. The 1st Far Eastern Army Group was one of three army groups eventually deployed against Japan, the others being led by General Purkaev and Marshal Malinovskii. Although Meretskov was hardly the most successful of Stalin's marshals, the relevant point was probably that by the late autumn of 1944, his headquarters was available for redeployment.

8. On operations on the central front from the autumn of 1943 to the spring of 1944, see M. A. Gareev in *VOV/VIO*, vol. 3, pp. 10–19; Frieser in *DRZW*, vol. 8, pp. 297–338; and Ziemke, *Stalingrad to Berlin*, pp. 189–96.

9. For the Stavka directives for a westward advance in the autumn of 1943, see *RA/VO*, vol. 5(5), pp. 213 [1 October], 215 [1 October], 218–9 [8 October], 219 [8 October], 220 [10 October], 222 [15 October], 223–4 [15 October 1943]; *SDVG*, vol. 3, pp. 219 [20 September], 235 (1 October). The advance of northern wing, towards Ostrov, was discussed in Chapter 10.

10. Mendelsohn, *Covert Warfare*, vol. 6, p. 111.

11. For excerpts from the report, see *VOV/VIO*, vol. 3, pp. 441–53. Sokolovskii later became Konev's chief of staff in the very successful 1st Ukrainian Army Group. He recovered from this setback to become Chief of the General Staff in 1952–60, and a famous strategic textbook appeared under his name in 1962.

12. Zhukov, *ViR*, vol. 3, p. 124.

13. The best account from the German side is Frieser in *DRZW*, vol. 8, pp. 493–603; also useful is Ziemke, *Stalingrad to Berlin*, pp. 312–45. For the Russian perspective, see I. V. Timokhovich in *VOV/VIO*, vol. 3, pp. 54–80, and Erickson, *Road to Berlin*, pp. 196–247.

14. The name of the prince (and the operation) is often mispronounced by English-language speakers. It is 'Bagrah-tee-on', not 'Bagra-shon'.

15. The geography is complicated here. Bobruisk, the southern 'fortress town' is actually on the Berezina River, which is a tributary of the Dnepr, flowing into it from the west. Mogilev, Orsha and Vitebsk were considerably to the east of the Berezina.

16. The Red Army's operations in the south coincided with its L'vov–Sandomierz operation on the Ukrainian–Polish border. This began on 13 July and involved the left flank of Rokossovskii's 1st Belorussian Army Group as well as Konev's 1st Ukrainian Army Group. It will be discussed in Chapter 12.

17. The Soviet 'official' end point of the Belorussian operation was 29 August, which was when the four Soviet army groups were ordered onto the defensive. The main objectives, except in northeastern Poland, had been achieved four weeks earlier.

18. Ziemke, *Stalingrad to Berlin*, p. 312, n. 55. See also Frieser in *DRZW*, vol. 8, pp. 527–35.

19. Vasilevskii, *Delo*, vol. 2, p. 169.

20. V. N. Kiselev and G. A. Kumanev in *VOV/VIO*, vol. 3, pp. 285, 341; Frieser in *DRZW*, vol. 8, p. 517.

21. *VOVE*, p. 84; *Poteri*, p. 268.

22. The German intelligence failure is discussed in detail in Frieser, *DRZW*, vol. 8, pp. 493–516.

23. *Hitlers Weisungen*, pp. 243–50 [8 March].

24. K. von Tippelskich, *Geschichte des zweite Weltkriegs* (Bonn: Athenäum-Verlag, 1951).

25. Klink in *GSWW*, vol. 4, pp. 366, 528; Frieser in *DRZW*, vol. 8, pp. 531–3.

26. Bugai, *Beriia – Stalinu*, pp. 209–13, 219.

27. Vasilevskii, *Delo*, vol. 2, p. 136.

28. A. Price, *Luftwaffe Data Book* (London: Greenhill, 1997), pp. 92–128; *VOVE*, p. 84, *The Rise and Fall of the German Air Force (1933 to 1945)* (London: Public Record Office, 2001), p. 357.

29. Overmans, *Verluste*, pp. 239, 278, 322; *VOV/VIO*, vol. 3, p. 76.

30. *Poteri*, pp. 296, 486. The Russian published figure of 179,000 losses took in the whole period from 23 June to 29 August 1944, and included operations in Latvia, Lithuania and eastern

Poland. It extended to the Lublin–Brest operation, which continued through August and involved heavy fighting in front of Warsaw and in the bridgeheads on the Vistula River. F. Pogue, *The Supreme Command* (Washington, DC: Office of the Chief of Military History, 1952), and L. Ellis, *Victory in the West* (London: HMSO, 1962), vol. 1, p. 493, give losses in Normandy.

31. Beria's report on the 'parade' was printed in *VOV/VIO*, vol. 3, pp. 457–8.

32. In Soviet military historiography, the 'Baltic [*Pribaltiiskaia*] operation' runs from 14 September (with the first attacks on Riga) to 24 November 1944 (when the Moon Sound amphibious operation was completed). It would be more logical to begin the campaign much earlier, in early August, with Bagramian's unsuccessful attack on Riga and with the Soviet Madona and Tartu operations of early August. This does, however, become confused with the end of the so-called 'Belorussian operation', which runs to 29 August.
    On the 1944–5 Baltic operations, however defined, see: Ziemke, *Stalingrad to Berlin*, pp. 403–10; Frieser in *DRZW*, vol. 8, pp. 623–78; and P. Ia. Tsygankov in *VOV/VIO*, vol. 3, pp. 155–71.

33. These were the 15th, the 19th and the 20th Waffen-SS Grenadier Divisions. Himmler did not want to create Lithuanian formations, as he regarded the Lithuanians as racially unacceptable.

34. M. Iu. Krysin, *Pribaltika mezhdu Stalinym i Gitlerom* (Moscow: Veche, 2004), provides extensive detail of the German occupation set-up; the book is a heavy-handed attempt to show the collaboration of the nationalists with the Nazis and to counter the Baltic nationalist historiography of the 1990s. For an updated émigré account, see T. U. Raun, *Estonia and the Estonians*, 2nd edn (Stanford, CA: Hoover Institution Press, 2001), pp. 157–68.

35. See G. Jukes, 'Ivan Khristoforovich Bagramian', in Shukman, *Stalin's Generals*, pp. 25–32.

36. Shtemenko, *General'nyi shtab*, p. 340.

37. The attack in Estonia developed more slowly than the Stavka expected. On 28 July the Leningrad Army Group had been ordered to reach Rakvere, well to the west of Narva, by 5–8 August at the latest, with the intention of moving rapidly on to Tallin and Parnau (*RA/VO*, vol. 5(4), p. 116).

38. *RA/VO*, vol. 5(4), p. 116 [28 July].

39. It is possible, however, that the unsuccessful outcome for the Soviets at Riga actually favoured the Red Army (although this could not have been predicted in advance). Hitler did not want to give up Kurland, and a large number of German divisions, some of good quality, were tied up there, while the heart of the Reich was under attack.

40. *RA/VO*, vol. 5(4), p. 161 [19 October]; *SDVG*, vol. 4, pp. 458–9 [22 October].

41. *Poteri*, p. 515.

42. On repression and deportations from the Baltic in 1944–5, see Bugai, *Beriia – Stalinu*, pp. 212–15, 218–19.

43. Stalin, *OVOVSS*, p. 168 [6 November]. The reconquest of the Moldavian SSR (Bessarabia), which took place in late August 1944, will be discussed in Chapter 12.

Chapter 12

1. Stalin, *OVOVSS*, p. 145 [1 May 1944].

2. Zhukov was in charge of the 1st Ukrainian Army Group and the 1st and the 2nd Belorussian Army Groups, while Vasilevskii led (from south to north) the 3rd Belorussian Army Group and the 1st and 2nd Baltic Army Groups (*RA/VO*, vol. 5(4), p. 120 [29 July 1944]).

3. This paradigm comes from Zubok and Pleshakov, *Inside the Kremlin's Cold War*; see also Chapter 1. Geoffrey Roberts' overview of Soviet policy towards eastern Europe and Germany in 1944–5 is in *Stalin's Wars*, pp. 228–53; see also his *Molotov: Stalin's Cold Warrior* (Washington: Potomac Books, 2012).

4. The 'Commission on Questions concerning the Peace Treaties and Post-War Situation [*ustroistvo*]' was set up under Litvinov after a Politburo decision of 4 September 1943. There was also a 'Commission Concerning Armistice Questions' under Voroshilov and including Maiskii. A 'Commission for the Compensation of Losses suffered by the Soviet Union', usually referred to as the 'Commission on Reparations', was created under Maiskii on 22 November 1944.

   Litvinov's paper was concerned mainly with Germany, which will be discussed in greater detail in Chapter 13. Neither paper actually expressed the 'official' policy of the USSR, but they are among the broadest overviews available from within the Soviet elite. Maiskii and Litvinov were very unlikely to have put forward views that differed markedly from what they took to be those of either Stalin or Molotov. For a further discussion, see G. Roberts, 'Ideology, Calculation, and Improvisation: Spheres of Influence and Soviet Foreign Policy, 1939–1945', *Review of International Studies*, vol. 25, 1999, pp. 655–73, and A. M. Filatov, 'Problems of Post-War Reconstruction in Soviet Foreign Policy Conceptions during World War II', in Gori and Pons, *Soviet Union and Europe in the Cold War*, pp. 3–22.

5. G. P. Kynin and I. Laufer (eds), *SSSR i germanskii vopros. 1941–1949. Dokumenty iz Arkhiva vneshnei politiki Rossiiskoi Federatsii*, 3 vols (Moscow: Mezhdunarodnye otnosheniia, 1996–2000), vol. 1, pp. 333–60 [11 January 1944]; Chuev, *Sto sorok besed s Molotovym*, p. 8.

6. *SSSR i germanskii vopros*, vol. 1, pp. 336, 352; Dimitrov, *Diary*, p. 124 [21 January 1940]. The Finns did in fact sign a 'long-term pact' with the USSR in 1948.

7. Malyshev, 'Dnevnik', p. 128 [28 March 1945].

8. *SSSR i germanskii vopros*, vol. 1, pp. 348–9 [11 January 1944].

9. The revolutionary nature of the Soviet state is a very complex question, bringing in the divisions between right and left in the Soviet Communist Party and Stalin's personality. An important factor was the Great Terror of the 1930s, which particularly affected the Comintern. It is still, eighty years after the fact, a hotly debated subject.

10. *15-ia konferentsiia Vsesoiuznoi Kommunisticheskoi partii (B): 26 oktiabria – 3 noiabria 1926 g.: Stenograficheskii otchet* (Moscow: GIZ, 1927), p. 674; Chuev, *140 besed*, pp. 91–2.

11. Dimitrov, *Diary*, p. 358 [28 January 1945]; M. Djilas, *Conversations with Stalin* (Harmondsworth: Penguin, 1962), p. 90. It could be argued, however, that Stalin said one thing to revolutionary firebrands like Dimitrov and Djilas and another to the diplomats at the Foreign Commissariat or the generals. Which was the 'real' Stalin is not at all easy to determine, and the Soviet dictator probably did not have one simple view.

12. Volokitina, *Sovetskii faktor*, vol. 1, p. 481.

13. This discussion leaves out consideration of any awareness the Soviet leaders may have had, even during the war years, of the potential of US nuclear weapons. On this, see D. Holloway, *Stalin and the Bomb* (New Haven, CT: Yale University Press, 1994), pp. 82–4, 90–5, 103–8, 116–18.

14. Djilas, *Conversations*, p. 61; *RA/VO*, vol. 3(2), p. 196 [24 April 1944].

15. For the best discussion of these policy disputes, see G. Swain, 'The Cominform: Tito's International', *Historical Journal*, vol. 35, 1992, no. 2, pp. 641–64.

16. Loewenheim, *Roosevelt and Churchill*, p. 503 [31 May]. At this time, both Romania and Greece were still within the German sphere.

17. O. Rzheshevskii, *Stalin i Cherchill* (Moscow: Nauka, 2004), pp. 412–87. The 'percentages agreement' did not deal with Poland or Czechoslovakia.

18. A. F. Noskova et al. (eds), *Iz Varshavy* (Moscow: Institut slavianovedeniia RAN/Sibirskii khronograf, 2001), pp. 351–2.

19. Dimitrov, *Diary*, pp. 124–5 [21 January 1940].

20. In describing the 1944–5 situation, I have used the Curzon Line (see below) as the eastern frontier of 'ethnic' Poland and counted East Prussia, Pomerania and Silesia as 'German'. I appreciate that this terminology will not satisfy everyone.

21. Dimitrov, *Diary*, p. 116 [7 September 1939]; J. Ciechanowski, *The Warsaw Rising of 1944* (Cambridge: Cambridge University Press, 1974), p. 4.

22. *SSSR i germanskii vopros*, vol. 1, pp. 341–2, 353 [11 January 1944]. As we will see, 'the strict principle of the ethnographic border' applied only in the east, not in the west or north. In the same paragraph, Maiskii proposed transferring East Prussia and Silesia to Poland, after the expulsion of the German population.

23. In Russian histories, the initial Soviet operations in northeastern Poland are dealt with as part of the so-called Belorussian operation. In a broad sense this was appropriate; the BAGRATION offensive opened on the Vitebsk–Orsha–Mogilev–Bobruisk line on 22 June 1944 and continued without significant pause until the end of August. In the terminology of the time, Operation BAGRATION was the fifth Stalinist 'crushing blow'; the sixth 'crushing blow' was the L'vov–Sandomierz operation.
    For the campaigns in Poland in 1944, see Ziemke, *Stalingrad to Berlin*, pp. 335–45; Frieser in *DRZW*, vol. 8, pp. 558–87, 604–12; and I. V. Timokhovich in *VOV/VIO*, vol. 3, pp. 71–6.

24. Shortly after the 1939 advance, the USSR ceded to Nazi Germany the most western part of the Polish territory it had occupied, including the city of L'vov, in exchange for Lithuania.

25. R. Woff, 'Konstantin Konstantinovich Rokossovsky', in Shukman, *Stalin's Generals*, pp. 177–96; Iu. V. Rubtsov, '"Sovetskii Bagration" Marshal K. K. Rokossovskii (1896-1968)', *NNI*, 2004, no. 6, pp. 148–74. The latest (1997) version of the Marshal's memoirs includes extensive comments that were deleted in the Soviet era: Rokossovskii, *Soldatskii dolg*.

26. Stalin was acutely aware of the 'national question', but it would be going too far to say that he put Rokossovskii in charge of the central Polish operation because he was a Pole. It happened that Rokossovskii's force had ended up here. Rokossovskii would, as we will see, be removed from this central command before the Soviet offensive into central Poland began in January 1945. Central and western Poland would be liberated by ethnic Russian marshals, Zhukov and Konev.

27. The town of Vil'nius/Wilno (in Lithuania) had been captured slightly earlier (see Chapter 11). Vil'nius had been outside the USSR in August 1939, but it was inside the territory Stalin annexed before June 1941.

28. *RA/VO*, vol. 5(4), p. 113 [21 July 1944].

29. Ziemke, *Stalingrad to Berlin*, pp. 336–7. Josef Harpe was one of the lesser known Eastern Front commanders. He commanded a panzer corps in Russia from January 1942, then took over the 9th Army in November 1943. Harpe had only in June 1944 assumed command of German Army Group North Ukraine, when Model was transferred to Army Group Centre.

30. Ziemke, *Stalingrad to Berlin*, pp. 336–7; Frieser in *DRZW*, vol. 8, pp. 568–9.

31. For Frieser's argument, see *DRZW*, vol. 8, pp. 570–87, 602–3. M. I. Mel'tiukhov, 'Operatsiia "Bagration" i Varshavskoe vosstanie 1944 goda', *VI*, 2004, no. 11, pp. 43–57, provided new information from the Russian point of view. See also Glantz, 'Forgotten Battles', pp. 415–18.

32. Zhukov, *ViR*, vol.3, pp. 152–3 [19 July]; *RA/VO*, vol. 5(4), pp. 118–9 [28 July]. The 3rd Belorussian Army group – on the far side of East Prussia and comparable to General Rennenkampf's army in the 1914 Tannenberg campaign – was not under Zhukov's direct control. Zhukov suggested another mission for his own third army group, 1st Ukrainian.

33. Zhukov, *ViR*, vol. 3, p. 154.

34. *RA/VO*, vol. 5(4), pp. 115 [24 July], 115–6 [27 July], 199 [28 July], 294 [23 July], 294–5 [26 July 1944].

35. *RA/VO*, vol. 5(4), pp. 136–7 [29 August]. The Stavka sent similar orders on this day to the Leningrad and Karelian Army Groups. These 'defensive fronts' were also ordered to economize on their use of ammunition (*RA/VO*, vol. 12(4), pp. 389–90).

36. *RA/VO*, vol. 5(4), pp. 130–1 [26 August], 132–3 [29 August]; *SDVG*, vol. 4, pp. 405–6 [3 August 1944].

37. Zhukov, 'Chego stoiat polkovodcheskie kachestva Stalina', p. 153. Some 35,000 Soviet troops were lost in the Serock and Łomza–Rózan operations of September and October 1944 (*Poteri*, p. 316).

38. The best account is in N. Davies, *Rising '44: The Battle for* Warsaw (Basingstoke: Macmillan, 2003). See also Ciechanowski, *Warsaw Uprising*.

39. The existence of these inflammatory messages were confirmed on 23 September in an internal report by G. Aleksandrov to Shcherbakov (*RA/VO*, vol. 3(2), pp. 434–5); see also *RA/VO*, vol. 3(1), pp. 199–200 [26 July]. Officially the Russians denied such messages.

40. Operation TEMPEST (BURZA), under which the Home Army's Warsaw rising was carried out, was actually a plan for increased anti-German diversionary activity *outside* Warsaw.

41. A. Werth, *Russia at War 1941–1945* (London: Barrie and Rockliff, 1964), p. 878.

42. *RA/VO*, vol. 5(4), pp. 118–9; Vasilevskii, *Delo*, vol. 2, p. 161. In early October Stalin told a visiting PKWN delegation that 'the Soviet High Command had hoped to take Warsaw, making use of the panic generated and counting on confusion to delay the construction of defences. Unfortunately ammunition supplies arrived two days late and the Germans had time to bring up their reserves' (A. Polonsky and B. Drukier (eds), *The Beginnings of Communist Rule in Poland* (London: Routledge & Kegan Paul, 1980), p. 298 [9 October 1944]).

43. *RA/VO*, vol. 3(2), pp. 420–1 [8 August].

44. *SDVG*, vol. 4, p. 152 [21 August]; *RA/VO*, vol. 5(4), p. 137 [29 August].

45. *RA/VO*, vol. 3(2), p. 433 [21 September].

46. Polonsky and Drukier, *Beginnings*, p. 301 [9 October].

47. *RA/VO*, vol. 3(2), p. 442.

48. Zhukov, *ViR*, vol. 3, pp. 148, 170, 179–80.

49. Polonsky and Drukier, *Beginnings*, pp. 297–8 [9 October 1944].

50. Zhukov, *ViR*, vol. 3, pp. 173–4. There is no reference to this conference in Stalin's appointments diary, but as mentioned in Chapter 6, that source does not give a complete picture of the Soviet dictator's activities.

51. For the Vistula–Oder operation, see Ziemke, *Stalingrad to Berlin*, pp. 419–28; R. Lakowski in *DRZW*, vol. 10.1, pp. 491–531; and V. N. Kiselev in *VOV/VIO*, vol. 3, pp. 230–44.

52. Zhukov, *ViR*, vol. 3, pp. 179, 183. This is discussed further in Chapter 13.

53. The alternative would have been to make one officer responsible for all three army groups, under Stalin. Zhukov linked Stalin's decision to the October 1944 disagreement about

strategy in Poland; see Zhukov, *ViR*, vol. 3, p. 172, and Simonov, *Glazami cheloveka moego pokoleniia*, pp. 326–7.

54. Zhukov, *ViR*, vol. 3, p. 173.

55. Zakharov was 'demoted' to command the 4th Guards Army, which was being deployed from the Stavka reserve to fight in Hungary.

56. *VOVE*, p. 130. German Army Group 'A' bore the main brunt of the Vistula–Oder operation. Lakowski in *DRZW*, vol. 10.1, pp. 502–4, gives it a strength of 401,000 men in its operational units on 1 January 1945, along with 318 AFVs, 616 field guns and 793 AT guns. Luftwaffe strength was 800 aircraft, including 300 fighters and 400 fighter-bombers.

57. The fighting in 'German' Silesia will be covered in Chapter 13.

58. Zhukov, *ViR*, vol. 3, p. 209.

59. *RA/VO*, vol. 3(2), p. 454 [29 January].

60. *Poteri*, pp. 296, 297, 303, 449. Defining what is meant by 'Poland' is only part of the problem. The Russians have published casualty figures specific to the L'vov–Sandomierz and Vistula–Oder operations – total 108,000 killed – but not for the Lublin–Brest operation. Russian-published figures lump losses for the Lublin–Brest operation (8 July to 2 August 1944) in with those of the whole 'Belorussian strategic offensive operation' (23 June to 29 August 1944). Within those Belorussian-offensive figures, the share of losses was 66,000 for the 1st Belorussian Army Group; this was the main force involved in the Lublin–Brest operation, and it was only peripherally involved in Belorussia. So a figure of 150,000 lost in Poland is probably about right.

61. *FRUS: Malta and Yalta*, p. 670; Noskova, *Iz Varshavy*, p. 26. By this time the Home Army was burned out. The German war was over. The Russians, seeking to attain Western recognition for the Warsaw government, had broadened its basis by including Mikołajczyk.

62. *SSSR i germanskii vopros*, vol. 1, pp. 336, 342–4, 352–3 [11 January 1944].

63. *RA/VO*, vol. 5(4), p. 82 [3 May 1944]. In an abrupt change of line from the Stavka, the 3rd and the 2nd Ukrainian Army Groups were ordered to 'strict defence' on 6 May 1944. On the 15th, the commanders were reshuffled, Malinovskii replacing Konev in the 2nd Ukrainian, and Tolbukhin replacing Malinovskii in the 3rd Ukrainian. At the end of May, the 5th Guards Tank Army and the 8th Guards Army were withdrawn into the Stavka reserve. Both ended up in Belorussia (*RA/VO*, vol. 5(4), pp. 84–5 [6 May], 86 [15 May]; vol. 12(4), pp. 213–4 [27 May], 216–7 [27 May]).

    This proposed Romanian offensive is not mentioned in Marshal Zhukov's account of the Stavka conference of 22–23 April 1944 (Zhukov, *ViR*, vol. 3, pp. 122–7). See also Glantz, *Red Storm over the Balkans*.

    Hardesty and Grinberg, *Red Phoenix Rising*, pp. 286–95, detail the major air battles over Iaşi in May and June 1944.

64. Schörner himself had only taken over the Army Group South Ukraine from Field Marshal Kleist in late March 1944. Friessner would not be held personally responsible for the Romanian disaster. He remained in command of Army Group South Ukraine until the crisis at Budapest at the end of December 1944.

65. The reputation of Timoshenko had been in decline since the 1942 Khar'kov disaster, and he was sidetracked following the failure of his advances northwest of Moscow at the start of 1943.

66. For the campaign in Romania in August and September 1944, see: Ziemke, *Stalingrad to Berlin*, pp. 346–56; K. Schönherr in *DRZW*, vol. 8, pp. 731–815; B. I. Nevzorov and V. V. Mar'ina in *VOV/VIO*, vol. 3, pp. 81–99.

67. *RA/VO*, vol. 3(2), p. 64 [21 October].

68. Loewenheim, *Roosevelt and Churchill*, pp. 660–1 [8 March].

69. Even the figure of 69,000 for overall Soviet losses is hard to square with the individual operations. The Bucharest–Arad operation (30 August to 3 October), that is, the overrunning of central and western Romania, claimed only 8,500 Soviet lives (*Poteri*, pp. 297–8, 316, 449). Combined with the Iaşi–Kishenev operation, that gives a total of less than 22,000.

70. *SSSR i germanskii vopros*, vol. 1, pp. 343–4, 353 [11 January 1944].

71. Ziemke, *Stalingrad to Berlin*, pp. 368–71; K. Schönherr in *DRZW*, vol. 8, pp. 815–9; B. I. Nevzorov and V. V. Mar'ina in *VOV/VIO*, vol. 3, pp. 99–107.

72. Zhukov, *ViR*, 3, pp. 164ff. The decision to send Zhukov was all the more surprising, as Marshal Timoshenko was already present, co-ordinating the 2nd and the 3rd Ukrainian Army Groups. General Tolbukhin, the commander of the formation which invaded Bulgaria – the 3rd Ukrainian Army Group – had already proven his considerable military talent.

73. *Poteri*, p. 449.

74. *SSSR i germanskii vopros*, vol. 1, pp. 343–4, 353 [11 January 1944].

75. For the Soviet–German military campaign in Yugoslavia, see: Ziemke, *Stalingrad to Berlin*, pp. 371–8; Nevzorov and Mar'ina in *VOV/VIO*, vol. 3, pp. 107–14; and K. Schmider in *DRZW*, vol. 8, pp. 1047–70.

76. S. M. Shtemenko, *General'nyi shtab v gody voiny* (Moscow: Voenizdat, 1989), p. 399. The General Staff argued that the more northerly advance would also open the road to Bohemia; the northern route also required shorter supply lines from the western USSR. The political advantage of an advance west into Croatia was presumably that it would pre-empt a possible British–American landing in Istria.

77. *FRUS: Malta and Yalta*, pp. 600f. The Ljubljana Gap was the relatively easy route from northeastern Italy across northwestern Yugoslavia (Slovenia) to Austria. Antonov noted, however, that 'he now understood that [such an offensive] was not possible'; this was evidently due to the fact that the Americans were withdrawing divisions from northern Italy.

78. *Poteri*, pp. 300–1, 449; Maslov, *Fallen Soviet Generals*, pp. 163, 206–8.

79. D. Cornelius, *Hungary in World War II: Caught in the Cauldron* (New York: Fordham University Press, 2011), pp. 226–383, deals with the situation in 1944–5. For the campaign in Hungary in 1944–5, see also: Ziemke, *Stalingrad to Berlin*, pp. 379–84, 433–7, 450–4; K. Schönherr in *DRZW*, vol. 8, pp. 819–48; K. Ungvary in *DRZW*, vol. 8, pp. 849–958; and B. I. Nevzorov and B. Zhelitski in *VOV/VIO*, vol. 3, pp. 131–41.

80. *SSSR i germanskii vopros*, vol. 1, p. 342 [11 January 1944].

81. Tolbukhin's 37th Army, under General Biriuzov, was left behind to occupy Bulgaria. The 5th Shock Army was transferred in October 1944 to the 1st Belorussian Army Group in Poland, in anticipation of the big offensive there.

82. *RA/VO*, vol. 3(2), p. 290, vol. 5(4), p. 160 [18 October].

83. *RA/VO*, vol. 3(2), pp. 314 [2 November], 329 [21 November].

84. *RA/VO*, vol. 5(4), p. 162 [24 October].

85. *RA/VO*, vol. 5(4), p. 194 [21 January]. Before 21 January 1945, Timoshenko co-ordinated Malinovskii's operations with those of his neighbour to the north of the Carpathians, Petrov's 4th Ukrainian Army Group.

86. *SDVG*, vol. 4, pp. 482–4 [17 December].

87. K. Ungváry, *Battle for Budapest: 100 Days in World War II* (London: Tauris, 2003), provides a full account.

88. *RA/VO*, vol. 3, pp. 362–3 [31 January].

89. Shtemenko, *General'nyi shtab*, p. 216; *Poteri*, pp. 317, 449, 486.

90. Dimitrov, *Diary*, p. 222 [5 June 1942].

91. For Stalin and other older Soviet leaders, there were distressing associations with another Russian-sponsored formation of Czechoslovak POWs. The Czechoslovak Legion was created by the Tsarist government in the First World War, mostly from Austro-Hungarian POWs. It created great difficulties in 1918–19, during the Russian Civil War, when it fought against the Communist government.

92. Russia had no historic claim to the region; Sub-Carpatho Ruthenia had been within Austria–Hungary before 1918. Aside from its Ukrainian population, Sub-Carpatho Ruthenia was strategically important to the Russians because of the L'vov–Užgorod–Debrecen railway, which connected Poland to Hungary. Control of the region also gave the USSR a common border with Hungary.

93. *SSSR i germanskii vopros*, vol. 1, p. 342 [11 January 1944]. The Czechoslovakia–USSR treaty was signed in July 1941. Teschen (Těšín) was a disputed border region between Poland and Czechoslovakia, which had been taken by the Poles in 1938. The eventual Soviet annexation of Sub-Carpatho Ruthenia went against the spirit of this proposal. It lopped off the eastern tip of Czechoslovakia. Elsewhere, the paper proposed modifying the Polish or Romanian borders to give the USSR a common border with Czechoslovakia (p. 336).

94. The émigré author Rezun-Suvorov mentioned pre-war plans to send the Red Army over the Carpathians, but so far this has not been supported by the published Russian documents: Suvorov, *Icebreaker*, pp. 158–62.

95. The original 4th Ukrainian Army Group, under Tolbukhin, had been disbanded in May 1944 after the completion of the Crimean operation.

96. *SDVG*, vol. 4, pp. 156 [26 August], 415 [13 August].

97. K. Schönherr in *DRZW*, vol. 8, pp. 719–24; B. I. Nevzorov and V. V. Mar'ina in *VOV/VOI*, vol. 3, pp. 118–30.

98. In one sense, the Slovak uprising was redundant, as Axis defences south of the Carpathians crumbled so quickly, at the end of August and in September. Had Romania not changed sides, and had Germany been able to hold a line in central Romania, then a Red Army threat to the rear of this position through the Dukla Pass and the Carpathians would have been very important.

99. In November and December 1944, with the 1st Hungarian Army under its command, the German 8th Army headquarters was called Army Group Wöhler. Wöhler's command was under German Army Group South and Heinrici's under Army Group 'A'.

100. *RA/VO*, vol. 5(4), pp. 330–3 [13 February]. For Stalin's condemnation of the 4th Ukrainian Army Group command, see *RA/VO*, vol. 5(4), p. 210 [17 March]. General Petrov continued his career in the post-war Soviet Army; he was deputy commander of Ground Forces in the 1950s.

101. *Perepiska*, vol. 2, p. 222 [7 April].

102. The details of the German capitulation in May 1945 will be discussed in Chapter 13.

103. Kiselev in *VOV/VIO*, vol. 3, pp. 290–4. For a recent balanced discussion of the role of Vlasov, see B. N. Petrov, 'Kto osvobozhdal Pragu?', *VIA*, vol. 2001, no. 19, pp. 169–76.

104. Ehrman, *Grand Strategy*, vol. 6, pp. 157–9. Eisenhower's options and strategic decisions in April 1945 will be discussed further in Chapter 13.

105. *Poteri*, p. 308.

106. This headquarters could not actually trace its history back to the Army Group Centre of 1941. The original Army Group Centre had been driven back from Belorussia in 1944 and into northern Poland and East Prussia, where in late January 1945 it was renamed Army Group North. Schörner's Army Group Centre of May 1945 was the renamed Army Group 'A', which was originally part of the 1941 Army Group South.

107. *Poteri*, p. 515.

108. The number of trucks in the active army had risen from 217,000 on 1 June 1944 to 268,000 on 1 January 1945; the number in the strategic reserve (*rezerv VGK*) decreased from 22,000 to 14,000 (Zolotarev, *Deistvuiushchaia armiia*, pp. 568, 573).

109. *Poteri*, p. 449; Pogue, *Supreme Command*, p. 543.

110. Overmans, *Verluste*, pp. 239, 278–9. Overmans links these high losses with the destruction of Army Group South Ukraine in Moldavia. However, in view of the relative losses of the Red Army (13,000 in Iaşi–Kishenev vs. 65,000 in L'vov–Sandomierz and 179,000 in Belorussia), the bulk of the German losses must have been further north.

111. Dear and Foot, *Oxford Companion*, p. 52. Using normal loss assumptions, there would have been about 25,000 German deaths out of 100,000 casualties.

112. Maiskii also envisaged a Germany that had been broken up into smaller states and would be occupied by Allied forces for at least ten years.

113. J. Hanhimäki and O. Westad, *The Cold War: A History in Documents and Eyewitness Accounts* (Oxford: Oxford University Press, 2003), p. 48.

Chapter 13

1. Kershaw, *The End*, provides a valuable study of the last year of the Reich, with an emphasis on explaining why the resistance organized by the Nazi Party continued for such a long time. See also the articles in *GSWW*, vol. 9.

2. *Goebbels Reden 1932-1945*, p. 178 [18 February 1943]; Loewenheim *Roosevelt and Churchill*, pp. 603–5 [24 November 1944].

3. Domarus, *Hitler: Reden*, vol. 1, pp. 1312–17 [1 September 1939], vol. 2, p. 1935 [8 November 1942]. See M. Geyer, 'Insurrectionary Warfare: The German Debate about a *Levée en Masse* in October 1918', *Journal of Modern History*, vol. 73, 2001, no. 3, p. 509, also B. Wegner, 'Hitler, der Zweite Weltkrieg und die Choreographie des Untergangs', pp. 493–518. I am indebted to William Mulligan for these references.

4. *Germanskii vopros*, vol. 1, pp. 333–60 [11 January], 419–49 [9 March]. For a background to the Maiskii and Litvinov papers, see Chapter 12.

5. This summary skates over a great deal of diplomatic ice. Even in late May 1944, President Roosevelt tried to renegotiate the occupation zones, although he was more concerned about the British than the Russians. The zones were originally premised on a single German state. In February 1945, at Yalta, the Big Three actually agreed in principle to the dismemberment of Germany, and that this dismemberment would not necessarily coincide with the agreed occupation zones. In any event, this was not carried out. At Yalta the Russians agreed to the creation of a French zone, but only if it was carved out of the American and British ones.

6. The policies of the Comintern and its successors in eastern Europe were discussed in Chapter 12.

7. Voroshilov, *Stalin i vooruzhennye sily*, pp. 120, 123. See Chapter 9, n. 3.

8. For a discussion of the planning of the final operations against Germany, see V. N. Kiselev in *VOV/VIO*, vol. 3, pp. 230–37, and Lakowski in *DRZW*, vol. 10.1, pp. 510–15. Chapter 12 covers operations in Poland in January 1945, which were the beginning of the assault on Germany.

9. Specific end dates for this first Berlin operation were evidently not given. The time period of fifteen and thirty days has been added here to the 'orientation' starting date of 20 January 1944. Zhukov's initial directive, dated 27 December 1944 and evidently approved by Stalin on that date, was for an advance to Łódź in central Poland, which is only about 75 miles southwest of Warsaw. (*RA/VO*, vol. 5(4), pp. 320–6; *VOV/VIO*, vol. 3, p. 234).

10. Shtemenko, *General'nyi shtab*, pp. 216–19.

11. General Antonov would tell the British and American planners at Yalta that 'the Soviet forces would press forward until hampered by weather'. 'The most difficult season from the point of view of weather was the second part of March and the month of April. This was the period when roads became impassable' (*FRUS: Malta and Yalta*, p. 579 [4 February]). He was saying this at the moment the Soviet general plan was changing, but the reckoning on the weather was presumably a constant for the planners.

    This prediction was based on the Russians' experience of the past three years with the *rasputitsa*. For Antonov's comparable directive from the late winter of 1943–4, see *RA/VO*, vol. 12(4), p. 83 [25 February 1944]. The Russian command evidently assumed that the same conditions would apply to battlefields and supply lines in Poland. And yet in 1945 it was precisely during this *rasputitsa* period that the British and Americans were planning their own Rhine crossings, and they told the Russians this.

12. For the start of the Vistula–Oder operation, see Chapter 12.

13. Shtemenko, *General'nyi shtab*, pp. 221–3.

14. *FRUS: Malta and Yalta*, pp. 581, 588 [4 February].

15. The Russian historian V. N. Kiselev was the first to make this important point about the intended early January start of the Vistula–Oder operation. He cited army-group documents from the Russian military archives. According to these, Zhukov's first-echelon rifle divisions were to be in position on the Vistula bridgeheads by the morning of 8 January. Konev was to begin his offensive on the 9th, Rokossovskii on the 10th; see V. N. Kiselev, 'Visla-Ardenny, 1944–1945', *VIZh*, 1993, no. 6, p. 30; *VOV/VIO*, vol. 3, p. 236.

    We also know that the central Soviet army groups had been ordered at the end of November 1944 to prepare their plans (*RA/VO*, vol. 5(2), pp. 174–7 [28 November]). General Petrov, at the 4th Ukrainian Army Group, was instructed on 30 November that his operation against Kraków, in co-operation with Marshal Konev, was to take the city 'no later than *the beginning of January 1945*' [my emphasis] (*RA/VO*, vol. 5(4), pp. 178–9). Rokossovskii's attack directive was dated 17 December, Konev's directive the 23rd and Zhukov's the 27th (*RA/VO*, vol. 5(4), pp. 311–26). Presumably the four-day delay in the start date, from 8 to 12 January, was set by the Stavka some time at the very end of 1944. On 7 January Stalin informed Churchill that the weather was poor, affecting Soviet aviation and artillery, but that preparations would be accelerated (*Perepiska*, vol. 1, p. 341).

16. Zhukov maintained that the Stavka approved this suggestion, but no document giving approval was published in *RA/VO*, vol. 5(4). Zhukov also claimed that Konev made a similar proposal on 28 January to destroy the Breslau group and reach the lower Elbe by 25–28

February, while the forces on his right flank co-operated with those on Zhukov's left to take Berlin (Zhukov, *ViR*, vol. 3, p. 199).

17. 'Marshal G. K. Zhukov: "... [*sic*] nastuplenie na Berlin mogu nachat' 19–20.2.45"', *VIZh*, 1995, no. 2, pp. 4–6. This important signal was not published in the document collection *RA/VO*.

18. Zhukov's general report of 21 March 1945 to the Stavka regarding his operations since 14 January was less than candid. This stressed 'the liberation from Germany of our ally, the Polish republic', and there was no mention of his requests to continue to Berlin (*RA/VO*, vol. 12(4), pp. 458–61).

19. Shtemenko, *General'nyi shtab*, p. 220; Zhukov, *ViR*, vol. 3, p. 199. Neither Konev's signal nor the Stavka response was published in *RA/VO*.

20. This argument has been put forward in a book which, although published in 1979, remains an important treatment of Stalin's late wartime foreign policy: V. Mastny, *Russia's Road to the Cold War: Diplomacy, Warfare, and the Politics of Communism, 1941–1945* (New York: Columbia University Press, 1979), pp. 237, 243–4.

21. Opinions vary about the effectiveness of Army Group Vistula. The most recent general Russian account, by Kiselev, suggests that 'Himmler quickly created in Pomerania a powerful grouping of forces'; Zhukov's intelligence discovered 'Himmler's concentration of forces' (*VOV/VIO*, vol. 3, pp. 242–3). In reality, Army Group Vistula was a weak force.

22. Hinsley, *British Intelligence*, vol. 3(2), p. 649, 655, 850; *FRUS: Malta and Yalta*, p. 648; *RA/VO*, vol. 12(4), p. 633; *Perepiska*, vol. 2, p. 223 [7 April 1945]. Although this would not have caused the initial pause, the British mistakenly told the Russians in early February 1945 that the Germans were sending panzer divisions to Pomerania, when they were actually going south to Hungary. See V. I. Lota, 'Razvedyvatel'noe obespechenie Balatonskoi oboronitel'noi operatsii Krasnoi armii v gody Velikoi Otechestvennoi voiny', *VIZh*, 2006, no. 5, pp. 16–20.

23. This interpretation, stressing the importance of East Prussia in the development of Soviet operations, owes much to the account in C. Duffy, *Red Storm on the Reich: The Russian March on Germany, 1945* (London: Routledge, 1991).

24. Danzig had had a special status as a 'free city'.

25. Dimitrov, *Diary*, p. 193 [8 September].

26. Loewenheim, *Roosevelt and Stalin*, p. 445 [20 February]. What Stalin offered at Tehran as an exchange for the northern part of East Prussia (including Königsberg) was the area around Belostok (Białystok) and Pshemysl' (Przemyśl) in the western Ukraine/southeast Poland.

27. East Pomerania (Hinterpommern) takes in the region east of Stettin and the Oder. West Pomerania (Vorpommern) is west of the Oder.

28. Operations in Pomerania and West Prussia in January and February are dealt with in Lakowski, *DRZW*, vol. 10.1, pp. 550–68, and Kiselev in *VOV/VIO*, vol. 3, p. 244–52.

29. *RA/VO*, vol. 5(4), p. 193 [21 January]; K. K. Rokossovskii, *Soldatskii dolg* (Moscow: Voennoe izdatel'stvo, 1997), pp. 373–4 (where the order is dated 20 January). The order did indicate that this was to be a *temporary* diversion. 'In the future' the 2nd Ukrainian was to advance 'the main part of its forces' to Danzig and Stettin; Rokossovskii was supposed to capture by 2–4 February his objectives at the mouth of the Vistula (the towns of Deutsch Eylau, Elbing and Marienburg).

30. *RA/VO*, vol. 5(4), pp. 328–9 [16 February], 200 [17 February].

31. In mid-February 1945 General Wenck was assigned to take effective command of this army group, and in late March, General Heinrici formally replaced Himmler.

32. Ziemke, *Stalingrad to Berlin*, pp. 445–8; Lakowski in *DRZW*, vol. 10.1, pp. 553–5; and Kiselev in *VOV/VIO*, vol. 3, pp. 250.

33. The 3rd Panzer Army headquarters, evacuated from East Prussia, was given control of the forces of the 11th SS Panzer Army, in another of the confusing name changes of the last weeks of the war. The 11th SS Panzer Army was one of the shorter-lived formations in Hitler's armed forces. The only other SS Panzer Army was the much more powerful 6th SS (under Sepp Dietrich), which had four well-equipped panzer divisions. Control of the 2nd Army in West Prussia was transferred from Army Group Vistula to Army Group North (with its headquarters in Königsberg) in mid-March 1945.

34. Zhukov, *ViR*, vol. 3, pp. 148, 149, 150–4, 179–80. See fuller discussion in Chapter 12.

35. Ziemke, *Stalingrad to Berlin*, pp. 428–33, 444–5; Frieser in *DRZW*, vol. 8, pp. 612–9; Lakowski in *DRZW*, vol. 10.1, p. 531–50; Kiselev in *VOV/VIO*, vol. 3, pp. 244–52.

36. *Poteri*, p. 316. For the 3rd Belorussian Army Group's directive to attack East Prussia, see *RA/VO*, vol. 5(4), pp. 154–5 [3 October]. The 2nd and the 3rd Belorussian Army Groups were ordered to go over to a defensive posture on 5 November; the 1st Belorussian followed on the 12th. See *RA/VO*, vol. 5(4), pp. 166 [5 November], 167 [5 November], 169 [12 November].

As early as 21 August, Stalin himself had stressed the importance of the Narew as the route to East Prussia: see *SDVG*, vol. 4, p. 152 [21 August], and *RA/VO*, vol. 3(2), pp. 426–7 [21 August]. This aborted Soviet operation against East Prussia may also partly explain the gap in Soviet operations in November and December 1944.

37. Frieser in *DRZW*, vol. 8, pp. 619–22; there an epilogue section entitled 'Nemmersdorf: The writing on the wall [*Menetekel von Nemmersdorf*]'. Kershaw discusses the Nemmersdorf massacre and its implications in *The End*, pp. 110–22.

38. Soviet 1st Baltic Army Group was disbanded. Its headquarters had briefly been moved to Insterburg.

39. Confusingly, although logically enough, on 26 January 1945 the German army groups were renamed again. Army Group North became Army Group Kurland, Army Group Centre became Army Group North, and Army Group 'A' became Army Group Centre.

40. According to Molotov, Marshal Vasilevskii advised Stalin that Königsberg could be taken in two or three weeks. For Molotov, it was a mark of Zhukov's superior generalship that he correctly advised it would take two or three *months* (Chuev, *Sto sorok besed s Molotovym*, p. 58). These contrasting views of the time needed for the capture of Königsberg may have been put forward in mid-January 1945, when the winter offensive began. Alternately, they may have related to mid-February, when Vasilevskii was ordered to sort things out. In any event, Zhukov may have stressed the possible length of the operation because he was trying to avoid tying down forces on a secondary front.

41. *RA/VO*, vol. 5(4), p. 199 [9 February]; Maslov, *Fallen Soviet Generals*, pp. 176–7.

42. *Poteri*, pp. 304–5, 486.

43. I. S. Konev, *Sorok piatyi* (Moscow: VIMO, 1966), p. 4.

44. Chapter 12 includes a discussion of the Sandomierz–Silesia operation in Poland. For operations in Silesia proper, see: Ziemke, *Stalingrad to Berlin*, pp. 424–5, 440–44, 465–6; Lakowski in *DRZW*, vol. 10.1, pp. 568–88; and Kiselev in *VIV/VIO*, vol. 3, pp. 251–2.

45. N. Davies and R. Moorhouse, *Microcosm: Portrait of a Central European City* (London: Jonathan Cape, 2002), pp. 13–37, provides an account of the 1945 siege of Breslau.

46. This, at least, was Konev's interpretation of the escape of the German 17th Army. If there was a conscious decision to leave an escape route, it made sense. The Stavka's directive of 17 January 1945 had ordered Konev, after taking Kraków, 'to continue the offensive towards the Dabrowa coal region [i.e. the Katowice area], bypassing it from the north and with part of your strength from the south' (*RA/VO*, vol. 5(4), pp. 190–1). The directive did not anticipate the involvement of the Soviet 3rd Guards Tank Army. Whatever the cause, the German 17th Army escaped to fight another day in northern Moravia.

47. This dubious honour of the 'last offensive' might also be applied to the larger 6 March offensive in Hungary, but that operation did not achieve anything. The Stavka criticized local Red Army formations for the defeat inflicted at Lauban by a numerically inferior enemy; see *RA/VO*, vol. 12(4), p. 654 [12 March 1945].

48. On Petrov's Vltava offensive, see Chapter 12. The Stavka's intention in early March 1945 was to reach the Vltava River valley and Prague from the east. Western Czechoslovakia was an objective of first-rate political and economic importance to the Kremlin. Petrov was ordered to achieve this objective by mid-April; after that, presumably in early or mid-May, the offensive on Berlin would have begun. In reality, priorities changed when the Americans achieved their unexpectedly rapid advance beyond the Rhine. The slow pace of the Soviet advance in northern Moravia in the last weeks of March may also have been the explanation for Konev's attack on Opole.

49. *RA/VO*, vol. 5(4), pp. 202–3 [17 February].

50. See Chapter 12.

51. Ziemke, *Stalingrad to Berlin*, pp. 452–6, and B. I. Nevzorov in *VOV/VOI*, vol. 3, pp. 141–3, outline the advance into Austria from Hungary.

52. The 2nd Panzer Army was transferred from Army Group South to Army Group Southeast, in the northern Balkans.

53. *RA/VO*, vol. 3(2), p. 631 [April 1945]; *Poteri*, p. 306. Remnants of these Waffen-SS divisions survived to surrender to the Americans.

54. C. Ryan, *The Last Battle* (London: Collins, 1966); A. Beevor, *Berlin: The Downfall* (London: Viking, 2002). On military aspects see: T. Le Tissier, *Race for the Reichstag: The 1945 Battle for Berlin* (London: Frank Cass, 1999); Ziemke, *Stalingrad to Berlin*, pp. 474–94; Lakowski in *DRZW*, vol. 10.1, pp. 588–680; and Kiselev in *VOV/VIO*, vol. 3, pp. 267–90.

55. A number of other high commands still existed, away from the core area: Army Group 'G' (Schulz) in Bavaria, Army Group Northwest (Busch) around Hamburg, Army Group 'F' (Weichs) in Croatia, Army Group Kurland (Rendulic) and Army Group South/Ostmark (Wöhler) in Austria. Army Group 'B' surrendered in the Ruhr pocket. See Müller-Hillebrand, *Das Heer*, vol. 3, pp. 275–7.

56. The 7th Army headquarters had played a prominent part in the Battle of Normandy.

57. Zhukov, *ViR*, vol. 3, pp. 213–4.

58. *FRUS: Malta and Yalta*, pp. 607, 635, 656.

59. Shtemenko, *General'nyi shtab*, p. 220.

60. Stalin, *OVOVSS*, p. 168 [6 November]. Antony Beevor has suggested another factor making the capture of Berlin imperative to Stalin: the resources of the German nuclear programme (*Berlin*, pp. 138–9, 210, 232, 324–5). While this may well have been a background consideration at the very highest level, it was probably secondary to prestige and other factors. Eisenhower's biographer suggested back in 1967 that the inconsistency of the Russians' statements came about because they changed their plans in the middle

of the battle (S. Ambrose, *Eisenhower and Berlin, 1945: The Decision to Halt at the Elbe* (New York: W. W. Norton, 1967), p. 67, n. 3). This seems a little naive; Stalin lied.

61. The Remagen coup on its own did not totally transform the strategic situation from Stalin's point of view. The British and Americans had demonstrated their considerable military potential in northern France, and the Russians may well have known of Montgomery's impending (late March) Rhine crossing. Remagen only advanced the strategic timetable by a few weeks.

62. Malyshev, 'Dnevnik', p. 128 [28 March]; *Perepiska*, vol. 2, pp. 219–20 [3 April]; *FRUS*, 1945, vol. 3, p. 746 [4 April].

63. Ziemke, *Stalingrad to Berlin*, p. 467; Ehrman, *Grand Strategy*, vol. 6, p. 157.

64. Eisenhower, a theatre commander, was communicating directly with Stalin and appeared to be making decisions about grand strategy; this did not please the British, as partners in the Combined Chiefs of Staff. The Americans justified this contact by military expediency (the CCS mechanism would have been too slow) and also on the grounds that Marshal Stalin was in effect the theatre commander on the Soviet side. On the disagreements between the British and the Americans, see Stoler, *Allies in War*, Chapter 10.

    We can only speculate about what 'might have been'. The agreed American–British plan was for the main thrust to be mounted north of the Ruhr. What would have happened had this not been changed by the unexpected American success south of the Ruhr (after the Remagen incident)? Although on the map, the northern route is the shortest one to Berlin, there is no reason to think that an offensive in this area would have made more rapid progress towards the Reich capital had the German line to the south held out. If anything, the Remagen breakthrough (and the unexpected crossing even further south at Oppenheim by Patton's American 3rd Army) made possible the encirclement of Model's army group on the Ruhr. This in turn accelerated the progress of the entire front, including that of Montgomery's British 21st Army Group in the north.

65. C. von Clausewitz, *On War* (London: David Campbell, 1993), p. 731.

66. *RA/VO*, vol. 5(4), p. 228 [17.50 hrs, 17 April]. Zhukov's original signal has evidently not been published; it was presumably sent earlier on 17 April, on the second day of the Seelow battle in front of Berlin.

67. 'Posetiteli', *IA*, 1996, no. 4, p. 96; Shtemenko, *General'nyi shtab*, pp. 228–9.

68. *Poteri*, p. 307.

69. Ziemke, *Stalingrad to Berlin*, pp. 470–2, 479; *Poteri*, p. 307.

70. *RA/VO*, vol. 5(3), p. 223. It is likely that this direct approach to Berlin was worked out with Zhukov at the Stavka. The Stavka thus approved the overall approach to the battle, and that to some extent preordained the crisis at Seelow. In contrast, in his January 1945 plan, Zhukov's intention was to use his tank armies in a more indirect approach, outflanking Berlin from the north.

71. Antony Beevor states – without giving a source – that Zhukov lost 30,000 killed 'in his desperation to capture the Seelow Heights' (*Berlin*, p. 244). Given the weak strength and low quality of the German defenders and the lack of fixed defences, this figure seems an unlikely one. The Seelow attack involved four Soviet armies and two days of action. According to the most recent Russian source, the losses of *all* the armies of Zhukov's 1st Belorussian Army Group *over the whole three weeks* of the 'Berlin operation' was 38,000 (*Poteri*, p. 307).

72. *RA/VO*, vol. 5(4), pp. 225 [3 April], pp. 225–6 [6 April], 229 [18 April], 232 [25 April]; Shtemenko, *General'nyi shtab*, p. 228. It could be added that Konev's army group became available for Berlin when it became clearer that Hitler was going to make his last-ditch stand in the capital, and not in southern Germany.

73. *Poteri*, pp. 307, 487; Ziemke, *Stalingrad to Berlin*, p. 489.

74. In view of the fact that the Luftwaffe had largely been destroyed, the Soviet loss of 920 combat aircraft in the Berlin operation was remarkably high. The Red Army Air Force lost only 820 combat aircraft in the 1944 Belorussian operation, and 340 in the 1945 Vistula–Oder operation (*Poteri*, pp. 486–7).

75. *Poteri*, p. 307. The 1st Belorussian Army Group began the Berlin operation with 908,500 troops and lost 37,610 (4.1 per cent); the 1st Ukrainian began with 550,900 and lost 27,580 (5.0 per cent).

76. Kershaw, *Hitler*, vol. 2, pp. 763, 1020, n. 45; Merridale, *Ivan's War*, pp. 267–77; M. Zeidler in *DRZW*, vol. 10.1, pp. 681–775.
   Beevor gives a figure of two million rape victims (*Berlin*, p. 410). The fullest and fairest discussion is in N. Naimark, *The Russians in Germany: A History of the Soviet Zone of Occupation, 1945–1949* (Cambridge, MA: Belknap Press, 1995), pp. 69–140. This is a 'blank page' in Russian histories of the war. For a rare reference to this (*sluchai maroderstva i nasiliia*) in a Russian military source, see the short discussion by V. N. Kiselev in *VOV/VIO* (vol. 3, p. 242). Among the causes cited was the failure of the army political organs to 'reconstruct themselves'. O. A. Rzheshevskii, '… [*sic*] izmenit' otnoshenie k nemtsam kak i voennoplennym, tak i k grazhdanskim', *VIZh*, 2003, no. 5, pp. 31–3, is a rejoinder to Beevor.

77. Discipline (and indiscipline) in the Red Army are also discussed in Chapter 7.

78. *RA/VO*, vol. 5(4), p. 229 [20 April].

79. *RA/VO*, vol. 5(4), p. 232 [2 May].

80. *RA/VO*, vol. 5(4), pp. 234–5 [8 May]. Despite apparently committing a gross diplomatic error, General I. A. Susloparov evidently went unpunished; he served on for four months as head of the Soviet military mission to France and then in a number of senior Red Army training posts. He had held a number of intelligence and administrative posts; in 1939–41 he was military attaché in France (*SSSR i germanskii vopros*, vol. 1, p. 759).

81. Stalin, *OVOVSS*, p. 192. For a discussion of the two surrenders, see J. Wheeler-Bennett and A. Nichols, *The Semblance of Peace: The Political Settlement after the Second World War* (London: Macmillan, 1972), pp. 261–5. A fuller surrender document, worked out by the European Advisory Committee, was signed on 5 June 1945. This was the Declaration on Defeated Germany and replaced the 7–8 May capitulation documents; there was no German involvement.

82. *Poteri*, p. 515. These figures are described as 'military personnel of the armed forces of Germany', but not all can have been ethnic Germans from the Wehrmacht.

Chapter 14

1. Naumov *1941 god*, vol. 2, p. 434 [22 June]; W. Murray, *German Military Effectiveness* (Baltimore, MD: Nautical and Aviation, 1999), p. 1.

2. J. Armstrong, *Soviet Partisans*, p. 138. Armstrong's explanation was 'the better organisation, leadership, discipline and military qualities of the lower ranks of the Wehrmacht' (pp. 137–8).

3. Stalin, *OVOVSS*, pp. 42–3 [23 February 1942]. When Stalin spoke of Germany's enemies, he did not specify whether he was talking about Russia or the whole anti-German Alliance. Although concise, this was perhaps Stalin's most systematic analysis of the war. For a time it became part of Soviet military orthodoxy; for a fuller post-war elaboration, see Voroshilov, *Stalin i vooruzhennye sily*, pp. 108–18.

4. Stalin did not write at length about the 'stability of the rear' in February 1942. He made the point more fully elsewhere, notably in his Revolution Day speech of 6 November 1941, where he spoke of the instability (*neprochnost'*) of the 'European rear' and the 'German rear' (Stalin, *OVOVSS*, pp. 31–2). To be sure, the standard of living – and stability – of the Reich (the 'German rear') were partly sustained by increased Nazi exploitation of the occupied territories (the 'European rear'), but this had the effect of reducing support for the German cause in those territories.

5. Stalin, *OVOVSS*, pp. 196–7 [24 May].

6. I. V. Stalin, *Sochineniia* (Stanford, CA: Hoover Institution, 1967), vol. 3(16), pp. 4–5 [9 February 1946], Stalin, *OVOVSS*, pp. 119–20 [6 November 1943].

7. *Hitlers Politisches Testament*, p. 72 [14 February].

8. Khrushchev, 'O kul'ta lichnosti', pp. 148–9; Ziemke *Stalingrad to Berlin*, p. 502; Erickson, *Road to Berlin*, p. 123.

9. Stalin's February 1942 order was made at a point when he felt little need for allies. There is no reference to the British or the Americans. In earlier and later speeches, he made more of his alliance partners.

10. A. A. Pechenkin (ed.), 'Sovremennaia armiia – armiia nastupatel'naia', *IA*, 1995, no. 2, p. 28 [5 May]; Stalin, *OVOVSS*, pp. 31–2 [6 November]. The other two factors in Stalin's November 1941 speech were the instability of the (German-occupied) European rear and the instability of the rear in Germany itself.

11. Domarus, *Hitler: Reden*, p. 1979 [30 January].

12. Stalin, *OVOVSS*, p. 156 [6 November 1944]; Voroshilov, *Stalin i vooruzhennye sily*, p. 99.

13. This is the judgement of Ziemke, *Stalingrad to Berlin*, p. 503. As the second edition of *Thunder in the East* was going to press a stimulating new book raised again the question of the relative importance of the Eastern and Western fronts: P. O'Brien, *How the War was Won: Air-Sea Power and Allied Victory in World War II* (Cambridge: Cambridge University Press, 2015). The author argues that the war in Europe was won by the Western Allies, and in particular by the American and British air forces. This is not the place to discuss the book's thesis in detail, but readers might also consider a contrary overview: E. Mawdsley, 'The Allies from Defeat to Victory', in R. Overy (ed.), *The Oxford Illustrated History of World War II* (Oxford: Oxford University Press, 2015), pp. 168–201.

14. Stalin, *OVOVSS*, p. 157 [6 November].

15. Geldern and Stites, *Mass Culture in Soviet Russia*, p. 318. The term 'little cost' is used here only in a relative sense. Both America and Britain lost hundreds of thousands of servicemen. The point is that Russian and German losses were very much higher.

16. 'Z' [Martin Malia], 'To the Stalin Mausoleum', *Daedalus*, vol. 119, 1990, no. 1, p. 316. Malia added, however: 'And at that point, the essentially military command structure of the Party-state indeed proved effective in relocating factories, mobilising the economy, and mounting its counterattack for victory.'

17. *Poteri*, pp. 248–59, 453–64. See the (improbably) higher figures suggested in B. Sokolov, 'Estimating Soviet War Losses on the Basis of Soviet Population Censuses', *JSMS*, vol. 27, 2014, no. 3, pp. 467–92.
    Timothy Snyder examined the results of state-sponsored mass murder in East Central Europe in *Bloodlands: Europe Between Hitler and Stalin* (New York: Basic Books, 2010). He argued that modern 'Russian leaders' – by which he presumably meant the leaders of the post-1991 Russian Federation – 'associate' their country with 'the more or less official numbers [figures] of Soviet victims', that is, 9 million military and 14–17 million civilians.

'Whatever the correct Soviet figures, Russian figures must be much, much [sic] lower. The high Soviet numbers include Ukraine, Belarus, and the Baltics' (pp. 402–3).

It is worth pointing out that the Soviet armies which fought Nazi Germany, both the 'old' army destroyed in 1941 and the new army which eventually defeated the Third Reich, were recruited primarily from parts of the USSR inhabited by ethnic Russians. One figure given for the number of Russians who died while serving in the Red Army was 5,747,100, out of 8,668,400 (G. F. Krivosheev, 'Ob itogakh statisticheskikh issledovanii poter' Vooruzhennykh sil SSSR v Velikoi Otechestvennoi voiny', in R. B. Evdokimov (ed.), *Liudskie poteri SSSR v period vtoroi mirovoi voiny: Sbornik statei* (St Petersburg: IRI RAN, 1995), pp. 79–80). Russians probably did make up 60–70 per cent of Red Army losses.

18. On this, see two comparative studies by B. V. Sokolov: 'The Cost of War: Human Losses for the USSR and Germany, 1939 1945', *JSMS*, vol. 9 (March 1996) no. 1, pp. 152–93, and 'How to Calculate Human Losses during the Second World War', *JSMS*, vol. 22, 2009, no. 3, pp. 437–58.

19. A. Sella, *The Value of Human Life in Soviet Warfare* (London: Routledge, 1992), argues against such an oversimplification.

20. Dear and Foot, *Oxford Companion to the Second World War*, p. 290. On civilian deaths, see also M. Ellmann and S. Maksudov, 'Soviet Deaths on the Great Patriotic War: A Note', pp. 674–80, *EAS*, vol. 46, 1994, no. 4, pp. 671–80; Evdokimov, *Liudskie poteri*, pp. 124–88; and M. Haynes, 'Counting Soviet Deaths in the Great Patriotic War: A Note', *EAS*, vol. 55, 2003, no. 2, pp. 303–9. This issue also relates to Timothy Snyder's argument (n. 17) about 'Russian' losses; although the majority of direct civilian victims of German occupation policies (including deliberate genocide) were non-Russians, the figure of 17,000,000 civilian deaths certainly includes a large number of ethnic Russians who died as a result of worsening conditions on both sides of the front line, including the area east of the 'Bloodlands'.

21. Kumanev in *VOV/VIO*, vol. 3, p. 342; Harrison, *Accounting for War*, p. 172.

22. Stalin, *OVOVSS*, p. 162 [6 November]. A *pogrom* was a riot, normally thought of as one against a minority, especially the Jews. A *pogromshchik* was a rioter, or an instigator of riots.

23. Ziemke, *Stalingrad to Berlin*, p. 425. This was written during the Cold War (in 1968), but similar sentiments can be found in later debates among West German historians. For a thoughtful recent comparison between Nazi Germany and Soviet Russia, see M. Edele and M. Geyer, 'The Nazi-Soviet War as a System of Violence, 1939-1945', in Geyer and Fitzpatrick, *Beyond Totalitarianism*, pp. 345–395.

SELECT BIBLIOGRAPHY

This bibliography only includes major sources, and sources listed more than once in the notes.

ABBREVIATIONS OF SOURCES USED

DRZW	*Das Deutsche Reich und der Zweite Weltkrieg*
EAS	*Europe-Asia Studies* (journal)
FRUS	*Foreign Relations of the United States* (document collection)
GSWW	*Germany and the Second World War*
IA	*Istoricheskii arkhiv* (journal)
IHR	*International History Review* (journal)
ITsK	*Izvestiia Tsentral'nogo komiteta KPSS* (journal)
JCH	*Journal of Contemporary History* (journal)
JMilH	*Journal of Military History* (journal)
JSMS	*Journal of Soviet [Slavic] Military Studies* (journal)
NNI	*Novaia i noveishaia istoriia (journal)*
OI	*Otechestvennaia istoriia* (journal)
Perepiska	Gromyko, *Perepiska Predsedatelia* (document collection)
Poteri	Krivosheev, *Rossia i SSSR v voinakh XX veka: Poteri vooruzhennykh sil*
RA/VO	Series *Russki arkhiv*; sub-series *Velikaia Otechestvennaia* (document collection)
RI	*Rossiiskaia istoriia* (journal)
SDVG	*Sbornik dokumentov Verkhovnogo glavnokomandovaniia* (document collection)
SM	*Svobodnaia mysl'* (journal)
VI	*Voprosy istorii* (journal)
VIA	*Voenno-istoricheskii arkhiv* (journal)
VIZh	*Voenno-istoricheskii zhurnal* (journal)
VOVE	*Velikaia Otechestvennaia voina: 1941–1945: Entsiklopediia*
VOV/VIO	*Velikaia Otechestvennaia voina: Voenno-istoricheskie ocherki*
Weisungen	Hubatsch, *Hitlers Weisungen für de Kriegführung*
WH	*War in History* (journal)

PUBLISHED DOCUMENTS

Army Security Agency, *European Axis Signal Intelligence in World War as Revealed in TICOM Investigations* [etc] (9 vols, Washington, 1946 [declassified. January 2009]) http://www.nsa. gov/public_info/declass/european_axis_sigint.shtml.

Bidlack, Richard and Lomagin Nikita. *The Leningrad Blockade, 1941-1944: A New Documentary History from the Soviet Archives*. New Haven, CT: Yale University Press, 2012.

Dzeniskevich, A. R. (ed.). *Leningrad v osade: Sbornik dokumentov o geroicheskoi oborone Leningrada v gody Velikoi Otechestvennoi voiny, 1941–1944*. Sankt-Peterburg: Liki Rossii, 1995.

Foreign Relations of the United States, 1945: The Conferences at Malta and Yalta. Washington, DC: GPO, 1955.

Gavrilov, V. A. (ed.). *Voennaia razvedka informiruet: Dokumenty razvedupravleniia Krasnoi Armii, ianvar' 1939-iiun' 1941 g*. Moscow: MF 'Demokratiia', 2008.

Geldern, J. von and Stites, R. (eds). *Mass Culture in Soviet Russia: Tales, Poems, Songs, Movies, Plays and Folklore, 1917–1953*. Bloomington, IN: Indiana University Press, 1995.

Greiner, H. and Schramm, P. (eds). *Kriegstagebuch des Oberkommandos der Wehrmacht (Wehrmachtführungsstab) 1940–1945*, 4 vols. Frankfurt: Bernard & Graefe, 1961–79. *(KTB OKW)*

Gromyko, A. A. et al. (eds). *Perepiska Predsedatelia Soveta Ministrov SSSR s prezidentami SShA i prem'er-ministrami Velikobritanii vo vremia Velikoi Otechestvennoi voiny, 1941–1945 gg.*, 2 vols. Moscow: Politizdat, 1986 (*Perepiska*).

Gurov, A. A. et al. (eds). *Stalingrad 1942–1943: Stalingradskaia bitva v dokumentakh*. Moscow: Biblioteka, 1995.

Grylev, A. N. (ed.). *Boevoi sostav Sovetskoi armii*, 5 vols. Moscow: VNU GSh, 1963–90.

Hill, A. *The Great Patriotic War of the Soviet Union, 1941-45: A Documentary Reader*. London: Routledge, 2009.

Hubatsch, W. (ed.). *Hitlers Weisungen für die Kriegführung 1939–1945: Dokumente des Oberkommandos der Wehrmacht*. Frankfurt: Bernard & Graefe, 1962.

Khaustov, V. N., Naumov, V. P., and Plotnikova N. S. (eds). *Lubianka: Stalin i NKVD-NKGB-GUKR 'Smersh', 1939 – mart 1946*. Moscow: MF 'Demokratiia', 2006.

Kokurin, Iu. N. and Petrov, N. V. (eds). *GULAG (Glavnoe upravlenie lagerei), 1918-1960*. Moscow: MF 'Demokratiia', 2002.

Kokurin, Iu. N. and Morukov, Iu. N. (eds). *Stalinskie stroiki GULAGa, 1930-1953*. Moscow: MF 'Demokratiia', 2005.

Korotkov, A. V. et al. (eds). 'Posetiteli kremlevskogo kabineta I. V. Stalina: Zhurnaly (tetradi) zapisi lits, priniatykh pervym gensekom 1924–1953 gg.'. *IA*, 1996, no. 2, pp. 72, no. 3, pp. 3–86, no. 4, pp. 66.

Koval'chenko, I. D. et al. (eds). *Moskva voennaia, 1941–1945. Memuary i arkhivnye dokumenty*. Moscow: Mosgorarkhiv, 1995.

Kudriashov, S. (ed.). *Voina: 1941-1945*. Moscow: Vestnik APRF, 2010.

Kynin, G. P. and Laufer, I. (eds). *SSSR I germanskii vopros. 1941–1949: Dokumenty iz Arkhiva vneshnei politiki Rossiiskoi Federatsii*, 3 vols. Moscow: Mezhdunarodnye otnoshneiia, 1996–2000.

Livshin, A. Ia. and Orlov I. B. (eds). *Sovetskaia propaganda v gody Velikoi Otchestvennoi voiny: Kommunikatsiia ubezhdeniiia i mobilizatsionnye mekhanizmy*. Moscow: Rosspen, 2007.

Loewenheim, F. I. et al. (eds). *Roosevelt and Churchill: Their Secret Wartime Correspondence*. London: Barrie & Jenkins, 1975.

Naumov, V. P. et al. (eds). *1941 god*, 2 vols. Moscow: Mezhdunarodnyi Fond 'Demokratiia', 1998.

Naumov, V. P. et al. (eds) *Georgii Zhukov: Stenogramma oktiabr'skogo (1957g.) plenuma TsK KPSS i drugie dokumenty*. Moscow: Demokratiia, 2001.

Noakes, J. and Pridham, G. (eds). *Documents on Nazism, 1919–1945*. New York: Viking, 1975.

Noakes, J. and Pridham, G. (eds). *Nazism 1919–1945: A Documentary Reader*, vol. 3, *Foreign Policy, War and Racial Extermination*, 3 vols. Exeter: Exeter University Press, 1988.

Noskova, A. F (ed.). *NKVD i pol'skoe podpol'e (1944–1945 gg). (Po 'Osobym papkam' I. V. Stalina)*. Moscow: Institut slavianovedeniia i balkanistiki RAN, 1994.

Pobol', N. L. and Polian, P. M. (eds). *Stalinskie deportatsii, 1928-1953*. Moscow: MF 'Demokratiia', 2005.

Pogonii, Ia. F et al. (eds). *Stalingradskaia epopeia: Materialy NKVD SSSR i voennoi tsenzury iz Tsentral'nogo arkhiva FSB RF*. Moscow: Zvonnitsa-MG, 2000.

Polonsky, A. and Drukier, B. (eds). *The Beginnings oj Communist Rule in Poland*. London: Routledge Kegan Paul, 1980.

Reemtsma, J. P. et al. (eds). *Verbrechen der Wehrmacht: Dimensionen des Vernichtungskneges 1941–1944. Ausstellungskatalog.* Hamburg: Hamburger Edition, 2002.

Russkii arkhiv. Velikaia Otechestvennaia. Moscow: Terra, 1993– *(RA/VO).*

  vol. 1(1) *Nakanune voiny: Materialy soveshcheniia vysshego rukovodiashchego sostava RKKA 23–31 dekabria 1940 g.,* 1993.

  vol. 2(2) *Prikazy Narodnogo Komissara Oborony SSSR: 22 iiunia 1941 g. – 1942 g.,* 1997.

  vol. 2(3) *Prikazy Narodnogo Komissara Oborony SSSR: 1943–1945gg.,* 1997.

  vol. 3(1) *SSSR i Pol'sha, 1941-1945: K istorii voennogo soiuza: Dokumenty i materialy,* 1994.

  vol. 3(2) *Krasnaia Armiia v strankakh Tsentral'noi, Severnoi Evropy i na Balkanakh: Dokumenty i materialy: 1944-1945,* 2000.

  vol. 4(1) *Bitva pod Moskvoi: Sbornik dokumentov,* 1997.

  vol. 4(3) *Preliudiia Kurskoi bitvy: Dokumenty i materialy: 6 dekabria 1942 g. 25 aprelia 1943 g.,* 1997.

  vol. 5(1) *Stavka VGK: Dokumenty i materialy: 1941 god,* 1996.

  vol. 5(2) *Stavka VGK: Dokumenty i materialy: 1942 god,* 1996.

  vol. 5(5) *Stavka VGK: Dokumenty i materialy: 1943 god,* 1999.

  vol. 5(4) *Stavka VGK: Dokumenty i materialy: 1944-1945,* 1999.

  vol. 6 *Glavnye politicheskie organy vooruzhennykh sil SSSR v Velikoi Otechestvennoi voine. 1941-1945 gg.: Dokumenty i materialy,* 1996.

  vol. 9 *Partizanskoe dvizhenie v gody Velikoi Otechestvennoi voiny 1941–1945 gg.: Dokumenty i materialy,* 1999.

  vol 12(1) *General'nyi shtab v gody Velikoi Otechestvennoi voiny: Dokumenty i materialy: 1941 god,* 1997.

  vol. 12(2) *General'nyi shtab v gody Velikoi Otechestvennoi voiny: Dokumenty i materialy: 1942 god,* 1999.

  vol. 12(3) *General'nyi shtab v gody Velikoi Otechestvennoi voiny: Dokumenty i materialy: 1943 god,* 1999.

  vol. 12(4) *General'nyi shtab v gody Velikoi Otechestvennoi voiny: Dokumenty i materialy: 1944–1945 gg.,* 2001.

  vol. 13(2) *Nemetskie voennoplennye v SSSR 1941–1955 gg.: Sbornik dokumentov,* 1999.

  vol. 14 *Tyl Krasnoi Armii v Velikoi Otechestvennoi voine 1941–1945 gg: Dokumenty i materialy,* 1998.

Rzheshevskii, O. A. (ed.). *Stalin i Cherchill: Vstrechi, besedy, diskussii.* Moscow: Nauka, 2004.

Rzheshevskii, O. A. (ed.). *Voina i diplomatii: Dokumenty, kommentarii 1941-1942.* Moscow: Nauka, 1997.

Sbornik dokumentov Verkhovnogo glavnokomandovaniia za period Velikoi Otechestvennoi voiny, 4 vols. Moscow: VIMO, 1968 (SDVG).

Skrytaia pravda voiny: 1941 goda: Neizvestnye dokumenty. Moscow: Russkaia kniga, 1992.

Stalin, I. V. *Sochineniia [Tom 15],* 3 vols. Moscow: ITPK, 2010.

Stepashin, S. V. et al. (eds). *Organy gosudarstvennoi bezopasnosti SSSR v Velikoi Otechestvennoi voiny. Sbornik dokumentov,* 5 vols. Moscow: Kniga v biznes/Rus', 1995.

Volokitina, T. V. et al. (eds). *Sovetskii faktor v Vostochnoi Evrope 1944–1953: Dokumenty,* 2 vols. Moscow: Rosspen, 1999.

Volokitina, T. V. et al. (eds). *Vostochnaia Evropa v dokumentakh rossiiskikh arkhivov, 1944–1953 gg.,* 1997, vol. 1, 1944–1948. Moscow-Novosibirsk: Sibirskii khronograph, 1997.

Zagorul'ko, M. M. (eds). *Voennoplennye v SSSR, 1939-1956: Dokumenty i materialy.* Moscow: Logos, 2000.

Zhilin, V. A. et al. (eds). *Bitva pod Moskvoi: Khronika, fakty, liudi,* 2 vols. Moscow: Ol'ma-Press, 2002.

Zolotarev, V. A. et al. (eds). *G. K. Zhukov v bitve pod Moskvoi: Sbornik dokumentov.* Moscow: Mosgosarkhiv, 1994.

BOOKS AND ARTICLES

Abalikhin, B. S. (ed.). *Stalingradskaia bitva*. Volgograd: Vale, 1994.

Addison, P. and Calder, A. (eds). *Time to Kill: The Soldiers' Experience in the West*. London: Pimlico, 1997.

Afanas'ev, Iu. N. (ed.). *Drugaia voina: 1939–1945*. Moscow: RGGU, 1996.

Andrew, C. and Gordievsky, O. *KGB: The Inside Story of its Foreign Operations*. London: Sceptre, 1991.

Anfilov, V. A. *Doroga k tragedii sorok pervogo goda*. Moscow: Akopov, 1997.

Anfilov, V. A. *Groznoe leto 41 goda*. Moscow: Izdatel'skii tsentr Ankil-Voin, 1995.

Anfilov, V. A. *Krushenie pokhoda Gitlera na Moskvu 1941*. Moscow: Nauka, 1989.

Anfilov, V. A. "'… Razgovor zakonchilsia ugrozoi Stalina": Desiat' besed s marshalom G. K. Zhukovym v mae-iiune 1965 goda', *VIZh*, 1995, no. 2, pp. 39–46.

Arad, Y. *The Holocaust in the Soviet Union*. Lincoln, NE: University of Nebraska Press, 2009.

Armstrong, J. A. (ed.). *Soviet Partisans in World War II*. Madison, WI: University of Wisconsin Press, 1964.

Barber, J. and Dzeniskevich, A. (eds). *Life and Death in Besieged Leningrad, 1941-1944*. Basingstoke: Palgrave, 2004.

Barber, J. and Harrison M. *The Soviet Home Front, 1941-1945: A Social and Economic History of the USSR in World War II*. Harlow: Longman, 1991.

Barber, J. and Harrison M. (eds). *The Soviet Defence-Industry Complex from Stalin to Khrushchev*. Basingstoke: Macmillan, 2000.

Barnett, C. *Hitler's Generals*. London: Phoenix, 1995.

Bartov, O. *The Eastern Front, 1941–45: German Troops and the Barbarization of Warfare*. New York: St Martin's Press, 1985.

Bartov, O. *Hitler's Army: Soldiers, Nazis, and War in the Third Reich*. New York: OUP USA, 1991.

Beevor, A. *Berlin: The Downfall*. London: Viking, 2002.

Beevor, A. *Stalingrad: The Fateful Siege: 1942-43*. New York: Viking, 1999.

Bellamy, C. *Red God of War: Soviet Artillery and Rocket Forces*. London: Brassey's, 1986.

Beorn, W. *Marching into Darkness: The Wehrmacht and the Holocaust in Belarus*. Cambridge, MA: Harvard University Press, 2014.

Berkhoff, K. C. *Harvest of Despair: Life and Death in Ukraine under Nazi Rule*. Cambridge, MA: Harvard University Press, 2004.

Berkhoff, K. C. *Motherland in Danger: Soviet Propaganda during World War II*. Cambridge, MA: Harvard University Press, 2012.

Bezborodova, I. V. 'Inostrannye voennoplennye i internirovannye v SSSR (1945–1953)', *OI*, 1997, no. 5, pp. 165–73.

Bezborodova, I. V. *Voennoplennyi vtoroi mirovoi voiny: Generaly Vermakhta v plenu*. Moscow: RGGU, 1998.

Birstein, V. *Smersh, Stalin's Secret Weapon: Soviet Military Counterintelligence in World War II*. London: Biteback Publishing, 2011.

Blood, P. *Hitler's Bandit Hunters: The SS and the Nazi Occupation of Europe*. Dulles,VA: Potomac, 2006.

Brandenberger, D. *National Bolshevism: Stalinist Mass Culture and the Formation of Modern Russian National Identity, 1931-1956*. Cambridge, MA: Harvard University Press, 2002.

Brandenberger, D. *Propaganda State in Crisis: Soviet Ideology, Indoctrination, and Terror under Stalin, 1927-1941*. New Haven, CT: Yale University Press, 2012.

Braithwaite, R. *Moscow 1941: A City and Its People at War*. London: Profile Books, 2006.

Brandon, R. and Lower, W. (eds). *The Shoah in Ukraine: History, Testimony, Memorialization*. Bloomington, IN: Indiana University Press, 2010.

Bugai, N. F. L. *Beriia – I. Stalinu: 'Soglasno Vashemu ukazaniiu'*. Moscow: AIRO-XX, 1995.

Carver, M. (ed.). *The War Lords: Military Commanders of the Twentieth Century*. London: Weidenfeld & Nicolson, 1976.

Citino, R. *Death of the Wehrmacht: The German Campaigns on 1942*. Lawrence, KS: University Press of Kansas, 2009.

Citino, R. *The German Way of War: From the Thirty Years' War to the Third Reich*. Lawrence, KS: University Press of Kansas, 2005.

Citino, R. *The Wehrmacht Retreats: Fighting a Lost War*, 1943. Lawrence, KS: University Press of Kansas, 2011.

Chuev, F. (ed.). *Sto sorok besed s Molotovym: Iz dnevnika F. Chueva*. Moscow: Terra, 1991.

Cohen, Laurie. *Smolensk under the Nazis: Everyday Life in Occupied Russia*. Rochester, NY: University of Rochester Press, 2013.

Collingham, L. *The Taste of War: World War Two and the Battle for Food*. London: Penguin, 2011.

Cooper, M. *The Phantom War: The German Struggle against Soviet Partisans, 1941–1944*. London: Macdonald and Janes, 1979.

Cornelius, D. *Hungary in World War II: Caught in the Cauldron*. Oxford: Oxford University Press, 2010.

Creveld, M. Van. *Fighting Power: German and U.S. Army Performance, 1939–1945*. Westport: CT, Greenwood Press, 1982.

Daines, V. O. *Shtrafbaty i zagradotriady Krasnoi Armii*. Moscow: Eksmo, 2008.

Dallin, A. *German Rule in Russia, 1941–1945, A Study of Occupation Policies*, 2nd edn. London: Macmillan, 1981.

Dear, I. C. B. and Foot, M. R. D. (eds). *The Oxford Companion to the Second World War*. Oxford: Oxford University Press, 1995.

Das Deutsches Reich und der Zweite Weltkieg, 10 vols. Stuttgart and Munich: Deutsche Verlags-Anstalt, 1979–2008 (DRZW).

Dimitrov, G. *The Diary of Georgi Dimitrov, 1933–1949*, ed. Ivo Banac. New Haven, CT: Yale University Press, 2003.

DiNardo, R. *Germany and the Axis Powers: From Coalition to Collapse*. Lawrence: U Press of Kansas, 2005.

Djilas, M. *Conversations with Stalin*. Harmondsworth: Penguin, 1962.

Domarus, M. (ed.). *Hitler: Reden und Proklamationen 1932–1945*, 4 vols. Wiesbaden: R. Löwit, 1973.

Dunn, W. *Hitler's Nemesis: The Red Army, 1930–1945*. New York: Greenwood Press, 1994.

Dunn, W. *The Soviet Economy and the Red Army, 1930–1945*. Westport, CT: Praeger, 1995.

Dunn, W. *Stalin's Keys to Victory: The Rebirth of the Red Army*. Westport, CT: Praeger Security International, 2006.

Dzeniskevich, A. R. *Blokada i politika: Oborona Leningrada v politicheskoi kon'iunkture'*. St. Petersburg: Nestor, 1998.

Edele, M. *Stalinist Society, 1928-1953*. Oxford: Oxford University Press, 2011.

Ehrman, J. *Grand Strategy*, 6 vols. London: HMSO, 1956.

Erickson, J. *The Road to Berlin*. London: Weidenfeld & Nicolson, 1983.

Erickson, J. *The Road to Stalingrad*. New York: Harper & Row, 1975.

Evans, R. *The Third Reich at War: How the Nazis Led Germany from Conquest to Disaster*. London: Allen Lane, 2008.

Evdokimov, R. B. (ed.). *Liudskie poteri SSSR v period vtoroi mirovoi voiny: Sbornik statei*. St Petersburg: IRI RAN, 1995.

Fritz, S. *Endkampf: Soldiers, Civilians, and the Death of the Third Reich*. Lexington, KY: University Press of Kentucky, 2004.

Fritz, S. *Frontsoldaten: The German Soldier in World War II*. Lexington, KY: University Press of Kentucky, 1995.

Fritz, S. *Ostkrieg: Hitler's War of Extermination in the East*. Lexington, KY: University Press of Kentucky, 2011.

Gellately, R. *Stalin's Curse: Battling for Communism in War and Cold War*. New York: Knopf, 2012.

Gerasimova, S. *The Rzhev Slaughterhouse: The Red Army's Forgotten 15-month Campaign against Army Group Center, 1942-1943*. Solihull, UK: Helion, 2013.

Germany and the Second World War. Oxford: Clarendon Press, 1990- (*GSWW*).

Geyer, M. and Fitzpatrick, S. (eds). *Beyond Totalitarianism: Stalinism and Nazism Compared*. Cambridge: Cambridge University Press, 2009.

Glantz, D. *After Stalingrad: The Red Army's Winter Offensive 1942-1943*. Solihull, UK: Helion, 2009.

Glantz, D. *Armageddon in Stalingrad, September-November 1942*. Lawrence, KS: University Press of Kansas, 2009.

Glantz, D. *Barbarossa: Hitler's Invasion of Russia 1941*. Stroud: Tempus, 2001.

Glantz, D. *Barbarossa Derailed: The Battle for Smolensk, 10 July-10 September 1941*, 3 vols. Solihull, UK: Helion, 2012–14.

Glantz, D. *The Battle for Leningrad, 1941–1944*. Lawrence, KS: University Press of Kansas, 2002.

Glantz, D. *Colossus Reborn: The Red Army at War*. Lawrence, KS: University Press of Kansas, 2005.

Glantz, D. *Companion to Colossus Reborn: Key Documents and Statistics*. Lawrence, KS: University Press of Kansas, 2005.

Glantz, D. *Endgame at Stalingrad*, 2 vols. Lawrence, KS: University Press of Kansas, 2014.

Glantz, D. 'Forgotten Battles of the German-Soviet War (1941-1945)', *JSMS*, vol. 8, 1995, no. 4, pp. 768–808.

Glantz, D. *From the Don to the Dnepr: Soviet Offensive Operations, December 1942 – August 1943*. London: Frank Cass, 1991.

Glantz, D., *Red Storm over the Balkans: The Failed Soviet Invasion of Romania, Spring 1944*. Lawrence, KS: University Press of Kansas, 2006.

Glantz, D. *The Soviet Airborne Experience*. Fort Leavenworth, KS: USA CGSC, 1985.

Glantz, D. *Stumbling Colossus: The Red Army on the Eve of World War*. Lawrence, KS: University Press of Kansas, 1998.

Glantz, D. *To the Gates of Stalingrad: Soviet-German Combat Operations, April-August 1942*. Lawrence, KS: University Press of Kansas, 2009.

Glantz, D. and House, J. *The Battle of Kursk 1943*. Lawrence, KS: University Press of Kansas, 1999.

Glantz, D. and House, J. *When Titans Clashed: How the Red Army Stopped Hitler*. Lawrence, KS: University Press of Kansas, 1995.

Goebbels, J. *Goebbels Reden 1932–1945*. Düsseldorf: Droste Verlag, 1972.

Goebbels, J. *Die Tagebücher von Joseph Goebbels*. Munich: K. G. Saur, 1998.

Gori, F. and Pons S. (eds). *The Soviet Union and Europe in the Cold War, 1943–53*. Basingstoke: Macmillan, 1996.

Gor'kov, Iu. A. *Gosudarstvennyi komitet oborony postanovliaet (1941–1945): Tsifry, dokumenty*. Moscow: Olma-Press, 2002.

Gor'kov, Iu. A. *Kreml'. Stavka. Genshtab*. Tver': RIF LTD, 1995.

Gorodetsky, G. *Grand Delusion: Stalin and the German Invasion of Russia*. New Haven, CT: Yale University Press, 1999.

Gotovil li Stalin nastupatel'nuiu voiny protiv Gitlera? Nezaplanirovannaia diskussiia. Sbornik materialov. Moscow: AIRO-XX, 1995.

Guderian, H. *Erinnerungen eines Soldaten*. Heidelberg: Kurt Vowinckel, 1951.

Halder, F. *Kriegstagebuch: Tägliche Aufzeichnungen des Chefs des Generalstabes des Heeres, 1939–1942*, 3 vols. Stuttgart: Kohlhammer, 1965.

Hardesty, V. and Grinberg I. *Red Phoenix Rising: The Soviet Air Force in World War II*. Lawrence, KS: University Press of Kansas, 2012.

Harrison, M. *Accounting for War: Soviet Production, Employment, and the Defence Burden, 1940–1945*. Cambridge: Cambridge University Press, 1996.

Harrison, M. (ed.). *The Economics of World War II: Six Powers in International Comparison*. Cambridge: Cambridge University Press, 1998.

Hartmann, C. *Operation Barbarossa: Nazi Germany's War in the East, 1941-1945*. Oxford: Oxford University Press, 2013.

Hayward, J. *Stopped at Stalingrad: The Luftwaffe and Hitler's Defeat in the East, 1942–1943*. Lawrence, KS: University Press of Kansas, 1998.

Heer, H. and Naumann K. (eds). *War of Extermination: The German Military in World War II*. Oxford: Berghahn, 1999.

Hilberg, R. *The Destruction of the European Jews*, 3 vols, 3rd edn. New Haven, CT: Yale University Press, 2003.

Hinsley, F. H. *British Intelligence in the Second World War: Its Influence on Strategy and Operations*, 5 vols. London: HMSO, 1979–90.

Hitler, A. *Hitler's Politisches Testament: Die Bormann Diktate vom Februar und April 1945*. Hamburg: Albrecht Knaus, 1981.

Hitler, A. *Hitler's Table Talk, 1941–1944*. London: Weidenfeld & Nicolson, 1953.

Istoriia Velikoi Otechestvennoi voiny Sovetskogo Soiuza, 1941–1945, 6 vols. Moscow: Voennaia izdatel'stvo, 1960-4.

Istoriia vtoroi mirovoi voiny 1939–1945, 12 vols. Moscow: Voenizdat, 1973–82.

Kay, A. *Exploitation, Resettlement, Mass Murder: Political and Economic Planning for German Occupation Policy in the Soviet Union, 1940-1941*. Oxford: Berghahn Books, 2006.

Kay, A., Rutherford, J., and Stahel, D. *Nazi Policy on the Eastern Front, 1941: Total War, Genocide, and Radicalization*. Rochester, NY: University of Rochester Press, 2012.

Kershaw, I. *The End: Hitler's Germany, 1944–1945*. London: Allen Lane, 2011.

Kershaw, I. *Hitler 1936–45: Nemesis*. London: Allen Lane, 2000.

Khrushchev, N. S. 'Memuary', *Voprosy istorii*, 1990, nos. 9–12; 1991, nos. 1–8.

Khrushchev, N. S. 'O kul'te lichnosti i ego posledsviiakh [25 February 1956]', *ITsK*, 1989, no. 3, pp. 128–70.

Konev, I. S. 'Nachalo Moskovskoi bitvy', *VIZh*, 1966, no. 10, pp. 56–67.

Krivosheev G. F. et al. (eds). *Rossiia i SSSR v voinakh XX veka: Poteri vooruzhennykh sil. Statisticheskoe issledovanie*. Moscow: OLMA-Press, 2001 (*Poteri*).

Krylova, A. *Soviet Women in Combat: A History of Violence on the Eastern Front*. Cambridge: Cambridge University Press, 2010.

Kumanev, G. A. *Riadom so Stalinym: Otkrovennye svidetel'stva*. Moscow: Bylina, 1999.

Kumanev, G. A. *Voina i zheleznodorozhnyi transport SSSR 1941-1945*. Moscow: Nauka, 1988.

Lopukhovsky, L. *The Viaz'ma Catastrophe, The Battle of the Viaz'ma-Briansk: The Red Army's Disastrous Stand against Operation Typhoon*. Solihull, UK: Helion, 2013.

Lower, W. *Nazi Empire-Building and the Holocaust in Ukraine*. Chapel Hill, NC: University of North Carolina Press, 2005.

Luther, C. *Barbarossa Unleashed: The German Blitzkrieg Through Central Russia to the Gates of Moscow: June-December 1941*. Altglen, PA: Schiffer, 2013.

Miagkov, M. Iu. 'Bitva pod Moskvoi: Ot oborony k kontrnastupleniiu', *NNI*, 2010, no. 3, pp. 2–61.

Malyshev, V. A. 'Dnevnik narkoma', *Istochnik*, 1997, no. 5, pp. 103–47.

Manstein, E. Von. *Verlorene Siege*. Bonn: Athenäum-Verlag, 1958.

Markwick, R. and Cardona, E. *Soviet Women on the Frontline in the Second World War*.
Houndmills: Palgrave Macmillan, 2012.

Maslov, A. A. *Captured Soviet Generals: The Fate of Soviet Generals Captured in Combat 1941–45*.
London: Frank Cass, 2001.

Maslov, A. A. *Fallen Soviet Generals: Soviet General Officers Killed in Battle 1941–1945*. London:
Frank Cass, 1998.

Mawdsley, E. 'Crossing the Rubicon: Soviet Plans for Offensive War in 1940–1941', *IHR*, vol. 24,
2003, no. 4, pp. 818–65.

Mawdsley, E. *December 1941: Twelve Days that Began a World War*. New Haven, CT: Yale
University Press, 2011.

Mazower, M. *Hitler's Empire: Nazi Rule in Occupied Europe*. London: Allen Lane, 2008.

May, E. (ed). *Knowing One's Enemy: Intelligence Assessment Before the Two World Wars*.
Princeton: Princeton UP, 1986.

Megargee, Geoffrey P. *Inside Hitler's High Command*. Lawrence, KS: University Press of Kansas,
2000.

Megargee, Geoffrey P. *War of Annihilation: Combat and Genocide on the Eastern Front, 1941*.
Lanham, MD: Rowman & Littlefield, 2005.

Mel'tiukhov, M. I. 'Operatsiia "Bagration" i Varshavskoe vosstanie 1944 goda', *VI*, 2004, no. 11,
pp. 43–57.

Melvin, M. *Manstein: Hitler's Greatest General*. London: Weidenfeld and Nicolson, 2010.

Mendelsohn, J. (ed.). *Covert Warfare: Intelligence, Counterintelligence and Military Deception
in the World War II Era*, vol. 6, *German Radio Intelligence and the Soldatsender*. New York:
Garland Press, 1989.

Merridale, C. *Ivan's War: The Red Army, 1939-1945*. London: Faber and Faber, 2005.

Mikoian, A. *Tak bylo: Razmyshleniia o minuvshem*. Moscow: Bagrius, 1999.

Millett, A. and Murray, W. (eds). *Military Effectiveness*, 3 vols. Boston: Unwin Hyman, 1987.

Miner, S. *Stalin's Holy War: Religion, Nationalism, and Alliance Politics, 1941-1945*. Chapel Hill,
NC: University of North Carolina Press, 2003.

Muller, R. *The German Air War in Russia*. Baltimore, MD: Nautical and Aviation Publishers,
1992.

Muller, R.-D. *The Unknown Eastern Front: The Wehrmacht and Hitler's Foreign Soldiers*. London:
I. B. Tauris, 2012.

Muller, R.-D. and Ueberschär, G. R. *Hitler's War in the East, 1941–1945: A Critical Assessment*.
Oxford: Berghahn. 1997.

Müller-Hillebrand, B. *Das Heer, 1933–1945: Entwicklung des organisatonschen Aufbaues*, 3 vols.
Darmstadt: E. S. Mittler, 1954–69.

Mulligan, T. *The Politics of Illusion and Empire: German Occupation Policy in the Soviet Union,
1942–1941*. New York: Greenwood Press, 1988.

Murphy, D. *What Stalin Knew: The Enigma of Barbarossa*. New Haven, CT: Yale University Press,
2005.

Naumov, V. P. 'Sud'ba voennoplennykh i deportirovannykh grazhdan SSSR: Materialy Komissii
po reabilitatsii zhertv politicheskikh repressii', *NNI*, 1996, no. 2, pp. 92–112.

Neitzel, S. and Welzer, H. *Soldaten: On Fighting, Killing and Dying: The Secret Second World War
Tapes of German POWs*. London: Simon and Schuster, 2012.

Neitzel, S. (ed.). *Tapping Hitler's Generals: Transcriptions of Secret Conversation, 1942-45*.
Barnsley: Frontline Books, 2007.

Overmans, R. *Deutsche militärische Verluste im Zweiten Weltkrieg*. Munich: R. Oldenbourg, 1999.

Overy, R. *The Bombing War: Europe, 1939-45*. London: Allen Lane, 2013.

Parrish, M. *Sacrifice of the Generals: Soviet Senior Officer Loses, 1939-1953*. Westyport, CT:
Greenwood, 2001.

Pechenkin, A. A. (ed.). '"Sovremennaia armiia armiia nastupatel'naia". Vystupleniia I. V. Stalina na prieme v Kremle pered vypusknikami voennykh akademii. Mai 1941 g.', *IA*, 1995, no. 2, pp. 23–31.

Pedosov, A. D. 'Vospominaniia A. D. Pedosova o vystuplenii Marshala G. K. Zhukova v Akademii Obshchestvennykh Nauk (1966)', *Arkheograficheskii ezhegodnik*, 1995, pp. 282–9.

Philippi, A. and Heim, F. *Der Feldzug gegen Sowjetrußland 1941 bis 1945: Ein operativer Überblick*. Stuttgart: W. Kohlhammer, 1962.

Pogue, F. *The Supreme Command*. Washington, DC: Office of Chief of Military History, 1952.

Pons, S. *Stalin and the Inevitable War, 1936–1941*. London: Frank Cass, 2002.

Portugal'skii, R. M. *Marshal S. K. Timoshenko*. Moscow: MOF-Pobeda, 1994.

Post, W. *Unternehmen Barbarossa: Deutsche und sowetische Angriffspläne 1940/41*. Hamburg: Mittler, 1995.

Reese, R. *Stalin's Reluctant Soldiers: A Social History of the Red Army, 1918–1941*. Lawrence, KS: University Press of Kansas, 1996.

Reese, R., *Why Stalin's Soldiers Fought: The Red Army's Military Effectiveness in World War II*. Lawrence, KS: University Press of Kansas, 2011.

Reinhardt, K. *Moscow: The Turning Point*. Oxford: Berg, 1992.

Roberts, G. *Molotov: Stalin's Cold Warrior*. Washington, DC: Potomac Books, 2012.

Roberts, G. *The Soviet Union and the Origins of the Second World War: Russo-German Relations and the Road to War, 1933–1941*. Basingstoke: Macmillan, 1995.

Roberts, G. *Stalin's General: The Life of Georgy Zhukov*. London: Icon Books, 2012.

Rokossovskii, K. K. *Soldatskii dolg*. Moscow: Voennoe izdatel'stvo, 1997.

Rutherford, J. *Combat and Genocide on the Eastern Front: The German Infantry's War, 1941–1944*. Cambridge: Cambridge University Press, 2014.

Sapir, J. 'The Economics of War in the Soviet Union during World War II', in I. Kershaw and M. Lewin (eds). *Stalinism and Nazism: Dictatorships in Comparison*. Cambridge: Cambridge University Press, 1997.

Shepherd, B. *War in the Wild East: The German Army and Soviet Partisans*. Cambridge, MA: Harvard University Press, 2004.

Shtemenko, S. M. *General'nyi shtab v gody voiny*. Moscow: Voenizdat, 1989.

Showalter, D. *Armor and Blood: The Battle of Kursk: The Turning Point of World War II*. New York: Random House, 2013.

Shukman, H. (ed.). *Stalin's Generals*. London: Weidenfeld & Nicolson, 1993.

Simonov, K. *Glazami cheloveka moego pokoleniia: Razmyshleniia o I. V. Staline*. Moscow: Kniga, 1990.

Simonov, N. *Voenno-promyshlennyi kompleks SSSR v 1920–1950-e gody: Tempy ekonomicheskogo rosta, struktura, organizatsiia proizvodstva i upravelenie*. Moscow: Rosspen, 1996.

Slepyan, K. *Stalin's Guerrillas: Soviet Partisans in World War II*. Lawrence, KS: University Press of Kansas, 2006.

Smith, B. *Sharing Secrets with Stalin: How the Allies Traded Intelligence, 1941–1945*. Lawrence, KS: University Press of Kansas, 1996.

Snyder, Timothy. *Bloodlands: Europe Between Hitler and Stalin*. London: Bodley Head, 2010.

Sokolov, Boris V. *The Role of the Soviet Union in the Second World War: A Re-Examination*. Solihull, UK: Helion, 2012.

Stahel, D. *Kiev 1941, Hitler's Battle for Supremacy in the East*. Cambridge: Cambridge University Press, 2011.

Stahel, D. *Operation Barbarossa and Germany's Defeat in the East*. Cambridge: Cambridge University Press, 2009.

Stahel, D. *Operation Typhoon: Hitler's March on Moscow, October 1941*. Cambridge: Cambridge University Press, 2013.

Select Bibliography

Stalin, I. *O Velikoi Otechestvennoi voine Sovetskogo Soiuza*, 5th edn. Moscow: GIPL, 1951 (Stalin, *OVOVSS*).

Statiev, A. 'Blocking Units in the Red Army', *JMilH*, vol. 75, 2012, no. 2, pp. 475–95.

Statiev, A. *The Soviet Counterinsurgency in the Western Borderlands*. Cambridge: Cambridge University Press, 2010.

Stoler, M. *Allies in War: Britain and America against the Axis Powers, 1941–1945*. London: Arnold, 2005.

Stolfi, R. *Hitler's Panzers East: World War II Reinterpreted*. Norman, OK: University of Oklahoma Press, 1991.

Stone, D. (ed.). *The Soviet Union at War, 1941-1945*. Barnsley, UK: Pen and Sword, 2010.

Streit, C. *Keine Kameraden: Die Wehrmacht und die sowjetischen Kriegsgefangenen 1941–1945*, 3rd edn. Bonn: J. H. W. Dietz, [1978] 1997.

Suvenirov, O. F. *Tragediia RKKA 1937–1938*. Moscow: Terra, 1998.

Suvorov, V. *The Chief Culprit: Stalin's Grand Design to Start World War II*. Annapolis: Naval Institute Press, 2008.

Suvorov, V. *Icebreaker: Who Started the Second World War?* London: Hamish Hamilton, 1990.

Svetlishin, N. A. *Krutye stupeni sud'by: Zhizn' i ratnye podvigi marshala G. K. Zhukova*. Khabarovsk: Khabarovskoe knizhnoe izdatel'stvo, 1992.

Thurston, R. *Life and Terror in Stalin's Russia, 1934-1941*. New Haven, CT: Yale University Press, 1996.

Thurston, R. and Bonwetsch, B. (eds). *The People's War: Responses to World War II in the Soviet Union*. Urbana: University of Illinois Press, 2000.

Tippelskirch, K. von. *Geschichte des zweiten Weltkriegs*. Bonn: Athenäum-Verlag, 1951.

Tooze, A. *The Wages of Destruction: The Making and Breaking of the Nazi Economy*. London: Allen Lane, 2006.

Tumarkin, N. *The Living and the Dead: The Rise and Fall of the Cult of World War II in Russia*. New York: Basic Books, 1994.

Tuyll, H. van. *Feeding the Bear: American Aid to the Soviet Union, 1941–1945*. New York: Greenwood, 1989.

Ungváry, K. *Battle for Budapest: 100 Days in World War II*. London: I. B. Tauris, 2004.

Vasilevskii, A. M. *Delo vsei zhizni*, 2 vols, 6th edn. Moscow: IPL, [1975] 1989.

Velikata Otechestvennaia voina: 1941–1945: Entsiklopediia. Moscow: Sovetskaia entsiklopediia, 1985 (*VOVE*).

Velikaia Otechestvennaia voina, 1941–1945: Voenno-istoricheskie ocherki, 4 vols. Moscow: Nauka, 1998-9 (*VOV/VIO*).

Voroshilov, K. E. *Stalin i vooruzhennye sily SSSR*. Moscow: GIPL, 1951.

Wegner, B. 'Hitler, der Zweite Weltkrieg und die Choreographie des Untergangs', *Geschichte und Gesellschaft*, vol. 26, 2000, no. 3, pp. 493–518.

Werth, A. *Russia at War 1941–1945*. London: Barrie and Rockliff, 1964.

Wette, W. *The Wehrmacht: History, Myth, Reality*. Cambridge, MA: Harvard University Press, 2007.

Zaloga, S. and Grandsen, J. *Soviet Tanks and Combat Vehicles of World War II*. London: Arms and Armour Press, 1984.

Zamulin, V. *Demolishing the Myth. The Tank Battle at Prokhorovka, Kursk, July 1943: An Operational Narrative*. Solihull: Helion, 2011.

Zemskov, V. N. 'K voprosu o repatriatsii sovetskikh grazhdan. 1944–1951 gody', *ISSSR*, 1990, no. 4, pp. 26–41.

Zetterling, N. and Frankson, A. *The Drive on Moscow, 1941: Operation Taifun and Germany's First Great Crisis in World War II*. Havertown, PA: Casemate, 2012.

Zetterling, N. and Frankson, A. *The Korsun Pocket: The Encirclement and Breakout of a German Army in the East, 1944*. Havertown, PA: Casemate, 2008.

Zetterling, N. and Frankson, A. *Kursk 1943: A Statistical Analysis*. London: Frank Cass, 2000.

Zharskii, A. P. *Sviaz' v vysshikh upravleniia Krasnoi armii v Velikoi Otechestvennoi voiny 1941–1945*. St. Petersburg: Evropeiskii dom, 2011.

Zhukov, G. K. 'Chego stoiat polkovodcheskie kachestva Stalina: Neproiznesennaia rech' marshala G. K. Zhukova', *Istochnik*, 1995, no. 2, pp. 143–59.

Zhukov, G. K. *Vospominaniia i razmyshleniia*, 3 vols, 10th edn. Moscow: APN, 1990 (Zhukov, *ViR*).

Ziemke, E. *Stalingrad to Berlin: German Defeat in the East*. Washington, DC: Center of Military History, [1968] 1987.

Ziemke, E. *The Red Army, 1918–1941: From Vanguard of World Revolution to America's Ally*. London: Frank Cass, 2004.

Ziemke, E. and Bauer, M. *Moscow to Stalingrad: Decision in the East*. Washington, DC: Center of Military History, 1989.

Zolotarev, V. A. (ed.). *Istoriia voennoi strategii Rossii*. Moscow: Kuchkovo pole and Poligrafresursy, 2000.

Zolotarev, V. A. (ed.). *Velikaia Otechestvennaia voina 1941-1945 gg.: Deistvuiushchaia armiia*. Moscow: Animi Fortitudo and Kuchkovo pole, 2005.

Zubok,V. and Pleshakov, C. *Inside the Kremlin's Cold War: Soviet Leaders from Stalin to Khrushchev*. Cambridge, MA: Harvard University Press, 1996.

INDEX

Abakumov, V. S.   64, 211
Air Force, German (Luftwaffe)   6, 25, 28, 54–5,
   97–8, 125–6, 134, 145, 169, 300
   airborne forces   23–4
   aircraft   26–7, 216
   doctrine   215–16
   field divisions   207
   losses   55, 264
   structure   24
Air Force, Red Army (VVS)   29, 72, 95, 204, 322
   aircraft   26–7, 195–7, 277
   doctrine   24, 38, 217–18, 258
   June 1941 disaster   54–5
   leadership   27
   losses   58–9, 201–2, 264, 379
   structure   24, 217
Allenstein   361
Allied Control Commission
   Finland   288
   Romania   333
All-Slavic Committee   310
anti-Communism   6–7
anti-Slav policies, Nazi   9–10
Antonescu, Field Marshal Ion   159, 174, 331–2
Antonov, Gen. A. I.   75, 204, 212, 217, 259, 286,
   295, 323, 336, 346, 352, 354, 356–7, 364,
   372–4, 377
Arctic convoys   174, 187, 238
Ardennes offensive (1944)   308, 327, 348, 354–5
Armenia   153
Army, German   *see also* Wehrmacht
   airborne forces *see* Air Force, German
   anti-Nazi movement   5
   anti-partisan operations   224, 231
   artillery   24, 26, 134, 141, 189–91
   communications   28, 198
   discipline   29
   doctrine   19, 207–8
   General Staff   5, 158, 276
   High Command (OKH)   3–6, 8, 11, 107, 157–9,
      199–200, 369–71
   Hiwis   207, 225
   infantry weapons   24, 189–90
   morale   385
   National Socialist leadership officers   206, 303
   officer corps   181–9, 206
   Osttruppen   225–6

   personnel   23–4, 206–8
   structure   23–4, 207
   tanks   25, 193, 258
   training   19
   transport   25, 194
   war crimes   10–11, 29, 99–101
Army, Soviet (Red Army)
   airborne forces   23–4, 119–20, 214–15,
      271–2, 368
   artillery   24–5, 190–2, 277
   blocking detachments (*zagraditel'nye
      otriady*)   31, 64, 163, 211
   cavalry   63, 103, 119, 213–14
   commissars   63, 70, 77, 97, 100, 135, 208
   communications/signals   27–8, 198
   deception (*maskirovka*)   171, 296
   Directorate of Communications/Transport
      (*Upravlenie voennykh soobshchenii*)   63
   discipline   31–2, 110–11, 210–11, 380
   doctrine   21–2, 34–5, 74–5, 217–8
   engineers   93
   General Staff   21, 60, 64, 93–4, 202–5, 352
   Guards   70, 214
   High Command (*Stavka*)   62, 96, 113, 123,
      166–7, 202, 205
   High Command Reserve (*RVGK*)   191
   infantry weapons   24, 189
   intelligence   32–7, 123, 205, 355–6
   Main Political Administration   63, 93,
      135–6, 203
   military tribunals   211
   morale   30–2, 385
   Moscow conference (1940)   60
   officer corps   19–20, 84–5, 208–9
   penal units   163, 211
   personnel   208–13
   pre-1941 war plans   12, 19–20, 37–41
   pre-war purges   12, 19–20
   reserves   39, 107–8, 164, 191, 208–10
   Signals Directorate (*Upravlenie sviazi*)   28
   signals intelligence   205–6
   Special Section (*OO*)   63–4, 163, 211
   and spreading revolution   313
   Stavka representatives   167, 204–5
   structure   23–4, 213–15
   supply   277, 297
   tanks   21, 23, 25–6, 143, 192–3, 277

training   30
transport   25, 195, 277, 347
Artem'ev, Gen. P. A.   65, 92
Atlantic Charter (1941)   240, 243, 302, 309
Auschwitz   100, 317, 344
Austria   368–9
Azerbaidzhan   153

Babii Iar massacre (1941)   98
Bagramian, Gen. I. Kh.   78, 137, 139, 263, 294, 296, 302–5, 362
BAGRATION, Operation (1944)   218, 289–301
Balkan campaign (1941)   107
Baltic islands   304
Baltic operation (1944)   301–5
Baltic states   14–15, 224, 302, 310, see also Estonia; Latvia; Lithuania
Banská Bystrica   343–4
BARBAROSSA, Operation (1941)   3, 58, 32, 41–5, 53–84, 113
Barkhorn, Col. Gerhard   198
Barvenkovo–Lozovaia operation   138
Barvenkovo salient (1942)   138–40
battle of annihilation (Vernichtungschlacht)   8–10, 41–5
BEAST OF PREY, Operation (1942)   128
Beck, Gen. Ludwig   5, 53
Belgorod   249, 253
Belgorod–Khar'kov operation (1943)   264–5, 271
Belgrade operation (1944)   336
Belorussia   39–40, 299
Belorussian defensive operation (1941)   58–66
Belorussian operation (1944)   299, see also BAGRATION, Operation
Belostok   58, 60–1, 294–5
Belov, Gen. P. A.   103, 113, 119–20, 123
Beneš, Edvard   341–2, 347
Berezina River   65, 115, 293
Beria, L. P.   62–3, 94, 168, 233, 313
Berlin, Battle of (1945)   352–7, 369–80
Berling, Gen. Z.   323
Bessarabia, see Moldavia
Bierut, Bolesław   311, 328
BIRCH TREE, Operation   288
Blitzkrieg   8, 113–4, 182, 207
Blomberg, Field Marshal Werner von   5
BLÜCHER II, OPERATION   154
BLUE, Operation (1942)   150–7, 177
Bobruisk   65, 293, 298
Bobruisk operation (1944)   293
Bock, Field Marshal Fedor von   55, 58, 61, 68–9, 91, 106–7, 150, 152, 158–9
Bogdanov, Gen. I. A.   65
Bogdanov, Marshal S. I.   277, 317, 326, 377
Bolkhov operation (1942)   124

Boris, King of Bulgaria   333
Bór-Komorowski, Gen. Tadeusz   321
Botoşani   273
Bradley, Gen. Omar   375
Bratislava   341, 343, 345
Bratislava–Brno operation (1945)   345
Brauchitsch, Field Marshal Walter von   5, 68, 107, 157, 200–1
Bräutigam, Otto   224
Breslau   356, 366–7, 382
Brest   58–9, 61, 294, 318
Brest Fortress, defence of (1941)   61
Brezhnev, L. I.   267, 342
Briansk   91
BRIDGE-BUILDING, Operation (1942)   122
Britain   6, 13, 235–43, 389
British-Soviet Treaty (1942)   235
Brno   345
BRUNSWICK, Operation, see BLUE, Operation
Bucharest   212, 332–3
Budapest, Battle of   339–40
Budennyi, Marshal S. M.   64, 66, 72, 76, 78, 91, 95, 111, 154, 166, 204
BUFFALO, Operation (1943)   149–50, 251–2
Bukrin operation (1943)   271
Bulganin, N. A.   64, 67, 96, 112, 203–4, 252, 292, 317
Bulgaria   212, 242, 307–8, 312, 329, 333–6
Bulge, Battle of the, see Ardennes offensive
Burmistenko, M. A.   78
Busch, Field Marshal Ernst   289, 297–8, 300
Busse, Gen. Theodor   360, 371, 378
BUSTARD HUNT, Operation (1942)   135

Cairncross, John   260
Cannae, Battle of (216 BC)   58, 165
Carpathian-Dukla operation (1944)   343
Central Asia   48, 50, 210, 225
central Soviet offensive (1943)   249–52
Central Staff of the Partisan Movement (TsShPD)   230
Chankufeng, see Khasan, Lake, incident
Chechen-Ingush peoples, deportation of (1944)   228
Chełm   317
Cherevichenko, Gen. Ia. T.   87, 117, 121, 252
Cherkassy   271–2
Cherniakhovskii, Gen. I. D.   253, 274, 294–6, 326, 361–4
Chernigov–Poltava operation (1943)   271
Chernovitsy   274
Chuikov, Gen. V. I.   155–6, 168, 171, 317, 355, 378
Churchill, Winston   33, 36, 236–41, 312–13, 333, 345, 348–9, 359, 375
CITADEL, Operation (1943)   257–63

Index

Clausewitz, Carl von   68, 375
CLAUSEWITZ, Operation (1942), *see* BLUE, Operation
collaborators (with Germans)   225–8, 232, 299, 302
collective farms   31, 51, 185, 225
Comintern (Communist International)   12, 94, 222, 241–2, 311–12
'commissar order' (1941)   11, 100
Communist Party of the Soviet Union   19, 21, 45, 208, 223
   Central Committee   93
   International Information Department (*OMI*)   312
   Komsomol (Communist Youth)   108, 309
   Politburo   12
Crimea   87, 99, 131–6, 278–80
Crimean operation (1944)   278–80
Crimean Tatars, deportation of (1944)   228, 280
Curzon line   314–16
Czechoslovakia   212, 341–7
   Czechoslovak personnel in Red Army   341, 343
Częstochowa   319

Danzig   359, 361
Daugavpils   80, 294
Debrecen operation (1944)   337–8, 341
'deep battle'   21, 23–4, 119, 213–14, 217–18, 272
Demiansk   121–2, 124, 147, 149, 248–9
deportations, by Germans   100–2, 150, 280–1
deportations, by Soviets   227–8, 299, 314–5
Dietrich, Gen. Josef ('Sepp')   87, 340, 369
Dimitrov, Georgi   241, 334
Djilas, Milovan   311–12
Dnepr airborne operation (1943)   271–2
Dnepropetrovsk   253, 266
Dnepr Power Station   75
DON, Operation (1943)   157, 171, 244, 246
Donbass   50, 87, 99, 150
Donbass defensive operation (1942)   50, 87, 99, 150
Donbass operation (1943)   271
Donbass–Rostov defensive operation (1941)   86–7
Dovator, Gen. L. M.   103
Dukla Pass   343
Dvina River   8, 32, 42, 61, 65–6, 79–80, 289–90, 294
Dzhugashvili, Sr. Lt. Ia. I.   66

East Carpathian operation (1944)   344
East Pomeranian operation (1945)   352, 360–1
East Prussia   40, 79, 305, 319, 322, 358
East Prussian operation (1945)   361–6
EDELWEISS, Operation   153, 160
Eden, Anthony   241
Efremov, Gen. M. G.   119–20
Einsatzgruppen, see SS
Eisenhower, Gen, Dwight D.   237, 346, 372, 374–5, 381

El'nia operation (1941)   70
Eremenko, Gen. A. I.   66, 70, 91, 95, 111, 152, 156, 167–9, 244, 266, 279, 290, 303, 344–5
Ershakov, Gen. F. A.   92
Estonia   14–5, 80–1, 301–4, 306, 319

Fatherland Front (Bulgaria)   334
Fediuninskii, Gen. I. I.   281
Finland   15, 173–4, 286–9, 310
FIRE MAGIC, Operation (1942)   172
Flerov, Captain I. A.   92
Focşani Gap   275, 329, 331–2
forced labour (used by Germans)   101, 226
forced labour (used by Russians), *see* GULAG
Foreign Affairs, People's Commissariat of (*NKID*)   309
'fortified places' strategy (1944)   274, 293, 297–8
France, invasion of (1940)   9, 14, 17–18, 20, 34
Free Germany Committee   234, 242
FRIDERICUS, Operation (1942)   138–40
Friessner, Gen. Johannes   303, 331–2, 338
Fritsch, Gen. Werner von   5

GALLOP, Operation (1943)   253, 255, 266
Gapich, Gen. N. I.   28
Gdynia   361
Gehlen, Gen. Reinhard   53, 205
Generalplan Ost   9
Georgia   153
German–Soviet Non-Aggression Pact (1939)   13, 35, 39
German–Soviet peace feelers   242
Germany
   armaments production   43, 51–2, 183f., 187, 386
   economy   51–2, 182–4
   food supply   50–1, 185
   geography   350–1
   impact of war on   391
   internal stability, morale   29, 220–1, 350, 384
   occupation policy in USSR   9–11, 223–6
   population   46
   post-war division   351
GKO, *see* State Defence Committee
GNEISENAU line (1944)   279
Goebbels, Joseph   7–8, 181–4, 199, 221, 242, 349, 362, 367
Goering, Hermann   4, 6, 9, 51–2, 129, 162, 216, 223
Golikov, Gen. F. I.   33–6, 103, 111, 121, 139, 150, 214, 246, 253–6
Gordov, Gen. V. N.   152, 168, 315
Gorodnianskii, Gen. A. M.   138–9
GOTH'S HEAD position (1943)   267
Gottwald, Klement   241, 347
Govorov, Marshal L. A.   128, 173–4, 280–1, 283, 286–7, 303

500

GPU, *see* NKVD

Graz 369

Grechko, Gen. A. A. 344

Greim, Field Marshal Robert 297–9, 373

Grigor'ev, Gen. A. T. 28

Grodno 58, 294–5

Groza, Petru 333

Groznyi 50, 153–4

Guderian, Gen. Heinz 58, 65, 68, 70, 77–9, 91–2, 103, 107, 113, 201, 257, 318, 360, 370

GULAG (Soviet labour camp system) 31, 49, 101, 195, 227, 234, 351

Gumbinnen–Goldap operation (1944) 362

HAGEN line (1943) 264

Halder, Gen. Franz 5–6, 8, 61–2, 68, 81, 83, 97, 104, 106–7, 117, 157–9

Hanke, Karl 367

HANNOVER, Operation (1942) 120

Harpe, Gen. Josef 318, 325, 327

Hartmann, Col. Erich 198, 347

Heiligenbeil pocket (1945) 364

Heinrici, Gen. Gotthard 119–20, 124, 342, 344, 371

HERON, Operation (1942) 160

Himmler, Heinrich 201, 206–7, 226, 268, 302, 360, 367, 369, 371

Hitler, Adolf

    foreign policy, world view 6–8, 15–16, 242–3

    decision to invade USSR 3–4, 6, 8

    summer–autumn 1941 decisions 67–72, 81–3, 87–8, 106–7

    reaction to Moscow defeat (1941–2) 103, 117–18, 122, 124, 140, 143

    'second campaign' and Stalingrad (1942) 144–5, 154, 157–62, 172–3, 175, 200, 251

    1943 offensive 254, 257–8

    1943–4 static defence in Ukraine, Baltic and Belorussia 268–9, 271, 273–6, 278, 285, 297, 302

    1944 bomb plot against 201–2, 221, 318

    1944–5 in southeastern Europe 332, 339

    1945 campaign 200, 337, 339, 349–50, 369–70

    Testament (1945) 6–7, 104, 186, 386

    no surrender policy (1945) 350, 370

    and Axis allies 159

    and 'Bolsheviks' 45, 183

    and German home front 221

    and Jews 6, 97–9

    as supreme commander 3–11, 15–16, 199–200

Hoepner, Gen. Erich 79, 91–3, 102, 107

Hollidt, Gen. Karl 253, 265, 271, 273

Holocaust 10–11, 97–9

Home Army, Polish 313, 315, 320–3, 328

Horthy, Regent Miklós 159, 337–8

Hossbach, Gen. Friedrich 362–3

Hoth, Gen. Hermann 58, 66, 81, 91–2, 138, 156, 160, 254, 257, 260–2, 264, 271–2

Hube, Gen. Hans 77, 273, 275

Hungary 159, 337–41

    Army 246, 338

Iaşi–Kishinev operation (1944) 331–3

Insterburg–Königsberg operation 326, 362–4

Iran 553, 187

IRON HAMMER, Operation (1943) 216

Italian campaign (1943–5) 238–9, 249

Italy 110, 160, 235

    Army 46, 159

    POWs 233

Izium–Barvenkovo operation (1943) 265

Jänecke, Gen. Erwin 278–9

Jankowski, Jan 328

Japan 15–16, 71, 110, 165, 187, 235, 387

Jodl, Gen. Alfred 5, 158, 200, 254, 257, 370–1, 381

Jordan, Gen. Hans 297

JUPITER, Operation (1942) 148–9

'jurisdiction decree' of OKW 11

'K' (KÖNIGSBERG) line (1941) 117–18

Kachalov, Gen. V. Ia. 77

Kachanov, Gen. K. M. 82

Kaganovich, L. M. 27, 97, 154

Kaganovich, M. M. 27

Kalach 156, 162, 170

Kalinin 102–3

Kaluga 103, 118

Kandalaksha 173–4

Kanev 271

Karelia, Battle of (1944) 286–7

Karlshorst surrender (1945) 381

Katowice 327, 367

Katukov, Gen. M. A. 111, 248, 254, 259, 261, 264, 277, 319, 326, 377

Katyn massacre (1940) 314

Keitel, Field Marshal Wilhelm 5, 158, 200, 229, 288, 370–1, 381

Kempf, Gen. Werner 257, 260–1, 264

Kerch' 133, 278

Kerch'–El'tigen operation (1943) 278

Kerch'–Feodosiia operation (1941–2) 134

Kerch' Strait 131, 134, 154, 267, 278

Kesselring, Field Marshal Albert 95, 110

Khalkhin Gol incident (1939) 15, 30, 111, 169

Khar'kov 87, 138, 253–4, 264

Khar'kov, Battle of (1942) 136–41

Khasan, Lake, incident (1938) 15, 30

Kholm 118, 121–2, 147, 162

Index

Khozin, Gen. M. S.   117, 125, 128, 248–9

Khrushchev, N. S.   42–3, 64, 76, 78, 137, 139, 166, 168–9, 202, 227, 259, 386, 389

Kiev   72–3, 98, 279

Kinzel, Gen. Eberhard   52–3

Kirkenes   288

Kirovograd   272

Kirponos, Gen. M. P.   72–80

Kishenev   275, 329, 331

Kleist, Field Marshal Ewald von   74–5, 86–7, 138–40, 153–4, 244, 269, 287

Klimovskikh, Gen. V. E.   59

Klin   102–3

Kluge, Gen. Günther   106–7, 120, 124, 146–7, 159, 201, 250, 262, 266, 297

Konev, Marshal I. S.   66, 89–92, 95–7, 102–4, 111, 113, 118, 124, 146–9, 166, 249, 252, 261, 271–5, 277, 315–7, 319, 322, 325–7, 329, 331, 342–6, 352, 355–6, 366–8, 376–80

Königsberg   326, 358–9, 362, 365, 367–8

KONRAD, Operation (1945)   339

Kopets, Gen. I. I.   27, 54

Korneichuk, A. E.   208

Korobkov, Gen. A. A.   59

Korsun'–Shevchenkovskii operation (1944)   272–3

Košice   343, 347

Kosmodem'ianskaia, Z. A.   108

Kostenko, Gen. F. I.   139

Kotov, Gen. G. P.   336–7

Kozhedub, Major I. N.   198

Kozlov, Gen. D. T.   116, 134–6

Kraków   40, 317, 319, 327, 344

Krasnoe selo–Ropsha operation (1944)   281–2

Kravchenko, Gen. A. G.   277, 331–2, 340

Krebs, Gen. Hans   201, 370–1

Kreizer, Gen. Ia. G.   279

KREML deception plan (1942)   140, 145

Krivoi Rog   50, 75, 271, 273

Kronshtadt   81, 281

Kruglov, S. N.   306

Kuban'   154

Küchler, Field Marshal Georg von   125, 128, 159, 172, 280–2

Kuibyshev   93

Kulik, Marshal G. I.   60, 133

Kurland   118, 224, 302, 305–6, 327, 369, 382

Kurochkin, Gen. P. A.   103, 117, 121–3, 141, 290

Kursk, Battle of (1943)   257–66

Küstrin   326, 370

Kuzbass   50

Kuznetsov, Gen. F. I.   74, 79–80, 133

Kuznetsov, Admiral N. G.   204

Kuznetsov, Gen. V. I.   103, 122

Ladoga, Lake   82–3, 129

Lasch, Gen. Otto   365

Latvia   14–15, 292, 301–6

Lauban offensive (1945)   367

Leeb, Field Marshal Wilhelm von   78, 82–3, 107

Leliushenko, Gen. D. D.   111, 277, 315, 326, 378

Lend-Lease   187–9, 191, 194–5, 198, 347

Lenin, V. I.   9, 12

Leningrad Blockade   125–31

Leningrad defensive operation (1941)   81–3

Leningrad–Novgorod operation (1944)   280–3

Liepaia   305

Lindemann, Gen. Georg   125, 172, 174, 248, 281, 303

List, Field Marshal Wilhelm   152–4, 158–9

Lithuania   14–15, 292, 294, 299, 302, 306

LITTLE SATURN, Operation (1942)   157, 160, 171, 246, 248

Litvinov, M. M.   309, 351

Liuban' operation (1942)   126–8

Liutezh operation (1943)   272

Łomza–Rózan operation (1944)   319–20

Lopatin, Gen. A. I.   168

losses, overall, civilian   391

losses, overall, military personnel   390–1

Lower Silesia operation (1945)   316

Lublin   40, 74, 317, 323

Lublin–Brest operation (1944)   313, 315, 317

Lublin government   317, 323, 328

Luftwaffe, see Air Force, German

Lukin, Gen. M. F.   92

Lüttwitz, Gen. Smilo von   337

L'vov   74

L'vov–Sandomierz operation (1944)   315–17

Mackensen, Gen. Eberhard von   87, 154, 254, 271

Magnuszew bridgehead (1944–5)   317, 319

Maikop   153

Maiskii, I. M.   309–12, 314, 329, 334–5, 337, 342, 348, 351

Majdanek   317

Malandin, Gen. G. K.   60

Malenkov, G. M.   62, 292

Malinovskii, Marshal R. Ia.   75, 116, 138–9, 150, 152, 165–6, 168, 171, 245, 265, 269, 271, 273, 276–8, 319, 329, 331–2, 337–40, 344–6, 368, 381

Malyshev, V. A.   192, 266–7

Manchuria (1945)   71, 289

Mannerheim, Field Marshal Carl Gustaf   174, 288

Mannerheim Line (1940)   40, 60, 73, 127, 288

Manstein, Field Marshal Erich von   80, 87, 133–6, 156–7, 159–60, 162, 172–3, 199, 201, 207–8, 219, 246, 249, 254–8, 260–2, 265–7, 271–6, 279

Manteuffel, Gen. Hasso von   371–2, 376

Marcks, Gen. Erich   8

Marshall, Gen. George C.   237, 346, 375

Maslennikov, Gen. I. I.   120, 168, 303
Mekhlis, L. E.   63, 135–6, 292, 342, 344
Mellenthin, Gen. Friedrich   255
Memel   304–5, 364
Memel operation (1944)   304–5
Meretskov, Marshal K. A.   21, 63, 88, 112, 127–8,
        173–4, 280–1, 283, 287–9
Mga   82, 266, 282
Michael, King of Romania   332
Miklós, Gen. Béla   338
Mikołajczyk, Stanisław   321, 328
Ministry for Occupied Eastern Territories
        (Ostministerium)   224
Mius operation (1943)   265
Minsk   58, 293
Mius River   87, 246
Mława–Elbing operation (1945)   326, 363
Model, Field Marshal Walter   77, 119, 124, 146,
        148, 206, 208, 257–8, 260, 262, 282, 284, 294,
        298, 315, 318–19, 321, 326, 347, 373
Mogilev   290, 293
Mogilev operation   293
Moldavia   15, 331
Moldavian defensive operation (1941)   58, 77
Mölders, Col. Werner   55
Molotov, V. M.   12, 35, 48, 59, 62, 93–5, 111, 204,
        228, 236–7, 241, 308, 311–12, 383
Molotov Line (1941)   22
Moltke, Field Marshal Helmuth von   8
Morava–Ostrava operation (1945)   355
Moscow   67–8, 79, 89, 92–3
        evacuation (1941)   93–4
Moscow, Battle of   87–97, 102–16
Moscow defensive operation (1941)   89, 104–6
Moscow offensive operation (1941–2)   89, 106, 119,
        120–2
Moscow–Volga Canal   102–3, 118
Moskalenko, Gen. K. S.   139, 253, 343–4
MOUNTAINS, Operation (1943)   171
Mozhaisk line (1941)   65, 92–4, 97, 102, 112
Müller, Gen. Vincenz   293
Munich crisis (1938)   13
Murmansk   173
Mussolini, Benito   159–60, 235, 258, 307–8
Muzychenko, Gen. I. N.   76

Nagykanizsa oil fields   337, 340
Napoleon Bonaparte   45, 104, 6, 115–16, 124, 141,
        228, 239
Narew offensive (1944)   318–22, 326, 259, 362
Narew River   318
Narva   283, 287, 303–4
National Committee for Free Germany
        (NKFD)   234, 242
'national redoubt', Nazi (1945)   350, 375
Navy, German   28, 217, 304, 350

Navy, Soviet   29, 75, 164, 209–10, 278
    Baltic Fleet   81, 305, 365
    Black Sea Fleet   81, 134–5, 278
Nazi Party (NSDAP)   7, 9–10, 29, 45, 182–3, 200,
        220–1, 232, 349–50, 389
Nazi–Soviet Pact, see German–Soviet
        Non-Aggression Pact
Nemmersdorf massacre (1944)   362
Nevel'   266, 298
Nikolaev   75, 274
Nikopol'   271, 273
NKVD (Soviet secret police)   36, 45, 59, 63–6, 79,
        93–4, 98, 101, 131, 168, 210–11, 228–30,
        233–4, 299, 306, 313–14, 328
Nomonhan, see Khalkhin Gol
Normandy invasion (1944)   299, 301
North Caucasus, campaign in   153–4, 176–7
NORTHERN LIGHTS, Operation (1942)   172–4
NORTHERN LIGHTS, Operation (1944)   289
Norway   173, 187, 289
Novgorod   282
Novikov, Marshal A. A.   365
Novorossiisk   267, 278

Odessa   75–6, 98, 273
OKH, see Army, German, High Command
Okulicki, Leopold   328
OKW, see Wehrmacht, High Command
Oppeln   367
Oranienbaum   281–2
Ordzhonidze   154
Orel operation (1943)   253
Orsha   65, 290, 293
Orsha conference (1941)   106–7
Osóbka-Morawski, Edward   328
Ostashkov–Pochep line (1941)   22, 89, 96
Ostrava–Prague operation (1945)   344–5
Ostrogozhsk-Rossoshan' operation (1943)   246
Ostrov   282, 290, 303
Ostwall (1943–4)   264, 266, 268–71, 280, 283–4,
        290, 293, 303

Paasikivi, Juho   288
Palanga   305
Panfilov, Gen. I. V.   102
PANTHER line (1943–4)   266, 268, 280–3
partisans, Soviet   62, 99, 108, 205, 228–32, 266,
        282, 299
Partisans, Yugoslav   311, 335–6
Pauker, Ana   311
Paulus, Field Marshal Friedrich   8, 137–8, 140, 152,
        154, 156, 160–2, 171, 234, 255
Pavlov, Gen. D. G.   58–63, 127
People's Army (Polish) (AL)   322
People's Militia (Narodnoe opol'chenie)   62, 65, 76,
        82, 92–4

'percentages agreement' (1944) 312
Perekop 133–4, 271, 278–9
Peter, King of Yugoslavia 335
Petrov, Gen. I. E. 136, 278, 342, 344, 367
Petrov, Gen. M. P. 92
Petrozavodsk 287
Petsamo 288
Petsamo–Kirkenes operation (1944) 288
Pfeffer-Wildenbruch, Gen. Karl von 339–40
Pillau 363–5
Pliev, Gen. I. A. 213–14
Ploesti 280, 329, 331–3
Podlas, Gen. K. P. 139
Pokryshkin, Col. A. I. 198
Poland 10–11, 14, 313–28
POLAR STAR, Operation (1943) 247–9
Poles'e (Pripiat' Marshes) 39, 289–90
Polish Committee of National Liberation
    (PKWN) 317, 322–3, 328
Polish forces in Red Army 322, 327
Polish government-in-exile (London) 314–16,
    321, 328
Polish Provisional Government 328
POLKOVODETS RUMIANTSEV, Operation
    (1943) 264, 267
Pomerania 352, 355–6, 358–61
Ponedelin, Gen. P. G. 76–7
Ponomarenko, P. K. 230, 299
Popov, Gen. M. M. 253–4, 263–4, 280–2
Potapov, Gen. M. I. 76, 78
Poznań 268, 326, 355–6
PQ17 (1942) 179, 187
Praga (Warsaw) 317, 320–2
Prague 345–7
prisoners-of-war, German-held 84, 99–102, 223–7
prisoners-of-war, Soviet-held 205, 233–5, 380, 382
Prokhorovka, Battle of (1943) 261–3
Proskurov–Chernovitsy operation (1944) 274
Pskov 69, 248, 282–3, 287
Pskov–Ostrov operation (1944) 303
Pukhov, Gen. N. P. 274
Puławy bridgehead 319
Purges, Soviet (1937–38) 12, 222, see also Army,
    Soviet, pre-war purges
Purkaev, Gen. M. A. 148

Radescu, Gen. Nicolae 333
Radio Kościuszko 320–1
Radzievskii, Gen. A. I. 317–18
Radzymin/Wołomin, Battle of 318, 326
Rákosi, Mátyás 311
Rakutin, Gen. K. I. 92
rasputitsa 47, 104–5, 117, 120, 277, 352
Raus, Gen. Erhard 305, 361
Red Army, see Army, Soviet
Red Orchestra 260

Reichenau, Field Marshal Walther von 86–7, 99, 161
Reichskommissariat for Ostland 224, 309
Reichskommissariat for Ukraine 224, 274
Reims surrender (1945) 345–6, 381–2
Reinhardt, Gen. Hans 102–3, 297–8,
    325, 363
Reiter, Gen. M. A. 246, 250, 252
Remagen bridge 373–4
Rendulic, Gen. Lothar 305, 363–4, 369
Rennenkampf, Gen. P. K. 361, 363
repatriation (of Soviet POWs and forced
    labourers) 226–7
revolutionary–imperial paradigm 12, 309–10, 313
Ribbentrop, Joachim von 13
Richtofen, Field Marshal Wolfram von 95, 135,
    155, 160
Riga 234, 283, 290, 304–5, 319
RING, Operation (1943) 157
'Road of Life' (Leningrad) 83, 129
Rodin, Gen. A. G. 261
Rokossovskii, Marshal K. K. 66, 75, 111,
    124, 156–7, 167–8, 204, 250–2, 256, 259,
    261–4, 269, 271, 290, 294, 296, 315–26, 355,
    358–64, 376–8
Romania 15, 50, 273, 310, 312, 328–33
    Army 98, 156, 159–60, 279, 332, 337
Roosevelt, Franklin D. 188, 236, 238–40, 309, 312,
    349–50, 374–5
Rosenberg, Alfred 11, 223–4
Rostov 87–8, 152, 157, 164
Rostov operation (1943), see DON, Operation
Rotmistrov, Marshal P. A. 261–4, 278
Rovno 224, 274
Rózan bridgehead (1944–5) 319, 326
Rundstedt, Field Marshal Gerd von 68–9, 74, 77,
    86–7, 99
Ruoff, Gen. Richard 153
Russia, see USSR
Russian Liberation Army (ROA) 345
Russian Orthodox Church 222–3
Rybalko, Marshal P. S. 246, 253, 263, 271, 277,
    315–16, 319, 326, 367, 378
Rychagov, Gen. P. V. 27, 55, 63
Ryti, Risto 288
Rzhev 148
Rzhev-Sychevka operation, first (1942) 145, 148
Rzhev-Sychevka operation, second (1942), see MARS,
    Operation
Rzhev-Viaz'ma operation (1942) 117, 120, 123
Rzhev-Viaz'ma salient 120, 124, 147, 149–50

Saaremaa Island 304–5
SALMON CATCH, Operation (1942) 173–5
Salmuth, Gen. Hans von 138
Samland Peninsula 363–5
Samsonov, Gen. A. V. 318, 371, 363

Sănătescu, Gen. Constantin 332–3

Sandomierz bridgehead 315–16, 319, 322, 325–6, 342

Sandomierz–Silesia operation (1945) 326–7, 376

SATURN, Operation 148, 171

Sauckel, Fritz 226

Saucken, Gen. Dietrich von 361

Schlieffen, Field Marshal Alfred von 8, 55

Schobert, Gen. Hugen von 133

Schörner, Field Marshal Ferdinand 206, 208, 273, 294, 303, 305, 326–7, 331, 344–5, 347, 367, 372, 382

Schulz, Gen. Friedrich 367

Schulze-Boysen, Harro ('Starshina') 36

'scorched earth' 50, 108, 150, 185, 271, 370

SEA, Operation (1943) 171

Sea of Azov, Battle on (1941) 87

'Second front', Allied plans for 142, 235–40

Seeckt, Gen. Hans von 19

Seelow 377–8, 380

Serock bridgehead (1944–5) 318–19, 326

Serov, Gen. I. A. 300, 313, 328

Sevastopol' 279

Sevastopol', siege of (1941–2) 131–6, see also Crimea

Sevsk operation (1943) 250–1

SEYDLITZ, Operation (1942) 122, 234

Seydlitz-Kurzbach, Gen. Walter von 122, 234

Shaposhnikov, Marshal B. M. 21–2, 60, 64, 66, 71, 78, 92, 96, 112, 116–17, 128, 137, 139, 166, 203–4

Shchadenko, Gen. E. A. 194

Shcherbakov, A. S. 251, 292

Shcherbakov, Gen. V. I. 288

Shlissel'burg 82, 125, 173, 175

Shlissel'burg corridor 125–6, 173–4, 281–4

Shtemenko, Gen. S. M. 259, 292, 303, 352–4

Shtern, Gen. G. M. 27

Sicily, invasion of (1943) 238, 262, 265

Silesia 363, 366–7

Simferopol' 134, 279

Simpson, Gen. William H. 375

Siniavino operation (1942) 173–4

Skorzeny, Col. Otto 338

Slovakia 16, 341–4

Slovak National Uprising (1944) 343–4

SMERSH 101, 211

Smirnov, Gen. A. K. 87

Smolensk 65, 266

Smolensk, Battle of (1941) 64–72

Smolensk operation (1943) 266, 290

Smolensk Proclamation (Vlasov) (1942) 226

Smushkevich, Gen. Ia. V. 27

Sobennikov, Gen. P. P. 82

Sofia 333–4

Sokolovskii, Gen. V. D. 60, 252, 263, 266, 290, 292

SOLSTICE, Operation (1945) 356, 360

Solzhenitsyn, A. I. 211

Sorge, Richard ('Ramsay') 36–7

Soviet–Finnish War (1939–40) 15, 30, 40, 59–60

Soviet–Japanese Neutrality Pact (1941) 15

Spaatz, Gen. Carl 382

Spanish Civil War 21, 27, 30

SPARK, Operation (1943) 174–5

Speer, Albert 52, 184, 216

Sponeck, Gen. Hans von 134

SPRING AWAKENING, Operation (1945) 340, 368

SS (Schutzstaffel) 10–11, 184
  Dirlewanger Brigade 320, 343
  Einsatzgruppen 97–8
  Kaminski Brigade 330
  Waffen-SS 87, 202, 254

Stalin
  and Red Army purge (1937–8) 20
  foreign policy, world view 11–15
  1939–41 policies 13–15, 32–41, 222
  response to 1941 invasion 59–60, 62–4
  Order No. 270 (1941) 77–8, 82, 101
  autumn 1941 defeats 95–6
  Battle of Moscow (1941) 108, 112–13
  offensive strategy (winter 1941–2) 107, 116–19, 122–3, 125–6, 136, 141–3
  'permanently operating factors' (1942) 220, 383–7
  summer 1942 plans 145–6, 163–4, 175–6
  Order No. 227 (1942) 162–3, 166
  Stalingrad 169, 202–3
  1943 offensive plans 202–3, 247, 250–2, 256, 258–9, 266–7
  'ten crushing Stalinist blows' (1944) 286, 288, 292, 301, 306, 331, 337
  and Warsaw Uprising 320–4
  1945 offensive 202–3, 212–13, 324, 352–7, 372–82
  and Czechoslovakia 13–14, 344
  and Finland 310, 313
  and Poland 14, 320–4, 328
  relations with Allies 142, 193, 235–41, 311–13, 381, 386–7
  views of Hitler and Germany 35–6, 141, 220–1, 241–2, 351, 357–9
  use of nationalism and pan-Slavism 222, 310
  and international Communism 12–13, 241, 310–11
  as supreme commander 20–1, 64, 67, 143, 167, 192, 202–3, 228–30, 267, 386

Stalin Line 22, 75, 76

Stalingrad 155

Stalingrad, Battle of (1942–3) 154–72
  Stalingrad defensive operation 166
  Stalingrad offensive operation (Operation URANUS) 156

Stalino   87, 266
STAR, Operation (1943)   253
Staraia Russa   121–2, 124, 249, 282
Stargard offensive (1945)   356, 358, 360
State Defence Committee (GKO)   20, 62–3, 95, 202
Stauffenberg, Col. Claus von   201–2
Stavka, see Red Army, High Command
Steiner, Gen. Felix   372
Stettin   355, 360–1
Stöbe, Ilse ('Al'te')   35
strategic bombing campaign,
        British-American   184, 238, 285, 300
Sub-Carpatho Ruthenia   341–2
Sukhinichi   118
Sumy–Khar'kov defensive operation (1941)   86–7
surrender negotiations in Switzerland (1945)   374
Susloparov, Gen. I. A.   381
SUVOROV, Operation (1943)   266, 290
Svechin, Komdiv A. A.   209
Svir'-Petrozavodsk operation (1944)   287
Svir' River   125, 287
Svoboda, Gen. Ludvik   341, 343
Sychevka   148–9

Taganrog   265
Tallin   80, 304
Tallin evacuation convoy   80–1
Taman' Peninsula   131, 154, 171, 278
Tannenberg, Battle of (1914)   318, 361, 363
Tartu operation (1944)   303, 319
TASS communiqué (June 1941)   39
Tedder, Air Marshal Arthur   382
Tehran Conference (1943)   239, 299, 314–15, 358–9
Telegin, Gen K. F.   323
theatres (military), Soviet   62, 64, 205
     northern   64
     southwestern   64, 76, 137
     western   64, 66
Tikhvin   88, 125
Timoshenko, Marshal S. K.   21, 33, 38, 59–60, 62,
        64, 66–7, 70, 72–3, 78, 88–9, 96–103, 111–12,
        137–9, 141, 149–50, 152, 165–6, 168, 203–4,
        248–9, 290, 331–2, 339, 344
Tippelskirch, Gen. Kurt von   165, 257–8, 297, 371
Tito, Josip Broz   241, 311–12, 335–6
Tiulenev, Gen. I. V.   75, 174, 171
Todt, Fritz   52, 184
Tolbukhin, Marshal F. I.   135, 156, 248,
        265, 269–71, 276, 279, 319, 331–2,
        334, 336–40, 368–9
TOLSTOY conference (1944)   312
TORCH, Operation (1942)   158, 170, 238
Torgau   380
Toropets salient   121–2, 138, 147, 250
total war   53, 182–3, 221
Triandafillov, V. K.   49, 218

Trubetskoi, Gen. N. I.   63
Tsanava, L. F.   313
Tukhachevskii, Marshal M. N.   21, 218, 357
Tula   103
Tupikov, Gen. V. I.   78
TYPHOON, Operation (1941)   67–9, 72, 91–2, 94,
        96–7, 99, 102, 113

Ukraine   7, 9, 40, 50–1, 60, 68, 219, 224
Ukraine, First Battle of (1941)   72–80, 86–7
Ukraine, Second Battle of (1943–4)   269–78
ULTRA   205, 260, 356
Uman' pocket (1941)   69, 72, 76–7, 99, 101
Union of German Officers (BDO)   234
Union of Polish Patriots (ZPP)   320
United Nations, Declaration of (1942)   235
Upper Silesia   40, 366–8
Upper Silesia operation (1945)   367–8, 376
Ural Mountains   50
URANUS, Operation (1942), see Stalingrad offensive
        operation
USSR
     armaments production   24–8, 42–5, 164–5,
          183–5, 189–99, 386, 391
     climate   46, 104–5, 388
     economy   7, 9, 48–9, 184–8
     evacuation of war industries (1941)   48
     food supply   7, 9, 50–1, 185, 188
     geography   46, 388–9
     impact of war on   391
     internal stability, morale   31, 188, 221–3, 384–5
     labour   49
     nationalism   222–3
     population   46–7
     railways   38, 47, 63, 68–9, 110, 188, 195,
          216–17, 231–2, 308
     resources   7, 9, 49–50, 188
Uzbekistan   280
Užgorod   341, 344

Vasilevskii, Marshal A. M.   64, 92, 95–6, 113, 122,
        125, 137, 139, 165–70, 202–5, 246, 251, 253,
        259–61, 265, 279, 281, 292, 295, 299, 303–5,
        308, 319, 324, 362, 364–5
Vatutin, Gen. N. F.   64, 80, 121, 150, 156, 167, 246,
        253–4, 259, 261, 265, 269, 271–4, 277, 290, 324
Velikie Luki   121, 145, 147, 148
VENUS, Operation (1942)   170
Viaz'ma-Briansk, Battle of (1941)   44, 88–97,
        99–100, 106
Vienna operation (1945)   368–9
Vietinghoff, Gen. Heinrich   305
Vil'nius   290, 294, 300, 314
Vishnevski, Gen. S. V.   92
Vistula–Oder operation (1945)   313, 324–8, 352–7
Vistula–Poznań operation (1945)   326

Vitebsk   67, 290, 293
Vitebsk operation (1944)   274
Vlasov, Gen. A. A.   75–8, 103, 128–9, 226, 345
Volga Germans, deportation of   99, 228
Volga River   8, 93, 164
Volkhov operation (1942)   119, 150
Volkhov River   88, 125–7, 281–3
Volkssturm   267, 349, 368, 379
Volodin, Gen. P. S.   55
Voronezh–Kastornoe operation (1943)   246, 250, 252
Voronezh–Khar'kov offensive operation
        (1943)   250, 258
Voronezh–Voroshilovgrad defensive operation
        (1942)   150
Vörös, Gen. János   338
Voroshilov, Marshal K. E.   18, 20, 60, 62, 64, 66, 80,
        82, 95, 111, 127, 155, 174, 193, 204, 230, 247,
        286, 340, 387
Voroshilovgrad   150, 246
VVS, *see* Air Force, Red Army
Vyborg   287
Vyshinskii, A. Ia.   333, 381

Waffen-SS, *see* SS
Wannsee Conference (1942)   99
war of annihilation   10, 52, 99, 242
Warsaw operation (plan) (1944)   322
Warsaw uprising (1944)   320–4
Wehrmacht (German Armed Forces), *see also* Air
        Force; Army; Navy, German
    High Command (OKW)   3–6, 201–2
    intelligence   41–2, 52–3, 107, 159, 161, 205–6, 296
    strategy   8, 200, 285, 299
    structure   5–6

Weichs, Field Marshal Maximilian von   69, 152,
        156, 159
Weidling, Gen. Helmuth   377–8
Weiss, Gen. Walter   297, 359–60, 363
Wenck, Gen. Walter   360, 371
West Carpathian operation (1945)   317, 344
West Prussia   358, 361, 365
WESTWALL   308, 373
Wilhelm Gustloff   365
WINTER STORM, Operation (1942)   157, 162, 171
Winter War, *see* Soviet–Finnish War
Wöhler, Gen. Otto   271, 275, 338, 344, 369
women   49, 131, 185, 209, 212, 226–7, 380
WOTAN position (1943)   266, 268, 271

Yalta conference (1945)   204, 226, 280, 328, 336,
        351–2, 354–6, 366
Yugoslavia   35, 212, 312, 335–6, 372

Zakharov, Gen. M. V.   279, 294–6, 325, 362
Zaporozh'e   253–4, 266
Zeitzler, Gen. Kurt   158, 201, 254, 257–8,
        276, 297, 318
Zhdanov, A. A.   64, 288
Zhitomir–Berdichev operation (1943–4)   272
Zhukov, Marshal G. K.   15, 21, 28, 30–1, 34, 36,
        38, 40, 60, 62, 64, 66–7, 70, 76–7, 82, 91, 93,
        95–6, 102–3, 105–6, 108, 111–14, 116–20,
        123–4, 136–7, 142, 146, 148–9, 152, 166–70,
        174, 192, 195, 202–5, 212–13, 217–18, 246,
        248–51, 254, 259–61, 264, 271–5, 292, 295,
        308, 315, 317–27, 334, 352, 355–6, 359–61,
        364–6, 372, 375–8, 380–1, 386
Zossen   378